JAMES BOND ENCYCLOPEDIA

JAMES BOND ENCYCLOPEDIA

JOHN CORK AND COLLIN STUTZ

CONTENTS

6   FOREWORD
8   INTRODUCTION
10 IAN FLEMING
12 THE BOND STYLE
22 THE ROLE OF BOND
36 BOND VILLAINS
108 BOND WOMEN
146 SUPPORTING CAST
196 VEHICLES
242 WEAPONS & EQUIPMENT
292 THE MOVIES
340 INDEX
352 ACKNOWLEDGMENTS

FOREWORD

When producing partners Albert R. Broccoli and Harry Saltzman began filming *Dr. No* in January 1962, they could not have imagined that the Bond series would be still going strong in the 21st century. Likewise, Ian Fleming, creator of the Bond character, would not have believed his secret agent would become a cinema legend delivering the most memorable line in film history—"Bond, James Bond."

John Cork and Collin Stutz have undertaken the monumental task of creating a Bond encyclopedia. Their research has been exhaustive. They have combed the MGM and Eon archives through documents, photographs, and film. They have interviewed actors and key production personnel and researched other archives and libraries. In short, they have been meticulous and thorough. The result is a definitive history of the Bond series over the past five decades.

Their effort is both a celebration and a tribute. It is a celebration of the Bond series and some of the best-loved and most exciting moments in cinema history. And it is a tribute to those who labored both in front and behind the camera to make Bond a legend. All are recognized, from the six exceptional actors who took up the challenge to play Bond and their magnificent leading ladies down to the day player and the background stunt artist. Directors, writers, designers, costumiers, cinematographers, camera crews, special effects, production, etc. are all acknowledged. Film is a collaborative process; every member of the team is essential right down to the most junior member of any department. This book is a tribute to their efforts, for which we are most grateful.

Michael G. Wilson
Barbara Broccoli

Broccoli and Saltzman in Jamaica, 1962

INTRODUCTION

Nobody does it better than Bond... James Bond. From the first reader who opened the first copy of *Casino Royale* in 1953 to the most recent viewer of the 23rd Bond film *Skyfall*, the public's imagination has been ignited by 007. What you hold in your hands is a visual encyclopedia, a window into the remarkable world of James Bond.

The first attempt to cover this ground was an unofficial tome written by Steven Jay Rubin, published nearly two decades ago. As the initial and often updated attempt at a Bond encyclopedia, all who follow must tip our hats to his mighty effort. We should note that this book looks at 007 quite differently. We have chosen to focus mainly on the world inside the Bond adventures, eschewing behind-the-scenes details in all but a few select areas. We also chose to focus only on the Bond films created by EON Productions, and not the two films made by other production companies: the 1967 parody version of *Casino Royale* and 1983 *Thunderball* remake, *Never Say Never Again*. This was not because of restrictions placed on us by EON, but because the central characters in these films are represented for the most part in the EON series and would make the composition of entries on a character like Emilio Largo or Vesper Lynd far more convoluted than necessary.

Like the Bond films themselves, this book is a collaborative effort. While we wrote the vast majority of the text, we certainly did not do it all alone. Bruce Scivally not only proofread all the text but also wrote a significant number of filmmaker profiles and many entries for the Vehicles and Weapons & Equipment sections. Music historian Jon Burlingame contributed the profile on John Barry. Alastair Dougall at DK took all the text and added his special magic. Jenni McMurrie at EON Productions, working with Michael G. Wilson and Barbara Broccoli, provided valuable guidance that helped us stay on target.

Through all 007's filmic adventures, the Bond series has prospered by both satisfying and defying audience expectations. It seems rather elementary to define James Bond's universe by creating categories such as listed in the table of contents of this book, but it is not quite so simple. We quizzed ourselves endlessly about the placement of and space devoted to every entry. Is Miss Taro a Bond villain or woman? Is General Moon a Bond villain or supporting character? Is a jet pack a vehicle or a piece of equipment? The Aston Martin DB5 is filled with gadgets, but, for this book, one needs to look in the Vehicles chapter to find them. We also decided that unless a gadget was utilized by Bond or a principle character in the field, it would not receive an entry in the Weapons & Equipment section. The many gadgets demonstrated in Q's lab, but never used by Bond in the field, are paid tribute to under Q's character entry in Supporting Cast. Nonetheless, we have tried to have fun with this book and make it somewhat like James Bond's world. The enjoyment is not in the logic, but in the discovery, the visual sweep, and the intricate details. Just as with Ian Fleming's novels, one shouldn't be able to anticipate exactly what one will find on the next page, but one should know it will be exciting, exotic, deadly, and beautiful. Welcome to the world of 007.

John Cork
Collin Stutz

Ian Fleming at Goldeneye, his Jamaican home

IAN FLEMING

BORN May 28, 1908
DIED August 12, 1964
FULL NAME Ian Lancaster Fleming

No other writer influenced popular literature in the 20th century more than Ian Fleming. His erudite, sensual, sardonic prose, coupled with the epic scope of his stories, captured a readership in the tens of millions in the 1950s and 1960s. While not the creator of the spy thriller, he so changed the genre that everything that came after was influenced by his twelve novels and nine short stories featuring James Bond.

Ian Lancaster Fleming entered the world cocooned by wealth and privilege. His grandfather Robert Fleming made millions creating overseas investment trusts. His father, Valentine, became part of the landed gentry and was elected to Parliament two years after Fleming's birth. Valentine died in combat in May, 1917, fighting in World War I. He left a modest fortune for his four sons in trust, although they would not have access to the funds until after their mother, Eve's, death or remarriage.

Fleming studied at Durnford School and then Eton, where he won the Victor Ludorum athletic prize twice. He left before the end of his final term, ostensibly to prepare to enter the Royal Military College at Sandhurst. He attended the Villa Tennerhof school in Kitzbuhel, Austria, where his teachers, Ernan Forbes-Dennis and Phyllis Bottome, encouraged his talent for creative writing. Fleming dropped out of Sandhurst before graduating after a scandal involving a London showgirl. He continued his education in Europe, hoping for a career in the Foreign Office, but did not test well enough for placement. He then turned to journalism and excelled in

VIP VISIT *Sean Connery (Bond) and Shirley Eaton (Jill Masterson) chat with Fleming on the set of* Goldfinger *at Pinewood Studios.*

> "To give my idle hands something to do... I decided one day to damned well sit down and write a book."

(the first child died shortly after birth), Anne left Rothermere and met Ian in Jamaica. As they awaited Rothermere's divorce decree, Fleming spent his mornings writing a spy novel he entitled *Casino Royale*.

For the next 14 winters, Fleming continued to write more James Bond adventures. Success was slow in coming. Although *Casino Royale* made quite a splash in 1953, culminating with a live television production on CBS in the US in 1954, the subsequent three novels did not see an increase in sales. However, Fleming gained some publicity when Sir Anthony Eden stayed at Goldeneye to recover from the fallout of the Suez Crisis. The *Daily Express* began serializing the Bond novels as comic strips. In the US, an endorsement from President J. F. Kennedy sent sales rocketing.

ON LOCATION *(left) Ursula Andress talks with Bond's creator in Jamaica while filming* Dr. No.

THE ORIGINAL *The first edition of* Casino Royale, *a book that changed the spy novel forever.*

By 1962, when *Dr. No* premiered in London, Bond had become a literary phenomenon.

Fleming always lived life on his own terms. He smoked up to 70 cigarettes a day and drank a half-bottle of spirits each evening. In 1964, with two heart attacks already behind him, Fleming suffered a coronary hemorrhage and died just weeks before the premiere of *Goldfinger*. He was 56 years old and the most-read author in the world.

GOLDEN YEARS *(from far left) Fleming's Jamaican home Goldeneye, where he wrote the Bond novels; Fleming, Pedro Armendariz, and Robert Shaw; Fleming with the crew of* From Russia With Love *in Istanbul; (below) Saltzman, Fleming, and Broccoli created a legacy of adventure and entertainment that inspires to this day.*

a brief career at Reuters. When his wealthy grandfather died, leaving nothing to Ian and his brothers, Fleming tried his hand at becoming a stockbroker. Traipsing to France and Austria on weekends and vacations, playing golf and seducing women, he wandered through his twenties. To many, he lived in the shadow of his brother Peter, an acclaimed writer, although the brothers always remained close.

In the months leading up to World War II, Fleming took on an assignment for *The Times* to report on a trade mission to Moscow. He turned over his observations to the Foreign Office and was soon employed as personal assistant to Admiral John Godfrey, Director of Naval Intelligence.

Fleming's work during World War II brought out the best in him. His imagination, forthrightness, and eye

for detail helped shape many important intelligence missions. While he did not see much active combat, he was at the forefront of the British espionage community.

For five winters after the war, Fleming traveled to his house Goldeneye on the north shore of Jamaica, living a life that was equal parts sybaritic and Spartan. In London, Fleming worked as foreign editor for Kemsley newspapers, managing reporters around the globe, much like a spymaster.

During this period, a long-term affair with Lady Anne Rothermere came to a head. He had known Anne while she was single and during her marriage to Lord O'Neill, who was killed during the war. She then married the press baron Lord Rothermere but continued her affair with Fleming. Eventually, pregnant with Ian's child for a second time

THE BOND STYLE

Bond's job consists of saving the world from chaos and catastrophe, so the order Bond places in his own life, from the way he ties his tie to the way he orders a drink, defines the world he fights so hard to save. Enter the world of Bond, James Bond, as seen through the details of his life, his many talents and his carefully acquired personal preferences. On the following pages you will dine, drink, and dress like a spy who knows that every pleasure may be his last. You will discover Bond's tastes, which, while easily copied, can only be fully savored by the embrace of adventure that serves as the main course of Bond's life.

CURRICULUM VITAE

THE JAMES BOND OF IAN FLEMING'S NOVELS is a veteran of World War II, whose path to becoming a "00" agent is shaped by his work with Naval Intelligence. The Bond of the early films appears to have a similar background, although he is too young to have served in any serious capacity in World War II. With *Casino Royale* (2006), the Bond filmmakers re-examined the character and his history for the post-Cold War era.

Fleming intended Bond to be a modern character, always in his thirties, always current, with a personal history as fluid as one might expect from a spy. Later Bond authors and historians have attempted to lock James Bond into a timeline, yet the best approach is clearly that taken by Fleming: Bond is, in the long run, timeless. He is old enough to be a seasoned professional, yet young enough to be in top physical condition.

In the films, Bond's age has changed as the series has progressed. Various passports have shown different dates that may or may not reflect Bond's actual birth date. For *Casino Royale*, Bond's birth date is set as April 13, 1968. This matches Bond's age to that of actor Daniel Craig, while the date of April 13 is the date of the publication of the novel *Casino Royale* in 1953. The filmmakers also set the location of Bond's birth in West Berlin.

Bond's pre-espionage life in the Bond movies, briefly mentioned in 1995's *GoldenEye,* is not fully explored until 2012's *Skyfall.* The novels record that his father, Andrew, a Scot working for Vickers Defence Systems, and his Swiss mother, Monique Delacroix, died during a climbing accident in the French Alps when Bond was 11 years old. Bond was raised by his Aunt Charmian and received a solid education, first at Eton College (from which he was soon expelled) and, from age 13, Fettes in Edinburgh, Scotland. *Skyfall* informs us that Bond grew up at Skyfall Lodge in Scotland. When his parents were killed, the gamekeeper Kincade informed young James of their deaths. Andrew and Monique were buried in the Bond family cemetery.

Fleming relates that Bond traveled to Austria in his youth. There he found a mentor in ski instructor Hannes Oberhausser, whom Bond described as a "second father." In the short story *Octopussy,* Oberhausser is killed by a British officer at the end of World War II during the theft of a cache of Nazi gold. Oberhausser's body is dumped in the crevasse of a glacier, only to reappear years later, revealing the identity of the killer—Major Dexter Smythe. Bond is given the assignment of confronting Smythe with the murder. The incident is also referenced in the film *Octopussy* (1983).

For *Casino Royale,* the filmmakers developed the following backstory: at the age of 17, Bond entered Britannia Royal Naval College. A quick learner, he was deemed a born leader. Bond served on the Type-42 destroyer HMS *Exeter* and the Trafalgar-class hunter-killer submarine HMS *Turbulent*. Bond volunteered for the Special Boat Service and later served with the elite commando 030 Special Forces Unit, undertaking covert assignments in Iraq, Somalia, Iran, and Libya. He also participated in combat operations in Bosnia. Having risen to the rank of Commander, Bond was recruited by the RNR Defence Intelligence Group. His assignments included gathering information on the Pan Am 103 case (the Lockerbie bombing), the S-300 missile crisis in Cyprus, the Hong Kong handover, Iraq's weapons programs, and a rescue mission in Taliban-controlled Afghanistan. Bond also studied at various universities, including Oxford and Cambridge, earning a First in Oriental Languages at the latter.

Around this time, Bond was recruited by the branch of Her Majesty's Secret Service known as MI6, based in the Ministry of Intelligence building, Vauxhall Cross, London. There have been various attempts to tell the story of how Bond became a spy. Fleming himself never detailed this part of Bond's career. What Fleming did record is how Bond became a "00" agent. In the novel *Casino Royale,* Bond achieves "00" status by assassinating a Japanese cipher expert in New York and then a Norwegian spying for the Germans. Bond has to perform the job silently and uses a knife to kill the man in an apartment in Stockholm. "He just didn't die very quickly," Bond recalls.

The film *Casino Royale* introduces Bond before he has achieved his licence to kill. After accomplishing two assassinations in rapid succession, he is elevated to double-0 status.

The first kill is a messy death and occurs in a public restroom in Pakistan. The second is "considerably" easier—Bond assassinates Dryden, an MI6 Section Chief selling secrets, in his office in Prague.

In the novel *On Her Majesty's Secret Service,* James Bond is confronted with a history of the Bond family of Bond Street fame, but disclaims any relationship. Despite being repelled by the snobbery associated with heraldry, Bond politely says he will adopt the crest's motto, *Orbis non sufficit*—"The world is not enough"— as his own. The phrase was used as the title of the 19th Bond film. In one scene, Bond proclaims it to be his family motto.

PERFECT HEALTH Bond's medical report indicates good blood pressure, perfect vision, excellent reflexes, and a date of birth of 6 May, 1961. Bond's birth date has changed as both the novels and films have progressed.

MEDI

BOND'S SKILLS

JAMES BOND MAINTAINS HIS ATHLETIC ABILITIES for one simple reason: his life depends on being in top physical condition. Bond possesses a high tolerance for pain and incredible stamina, two attributes not only vital to his survival, but also qualities that give him great confidence in taking on new physical challenges. 007's keen conditioning makes him a deadly foe on land, sea or in the air.

On the ground, Bond possesses legendary fighting skills. He has privately worked on a training manual for unarmed combat entitled *Stay Alive!* that he hopes will be added to the list of internal MI6 publications. He is skilled at karate, judo, jujitsu, tae kwon do, boxing, wrestling, and knows five ways to kill a man with a single blow. Whether battling enemies aboard speeding vehicles or in the confines of a lift or stairway, 007 knows how to inflict the most damage on an opponent. Because of his physical conditioning, he can adapt to new challenges. Although never trained in Free Running techniques, sheer determination allows him to keep pace with a highly skilled practitioner during one mission in Madagascar.

Bond learned to ski at an early age at the Hannes Schneider School in Arlberg, which is notable because Schneider is credited as the father of modern skiing. Hannes Oberhausser taught Bond the finer points of the sport during 007's school vacations in Austria during his teens, and his skills improved to championship level by his twenties. Bond can ski in extremely icy conditions, including in a bobsled run and on one ski. He has also mastered snowboarding. His skiing expertise helps him elude SPECTRE guards in Switzerland and KGB assassins in Austria, the Soviet Union, and Italy, as well as evade pursuing parahawks in the mountains of Azerbaijan. Bond has also spent time practicing the dangerous sports of bobsledding and the luge.

Bond's high-altitude skills include mountain climbing, another activity he learned in his youth while in Austria. Bond's mountaineering abilities have allowed him to scale sheer walls, cliff faces, and ice. His familiarity with climbing techniques, equipment, and safety procedures make it easy for him to learn commando skills utilizing ultra-fast rappelling, piton guns, and suction devices for 90°-plus ascents and descents.

Bond is just as proficient in water as he is on land. A superb swimmer and high diver, Bond excelled in underwater commando

Bond's driving skills have allowed him to survive some very close calls. From Jamaica to Iceland, Bond has driven under the most treacherous conditions. 007 feels comfortable and confident behind the wheel of virtually every type of vehicle, from an Aston Martin sports car to a prototype lunar rover or a military hovercraft.

training in the Royal Navy, becoming a champion scuba diver and an expert in underwater combat, as revealed during Operation Thunderball. On the water's surface, Bond excels at barefoot skiing and surfing. He employs both these skills during missions in the Caribbean and North Korea.

A confident pilot of all forms of watercraft, Bond drives both large and small boats at high speeds and can also operate military and personal submarines. His near instinctual feel for the operational limits of a craft serve him well during missions in all kinds of conditions and locations, including off the Dalmatian Coast, in Louisiana, Bangkok, the Mediterranean, Venice, Brazil, the River Thames, and off the coast of Haiti.

007's most remarkable set of skills reveal themselves in the air. In the Royal Navy, Bond undertook intensive parachute training, developing skills that save his life on numerous occasions. Bond relies on his aerial expertise when the assassin Jaws shoves him out of a chartered jet without a parachute. Bond maneuvers through the air to intercept an enemy skydiver and steal his chute, then battles Jaws in freefall. Bond's confidence in the air has allowed him to climb along the exterior of a helicopter being flown by remote control, to leap onto the exterior of a Beech 18 during takeoff, to be lowered by helicopter to snare the tail of a plane, and to parachute into a Bolivian sinkhole.

Bond has performed a High Altitude, Low Opening (HALO) jump in order to locate the sunken HMS *Devonshire* off the Vietnamese coast by jumping from the back of a plane at 29,000 ft (8,839 m), freefalling for 5 miles (8 km) using his oxygen tank to breathe, and then opening his parachute 200 ft (60.9 m) below Vietnamese radar. Bond has also participated in aided skydiving operations with Programmable High Altitude Single Soldier Transport units, also known as Switchblades. An excellent hang glider/paraglider pilot, Bond can maneuver these frail craft through extreme conditions, such as the updrafts from waterfalls.

Bond maintains his skills as a pilot, able to fly virtually any aircraft, from a rocket belt and attack helicopters to prop planes and jet fighters, even a decades-old Douglas DC-3 cargo plane.

Bond's unique combination of skills make him the most versatile and lethal secret agent to ever serve in Her Majesty's Secret Service, superbly equipped to face the deadliest of foes in the most challenging conditions imaginable. His determination to maintain his body in top physical condition is only matched by his drive to do the best work possible in the service of his country. Wherever 007's missions may take him, from icy slopes to the murky ocean depths, *nobody* does it better.

SURVIVAL INSTINCT *When in peril for his life, Bond knows his very existence depends on his ability to use his wits and never give up. Top: Bond pursues a terrorist bomber in* Casino Royale *in a lung-busting chase that also fully tests 007's agility and ability to think on his feet. Left to right: Bond uses martial arts training to fend off an assailant in* On Her Majesty's Secret Service; *Bond's mountain-climbing skills prove crucial to the mission's success in* For Your Eyes Only; *Bond performs a death-defying leap from a plane onto a tanker truck in* Licence To Kill; *Bond's years in the Royal Navy taught him numerous essential skills, enabling him to win through thanks to his courage and resourcefulness, not to good fortune or gadgets; Bond's skiing abilities save his life in* The World Is Not Enough.

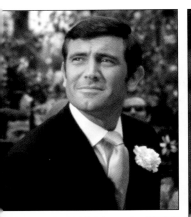

WARDROBE

COSTUME DESIGNER LINDY HEMMING, who has dressed 007 on numerous occasions, once commented: "When Bond enters a room, he has to have status. You have to believe he could enter a room anywhere in the world and be perfectly dressed for the occasion, but not stand out from his surroundings in a way that would make him a target of suspicion. He's kind of an elegant chameleon."

No moment better illustrates this point than Bond's transformation after he has planted explosives inside a heroin lab in Mexico in *Goldfinger* (1964). Bond strips off a waterproof suit to reveal an immaculate white dinner jacket and bow tie. He plucks a red carnation and places it in his lapel. The transformation from commando to connoisseur is complete.

James Bond's wardrobe redefined the look of a spy. Bond eschewed fedoras and trench coats, opting for finely tailored suits, stylish casual wear, and sleek commando gear. 007's clothes exude elegance through their practical durability. Their perfect styling echoes the inner confidence of Bond's character. Bond, of course, requires bespoke suits to hide the shape of his Walther PPK in its shoulder holster and to look good walking into a fine restaurant after a back alley fight.

The attention to the details of Bond's clothing in Ian Fleming's novels directly inspired Bond's cinematic wardrobe. Fleming's Bond always dressed for the occasion. In major cities and when traveling, Bond favored a dark-blue, single-breasted suit, often described as "navy serge" or "tropical worsted," with a black knitted tie, knotted with a simple four-in-hand knot (Bond was always suspicious of a man who used a Windsor knot to tie his tie).

In the early film adventures, Bond often wore gray suits and opted for lightweight tropical fabrics. By *Goldfinger*, 007's suits included waistcoats, a choice that gave way in the 1970s and 1980s to tailored sports jackets, reflecting a more casual era. In the late 1980s, Bond returned to wearing the kind of tailored suits that reflected both position and self-assurance.

Sean Connery is measured for one of James Bond's suits by Anthony Sinclair, a stylish Savile Row tailor of the 1960s, who provided many significant pieces of Bond's early wardrobe, including the tuxedo he wears in the opening scenes of *Dr. No*.

In 2006's *Casino Royale*, Vesper Lynd seems to mock Bond's style, correctly pegging him as an alumnus of Eton by the bespoke tailoring of his suit. She later presents him with the icon of 007's wardrobe, a tailored tuxedo. The moment Bond pulls his bow tie taut provides an important glimpse into the complementary nature of Bond to his wardrobe. While soldiers have their uniform, Bond's tuxedo serves as his battle gear as he engages his enemies in the most exclusive places in the world.

007's casual attire is just as important as his sartorial choices for formal situations. In Fleming's novels, Bond's regular visits to the tropics saw him wearing short-sleeved Sea Island cotton shirts—usually either white or dark blue—with dark slacks, leather sandals, or rope-soled shoes. These choices directly influenced Bond's look in the films. Bond's sky blue polo shirt and dungarees in *Dr. No* (1962) may have been a brighter color, but they come straight from the novel, and his dark blue tropical shirt, sandals, and slacks, as featured in *Thunderball* (1965), are taken nearly item for item from Fleming.

In the late 1960s and early 1970s, Bond dabbled in some of the styles of the time. Bond's golfing suit from 1969's *On Her Majesty's Secret Service* and safari suit from 1974's *The Man With The Golden Gun* stand out as prime examples. James Bond's identity, however, comes through in the way he wears his clothes, not in what he wears. When Bond dons a pink shirt in *Diamonds Are Forever* (1971) or a blue terrycloth one-piece bathing suit cover in *Goldfinger*, he does so with masculine confidence. He selects quiet sweaters that never bag, such as the one he wears while driving to Monaco at the beginning of *GoldenEye* (1995). From the silk shirts worn by Bond in Nassau and Venice in *Casino Royale* to the riding jacket he wears in *A View To A Kill* (1985), Bond's style choices reflect his acute sense of what is appropriate to the occasion.

At the end of *Casino Royale*, after the tragic loss of Vesper, Bond steels himself against the pain, literally armoring himself psychologically and physically as he tracks down Mr. White. Shooting him in the leg, Bond steps into view. His dark, bespoke three-piece suit would gain him the best table at any restaurant in the world. This is his armor. 007 is literally dressed to kill.

FOR EVERY OCCASION *Opposite page, top to bottom: an impeccably groomed Bond at his wedding in* On Her Majesty's Secret Service; *in* The Man With The Golden Gun, *Bond's look included a more casual, open-necked style befitting the steamy South China Sea climate; a leather-jacketed Bond readies his weapon in this publicity photo from* The Living Daylights; *Bond conveys elegance and danger with a gray Brioni suit and a silenced Walther P99 in this publicity shot from* The World Is Not Enough.
CLASSIC STYLE *Opposite page, right: Bond strides through* Casino Royale, *a man in his element in his ultimate uniform.*

LIFESTYLE

ACCORDING TO IAN FLEMING, James Bond lives in a "comfortable flat" in a converted Regency house in a square off King's Road in Chelsea, London. On the ground floor, Bond has a "book-lined sitting room" and an "ornate Empire desk" by a broad window. Upstairs, 007 sleeps in a double bed with a dark blue counterpane in a smallish bedroom with white and gold Cole wallpaper accented with deep red curtains. He has a large white-tiled bathroom with an American-style shower. He also employs a devoted elderly Scottish housekeeper named May.

The Bond of the films has moved on from Fleming's portrait of bachelordom 1950s-style. Throughout the series, Bond retains an acute appreciation of classic excellence and elegance in every aspect of his life, while at the same time remaining perfectly in tune with his times. Bond's London home is seen in two films. In *Dr. No* (1962), we can see that Bond has a penchant for prints of vintage cars, owns a television, and has a spectacular entrance hall. In *Live And Let Die* (1973), Bond lives in a modern, ground-floor flat with a bedroom that opens into the living room and a state-of-the-art kitchen with a coffee grinder and espresso machine.

Bond enjoys good food served without pretense. He explains his attitude to food in the novel *Casino Royale*: "I take ridiculous pleasure in what I eat and drink. It comes partly from being a bachelor, but mostly from a habit of taking a lot of trouble over details..." In the novels, Bond relishes asparagus with *sauce béarnaise*, eggs Benedict with mousseline sauce, avocado with French dressing (a delicacy in post-war Europe), *tagliatelle verdi* with pesto sauce, langouste, stone crabs with melted butter, and a good pâté. Bond also savors well-prepared basics. Fleming had 007 comment once that the best food in the world is English food when cooked properly.

In the films, Bond's knowledge of food sets him apart from the average tourist or business traveler. He knows what to order and why. In *Thunderball* (1965) and *You Only Live Twice* (1967), Bond chooses conch chowder and oysters respectively because of their reputation as aphrodisiacs. In *On Her Majesty's Secret Service* (1969), Bond tastes the caviar at the Palacio Estoril Hotel in Portugal and immediately knows it is Royal Beluga.

In foreign countries, Bond samples the local cuisine, such as Blue Mountain coffee in Jamaica, green figs and yogurt in Istanbul, preveza prawns, savara salad, and bourdetto in the village of

In the films, Bond's tastes in champagne are aligned with Dom Perignon, Taittinger, and Bollinger. He prefers his champagne no warmer than 38° Fahrenheit. Bond believes the best vintage champagne is Dom Perignon '53. He mentions this preference to Dr. No, who serves Dom '55, and also to Jill Masterson in *Goldfinger* (1964).

Gastouri outside of Corfu, and lobster with quail's eggs and sliced seaweed in Hong Kong. Bond cooks only once in the films, expertly preparing quiche for Stacey Sutton in *A View To A Kill* (1985). Bond's culinary knowledge extends to knowing where best to dine anywhere, from Miami Beach to Karachi.

The phrase, "shaken, not stirred" is synonymous with James Bond. Bond's opinion on how to prepare his vodka martini establishes him as a man who appreciates the subtle efforts that separate a mediocre drink from a remarkable cocktail. In both the novel and the film *Casino Royale* (2006), Bond orders a particularly fussy martini, which he names The Vesper: 3 measures Gordon's Gin; 1 measure vodka; a half measure Kina Lillet (now available as Lillet Blanc). Shake very well until ice-cold. Serve in a deep champagne goblet with a large thin slice of lemon peel. In Bond's other adventures, his martini is not quite so elaborate, and later in *Casino Royale,* Bond asks one bartender if he looks like he gives a damn if the drink is shaken or stirred.

In the novels, Bond enjoys champagne, particularly the best. He orders the famed Taittinger Blanc de Blanc Brut '43, "probably the finest champagne in the world," Dom Perignon '46, the '53 Taittinger Blanc de Blanc, Bollinger, Krug, and Pommery. Bond also drinks pink champagne, such as Cliquot rosé, and Black Velvet, a mix of champagne and Guinness. Fleming's Bond is happy to imbibe the local cocktail, liqueur, or brew. In the films, Bond largely confines himself to martinis or bourbon and branch water. However he does enjoy local specialties, such as a mint julep in Kentucky, raki in Turkey and saké in Japan. Bond is an infallible judge of brandy and sherry and a connoisseur of fine wines, his favorite being Château Mouton-Rothschild.

In the films, 007's winemanship has proved essential. In *From Russia With Love* (1963), Bond knows no self-respecting British agent would order red wine with fish, so he is not surprised when Captain Nash turns out to be SPECTRE assassin Donald Grant. In *Diamonds Are Forever* (1971), Bond's knowledge that Château Mouton-Rothschild is a claret allows him to spot the assassin Mr. Kidd posing as a wine steward.

James Bond is an expert gambler, noted as the best in MI6. He understands the strategy and odds in all casino games, knows how to spot cheats and, most importantly, how to handle himself when playing for very high stakes. Bond gambles in casinos in three novels and 11 films. He also plays roulette in the novels, and in the films shows his skills at baccarat, blackjack, craps and backgammon. Most importantly, Bond plays Texas Hold'em poker in the film *Casino Royale* for stakes totaling over £100 million.

THE BOND LIFESTYLE *Ian Fleming wrote, "There are moments of great luxury in the life of a secret agent." Top: 007 offers his assessment of a "rather disappointing brandy" in* Goldfinger; *(left to right) Bond enjoys a fine meal in India with Magda in* Octopussy; *Bond enjoys introducing Kara Milovy to the luxuries of the West in* The Living Daylights; *Bond drinks a vodka martini with "plenty of ice" in Graves's Ice Palace in* Die Another Day; *Bond tests his gambling skills against Le Chiffre in* Casino Royale.

THE ROLE OF BOND

It takes a special kind of man to convince the world he is James Bond. One can slip on a dinner jacket, drive an Aston Martin and drink vodka martinis, but it takes more than surrounding oneself with 007's props to look the world in the eye and convincingly utter the words, "The name is Bond, James Bond." This requires an inner, elusive quality not easily put into words. Each actor must not only look the part, but also bring something to the role beyond the requisite good looks, sense of timing, and ability to portray grace under pressure. Each of the six actors to play 007 has brought a unique personal touch to Ian Fleming's "blunt instrument." Each has interpreted 007 their own way yet remained true enough to the core of Bond's character to feel part of the cinematic continuum. Thanks to them, James Bond's name has ceased to be, as Fleming wrote, "flat and colorless." The very words "James Bond" define our fantasy of stylish masculinity thanks in large part to these men. Bond, through them, is our shorthand for urbane aplomb.

Meet the actors who made the man more than a number. Discover their journeys to the role that changed their lives and in some small way ours. Meet the men who became secret agent 007.

SEAN CONNERY

MISSIONS Dr. No (1962), From Russia With Love (1963), Goldfinger (1964), Thunderball (1965), You Only Live Twice (1967), Diamonds Are Forever (1971)

BORN 25 August, 1930, Edinburgh, Scotland

FULL NAME Thomas Sean Connery

Sean Connery defined the cinematic James Bond. His style, grace, sense of self, and sheer magnetism brought Ian Fleming's character to life. It was Connery's interpretation of 007 that helped establish the foundation of success upon which the entire James Bond series has been built.

Connery's upbringing in the working-class Fountainbridge neighborhood of Edinburgh was a far cry from the privileged British "old boy" network of Ian Fleming and James Bond. Connery's father, Joseph, was a lorry driver who prided himself on never missing a day's work.

After leaving school in his early teens, Connery worked on a milk delivery route which included Fettes, the exclusive Edinburgh boarding school where Ian Fleming placed a

young James Bond after expulsion from Eton. While the fictional Bond learned the classics at Fettes, Connery worked to support his family.

Connery had many jobs before he joined the Royal Navy, hoping to see the world. He served as an able seaman assigned to battleships, training in gunnery school. Discharged with ulcers, he returned to Edinburgh, where he trained as a French polisher before deciding to enter the Mr. Universe contest in

"The person who plays Bond has to be dangerous."

PLAYING THE GAME *(above left) James Bond meets Sylvia Trench (Eunice Gayson) in Dr. No at the Le Cercle gaming tables.*

BOND'S CREATOR *(above) Sean Connery and Ian Fleming deep in conversation on Dr. No's reactor set.*

CHECKING THE LIGHT *(left) Honor Blackman (Pussy Galore) and Sean Connery on the Auric Stud set at Pinewood Studios.*

BEACHCOMBER *(below left) 007 introduces himself to Honey Ryder (Ursula Andress) on Crab Key beach in Dr. No.*

London in 1953. Connery earned a bronze medal in his weight division, but it was clear that he had no future as a professional bodybuilder. Another competitor mentioned auditions for a touring company of *South Pacific*. They were looking for male dancers for the sailor's chorus. Connery, who had appeared as an extra in a play in Edinburgh, landed a role in the chorus and soon afterwards set off around the country as a professional actor.

Connery's new job as an actor almost lost out to a career as a professional footballer for Manchester United. On tour with *South Pacific* in Manchester, the production played against the football club's junior team. Matt Busby, the United manager, approached Connery and offered him a contract to play. Connery asked fellow actor Robert Henderson for advice. The older actor advised Connery to take the long view. Connery considered that a footballer's career would end by 30, but an actor could act forever. He dedicated himself to studying the classics at local libraries around the UK during his time off from his duties with the chorus.

Connery struggled to build his

reputation as an actor, barely earning enough to live on as part of a suburban London repertory company. However, the small company gave him the chance to perfom new dramatic roles each week. His developing skills and physical presence gained Connery roles in low-budget films, including 1957's *Action Of The Tiger*. The film's director, Terence Young, told Connery that the part would not do much for Connery's career, but that he would hire Connery for a better role one day.

Connery began working in BBC live drama productions and, when Jack Palance could not star in *Requiem For A Heavyweight*, Connery won the lead role. Rave reviews led to a contract with 20th Century-Fox, more television, and a role in the 1958 Lana Turner film, *Another Time, Another Place*, shot in England. The following year, Walt Disney and the director Robert Stevenson cast Connery in *Darby O'Gill And The Little People*, which brought him to Hollywood for the first time. The next two years provided a variety of television, theater, and small films but no break-out roles.

Then, in the summer of 1961, now free of his Fox contract, Connery entered the Mayfair offices of American film producer Albert R. Broccoli. Connery walked with smooth, graceful strides, learned in part from classes with the Swedish dancer and drama teacher Yat Malmgren. His working-class background was by then leavened by relationships with beautiful upper-class women such as Julie Hamilton and Diane Cilento, his future wife. His air of confidence stemmed from succeeding against the odds. The producer, Albert R. Broccoli, his producing partner, Harry Saltzman, and United Artists executive Bud Ornstein watched Connery stride across the street after leaving. "He moved," Saltzman recalled, "like a big jungle cat." He would, they felt, be perfect for the role of James Bond.

By the time Connery retired from playing 007 in EON Productions's Bond films, his 007 adventures had grossed over $600 million. He had also starred

LOVE SCENE *Bond gets to know Tatiana Romanova (Daniela Bianchi) better in* From Russia With Love.

in movies directed by Alfred Hitchcock, Sidney Lumet, and Martin Ritt. In the 1970s, Connery established himself as an actor who could bring success to diverse films. He took on larger-than-life roles, such as the Raisuli in *The Wind And The Lion* (1975), Kipling's legendary Daniel Dravot in *The Man Who Would Be King* (1975), and Robin Hood in *Robin And Marian* (1976). In the 1980s, he won an Academy Award for Best Supporting Actor in *The Untouchables* (1987) and played the irascible father of Indiana Jones in *Indiana Jones And The Last Crusade* (1989), for which he received Golden Globe and BAFTA award nominations in the Best Supporting Actor category.

By the 1990s, Connery could develop and produce films in which to star. He received a Lifetime Achievement award at the 1996 Golden Globes, a gala tribute at Lincoln Center, and praise from President Bill Clinton for his contribution to the arts. Connery received a knighthood on New Year's Day, 2000. In 2006, the American Film Institute awarded Connery a Lifetime Achievement award, and he is recognized as one of the most influential and successful actors of the past half century.

> **"I care about Bond and what happens to him."**

PUNCHED OUT *Bond and Red Grant (Robert Shaw) fight in* From Russia With Love.

GEORGE LAZENBY

OFFICIAL MISSIONS
On Her Majesty's Secret Service (1969)

BORN 5 September, 1939
Queanbeyan, Australia

FULL NAME George Robert Lazenby

George Lazenby has always pushed himself to the limit. His confidence, pride, striking good looks, and charm made him a natural choice to become the successor to Sean Connery as James Bond.

Growing up in Australia, George Lazenby always dreamed big. He moved to Canberra in his teens and through sheer perseverance became the leader of a rock 'n' roll band as well as a booker for larger acts coming from Sydney. Recalling that early success, Lazenby relates it to his one performance as 007:

"I was basically doing it just to get out there. I didn't know I wanted to be an entertainer at the time. But, what was in the back of my mind, I guess, was to show off, to be somebody. And that's why, I think, when Bond came up, the odds were I'd get it because I wanted it more than anybody else."

Lazenby came to London to reunite with a girlfriend, but by the time he arrived, she had moved on. He lined up a car salesman job and

GEORGE AND HARRY *Producer Saltzman championed Lazenby's casting and remained friends with him for years.*

then advanced to selling Mercedes on Park Lane in London. His looks gained the notice of photographer Chard Jenkins. Soon, Lazenby was one of the highest-paid male models in Europe. He starred in a series of television commercials for Big Fry's chocolates, which made his face recognizable around the UK.

A chance blind date with casting director Maggie Abbott led her to suggest he try out for James Bond. Lazenby liked the idea of playing Bond, and he set about becoming

> "People think: Let's go and see a Bond film. It's always entertaining."

the perfect candidate. Lazenby purchased a suit that had been made for Connery in You Only Live Twice (1967) but was never used. At the Dorchester Hotel, Lazenby visited Kurt the Barber and asked for a haircut like Sean Connery's. It turned out producer Albert R. Broccoli was in the next chair, but Broccoli thought Lazenby was simply a businessman. Sporting a Rolex watch like 007's, Lazenby appeared at the door of the casting director's office saying, "I heard you were looking for James Bond."

After a meeting with producer Harry Saltzman, Lazenby confessed to director Peter Hunt later that he had no real acting experience. Hunt told him that if they stuck together, he could turn him into the new Bond. During a particularly energetic screentest, Lazenby bloodied the nose of stuntman Yuri Borienko. Bond producer Harry Saltzman walked over and told him, "We're going with you."

Producer Cubby Broccoli wrote in his autobiography *When The Snow Melts*: "Lazenby, in my judgment, made a good James Bond. He could easily have fallen into the trap of doing a smart but fatal imitation of Sean. Instead, he fought his corner as a fledgling actor, avoided tricks and gave a surprisingly effective performance."

The aftermath of *On Her Majesty's Secret Service* was difficult for Lazenby. He failed to capitalize on the effort he had put into playing Bond. Following what he now feels was some very bad career advice, Lazenby walked away from any chance he had to return as 007.

READY FOR ACTION *Lazenby's physical grace made him a natural successor to Sean Connery.*

MONEYPENNY REPORTS *The actress Lois Maxwell remembers, "George was young and delicious and girls were falling in front of him like pieces of confetti."*

"At the time, I didn't know how big James Bond was. I didn't realize that no one's going to treat you the same again," Lazenby recalled. "All the doors open for you. I had that experience, and it was kind of fun. Later on, the opposite happened. They all closed. That was another part of life that I had to endure that wasn't so much fun."

He co-wrote, executive produced, and starred in the film *Universal Soldier* (1971), which died at the box office. By the mid-1970s, Lazenby was returning to Bond in a way. He appeared in a stylish commercial for Sony, playing a secret agent impressed by the technological

ON SET *Lazenby discusses a scene with director Peter Hunt and actor Telly Savalas on location at Schilthorn, Switzerland.*

"It's hard to top a Bond film. There's nothing bigger."

MRS. JAMES BOND *"Diana Rigg was a star in her own right from* The Avengers *series. And I was this young upstart guy who probably didn't know a tenth of what she knew about the business."*

wizardry of Sony's off-the-shelf products. Lazenby subsequently played Bond-like characters in several films and television shows, but he also demonstrated real strength as an actor, a strength that has all-too-rarely been tapped. He played a US senator in Peter Bogdanovich's moving film *Saint Jack* (1979) and appeared as General Pettigrew in *Gettysburg* (1993). Lazenby has played other iconic roles, including Superboy's father Jor-El, as well as providing the voice of the Batman villain King in the *Batman Beyond* television series.

Outside of acting, Lazenby has been tremendously successful in real estate and sports, particularly off-road motocross racing.

ACTION MAN *Lazenby enjoyed the role's physical challenges and complained when prevented from doing some of his own stunts.*

THE NEW 007 *Director Peter Hunt felt Lazenby had star quality. "He should've gone on and done the other Bonds. He would have made a very credible Bond and been very good indeed."*

ROGER MOORE

MISSIONS

Live And Let Die (1973), The Man With The Golden Gun (1974), The Spy Who Loved Me (1977), Moonraker (1979), For Your Eyes Only (1981), Octopussy (1983), A View To A Kill (1985)

BORN 14 October, 1927, London, England

FULL NAME Roger George Moore

Roger Moore's good looks, charm, and wit made him a natural for stardom. A worldwide star before being cast as Bond, Moore's easy sense of grace and savoir-faire brought the cinematic 007 unparalleled success in the 1970s and 80s. Moore's James Bond brought fantasy to the films at a time when movie audiences needed escapist entertainment of the highest caliber.

Born in Stockwell, South London, Moore excelled at art as a youth. After school, he took a job at an animation studio working on War Office short films in the middle years of World War II. Moore lost this job but quickly reentered the film world. His father was a detective sergeant with the London Police and an amateur actor himself. He had met director Brian Desmond Hurst while investigating a robbery. Moore's father took Roger to meet Hurst and asked him to help his son become an actor. Soon, Moore's strikingly handsome looks were noted when he worked as an extra on *Caesar And Cleopatra* (1945). With Hurst's

guidance, Moore found other small roles before joining the Royal Academy of Dramatic Arts, where one of his classmates was Lois Maxwell, the future Miss Moneypenny. Elocution lessons at RADA smoothed the rough edges of Moore's South London accent, enabling him to play sophisticated leading men convincingly.

In 1945, Moore was called up for military service. He has said he was recommended for officer training in part because of his good looks. After enduring postings in Germany, a car accident, and appendicitis, Moore transferred to the Combined Services Entertainment Unit, becoming friends with many other actors and future directors.

GLAMOR ON SET *Roger Moore poses with the actresses portraying Octopussy's beautiful but lethal girls.*

OTHERWISE ENGAGED *(above) 007 stalls M on the phone so that he can make love to Mary Goodnight (Britt Ekland) in* The Man With The Golden Gun.

TAKING A BREAK *(left) Albert R. Broccoli, Harry Saltzman, and new Bond Roger Moore relax before boat work begins for* Live And Let Die.

DEADLY DUEL *Bond pursues a mysterious assassin in* A View To A Kill.

HOW DOES THAT GRAB YOU? *(right) Jaws (Richard Kiel) has Bond in his grasp in* The Spy Who Loved Me.

as Simon Templar, the legendary adventurer created by Leslie Charteris, made him one of the most recognizable actors of the 1960s. As his fame grew, so did the interest in casting him as 007.

When Sean Connery announced he was leaving the role of Bond in 1966, producers Albert R. Broccoli and Harry Saltzman discussed casting Moore as Bond in *The Man With The Golden Gun*. The film was to have begun production soon after *You Only Live Twice* was completed, with Cambodia as a key locale. When political violence erupted in the country, the producers shelved the idea of making the film. Moore's commitment to *The Saint* prevented him from assuming the role when they decided to make *On Her Majesty's Secret Service* a year later. When the producers needed to replace George Lazenby, they again reached out to Moore, but his commitment to a new television series *The Persuaders* prevented him from taking the role. Finally, in 1972, the stars aligned, and Moore accepted the role of James Bond.

Roger Moore's first 007 film *Live And Let Die* significantly outgrossed

Connery's previous Bond, *Diamonds Are Forever*, firmly establishing Moore as a success as Bond. By the time Moore retired from the role of 007 in 1985, he had redefined the character of Bond and brought in over one billion dollars in worldwide box office. Moore earned a reputation for being an affable presence on the set, often engaging in practical jokes, or backgammon matches with producer Broccoli.

Moore continued to star in other films during his years as Bond, including numerous action-adventures, such as *Shout At The Devil* (1976) and *The Wild Geese* (1977). After 007, Moore continued to make film and television appearances, but at the request of his friend Audrey Hepburn, he began work as a Goodwill Ambassador for UNICEF (the United Nations International Children's Emergency Fund). Moore's work has taken him around the world, helping to raise money and awareness for global issues facing the planet's children. As James Bond, Roger Moore saved the world onscreen. As a UNICEF Goodwill Ambassador, his efforts have helped save real lives on a global scale.

After leaving military service, Roger Moore acted in various television and stage productions in London and New York. His New York work attracted the attention of MGM Studios, who signed him to a contract to begin work on April 1, 1954. His first significant role was in *The Last Time I Saw Paris* (1954) opposite Elizabeth Taylor. Moore quickly became friends with many top names in show business, including Frank Sinatra, a good friend of Bond producer Albert R. Broccoli. His contract lasted only three years, but it gave Moore a foothold in the film industry.

Moore appeared in many films in the 1950s, but he really made his mark on television. In 1957, he starred in *Ivanhoe*, which was followed by *The Alaskans, Maverick*, and then *The Saint*, which lasted from 1962 to 1969. Moore was one of the names considered for the role of James Bond in 1961 when Connery was cast. Moore's worldwide success

"I'm not that cold-blooded killer type. Which is why **I play it mostly for laughs.**"

TIMOTHY DALTON

OFFICIAL MISSIONS
The Living Daylights (1987),
Licence To Kill (1989)
BORN 21 March, 1946,
Colwyn Bay, Wales
FULL NAME Timothy Peter Dalton

Timothy Dalton approached the role of Bond with the desire to bring the character of 007 as written by Ian Fleming to the screen. Dalton made the role his own by rereading all the Fleming novels and emphasizing the undercurrent of bitterness and ruthlessness that he felt defined the literary Bond while still embracing Bond's élan and extraordinary skills and determination.

Timothy Dalton was born in the coastal town of Colwyn Bay in North Wales where his father was stationed during World War II. The oldest of five children, Dalton came from a show business family. Both of his grandfathers were vaudevillians, while his grandmother was a theatrical agent who was once a variety performer with Charlie Chaplin. In the late 1940s, Dalton's father moved his American wife and growing family to Belper in Derbyshire, England, near Manchester where he could work in advertising. This is where the young Dalton soon found himself attracted to the cinema. Dalton remembers seeing *The Red Beret* in 1953, and imitating the soldiers with his friends. *The Red Beret* was the first UK production of the future Bond producer Albert R. "Cubby" Broccoli. At the age of 16, Dalton saw a production of *Macbeth* at the famous Old Vic theater and decided that he wanted to become an actor.

Dalton began his training at London's Royal Academy of Dramatic Art (RADA) in 1964 and spent his summers studying at the National Youth Theatre. He made his debut on stage in Shakespeare's *Coriolanus* at the Queen's Theatre. He left RADA after almost two years and joined the Birmingham Repertory Theatre. Actor John Rhys-Davies, a classmate of Dalton's at RADA and later his co-star in The

> **" I tried to bring the movies back to something that was more like Ian Fleming. "**

Living Daylights, has commented on Dalton's incredible sexual presence on stage during the late 1960s and how women would wait outside the stage door for him.

It wasn't long before movie producers came calling. He made his film debut in 1968's *The Lion In Winter*, starring Peter O'Toole and Katharine Hepburn, and went on to star in such films as *Wuthering Heights* (1970), *Cromwell* (1970), and *Mary, Queen Of Scots* (1971). Dalton commented in 1987 that after these films, he had felt "the need to go back to the stage." Devoting himself to the theater, Dalton made only one film between 1972 and 1978.

In 1987, after being cast as Bond, Timothy Dalton spoke about his long path to slipping on the shoulder-holster. "When I was about 25, Mr. Broccoli kindly asked me if I would be interested in taking over from Sean Connery who was about to relinquish Bond," he recalled. "It was not a firm offer, but an expression of interest. Frankly, I thought it would have been a stupid move for me. I was too young—Bond should be between 35 and 40 years old." Dalton continued acting, playing a wide variety of roles. "Then, several years ago, when Roger Moore was uncertain about continuing as 007, I was approached again. The situation was very vague, there wasn't a script yet, and I had already been asked to do *Flash Gordon*. But I was pleased to have been considered. When I was asked in early 1986, I was unavailable. I was doing my own stage productions of *Antony And Cleopatra* and *The Taming Of The Shrew* so the schedules conflicted and the idea went out the window again." Dalton's inability to sign in early 1986 led the filmmakers to pursue Pierce Brosnan, but when Brosnan proved unavailable

> "I don't think anyone except the few people who have played James Bond can tell you how strange and special it is."

BETTER MAKE THAT TWO *(left) Bond prepares to spend some quality time with Linda (Kell Tyler) in* The Living Daylights.

GONE FISHING *007 uses a Coast Guard helicopter's winch to capture drug baron Franz Sanchez in mid-air in* Licence To Kill.

LATE ARRIVAL *(below center) In* Licence To Kill, *007 parachutes in to Felix and Della Leiter's wedding in Key West, Florida.*

PUT-UP JOB *In* The Living Daylights, *Bond "assassinates" General Pushkin at the North African Trade Convention.*

EYE ON THE TARGET *(left) In a deleted scene from* Licence To Kill, *Bond watches Franz Sanchez on TV in his Key West hotel room.*

AFGHAN NIGHTS *(right) In* The Living Daylights, *007 assures Kara Milovy (Maryam d'Abo) that she will see him again.*

owing to the renewal of his *Remington Steele* television contract, producers Cubby Broccoli and Michael G. Wilson returned to Dalton, who again had conflicts, as he was working on the film *Brenda Starr*, released in 1989. The producers agreed to delay the start of production of *The Living Daylights* if Dalton were willing to start immediately after *Starr* wrapped. Dalton accepted, becoming the fourth James Bond.

From the set of the TV mini-series *Scarlett* in April 1994, Dalton announced that he would not portray James Bond for a third time. He continued to alternate between film, television, and stage work. Highlights included the comedy *The Beautician And The Beast* (1997), the western *American Outlaws* (2001), the animated/live-action film *Looney Tunes: Back In Action* (2003), the television epics *Cleopatra* and *Hercules*, and the comedy *Hot Fuzz* (2007). On stage, Dalton portrayed Lord Asrael in Philip Pullman's *His Dark Materials* at London's National Theatre.

In 2014, Dalton starred with Bond alumni Eva Green, Rory Kinnear, and Helen McCrory in the *Penny Dreadful* TV series created by Bond screen writer John Logan and produced by Logan and Sam Mendes.

PIERCE BROSNAN

MISSIONS
GoldenEye (1995), Tomorrow Never Dies (1997), The World Is Not Enough (1999), Die Another Day (2002)
BORN 16 May, 1953, Drogheda, County Louth, Ireland
FULL NAME Pierce Brendan Brosnan

Pierce Brosnan successfully brought James Bond into the 1990s and the 21st Century. His portrayal of 007 in 1995's *GoldenEye* ensured Bond's relevance after the end of the Cold War, and the success of *Die Another Day* in 2002 showed 007's enduring appeal after 9/11.

Pierce Brendan Brosnan was born in Ireland in 1953. Pierce's father left his mother May shortly after the birth. When May moved to London to study nursing, Pierce was raised by his maternal grandparents. They died when Pierce was six, so various relatives raised him until boarding house owner Eileen Reilly took him into her home.

On the day Ian Fleming died, August 12, 1964, eleven year old Pierce arrived in London to live with his mother. One month later, his mother took him to see his first movie since arriving in England,

Goldfinger. Young Pierce was mesmerized by what he saw on the big screen. "I was an 11-year-old boy from the bogs of Ireland and there was this beautiful gold lady on a bed—naked. It made quite an impression on me," Brosnan recalled in 1995.

After attending Elliot School in London, Pierce worked as a commercial artist and a circus fire eater before studying at the London Drama Centre for three years. After graduating in 1976, he became assistant stage manager at the Theatre Royal, York, where he was handpicked by playwright Tennessee Williams to star in the British premiere of *The Red Devil Battery Sign*. Brosnan received rave reviews—his acting career had begun.

During this time, Brosnan fell in love with Australian actress Cassandra Harris, a divorced mother of two young children. They married on December 27, 1980, a few months after Cassandra had completed filming in Corfu as one of Bond's leading ladies in *For Your Eyes Only*. When

Pierce visited Cassandra on the set, a number of people, including producer Albert R. "Cubby" Broccoli and actor Julian Glover, felt that Brosnan had the looks and bearing of a future 007.

While in Corfu, Brosnan received the script for a six-hour US TV mini-series *The Manions Of America*. When he returned to London and auditioned, he won a key role.

The show aired on ABC in September 1981, and Pierce and Cassie flew to Hollywood for Pierce to go on a round of auditions. During the trip, Pierce and Cassie dined at Cubby Broccoli's house in Beverly Hills. Driving back to their hotel, Pierce couldn't resist attempting the famous line, "The name is Bond, James Bond."

Brosnan soon signed a seven year contract with NBC, and, in the fall of 1982, *Remington Steele* premiered. After *Octopussy* was released in cinemas in June 1983, Roger Moore made noises about retiring as Bond. In numerous polls asking who people thought should be the next 007, Brosnan won by a landslide. However, Moore announced that he would make another Bond film, *A View To A Kill*. Meanwhile, Brosnan enjoyed continued success as Steele as well as the personal joy of the birth of his son Sean in September 1983.

When Moore finally resigned from the role, the world's press touted numerous actors, including Pierce, as the next 007. NBC announced the cancellation of *Steele* on May 15, 1986—although the network kept a 60-day option to renew the show.

On the day of cancellation, *The New York Post* announced that Brosnan would become the fourth actor in the EON Bond series to play 007. As a result of all the publicity, summer reruns of *Steele* posted record-breaking ratings for the series. On July 15, 1986—the 59th day of the option period—NBC head Brandon Tartikoff changed his mind and renewed *Remington Steele*, just as Brosnan was celebrating his selection as the next Bond with Cubby. Although Tartikoff offered to film *Steele* in conjunction with the Bond film, Broccoli refused. On August 6, 1986, Timothy Dalton was announced as the fourth 007.

A devastated Brosnan made three *Remington Steele* TV movies before NBC cancelled the series. Brosnan pursued film roles, but heartbreak followed when his wife, Cassie, was diagnosed with cancer. Brosnan's career took a backseat while he helped care for his wife, who sadly passed away on December 28, 1991. Brosnan became an advocate for women's health issues, working with numerous charities and lobbying the US Congress for research funding for ovarian cancer.

On April 11, 1994, Timothy Dalton announced his resignation as Bond. Although Brosnan found himself again in negotiations to play Bond, Brosnan was reluctant to get his hopes up, despite numerous polls that showed him as the top choice to be the new 007. Finally, on June 1, 1994, at 12:35 p.m., Brosnan received a phone call from his agent, Fred Spektor, saying "Hello, Mr. Bond, you've got the part." At a press event on June 8, 1994 in London, producers Michael G. Wilson and Barbara Broccoli announced Brosnan as the fifth James Bond.

> ## "Bond is an enigma."
> ### Pierce Brosnan

DRESSED TO KILL
A tuxedo-clad Brosnan poses in the traditional 007 uniform for GoldenEye.

SURE SHOT *Lee Tamahori gives Brosnan direction while filming the virtual reality scene in* **Die Another Day.**

LOOKING COOL *Brosnan and Michelle Yeoh break from shooting the Saigon motorcycle chase, filmed in Bangkok in 110°F heat for* **Tomorrow Never Dies.**

Brosnan is married to Keely Shaye-Smith, and they have two children. He has his own production company, Irish Dreamtime and, since retiring as 007, has starred in diverse movies, including *Laws of Attraction* (2004), *After the Sunset* (2004), *The Matador* (2005), for which he was nominated for a Golden Globe for Best Actor in a Musical or Comedy, *Seraphim Falls* (2007), the smash-hit film adaptation of the Abba musical *Mamma Mia!* (2008), opposite Meryl Streep, Roman Polanski's *The Ghost Writer* (2010), and *The Love Punch* (2013), alongside Emma Thompson.

In July 2003, Queen Elizabeth II awarded Brosnan an honorary OBE (Order of the British Empire) for his "outstanding contribution to the British film industry." In September 2004, he became a citizen of the United States, although he has retained his Irish citizenship. He has also become an advocate for environmental issues, lending his name, time, and stature to a wide array of initiatives.

DANIEL CRAIG

OFFICIAL MISSIONS
Casino Royale (2006),
Quantum Of Solace (2008),
Skyfall (2012)
BORN 2 March, 1968,
Chester, England
FULL NAME
Daniel Wroughton Craig

"It is important that we see this character go places that excite you... For me, as a kid, the Bond movies transported you to another world."

BRAND NEW BOND *Daniel Craig wanted to develop and expand the role of Bond: "It's a question of taking it somewhere where it's never gone before."*

Daniel Craig redefined the character of James Bond in *Casino Royale* and *Quantum Of Solace,* stepping out of the shadows cast by his predecessors in the role and making 007 feel new, fresh, and dangerous. Craig brought a physical rawness, emotional focus, and darkly seductive air to Ian Fleming's creation; critics, fans, and moviegoers around the world embraced his interpretation, which has helped to make *Casino Royale, Quantum of Solace,* and *Skyfall* the three highest-grossing Bond films.

Daniel Craig decided that he wanted to be an actor at the age of six when his mother took him to the Everyman Theatre in Liverpool, England. At 16 he had made up his mind and applied to study at the National Youth Theatre in London. There he earned a reputation as a diverse and dedicated actor.

Craig appeared in numerous television productions, and in 1996 took a role in BBC television's political and social drama *Our Friends In The North.* In 1998, his performance as a petty crook who becomes the lover of the artist Francis Bacon in *Love Is The Devil* won critical accolades. The size and quality of the roles offered to him steadily grew, and he worked with such respected film directors as Steven Spielberg (*Munich*), Sam Mendes (*Road to Perdition*), and Roger Michell (*The Mother, Enduring Love*). The lead in the underworld thriller *Layer Cake* (2004) brought Craig worldwide acclaim. Three fans of the film were Michael G. Wilson and Barbara Broccoli, producers of the Bond films, and casting director Debbie McWilliams.

"He's a phenomenal

With the decision in early 2004 to recast the role of James Bond, the filmmakers' thoughts soon turned to Daniel Craig. Broccoli recalls, "When we decided we were going to make *Casino Royale*, it was obviously a big decision who we were going to use, and he [Craig] was always in the forefront of our minds." Craig was not so certain. Michael G. Wilson recalled, "He said to us, 'If I take this part, I will do it wholeheartedly. But I can't say I will till I've read the script.'" It was many months after that meeting before the script was completed, but the Bond producers kept in touch. When the filmmakers finally had a script they felt was ready to show, they sent it to Craig. "Once I sat down and read the story, I just thought that I wanted to tell this story," recalled Craig. "I'm a big Bond fan."

During 2005, MGM, the distributor of the Bond films, was sold to a consortium that included Sony Pictures, and Sony became the studio that would distribute *Casino Royale* around the globe. This meant the producers needed the approval of Sony's production executives on their choice for a new 007.

The screen test showed Craig's remarkable ability to transform himself into Bond and make the character his own. Sony chief production executive Amy Pascal watched the test and commented, "He has a kind of intensity, and a sexuality, and a roguishness." Sony gave the producers the green light to his casting, and on October 14, 2005, Daniel Craig arrived at the banks of the River Thames, stepped onto a

rigid raider boat piloted by a Royal Navy escort, and raced across the water to HMS *President* for his introduction to the world's media.

Just over 14 months later, Craig became the only 007 actor to have starred in a Bond film which took over $593 million in worldwide box office. Craig's portrayal of Bond has the sense that beneath the veneer of 007's implacable outer shell exists a dark, damaged, and extraordinary man. His remarkable transformation of the character has brought a new sense of emotional reality and danger to the Bond films.

After *Casino Royale's* release, Craig continued to take diverse film roles. He played the character of Lord Asriel in *The Golden Compass* (2007),

opposite Nicole Kidman. He also starred in and executive produced the film *Flashbacks of a Fool* (2008). Before filming *Quantum of Solace*, Craig played Jewish resistance leader Tuvia Bielski in Ed Zwick's World War II drama, *Defiance* (2008).

Between *Quantum of Solace* and *Skyfall*, Craig starred in *A Steady Rain* with Hugh Jackman on Broadway and in several films including *Cowboys & Aliens* (2011) and David Fincher's *The Girl with the Dragon Tattoo* (2011). After *Skyfall's* enormous success, he returned to Broadway to star in a production of Harold Pinter's play *Betrayal* directed by Mike Nichols and working alongside his wife, Rachel Weisz, and British actor Rafe Spall.

ACTION HERO *(above) Craig performed many of his own stunts in* Casino Royale.

OUT IN THE OPEN *(below) Bond goes after Dominic Greene in Bolivia in* Quantum of Solace.

"If you don't get bruised playing Bond, you're not doing it properly."

STOPPING AT NOTHING *(left) Bond borrows a Turkish merchant's Honda bike to pursue the assassin Patrice in* Skyfall.

BOND
VILLAINS

"Goodbye, Mr. Bond." The absolute certainty with which Goldfinger dismisses 007 is but the pride that goeth before the fall. All Bond villains must fail in their schemes, but still, let us pay our respects to the greatest minds to ever twist an evil plot. Bond villains are towering figures, billionaires, captains of industry, born leaders, visionaries. Bond villains such as Ernst Stavro Blofeld, Karl Stromberg, and Hugo Drax embark upon monumental undertakings that could only be realized by individuals capable of changing the world. That is their dream. To accomplish it, to wipe away our comfortable lives in one stroke, they employ hordes of slavishly devoted henchmen, drawn to their magnetic personalities. On the following pages, meet the men and women whose ambitions proved too big for this world.

ADAM

APPEARANCE
Live And Let Die (1973)
STATUS Dead; killed in a boating accident while pursuing 007
CHARACTERISTICS Stern, determined
PLAYED BY Tommy Lane

Dr. Kananga/Mr. Big henchman Adam confronts Bond at Lakeside Airport. Bond escapes in a speedboat headed for the Irish Bayou, and Adam pursues him by car. Adam first eludes Sheriff Pepper, then steals the fastest boat on the river from Pepper's brother-in-law, Billy Bob. Adam chases Bond through the bayou until Bond throws fuel in Adam's eyes and his boat crashes into the rusting hulk of a ship.

ALVAREZ, DR.

APPEARANCE
Die Another Day (2002)
STATUS Dead; shot by Jinx
CHARACTERISTICS Proud, pompous
PLAYED BY Simón Andreu

Based in a clinic on Los Organos off the coast of Cuba, Dr. Alvarez is a leader in the field of gene therapy, genetically transforming individuals into other races. He also "increases the life expectancy of our beloved leaders and the richest westerners." Having successfully transformed Colonel Moon into Gustav Graves, Alvarez is in the process of turning North Korean Zao into a Caucasian when NSA agent Jinx assassinates him and destroys his clinic with a cell phone bomb.

LAST WORDS *Dr. Alvarez explains that his research depends on a supply of healthy donors, such as "orphans, runaways, people that won't be missed." He believes NSA agent Jinx is a new patient, but she is his assassin.*

APOLLO JET CREW

APPEARANCE
Moonraker (1979)
STATUS Pilot dead; fate of hostess unknown
CHARACTERISTICS Service—and death—with a smile
PLAYED BY Jean-Pierre Castaldi (pilot), Leila Shenna (hostess)

The villainous Apollo jet crew hijack Bond's chartered Dakar—London flight. They hope to stage a plane crash in which Bond's body will be found. After kissing Bond, the hostess produces a gun and trades her weapon for a parachute held by the pilot, who shoots out the controls. Bond shoves the pilot out of the plane, but is then himself pushed out by Jaws. Bond skydives after the pilot, steals his parachute, and evades Jaws. The pilot dies on impact, although the hostess probably survives.

HAVE A SAFE FLIGHT *The flight crew on Apollo demonstrates the proper use of a parachute in case of an in-flight emergency.*

APOSTIS

APPEARANCE
For Your Eyes Only (1981)
STATUS Dead; killed by Bond
CHARACTERISTICS Silent, restrained, merciless, relentless
PLAYED BY Jack Klaff

Apostis serves not only as a chauffeur for intelligence informant Kristatos, but also as a fierce killer in Kristatos's organization. Kristatos invites Bond to utilize Apostis as a chauffeur one evening and Apostis apparently informs Kristatos and killer Emile Locque of Bond's location, resulting in an attack that causes the death of Columbo's mistress Countess Lisl Von Schlaf.

Bond confronts Apostis when climbing to Kristatos's clifftop hideaway. Apostis kicks Bond over a cliff and begins to dislodge the pitons securing Bond's climbing ropes. Bond hurls a piton into Apostis, causing him to fall to his death.

ARKOV, DR.

APPEARANCE
The World Is Not Enough (1999)
STATUS Dead; identity used by others
CHARACTERISTICS Apprehensive, hesitant, worried, distressed
PLAYED BY Jeff Nuttall

A scientist in league with terrorist Renard and Elektra King, Arkov provides Renard with the Parahawks that attack Bond. However, when Bond destroys the Parahawks, Arkov blames the failure to kill Bond on Elektra's sidekick Davidov. Renard has Arkov killed for failing "his test of devotion." Bond later uses Arkov's identity to enter a nuclear site in Kazakhstan.

ASIAN CARTEL

APPEARANCE
Licence To Kill (1989)
STATUS Living; whereabouts unknown
CHARACTERISTICS Ruthless but cowardly; eager to profit from drugs trade, but unwilling to get hands dirty
PLAYED BY Unknown

Drug lord Franz Sanchez hopes to create an Asian drug cartel with members from Japan, Taiwan, South Korea, and Malaysia. To create a drug empire from Chile to Alaska, Sanchez prepares to grant them exclusive cocaine franchises in Asian territories and guarantee prices for five years. At the Olympatec Meditation Institute, he asks each cartel member to pay $100 million in negotiable bearer bonds. When Bond destroys the institute, the members escape.

BAMBI & THUMPER

APPEARANCE
Diamonds Are Forever (1971)
STATUS Arrested by the CIA
CHARACTERISTICS Great gymnasts, powerful hand-to-hand combatants
PLAYED BY Lola Larson (Bambi), Trina Parks (Thumper)

Bambi and Thumper work for the unscrupulous casino manager Bert Saxby and less directly Ernst Stavro Blofeld. They guard millionaire recluse Willard Whyte, keeping him a prisoner in his desert home.

When James Bond arrives, Bambi and Thumper greet him with mocking insouciance and seductive warmth. It is all just a ploy to get Bond in a position where they can hurt him. Both trained gymnasts, they use their lithe but powerful bodies to knock Bond around. After throwing Bond into a pool, they dive in after him, only to discover that Bond's superior swimming skills put them both at a grave disadvantage. Rather than drown, they confess Whyte's true location before Felix Leiter and CIA agents arrest them.

BARSOV, SERGEI

APPEARANCE
The Spy Who Loved Me (1977)
STATUS Killed by Bond
CHARACTERISTICS Experienced KGB agent and assassin; superb skier
PLAYED BY Michael Billington

KGB agent Sergei Barsov attempts to chase and shoot James Bond on skis near Berngarten in the Austrian Alps, but Bond whirls around and eliminates him with a ski-pole rocket gun. Despite his death, Barsov still poses a danger to Bond. On his next mission, Bond finds himself working with Major Anya Amasova, Barsov's former lover.

GUNNING FOR BOND *KGB agent Sergei Barsov, the lover of Major Anya Amasova, takes on 007 in the Austrian Alps and loses.*

Bambi: Hi, there. I'm Bambi. Thumper: And I'm Thumper. Is there something we can do for you?

BLOFELD, ERNST STAVRO

APPEARANCES From Russia With Love (1963), Thunderball (1965), You Only Live Twice (1967), On Her Majesty's Secret Service (1969), Diamonds Are Forever (1971), For Your Eyes Only (1981)

STATUS Presumed dead

CHARACTERISTICS A brilliant criminal mind; ruthless, calculating, enigmatic, snobbish, messianic, erudite

PLAYED BY Anthony Dawson (body in From Russia With Love, Thunderball), Eric Pohlmann (voice in From Russia With Love, Thunderball), Donald Pleasence (You Only Live Twice), Telly Savalas (On Her Majesty's Secret Service), Charles Gray (Diamonds Are Forever), John Hollis (body in For Your Eyes Only), Robert Rietty (voice in For Your Eyes Only)

Ernst Stavro Blofeld, founder of the terrorist organization SPECTRE, remains one of the greatest geniuses in the history of crime. He would be one of the world's richest and most influential men if it were not for James Bond. Blofeld has hijacked hydrogen bombs, built two operational space weapons, and developed a powerful bacteriological weapon. He has mounted numerous smaller criminal operations and inspired slavish loyalty in hundreds of associates, many of whom have been willing to go to their deaths on his behalf. He eluded capture for years. MI6 even launched a major campaign to capture or kill Blofeld—Operation Bedlam—which ended

> "Allow me to introduce myself.
> I am **Ernst Stavro Blofeld.**"

with uncertain results.

Blofeld has the remarkable ability to significantly alter his appearance, both in the James Bond novels and films. According to Fleming, Blofeld was born on 28 May, 1908 in what is now Gdynia, Poland to a Greek mother and Polish father. Athletic as a youth, he competed in amateur weight-lifting contests. Blofeld studied economics and political history at the University of Warsaw. Realizing that wealth and power flow to those who have early access to information, he took a job at the Ministry of Posts and Telegraphs. In the build-up to World War II, Blofeld, using top secret communications, formed a fictional spy network—TARTAR—and began selling secrets. He sold to the Germans, the Americans, and the Swedish, amassing a small fortune.

Blofeld destroyed his birth records and left Poland before Germany invaded. In Istanbul, Blofeld worked for Ankara Radio. Once it became clear that the Germans were losing

FIRST APPEARANCE *Blofeld briefs subordinates Rosa Klebb, Morzeny, and Kronsteen in* **From Russia With Love.**

the war, he set up another fake spy ring and sold government communications to the Allies. Blofeld finished the war rich and decorated by the Allies.

After years in South America, Blofeld returned to Europe ready to make his mark. He formed SPECTRE, which made him tremendously powerful.

By the early years of SPECTRE, he weighed roughly 280 lbs and sported a crew-cut. His eyes showed whites all the way around above a squat nose. A mere two years later, Blofeld looked very different. His now long, white hair was carefully groomed. He had lost over 100 lbs, and his formerly even voice sounded more animated. His eyes looked normal behind green contacts and his nose, reshaped by surgery, appeared aquiline but damaged by tertiary syphilis. Nine months later, Blofeld had again altered his

FACE TO FACE *Cradling his white Persian cat, Blofeld confronts Bond in SPECTRE's volcano rocket base.*

COUNT DOWN *Blofeld briefly showed a romantic side to Tracy in* On Her Majesty's Secret Service.

MAN OF MYSTERY *An attack on Bond in* For Your Eyes Only *may or may not have been masterminded by Blofeld.*

appearance, repairing the damage to his nose and growing a drooping black mustache. The literary Blofeld dies at the end of the novel *You Only Live Twice*, when Bond strangles him at his Castle of Death in Japan.

In the films, Blofeld first appears in *From Russia With Love*, demonstrating his philosophy of letting two competing forces think they are battling each other before opportunistically attacking the weakened victor. He has medium length black hair, but his face remains unseen. He wears a signet ring with an octopus design and strokes a white Persian cat that reflects his relaxed but predatory indifference to all that surrounds him.

The Blofeld of *Thunderball* is nearly bald, lean, and fit. He is briefly glimpsed, face obscured, at the SPECTRE board meeting in Paris, once again stroking his white cat.

In *You Only Live Twice*, Blofeld moves his operation to Japan where,

> "I shall look forward personally to exterminating you, Mr. Bond."

with financing from Communist China, he builds a rocket base inside a hollowed-out volcano. When he reveals his face to Bond for the first time, he has a scar down the right cheek and around one eye. Wearing a traditional Mao jacket and slacks, he obsessively strokes his cat. His decrepit physique appears to be an outward expression of his mental perversions.

By *On Her Majesty's Secret Service*, Blofeld is unscarred, physically robust and sexually aggressive. He confidently fights, skis, and handles a bobsled. In *Diamonds Are Forever*, Blofeld not only endures numerous plastic surgeries, but also convinces many others to have their appearance and voice altered to double him. He seems to have modeled his looks on

Dikko Henderson, Bond's contact in Japan in *You Only Live Twice*—if, in fact, the character Bond battles at the end of the film *is* Blofeld. Certainly the assassination attempt on Bond at the end of *Diamonds Are Forever* after Blofeld's apparent demise would seem to imply that the master criminal may have survived through sheer stamina or cunning.

In *For Your Eyes Only*, a wheelchair-bound, bald man holding a white cat attempts to assassinate Bond. Despite his physical similarity to Blofeld from *On Her Majesty's Secret Service*, it is unclear if the man in the wheelchair is indeed the notorious mastermind. It is possible Blofeld has gone half-mad while plotting Bond's death, totally losing his sophisticated veneer. He makes brittle jokes for his own pleasure and laughs maniacally. Despite being dropped down a gasworks chimney, no positive identification has ever been made of Blofeld's corpse. His ultimate fate remains a mystery.

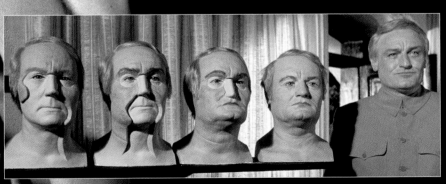

CHANGING FACES *A series of medical models reveals the extent of Blofeld's plastic surgery from* You Only Live Twice *to* Diamonds Are Forever.

SWORN ENEMIES *Bond eliminates one of Blofeld's doubles at the beginning of* Diamonds Are Forever. *Thinking he has avenged the murder of his wife, Bond soon finds he has a seemingly limitless number of Blofelds to kill.*

A LADY'S TOUCH *Boitier, dressed in drag for his own funeral, attacks 007 with a poker.*

BOITIER, COL. JACQUES

APPEARANCE
Thunderball (1965)
STATUS Beaten, whipped, and throttled
CHARACTERISTICS Looks good in
a dress
PLAYED BY Rose Alba, Bob Simmons

SPECTRE No. 6, Colonel Jacques Boitier (pronounced "Boovarr"), is a murderer of two British Secret Service agents. The wealthy Boitier attempts to alter his identity and thus elude authorities and James Bond. He stages his own death and poses as his widow at the funeral. Bond becomes aware of his deception and waits for the Colonel in the drawing room of his chateau. There, the two engage in a brutal fight, destroying many priceless antiques in Boitier's collection. Bond eventually kills Boitier with a fire poker, choking the life out of him over the hearth.

> " My dear Colonel Boitier, I don't think you should have opened that car door by yourself. "
> 007 to Boitier

NICE MOVES *Bonita dances the tarantella before an explosion at Mr. Ramirez's heroin lab interrupts her show.*

BONITA

APPEARANCE
Goldfinger (1964)
STATUS Living; whereabouts unknown
CHARACTERISTICS Deceitful dancer
PLAYED BY Nadja Regin

Bonita, a young woman from Turkey, dances the tarantella at the El Scorpio nightclub in coastal Mexico. She works with Mr. Ramirez, a major heroin smuggler with a local base of operations. After Bond destroys a heroin lab at the Ramirez Export Compania grounds, he visits Bonita, only to discover she has enticed him into a trap in her dressing room. As Bond and Bonita embrace, Bond sees a capungo—a Mexican thug—reflected in Bonita's eyes. Bond flings her into the path of the capungo's cosh, knocking her out. After killing the Mexican bandit, Bond leaves Bonita nursing her sore head.

BRANDT, HELGA

APPEARANCE
You Only Live Twice (1967)
STATUS Dead; fed to piranhas
CHARACTERISTICS Cunning, but
not ruthless enough for SPECTRE
PLAYED BY Karin Dor

SPECTRE No. 11, Helga Brandt, is the confidential secretary to chemical tycoon and SPECTRE operative, Mr. Osato. An accomplished pilot, seductress, and murderess, she aids Ernst Stavro Blofeld in his plot to launch World War III on behalf of the Communist Chinese.

Brandt first meets Bond when he poses as Mr. Fisher, managing director of Empire Chemicals. She knows Bond engaged in the theft of documents in Osato's office the previous night, yet Brandt and Osato are uncertain of Bond's real identity, believing earlier newspaper reports of his death in Hong Kong. After the meeting, Osato orders Brandt to kill "Mr. Fisher," and she tries to accomplish this with a carload of assassins and no fewer than 25 assailants at the Kobe docks. When she captures Bond, Brandt insists on questioning him herself and pretends to be seduced. Bond claims to be an industrial spy and offers her $150,000 to help him escape. Brandt flies him to Tokyo the next day but, airborne, she triggers a device to pin Bond in his seat, tosses a lipstick magnesium flare into the cockpit and parachutes away, sending Bond to what she believes will be certain doom. Later, Brandt and Osato learn from Blofeld that Mr. Fisher is in fact James Bond and is very much alive. Blaming Brandt for the failure to eliminate Bond, Blofeld feeds her to a school of hungry piranhas.

BRAUN

APPEARANCE Licence To Kill (1989)
STATUS Fried
CHARACTERISTICS Silent; obeys orders without question
PLAYED BY Guy De Saint Cyr

NO HEART *Braun holds Lupe Lamora's boyfriend Alvarez helpless.*

Braun is a henchman of drug lord Franz Sanchez. With Sanchez, Perez, and Dario, he participates in the murder of Alvarez, lover of Sanchez's girlfriend Lupe. He also aids in the stabbing of Della Leiter and the maiming of Felix Leiter. When Sanchez's security chief, Heller, tries to steal Sanchez's stinger missiles, Braun drives a forklift blade through Heller's chest. Later, on a winding road, Braun's flame-engulfed truck careens off a cliff, just missing Pam Bouvier's plane.

BULL, THE

APPEARANCE
The World Is Not Enough (1999)
STATUS Dead; shot by Zukovsky
CHARACTERISTICS Smug, cocky, deceitful; not as tough as he looks
PLAYED BY Goldie

The Bull, alias Mr. Bullion, works for Valentin Zukovsky as his bodyguard. He is secretly in the employ of Elektra King and her terrorist lover, Renard.

When Elektra is convinced Bond has died in an explosion, The Bull calls to inform her that Bond is in fact alive. Elektra orders an attack on Bond and Dr. Christmas Jones at Zukovsky's caviar factory. When this fails, The Bull sabotages the Istanbul building where Bond, Jones, and Valentin meet. The explosion injures Valentin, but Bond and Christmas escape. The Bull captures Bond and Jones and takes them to Elektra's base at Maiden's Tower, Istanbul. Zukovsky soon arrives and promptly shoots The Bull.

NAME CHANGE *In an early script draft, The Bull was known as "The Boa."*

BUNT, IRMA

APPEARANCE On Her Majesty's Secret Service (1969)
STATUS Living; whereabouts unknown
CHARACTERISTICS Humorless and determined; blindly loyal to Blofeld
PLAYED BY Ilse Steppat

Irma Bunt is the personal secretary of Ernst Stavro Blofeld. She actively participates in his plot to threaten the world with the biological warfare agent, Virus Omega.

Bunt watches over the female allergy patients at Bolfeld's clinic, Piz Gloria. To help Blofeld secure an hereditary title, she escorts James Bond (posing as Sir Hilary Bray of the Royal College of Arms), to Blofeld's mountain clinic. After Blofeld learns from British agent Campbell that Bray is in fact James Bond, Bunt aids in his capture. She sneaks into Ruby Bartlett's bed where she knows Bond will come to visit. When Bond enters, she has a guard knock him over the head with a nightstick.

After Bond escapes Piz Gloria on skis and arrives in the village below, Bunt supervises the pursuit, but she narrowly escapes with her life when her car overturns and explodes. When Bond marries Tracy, it is Bunt, not Blofeld, who fires the machine gun burst that kills Bond's bride.

Irma Bunt appears in the novels *On Her Majesty's Secret Service* and *You Only Live Twice*. In the former, Bond quickly becomes annoyed with her and it is "quite an effort to restrain his right shoe from giving Irma Bunt a really tremendous kick in her tight, bulging behind."

In the latter, Bond knocks her unconscious in a Kyushu castle, strangles Blofeld to death, and then rigs a geyser to destroy the castle.

"Bunt. Interesting name... Nautical term meaning the baggy or swollen parts of a sail. **Nothing personal, of course.**"
007 to Bunt

BUTCHER, PROFESSOR JOE

APPEARANCE
Licence To Kill (1989)

STATUS Living, still blessing people's hearts for cash

CHARACTERISTICS Lecherous conman

PLAYED BY Wayne Newton

American televangelist Professor Joe Butcher, whose catchphrase is "Bless your hearts," secretly works as a cocaine price fixer for drug baron Franz Sanchez. The author of a self-help book, *The Secrets Of Cone Power Revealed*, Butcher hosts his television program from the Olympatec Meditation Institute near Isthmus City. The Institute also houses Sanchez's cocaine labs. Butcher helps set the price of Sanchez's cocaine in an ingenious way.

When Butcher announces a fundraising goal for his meditation chapters, he is actually informing drug dealers around the world of the current month's cost per kilo. The drug dealers then call 555 LOVE with their orders disguised as pledges. CIA contract pilot Pam Bouvier pretends to be infatuated with Butcher to gain access to the cocaine labs and help Bond destroy Sanchez's operation.

TV SHOPPING *A pledge of $100 to Professor Butcher's Institute secures the pledger a copy of his book, valued at $49.95, for free.*

CAPUNGO

APPEARANCE
Goldfinger (1964)

STATUS Dead, gone in a flash

CHARACTERISTICS Brutal, evil

PLAYED BY Alf Joint

"A capungo is a bandit who will kill for as little as forty pesos," writes Ian Fleming in the novel *Goldfinger*. In the film, the capungo, a thug working for the heroin producer and smuggler Mr. Ramirez, attacks Bond in the dressing room of the tarantella dancer Bonita in an unnamed coastal Mexican town. Bond spies the capungo's reflection in Bonita's betraying eyes as he sneaks up behind with a club. Bond hurls Bonita into the path of the club, then, after a brutal fight, tosses the thug into Bonita's filled bathtub, knocking in a portable heater and electrocuting the capungo with a crackling flash.

SNEAK ATTACK
The capungo prepares to strike, but Bond is not to be caught off guard so easily.

CARLOS

APPEARANCE
Casino Royale (2006)

STATUS Dead, detonated

CHARACTERISTICS Silent, cold, skilled driver under pressure

PLAYED BY Claudio Santamaria

Carlos contracts with Dimitrios to destroy the Skyfleet S570 prototype passenger plane in Miami. With a uniform, ID and pass code, Carlos enters the secure area of the airport and sets off fire alarms, using the distraction to steal a tanker truck. Armed with a detonator disguised as a keyfob (triggered by his mobile phone), he can turn the truck into a powerful bomb.

Bond tracks and chases Carlos, resulting in a brutal fight as the tanker truck races for the plane. Although Carlos leaps to safety and

Bond stops the truck short of the plane, both men know the keyfob detonator could still ignite a lethal explosion. After entering the trigger code, Carlos discovers the keyfob is attached not to the tanker, but to his own pants. His fiery death prompts a wry smile from 007.

CARVER, ELLIOT

APPEARANCE
Tomorrow Never Dies (1997)
STATUS Dead; according to press
reports, committed suicide
CHARACTERISTICS Power-hungry,
flamboyant, seething with rage
PLAYED BY Jonathan Pryce

Worldwide media mogul Elliot
Carver may be the most powerful
man on the planet. According to
James Bond, Carver can "topple
governments with a single broadcast."
This stylish villain plans to create war
between Britain and China and
install a sympathetic government in
China that will grant his Carver
Media Group Network (CMGN)
exclusive satellite transmission rights
for the next 100 years.

Carver was born in Hong Kong,
the illegitimate son of a German

woman, who died in childbirth, and
press tycoon Lord Roverman. A
Chinese family subsequently paid
£50 for the boy. Aged 16, he went to
work for a Hong Kong paper, whose
editor taught him the key to any
great story: "Why?"

When he turned
30, Carver took
revenge against his
father by building a
rival chain of
newspapers that
drove Roverman to
bankruptcy and
suicide.

Now in his fifties,
Carver, nicknamed
"The Emperor of the Air" by his
wife Paris, lives the life of a media
baron. He views himself as a
modern-day Caesar or Napoleon;
instead of legions and armies, he
commands television channels,
newspapers, magazines, and 8,000

MEDIA MOGUL *Carver proudly announces
the launch of his satellite news network.*

journalists in 132 countries. He uses
information as a weapon. For
example, he hopes to blackmail a US
President into signing a bill lowering
cable rates by
threatening to release a
compromising tape of
him with a cheerleader.
After the President
signs, Carver releases
the tape anyway.

Carver has
everything he could
want except for
exclusive broadcasting
rights in China.
Working from a stealth ship invisible
to radar, Carver uses a stolen GPS
encoder to send HMS *Devonshire* off
course into Vietnamese waters. The
Chinese, believing the ship is in their
waters, respond by sending two MiG
fighters to fly over the *Devonshire*.

> "Words are the
> new weapons,
> **satellites**
> the new artillery."
>
> **Elliot Carver**

Carver orders the sinking of the ship
with his Sea-Vac underwater drill and
the killing of any survivors. He also
orders the shooting down of a
Chinese MiG fighter.

Searching through the wreckage of
the *Devonshire*, Carver's men recover
a Tomahawk-class missile, which
Carver plans to fire at the building
hosting an emergency meeting of the
Chinese high command in Beijing.
A member of the high command,
General Chang, who is in league
with Carver, will deliberately delay
his arrival, allowing him to survive
the attack and ascend to power.

The suspiciously early reporting by
Carver's media empire of the
Devonshire's sinking, plus the fact that
his satellites were the source for the
GPS signals that sent the ship off
course, make Carver and his media
empire the focus of British and
Chinese investigations, led by James
Bond and Colonel Wai Lin.

Bond's past relationship with
Carver's wife Paris makes Bond a
particular target of Carver's wrath,
resulting in Carver ordering the
murders of Paris and Bond. When
Bond steals the incriminating GPS
encoder, Carver pulls no punches
trying to have Bond killed. Carver
fails and his men later find Bond and
Wai Lin searching the wreckage of
the *Devonshire*.

Carver confronts Bond in Vietnam,
but once again fails to kill him and
Wai Lin before they escape.
Regardless, Carver travels to his
stealth ship to instigate his war. Bond
and Wai Lin infiltrate the ship and
Bond eventually kills Carver using
the Sea-Vac drill to chew him to
pieces. The media report that Carver
has committed suicide on his luxury
yacht in the South China Sea.

CARVER, ROSIE

APPEARANCE
Live And Let Die (1973)
STATUS Killed by Kananga's scarecrows
CHARACTERISTICS naive secret agent, naive double agent, very superstitious
PLAYED BY Gloria Hendry

Rosie Carver works as a double agent for Dr. Kananga, prime minister of the Caribbean island of San Monique. Kananga, as "Mr. Big," schemes to corner the US drugs market with supplies of heroin produced on the island. Rosie feeds his organization valuable intelligence from her other job—field agent for the CIA. She does little to inspire confidence from James Bond. Her superstition and fear seem genuine, but her motivations remain unclear.

Rosie takes the liberty of checking into Bond's San Monique hotel as his wife and tries to sneak into his suite with her Smith & Wesson .38 drawn. Rosie later finds a voodoo sign in her bedroom—a small top hat with bloody feathers—and is so frightened that she begs Bond not to leave her alone for the night.

The next morning, Bond receives a Queen of Cups tarot card in an upside-down position (anonymously sent by Solitaire)—a sign that Rosie is not to be trusted. Bond and Rosie travel by boat to Kananga's plantation, and Bond tries to get her to take him to the spot in the hills where the authorities recovered the body of Baines, another British agent (whom Rosie, on her first CIA assignment, previously betrayed). Rosie appears afraid and confused, although her assignment from Kananga is clear: to lead Bond into a trap.

After making love to Rosie in a jungle clearing, Bond confronts her with the incriminating tarot card. She says she dare not tell him anything saying, "They'll kill me if I do." When Bond aims his gun at her, Rosie runs away in a panic. A gun concealed in the mouth of one of Kananga's scarecrows shoots her dead.

CHANG

APPEARANCE
Moonraker (1979)
STATUS Dead; fell through a clockface
CHARACTERISTICS Good at aikido and other martial arts, but not good enough
PLAYED BY Toshiro Suga

TIME TO KILL *Bond and Chang fight to the finish in Venice's historic Torre dell'Orologio. Chang's death prompts Hugo Drax to hire a new henchman, Jaws.*

Chang is billionaire Hugo Drax's loyal manservant and hitman. Drax orders him to prevent Bond from prying into his affairs. Chang's first attempt to kill Bond occurs when he deliberately over-revs a centrifuge Bond tests at Drax's technical facilities. Later, Chang releases Drax's pet Doberman dogs to hunt and kill Bond's ally and lover, Corinne Dufour, in the woods of Drax's country estate.

Finally, Chang, dressed in full Aikido gear, confronts Bond outside the showrooms of Venini Glass in Piazza San Marcos, Venice. He battles Bond inside the gallery, smashing shelves of priceless glassworks. The fight proceeds into the Torre dell'Orologio—the St. Mark's Clocktower—where Bond throws Chang through the famed stained-glass clockface. Chang crashes down onto a grand piano, fatally disrupting a classical music recital.

> "Look after Mr Bond. See that **some harm** comes to him."
>
> **Drax to Chang**

CHULA

APPEARANCE
The Man With The Golden Gun (1974)
STATUS Living
CHARACTERISTICS Karate expert
PLAYED BY "Charlie" Chan Yiu Lam I

MARTIAL ARTIST *Bond is faced by Chula, the star of Hai Fat's school. Fortunately, Bond has a few moves Chula does not anticipate.*

After being knocked unconscious by Scaramanga's assistant, Nick Nack, Bond awakens at a Bangkok martial arts academy run by tycoon Hai Fat. Bond soon realizes he is to be used as sport by assassins–in–training at the academy. After Bond seriously injures one student in an initial bout, the others chant for Chula, the school's most deadly student, who sits at the right hand of the master. Chula initially inflicts a great deal of pain on Bond but, using judo and kick-boxing techniques, Bond floors him. While Chula recovers, Bond breaks out of the fighting school. After Bond's ally Lt. Hip and his nieces, Cha and Nara, battle a swarm of pursuing students, Bond steals a longtail boat and races down Bangkok's klongs with Chula and other students in pursuit. Bond eventually lies in wait and, when Chula and crew stop, guns his engine and splits their boat in two. Chula is last seen flailing in the klong as Bond drives safely away.

CIGAR GIRL

APPEARANCE
The World Is Not Enough (1999)
STATUS Dead; blown to pieces
CHARACTERISTICS Accomplished assassin; totally committed to the cause
PLAYED BY Maria Grazia Cucinotta

KILLER ON THE RIVER *The assassin known as Cigar Girl takes aim at 007 during a chase on the river Thames.*

The Cigar Girl is the nickname for an extremely accomplished assassin working for anarchist Renard. She is first seen bringing Bond a cigar in Lachaise's office in Bilbao, Spain. Just as Lachaise is about to reveal to Bond the identity of the person who sold Sir Robert King a stolen Soviet Atomic Energy Commission report, she expertly throws a knife, hitting Lachaise in the neck.

After an explosion inside the MI6 building blasts a massive hole in a wall facing the River Thames, Bond spots the Cigar Girl on board a Sunseeker powerboat. She fires at Bond, but misses him.

Determined to catch her, Bond jumps into a prototype Q boat and speeds out of the rubble onto the

Cigar Girl: Would you like to check my figures?

007: Oh, I'm sure they're perfectly rounded.

Thames in pursuit. Bond and the Cigar Girl engage in a hair-raising high-speed chase, each attempting to outmaneuver the other. Spotting the launch of a hot-air balloon at the nearby Millennium Dome, Cigar Girl beaches her vessel and leaps out of the boat, shooting the balloon pilot.

As she ascends in the balloon, Bond jumps the Q boat into the air and seizes one of the balloon's tethers. Bond offers to protect her if she will reveal the identity of her employer. But the Cigar Girl, believing that Bond would never be able to protect her from Renard, fires a bullet into a propane gas tank, blowing herself up. Bond falls onto the Millennium Dome roof, dislocating his collar bone.

COLONEL OF POLICE

APPEARANCE
Quantum Of Solace (2008)
STATUS Dead; shot by 007
CHARACTERISTICS Calm, deceitful, money-grabbing
PLAYED BY Fernando Guillén-Cuervo

Bolivian Colonel of Police Carlos partners with Dominic Greene and General Medrano, unbeknownst to old friend René Mathis. After ordering Mathis's death, he receives a large payoff from Greene to ignore the upcoming Bolivian political coup. Bond kills Carlos, reminding him the two had a "mutual friend."

CONLEY, BOB

APPEARANCE
A View To A Kill (1985)
STATUS Mining disaster victim
CHARACTERISTICS Corrupt
PLAYED BY Manning Redwood

Bob Conley works as Max Zorin's mining engineer for Operation Main Strike. In addition, he handles Zorin's oil interests in the East Bay. Before linking with Zorin, Conley worked as chief engineer for a South African gold mine where a cave-in killed 20 miners. This led to his hasty departure from South Africa.

When Conley realizes that Zorin intends to betray assassin May Day and his fellow loyal miners, he objects. Zorin's chief henchman Scarpine knocks Conley unconscious, and he drowns in the flooding of the mine.

DAMBALA

APPEARANCE
Live And Let Die (1973)
STATUS Dead; shot by 007
CHARACTERISTICS Good with reptiles; has a flair for showmanship
PLAYED BY Michael Ebbin

Dambala is the high priest of a voodoo cult on the Caribbean island of San Monique. He dresses in a goat's head cowl and performs deadly rituals at the behest of Kananga, the island's despotic ruler.

Dambala does not participate in any of the more mundane criminal activities associated with Kananga's plot to flood the US with heroin. His role is to perform ceremonial sacrifices of anyone that Kananga wishes to have killed, such as the British secret agent Baines.

Dambala's voodoo ceremonies involve him leading crowds of excited believers in trance-like dancing and chanting. Dambala then carefully selects a poisonous snake from a coffin and waves the snake in the face of his victim until the enraged creature strikes. Fortunately, Bond arrives in time to prevent Dambala visiting this grisly fate on the beautiful Solitaire.

DARIO

APPEARANCE
Licence To Kill (1989)
STATUS Pulverized
CHARACTERISTICS Cocky, menacing, pitiless; handy with a knife
PLAYED BY Benicio Del Toro

Dario works as a key enforcer for Franz Sanchez, a Central American drug lord. Sanchez treats Dario, the youngest member of his inner circle, like a younger brother.

Dario demonstrates his skill with a Bowie knife when he arrives in Cray Cay with Sanchez to retrieve the drug lord's girlfriend, Lupe Lamora. Dario removes the heart of her illicit lover, Alvarez, and provides Sanchez with a "little valentine." After DEA agent Felix Leiter, who has been hunting Sanchez for years, finally captures him, Dario exacts revenge by stabbing Della, Felix's bride. Dario then helps Sanchez lower Leiter into a shark tank.

Dario acquires Leiter's secret files and eliminates all of Leiter's contacts in his investigation of Sanchez except one—Pam Bouvier. Dario travels to the Barrelhead Bar in Bimini to kill her and shoots her in the back as she speeds away in a boat with 007. Dario thinks she is dead, unaware that her Kevlar vest stopped the bullets.

When Bond participates in a tour of Sanchez's drug processing plant, Dario reconizes him. His cover exposed, Bond sets the lab ablaze, but Sanchez captures and interrogates him. When Bond refuses to speak, Dario throw him onto a conveyor belt leading to a pulverizer. Before Dario can kill Bond, Pam appears through the cocaine mist and Dario momentarily thinks she is a ghost. Pam shoots Dario, and Bond hurls him into the pulverizer.

MENACING MAN
Totally loyal to Sanchez, Dario enjoys inflicting pain and terrorizing victims of his boss's displeasure.

DAVIDOV

APPEARANCE
The World Is Not Enough (1999)
STATUS Dead; killed by Bond
CHARACTERISTICS Quiet, nervous
PLAYED BY Ulrich Thomsen

Sasha Davidov runs security for King Industries. Although he acts out the charade that terrorist Renard is threatening Elektra King's life, Davidov, in fact, is in league with Elektra, Renard, and Dr. Arkov in a plot to steal a nuclear bomb from an abandoned facility in Kazakhstan. When Renard orders Arkov's death, Davidov takes Arkov's place to gain entry to the nuclear facility. Bond shoots Davidov and assumes Arkov's identity.

DAY, MAY

APPEARANCE
A View To A Kill (1985)
STATUS Dead; blown up
CHARACTERISTICS Strong,
dedicated, stylish, deadly
PLAYED BY Grace Jones

Of all the foes faced by 007, none can claim to be more exotic than the couture killer May Day. With strength allowing her to lift a grown man over her head and the poise to base jump from the top of the Eiffel Tower, May Day appears to be the perfect ally and lover for Max Zorin. Both have near-total disregard for human life and manic personalities.

May Day's main role in

Zorin's plot appears to be killing his opponents. She murders French private detective Aubergine, MI6 agent Sir Godfrey Tibbett, and CIA agent Chuck Lee. She makes love to Bond on her terms, but remains perfectly willing to kill him. Yet, events at the Main Strike mine change her mind. After loyally murdering Zorin's potential enemies, she discovers that Zorin sees her as expendable. He floods the Main Strike mine with her in it, killing numerous other associates. Overcome with a newfound sense of decency, she helps Bond disrupt Zorin's plan to set off a double earthquake, flood Silicon Valley, and monopolize microchip production. Using her enormous upper body strength, May Day cranes up a detonator from a pit of explosives, then personally guides the timed device outside the mine. Knowing she will die when the detonator explodes, May Day asks one favor from Bond: "Get Zorin for me!"

007: I can see you're a woman of very few words.
May Day: What's there to say?

DENT, PROF.

APPEARANCE
Dr. No (1962)
STATUS Dead; shot by 007
CHARACTERISTICS Suspicious,
rash; dislikes doing his own dirty work
PLAYED BY Anthony Dawson

According to the script of *Dr. No*, Professor R. J. Dent is "40, distinguished-looking, and a metallurgist by profession." He is also the leader of Dr. No's organization in Jamaica. He oversees the murder of anyone too curious about Dr. No's activities on his island Crab Key, such as British agent Strangways and his secretary, Mary.

When James Bond arrives in Jamaica to investigate Strangways's disappearance, Dent sends an assassin, Mr. Jones, to intercept him. Jones, confronted by Bond, ends up dead, weakening Dent's suggestion that Strangways might simply have run off with his secretary.

Bond's discovery of a receipt from Dent's metallurgist lab forces Dent to lie about the radioactive rock samples Strangways brought to him from Crab Key. Knowing Bond may discover the truth, Dent plots several attempts on Bond's life. He arranges for a tarantula to be placed in Bond's bed and, when this fails, he instructs his associate, Miss Taro, to invite Bond to her house, ordering the Three Blind Mice assassins to attack Bond on the way.

Bond survives and arrives at Miss Taro's unscathed, much to her surprise. She phones Dent, who tells her to delay Bond. Suspecting a trick, Bond makes love to Miss Taro before having her arrested. He then waits for Dent to arrive. After Dent fires all his bullets into pillows Bond has placed under the bedclothes to resemble his body, Bond coolly shoots Dent twice.

DOCTOR'S ORDERS *Summoned by Dr. No, Professor Dent takes delivery of a deadly tarantula with which to eliminate 007.*

49

DIMITRIOS, ALEX

APPEARANCE
Casino Royale (2006)
STATUS Dead; killed by Bond
CHARACTERISTICS Quick-tempered, jealous, sleazy, vengeful
PLAYED BY Simon Abkarian

Dimitrios organizes professional saboteurs for terrorist banker Le Chiffre in his plot to manipulate the stock price of the aircraft manufacturer Skyfleet. According to the MI6 database, Dimitrios has been a government contractor in Iraq, Afghanistan, Chechnya, Rwanda, Nicaragua, and El Salvador for the past 30-odd years. Working as an arms dealer, Dimitrios has ties to death squads and right-wing paramilitary groups. MI6 Intelligence believes most of Dimitrios's associates have been killed, including the very much alive Le Chiffre.

When Bond finds a cell phone number in the belongings of bomb-maker Mollaka, he traces a mysterious text message to Dimitrios in the Bahamas. There, Bond humiliates Dimitrios at poker, wins possession of his vintage Aston Martin DB5, and seduces his wife, Solange. When Dimitrios has to travel to Miami to provide payment to another saboteur, Carlos, Bond follows him. Dimitrios tries to kill Bond at the Body Worlds Exhibition, but Bond turns the tables on him, stabbing Dimitrios with his own stiletto.

DRAX, HUGO

APPEARANCE
Moonraker (1979)
STATUS Dead; orbiting
CHARACTERISTICS Dignified, messianic, brilliant, softly spoken, cultured
PLAYED BY Michael Lonsdale

Aerospace mogul Hugo Drax secretly launches a deadly attack on humanity in order to eradicate the human race from the earth. He plans to repopulate it with hand-picked, genetically ideal humans and create an "ultimate dynasty."

Drax is, as James Bond notes, "obsessed with the conquest of space." He has built an aerospace empire in Southern California, including a state-of-the-art manufacturing facility for the

> ## "James Bond. You appear with the tedious inevitability of an **unloved season.**"
>
> ### Drax to 007

Moonraker, a space shuttle created ostensibly for NASA. Drax has also launched a personally funded training program for a new astronaut corps, reputedly to man the *Moonraker* fleet. In fact, he has built the shuttles and trained the astronauts to help him carry out his masterplan.

Little of Drax's background is known, but the scale of his operation provides evidence that he has built his empire over many years. Drax's austere, emotionless manner masks an inner belief in himself as a godlike figure. His aristocratic lifestyle rivals that of King Louis XIV of France—

RENAISSANCE MAN
Drax prides himself on being a man of culture and taste. When Bond first meets him, he is playing the piano for two guests, Countess Labinsky and Lady Victoria Devon.

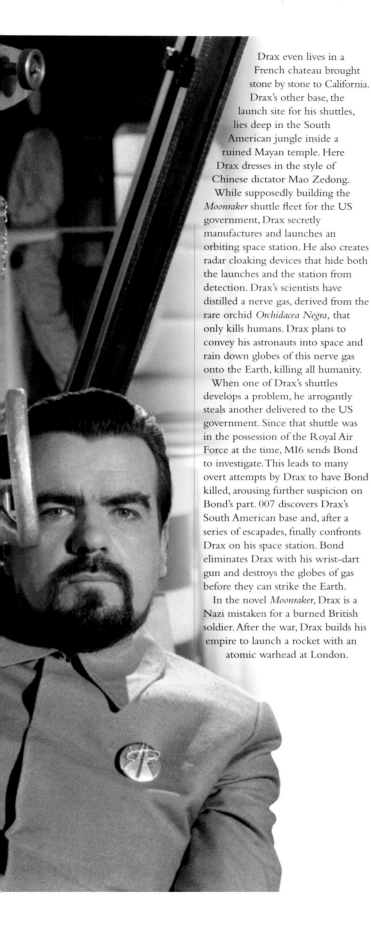

Drax even lives in a French chateau brought stone by stone to California. Drax's other base, the launch site for his shuttles, lies deep in the South American jungle inside a ruined Mayan temple. Here Drax dresses in the style of Chinese dictator Mao Zedong. While supposedly building the *Moonraker* shuttle fleet for the US government, Drax secretly manufactures and launches an orbiting space station. He also creates radar cloaking devices that hide both the launches and the station from detection. Drax's scientists have distilled a nerve gas, derived from the rare orchid *Orchidacea Negra,* that only kills humans. Drax plans to convey his astronauts into space and rain down globes of this nerve gas onto the Earth, killing all humanity.

When one of Drax's shuttles develops a problem, he arrogantly steals another delivered to the US government. Since that shuttle was in the possession of the Royal Air Force at the time, MI6 sends Bond to investigate. This leads to many overt attempts by Drax to have Bond killed, arousing further suspicion on Bond's part. 007 discovers Drax's South American base and, after a series of escapades, finally confronts Drax on his space station. Bond eliminates Drax with his wrist-dart gun and destroys the globes of gas before they can strike the Earth.

In the novel *Moonraker,* Drax is a Nazi mistaken for a burned British soldier. After the war, Drax builds his empire to launch a rocket with an atomic warhead at London.

DRYDEN

APPEARANCE
Casino Royale (2006)
STATUS Dead; shot by Bond
CHARACTERISTICS Devious, fatalistic
PLAYED BY Malcolm Sinclair

Prague station chief Dryden becomes James Bond's second kill in his progress to become a double-0 agent. Dryden has turned traitor, selling MI6 secrets through a network that includes Fisher, a contact in Pakistan. After Bond kills Fisher, he visits Dryden and assassinates him in his office.

ELVIS

APPEARANCE
Quantum Of Solace (2008)
STATUS Dead; blown up
CHARACTERISTICS Inefficient
PLAYED BY Anatole Taubman

Elvis is Dominic Greene's right-hand man. At a Greene fundraiser in Bolivia, Elvis tries to follow Bond, but Agent Fields trips him up, sending him and his bowl-cut wig down a flight of stairs. When Bond wreaks havoc at the Perla de las Dunas hotel, a hydrogen tank explodes, taking Elvis with it.

FAT, HAI

APPEARANCE
The Man With The Golden Gun (1974)
STATUS Interred in his own mausoleum
CHARACTERISTICS Ruthless, arrogant, fatally over-confident
PLAYED BY Richard Loo

Bangkok businessman Hai Fat hopes to monopolize the solar energy market by obtaining a highly efficient solar cell, the Solex. To this end, he partners with hit man Scaramanga, finances a solar power plant on a remote Chinese island, and lures expert Gibson away from the British. When Bond investigates, Fat expresses regret at involving Scaramanga in his plan. In response, Scaramanga shoots Fat dead.

FEYADOR, COL.

APPEARANCE
The Living Daylights (1987)
STATUS Dead; blown up
CHARACTERISTICS Corrupt comrade
PLAYED BY John Bowe

Colonel Feyador is commander of a Soviet airfield in Afghanistan. An old comrade-in-arms of Soviet General Georgi Koskov, Feyador is the only one on his base aware of Koskov's duplicitous defection to the West. He is involved with Koskov and Whitaker's opium-smuggling scheme. When Kamran Shah and his mujahedeen rebels attack the base, Shah throws a grenade under former captor Feyador's petrol truck, blowing him up.

FILLET OF SOUL WAITER

APPEARANCE
Live And Let Die (1973)
STATUS Living
CHARACTERISTICS Outwardly deferential, but capable of nasty turns
PLAYED BY Dan Jackson

The Fillet of Soul waiter works for Kananga/Mr. Big. When Bond orders a bourbon and water "neat" (no ice), the waiter tells him this will cost him extra. The same waiter delivers Bond into Mr. Big's clutches at two different clubs: once by seating Bond in a pivoting booth and second at a sinking table.

FISHER

APPEARANCE
Casino Royale (2006)
STATUS Dead; killed by Bond
CHARACTERISTICS Hard to kill
PLAYED BY Daud Shah

Fisher is in league with MI6 station chief Dryden selling British government secrets. As such, he becomes James Bond's first assassination assignment, one of two government-sanctioned killings necessary to achieve "00" status.

In a bathroom at a cricket stadium in Pakistan, Bond believes he has drowned Fisher and turns away. Fisher, still alive, grabs his gun and takes aim. Bond's lightning reactions serve him well as he turns and shoots Fisher dead.

FLEX, JENNY

APPEARANCE
A View To A Kill (1985)
STATUS Dead; submerged
CHARACTERISTICS Charming, cruel
PLAYED BY Alison Doody

Jenny Flex works as one of Max Zorin's deadly female accomplices. An avid horsewoman, Flex meets James Bond at Zorin's French chateau. She assists in the kidnapping and murder attempt on Bond in France as well as starting the fire in San Francisco City Hall.

In Zorin's Main Strike Mine, Flex delivers a bomb disguised as a coffee thermos to Scarpine and helps position the detonator Zorin plans to use to create a double earthquake. She chases after Bond and geologist

Stacey Sutton when Zorin finds them hiding in the mine. Along with many others, Zorin betrays Flex, flooding the mine with her in it.

FRANKS, PETER

APPEARANCE
Diamonds Are Forever (1971)
STATUS Dead; killed by Bond
CHARACTERISTICS Experienced smuggler; skilled at close quarters combat
PLAYED BY Joe Robinson

Smuggler Peter Franks unwittingly provides cover for Bond to infiltrate Blofeld's diamond smuggling operation. Before Franks can move a hoard of diamonds from Amsterdam to Los Angeles for $50,000, British officials arrest him. Bond poses as Franks, complete with fake fingerprints, to meet his contact Tiffany Case. When Franks escapes custody, Bond must prevent him from contacting Case. Bond and Franks fight in the elevator in Case's apartment building and, after a brutal struggle, Bond kills Franks. Bond convinces Case that the dead man is 007 and smuggles the diamonds into the US in Franks's coffin.

FROST, MIRANDA

APPEARANCE
Die Another Day (2002)
STATUS Dead; killed by Jinx
CHARACTERISTICS Aloof, articulate
PLAYED BY Rosamund Pike

Cold-hearted Miranda Frost is an MI6 agent, Olympic fencer, and the secret lover of Gustav Graves/Colonel Moon.

Miranda meets Colonel Moon when they both compete for the Harvard Fencing Team. They fall in love, and, after completing his education, Moon returns to North Korea corrupt and power-hungry. Miranda wins the 2000 Olympic Gold Medal in Fencing by default when Moon arranges for the true victor to overdose on steroids. Frost is soon recruited by MI6 and the three years she spends working in cryptology place her in the ideal position to keep her lover abreast of ministry secrets.

Miranda betrays Bond in North Korea by informing Moon's associate Zao of his true identity. Bond's infiltration of Moon's organization forces Moon to change his identity to Gustav Graves via DNA replacement therapy. Although his face is different, Miranda still loves him and pretends to spy on him for MI6 while working as his publicist. She battles NSA agent Jinx aboard Graves's Antonov plane using various knives and swords until Jinx fatally stabs her in the heart.

> "I know all about you 007. **Sex for dinner, death for breakfast.** Well it's not going to work with me."
>
> **Miranda Frost**

GABOR

APPEARANCE
The World Is Not Enough (1999)
STATUS Dead; guarded
CHARACTERISTICS Silent, protective
PLAYED BY John Seru

Gabor is the loyal bodyguard of Elektra King and has been at her side since her kidnapping by the terrorist Renard. Gabor follows Elektra wherever she travels and also works to protect her more nefarious interests.

Bond shoots Gabor dead at the Maiden's Tower, Istanbul, immediately after Baku-based casino and caviar factory owner Valentin Zukovsky frees Bond from Elektra's torture chair.

GETTLER

APPEARANCE
Casino Royale (2006)
STATUS Dead; killed by Bond
CHARACTERISTICS Methodical killer
PLAYED BY Richard Sammel

Gettler, distinguished by his Panama hat and glasses with one dark lens, works for terrorist Mr. White, who sends him to Venice to acquire the money Vesper Lynd has embezzled from Bond's holding account. Bond discovers Vesper's treachery and pursues her through the streets, but Gettler spots him and takes Vesper hostage in a building under restoration on one of Venice's canals. Bond kills Gettler by firing a nail gun into the dark lens of his glasses.

In the novel, SMERSH agent Gettler hunts down Vesper when she refuses to cooperate with SMERSH.

GOLDFINGER

APPEARANCE
Goldfinger (1964)
STATUS Dead; depressurized
CHARACTERISTICS The personification of greed, a compulsive cheater, brilliant criminal strategist
PLAYED BY Gert Frobe

One of the most audacious criminal masterminds in history, Auric Goldfinger assaults and successfully penetrates the United States Bullion Depository at Fort Knox, nearly succeeding in his Operation Grand Slam to irradiate $15 billion of gold—the entire Federal Gold Reserve.

One of the world's richest men, obsessed with gold and its acquisition, Goldfinger, a British citizen, owns gold deposits in Zurich, Amsterdam, Hong Kong, and Caracas worth roughly £20 million. According to the Fleming novel, Goldfinger's father and grandfather worked for Gustav and Carl Fabergé, jewelers to the Imperial Court of Russia. Born in 1916, Auric immigrated to England from Riga, Lithuania, at the age of 21. By purchasing gold coins and jewelry through a chain of pawn shops, Goldfinger amassed a fortune.

In the film, Goldfinger plots to place an atomic device, obtained from the Communist Chinese government, inside Fort Knox. By

GOBINDA

APPEARANCE
Octopussy (1983)
STATUS Dead; fell from airplane
CHARACTERISTICS Commanding, silent, murderous, exceptionally loyal; practiced with various antique weapons
PLAYED BY Kabir Bedi

Gobinda works in the service of amoral exiled Afghan prince Kamal Khan. He grimly eliminates anyone who interferes with Khan's plans.

Described in the script as a "tall, imposing Sikh in Indian suit and turban," Gobinda demonstrates his strength when, after Bond defeats Kamal Khan at backgammon using Khan's own loaded dice, he crushes the dice into sand in front of Bond.

Gobinda attempts to kill Bond numerous times—firing a blunderbuss at him from a tuk-tuk taxi, shooting at him during a supposed tiger hunt, and attempting to cut him in half with a sword while on top of smuggler Octopussy's circus train. Despite his repeated failures to end Bond's life, Gobinda

GUNNING FOR 007 Gobinda attempts to bring down Bond with his blunderbuss during a spectacular chase through a crowded market.

remains undeterred and implacable.

Gobinda and Khan hire a band of local thugs, led by the sinister Mufti, to assassinate Bond. The thugs make their attempt on Bond's life while Bond visits Octopussy's magnificent floating palace. Under Gobinda's command, the thugs kill Bond's contact Vijay with a deadly yo-yo buzz saw and then use snorkels disguised as lilypads to cross the lake surrounding the palace. They then sneak into the palace, unsuccessfully attempting to kill Bond with the same buzz saw while he and Octopussy make love.

Although Khan betrays Octopussy and Magda, he remains loyal to Gobinda until he orders him to climb out of his Beech 18 plane in mid-air and battle Bond, at which point Gobinda realizes that Khan will even sacrifice him. As Gobinda and Bond struggle, Bond bends back an antenna on top of the plane's fuselage and whips it into Gobinda's face, causing him to lose his grip and fall to his death.

AN ODD COUPLE *Goldfinger and his Korean manservant and caddy Oddjob calmly prepare for a round of golf.*

this coup, Goldfinger plans to increase the market value of his own sizeable gold hoard tenfold; the Communist Chinese hope to induce economic chaos in the West.

Bond gains a valuable insight into Goldfinger's ultra-competitive, devious, and ruthless nature when he catches him cheating at gin rummy in Miami Beach. Goldfinger's anger that his paid companion Jill Masterson betrayed him to Bond results in her horrific death from skin suffocation; he has her painted gold.

Rumors that Goldfinger has been smuggling gold ignite the interest of the British Secret Service and MI6 sets Bond on Goldfinger's

tail. Bond infuriates Goldfinger by out-tricking him in a golf match and then follows him to his factory in Switzerland. There Bond discovers that Goldfinger has been smuggling gold from England in the body panels of his Rolls-Royce.

Goldfinger then kidnaps Bond, who, having chanced to overhear mention of "Operation Grand Slam," convinces Goldfinger to keep him alive, instead of cutting him in half with an industrial laser.

Using most of the organized crime families in the US to smuggle in the components he needs to carry out his plan, Goldfinger gathers the crime bosses together at his stud farm in Kentucky, boastfully informs

GRAND SLAM *Auric Goldfinger explains his masterplan to a convention of American hoods. He twists the details to make them think he plans to steal the gold in Fort Knox.*

them of some of the details of Operation Grand Slam, and then proceeds to gas them all.

One ally he cannot afford to betray, Pussy Galore, proves to be his downfall. Goldfinger enlists Galore's pilots from her Flying Circus to spray Delta-9 nerve gas over the Fort Knox area. Bond convinces Galore to reconsider. She works with the authorities to replace the deadly gas in the canisters. When Goldfinger makes his assault, he finds himself

involved in a battle. Nevertheless, he manages to get his atomic device locked inside the depository, with Bond handcuffed to it, before escaping. The authorities defuse the bomb, but Goldfinger has one last trick. He hijacks a presidential jet flying Bond to the White House. During a fight on board, Goldfinger fires his pistol. The shot shatters a window. As the cabin depressurizes, Goldfinger is sucked through the opening to his doom.

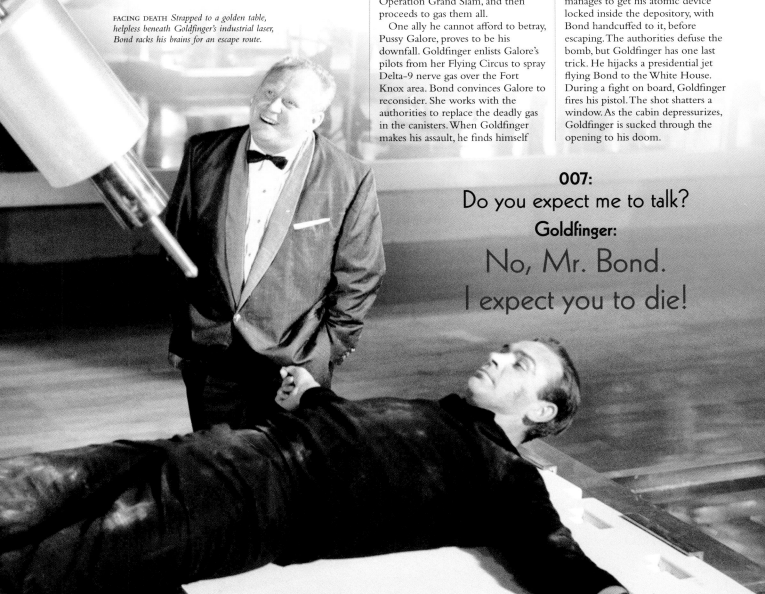

FACING DEATH *Strapped to a golden table, helpless beneath Goldfinger's industrial laser, Bond racks his brains for an escape route.*

007:
Do you expect me to talk?
Goldfinger:
No, Mr. Bond.
I expect you to die!

GONZALES, HECTOR

APPEARANCE
For Your Eyes Only (1981)
STATUS Assassinated
CHARACTERISTICS Arrogant and
deadly assassin-for-hire
PLAYED BY Stefan Kalipha

Cuban hit man Hector Gonzales
poses as a pilot for the Athens-based
Kerkyra Charter Service in order to
murder British agent Sir Timothy
Havelock and his wife, Iona.
Gonzales flies Timothy and Iona's
daughter Melina to her parents'
research ship, *Triana* in Corfu
Harbour. He then turns his seaplane
around and guns down her parents.

The Greek police identify
Gonzales using Melina's description.
Through a detective agency, Melina
tracks Gonzales to a villa outside
Madrid, Spain. After Gonzales
receives a payment from henchman
Locque for the Havelock murders,
Melina, hiding in nearby bushes,
shoots him with her crossbow.

Major Hector Gonzales appears in
the short story *For Your Eyes Only*, set
in Jamaica and Vermont. Working for
a man named Von Hammerstein,
Gonzales murders the Havelocks
when they refuse to sell their land.

GRANT, DONALD "RED"

APPEARANCE
From Russia With Love (1963)
STATUS Dead; eliminated by 007
CHARACTERISTICS A cunning killer
who enjoys playing a waiting game; very
fit, bitter, psychotic, greedy for money
PLAYED BY Robert Shaw

Donald Grant is SPECTRE's
ultimate killing machine. His physical
strength and methodical
determination set him apart from
other assassins.

Named Donovan Grant in Ian
Fleming's novel, he hails from
Northern Ireland where he won a
boxing title in 1945. Defecting in
Berlin, Grant works as the chief
executioner for SMERSH and has
adopted the Russian name Krassno
Granitski. His murderous moods are
linked to lunar cycles.

In the film, Grant is a convicted
murderer who escaped from
Dartmoor Prison in 1960.
SPECTRE recruited him in Tangier
in 1962. A homicidal paranoiac,
Grant responded well to SPECTRE
training, changing his crude killing
techniques. He has one affectation:
he pulls on gloves before committing
a murder. He also often garrotes his
victims with a wire concealed inside
his watch.

SPECTRE member Rosa Klebb
selects Grant to carry out Kronsteen's
plot to humiliate the British Secret
Service, exact vengeance on James
Bond for the death of Dr. No, and
sell a Lektor decoder back to the
Soviets.

Grant initially serves as Bond's
guardian angel, protecting him from
assassination until Bond can steal the
decoder. Grant then isolates Bond by
murdering both Head of Station T
Kerim Bey and Soviet security agent
Benz aboard the Orient Express. He
assassinates the British agent sent by
M to meet Bond in Zagreb and takes
the alias of Captain Nash. Bond
becomes suspicious when Grant
orders red wine with fish at dinner.
Grant drugs Soviet cipher clerk
Tatiana Romanova before
confronting Bond on board the train.
Faced with certain death, Bond
exploits Grant's greed by telling him
that his attaché case and another one
in the compartment both have gold
sovereigns in them. When Grant
opens the second case, he sets off a
tear-gas canister. After a brutal fight,
Bond strangles Grant with the
garrote-wire watch.

THE IMPOSTER *To get the drop on Bond
aboard the Orient Express, Grant pretends to
be a British agent named Captain Nash.*

> "He seems fit enough.
> # Have him report to me
> in Istanbul in 24 hours."
>
> Rosa Klebb

GRAVES, GUSTAV / MOON, COLONEL

APPEARANCE
Die Another Day (2002)
STATUS Dead; electrocuted
CHARACTERISTICS Suffers from
anger-management issues; obsessed
with victory; cannot sleep so he
attempts to live his dreams.
PLAYED BY Toby Stephens/
Will Yun Lee

ON THE TAKE *Moon abuses his position in the North Korean army to gain considerable wealth for himself.*

Colonel Tan-Sun Moon, alias Gustav Graves, is a psychotic North Korean officer who hopes to forcefully unite South Korea with the North and form a new superpower. Moon is the son of peaceful North Korean General Moon, who wishes to form a bridge between his country and the West by sending his son to Harvard to receive a Western education. There, the younger Moon falls for beautiful British fencer Miranda Frost and becomes consumed with dreams of power. After further study at Oxford University, Moon returns to North Korea where his father awards him the rank of Colonel.

Moon subsequently arranges for the winner of the fencing gold medal at the Sydney Olympics to overdose on steroids so that the runner-up, Miranda Frost, can claim the gold by default. In return for this service, Miranda gives Graves full access to the Ministry's secrets when she begins working for MI6.

When 007 arrives in North Korea to stop Moon's trade in African conflict diamonds, Miranda tips off Moon's henchman Zao to Bond's real identity via PDA mobile phone. Bond and Moon battle on board a hovercraft amid the minefields of the Korean Demilitarized Zone (DMZ), resulting in Moon plunging over a high waterfall.

Moon is thought dead, but he is actually only injured. He secretly travels to Dr. Alvarez's Cuban clinic to undergo painful DNA replacement therapy. Several months later, he emerges with a new face and identity. He reappears as Argentinean orphan Gustav Graves, an engineer who has discovered a fortune in diamonds in Iceland (they are really African conflict diamonds). Graves amasses great wealth and presents himself as an environmentalist, a humanitarian and a relentless sportsman training for the British Olympic fencing team. Only the latter is true, but soon his adoptive nation of Britain offers him a knighthood.

With his great wealth, he announces a grand humanitarian project at a party at his Ice Palace in Iceland: the Icarus space mirror. Graves claims the Icarus will act as a second sun, growing crops and preventing hunger. In fact, Icarus is a deadly weapon capable of destruction on a massive scale. Bond eventually battles Graves to the death aboard his Antonov plane, electrocutes Graves with his own battlesuit, and sends him into the jet engines.

Graves/Moon is based on the character of Hugo Drax in the novel *Moonraker*—a Nazi who changes his face and lives as a knighted Englishman with plans to use his Moonraker rocket to destroy London. The name Colonel Moon is a nod to the first non-Fleming James Bond novel *Colonel Sun* by Kingsley Amis (under the pseudonym Robert Markham), in which the villain's name is Colonel Sun Liang-tan.

> "You see, Mr. Bond, you can't kill my dreams. **But my dreams can kill you.**"
>
> Gustav Graves

ELECTRIC WARRIOR *Graves's battlesuit, possessing a taser defense system and allowing Graves to control his Icarus superweapon, greatly enhances his strength.*

CROSSING SWORDS *Bond gets under the skin of Gustav Graves by defeating him in a spectacular duel at Blades, Graves's fencing club.*

GREENE, DOMINIC

APPEARANCE
Quantum Of Solace (2008)
STATUS Dead; executed by Quantum
CHARACTERISTICS Smooth-talking, wily, sophisticated, ruthless, vindictive
PLAYED BY Mathieu Amalric

Dominic Greene, utilities company Greene Planet CEO and high-ranking Quantum member, plots with deposed Bolivian dictator General Medrano to stage a political coup in exchange for a barren piece of land.

Little is known about Greene's early life except that at age 15 he had a crush on one of his mother's piano students. He burned her with an iron after overhearing her saying unkind things about him. How Greene became a member of Quantum remains a mystery. Masquerading as a committed environmentalist, Greene claims to perform philanthropic work by purchasing large tracts of

> "**Friends talking behind my back feels like ants under my skin.**"
>
> **Greene to Camille**

SMILING VILLAIN *Greene and his henchman Elvis arrive at the opera house in Bregenz, Austria, for a secret, top-level Quantum meeting, planned to take place during the performance.*

land for ecological purposes.

When Greene learns his lover and employee, Camille, has attempted to buy secret reports from one of his top geologists regarding a seemingly barren Bolivian property known as the Tierra Project, he orders the geologist killed and sends the assassin Slate to eliminate her.

Bond kills Slate before he can carry out Greene's orders. When Greene and Medrano meet, Greene gives Camille to Medrano to "sweeten the deal," advising Medrano to "throw her over the side" when he's finished with her.

Greene then finalizes a deal with CIA South American Section Chief Gregory Beam to ignore the Bolivian coup in exchange for rights to any oil discovered under Greene's land. He also asks Beam to eliminate "a pest"—James Bond.

At a top-secret Quantum meeting in Austria, Quantum members express concern regarding Greene's Tierra Project. Greene insists Bolivia must be Quantum's top priority. When Bond and Camille investigate the Tierra Project, they discover that Greene has been inhibiting the delivery of fresh water, damming it in a vast reservoir underground. Greene and Quantum want control of Bolivia's water supply, convinced that whoever controls this vital natural resource will be more powerful than the government.

DANGEROUS GAMES *Camille vainly attempts to convince Greene that she is still loyal to him.*

THROWN TO THE WOLVES *Bond abandons Greene in the Bolivian desert.*

> "MI6 says he is difficult to control. Nice way of saying that everything he touches seems to wither and die."

Greene to Camille, concerning James Bond

At the Perla de las Dunas Hotel in Bolivia, Greene bribes the Colonel of Police and informs Medrano that the country's already expensive water costs will double when Greene Planet becomes the exclusive provider. Medrano is faced with a stark choice: to agree to this proposal or face certain death.

Bond follows Greene to the hotel After an explosive clash, Bond extracts information from Greene regarding Quantum before leaving him in the desert with just a can of motor oil—an ironic revenge for the cruel murder of Agent Fields. M later informs Bond that Greene has been found, motor oil in his stomach and two bullets in the back of his skull.

A BEATEN MAN *The smooth operator calmly taking his seat in the Bregenz opera house in Austria (right) becomes bruised, battered, and bloodstained at Bond's hands in Bolivia (above).*

GRISHENKO, BORIS

APPEARANCE
GoldenEye (1995)
STATUS Dead; frozen stiff
CHARACTERISTICS Talented
computer programmer, highly inflated
opinion of himself, not invincible
PLAYED BY Alan Cumming

Boris Grishenko provides former
MI6 agent Alec Trevelyan with the
hacker skills to carry out a plot to
zap London with an electromagnetic
pulse weapon named GoldenEye and
illegally transfer billions of pounds
from the Bank of England.

Grishenko works at the Severnaya
Space Weapons Control Centre in
Siberia as the senior computer
programmer. In his spare time, he
hacks into secure computers around
the world. He loves riddles, which he

PASSWORD PROTECTED *Boris teases Natalya with another prank on her computer, making her guess the password—"Knockers."*

uses to create passwords. Boris, who
has the maturity of a pre-adolescent,
sees the world as though it is a
computer game, with little or no
moral consequences to his action.
His victory yell is, "I am invincible!"

Boris gives the signal for General
Ourumov and Xenia Onatopp to
start the massacre at Severnaya and

later lures programmer
Natalya Simonova into
a trap in St. Petersburg.
In Cuba, Boris not only
programs the surviving
GoldenEye satellite to
detonate over London,
but he also hacks into
the Bank of England
mainframe. When Bond
and Natalya infiltrate
the Cuban control
complex, Boris seems
happy to see Simonova alive and is
unprepared for her anger at his actions.

More worrisome for Boris,
Simonova alters the GoldenEye's
course, programming the satellite to
burn up over the Atlantic. Boris tries
to break her pass codes as Bond and
Simonova work to destroy the
satellite control station. He survives
the crash of the transmitter and
antenna through the complex's roof,
but as he celebrates, a cascade of
liquid nitrogen freezes him solid.

BLIND AMBITION *Boris Grishenko believes he is the best hacker in the world, and with Trevelyan's grand scheme, he plans to prove it.*

> ## "I am invincible!"
> **Boris Grishenko**

GRUNTHER

APPEARANCE
On Her Majesty's Secret Service (1969)
STATUS Dead; reached a prickly end
CHARACTERISTICS Quiet, merciless
PLAYED BY Yuri Borienko

SIDEKICK *Grunther helps Blofeld in the brainwashing of his 12 allergy patients.*

Described in the script as a
"professional winter-sports man,"
Grunther is security chief at Ernst
Stavro Blofeld's allergy clinic Piz
Gloria. He prevents Bond's contact
Campbell from boarding the cable
car leading to Blofeld's mountaintop
retreat and later leads Blofeld's men
down the alpine slopes in a frantic
race to kill 007, who is armed with
information regarding Blofeld's
bacteriological warfare plot.
Grunther eventually dies struggling
with Bond's fiancée Tracy at Piz
Gloria. She defeats him by spinning
him into a spiked wall decoration.

GUPTA, HENRY

APPEARANCE
Tomorrow Never Dies (1997)
STATUS Dead; shot by Elliot Carver
CHARACTERISTICS A dedicated
anarchist, mild-mannered, cunning
PLAYED BY Ricky Jay

Employed by media mogul Elliot
Carver, Henry Gupta plays a key
role in Carver's plot to foment war
between Britain and China.
Formerly a student radical at
Berkeley in the 1960s, Gupta
developed the concept of techno-
terrorism. He purchases a GPS
encoder and barely escapes with his
life when Bond raids a terrorist arms
bazaar in the Khyber Pass. With the
aid of Carver's satellites, Gupta uses
the GPS encoder to send HMS
Devonshire off course into Vietnamese
waters, igniting an international
incident. He also acts as a security

advisor to Carver, declaring Bond to be a government agent and showing Carver a security camera recording of his wife, Paris, admitting that she once had an affair with 007. Carver kills Gupta when he outlives his usefulness.

HAINES, GUY

APPEARANCE
Quantum Of Solace (2008)
STATUS Living; whereabouts unknown
CHARACTERISTICS Clever politician; keeps a low profile
PLAYED BY Paul Ritter

Guy Haines, advisor to Britain's Prime Minister, is one of Quantum's high-ranking members. During a secret Quantum meeting at the opera house in Bregenz, Austria, Haines is asked what will happen when the CIA learns it has been duped and there is no Bolivian oil. He replies that he is "working on that." When Bond makes his presence known, Haines and other Quantum members get up from their seats and leave, allowing Bond to snap shots of them with his nano-surveillance camera phone.

HANS

APPEARANCE
You Only Live Twice (1967)
STATUS Dead; eaten by piranhas
CHARACTERISTICS Strong, impassive
PLAYED BY Ronald Rich

Hans serves as Ernst Stavro Blofeld's bodyguard during Blofeld's time in Japan. Tall, quiet, and tremendously strong, Hans performs a demonstration feeding of Blofeld's piranhas for the representatives of the Communist Chinese government to encourage them to pay Blofeld in advance for his services.

During the Japanese SIS ninja attack on the rocket base, Blofeld entrusts Hans with the key to the *Bird 1* exploder button so that Hans can destroy the spacecraft once it has engulfed the US *Jupiter* orbiter. James Bond confronts Hans, steals the exploder key, and flips him into Blofeld's piranha pool where the fish promptly eat him.

WRESTLING MATCH *Bond tangles with Hans in Blofeld's apartment, trying to grab the key that will blow up Blofeld's* Bird 1 *rocket.*

HELLER

APPEARANCE
Licence To Kill (1989)
STATUS Forked; came to a dead end
CHARACTERISTICS Protective, aggressive
PLAYED BY Don Stroud

Heller, an ex-Green Beret colonel, is drug lord Franz Sanchez's security chief. He inadvertently saves Bond's life when he attacks a safe house run by narcotics agents Kwang and Loti.

Pam Bouvier gives Heller a letter from the US Attorney General granting him immunity if he safely returns four Stinger missiles bought by Sanchez from the Contras. Bond later uses this information to further the distrust between Sanchez and his men. Pam and Bond discover Heller impaled on a forklift blade, courtesy of Sanchez's henchman Braun.

HOWE, W. G.

APPEARANCE
A View To A Kill (1985)
STATUS Dead; shot by Zorin
CHARACTERISTICS A weak-willed yes-man, misguidedly loyal to Zorin
PLAYED BY Daniel Benzali

Based at San Francisco City Hall, office of the State Department of Conservation, Division of Oil and Mines, W. G. Howe unwittingly aids industrialist Max Zorin in his plot to destroy California's Silicon Valley. He barely tolerates State Geologist Stacey Sutton, and when she continues to question Zorin's activities, Howe fires her at Zorin's request. Zorin does not reward Howe for his help; he kills him with Bond's Walther PPK in order to frame Bond for Howe's murder.

HO, PAN

APPEARANCE
A View To A Kill (1985)
STATUS Dead; drowned in a mine
CHARACTERISTICS Calculating; ruthless in the execution of her duties
PLAYED BY Papillon Soo Soo

Pan Ho, along with Jenny Flex, is one of Max Zorin's many assistants. She greets Bond at Zorin's French chateau, carefully checking 007's

invitation to a sale of racehorses. She later pours gasoline all over the floors of San Francisco City Hall, which Zorin then sets ablaze in order to kill Bond and geologist Stacey Sutton.

When Zorin floods his Main Strike Mine, Pan Ho and Jenny both drown in the torrent, leaving May Day grief-stricken at their deaths.

IMPOSTER 00 AGENT

APPEARANCE
The Living Daylights (1987)
STATUS Dead; cover blown
CHARACTERISTICS Determined
PLAYED BY Carl Rigg

The Imposter 00 Agent works for General Koskov to ignite a secret war between Britain and the Soviet Union. He infiltrates a training mission for three 00 agents who parachute onto Gibraltar for a routine training exercise with the SAS. The Imposter kills an SAS guard and 004. This is the beginning of the *Smiert Spionam*—"Death to Spies"—plot hatched by Koskov and US arms dealer Brad Whitaker to convince the British that KGB head General Pushkin should be killed. Bond battles the Imposter in a stolen, explosive-filled British Army Land Rover, which eventually plummets over a cliff toward the water. Bond deploys his back-up parachute, escaping the vehicle as its cargo explodes over the Mediterranean.

JAILER

APPEARANCE
The Living Daylights (1987)
STATUS Unknown
CHARACTERISTICS Sadistic and
brutal; laughs at his own jokes
PLAYED BY Ken Sharrock

The jailer working for Colonel
Feyador at a Soviet air base in
Afghanistan is charged with holding
Bond and cellist Kara Milovy before
sending them to Moscow. After
threatening mujaheddin leader
Kamran Shah with execution and
Kara with a strip search, the jailer beats
Bond before taking his key fob from
him. However, when Bond whistles
Rule, Britannia! his key fob emits a
cloud of stun gas, dazing the Soviet
jailer long enough for 007 to get the
better of him and escape with Kara.

WHISTLE WHILE YOU WORK *The Soviet
army jailer plays with Bond's key fob.*

JANNI

APPEARANCE
Thunderball (1965)
STATUS Dead; killed in explosion
CHARACTERISTICS Likes his dirty work
PLAYED BY Michael Brennan

Janni works for SPECTRE No. 2,
Emilio Largo, and is often paired
with Vargas. Janni helps Vargas kidnap
James Bond's Nassau contact Paula
Caplan and also searches for Bond in
the Junkanoo parade. Janni dies when
the hydrofoil portion of Largo's
yacht, *Disco Volante*, crashes into a
coral reef and explodes.

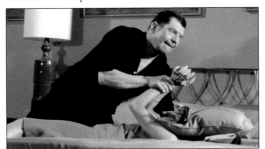

JAWS

APPEARANCE
The Spy Who Loved Me (1977);
Moonraker (1979)
STATUS Alive and living large
CHARACTERISTICS Orally fixated,
deadly bite; seemingly indestructible
PLAYED BY Richard Kiel

This seven-foot-two-inch monster of
a man with steel teeth is one of the
most awe-inspiring figures in the
history of villainy.

Nothing of the background of
Jaws exists in the Bond films, but
screenwriter Christopher Wood
reveals quite a bit of the history of
Jaws in his novelization of *The Spy
Who Loved Me*. Born Zbigniew
Krycsiwiki in Poland, his father was a
circus strongman and his mother a
prison warden. A police arrest in
1972 led to a beating that destroyed
his teeth and jaw. Eventually, the
megalomaniac Karl Stromberg found
him and coerced a former
concentration camp doctor into
saving Krycsiwiki. Fourteen
operations later, Krycsiwiki's jaw
worked again, but now with razor-
sharp steel teeth.

Working as an enforcer for
Stromberg, Jaws initially attempts to
obtain a microfilm of the plans of
Stromberg's submarine tracking
system from Max Kalba in Cairo.
James Bond and Major Anya
Amasova steal it back that evening.
Jaws later attacks them on a train, but
Bond kicks him out a window.

Jaws is nothing if not persistent. In
Sardinia, Bond sprays his windshield

"He just dropped in for a quick bite."

Bond to Anya Amasova

TIED UP *Janni works
enthusiastically with Vargas
to kidnap Paula Caplan.*

HIGH AMBITION *(top) Jaws prepares to try to kill James Bond again in* Moonraker.

HOT SHOTS *(top right) Jaws and a henchman fire gunshots at Bond and Anya Amasova in* The Spy Who Loved Me.

HEAVY WEIGHT *(above) Jaws moments before he accidentally drops a stone block on his own foot in* The Spy Who Loved Me.

PERFECT MATCH *(right) Jaws with the petite Dolly, his true love, in orbit in* Moonraker.

with cement, sending his car full of killers off a cliff. Later, in Stromberg's *Atlantis* base, Bond uses an electromagnet to lift Jaws by his teeth and drop him in a shark tank. Somehow Jaws survives all of these indignities.

Later, working for an unnamed employer, Jaws shoves 007 out of a charter jet, then skydives after him, only to tear loose his own ripcord and plunge into a circus tent. The industrialist Hugo Drax soon hires Jaws to work for him. Jaws attempts to kill Bond at Rio's Carnival and then tries to end 007's life on the cable cars at Sugarloaf Mountain. For his troubles, Jaws crashes at high speed into the control station. In the rubble, he meets Dolly, and the pair immediately falls in love.

Jaws travels with Drax to his secret rocket base, where he helps Drax

with security issues, such as chasing Bond over a waterfall in a boat and later policing 007 while Drax gives Bond a tour of his control room.

Jaws soon travels to Drax's space station with Dolly. After capturing Bond and Dr. Holly Goodhead, he eventually realizes that, when Drax has accomplished his plan to repopulate the earth with beautiful people, both he and Dolly will be eliminated. He fights Drax's men alongside Bond and then frees a *Moonraker* shuttle so that Bond and Holly can escape Drax's exploding space station. When it looks like Jaws will die in space, he shares a bottle of champagne with his lover, speaking his only words, "Well, here's to us." Space Marines later rescue him and Dolly from the wreckage of the station.

JONES, MR.

APPEARANCE
Dr. No (1962)
STATUS Dead; suicide by poison
CHARACTERISTICS Shifty, fearful
PLAYED BY Reginald Carter

One of Dr. No's agents, Mr. Jones, poses as a chauffeur in an attempt to kidnap James Bond. Jones meets 007 at Jamaica's Palisadoes Airport claiming Government House has sent him. Bond confirms that government official Pleydell-Smith did not send a car but nevertheless agrees to ride with Jones. After losing a car that tails them, Bond demands to know who really sent Jones. A fight ensues, which Jones loses. Rather than betray his terrifying employer, Jones opts to kill himself. Biting into a cigarette that contains a cyanide capsule, he tells Bond to "go to hell" and dies instantly.

KANANGA, DR.

APPEARANCE
Live And Let Die (1973)
STATUS Dead; exploded
CHARACTERISTICS Immensely ambitious, contemptuous, superstitious
PLAYED BY Yaphet Kotto

Dr. Kananga serves as Prime Minister of the Caribbean nation of San Monique while maintaining another identity as Mr. Big, underworld boss and head of the chain of Fillet of Soul clubs. Having created a pipeline for heroin into the US, Kananga plans to flood the country with the drug and monopolize the market. Kananga supports his bold ambition with a surprisingly large underworld network of willing followers.

Kananga encourages a belief in voodoo among the local population. He also maintains an interest in Obeah, the Caribbean folk religion that includes spells, fortune-telling, and black magic. Kananga travels with a man

claiming to be the human embodiment of Baron Samedi, one of the most feared figures in voodoo culture and chief of the legion of the dead.

Over the years, Kananga employs at least two women whom he believes have the power to tell the future with tarot cards: Solitaire and, previously, her mother. He has done everything possible to cut these women off from outsiders, declaring that their power exists only to serve him.

All of this dabbling in the occult and folk religions appears to play a key role in creating a vast network of followers of Kananga, both in San Monique and the US. When the British Secret Service and CIA investigators begin to suspect that Dr. Kananga and Mr. Big may both

be linked to drug smuggling, Kananga pulls off a triple killing of British agents—Dawes at the UN, Hamilton in New Orleans, and Baines in San Monique.

The killings naturally draw more attention to Kananga's activities, most notably bringing James Bond to New York to investigate. Kananga immediately orders Bond's death. Bond survives numerous attacks during the visit, which includes a brief meeting with Kananga disguised as Mr. Big. Kananga returns to San Monique and Bond immediately follows. On the island, Kananga attempts to have his CIA mole Rosie Carver lead Bond to a location where he will be killed. Not only does Bond foil this plot, he also escapes San Monique with Solitaire.

MAN OF THE PEOPLE *To the world at large, Dr. Kananga presents himself as a humanitarian politician, campaigning for San Monique at the United Nations.*

"The question still stands, Mr. Bond... Did you touch her?"

Kananga to 007

Kidnapping them both in New Orleans, Kananga discovers Solitaire has slept with Bond, negating her supposed power to see the future, which was linked to her virginity.

Bond again escapes from Kananga's men, destroying Kananga's heroin processing lab along the way. Kananga returns to San Monique and stages a massive voodoo ceremony at which his High Priest Dambala will execute Solitaire. He correctly believes this will draw Bond, allowing him one more chance to kill 007. Not only does Bond save Solitaire, but he also blows up Kananga's poppy fields, kills Dambala and, seemingly, Baron Samedi. Kananga's trap nonetheless snares Bond and Solitaire. He has the pair tied to a winch platform so they can be lowered into a shark tank and eaten by the sharks. Bond escapes and fights Kananga. They fall into the shark pool, but Bond shoves a compressed-air shark pellet into Kananga's mouth. Kananga's body fills with carbon dioxide gas, causing

"Drown, Mr Bond? I doubt you'll get the chance to drown!"

Kananga to 007

SHARK BAIT *Kananga looks forward to the imminent deaths of Bond and Solitaire.*

him to literally explode.

Mr. Big, but not the alter-ego Dr. Kananga, exists in the Ian Fleming novel. A Haitian of French and African ancestry and named Buonaparte Ignace Gallia, Mr. Big is an agent for SMERSH, financing Communist interests in the US through the sale of gold coins from treasure discovered in Jamaica. Mr. Big sees himself as "a wolf, and I live by a wolf's laws. Naturally, sheep describe such a person as a 'criminal'." Mr. Big suffers from heart disease, which has turned his skin grey.

KANANGA'S CAB DRIVER

APPEARANCE
Live And Let Die (1973)
STATUS Unknown
CHARACTERISTICS Good natured and humorous with a winning smile
PLAYED BY Arnold Williams

If only all cab drivers had the cheerful personality of Kananga's unnamed cab driver, who is assigned to pick up 007 in New York and New Orleans. He delivers Bond to the Fillet of Soul in Harlem and subsequently kidnaps Bond and Solitaire in New Orleans.

KAUFMAN, DR.

APPEARANCE
Tomorrow Never Dies (1997)
STATUS Dead; killed by Bond
CHARACTERISTICS Professor of forensics; expert marksman; sadistic, arrogant
PLAYED BY Vincent Schiavelli

Dr. Kaufman is a softly spoken hitman employed by media mogul Elliot Carver to assassinate those who betray him, such as his wife, Paris. At the time of his death, Kaufman was schooling Carver's henchman Stamper in Chakra torture. Kaufman has kept a victim alive for 52 hours, a record Stamper, who views Kaufman as a father figure, hopes to break.

KHAN, KAMAL

APPEARANCE
Octopussy (1983)
STATUS Dead; killed in plane crash
CHARACTERISTICS Charismatic, thoroughly corrupt, enjoys cheating
PLAYED BY Louis Jourdan

Exiled Afghan prince Kamal Khan is an international art dealer and marginal politician who works with Soviet General Orlov to stage a nuclear "accident" on a US Air Force base in West Germany.

Based in Udaipur, India, Khan is a sportsman, hunter, and backgammon player. He and his partner Octopussy steal Soviet art treasures from the

BIDDING WAR *Kamal Khan and Magda watch as Bond raises his bid on a Fabergé egg. Khan must win the auction or risk exposing his smuggling operation.*

"Mr. Bond is indeed a very rare breed. Soon to be made extinct."

Kamal Khan

Kremlin Art Repository and replace them with near perfect forgeries designed in the basement workshop of his Monsoon Palace. After smuggling the real treasures into the West via Octopussy's train, Khan and Orlov betray her by removing the treasures, replacing them with a nuclear bomb, and leaving her to die. Khan's reward will be the treasure all for himself.

After Bond foils Khan's and Orlov's plot, Khan kidnaps Octopussy and escapes in his plane with international monies that he can reprint. Bond rescues Octopussy from Kamal's plane seconds before it crashes.

KIL, MR.

APPEARANCE
Die Another Day (2002)
STATUS Dead; lasered by Jinx
CHARACTERISTICS Has a name to die for, incredibly strong, silently intimidating
PLAYED BY Lawrence Makoare

Mr. Kil works for Gustav Graves as head of security at Graves's Ice Palace in Iceland. Mr. Kil's job encompasses everything from carrying Bond's luggage to attempting to decapitate Bond's ally, NSA agent Jinx, with a diamond-cutting laser. When Bond arrives to rescue Jinx, he and Kil fight in a laser fire maze, with Kil trying to stab Bond with his Maori bone hair comb. A tied-down Jinx reaches the remote control switch and fires a laser through Kil's head. She later lasers off Kil's hand and uses his palm print to gain access to other areas of Graves's diamond mine.

KILLIFER

APPEARANCE
The World Is Not Enough (1999)
Licence To Kill (1989)
STATUS Dead; shark bait
CHARACTERISTICS Opportunistic
and devious; not as clever as he thinks
PLAYED BY Everett McGill

Ed Killifer is a cigar-chomping DEA agent and a friend of Felix Leiter, who turns traitor when he accepts a $2 million bribe to free drug baron Franz Sanchez from US custody. Killifer crashes the van carrying Sanchez off Key West's Seven Mile Bridge into the sea, and they escape in a Shark Hunter two-man submersible, courtesy of Sanchez's associate, Milton Krest.

After Killifer frees Sanchez, he enters the murky world of drug lord justice. He collects his payment, but then must endure watching Leiter lowered into a shark tank.

Waiting to be picked up at Krest's Ocean Exotic warehouse, Killifer hears gunshots and finds Bond has killed all the guards. Knocked off balance by Leiter's fisherman friend Sharky, Killifer offers Bond a million dollars to save him from falling into the shark tank. Bond refuses, slinging Killifer's heavy suitcase full of bribe money at him, and sending the treacherous DEA agent to his death.

KING, ELEKTRA

APPEARANCE
The World Is Not Enough (1999)
STATUS Dead; shot by Bond
CHARACTERISTICS Bitter, vengeful, ambitious; virtually irresistible to men.
PLAYED BY Sophie Marceau

Elektra Vavra King secretly teams with her terrorist kidnapper Renard in a scheme to kill her father, Sir Robert King, monopolize oil distribution from the Caspian Sea, and destroy Istanbul.

Elektra's great-grandfather discovered oil in the Caspian at the turn of the 20th Century. The Bolsheviks slaughtered him and many of his people, the Vavras, in order to gain control of the reserves. British industrialist Robert King married into the Vavra family, and, after the Soviet Union collapse, the renamed family business King Industries established a strong presence in the Caspian.

Before the film begins, international terrorist Renard kidnaps Elektra, holds her in Cyprus, and demands $5 million for her release. During captivity, Elektra realizes her father refuses to pay her ransom. Fueled by a sense of betrayal, Elektra turns Renard toward a much darker and more far-reaching plot. First, she makes it appear that Renard cut off part of her ear and that she killed two captors to escape. In the aftermath of the kidnapping, MI6 agent 009 shoots Renard. The bullet lodges in his brain, slowly destroying his tactile senses and condemning him to certain death. With his fate sealed, Elektra knows that the obsessed Renard will undertake any risk for her.

> **"There's no point in living if you can't feel alive."**
>
> Elektra to 007

Elektra and Renard then arrange a complex financial transfer that results in Sir Robert blowing himself up with a bomb concealed inside a case of money at MI6 headquarters. With the death of her father, Elektra sets her sights on two goals: killing M for persuading Sir Robert not to pay the ransom and gaining complete control of Caspian Sea oil distribution.

Elektra anticipates that her father's death will result in M sending someone to protect her. She soon finds herself in the company of James Bond. Taking advantage of Bond's protective impulses, she uses him to convince M that Renard continues to pose a threat. Elektra sleeps with Bond, drawing him in emotionally. She is attracted to him but even more enchanted by her own power over men. Next, she convinces M that a nuclear warhead stolen by Renard has been used to blow up her pipeline. Elektra then obtains a Russian nuclear submarine and crew for her plot to destroy Istanbul—the only other channel for Caspian Sea oil to reach the West, apart from her pipeline.

As a final act of devotion, Renard plans to place part of the stolen warhead's plutonium in the submarine's reactor, turning the sub into a nuclear bomb.

Elektra takes Bond prisoner at the Maiden's Tower on the Bosphorus. When Russian casino and caviar factory owner Valentin Zukovsky confronts her, she shoots him. However, he fires one final shot, which frees 007.

ACCESSING THE FILES (right) Bond searches the MI6 archives to search for clues related to Elektra's kidnap ordeal.

ACT OF BETRAYAL (far right) M lashes out at Elektra, furious at the duplicity of a young woman she looked on as a daughter. Elektra responds by imprisoning M in Istanbul's Maiden's Tower.

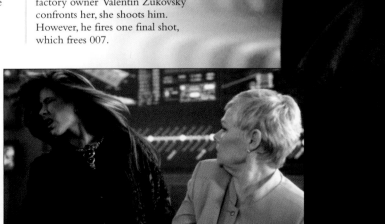

TURN OF THE SCREW *Elektra taunts Bond, held captive in an antique torture chair.*

"You should have killed me when you had the chance. But you couldn't —not me— not a woman you've loved."

Elektra to 007

FINAL FAREWELL *Elektra and Renard share a last embrace before he goes to his death. "The future is yours—have fun with it," he tells her.*

Elektra, unarmed, faces Bond at the top of the tower. Bond trains a gun on her, making it clear he will spare her life if she calls off Renard's attack. She feels certain Bond will not kill her—a former lover—in cold blood. The moment she gives the final command to Renard via radio, Bond shoots her in the heart.

KISCH

APPEARANCE
Goldfinger (1964)
STATUS **Dead; killed by Oddjob**
CHARACTERISTICS **Quiet, efficient**
PLAYED BY **Michael Mellinger**

Goldfinger uses Kisch, his loyal lieutenant, for many key tasks. Kisch shoots Bond with a tranquilizer gun, gasses a group of American gangsters, and handcuffs Bond to an atomic device inside the vault at Fort Knox. When Goldfinger seals Kisch inside the depository, Kisch makes a dash to remove the bomb's fuse, but Oddjob hurls him off a gangway to his death. Bond retrieves the handcuff key from Kisch's body and frees himself to battle Oddjob.

TIME BOMB *Kisch prepares to lock James Bond to an atomic device inside Fort Knox.*

KLEBB, ROSA

APPEARANCE
From Russia With Love (1963)
STATUS Dead; shot by Tatiana Romanova
CHARACTERISTICS Viciously cruel, phlegmatic, repulsive
PLAYED BY Lotte Lenya

Colonel Rosa Klebb, a.k.a. SPECTRE Number 3, is the former head of operations for SMERSH. She relishes the mechanisms of authoritarian structure with a sadomasochistic delight. In the presence of Blofeld, she obsequiously hangs on his every word. Outside Blofeld's presence, Klebb becomes a dominatrix, issuing orders with glee and luxuriating in her power.

Klebb, as described by Ian Fleming, is a squat, toadlike woman with her orange hair tightly scraped back. She is bisexual and makes a crude pass at Tatiana Romanova in both the novel and film.

Klebb defected from the Soviet Intelligence apparatus to run operations for SPECTRE. She implements Kronsteen's plan by selecting assassin Donald Grant and recruiting Soviet cipher

clerk Tatiana Romanova to entice Bond to steal a Lektor decoder. She also guides Grant to commit acts of sabotage and murder to heat up the Cold War in Istanbul. When Bond survives Grant's attempt to kill him on the Orient Express, Klebb, under personal orders from Blofeld, goes after Bond herself in Venice. Disguised as a hotel maid, she tries to steal the Lektor and assassinate Bond. Tatiana knocks the gun away, leading to Klebb's attack with the poison-tipped blade in her shoe. Tatiana shoots Klebb before she can fatally kick Bond.

In the novel, Klebb is one of the most powerful and feared women in the Soviet Union. She rose to power working for Moscow during the Spanish Civil War. In 1953, she became the head of operations for Otdyel II, SMERSH, where she reportedly let no torture take place without her presence and had a special blood-spattered smock for such occasions. She is said to have killed—or ordered the killing of—more people than anyone in the world. She attempts to stab Bond with poisoned knitting needles at the Ritz in Paris but fails. As French authorities arrest her, she nearly kills 007 with a kick from the poison-tipped blade in her shoe. M later reports that Klebb died in custody.

> "You are not here to ask questions!"
> Rosa Klebb to Tatiana Romanova

KOSKOV, GENERAL

APPEARANCE
The Living Daylights (1987)
STATUS Arrested; probably executed by the KGB
CHARACTERISTICS Veneer of charm conceals a cunning criminal brain
PLAYED BY Jeroen Krabbe

Soviet mastermind General Georgi Koskov plots an elaborate scheme with American arms dealer Brad Whitaker to take over the KGB for personal gain.

When Koskov informs the British Secret Service that he wishes to defect to the West, he specifically asks for James Bond to protect him from a KGB sniper assigned to watch him. In actuality, Koskov's defection is part of an elaborate plot to convince MI6 to assassinate General Leonid Pushkin, the new head of the KGB. He sets up his cellist girlfriend Kara Milovy as the supposed sniper so that Bond will assassinate her. He wants her out of the way, since she knows too much about his operations. Sensing Kara doesn't know what she's doing, Bond shoots the rifle out of her hands and successfully brings Koskov to England.

At MI6's Blayden safe house, Koskov claims to M, the Minister of Defense, and Bond that General Pushkin is "sick like Stalin" and has restarted the assassination program Smiert Spionam ("Death to Spies"), deactivated for 20 years, to eliminate British and American agents. Minutes later, the KGB supposedly recaptures Koskov. Actually, Koskov's accomplice Necros captures him and delivers him safely to Brad Whitaker's palatial home in Tangier.

Once Bond eliminates Pushkin,

LIVING IT UP *Georgi Koskov relaxes poolside at arms dealer Brad Whitaker's luxurious mansion in Tangier.*

Koskov and Whitaker plan to use the down payment on a large Soviet order of American high-tech weapons to buy a vast supply of opium from Afghan drug dealers the Snow Leopard Brotherhood. They will make a fortune when they sell the opium to various parts of the world and still be able to supply the Soviets with their initial arms order. Claiming his defection was just a clever ruse, Koskov will then heroically return to the Soviet Union with Bond, Pushkin's killer, in line to become the next head of the KGB.

Bond, however, does not believe that Pushkin is a psychopath, and the two men join forces to turn the tables on Koskov and Whitaker by

> **"I'm sorry, James. For you I have great affection, but we have an old saying: duty has no sweethearts."**
>
> **Koskov to 007**

faking Pushkin's assassination. When Koskov convinces Kara to drug Bond, claiming he is a KGB agent pursuing him, Bond proves Koskov is a liar by revealing that he was assigned to kill her by British Intelligence but spared her life.

Koskov captures Bond and takes him and Kara to Colonel Feyador's airbase in Afghanistan. Bond and Kara escape custody, and Bond destroys Koskov's and Whitaker's opium shipment. Bond then returns to Tangier to eliminate Whitaker. Pushkin recaptures Koskov and ships him in a "diplomatic bag" back to Moscow, where he faces execution.

KRA

APPEARANCE
The Man With The Golden Gun (1974)
STATUS Dead; killed by Goodnight
CHARACTERISTICS Skilled with machines
PLAYED BY Sonny Caldinez

Kra works in maintenance and security for Scaramanga, operating his solar energy system. He finds life lonely on Scaramanga's island, and the sight of Mary Goodnight in a bikini proves too much for him. She hits him over the head with a spanner, sending his body into the temperature-controlled vats. The heat from Kra's body sets off a series of explosions that destroy the island.

KRATT

APPEARANCE
Casino Royale (2006)
STATUS Dead; shot by Mr. White
CHARACTERISTICS Intimidating and watchful; good with a knife
PLAYED BY Clemens Schick

Le Chiffre's shaven-headed bodyguard Kratt accompanies his boss to Uganda to make a deal with terrorist leader Steven Obanno. Back in the Bahamas, Kratt informs Le Chiffre that MI6 has eliminated the bomber Mollaka. Later, using a knife, Kratt cuts a tracking device from Bond's arm and the seat from a cane-bottomed chair. He strips 007 and places him in the chair so Le Chiffre can torture him. Kratt dies when Mr. White arrives, killing Le Chiffre and his men.

KREST, MILTON

APPEARANCE
Licence To Kill (1989)
STATUS Dead; killed by Sanchez
CHARACTERISTICS Frequently drunk, belligerent, extremely unlucky
PLAYED BY Anthony Zerbe

American Milton Krest owns the Ocean Exotica Warehouse in Key West and the *Wavekrest*, a marine research vessel. Both serve as covers for drug lord Franz Sanchez's US and Caribbean drug operations.

Once an imposing man, Krest is now Sanchez's alcoholic puppet, who peeks through windows at his boss's girlfriend Lupe Lamora. After aiding in Sanchez's escape from US custody, Krest becomes a pawn in Bond's vengeance plot to turn the drug lord against his many underlings. Bond steals $5 million in drug money from Sanchez and plants the money on the *Wavekrest* in Isthmus City. Krest pleads his innocence to his boss,

CRUEL DEATH *Sanchez metes out the ultimate punishment to his associate Krest.*

claiming that he has no idea how the money ended up there, but Sanchez believes Krest stole the money to pay a freelance hit team to kill him. Sanchez throws Krest into the ship's decompression chamber, causing his head to explode.

Krest appears in Fleming's short story *The Hildebrand Rarity*. Bond helps Krest and fisherman Fidele Barbey capture a rare fish, the Hildebrand Rarity, in the Seychelles for the Smithsonian Institute. Bond dislikes Krest, whom he discovers whips his wife with a stingray tail known as "The Corrector." Bond later finds Krest dead with the rare fish stuffed in his mouth.

KRIEGLER, ERICH

APPEARANCE
For Your Eyes Only (1981)
STATUS Dead; shoved out the window by 007
CHARACTERISTICS Extremely fit, quietly menacing; expert skier and shot
PLAYED BY John Wyman

KGB agent Erich Kriegler is an assassin as well as the East German biathlon champion, who, according to Bibi Dahl, "doesn't smoke, only eats health foods, and won't even talk to girls." The KGB assigns Kriegler to help their agent Aris Kristatos salvage the Automatic Targeting Attack Communicator (ATAC) from the wreck of the *St. Georges*.

Bond encounters Kriegler while the latter competes on a biathlon course at Cortina D'Ampezzo in the Italian Alps. Kriegler first pursues Bond on skis and then chases him on the snow and down a bobsled run while riding a Yamaha XJ500 motorcycle equipped with machine guns. Bond escapes, but Kriegler crashes the motorcycle.

When Kristatos retrieves the ATAC from Bond, Kriegler guards it until the KGB arrives at St. Cyril's Monastery to pay for its delivery. Bond then raids the monastery and uses a heavy spiked candelabra to push Kriegler headlong through a window, causing the KGB assassin to fall to his death.

KRILENCU

APPEARANCE
From Russia With Love (1963)
STATUS Assassinated by Kerim Bey
CHARACTERISTICS Enjoys killing
PLAYED BY Fred Haggerty

Bulgarian Krilencu works as a killer for the Soviets in the Balkans. He twice attempts to assassinate Kerim Bey. He plants a limpet mine outside Bey's office and, during a gun battle at a gypsy camp, he shoots Bey in the arm. The next night, Kerim Bey sets a trap. He brings Bond to Krilencu's home, a building with a poster for the Bob Hope comedy *Call Me Bwana* (1963) painted on the side. Bey's sons, dressed like police, ring the doorbell. Bey and Bond watch as a secret trapdoor, concealed in Anita Ekberg's mouth, opens. As Krilencu escapes, Bey shoots him.

In the novel, Marilyn Monroe's mouth on the poster of *Niagara* (1953) hides the trapdoor.

> " This man **kills for pleasure.** "
>
> **Kerim Bey on Krilencu**

KRISTATOS, ARIS

APPEARANCE
For Your Eyes Only (1981)
STATUS Dead; knifed by Columbo
CHARACTERISTICS Cultured manner hides a cruel and ruthless nature
PLAYED BY Julian Glover

Aristotle Kristatos leaves a trail of murder and mayhem in his quest to obtain the British Automatic Targeting Attack Communicator (ATAC) transmitter and sell it to the Soviets.

Originally from Kefalonia, Greece, Kristatos appears to be an Anglophilic shipping magnate with additional businesses in insurance and oil exploration. The British awarded him the King's Medal for his resistance fighting against the Nazis on Crete during World War II, but in actuality Kristatos worked as a double agent during the war and the Greek Civil War. His arch-rival, smuggler Milos Columbo, knows his secret history and his current work of smuggling

heroin from Albania into England through newsprint rolls. The proud sponsor of Olympic hopeful ice skater Bibi Dahl, Kristatos lives for the day she will win the gold medal. According to British agent Luigi Ferrara, Kristatos spends a few months every year at his chalet in Cortina d'Ampezzo and "knows everything going on."

To obtain the ATAC, Kristatos apparently arranges for a World War II–era contact mine to be placed in the fishing nets of the *St. Georges*, a British vessel that secretly serves as an electronic surveillance ship. The mine explodes, but the *St. Georges* sinks in water too deep for Kristatos to mount a recovery operation. The British send marine archaeologist Sir Timothy Havelock to secretly locate the ATAC. Kristatos orders his murder, failing to account for the vengeful dedication of Havelock's daughter, Melina.

When Kristatos meets Bond in Cortina, he stages the murder of British agent Ferrara and orders assassination attempts on Bond and Melina Havelock. Kristatos temporarily misleads Bond into believing that Columbo, Kristatos's hated rival, ordered the Havelock assassination, but finds the tables have turned when Bond and Columbo raid his Albanian warehouse. Realizing Bond and Melina will lead him to the location of the ATAC, he has them shadowed. Once Bond and Melina recover the ATAC, he seizes it and attempts to murder them by dragging them over a coral reef in shark-infested waters.

Kristatos retires to St. Cyril's Monastery in Greece, where he awaits payment from the KGB. After he completes the transaction, he plans to leave Greece for Cuba. He never gets the chance. Bond, Melina, and Columbo raid the monastery as General Gogol arrives with the payment for the ATAC. Before Kristatos can complete the transaction, Columbo hurls a knife in his back, killing him. Kristatos dies surrounded by those he betrayed.

> "Leave the legs free.
> They'll make appetizing bait."
> **Kristatos**

KRONSTEEN

APPEARANCE
From Russia With Love (1963)
STATUS Assassinated by Morzeny
CHARACTERISTICS Tactical genius; methodical, arrogant, vain
PLAYED BY Vladek Sheybal

> "I have anticipated every possible variation of counter move."
> **Kronsteen**

Czechoslovakian chess champion Kronsteen secretly serves as SPECTRE's Number 5, the director of planning. He devises a plan to have the British Secret Service steal a Lektor decoder with the aid of Soviet cipher clerk Tatiana Romanova, who believes she is on a top-secret mission for SMERSH, the murder apparat of the Soviet Union.

SPECTRE plans to recover the decoder and sell it back to the Soviets. But first, Kronsteen's plan calls for the humiliating death of James Bond to avenge his killing of SPECTRE operative Dr. No.

Kronsteen's scheme would ultimately encompass the faked suicide of Bond and a letter, supposedly from Tatiana, threatening to turn over to the press a film of her making love to Bond if he does not marry her. When Kronsteen's cunning plot fails, SPECTRE Number 1 Ernst Stavro Blofeld orders his death. In the novel, Kronsteen is known as the "Wizard of Ice" for his emotionless chess style, which has helped him win the title of Champion of Moscow twice.

KUTZE, LADISLAV

APPEARANCE
Thunderball (1965)
STATUS Presumed dead; lost at sea
CHARACTERISTICS Meticulous
PLAYED BY George Pravda

Polish nuclear physicist Ladislav Kutze is Emilio Largo's chief technical engineer, preparing hijacked nuclear weapons to extort money from the West. Kutze becomes increasingly ambivalent about his role and disturbed when he finds Largo torturing Domino Derval. When Largo later tries to escape the Royal Navy in the *Disco Volante*, Kutze frees Domino and tells her that he has thrown the arming device for the one remaining bomb into the sea. Kutze leaps from the *Disco Volante* hydrofoil before it explodes, never to be seen again.

LACHAISE

APPEARANCE
The World Is Not Enough (1999)
STATUS Dead; knifed in the neck
CHARACTERISTICS Well-groomed, tight-lipped, professional, procedural
PLAYED BY Patrick Malahide

An executive at La Banque Suisse de L'Industrie in Bilbao, Spain, Lachaise operates as a middleman, baiting a trap set by Elektra King and terrorist Renard to kill Sir Robert King, Elektra's father. Lachaise contacts MI6, offering to return money paid by Sir Robert for a secret Russian Atomic Energy Commission Report that turned out to be worthless. Just as Lachaise is about to reveal the name of the person behind the scam to Bond, another Renard agent— The Cigar Girl—kills him.

LARGO, EMILIO

APPEARANCE
Thunderball (1965)
STATUS Dead; harpooned
CHARACTERISTICS Authoritative, arrogant, amoral, cruel; enjoys impressing others with his beautiful possessions
PLAYED BY Adolfo Celi

SPECTRE Number 2 Emilio Largo leads a plot to hijack a bomber carrying two hydrogen bombs and extort $280 million (£100 million) from the NATO nations. According to Ian Fleming in his novel *Thunderball*, Largo hails from Rome. His ruthlessness, social position, nerves of steel, and most of all, his "exquisite fineness" make him a perfect match for SPECTRE.

Largo has seduced Dominique (Domino) Derval in Capri. She is the sister of François Derval, a NATO pilot whom SPECTRE eventually murders. Domino proves to be Bond's avenue to Largo.

BAD LOSER *Bond defeats Largo at the baccarat tables while Domino looks on.*

After arranging for the hijacked NATO bomber to crash-land at sea, Largo kills SPECTRE-hired pilot Angelo Palazzi. Largo's men then camouflage the bomber at rest on the seabed and transport the nuclear weapons to a sealed underwater cave.

In Nassau, Largo discovers Bond has been dispatched to observe him. Both know they are watching each other. Both also know that Largo has nothing to fear directly from 007 as long as Bond does not know where the nuclear warheads are hidden.

As the deadline approaches, Largo retrieves the bombs but discovers 007 has infiltrated his underwater crew. Largo traps Bond behind the hydraulic doors of the underwater pen. He then takes the *Disco Volante* to Biscayne Bay but discovers that Domino has betrayed him by trying to signal to the CIA that the bombs are on board. Furious, he tortures her. Largo and his crew slip out through the underwater hatch to plant one bomb to be used should the NATO nations fail to pay up. However, as he guides his men underwater, Aquaparas from the US Navy attack them. Bond joins them, and they capture one bomb.

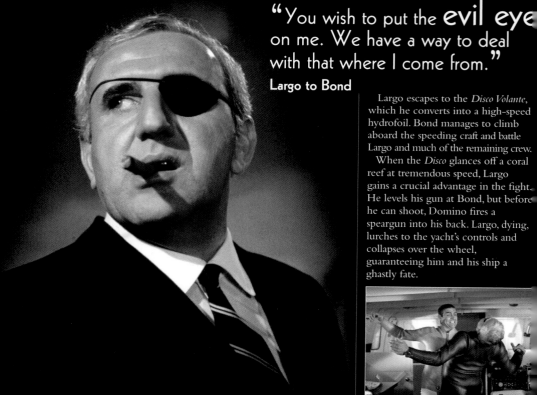

"You wish to put the **evil eye** on me. We have a way to deal with that where I come from."
Largo to Bond

Largo escapes to the *Disco Volante*, which he converts into a high-speed hydrofoil. Bond manages to climb aboard the speeding craft and battle Largo and much of the remaining crew.

When the *Disco* glances off a coral reef at tremendous speed, Largo gains a crucial advantage in the fight. He levels his gun at Bond, but before he can shoot, Domino fires a speargun into his back. Largo, dying, lurches to the yacht's controls and collapses over the wheel, guaranteeing him and his ship a ghastly fate.

FINAL RECKONING *Largo and Bond grapple aboard the* **Disco Volante.**

Fiona Volpe: You Would like **Bond dead?**
Largo: I can think of no **better arrangement!**

LE CHIFFRE

APPEARANCE
Casino Royale (2006)
STATUS Dead; shot by Mr. White
CHARACTERISTICS Conniving, ruthless, enigmatic
PLAYED BY Mads Mikkelsen

Le Chiffre provides private banking services for the world's terrorists. He invests their money, then gives them access to it wherever they need it. To make his personal fortune, he employs terrorists to manipulate stock values.

Le Chiffre's background remains murky. MI6 knows him only as Le

BUSINESS TALKS *Le Chiffre and the mysterious Mr. White meet with Steven Obanno, leader of the Lord's Resistance Army, to discuss Obanno's substantial investment.*

Chiffre, or "the cipher." Born, it is believed, in Albania, Le Chiffre earned a reputation as a chess prodigy and mathematical genius. As a poker player, his ability to quickly determine the odds made him a formidable opponent. Le Chiffre associated with Saddam Hussein, but the Iraqi leader reportedly turned against him after the 1991 Gulf War and ordered him beheaded. Although MI6 long believed Le Chiffre to be dead, he remained alive and prospered as terrorist networks grew during the 1990s.

Le Chiffre's distinguishing features include a scar surrounding his left eye and "a derangement of the tear duct" that causes him to weep blood. He often uses an inhaler.

After receiving a large investment from Steven Obanno, leader of the Lord's Resistance Army in Uganda, Le Chiffre writes put options on Skyfleet (a "put option" is an agreement to buy a stock at a certain price), an aerospace consortium about to unveil the world's largest airliner. He plans to destroy the

plane, but Bond foils the plot, causing Le Chiffre to lose over $100 million. To win back the money, Le Chiffre sets up a high-stakes poker tournament in Montenegro.

Bond, staked first by the British government and later by the CIA, defeats Le Chiffre. Facing financial ruin, Le Chiffre captures and tortures Bond, but 007 refuses to give him the password to access the account holding the winnings. Before Le Chiffre can kill Bond, Mr. White, a shadowy figure from the terrorist underworld, murders Le Chiffre, leaving Bond alive.

In the Ian Fleming novel, Le Chiffre works as a Soviet operative in France.

> "The only question remains. Will you yield... in time?"
>
> Le Chiffre to Bond

LING, MR.

APPEARANCE
Goldfinger (1964)
STATUS Dead; killed by Goldfinger
CHARACTERISTICS A methodical man
PLAYED BY Burt Kwouk

COUNTDOWN *Outside the Fort Knox vault, Mr. Ling sets the timer on the atomic device.*

Nuclear fission specialist Mr. Ling accompanies the atomic device provided to Auric Goldfinger by the Communist Chinese. Bond overhears Goldfinger speak the phrase "Operation Grand Slam" to Ling in Switzerland. When Goldfinger captures Bond, Ling advises keeping him alive. When the atomic device arrives at Fort Knox, Ling primes it to explode in four minutes. Goldfinger shoots Ling dead when US Army troops attack.

LIPARUS CAPTAIN

APPEARANCE
The Spy Who Loved Me (1977)
STATUS Dead; killed in an explosion
CHARACTERISTICS Loyal to his chief, good at complex tasks
PLAYED BY Sydney Tafler

The captain of the *Liparus* manages one of the most complex ships ever built—a craft large enough to hold an operations center to launch a nuclear war, three Polaris-class submarines, and hundreds of prisoners and crew. The captain nervously reports to shipping magnate Karl Stromberg that fighting has broken out among his crew and the captured sailors. When Bond attacks the operations center, an explosion fatally injures the captain. He tells Bond that only four minutes remain before nuclear missiles launch to destroy New York and Moscow.

LIPPE, COUNT

APPEARANCE
Thunderball (1965)
STATUS Dead; killed by Fiona Volpe
CHARACTERISTICS Cruel, rash
PLAYED BY Guy Doleman

Count Lippe recruits and coaches Angelo Palazzi to impersonate NATO pilot Major François Derval as part of a plot to hijack two atomic weapons. A SPECTRE agent, Lippe stays with Palazzi at the Shrublands health clinic, where James Bond notices the symbol of the Red Dragon of Macau Tong tattooed on his wrist. Lippe, aware of Bond's suspicion about the tattoo, tries to kill him on a motorized traction machine. Bond survives and traps Lippe in a steam cabinet with the heat turned up high.

After helping switch Palazzi for Derval, Lippe tries once more to kill Bond. Yet, Lippe is unaware that Blofeld has ordered his death. As he chases and fires at Bond's Aston Martin DB5, SPECTRE killer Fiona Volpe shoots rockets into his car, incinerating him.

LOCQUE, EMILE LEOPOLD

APPEARANCE
For Your Eyes Only (1981)
STATUS Dead; killed by Bond
CHARACTERISTICS Silent, psychotic, murderous, unemotional
PLAYED BY Michael Gothard

Emile Leopold Locque commits murders for corrupt smuggler Kristatos. A former enforcer for the Brussels underworld, Locque escaped a murder sentence at Namur prison after strangling his psychiatrist.

Locque pays Hector Gonzales in Spain for assassinating Sir Timothy Havelock and his wife. When daughter Melina Havelock kills Gonzales, Locque takes back the cash. Locque aids Kristatos in convincing James Bond that rival Milos Columbo murdered the Havelocks. Locque kills MI6 contact Luigi Ferrara, leaving a columbo (dove) pin on his body. He later runs over Columbo's mistress Countess Lisl Von Schlaf. Locque faces Bond in Albania, where 007 shoots him and then kicks him and his car off a cliff.

"He had **no head for heights.**"
007

EYES OF A KILLER *Locque's unusual octagonal glasses help Bond identify him using Q's Visual Identagraph machine.*

LOG CABIN GIRL

APPEARANCE
The Spy Who Loved Me (1977)
STATUS Living; whereabouts unknown
CHARACTERISTICS Stunning, passionate, duplicitous
PLAYED BY Sue Vanner

James Bond makes love to a beautiful woman in a cabin near Berngarten, Austria, unaware that she works for the KGB. Her passion seems genuine enough. However, when Bond receives word that M needs him and quickly leaves, she notifies agent Sergei Barsov and his team of assassins via radio, igniting a dangerous and deadly chase on skis culminating in Bond leaping off the side of a mountain.

MEDRANO, GENERAL

APPEARANCE
Quantum Of Solace (2008)
STATUS Dead; shot by Camille
CHARACTERISTICS Calculating, brutal
PLAYED BY Joaquín Cosio

General Medrano is a deposed Bolivian dictator dealing with Dominic Greene and Quantum to overthrow the existing government and return him to power in exchange for what appears to be a tract of valueless desert.

Early in his career, Medrano killed Ernesto Montes, a powerful figure in the Bolivian military junta. After killing Montes, he raped and strangled his wife and older daughter, allowing Montes's younger daughter Camille to watch before burning the house down. He is surprised and

delighted when Greene offers him the very same Camille to help seal their bargain.

At the Perla De Las Dunas Hotel, Medrano meets with Greene to sign the final paperwork. Medrano refuses to do so when he learns that water costs in Bolivia will double when he takes office. The tract of desert

Greene has acquired by the deal conceals a vast underground reservoir of water—60 per cent of the entire country's water supply. Greene tells Medrano that if he doesn't sign, he will be deposed and killecd; Medrano duly signs.

Medrano returns to his suite and attempts to rape the hotel receptionist. Camille stops the rape and Medrano attacks her instead. She kills him with a single gunshot.

THE DEAL SWEETENER In Haiti, General Medrano and his men take Camille aboard his boat.

MURDER IN MIND General Medrano vents his brutal rage on Camille, but she will soon have her revenge.

MARKOVITZ & BECHMANN

APPEARANCE
The Spy Who Loved Me (1977)
STATUS Dead; blown up
CHARACTERISTICS Nervous, greedy
PLAYED BY Milo Sperber (Markovitz), Cyril Shaps (Bechmann)

The two brilliant scientists Professor Markovitz and Dr. Bechmann develop a submarine tracking system for shipping magnate Karl Stromberg. After the successful capture of HMS *Ranger* and the *Potemkin*, Stromberg instructs his assistant to pay $10 million each into the scientists' Swiss bank accounts. But as they fly from his ocean laboratory, *Atlantis*, Stromberg blows up the helicopter in which they are riding.

METZ, DR.

APPEARANCE
Diamonds Are Forever (1971)
STATUS Missing; presumed dead
CHARACTERISTICS Brilliant scientist; idealistic, pompous, gullible
PLAYED BY Joseph Furst

Known as the world's leading expert on laser refraction, Metz builds Ernst Stavro Blofeld the ultimate weapon, a diamond-encrusted satellite laser. Metz believes he and Blofeld have the same goal: total disarmament of the nuclear powers, resulting in world peace. Once Metz's satellite begins blasting military targets, Metz foresees war and begs Blofeld to surrender. With horror, he realizes Blofeld wants world domination. Metz dies in the assault on Blofeld's oil rig command center.

MISCHKA & GRISCHKA

APPEARANCE
Octopussy (1983)
STATUS Dead; both killed by Bond
CHARACTERISTICS Fiercely loyal to
each other; implacable killers
PLAYED BY David and Tony Meyer

Twin knife throwers Mischka and
Grischka feature prominently in
Octopussy's circus. Kamal Khan and
General Orlov also secretly employ
the pair as assassins.

When Agent 009, disguised as a
circus clown, steals a fake Fabergé
egg from Octopussy's circus in East
Berlin, Mischka and Grischka give
chase. They eventually throw a knife
into his back, fatally wounding him.
009's murder and the recovery of the
fake Fabergé egg from his body bring
James Bond to investigate.

Later, on board Octopussy's train,
Mischka uses a welding torch to
attack Bond as he enters a car
housing Khan's and Orlov's atomic
bomb. Momentarily blinded, Bond
pulls a lever just in time, bringing
the circus's heavy cannon down on
Mischka, instantly killing him. Bond
then disguises himself in Mischka's
clothes. When Grischka sees Khan's
henchman Gobinda battling Bond,
who is dressed in his brother's
clothes, he realizes his brother has
been murdered. Bond and Grischka
fight and fall off the train. Grischka
pursues 007, pinning him to a cabin
door with his knives. Bond turns
the tables on the vengeful twin by
throwing one of Grischka's own
knives into his stomach, avenging
the murder of 009.

The origins of Mischka and
Grischka stem from an early script
draft of *The Spy Who Loved Me* (1977).

MITCHELL

APPEARANCE
Quantum Of Solace (2008)
STATUS Dead; shot by Bond
CHARACTERISTICS Expert at
passing security tests; non-smoker
PLAYED BY Glenn Foster

Under interrogation in Siena, Italy,
Mr. White reveals to M and Bond
that his organization has people
"everywhere." Craig Mitchell, 45, has
worked for M for eight years, five as
her personal bodyguard. He suddenly
shoots an MI6 guard and fires at M,
wounding Mr White. Bond pursues
Mitchell through Siena's cisterns,
through the Palio horserace crowds,
and across rooftops. They crash
through a art gallery's glass dome
onto scaffolding. After a struggle,
Bond is forced to shoot Mitchell.
Mitchell's intervention has allowed

DOUBLE AGENT *Mitchell takes a shot at Bond in Siena.*

White, though wounded, to escape.
M is desperate to discover who
Mitchell and Mr. White are
working for. MI6 Forensics
find a clue in Mitchell's
apartment: a bank bill
with links to Le Chiffre.
Similar bills have also
been traced to an
assassin named Edmund
Slate currently in Port-
Au-Prince, Haiti.

SMOOTH MOVES *Mollaka races through a construction site in Madagascar to elude Bond.*

MOLLAKA

APPEARANCE
Casino Royale (2006)
STATUS Dead, shot by Bond
CHARACTERISTICS Fast on his feet;
amazing free runner; burn scars on body
PLAYED BY Sébastien Foucan

Mollaka earns his living as a bomb-maker and saboteur. Alex Dimitrios, a middleman working with terrorist banker Le Chiffre, contacts him to destroy the prototype of the world's largest airliner, built by Skyfleet.

In Madagascar, Mollaka realizes that MI6 operative Carter has him under surveillance and knowing that the bomb in his backpack will incriminate him, he runs. He eludes Carter, leaping through an empty swimming pool where a cobra-mongoose fight takes place. Carter falls foul of the cobra, but Mollaka soon discovers that another

MI6 agent is pursuing him—James Bond. Racing for the sanctuary of the Nambutu Embassy, Mollaka charges into a construction site. An expert free runner, Mollaka races up the girders forming the skeleton of a building, assuming that Bond will be forced to remain on the ground. Bond, however, refuses to quit, doggedly pursuing his quarry even when Mollaka scales a construction crane, springs across to another crane, and then leaps down onto a rooftop.

Bond follows Mollaka into the Nambutu Embassy, determined not to let him escape. When embassy guards finally corner Bond, he shoots Mollaka dead and escapes in a cloud of flame and smoke with Mollaka's backpack. This explosive incident, faithfully captured on the embassy's security cameras, becomes front-page news in England. Mollaka's death forces Dimitrios to hire Carlos, a new bomber.

MOON, GENERAL

APPEARANCE
Die Another Day (2002)
STATUS Dead; victim of patricide
CHARACTERISTICS Dignified; over-indulgent parent
PLAYED BY Kenneth Tsang

"The son I knew died long ago."
General Moon to Gustav Graves

North Korean General Moon yearns for peace between North Korea and the West, but his son has other plans. Moon hoped his son's Western education would broaden his mind, but it only corrupted him. Colonel Moon's apparent death, during a hovercraft chase with 007, crushes his father. General Moon takes Bond prisoner and discovers that Bond's incursion into North Korea has given a stronghold to a group of warmongering generals in the North Korean government. He also believes Bond knows his son's Western ally. He learns nothing from 007 and eventually frees him for Zao in a prisoner exchange. The General later learns that his son has used gene therapy to transform himself into Gustav Graves and plans to launch a war with South Korea. When General Moon rejects the plan and his son, Graves murders him.

MORTNER, DR.

APPEARANCE
A View To A Kill (1985)
STATUS Dead; killed in airship explosion
CHARACTERISTICS Protective, paternal
PLAYED BY Willoughby Gray

Dr. Carl Mortner's real name is Hans Glaub, a Nazi scientist who experimented with steroids on pregnant Jewish women in concentration camps to enhance intelligence. A number of women aborted, although several children were produced with phenomenal IQs. The only side-effect was that the children, who included Max Zorin, matured into psychotics. The Soviets then grabbed Glaub and had him develop steroids for their athletes. Glaub eventually appears in the West with Zorin as Dr. Carl Mortner, a horse breeding consultant who injects steroids into Zorin's horses. Mortner is later distraught at his "creation's" death and dies when Zorin's airship explodes.

MORZENY

APPEARANCE
From Russia With Love (1963)
STATUS Unknown
CHARACTERISTICS Lethal, bureaucratic
PLAYED BY Walter Gotell

Morzeny trains personnel on SPECTRE Island, where he introduces SMERSH defector Rosa Klebb to assassin Donald Grant. Under orders from Blofeld, Morzeny kills SPECTRE No. 5, Kronsteen, when his plan to acquire the Lektor decoder fails. Klebb orders Morzeny to complete the mission. He suffers burns when Bond ignites a fuel slick around his boat off the Dalmatian coast. It is rumored he returned to the Soviet Union and had a career with the KGB.

KILLER TACTICS *Morzeny, Rhoda, and Klebb plot the demise of 007.*

NAOMI

APPEARANCE
The Spy Who Loved Me (1977)
STATUS Dead; blasted out of the sky
CHARACTERISTICS Great helicopter pilot, even better at flirting
PLAYED BY Caroline Munro

Naomi works for Karl Stromberg as his beautiful but murderous helicopter pilot/assistant. Naomi's dazzling smile and sparkling eyes conceal a deadly fascination with killing. She collects James Bond and Anya Amasova at the Hotel Cala di Volpe and brings them to *Atlantis*, Stromberg's ocean laboratory. Her flirtations with Bond raise Anya's ire. When Bond and Anya later drive in 007's Lotus Esprit, Stromberg's assassins, including Naomi, set upon them. Naomi blasts the Lotus with the machine guns mounted on her Bell Jet Ranger helicopter. She appears to drive Bond and Anya into the sea, unaware that Bond's Lotus can transform into a well-armed submarine. She ends up a sitting duck, blown away by a sea-air missile.

NECROS

APPEARANCE
The Living Daylights (1987)
STATUS Dead; given the boot by 007
CHARACTERISTICS Extremely strong, fit, and cunning; often employs disguise
PLAYED BY Andreas Wisniewski

Soviet assassin Necros works for KGB General Koskov and arms dealer Brad Whitaker. A true chameleon, he convincingly adopts various accents and impersonates a runner, a milkman, a doctor, a balloon vendor, and a lighting technician to accomplish his various objectives. He uses his Walkman headphone wires as a garrote to assassinate his victims.

Necros plays a central role in Koskov's kidnapping from the Blayden safe house. He also kills Saunders, head of Section V, and kidnaps Bond in Tangier, helping to transport him to Afghanistan.

Necros assists in Koskov's opium smuggling scheme and fights with Bond on a cargo net hanging out of the back of a Soviet transport plane. The assassin grabs Bond's boot to prevent himself from falling, but Bond cuts his boot's laces, causing Necros to plummet to his death.

NICK NACK

APPEARANCE
The Man With The Golden Gun (1974)
STATUS Living; serving a life sentence in a very small cell
CHARACTERISTICS Impish, conniving
PLAYED BY Hervé Villechaize

Nick Nack works for master assassin Francisco Scaramanga as a most evil gentleman's gentleman, serving the functions of butler, chef, accomplice, and occasional assailant.

Nick Nack resides on Scaramanga's island in the South China Sea. He arranges for hitmen to try to kill Scaramanga in his private fun house maze. These exercises help to keep his boss in peak condition for killing. On one occasion, Nick Nack remarks that, should Scaramanga die, the island will become his.

Nick Nack helps Scaramanga in his mission to auction off the world's first solar energy system. He also steals the vital Solex Agitator from the lifeless body of the scientist Gibson after Scaramanga kills him.

When Bond faces off with Scaramanga on the island, Nick Nack officiates the duel. After Bond kills Scaramanga and escapes with Mary Goodnight in Scaramanga's junk ship, Nick Nack attacks. Bond shuts Nick Nack in a suitcase and places him in a wicker basket hung from the boat's mainmast.

"I may be small, but I never forget."

Nick Nack to 007

NO, DR.

APPEARANCE
Dr. No (1962)
STATUS Dead; boiled alive
CHARACTERISTICS A scientific genius, egotistical, impassive, commanding; rules subordinates by fear
PLAYED BY Joseph Wiseman

Dr. No masterminds a plot to sabotage or "topple" American rocket launches from Cape Canaveral. Using a secret base on the Caribbean island of Crab Key off the coast of Jamaica, Dr. No employs a nuclear reactor to beam radio signals that interfere with the rockets' gyroscopic controls.

By Dr. No's own account, he is "the unwanted son of a German missionary and a Chinese girl of good family." He became "treasurer of the most powerful criminal society in China," before stealing $10 million of their money and escaping to the US. Rejected by the scientific communities of both East and West, Dr. No joined the terrorist organization SPECTRE and became one of their top operatives. He now plans to exact revenge against East and West, with SPECTRE deciding which side will win the Cold War and be first to reach the moon.

Dr. No's great strength is his ability to instill fear into the men and women he employs. Metallurgist Professor Dent heads his criminal organization in Jamaica. Dr. No, through Dent, apparently controls the actions of the so-called Three Blind Mice killers, Mr. Jones, a

MASTER VILLAIN *Dr. No congratulates 007 for damaging his organization and his pride before calling him "a stupid policeman."*

> ## "I never fail, Mr. Bond."
> ### Dr. No to 007

woman posing as a *Daily Gleaner* photographer, Miss Taro, and likely others. Together, they keep a watchful eye on anyone in the Jamaica area who shows interest in Dr. No or Crab Key. It is this team who is responsible for the deaths of Commander John Strangways and his secretary Mary Prescott. Dr. No's guards on the island also killed Honey Ryder's father and several of Quarrel's friends.

On Crab Key, Dr. No employs a small army of guards. He also uses a flame-throwing swamp vehicle painted to resemble a dragon to frighten away or kill any curious visitors.

Equipped with mechanical hands as a result of radiation experiments gone wrong, Dr. No considers himself one of the great radiation power experts in the world. Possessing Goya's portrait of Wellington, stolen in August 1961 from London's National Gallery, Dr. No exhibits impeccable taste, expertly mixing antiques and modern design. (The real painting was recovered in May, 1964.)

Dr. No's men capture Bond and Honey, and at first they treat them well, since Dr. No hopes 007 will join his organization. Bond refuses, and Dr. No incarcerates him and Honey. Dr. No prepares to topple a NASA moon launch, unaware that 007 has escaped and entered the nuclear reactor room disguised as a technician. When Dr. No realizes Bond is overheating the reactor, he

charges. The pair battle on the fuel elements carriage as it is lowered into the reactor core. Bond knocks Dr. No into the reactor pool. Dr. No's metal hands uselessly claw at the carriage as the genius scientist boils to death in the churning water.

In the novel, Fleming describes Dr. No as "a giant venomous worm wrapped in grey tin-foil." When Dr. No steals $1 million in gold from the Tongs, they catch him, cut off his hands, and shoot him through the heart. However, Dr. No is one of those rare individuals whose heart is on the right hand side of his body. He miraculously survives and invests the stolen gold in rare stamps, so that his money can be easily moved. He changes his appearance and takes the name Julius No: "Julius," after his father; "No," for his rejection of him and all authority. Backed by the Soviets, he buys the island of Crab Key and plans to destroy American rockets. The great doctor meets his demise when Bond buries him under a giant mound of guano.

TOPPLING TIME *Attired in protective clothing, Dr. No prepares to send a moon launch from Cape Canaveral off course.*

DOCTOR'S ORDERS *(below left) Dr. No brings Bond and Honey into his inner sanctum; (below) Dr. No demonstrates the power of his mechanical hands, crushing a metal Buddha figurine.*

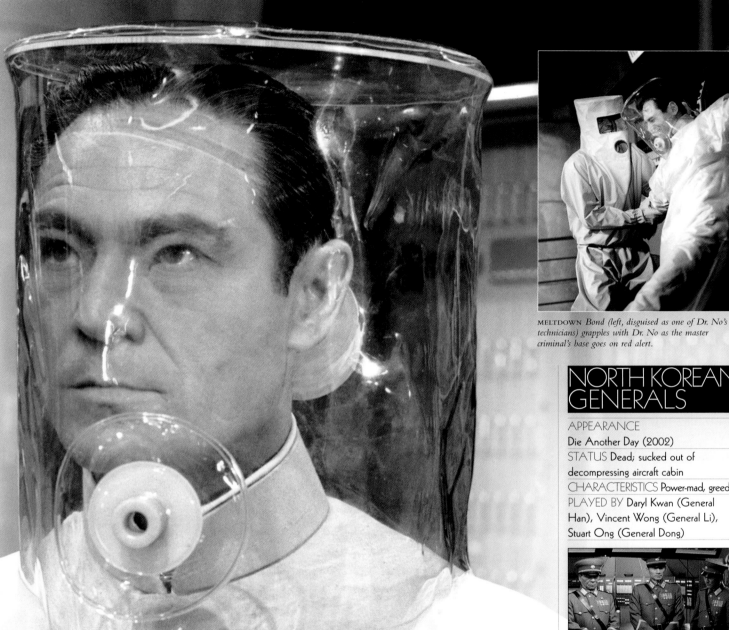

MELTDOWN *Bond (left, disguised as one of Dr. No's technicians) grapples with Dr. No as the master criminal's base goes on red alert.*

NORTH KOREAN GENERALS

APPEARANCE
Die Another Day (2002)
STATUS Dead; sucked out of decompressing aircraft cabin
CHARACTERISTICS Power-mad, greedy
PLAYED BY Daryl Kwan (General Han), Vincent Wong (General Li), Stuart Ong (General Dong)

WARMONGERS *The generals plan to make North Korea a dominant Asian power.*

Han, Li, and Dong are three top North Korean generals who stage a coup to remove General Moon from power so that his psychotic son can use the Icarus satellite to destroy the Korean DMZ. Once this occurs, they plan to attack South Korea and then Japan. When James Bond's Walther P99 accidentally fires inside the flying command center, the plane depressurizes, sucking the generals into the upper atmosphere.

> " The successful criminal brain is **always superior.** It has to be! "

Dr. No to 007

OBANNO

APPEARANCE
Casino Royale (2006)
STATUS Dead; throttled by Bond
CHARACTERISTICS Callous; rules
by inflicting violence and creating terror
PLAYED BY Isaach de Bankole

Steven Obanno leads the Lord's Resistance Army, an actual rebel force based in Uganda accused of acts of terrorism and war crimes. The real leader of the LRA, Joseph Kony, partly inspired the character of Obanno in *Casino Royale*.

Obanno entrusts an investment of millions of dollars to Le Chiffre, a banker to terrorists introduced to him by Mr. White. When that investment is lost by Le Chiffre, Obanno threatens him and his girlfriend Valenka during a break in Le Chiffre's poker tournament at Casino Royale. Obanno's lieutenant realizes that Bond has been listening in on Obanno's heated confrontation with Le Chiffre. Obanno and his lieutenant attack Bond, who, after a vicious struggle in a stairwell at the Hotel Splendide, kills them both.

ODDJOB

APPEARANCE Goldfinger (1964)
STATUS Dead; electrocuted
CHARACTERISTICS Martial arts expert, staunchly loyal, deadly aim
PLAYED BY Harold Sakata
(Tosh Togo)

Oddjob is the dean of all henchmen, a perfect combination of strength, skill, and loyalty. Ostensibly the manservant, chauffeur, and caddy of Auric Goldfinger, Oddjob is an impassive killer who knows seven ways to kill a man with one blow. For long range attacks, Oddjob throws his metal-rimmed hat, which can sever the head of a statue or break a person's neck.

Oddjob knocks Bond out at the Fontainebleau Hotel in Miami Beach. In England, Oddjob abets Goldfinger in his attempt to cheat during a golf match with Bond. Following Goldfinger's defeat, Oddjob crushes a golf ball with one hand as a show of strength.

When Bond and Tilly Masterson trip an alarm at Goldfinger's factory, Oddjob supervises their pursuit by Korean guards and kills Tilly with a throw of his hat. In Kentucky, Oddjob shoots Mr. Solo, the one gangster who opts out of Goldfinger's scheme, and has his body crushed inside a Lincoln Continental. After priming an atomic device to irradiate the US gold supply, Goldfinger locks Oddjob inside the vaults along with Bond and Kisch, a trusted lieutenant. Rather than join forces to try to escape, Oddjob kills Kisch and turns on Bond, who kills Oddjob by sending a surge of electricity through the brim of his hat.

FEAR FACTOR *Obanno and his henchman terrorize Le Chiffre's girlfriend Valenka.*

SHOCK TACTICS *Oddjob dies in a shower of sparks, electrocuted by Bond during their epic battle inside Fort Knox.*

ONATOPP, XENIA

APPEARANCE
GoldenEye (1995)
STATUS Crushed to death
CHARACTERISTICS Seductive, sadistic, outlandish, psychotic
PLAYED BY Famke Janssen

Ex-Soviet fighter pilot Xenia Onatopp is a key figure in the Janus crime syndicate run by Alec Trevelyan and one of the most beautiful and unusual femme fatales ever to seduce a man to his doom. Xenia gains great sexual pleasure from killing. She dresses in leather or in elaborate gowns, basking in her perverse sexuality.

Xenia first meets Bond in the South of France. Driving her red Ferrari, she races Bond's Aston Martin down the twisting corniche toward Monte Carlo. After a further brush with Bond in the casino, she kills Canadian Navy Admiral Chuck Farrel by crushing him between her thighs—her favored method of

> "This time, Mr. Bond, the pleasure will be all mine."
>
> Onatopp to 007

murder. She shoots two French pilots and steals the latest NATO helicopter, the Tiger, which is immune to all electronic interference. With General Ourumov, she participates in the mass murder of staff at the Severnaya satellite station in Siberia and the destruction of the area with the GoldenEye weapons system.

Xenia kidnaps Natalya Simonova in St. Petersburg and attempts to kidnap Bond. Following a sexually charged battle in his hotel's spa, Bond forces Xenia to take him to Trevelyan, then knocks her unconscious. Bond rescues Natalya, but Xenia helps Ourumov recapture her, bringing her on board an armored train and luring Bond to save her. Xenia later escapes with Trevelyan to Cuba. When 007 and Natalya arrive in Cuba, Xenia attacks them, abseiling from a helicopter. Bond shoots the pilot, sending the helicopter out of control and flinging Xenia into the fork of a tree. With the weight of the helicopter cinching her between the branches, Xenia discovers the reality of death by crushing.

GIRL POWER *In the Cuban jungle, Xenia Onatopp puts the squeeze on Bond.*

ORLOV, GENERAL

APPEARANCE
Octopussy (1983)
STATUS Killed as a traitor
CHARACTERISTICS Fanatical, warmongering, conniving, power-hungry
PLAYED BY Steven Berkoff

General Orlov is a war-obsessed Soviet general who is in league with exiled Afghan prince Kamal Khan in a scheme to detonate an atomic bomb on the American Air Force Base in Feldstadt, West Germany.

Failing in his never-ending attempt to convince the Soviet leadership council that the USSR can successfully invade Western Europe, Orlov secretly sets up his plot. He funnels precious jewels from The Kremlin Art Repository, replacing them with duplicates created by expert forger Lenkin. Working with smugglers Kamal Khan and Octopussy, Orlov offers the originals for auction in the West and uses some of the money to pay Khan. Orlov and Khan double-cross Octopussy by smuggling a nuclear weapon rather than jewels on her circus train when it travels from East Germany to West Germany, where it is to be detonated. If the world believes an American nuclear weapon blasted a base and town in West Germany, Orlov knows the US will be required to remove its nuclear deterrent from Europe. Soviet tanks and armies would be better positioned to invade the West.

Once Bond learns of Orlov's scheme, he races to stop the train with the bomb. Orlov pursues Bond, unaware that General Gogol has uncovered his jewel-smuggling racket. When the train crosses the border, Orlov runs after it, and East German guards gun him down. As Gogol stands over him, Orlov hints at his much larger plot as he dies.

DREAMS OF GLORY *Dismayed at improving political relations between East and West, Orlov plots to bring about World War III.*

GUNNED DOWN *Orlov races to catch and kill Bond, but East German guards shoot him first.*

> "Tomorrow I shall be the hero of the Soviet Union."
>
> Orlov to Gogol

OURUMOV, GENERAL

APPEARANCE
GoldenEye (1995)
STATUS Dead; shot by Bond
CHARACTERISTICS Unctuous, corrupt, self-serving, ruthless
PLAYED BY Gottfried John

General Ourumov conspires with Alec Trevelyan to use the GoldenEye weapon system to make himself tremendously wealthy. The head of the Arkangel Chemical Weapons Facility during the Soviet years, he helps to fake the death of 006 and then build and position the Janus crime syndicate.

After the fall of the Soviet empire, he is promoted from colonel to general and becomes Head of the Space Division of the Russian Army. The British believe Ourumov wants to be the next iron man of Russia. Along with Xenia Onatopp, he stages an unscheduled test of the Severnaya Space Weapons Control Centre to obtain command of the GoldenEye space weapons. He has Xenia kill everyone inside with the exception of accomplice Boris Grishenko. Ourumov informs the

TIGHT CORNER Osato and a gang of crowbar-wielding thugs confront Bond in the Tokyo docks when he tries to investigate the Ning-Po.

OSATO

APPEARANCE
You Only Live Twice (1967)
STATUS Dead; paid the price of failure
CHARACTERISTICS Ruthless, fearful
PLAYED BY Teru Shimada

Owner of Osato Chemicals & Engineering Co. Ltd., Mr. Osato provides Ernst Stavro Blofeld with liquid oxygen and various other components for his plot to launch World War III on behalf of the Communist Chinese.

As one of the leading manufacturers of chemicals in Asia, Osato manages his own empire. The depth and length of his relationship with SPECTRE remains unclear, but by the events depicted in *You Only Live Twice*, much of Osato's organization exists totally to serve SPECTRE's needs. His confidential secretary Helga Brandt also serves as SPECTRE No. 11, and Osato's assistant doubles as SPECTRE No. 4. Osato's freighter, *Ning-Po*, ships liquid oxygen and various other supplies to Blofeld. Despite his position of power, Osato views Blofeld with great respect and also with great fear.

Osato apparently helps arrange for the murder of Dikko Henderson, Bond's Tokyo contact. When Bond doubles as the assassin and pretends to be wounded, the getaway car driver delivers him to Mr. Osato's office. There, Bond kills the driver and steals important clues from Osato's safe.

Blofeld orders Osato to kill 007, but Bond survives numerous attempts on his life. When Blofeld captures Bond in his volcano rocket base and finds that Japanese SIS ninjas have followed, he shows 007 "the price of failure" and shoots Osato at point blank range.

FAKED DEATH *Ourumov tries to make Bond surrender by threatening his partner, 006.*

Minister of Defence, Dimitri Mishkin, and the Russian Defence Council that Siberian Separatists committed the crime.

After learning that programmer Natalya Simonova escaped Severnaya, Ourumov discovers Mishkin has arrested both James Bond and Natalya and plans to interrogate them. When Ourumov interrupts, Mishkin reveals that he now suspects Ourumov in the massacre at Severnaya. In response, Ourumov kills Mishkin. Natalya temporarily escapes with Bond, but Ourumov recaptures her and takes refuge in Trevelyan's train. He holds a gun to Natalya's head when 007 enters, but Bond shoots Ourumov anyway.

PALAZZI, ANGELO

APPEARANCE
Thunderball (1965)
STATUS Dead; drowned by Largo
CHARACTERISTICS Experienced pilot; efficient, but a little too greedy
PLAYED BY Paul Stassino

SPECTRE hires Angelo Palazzi to impersonate pilot Major Derval on a NATO training mission. His brief is to gas the crew and to fly the Vulcan bomber to waters off the Bahamas. The job requires two years of plastic surgery. Palazzi agrees to a fee of $100,000, but after killing the real Derval, he demands $250,000 instead. He accomplishes his mission and delivers the plane and its two nuclear warheads to Emilio Largo. While the plane rests underwater with Palazzi strapped into the cockpit, Largo renegotiates Palazzi's fee. He cuts his airhose, settling SPECTRE's account permanently.

> "Not enough. $100,000 is not enough."
>
> **Palazzi to Fiona Volpe**

DOUBLE TROUBLE *Palazzi (below) makes the fatal error of asking for more money from SPECTRE's Fiona Volpe for impersonating lovestruck NATO pilot Major Derval (above).*

PATRICE

APPEARANCE
Skyfall (2012)

STATUS Dead; fell from the 67th floor of a Shanghai skyscraper

CHARACTERISTICS mysterious, silent, murderous, menacing

PLAYED BY Ola Rapace

Patrice, an assassin employed by Silva, encounters James Bond in Istanbul and Shanghai. A 6ft 2in "ghost" mercenary with no known residence or country of origin, Patrice is secretly employed by Silva to steal a top-secret MI6 hard drive in Istanbul. This hard drive contains the names of almost every NATO

> ## "Who's got the list? Tell me! Who are you working for?"
>
> ### 007 to Patrice

Three months later, shrapnel from Bond's wound reveals that Patrice's bullet was a depleted military-grade uranium shell. Patrice is one of only three men worldwide known to use such bullets. The CIA is currently seeking Patrice for the murder of the Yemeni ambassador, and expects him to be in Shanghai in two days. Desperate to retrieve the hard drive and discover who masterminded its theft, M dispatches Bond to Shanghai to track Patrice down.

Bond picks up Patrice's trail at Shanghai airport and follows him to the 67th floor of a Shanghai skyscraper by clinging to the underside of the elevator. Bond watches as Patrice assembles a bolt-action-suppressed sniper rifle and proceeds to assassinate a man

who is admiring a painting in an adjacent apartment block. A beautiful woman calmly standing next to the man looks on as Bond attacks and disarms Patrice. Their fierce hand-to-hand fight ends with Patrice dangling from the skyscraper, held only by Bond. Bond is desperate to learn who has the list of NATO agents and who is employing Patrice but Patrice falls to his death.

A gambling chip—payment for the assassination—in Patrice's gun case, leads Bond to Macau's Floating Dragon Casino. Bond cashes in Patrice's chip and collects a case full of cash. At the same time, he observes the woman he saw earlier and her trio of sinister bodyguards. They are watching him.

FIREPOWER *(far left) Patrice blazes away with his 100-round Glock to avoid capture.*

FAST GETAWAY *(left) After gunning down two motorcycle cops, Patrice steals one of their bikes.*

CLOSE COMBAT *(below) Bond finally gets to grips with Patrice on top of a fast-moving train, but the assassin is no pushover.*

agent embedded in global terrorist organizations. Patrice eliminates MI6 operative Ronson, steals the hard drive, and flees in a black Audi, pursued by James Bond and MI6 field agent Eve Moneypenny in a Land Rover. Bond induces Patrice to crash the car in Eminonu Square. Patrice leaps out and fires a Glock 18 fitted with a 100-round magazine at Bond and Moneypenny. Failing to hit his target, Patrice seizes a Honda CRF 250R police motorbike and races across the rooftops of the Grand Bazaar, with Bond, mounted on a street-trader's bike, close behind.

Following in a Land Rover, Eve nearly catches Patrice at a road bridge, but Patrice abandons his bike and leaps over the bridge parapet onto a moving train. Bond executes a spectacular leap and clings onto the train as it speeds

along. Out of ammunition, Bond boards a Caterpillar 320D L excavator loaded on a flatbed truck to pursue Patrice. As Bond powers forward in the excavator, one of Patrice's bullets wounds him in the shoulder. Patrice then uncouples the truck carrying Bond and the excavator. Undaunted, Bond grabs onto the coach carrying Patrice with the excavator's bucket, runs along the vehicle's arm, and leaps through the gaping hole made by the bucket.

Bond and Patrice continue their fight atop the train as it rattles toward a tunnel. Eve is keeping up with the train in the Land Rover— until she runs out of road. Realizing that this is the last chance to stop Patrice, Eve, on M's order, attempts to shoot him as he grapples with Bond. She hits Bond instead and Patrice escapes with the hard drive.

IN HIS SIGHTS *From a vantage point in a Shanghai skyscraper, Patrice prepares to make another kill.*

PEREZ

APPEARANCE
Licence To Kill (1989)
STATUS Dead; flame-broiled
CHARACTERISTICS Loyal, sadistic
PLAYED BY Alejandro Bracho

Perez and fellow henchmen Dario and Braun are employed by drug lord Franz Sanchez to kill his enemies. Perez helps to maim DEA agent Felix Leiter and to kill his wife, Della. Perez later fires a Stinger missile at a tanker truck driven by 007 and gets covered with insecticide powder by CIA informer Pam

Bouvier. He is in Braun's truck when it is engulfed in flames and veers off a cliff, plunging to certain doom.

PHOTOGRAPHER, THE

APPEARANCE
Dr. No (1962)
STATUS A mystery
CHARACTERISTICS Defensive, scared
PLAYED BY Marguerite LeWars

This unnamed photographer, identified as Annabel Chung in the novel, works for Dr. No. She fails to take Bond's picture at Palisadoes International Airport, Jamaica, when he conceals his face with his hat, so she tries again at Puss-Feller's nightclub.

Local islander and 007 ally, Quarrel, grabs her and her camera, but she refuses to reveal the identity of her employer, cutting Quarrel's face with the broken lightbulb from her camera.

> "You'll be sorry. You'll all be sorry. You rats."
>
> **The Photographer to 007, Quarrel, and Leiter**

EXPOSED *Bond and Quarrel corner the photographer in Puss-Feller's club and try to discover the identity of her employer. Bond exposes the film she has taken, which contains shots of him.*

QUANTUM

APPEARANCES
Casino Royale (2006), Quantum Of Solace (2008)

Quantum is a mysterious and highly dangerous international terrorist and criminal organization dealing with extremists of left and right, with dictators and "liberators" alike. It specializes in staging political coups and blackmailing schemes. Mr. White, a prominent member who appears to act as Quantum's middleman, observed, seemingly without exaggeration, that

Quantum has "people everywhere."

One agent, Yusef Kabira, worked as a honeypot spy, romancing women in government or the intelligence services. Quantum then "kidnapped" him and blackmailed the women concerned, including Treasury official Vesper Lynd, into working for them.

MI6 agent Craig Mitchell was M's personal bodyguard for five years before revealing his allegiance to Quantum. Another Quantum member, Guy Haines, became one of the British Prime Minister's closest advisors. Other

Quantum suspects include Gregor Karakov, a former Russian government minister, who owns most of Siberia's mines and Moishe Soref, formerly a member of Mossad and now a telecom giant. At public functions, Quantum members have been spotted wearing a "Q" pin.

Quantum seeks to profit from destabilizing governments. When the Haitians elected a leader who raised the minimum wage, business corporations in Haiti contacted Quantum, who removed Aristide from office. Dominic Greene, a high-ranking Quantum member, plotted to restore Bolivian dictator General

> "We have people everywhere."
>
> **Mr White**

AT KNIFEPOINT *Cornered by Bond, Quantum agents threaten Vesper.*

PLANNING REVENGE *Le Chiffre is one of many Quantum associates to fall foul of 007.*

MORE QUESTIONS THAN ANSWERS *Quantum operative Mr. White is interrogated by M and Bond at an MI6 safe house in Siena, Italy.*

SNAP SHOT *Quantum double agent Mitchell tries to eliminate his unrelenting pursuer, James Bond.*

SEEING DAGGERS *Dominic Greene and his henchmen confront Bond at the Bregenz opera house.*

Medrano to power in exchange for control of the country's water supply—until Bond and former Bolivian secret service agent Camille ruined the plot.

Quantum does not tolerate failure. It executed banking associate Le Chiffre for betrayal of trust and for losing a fortune to Bond, and also Dominic Greene, whom Quantum suspect may have given Bond key information about the organization.

IN CONFERENCE *Quantum members secretly meet at the Bregenz opera.*

QUIST

APPEARANCE
Thunderball (1965)
STATUS Dead; eaten by sharks
CHARACTERISTICS Out of his depth; lacks the killer instinct
PLAYED BY Bill Cummings

IN THE DEEP END *Largo's men prepare to throw Quist (center) into the shark pool.*
Quist works for Emilio Largo in Nassau, shadowing his mistress Domino and performing other bits of dirty work. Largo sends Quist to investigate Bond at the Coral Harbour Hotel. While Quist snoops in Bond's hotel room, 007 returns and Quist hides in the shower. Bond cranks the hot water then knocks Quist about. Bond sends him back to Largo, calling him "the little fish I throw back into the sea." Largo does 007 one better, tossing Quist into his shark pool.

RAMIREZ

APPEARANCE
Goldfinger (1964)
STATUS Living; operation damaged
CHARACTERISTICS Powerful heroin manufacturer

One of the few unseen villains in the Bond films, Mr. Ramirez operates a heroin manufacturing lab in Mexico. The profits from the drug sales go to finance Communist revolutionaries in Central America and the Caribbean. Ramirez has a state-of-the-art lab in a fake oil storage tank, which Bond sabotages. Ramirez later sends one of his goons—a capungo—to try and kill Bond in dancer Bonita's dressing room. The damage Bond inflicts on Ramirez's operation effectively shuts down his political activities.

RENARD

APPEARANCE
The World Is Not Enough (1999)
STATUS Dead; killed by Bond
CHARACTERISTICS Detached, psychotic, apolitical, devoted, unrelenting
PLAYED BY Robert Carlyle

Viktor Zokas—alias Renard—wishes to spread anarchy, but he changes his goal when he falls in love with his kidnap victim Elektra King. While he previously spent his life creating chaos around the globe, now facing death, he devotes his remaining days to helping Elektra carry out a megalomaniacal plot of revenge that will leave her as one of the most powerful women in the world.

Renard once worked for the KGB, but his ruthless methods led them to declare him a liability after the Afghan conflict. He then became a freelance terrorist, working for anyone who would hire him. He operated in Pukch'ong, North Korea and in Moscow in 1996. He has, according to MI6 records, also been spotted in "all the romantic vacation spots," such as Bosnia, Iraq, Iran, Beirut, and Cambodia.

Renard kidnaps oil heiress Elektra King, but when Elektra's father, Sir Robert, refuses to pay, Elektra seduces Renard, turning him into a tool for her goals. She stages an escape with Renard's help. A week later, MI6 agent 009 shoots Renard in the head. However, the bullet does not kill him, but starts a slow path through his brain, gradually killing off his senses. Renard, now unable to feel agony or sensual pleasure, can push his

BOMB RAID *Renard steals a nuclear weapon from a former Soviet test site in Kazakhstan.*

SLOW DEATH *Viewing a hologram, Bond learns that a bullet fired by an MI6 agent is moving through Renard's brain, destroying his senses.*

FIGHT TO THE DEATH *Bond enrages Renard by telling him that his beloved Elektra is dead, but Renard refuses to be distracted from his deadly purpose: to blow up a nuclear submarine.*

body harder and for longer than a normal person. He will grow stronger until the day the bullet cuts off his entire nervous system, killing him.

Renard and Elektra first stage the killing of Elektra's father, by blowing him up with the exact amount of

> Renard: You can't kill me. I'm already dead.
> 007: Not dead enough for me.

explosive-laced money he refused to pay for Elektra's release. They anticipate this will lure M, Sir Robert's personal friend, into their trap, allowing them to kidnap her. Renard attempts to kill Bond when 007 stumbles on a plot to steal a nuclear weapon in Kazakhstan.

Renard next attempts to stage a small nuclear explosion in a pipeline controlled by Elektra King, an act designed to distract the world from her more deadly plot to destroy Istanbul. Using a stolen Russian nuclear submarine, Renard plans to place a rod made from the stolen weapon's plutonium core into the sub's reactor. This will cause the submarine to explode in the Bosphorus, creating a highly toxic dirty bomb, killing eight million people, and ensuring that Elektra's pipeline is the only source of oil from the Caspian to the West. Renard brings Dr. Christmas Jones, a nuclear physicist working with Bond, onboard to die with him. 007 gains access to the sub as it submerges, battles Renard, and eventually impales him on his own plutonium rod, bringing his fatalistic suicidal dream to an end.

RHODA

APPEARANCE
From Russia With Love (1963)
STATUS Unknown
CHARACTERISTICS Silent, obedient
PLAYED BY Peter Brayham

SPECTRE operative Rhoda serves as Morzeny's attaché, helping to coordinate agent training. Rhoda has an important role in SPECTRE's plot to kill 007 and sell a stolen Lektor decoder back to the Soviets. He creates a road block on the Orient Express train line, providing an escape route for Donald Grant. Bond, with Tatiana Romanova, takes Rhoda hostage and steals his truck, using Grant's escape plan. Bond sets off in SPECTRE's Fairy Huntress speedboat and shoves Rhoda overboard in the Gulf of Trieste.

SALES GIRL

APPEARANCE
Live And Let Die (1973)
STATUS Living, whereabouts unknown
CHARACTERISTICS Observant
PLAYED BY Kubi Chaza

The unnamed Sales Girl is another of Dr. Kananga/Mr. Big's US operatives. After the death of CIA driver Charlie in New York, James Bond tracks the assassin Whisper's white Corvorado to the Oh Cult Voodoo Shop at 33 E. 56th Street. Bond distracts the Sales Girl in order to slip into the store's garage, which is shared with Dr. Kananga's San Monique Embassy offices. Bond then follows a Cadillac with Texas plates out of the garage, but the Sales Girl reports his movements. She later briefly appears in New Orleans as a flight attendant on Mr. Big's personal jet.

SAMEDI, BARON

APPEARANCE
Live And Let Die (1973)
STATUS Unknown
CHARACTERISTICS Intimidating, with a deliberately threatening laugh
PLAYED BY Geoffrey Holder

The legendary figure of Baron Samedi is a mischief-maker who both tempts and punishes humans. The host at a show for tourists in San Monique describes Baron Samedi as the "voodoo god of cemeteries and Chief of the Legion of the Dead, the man who cannot die." Dr. Kananga employs a man who claims to be the Baron to instill fear in his minions and to protect his thousands of acres of poppy fields.

Bond and Solitaire briefly meet Baron Samedi in a graveyard. He later appears in New Orleans at Mr. Big's office taunting Kananga and Solitaire with a flaming High Priestess tarot card and a Death card.

On San Monique, Baron Samedi, painted with a skeleton design, rises from a grave. Bond shoots him, revealing that this Baron Samedi is just a mannequin. Another Baron Samedi, this time human, then rises from the grave. Bond tosses him into a coffin filled with poisonous snakes, apparently killing him. But nothing is certain where the God of Cemeteries is concerned, and Baron Samedi sits mocking human conceit on the front of the Crescent train at the film's end.

SANCHEZ, FRANZ

APPEARANCE
Licence To Kill (1989)
STATUS Dead; burned to death
CHARACTERISTICS Authoritative;
tendency towards violence and paranoia
PLAYED BY Robert Davi

Drug baron Franz Sanchez plans to create a cocaine cartel that stretches from Central America to the Far East. To Sanchez, loyalty is more important than money, and a vengeance-seeking James Bond seizes upon this belief to bring down the drug lord and his empire.

Under his personal law of *plomo o plata* (lead or silver), Sanchez has killed, intimidated, or bribed government officials in countries stretching from the US to Chile, and he faces 139 felony counts and 936 years in prison if caught by the US government. Constant pressure from the Drug Enforcement Agency (DEA) leads Sanchez to purchase four Stinger missiles from the Contras. He threatens to shoot down a US airliner if the DEA doesn't back off. Using the small nation of Isthmus as his operational base, Sanchez maintains full control over "President for life" Hector Lopez. Sanchez operates the world's largest, albeit illegal, private investment fund, which is linked to his illegal drug network. He sells cocaine worldwide through the coded sermons of televangelist Professor Joe Butcher,

and his casino operation enables him to launder large quantities of cash.

Sanchez makes a rare foray into US territory when he discovers his mistress Lupe Lamora has joined her illicit lover Alvarez. DEA agents, including Felix Leiter and MI6 "observer" James Bond, capture Sanchez in an aerial chase as he attempts to fly into international airspace.

Sanchez bribes DEA agent Ed Killifer with $2 million to spring him from US custody. He then exacts revenge on Leiter by having Felix's bride Della murdered and Felix himself lowered into a shark tank. He leaves Leiter maimed but alive as a warning of what happens to those who cross him. He then returns to Isthmus City

and restarts his drug manufacturing and smuggling operation.

Sanchez soon learns that a major cocaine shipment to the US has gone awry, with the cocaine ruined and the payment stolen by a mysterious stranger. He does not realize the stranger is Bond, now on a personal mission of vengeance. Armed with the drug lord's money, 007 arrives in Isthmus City and offers his services to Sanchez. He comes to trust Bond after wrongly concluding 007 foiled an assassination attempt against him. Realizing that Sanchez values loyalty above anything else, Bond cunningly sows the seeds of distrust between the drug lord and his henchmen.

Bond discovers Sanchez's master plan: a scheme with an Asian drug cartel to smuggle vast quantities of cocaine by dissolving the drug in ordinary gasoline, shipping it

LIZARD KING *Sanchez sees himself as calculating and cold-blooded—as reflected by his choice of an iguana as a pet. The creature wears a diamond-encrusted collar, advertising Sanchez's wealth.*

by ocean-going tanker, and then reconverting it to cocaine. In a spectacular battle, Bond, assisted by Pam Bouvier, destroys each tanker truck one-by-one. He then takes a cigarette lighter given to him by Felix and Della and uses it to torch a gasoline-soaked Sanchez.

THE FINAL CUT *Sanchez prepares to strike Bond with a machete seconds before the drug baron meets his own death.*

Felix Leiter: Killing me won't stop anything, Sanchez!

Sanchez: There are worse things than dying, *hombre.*

SANDOR

APPEARANCE
The Spy Who Loved Me (1977)
STATUS Dead; killed by Bond
CHARACTERISTICS Hugely strong, intimidating; kills without question
PLAYED BY Milton Reid

Sandor works for shipping magnate Karl Stromberg, who instructs him to travel with Jaws and eliminate anyone who comes into contact with the stolen microfilm of Stromberg's remarkable submarine tracking system. Sandor attempts to assassinate Bond at the house of middleman Aziz Fekkesh in Cairo but shoots Felicca instead. A fierce struggle with Bond leaves Sandor hanging precariously over the edge of a rooftop, clinging to Bond's tie. After Sandor tells Bond that Fekkesh can be found at the pyramids, Bond flips his tie away, sending Sandor to his death. "What a helpful chap," comments Bond.

TIGHT SQUEEZE *Despite his great strength, Sandor meets his match when he comes up against Bond in Cairo.*

SAXBY, BERT

APPEARANCE
Diamonds Are Forever (1971)
STATUS Dead; shot by the CIA
CHARACTERISTICS Gruff, businesslike, laconic, treacherous
PLAYED BY Bruce Cabot

Casino manager Albert R. Saxby is the reclusive billionaire Willard Whyte's right-hand man—until he decides to join Ernst Stavro Blofeld in a plot to kidnap Whyte, take over his empire, and use it to create the ultimate weapon. Saxby manages the Las Vegas end of Blofeld's diamond smuggling operation. When Whyte discovers that Saxby has betrayed him, he demands that Saxby be told he's fired, unaware that a CIA sharpshooter has just killed the traitorous employee.

SCARAMANGA, FRANCISCO

APPEARANCE
The Man With The Golden Gun (1974)
STATUS Dead; shot by Bond
CHARACTERISTICS Superb marksman, sophisticated manner hides a ruthless craving for power
PLAYED BY Christopher Lee

Francisco Scaramanga, known as The Man With The Golden Gun, plans to auction the world's most efficient solar energy system to the highest bidder. Already the world's highest paid assassin, Scaramanga schemes to transform himself into an immensely powerful underworld figure.

007: Six bullets to your one?
Scaramanga:
I only need one.

SIGN OF POWER *Andrea Anders dries off Scaramanga after a swim. Some believe his third nipple is a sign of invulnerability.*

Born to a Cuban ringmaster father and an English snake-charmer mother, Scaramanga grew up in the circus where he gained a reputation as a trick shot artist and where his only real friend was an African bull elephant. Scaramanga murdered the elephant's cruel handler and then, realizing he loved killing more than animals, he decided to devote his life to the "art" of murder.

The KGB recruited and trained him, turning him into an overworked and underpaid assassin. In the late 1950s, Scaramanga left the Soviets, offering his services to anyone who could afford his price—one million dollars a kill. No known photographs of him exist, although the CIA has his fingerprints on file. He has one distinguishing feature—a superfluous papilla—a third nipple.

Scaramanga kills his victims with golden bullets and uses a number of golden guns, including one made

SHOOTING MATCH *Scaramanga searches for James Bond in his fun house, failing to notice that 007's mannequin has regrown the fingers he previously shot off.*

from seemingly innocuous objects—a lighter, a pen, a cigarette case, and a cuff link.

Living on a remote island in Chinese waters with his valet Nick Nack and mistress Andrea Anders and traveling by Chinese junk, Scaramanga performs the occasional favor for his Communist landlords. To hone his assassin skills, Scaramanga instructs Nick Nack to bring in hitmen to engage him in shootouts in a specially designed fun house maze. The maze contains a lifelike mannequin of Bond, the only man Scaramanga sees as a peer.

Scaramanga becomes corrupt industrialist Hai Fat's junior partner in a scheme to monopolize a new solar energy process designed by British scientist Gibson. Hai Fat and Gibson house the test plant in the rock spires on Scaramanga's island.

Unknown to Scaramanga, Andrea wants him dead, and she sends the British Secret Service a golden bullet inscribed "007," hoping Bond will be dispatched to kill him.

Cracks appear in Scaramanga and Hai Fat's scheme when Gibson opts to re-defect to the British using the Solex Agitator, the key to converting solar energy into electricity, as a bargaining chip for immunity. Scaramanga assassinates the scientist and recovers the Solex, but Gibson's overtures launch Bond on Scaramanga's trail.

Scaramanga kills Hai Fat to consolidate his position as lone controller of the solar technology. He murders Andrea for betraying him, kidnaps Bond's assistant, Mary Goodnight, and sets up a showdown with James Bond.

Bond tracks Scaramanga to his island, where a duel of the titans—Scaramanga versus 007—occurs. Scaramanga leads Bond on a chase through Nick Nack's fun house, but Bond outwits him by posing as his own mannequin and shooting him.

In Fleming's novel, KGB assassin "Pistols" Scaramanga, who always uses a gold-plated Colt .45, operates in the Caribbean. M orders Bond to assassinate Scaramanga, who has eliminated numerous agents. It is Bond's first assignment since the Soviets captured and brainwashed him. Bond eventually kills Scaramanga in a Jamaican swamp.

SCARPINE

APPEARANCE
A View To A Kill (1985)
STATUS **Dead; killed in an airship explosion**
CHARACTERISTICS **Suave and well-dressed; a calm and ruthless mass killer**
PLAYED BY **Patrick Bauchau**

Scarpine, a French killer with a deep scar on his cheek, works as Max Zorin's trusted and valued head of security at his French chateau and at his oil pumping station in San Francisco. After Zorin betrays May Day in the Main Strike Mine, Scarpine becomes Zorin's number two man, machine-gunning Zorin's mineworkers and later piloting his airship. He prepares to kill Bond on the Golden Gate Bridge, but Stacey Sutton knocks him unconscious with a fire extinguisher. He meets his demise when Zorin's airship blows up over San Francisco Bay.

SCORPION GUARD

APPEARANCE
Die Another Day (2002)
STATUS **Alive; whereabouts unknown**
CHARACTERISTICS **Vicious, sadistic**
PLAYED BY **Tymarah**

This seemingly emotionless army officer in charge of a North Korean prison tortures Bond for 14 long months with the stings of *Parabuthus* and death stalker scorpions. She then provides Bond with an antiserum in an attempt to extract information from him. A defiant Bond, however, refuses to give away any MI6 secrets. His ironic nickname for her is "The Concierge."

SISTER LILY & SISTER ROSE

APPEARANCE
Dr. No (1962)
STATUS **Unknown**
CHARACTERISTICS **Duplicitous, over-friendly, and coy**
PLAYED BY **Yvonne Shima (Sister Lily), Michel Mok (Sister Rose)**

The script for *Dr. No* describes these two Chinese hostesses based in Dr. No's bauxite mine base as "bright, helpful, inquisitive." Sister Lily beams from ear to ear as she shows Bond and Honey their rooms in Dr. No's luxurious underground bunker. She seems to genuinely want her guests to feel as comfortable as possible, despite her knowledge that Bond and Honey are Dr. No's prisoners. Sister Lily's smile only becomes a trifle forced when Bond requests two tickets to London.

SLATE, EDMUND

APPEARANCE
Quantum Of Solace (2008)
STATUS **Dead; killed by Bond**
CHARACTERISTICS **Murderous**
PLAYED BY **Neil Jackson**

In Port-Au-Prince, Haiti, assassin Edmund Slate is hired by Greene Planet CEO Dominic Greene to eliminate his employee and lover Camille, whom he suspects of being a spy. Greene has discovered that Camille has tried to buy secret information from one of his top geologists. Greene has had the geologist killed and replaced with Slate. Meanwhile, MI6 has discovered a link between Slate and the double agent Mitchell. Bond arrives at Slate's hotel room, number 325, Hotel Dessalines, and a brutal fight ensues. Bond kills Slate and then takes a briefcase left for Slate in the lobby and heads out into the street. Camille

is waiting to pick him up in her car. She naturally assumes that Bond is the geologist Greene sent her to meet.

SLUMBER, MORTON

APPEARANCE
Diamonds Are Forever (1971)
STATUS **Living; whereabouts unknown**
CHARACTERISTICS **Solicitous, unctuously charming, unscrupulous**
PLAYED BY **David Bauer**

Morton Slumber, President of Slumber, Inc. Mortuary, plays a key role in Ernst Stavro Blofeld's diamond-smuggling operation. When Bond, using the identity of Peter Franks, arrives with a shipment of fake diamonds concealed in a coffin, Morton Slumber greets him effusively. The coffin is incinerated and Bond is presented with an urn containing the diamonds. The assassins Wint and Kidd then attack Bond as he collects his $50,000 fee, dump him in a coffin and send him to be cremated alive. Slumber and his accomplice, Shady Tree, discover that the diamonds are fake and manage to rescue Bond just in time. Bond remarks that he must have been given fake money, too, as no one would burn up 50,000 real dollars. "You get me the real money, and I'll bring you the real diamonds," is Bond's parting shot.

SILVA

APPEARANCE
Skyfall (2012)
STATUS Killed by 007
CHARACTERISTICS A step ahead of everyone else, theatrical, music-lover, revels in making people uncomfortable
PLAYED BY Javier Bardem

Silva, a brilliant cyber-terrorist who holds M responsible for betraying him, concocts a complex plan to humiliate and murder her. Born Tiago Rodriguez, he was one of M's best Hong Kong operatives from 1986–1997. As the handover of Hong

CLOSE ATTENTION
Silva attempts to persuade Bond to "change his nature" as he inspects his recent wound.

Kong from Britain to China approached, M learned that Rodriguez was operating beyond his brief, hacking the Chinese. Believing that Rodriguez was jeopardizing the handover, M traded him to the Chinese in exchange for six agents. Tortured for five months while refusing to reveal M's secrets, Rodriguez attempted suicide by biting into a cyanide capsule hidden in his back left molar. The cyanide burned his insides, but he survived. Eventually escaping, Rodriguez reinvented himself as cyber-criminal Silva, wearing a denture prosthetic to cover his ruined teeth and hold his jawbones in place. Silva captured an island off Macau and established a base. The entire population evacuated overnight, fooled by Silva into thinking that there was a deadly chemical plant leak.

Silva lined a vast factory space with supercomputers and grew rich by committing massive cyber-crimes—destabilizing multinationals by manipulating stocks, interrupting spy satellite transmissions over Kabul, or rigging a Ugandan election.

To implement his vengeful plan against M, Silva hires mercenary Patrice to steal an MI6 hard drive containing the names of virtually every NATO agent embedded in terrorist organizations, thus placing M on dangerous ground with her government overseers. He sends M a mysterious message, "Think on your sins," then hacks into MI6's environmental control system, locks out the safety protocols, turns on the gas, and causes an explosion at MI6 headquarters that kills eight civil servants. Silva decrypts the list of secret agents and posts the names of five of them on the web with the threat to

SOLITARY CONFINEMENT *(left)* Silva bides his time in MI6's high-security cell.

> ## "You're still clinging to your faith in that old woman when all she has done is lie to you."
>
> ### Silva to 007

expose five more every week. At least three agents are murdered, further jeopardizing M's standing in government circles.

Meanwhile, Bond's pursuit of Patrice leads him to Silva's mistress, Severine. She escorts Bond to Silva's island, where Silva tries to convince Bond that M has betrayed them both—Silva in Hong Kong and Bond in Istanbul. He proposes a partnership, which Bond refuses. Silva then reveals that M returned Bond

to the field, despite him failing physical and psychological tests and makes flirtatious advances to get under Bond's skin.

Silva tries to humiliate Bond further by forcing him to engage in a William Tell-style shooting competition, with Severine as the victim. Silva murders Severine for betraying him but Bond manages to shoot Silva's bodyguards just as MI6 helicopters, alerted by Bond's radio transmitter, arrive to rescue Bond and capture Silva.

Confined in MI6's new underground headquarters, Silva reveals his deep hatred for M. Meanwhile, Q attaches Silva's computer to his own, unwittingly allowing Silva to hack into MI6's

system, opening the bunker's electronic security hatches and allowing Silva to escape into the London underground system. Only then does Silva's elaborate plan become clear; he had allowed himself to be captured so that he could escape and target M at a public inquiry. Now impersonating a Metropolitan police officer, Silva tries to eliminate 007 by detonating explosives and causing a

subway train to crash into a service chamber. He then escapes and attempts to murder M at the public inquiry. The attempt fails but Silva escapes once more.

Bond realizes that MI6 has been one step behind Silva from the start and resolves to change the game. M agrees to act as bait in order to catch Silva and Bond takes her to his childhood home, Skyfall, in his Aston Martin DB5. Bond also arranges for Q to lay a cunning "breadcrumb trail" of clues for Silva to follow.

Silva's advance team's attack is repulsed by Bond, Skyfall's redoubtable gamekeeper Kincade, and M. However their victory is short-lived; Silva himself arrives with more men in an AgustaWestland AW101 helicopter.

Silva attempts to flush M and Bond from the house by tossing incendiary bombs though the ground-floor windows. When this tactic fails, he orders his helicopter to destroy Bond's beloved Aston Martin DB5, whose machine guns had earlier played an important part in repelling the previous assault by Silva's henchmen.

IN DISGUISE *(right)* Silva attempts to elude Bond on the London undergound.

NIGHT ATTACK *(below)* Silva leads his men during the assault on Skyfall.

Bond responds by exploding two gas cylinders, destroying both Skyfall and Silva's helicopter. M is wounded in the attack but, helped by Kincade, escapes the house via an ancient priest hole tunnel that leads onto the moor. Bond follows close behind.

Realizing that M has escaped the house, Silva and his remaining men give chase across the moor. Silva tracks M to a chapel, where he finally confronts her. Just as Silva is about to end both their lives with a single bullet, Bond appears and hurls his hunting knife into Silva's back. As Silva dies, Bond informs him that he, 007, is now the "last rat standing."

SMERSH

APPEARANCES From Russia With Love (1963), The Living Daylights (1987)

SMERSH, a real Soviet intelligence directorate, has a murky history. Even the date of its formation remains in dispute. SMERSH was a contraction of two words: *smiert spionam* (or *spionom),* meaning "death to spies." SMERSH's autonomy and ruthlessness gave it broad power and instilled fear in defectors.

SMERSH appears as the villainous organization in four of Ian Fleming's novels, although it was most likely disbanded by 1953. In the Bond films, Rosa Klebb is former head of operations for SMERSH in *From Russia With Love.* Although the word "SMERSH" is never used in the film, the concept of a Soviet murder organization is revived under the root phrase *smiert spionam* in *The Living Daylights.*

SOLO, MR.

APPEARANCE
Goldfinger (1964)
STATUS Dead; killed by Oddjob
CHARACTERISTICS Brash but sensible
PLAYED BY Martin Benson

Mr. Solo is the lone gangster who refuses Goldfinger's invitation to loot the Bullion Depository at Fort Knox. Goldfinger's owes Solo $1 million in gold for smuggling his industrial laser into the US. Goldfinger has Oddjob ostensibly drive Solo to the airport with the gold. Instead, Oddjob shoots Solo and has the car crushed. It is an expensive death since Goldfinger must then separate his gold from the car.

SPECTRE

APPEARANCES

Dr. No (1962), From Russia With Love (1963), Thunderball (1965), You Only Live Twice (1967), On Her Majesty's Secret Service (1969), Diamonds Are Forever (1971)

There stands but one criminal organization which can make governments tremble at the very mention of its name: SPECTRE.

The brainchild of Ernst Stavro Blofeld, SPECTRE stands for Special Executive for Counter-intelligence, Terrorism, Revenge and Extortion. This acronym should never be spelled with periods after each letter.

SPECTRE gleefully exploits global fears and international rivalries to make a profit. Aside from Blofeld, major operatives include Dr. No, Rosa Klebb, Donald Grant, Kronsteen, Jacques Boitier, Count Lippe, Emilio Largo, Fiona Volpe, Mr. Osato, Helga Brandt, and Irma Bunt, as well as hundreds of other associates. SPECTRE's symbol is an octopus, its tentacles able to work independently and together. Some agents have been known to wear an octopus signet ring. Fortunately for world peace, Bond has destroyed so many SPECTRE plots that the organization has all but ceased to exist.

In the novels, Ian Fleming introduces SPECTRE in *Thunderball* (1961), but his fascination with the name predates this. In *Diamonds Are Forever* (1956), he names a ghost town Spectreville, and in *From Russia With Love* (1957), Bond seeks an encoding machine called the Spektor.

CALLED TO ACCOUNT *The International Brotherhood for the Assistance of Stateless Persons is a front for SPECTRE's Paris base. It is here that top operatives, including SPECTRE No. 2 Emilio Largo (far left), gather to report to their chief, Blofeld.*

STAMPER

APPEARANCE
Tomorrow Never Dies (1997)
STATUS Dead; blown up
CHARACTERISTICS Sadistic killing machine; nearly impervious to pain
PLAYED BY Götz Otto

Stamper works as Elliot Carver's murderous assistant, abetting the media mogul in his plot to stage and profit from a military crisis between the UK and China. At well over 6 ft tall, with one blue and one brown eye, Stamper is a truly imposing presence. More than just muscle, he is a genuine psychopath, a protégé of the assassin Dr. Kaufman, who teaches him the fine arts of chakra torture.

Stamper oversees Carver's operation in the South China Sea by sending the Sea Vac drill from Carver's stealth ship into the hull of HMS *Devonshire.* When seventeen British sailors survive the sinking, Stamper personally machine-guns them in the water.

Stamper subsequently oversees numerous attempts to kill Bond and the Chinese agent Wai Lin. He captures them in Vietnamese waters and delivers them to Carver's Saigon headquarters. There, Elliot Carver instructs Stamper to kill Bond slowly using chakra torture tools. Stamper hopes to break Kaufman's 52-hour record of inflicting agony before the victim dies. Bond and Wai Lin manage to escape, with Bond burying a chakra blade deep in Stamper's thigh.

Stamper returns to Carver's stealth ship where he helps prepare the launch of a Tomahawk-class missile at Beijing. When Bond and Wai Lin board the ship, Stamper leads the hunt for them. After Carver's death, Stamper tries to stop Bond from sabotaging the missile. When the missile's engine explodes, the blast kills Stamper.

STROMBERG, KARL

APPEARANCE
The Spy Who Loved Me (1977)
STATUS Dead; shot by Bond
CHARACTERISTICS Webbed hands; misanthropic, impatient; obsessed with life beneath the sea
PLAYED BY Curt Jurgens

One of the richest men in the world, Karl Stromberg owns the Stromberg Shipping Line. He hopes to destroy humanity and rebuild civilization beneath the sea. If not for the alliance of James Bond and KGB agent Major Anya Amasova, Stromberg would very likely have achieved his dream.

Named Sigmun Stromberg in the film's novelization, he hails from Apvorst, Sweden, where his interest in marine life and immeasurably high IQ brought him respect and power. After first making a small fortune as a corrupt undertaker, Stromberg went into insurance following World War II, and took over a large shipping line.

Stromberg hires scientists Professor Markovitz and Dr. Bechmann to develop a submarine tracking system that he uses to capture the SLBM-equipped submarines, Britain's HMS *Ranger* and the Soviet *Potemkin*. With these, he plots nuclear strikes against New York and Moscow, counting on global nuclear warfare to follow and destroying a world he sees as irredeemably decadent.

Stromberg's plan begins to unravel close to home. He discovers his assistant has placed a microfilm of the tracking system up for sale. After killing the culprit, Stromberg

TAKING CONTROL *Stromberg confronts James Bond and Major Anya Amasova aboard his* Liparus *supertanker headquarters.*

D-DAY *Stromberg tells the* Liparus's *Captain to proceed with their plan for Armageddon.*

SEAFOOD SUPPER *Stromberg dines in his luxurious dining room aboard* Atlantis.

ATLANTIS RISING *Stromberg's marine research lab surfaces from the sea off the coast of Sardinia.*

> **007:** Don't you miss the outside world?
> **Stromberg:** For me, this is all the world. There is beauty... there is ugliness... and there is death.

launches a campaign to kill anyone who has come into contact with the microfilm. The microfilm draws the attention of Amasova and Bond, who arrange to visit Stromberg's marine research laboratory *Atlantis* off the coast of Sardinia undercover as a marine biologist and his wife. Stromberg, seeing through the charade, orders his personal henchman, the metal-toothed Jaws, to kill Bond and Amasova. The pair

survive a barrage of attacks.

The use of a Stromberg Shipping Line helicopter in one instance brings more attention to Stromberg's plot, as does a model of the *Liparus* with an all-too accurate depiction of its custom hull design. As a result, Bond and Amasova join the submarine USS *Wayne*, which is sent to attack the *Liparus*. Stromberg captures the *Wayne*, takes custody of Amasova, and orders the positioning of the *Ranger*

and *Potemkin* so that they may launch their SLBMs.

Stromberg retires to *Atlantis* to await Armageddon, an optimistic outlook considering the USSR, US, and British are by now fully cooperating. Bond leads an attack of British, American, and Soviet sailors that foils Stromberg's plot. 007 travels on the *Wayne* to *Atlantis*, confronting Stromberg and killing him with four shots from his Walther PPK.

SWISS GATEKEEPER

APPEARANCE
Goldfinger (1964)
STATUS Unknown
CHARACTERISTICS Friendly, unless told to kill; handy with a machine gun
PLAYED BY Varley Thomas

Working at Auric Enterprises, this grandmotherly gatekeeper politely lets the captured James Bond into the compound while under armed guard and escort. Later, after Bond ejects his unwelcome passenger out of his Aston Martin DB5, he charges for the gate. The gatekeeper fearlessly stands in 007's way, spraying Bond's windscreen with machine gun fire.

TEE HEE

APPEARANCE
Live And Let Die (1973)
STATUS Dead; disarmed by Bond
CHARACTERISTICS A smiling assassin; unswervingly loyal to Kananga
PLAYED BY Julius W. Harris

One could call Tee Hee the right-hand man for Dr. Kananga/Mr. Big—except he has neither a right hand nor a right arm. He lost the limb to Albert, an old crocodile. In its place, he boasts a deadly set of pincers that can grab, cut, or claw at a victim. The strength of these can be seen when Tee Hee twists the barrel of Bond's Walther PPK when they meet in New York. His nickname results from his omnipresent snicker.

In New Orleans, under orders from Dr. Kananga/Mr. Big, Tee Hee threatens to snip off Bond's little finger. He knocks Bond unconscious and escorts him to a drug lab outside the city. He then leaves 007 stranded on an island surrounded by hungry crocodiles.

After 007 escapes and destroys Kananga's operation, Tee Hee sneaks aboard a train, battles Bond, and slams him around with his mechanical arm. 007 uses nail clippers to force Tee Hee's claw to lock onto the window handle, then throws him out, ripping his prosthesis off in the process.

Bond kills a character named Tee-Hee Johnson in the Fleming novel.

DISARMING THE VILLAIN *Tee Hee attempts to avenge the death of his boss, Kananga, on* The Crescent *passenger train.*

"Funny how the least little thing amuses him."

007, after Tee Hee destroys his Walther PPK

THE PERFECT COVER *Three killers disguised as blind beggars approach The Queen's Club to assassinate Strangways.*

FAREWELL PERFORMANCE *Shady Tree and his Acorns perform at The Whyte House.*

THREE BLIND MICE, THE

APPEARANCE
Dr. No (1962)

STATUS Dead; killed in car crash

CHARACTERISTICS Sharp-eyed killers

PLAYED BY Eric Coverley (1st Beggar), Charles Edghill (2nd Beggar), Henry Lopez (3rd Beggar), Adrian Robinson (Hearse Driver)

These three blind beggars actually possess 20/20 vision and work for Dr. No. They shoot British Secret Service representative Strangways with silenced revolvers and later murder Mary Prescott, the secretary working with Strangways. The killings bring Bond to Jamaica to investigate. The Three Blind Mice attempt to eliminate Bond as he exits a taxi at his hotel. When this fails, they pursue Bond's Sunbeam Alpine through the mountains in their hearse. An adroit maneuver by Bond leads them to crash in flames.

TORO, COLONEL

APPEARANCE
Octopussy (1983)

STATUS Dead; blown up by Bond

CHARACTERISTICS Sure, authoritative

PLAYED BY Ken Norris

In an unnamed Latin American country, Bond impersonates army officer Colonel Toro in order to destroy a spy plane prototype housed

SEEING DOUBLE *Colonel Toro comes face to face with his lookalike, James Bond.*

in a hangar. Unfortunately, the real Colonel Toro arrives, and his men quickly capture 007. With his beautiful assistant Bianca's help, Bond plans his escape in the Acrostar Bede jet, but Toro's men fire a rapier surface-to-air missile at the jet. Bond flies through the hangar just before the doors close. The missile hits the doors, causing a massive explosion.

TREE, SHADY

APPEARANCE
Diamonds Are Forever (1971)

STATUS Dead; killed by Wint and Kidd

CHARACTERISTICS Crotchety, cynical; enjoys crossword puzzles

PLAYED BY Leonard Barr

Shady Tree is not only a comedian at The Whyte House's Lincoln Lounge but also a final link in Ernst Stavro Blofeld's complex diamond-smuggling pipeline.

Tree confronts James Bond, whom he believes to be smuggler Peter Franks, at Slumber Mortuary, cursing him for delivering a consignment of fake diamonds. Bond calmly tells Tree to get him the real money, instead of forged notes, and he will deliver the real diamonds.

At The Whyte House, the killers Mr. Wint and Mr. Kidd, posing as fans wishing to sell comedy material, visit Tree, who claims he hasn't changed his act for 40 years. Wint and Kidd shoot him before casino manager Bert Saxby informs them that Tree has yet to acquire the real diamonds. The killers reply, "That's most annoying."

> " On behalf of the Whyte House, I'd just like to say you've been a **lousy audience...** "
>
> **Shady Tree**

TREE ASSASSIN

APPEARANCE
Moonraker (1979)

STATUS Dead; shot by Bond

CHARACTERISTICS Good at climbing into and falling out of trees

PLAYED BY Guy Delorme

Little is known about this henchman who works for billionaire aerospace mogul Hugo Drax. Under orders from Drax, the marksman climbs

into a tree. When Bond appears, Drax sets him up to be killed, handing him a gun and asking him to shoot at a pheasant during a hunt on Drax's country estate.

Drax counts on the lack of interest of US police in hunting-related shooting deaths to cover up what he hopes will be Bond's death. The tree assassin fails to take his shot quickly, and Bond picks him off while pretending to shoot at a pheasant.

TREVELYAN, ALEC

APPEARANCE GoldenEye (1995)
STATUS Dead
CHARACTERISTICS Vengeful, highly skilled at the art of espionage
PLAYED BY Sean Bean

MISSION ACCOMPLISHED *006 convincingly fakes his own death with the help of Colonel Ourumov and his soldiers.*

Alec Trevelyan launches a plot to destroy London as an act of vengeance for the betrayal of his parents by the British Army at the end of World War II. Trevelyan's parents were Cossacks who opposed Stalin and fought with the Nazis. When the British captured many Cossacks near Lienz, Austria, they were turned over to the Soviets who swiftly executed them. Trevelyan's parents survived, but his father could not live with the shame and killed himself and his mother.

Trevelyan quickly rose through the ranks of MI6 to become 006. While MI6 knew about his parents' fate, the service believed that Trevelyan was too young to be affected by what

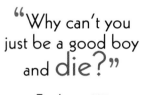

" Why can't you just be a good boy and die? "

Trevelyan to 007

had happened.

Trevelyan convinces MI6 to send Bond with him on a mission to the Soviet Union to destroy the Arkangel Chemical Weapons Facility, managed by Colonel Ourumov. In fact, the raid gives Trevelyan an opportunity to fake his own death. While the original plan anticipated the capture of Bond, 007 survives and causes explosions that scar Trevelyan.

After the fall of the Soviet Union, Trevelyan and Ourumov sell arms to illegal clients, such as Iraq. Trevelyan calls himself Janus after the two-faced Roman god and makes his residence on an armored train once used to transport nuclear missiles.

All this is a prelude to Trevelyan's master plan: to transfer billions of pounds from the Bank of England and set off the electromagnetic pulse space weapon GoldenEye over London to erase any record of the transaction. With the aid of hacker Boris Grishenko, assassin Xenia Onatopp, and Ourumov (now a General), he organizes a massacre of staff at the Russian Space Weapons Centre, Severnaya, in order to obtain his hands on the GoldenEye satellite system. A minor hitch occurs when one of the staff, Natalya Simonova, survives. This draws 007 to Russia. Trevelyan meets Bond once again after Xenia Onatopp fails to kill him. Through a series of cat-and-mouse maneuvers, Trevelyan ends up in Severnaya's sister control station in Cuba, where he and Bond fight to the death on a giant satellite dish transmitter. Competitive to the last, Trevelyan taunts 007: "I was always better." Bond responds by dropping his former friend and colleague from the antenna, which falls and crushes Trevelyan to death.

UNWANTED ATTENTIONS *Trevelyan toys with Natalya Simonova on his converted armored train.*

GUNNING FOR 007 *Trevelyan threatens to fire if Natalya does not reveal a passcode. "Shoot him. He means nothing to me," she replies.*

TRUMAN-LODGE

APPEARANCE
Licence to Kill (1989)
STATUS Dead; casualty of cutbacks
CHARACTERISTICS Whiny fiscal whiz
PLAYED BY Anthony Starke

Harvard Business School graduate William Truman-Lodge oversees the financial side of drug lord Franz Sanchez's cocaine empire. Wanted for insider trading on Wall Street, Truman-Lodge creates the business plan for Sanchez to supply an Asian drug cartel with cocaine. He also sets the prices for the US distribution of cocaine.

Eventually, Truman-Lodge's frequent nagging about money matters prompts Sanchez to "fire" him—using a submachine gun.

VALENKA

APPEARANCE
Casino Royale (2006)
STATUS Dead; shot by Mr. White
CHARACTERISTICS Devoted but lethal
PLAYED BY Ivana Milicevic

Le Chiffre's girlfriend Valenka revels in the luxurious life his illicit banking activities provide. She accompanies him to his high-stakes poker tournament in Montenegro. During the tournament, the Ugandan terrorist Obanno, who had entrusted Le Chiffre with a vast amount of money, attacks Valenka. Obanno and his lieutenant force Valenka to call Le Chiffre to his room. Obanno informs Le Chiffre that if he does not pay back the money he has lost, he will cut off Valenka's arm. Obanno notes that Le Chiffre raises no protest and sarcastically suggests that Valenka should find a new boyfriend.

Valenka ignores this advice and helps Le Chiffre in his bid to win the all-important poker game by poisoning Bond's "Vesper" martini.

TO YOUR HEALTH *Valenka looks on as a poisoned "Vesper" martini is delivered to 007.*
The poison sends 007 into cardiac arrest, and he only survives thanks to the quick thinking of his colleague, Treasury financial officer Vesper Lynd.

After Bond defeats Le Chiffre at poker, Valenka and her lover take Bond aboard a barge, where Le Chiffre tortures 007. Mr. White arrives and kills Le Chiffre and his entourage, including Valenka, but allows Bond to live.

VAN BIERK

APPEARANCE
Die Another Day (2002)
STATUS Serving time, per his sentence from the World Court
CHARACTERISTICS Debonair, smart
PLAYED BY Mark Dymond

Van Bierk, a South African trader of Sierra Leone conflict diamonds, bears a passing resemblance to James Bond. He sells the illegal diamonds to North Korean Colonel Moon in exchange for weapons. Bond uses a beacon device to divert Van Bierk's helicopter to his location and then impersonates Van Bierk to penetrate Moon's compound and plant an explosive device.

VARGAS

APPEARANCE
Thunderball (1965)
STATUS Dead; shot by Bond with a spear gun
CHARACTERISTICS Does not drink, smoke, or make love; his passion is killing.
PLAYED BY Philip Locke

Vargas works for Emilio Largo. His gaunt looks mirror his sinister nature. One of a group of SPECTRE thugs who toss Largo's hapless henchman Quist into a shark pool, Vargas later tries to kill Bond when 007 searches below the *Disco Volante*. He participates in the kidnapping of Bond's ally Paula Caplan and is interrogating her when she poisons herself. Vargas sees Bond talking to Domino on a beach and moves in for the kill. Bond shoots him with a speargun, saying, "I think he got the point."

VENICE ASSASSINS

APPEARANCE
Moonraker (1979)
STATUS One dead; one escaped
CHARACTERISTICS Ingenious at springing surprise attacks, but ineffective
PLAYED BY Unknown

Industrialist Hugo Drax sends two assassins to kill Bond while he travels through Venice in a gondola. One tries to murder 007 from a funeral boat, emerging like Dracula from a coffin and hurling knives at Bond's gondolier and 007. Bond retrieves the knife meant for him and kills the attacker. The other assassin fires a machine gun at Bond as he flees in his specially equipped gondola.

VLAD

APPEARANCE
Die Another Day (2002)
STATUS Dead; flying high
CHARACTERISTICS Keen, nervous
PLAYED BY Michael Gorevoy

Russian scientist Vladimir Popov, called Vlad by his associates, is the brains behind the Icarus space program. He also designs an ice dragster and an armored battlesuit that can control the Icarus satellite. Gustav Graves is surprisingly rude to Vlad, taking his amazing technical accomplishments for granted. Vlad dies when a shot from Bond's Walther P99 decompresses Graves's Antonov transport plane, sucking Vlad into the stratosphere.

"When the time is right, he will be killed. **I shall kill him.**"

Fiona Volpe to Largo, concerning 007

VOLPE, FIONA

APPEARANCE Thunderball (1965)
STATUS Dead; shot by her own men
CHARACTERISTICS Cunning strategist; weapons expert; often makes love to her victims before killing them
PLAYED BY Luciana Paluzzi

As the Head of SPECTRE's Execution Branch, Fiona Volpe serves as the ultimate femme fatale. She not only kills anyone deemed a security risk, she enjoys seducing her targets, teasing their egos and libidos, and sending them to their doom.

Volpe plays an important role in SPECTRE's plan to ransom two atomic weapons. She sets up NATO pilot François Derval to be killed by SPECTRE mercenary Angelo Palazzi, then kills her colleague Count Lippe for bringing the conniving Palazzi onboard.

Volpe bides her time rather than lashes out in anger. She scolds key SPECTRE figure Emilio Largo for trying to kill James Bond. As she points out, Bond's death would have led the British to discover SPECTRE's plan.

Volpe meets Bond when he flags down her car in the Bahamas. As she drives him to the Coral Harbour hotel, he notices her SPECTRE signet ring. She later orders the kidnapping of Bond's contact, Paula

DANCE OF DEATH *Fiona Volpe dies in Bond's arms at the Kiss Kiss Club.*

Caplan, seduces Bond, then arranges for him to be abducted. When Bond escapes, Volpe tracks him to a club where she plots for him to be shot as they dance. Bond sees the trap and spins her into the bullet's path.

WHISPER

APPEARANCE
Live And Let Die (1973)
STATUS Unknown
CHARACTERISTICS Methodical and slow-moving; soft-spoken to the extreme
PLAYED BY Earl Jolly Brown

Whisper works as one of Dr. Kananga's henchmen. He gets his nickname from his quiet, hoarse voice. Whisper tries to kill 007 upon his arrival in New York by firing a poison dart from the side mirror of his white Corvorado "pimpmobile" into the temple of Bond's driver. He hopes the car will crash, but Bond manages to bring it to a stop.

On the island of San Monique, Whisper delivers champagne to Bond's hotel bungalow shortly before 007 battles a desert kingsnake. Whisper later becomes the butt of one of Kananga's jokes when Kananga fires a CO_2 shark pellet into a sofa on which Whisper sits, making it explode. Bond later kicks Whisper into a drug shipment container and then locks him inside.

In the novel, he is known as The Whisper and runs Mr. Big's switchboard in Harlem, New York, which tracks the enemy's movements. His quiet voice is a result of a childhood illness that left him with only half a lung.

WHITAKER, BRAD

APPEARANCE
The Living Daylights (1987)
STATUS Dead; killed by Bond
CHARACTERISTICS Egotistical, war-hungry, brash, over-confident
PLAYED BY Joe Don Baker

Based in Tangier, American arms dealer Brad Whitaker has a museum containing statues of military leaders such as Hitler, Napoleon, and Caesar, —all in his own likeness—and dioramas of great battles. Expelled from West Point for cheating, Whitaker was a mercenary in the Belgian Congo and then worked with criminal organizations that financed his first arms deals. He now partners General Koskov in a scheme to eliminate KGB head Pushkin and misuse Soviet government funds to trade diamonds for opium.

"He met his Waterloo."

007

When Bond confronts him in his home, Whitaker nearly kills 007 with a high-tech assault rifle. Bond kills Whitaker by attaching his explosive key fob to a statue of Wellington. When Bond emits a wolf whistle, the statue explodes and crushes Whitaker into his diorama of the battle of Waterloo.

WHITE, MR.

APPEARANCE
Casino Royale (2006), Quantum of Solace (2008)
STATUS Fate unknown
CHARACTERISTICS Genius of betrayal
PLAYED BY Jesper Christensen

A representative for the mysterious Quantum organization, which helps finance chaos and instability, calls himself Mr. White. He introduces Steven Obanno of the Lord's Resistance Army to Le Chiffre, private banker to world terrorists. Le Chiffre loses Obanno's money by sponsoring his own financially-motivated terrorist plot that goes wrong. Mr. White's involvement and knowledge of Le Chiffre's attempt to regain his money through a poker tournament remain unclear. However, Quantum and Le Chiffre, using Financial Action Task Force liaison officer Vesper Lynd, weave an elaborate web to ensure the winnings end up in their possession.

When Bond wins the poker game, Le Chiffre kidnaps and tortures Bond, who refuses to reveal the password that will allow access to the tournament prize money. Mr. White arrives just as Le Chiffre is about to kill Bond. White kills Le Chiffre, but spares Bond's life, seemingly as part of a deal with Lynd to gain access to the winnings.

In Venice, when the transfer of funds between Lynd and Quantum operative Gettler goes wrong thanks to Bond's intervention, Mr. White collects the briefcase of cash. White appears to be Lynd's key contact in Quantum. Through White, she thinks her French–Algerian lover, Yusef Kabira, has been kidnapped, and should she fail to cooperate, she believes Kabira will be killed.

After Lynd drowns in a sinking Venetian house, she leaves White's cell phone number for Bond to find. He tracks White to an Italian lakeside villa. Bond calls White's mobile, shoots him in the leg, and introduces himself to White in preparation for his attack on Quantum.

Bond loads White into the trunk of his Aston Martin and drives him to an MI6 safehouse in Siena. After informing M and Bond that his organization has people "everywhere," (one of whom is M's bodyguard, Mitchell), White escapes and later reappears at a secret Quantum meeting during a performance of *Tosca* at the opera house in Bregenz, Austria. When Bond makes his presence known, White's fellow members foolishly depart the opera, enabling Bond to snap photos of them. White remains seated, however, and Bond does not spot him.

WINT, MR. & KIDD, MR.

APPEARANCE
Diamonds Are Forever (1971)

STATUS Dead; lost at sea

CHARACTERISTICS Methodical killers with a macabre sense of humor; able to finish each other's sentences

PLAYED BY Bruce Glover (Wint), Putter Smith (Kidd)

Wint and Kidd work as killers for Ernst Stavro Blofeld, murdering the members of Blofeld's diamond smuggling ring as the final consignment of stones works its way through the pipeline. Starting with Dr. Tynan in South Africa, Wint and Kidd follow the chain of smugglers to Amsterdam, Los Angeles, and Las Vegas, leaving a trail of corpses in their wake.

Although Wint and Kidd knock Bond unconscious at Slumber, Inc. and later place his body in a buried pipeline, Bond never sees the pair until the very end of the mission.

A homosexual couple, Wint and Kidd indulge in macabre banter as they work. For example, when Kidd takes pictures of police pulling Mrs. Whistler's body from the Amster River, he notes that she wanted photos of the canals for the children at her school.

Wint's liking for pungent cologne stays with 007, after he smells it on his clothes when he awakes in a desert pipeline. When Wint and Kidd, posing as stewards, try to kill Bond and Tiffany Case aboard Willard Whyte's cruise ship, Bond recognizes the scent. He mentions that it would have been more appropriate to serve a claret rather than Mouton Rothschild '55 with their meal. Wint apologizes, but Bond points out that Mouton Rothschild *is* a claret. Realizing their cover is blown, Wint and Kidd attack. Bond sets Kidd ablaze with brandy; he then tosses Wint over the side with the bomb (disguised as a dessert called a "Bombe Surprise") meant to kill him and Tiffany. Wint explodes before hitting the water.

Wint and Kidd appear in the novel as enforcers for The Spangled Mob. Bond kills them aboard a ship—the *Queen Elizabeth*.

> **"Everyone who touches those diamonds seems to die."**
>
> Mr. Wint

YUSEF

APPEARANCE
Quantum Of Solace (2008)

STATUS Living; whereabouts unknown

CHARACTERISTICS Devious charmer

PLAYED BY Simon Kassianides

French-Algerian Yusef Kabira works as a honeytrap spy, preying on women working in intelligence. Romantically involved with Treasury official Vesper Lynd, Quantum "abducts" Yusef, blackmailing Vesper into working as a double agent.

After her suicide, Quantum fakes Yusef's death, arranging for a body, with his ID and wallet, to wash up on an Ibizan beach, the face mutilated. M confirms it's not him through DNA testing. With information from Dominic Greene,

Bond tracks Yusef to Russia, where he's in the process of scamming Canadian Security Intelligence Service officer Corinne Veneau as he did Vesper. He has even given Corinne an identical Algerian love knot necklace. After Yusef confirms to Bond that he duped Vesper, MI6 takes Yusef into custody.

ZAO

APPEARANCE
Die Another Day (2002)

STATUS Dead; smashed by a lighting fixture while battling Bond

CHARACTERISTICS Experienced and sadistic assassin and terrorist

PLAYED BY Rick Yune

Zao is a North Korean terrorist in league with Colonel Moon, selling conflict diamonds and illicit weapons. At Moon's North Korean compound, Zao takes a PDA cell phone photo of Bond, who is posing as conflict-diamond trader Van Bierk, and transmits it to MI6 double agent Miranda Frost. She quickly identifies "Van Bierk" as Bond. Unmasked, Bond sets off an explosion that embeds diamonds in Zao's face. Bond then seemingly kills Moon before being taken prisoner.

Zao later attempts to blow up a summit meeting between South Korea and China, killing three Chinese agents before being captured. To secure Zao's release, Colonel Moon, altered by gene therapy and now known as Gustav Graves, asks Miranda Frost, his lover, to reveal to the North Koreans the identity of the top US agent in the North Korean High Command. The spy is executed, leading the US and British Secret Services to assume that Bond has cracked under torture and revealed this information. They hastily arrange

> **007:** Your time will come
>
> **Zao:** Not as soon as yours.

UNMARKED *Zao before Bond gives him the world's most expensive face (top).*

for Zao to be released in a prisoner exchange with Bond.

Zao travels to a Cuban medical clinic for DNA replacement therapy, which will morph him into a German Caucasian. Bond disrupts Zao's transformation, but Zao escapes in a helicopter, his face still pockmarked with diamonds, his body chalk white from the unfinished transformation. Zao arrives in Iceland and, driving a Jaguar XKR loaded with weaponry, attacks Bond in his Aston Martin Vanquish. Inside Gustav Graves's melting and crumbling Ice Palace, Bond tricks Zao into crashing his car. 007 then fires a single shot that severs a cable holding a giant ice chandelier. It comes crashing down upon Zao and kills him.

ZORIN, MAX

APPEARANCE
A View To A Kill (1985)
STATUS Dead; at the bottom of San Francisco Bay
CHARACTERISTICS Brilliant but unstable; relishes killing
PLAYED BY Christopher Walken

Max Zorin's boundless ambition leads him to create a plot to corner the world's microchip market. The result of Nazi steroid experiments on pregnant women in concentration camps, Zorin was born in Dresden and quickly deemed a genius (he speaks five languages without accent). But, like all the "steroid kids," he is a psychotic. According to the script, Zorin is "tall, slender, impeccably dressed, in his late thirties. Unusually handsome, he has one grey eye and one blue eye."

In the 1960s, Zorin fled East Germany for France with his "creator," Hans Glaub, the scientist who ran the steroid experiments and changed his name to Dr. Carl Mortner. Zorin built a fortune in oil and gas trading and then expanded into electronics. Gaining a reputation as a staunch anti-Communist and a penniless refugee who made good, Zorin acquired influential friends in European governments.

Zorin's success proves a perfect cover for his second life as a KGB agent who, working for General Gogol, funnels important technology into the Soviet Union. Zorin also works behind the KGB's back, providing technology to a group of microchip manufacturers whom he hopes will join him in a microchip production and distribution cartel. M becomes suspicious of Zorin when a microchip recovered by 007 in Siberia matches a chip impervious to electromagnetic pulse damage developed by a Zorin Industries company. Zorin plans to trigger a massive double earthquake that will flood the entire San Francisco Bay area, including Silicon Valley, home of 80 percent of world microchip production. Calling his plan Operation Main Strike, he foresees that his cartel's chips will then rule the market.

Zorin faces two obstacles. The first is his questionable obsession with

THE BOSS FROM HELL *Max Zorin ruthlessly guns down his loyal workers in his Main Strike mine prior to flooding it.*

THE IMPERFECT COUPLE *Super-intelligent but psychotic Max Zorin and super-strong but amoral May Day make a lethal partnership.*

horse racing. Zorin and Mortner use remote-triggered microchips to inject steroids in racehorses during competition. This draws attention to his activities and compels him to order his accomplice May Day to murder two investigators in France—Achille Aubergine and Sir Godfrey Tibbett—and to personally attempt to murder 007. Additionally, Zorin engages in an ugly battle for control of Sutton Oil. He takes over the company in a rigged proxy fight, but this sparks a legal challenge from oil heiress Stacey Sutton. Zorin offers her $5 million for her shares in the company, but Stacey tears up the check and vows to regain what is rightfully hers.

As Operation Main Strike nears, Zorin severs all ties with the KGB and commits grander crimes. He orders May Day to murder CIA agent Chuck Lee. He assassinates state geologist W. G. Howe and sets San Francisco City Hall afire. He even machine guns his own employees at his mine and betrays May Day. This final act proves the undoing of Operation Main Strike. May Day sacrifices her life to remove the detonator from the tons of explosives set to trigger the fateful earthquake.

When Zorin attempts to escape in his airship, Bond grabs onto the mooring line and ties it to the vertical struts of the Golden Gate Bridge, where Zorin and Bond battle. Bond gains the advantage, and Zorin falls to his death.

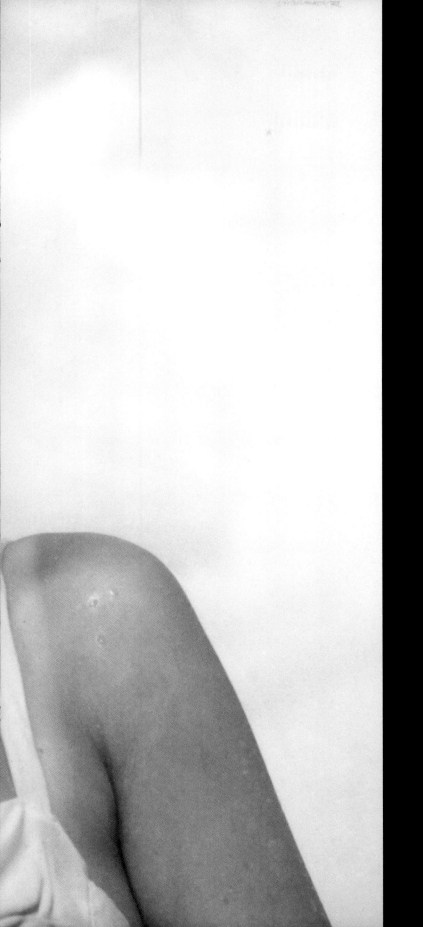

BOND
WOMEN

More than any other characters in the Bond ca[...]
often the women who issue Bond a challeng[...]
test his confidence. They demand he rise to their sta[...]
When Anya Amasova discovers that Bond killed her l[...]
must prove his integrity to her or be killed. The wome[...]
Bond films usually know what they want—and how t[...]
They understand the world and are not afraid of it. W[...]
secret agents or mistresses, smugglers or cellists, they [...]
smartest, most beautiful, most life-embracing women [...]
Some, such as NSA agent Jinx and Wai Lin of the [...]
People's External Security Force, are very much Bond's [...]
Bond represents masculinity, these women are the epi[...]
modern femininity: strong, sensual, brilliant, and self-pos[...]

AKI

APPEARANCE
You Only Live Twice (1967)
STATUS Poisoned in Bond's arms
CHARACTERISTICS Excellent spying skills; remains calm under pressure; superior driver and athlete
PLAYED BY Akiko Wakabayashi

The first Bond woman to be considered a comrade in arms to 007, Aki works for the Japanese Secret Service (SIS) as Agent 294. Aki makes contact with 007 at a sumo wrestling match in Tokyo. When Bond gives her the recognition signal, "I love you," she takes him to see British Secret Service operative Dikko Henderson at his home. An assassin kills Henderson before he can give 007 important information, and Aki trails Bond and the killer's accomplice in her Toyota 2000GT to the headquarters of Osato Chemicals & Engineering. She rescues Bond from Ostato's guards and delivers him to the office of Tiger Tanaka, head of the SIS.

The following day, Aki once again saves Bond from gunmen, and the two travel to the Kobe docks, escaping a multitude of attackers. Tanaka informs Bond he will have to take a wife as part of his cover as a Japanese fisherman. He forbids a disappointed Aki from playing the role, but she supervises Bond's cosmetic transformation into a Japanese fisherman. Bond and Aki then share a bed for the night. As they sleep, a SPECTRE assassin climbs above the bed and drips a deadly poison down a string directed at Bond's mouth. Aki, however, shifts in her sleep, and the poison drips onto her lips, killing her instantly.

AMASOVA, MAJOR ANYA

APPEARANCE
The Spy Who Loved Me (1977)
STATUS Living; whereabouts unknown
CHARACTERISTICS The KGB's top agent; graduate of a Siberian survival course; positive mental attitude; patriotic and vengeful
PLAYED BY Barbara Bach

Major Anya Amasova, Agent Triple X of the KGB, works with James Bond in an uneasy alliance to locate two hijacked nuclear submarines.

Anya arrives in Moscow after a period of leave with her KGB agent lover, Sergei Barsov. KGB chief General Gogol informs her that the nuclear submarine *Potemkin* has disappeared and instructs Anya to

"Then when this mission is over, I will kill you."

Anya to 007

pursue a connection in Cairo. He then tells her of Barsov's death in a British Secret Service operation. Anya replies, "I would very much like to meet whoever was responsible for his death."

In Egypt, Anya pursues the submarine tracking system microfilm offered for sale by Max Kalba. She encounters Bond at the Pyramids of Giza while meeting contact Aziz Fekkesh. She meets 007 again at the Mujaba Club, where the pair shares knowledge of each other's dossiers and attempt to bid for the microfilm. When a huge hulking figure—Karl Stromberg's henchman Jaws—kills

MAJOR PLAYER *Anya Amasova learns of the tragic death of her lover, Sergei Barsov, from her chief, General Gogol.*

THE LAST CALL *Anya decides Bond's fate at the end of their mission.*

Kalba, Anya and Bond follow and successfully battle the giant for the microfilm. Anya then wins the microfilm for the KGB by blowing narcotic dust from a trick cigarette into Bond's face.

When Anya contacts General Gogol, she discovers the Soviets and British have agreed to pool their resources. After another attack by Jaws, Anya and Bond give in to their romantic attraction, but when Anya discovers that 007 killed her lover, she vows to kill him when the mission is over. Realizing that shipping magnate Stromberg is behind the nuclear submarine hijack, Bond and Anya hunt Stromberg's *Liparus* supertanker on the USS *Wayne* submarine, but Stromberg captures the craft.

Stromberg takes Anya to *Atlantis*, his marine research laboratory. Having destroyed the *Liparus*, Bond rescues Anya as the *Wayne* torpedoes *Atlantis*, and they flee in Stromberg's escape pod. Anya must decide whether or not to fulfill her vow to kill Bond. She decides to put the Cold War behind her, and Gogol, M, Q, and the Minister of Defence catch the two spies making love, oblivious to their rescue by the Royal Navy.

ANDERS, ANDREA

APPEARANCE
The Man With The Golden Gun (1974)

STATUS **Dead; shot by Scaramanga**

CHARACTERISTICS **Desperate to free herself from a man she fears**

PLAYED BY **Maud Adams**

Trapped in a relationship with master assassin Francisco Scaramanga, Andrea Anders sends a golden bullet engraved with the number "007" to the British Secret Service. She hopes it will spur James Bond to come after Scaramanga, kill him, and free her from a life she loathes. Her plan succeeds but too late for her to reap the rewards.

When Bond appears at her hotel room in Hong Kong, Andrea pretends not to know Bond's identity. She suffers 007's rough treatment, eventually confessing that Scaramanga has an appointment at the Bottoms Up Club in Hong Kong. Andrea finds Bond again in Bangkok, slipping into his room to warn him that Scaramanga wants to kill him. She admits that she sent the bullet and offers to sleep with him if he will kill Scaramanga. Bond asks her to acquire for him the Solex Agitator, the key component of the world's most efficient solar energy system. She steals it for Bond, but Scaramanga discovers her betrayal and shoots her through the heart at their rendezvous, a Thai kick-boxing match.

BARTLETT, RUBY

APPEARANCE On Her Majesty's Secret Service (1969)
STATUS Living; whereabouts unknown
CHARACTERISTICS Good-natured
PLAYED BY Angela Scoular

Ruby Bartlett unwittingly helps 007 gain insight into Blofeld's operation at his Swiss mountain allergy clinic. In her room, Bond witnesses Blofeld's brainwashing techniques. Raised on a poultry farm in Morecambe Bay, Lancashire, England, Ruby became allergic to chickens. Blofeld has cured her allergy; however, brainwashing has now primed her to return to England and spread the bacteriological warfare agent Virus Omega among poultry populations.

BERGSTROM, PROF. INGA

APPEARANCE
Tomorrow Never Dies (1997)
STATUS Living; whereabouts unknown
CHARACTERISTICS Cunning linguist
PLAYED BY Cecilie Thomsen

Professor Inga Bergstrom is a Danish Professor at Oxford University with whom Bond brushes up on "a little Danish" and "learns a new tongue." Moneypenny disrupts their afternoon tryst with a phone call. She summons Bond to the Ministry of Defence to deal with a crisis in the South China Sea, where 17 British sailors have been murdered.

BIANCA

APPEARANCE
Octopussy (1983)
STATUS Living, whereabouts unknown
CHARACTERISTICS Resourceful; improvises on the spot
PLAYED BY Tina Hudson

Bond's colleague Bianca aids him when he arrives in a Latin American country to destroy a spy plane. She places a fake mustache on his upper lip and attaches a fake ID to his jacket to aid in his convincing disguise as Colonel Luis Toro.

Minutes later, Bianca notices Toro's paratrooper guards driving away with a captured Bond. She speeds up to the vehicle in a Range Rover Convertible and uses her feminine wiles to distract the guards, allowing Bond to pull the rip cords on the guards' parachute harnesses. Before Bond escapes in the Acrostar Bede jet, which he and Bianca have stowed in the back of a horsebox, 007 kisses Bianca goodbye, telling her he will see her in Miami.

DRESSED TO THRILL *Beautiful Bianca proves to be a resourceful and skilled accomplice on Bond's mission to destroy a spy plane.*

BLOFELD'S ANGELS OF DEATH

APPEARANCE On Her Majesty's Secret Service (1969)
STATUS Living; whereabouts unknown
CHARACTERISTICS International, impressionable, naïve
PLAYED BY Angela Scoular (Ruby), Catherina von Schell (Nancy), Julie Ege (Scandinavian Girl), Mona Chong (Chinese Girl), Sylvana Henriques (Jamaican Girl), Dani Sheridan (American Girl), Joanna Lumley (English Girl), Zara (Indian Girl), Anoushka Hempel (Australian Girl), Ingrit Back (German Girl), Helena Ronee (Israeli Girl), Jenny Hanley (Italian Girl)

Ernst Stavro Blofeld gathers twelve beautiful women from around the globe who will unwittingly act as his Angels of Death, spreading his Virus Omega to crops and livestock if his demands are not met.

"The first impression of them is of contestants in an international beauty contest." This is how these women are described in the script. They all suffer from different allergies, including sensitivities to chicken, potatoes, bananas, and rice. They convene in a Swiss clinic known as The Bleuchamp Institute for Allergy Research at Piz Gloria hoping to find a cure for their allergies. Blofeld, posing as the Count Balthazar de Bleuchamp, uses the clinic as cover

BREAKING AND ENTERING *Bond discovers Nancy in his bedroom at Piz Gloria. She circumvented the security doors with a nail file.*

to develop and distribute his bacteriological warfare agent. The twelve brainwashed women, along with several unidentified others, will return to their respective countries and, on his command, spray the deadly Virus Omega agent using innocent-looking atomizers, destroying crops and decimating livestock.

Bond arrives at Piz Gloria disguised as the genealogist Sir Hilary Bray, whom Blofeld has hired to prove his claim to the title of Comte de Bleuchamp. Bond seduces two women, Ruby and Nancy, and flirts with the Chinese woman in an attempt to discover Blofeld's plans. Although captured after sneaking into Ruby's room late at night, Bond uncovers the bacteriological warfare plot and escapes Piz Gloria on skis.

Bond returns later with his future father-in-law Marc Ange Draco and Draco's men, firstly to rescue his fiancée Tracy, who has been kidnapped by Blofeld, and secondly to destroy Blofeld's base, Piz Gloria. This communications center controls the women in their respective countries, and its destruction removes the world threat posed by the twelve "Angels of Death."

There are only ten beautiful women in Fleming's novel. Instead of arriving from all over the world, they come solely from the United Kingdom. All in their twenties, they are described as "working girls probably. Sort of air-hostess type."

"I'll tell you what to do,
I will tell you when, and
I will tell you how."

Ernst Stavro Blofeld

BOUVIER, PAM

APPEARANCE
Licence To Kill (1989)
STATUS Living; whereabouts unknown
CHARACTERISTICS Professional,
superb pilot; has a possessive streak
PLAYED BY Carey Lowell

in order to break into The Olympatec Meditation Institute, a cover for Sanchez's cocaine labs. She rescues Bond and then flies him above one of the tanker trucks to stop Sanchez. At a party celebrating the end of Sanchez's reign, Pam expresses disappointment when she sees Bond kissing Lupe. In the end, Bond chooses to be with Pam.

Pam Bouvier works as a CIA contract pilot and agent trying to contain drug lord Franz Sanchez's operation in Isthmus City.

Bond meets her at DEA agent Felix Leiter's wedding reception and then later at the Barrelhead Bar in Bimini where her drink of choice is "Bud with lime." While at the bar, she finds herself under attack from Sanchez's henchman Dario and his gang. She successfully defends herself with a 12 gauge shotgun. She escapes with Bond and informs him that she was an army pilot who has flown to the toughest hellholes in South America. Bond pays her $75,000 for a private flight to Isthmus City, where he continues to pay her to pose as his secretary, Ms. Kennedy. She even cuts her hair very short to look the part but keeps a Beretta in her garter belt for her own security.

Pam delivers a letter from the US Attorney General to Heller, Sanchez's Chief of Security, granting him immunity if he can retrieve the four Stinger missiles Sanchez purchased from the Contras. Pam harbors concern for Bond's safety during the mission but displays anger and jealousy when she learns Bond has had an affair with Lupe Lamora, Sanchez's girlfriend. She still comes to Bond's aid by posing as a Bible Belt churchgoer from Wichita Falls

STRAIGHT SHOOTER
Pam encounters Bond for the second time in a sleazy Bimini bar, where she proves herself adept with a shotgun.

"If it wasn't for me, your ass would've been nailed to the wall."
Pam Bouvier

CAROLINE

APPEARANCE GoldenEye (1995)
STATUS Retired from MI6, now a guidance counselor at Eton
CHARACTERISTICS Easily flustered
PLAYED BY Serena Gordon

A woman of impeccable background, Caroline works for MI6 evaluating the psychological health of agents. M sends her to report on 007, and she rides with him on a twisting corniche into Monaco in Bond's Aston Martin DB5. When 007 engages in a high-speed flirtatious chase with Ferrari-driving Xenia Onatopp, a terrified Caroline demands he stop. Bond pulls the car to the edge of a cliff overlooking Monaco and produces a bottle of Bollinger as Caroline melts into his arms.

CARUSO, MISS

APPEARANCE
Live And Let Die (1973)
STATUS Alive; whereabouts unknown
CHARACTERISTICS Covert worker
PLAYED BY Madeline Smith

Little is known about the secretive Miss Caruso. After helping James Bond on a mission in Rome, she leaves the country to spend time with him without informing her superiors. This causes the Italians to query M as to her whereabouts. When M arrives at Bond's home at 5:48 a.m. to give 007 an assignment, he asks Bond about her. 007 does not answer, since Caruso is hiding in his closet. Miss Moneypenny witnesses this and helps Bond keep Caruso concealed from M, allowing the pair to spend additional time together before 007 flies to New York.

Miss Caruso: Such a delicate touch.
007: Sheer magnetism, darling!

CARVER, PARIS

APPEARANCE
Tomorrow Never Dies (1997)
STATUS Assassinated
CHARACTERISTICS Sophisticated, cosmopolitan, unhappy; still carrying a torch for 007
PLAYED BY Teri Hatcher

Paris Carver is the stunning American wife of British media baron Elliot Carver and a former flame of James Bond.

Paris and 007 meet again at a party in Hamburg, Germany, celebrating the launch of Elliot Carver's new global satellite network. Paris slaps Bond hard when she sees him again, still angry that his last words to her were, "I'll be right back." When Bond knew her, she used to drink straight shots of tequila. Now she prefers to take a sip of her husband's champagne. She knows Bond very well, asking him if he still sleeps with a gun under his pillow. A jealous Elliot asks his wife how she knows Bond. She lies, saying that James dated her roommate in Zurich.

Paris later goes to Bond's hotel room and tells him that she used to look for his obituary in the papers every day. Bond confesses to her that the reason he backed out of their relationship was because she had become "too close for comfort." The two spend a passionate evening together, and with the help of Paris, Bond locates Elliot Carver's secret lab. When Carver learns of his wife's betrayal, he sends Dr. Kaufman, a professional hitman, to assassinate her. Bond returns to his hotel room to find Paris still in his bed—dead.

007: Was it something I said?
Paris: How about the words I'll be right back?

Camille: You lost somebody?
007: I did, yes.
Camille: You catch whoever did it?
007: No. Not yet.
Camille: Tell me when you do.
I'd like to know how it feels.

CAMILLE

APPEARANCE
Quantum of Solace (2008)
STATUS Living; whereabouts unknown
CHARACTERISTICS Feisty, vengeful,
PLAYED BY Olga Kurylenko

CAMILLE'S CONFESSION *In a sinkhole beneath the Bolivian desert, Camille explains to Bond her reasons for revenge.*

DUSTY AND DETERMINED *Having discovered Greene's plot to control Bolivia's water supply, Bond and Camille take a long, hot walk back to civilization.*

A chain of violent events leads Camille to ally with Bond in his mission against Dominic Greene and General Medrano. Camille is the daughter of Ernesto Montes, once a powerful figure in the Bolivian military junta, and a Russian dancer. As a girl she witnessed Medrano murder her father and strangle her mother and older sister. Medrano then burned their house down; Camille's back still bears the scars from her escape. Camille has vowed to have revenge on Medrano. She discovered a connection between Medrano and Greene and infiltrated Greene's organization by becoming his lover. Little else is known about her past, but Bond's sources tell him that she once belonged to the Bolivian secret service.

In Haiti, Bond enters Camille's life at a critical moment: Greene has discovered that she has tried to buy secret documents relating to the Tierra Project, a plot he is cooking up with Medrano. Greene sends an assassin, Slate, to kill her, but Bond, who is investigating Slate on behalf of MI6, kills him. Camille vainly tries to convince Greene that she is not a spy, but he hands her over to Medrano's tender mercies.

Camille is about to shoot Medrano, but Bond, believing she is being kidnapped, intervenes, unwittingly foiling Camille's assassination attempt. She and Bond join forces in Bolivia to investigate Greene's Tierra Project. Parachuting from their crippled Douglas DC-3 into a desert sinkhole, they discover Greene has been damming vast amounts of the country's water beneath the desert.

Camille confronts Medrano at the Perla de las Dunas hotel. She kills him, but fire engulfs the room. Paralyzed by her childhood fear of the flames, desperate to avoid being burned alive, she asks Bond to shoot her. Bond saves both their lives, igniting a fuel cell and blowing a hole in the wall.

Their very different missions accomplished, Camille and Bond go their separate ways at a train station.

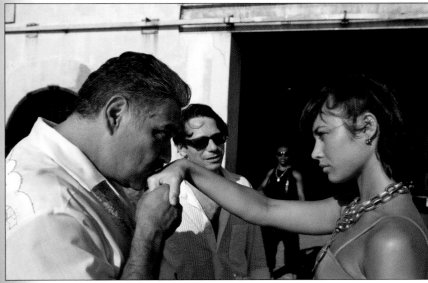

BITTER ENCOUNTER *General Medrano and Camille, the girl he savagely orphaned, meet again.*

CASE, TIFFANY

APPEARANCE
Diamonds Are Forever (1971)
STATUS Living; whereabouts unknown
CHARACTERISTICS Confident, mercenary, clever, seductive
PLAYED BY Jill St. John

Smuggler Tiffany Case plays a vital role in the downfall of Ernst Stavro Blofeld. Part of a smuggling pipeline of South African diamonds, Tiffany finds herself in the middle of a battle between Bond, the CIA, and Blofeld's organization—with world domination in the balance.

Tiffany reveals little of her background except that she was born on the first floor of Tiffany & Co. while her mother shopped for a wedding ring. She has grown up with a mercenary attitude toward wealth and uses her feminine wiles to get what she wants and to protect herself and her interests.

When she meets James Bond, he poses as smuggler Peter Franks. When Bond kills the real Franks, he convinces her the dead man is actually 007. She urges Bond to leave with her and the diamonds immediately. She parts ways with Bond in Los Angeles, only to be called back into service by her contacts in Las Vegas because Bond has delivered fake diamonds. After collecting the real diamonds and eluding over 30 US government agents, Tiffany discovers from Bond that someone is killing all the smugglers in the pipeline. The body of Plenty O'Toole, drowned in her pool, confirms that Tiffany herself is the next target.

Tiffany agrees to help Bond, leading him to the diamonds. She soon finds herself in a guarded suite in Las Vegas, uncertain if she will be rewarded or prosecuted. After Bond discovers Blofeld is behind the smuggling operation, Tiffany convinces the CIA of her willingness to cooperate.

When she sees a woman with a white Persian cat leaving the Whyte House, she follows, thinking it could be Blofeld in drag. It is, but Blofeld kidnaps Tiffany. She pretends to cooperate, traveling with Blofeld to the oil rig from where he launches his satellite attacks against military targets belonging to the world's

007: Weren't you a blonde when I came in?

Tiffany Case: Could be.

007: I tend to notice little things like that— whether a girl's a blonde or a brunette.

MORE THAN MEETS THE EYE *Tiffany Case schemes to obtain a cache of diamonds. Bond has other plans.*

SHOW OF LOYALTY *Tiffany pretends to side with Blofeld against Bond on the mastermind's oil-rig command center.*

superpowers. Case maintains the illusion of allegiance to Blofeld when Bond arrives, but surreptitiously tries to help 007.

At the end of the adventure, Tiffany and Bond go on a sea cruise together. After Bond has disposed of the assassins Wint and Kidd, Tiffany asks Bond: "James, how the hell do we get those diamonds down again?"

In Fleming's novel, Tiffany has led a troubled life. Her mother worked as a madam, and Tiffany became an alcoholic. After she saved a child from drowning, she turned her life around and became a smuggler for the Spangled Mob. At the story's conclusion, Tiffany moves in with Bond—the only woman to do so in the novels or films—but the affair soon ends.

CHEW MEE

APPEARANCE The Man With The Golden Gun (1974)
STATUS Living; whereabouts unknown
CHARACTERISTICS Enjoys swimming
PLAYED BY Françoise Therry

When Bond sneaks into industrialist Hai Fat's estate impersonating his employee Francisco Scaramanga, he meets beautiful Chew Mee swimming in Fat's pool. She invites Bond to join her. When Bond informs her he has no bathing suit, Chew Mee admits that neither has she. Bond starts to unbutton his shirt, but Hai Fat interrupts.

AUDIENCE CONCERN
Bibi and Bond observe East German biathlon champion Erich Kriegler's expert shooting.

DAHL, BIBI

APPEARANCE
For Your Eyes Only (1981)
STATUS Living; retired from ice-skating
CHARACTERISTICS Cute, libidinous
PLAYED BY Lynn-Holly Johnson

Bibi Dahl is an Olympic-caliber ice skater whose fresh-faced innocence belies her irrepressible sexual drive.

Bond meets the teenager at an ice rink in Cortina through her sponsor, Aris Kristatos, and her coach, Jacoba Brink. Bibi immediately falls for Bond and later tries to seduce him in his room at the Hotel Miramonte. Mindful of her youth, Bond politely, but firmly, shows her the door.

She is also a fan of East German biathlon champion Erich Kriegler (secretly a hitman working for Kristatos), who rudely ignores her.

Later, when Kristatos retreats with his entourage to an abandoned monastery in Greece, Bibi, sick of his bullying, tries to flee with Jacoba Brink. After Milos Columbo kills Kristatos, Columbo apparently becomes Bibi's new sponsor.

> *"She's completely absorbed in her skating, but innocent in the ways of the world."*
>
> Aris Kristatos to 007

DI VICENZO, TRACY

APPEARANCE On Her Majesty's Secret Service (1969)
STATUS The late, beloved wife of James Bond
CHARACTERISTICS Headstrong, susceptible to depression, athletic, honest
PLAYED BY Diana Rigg

ON THE BEACH *Bond rescues Tracy from drowning herself.*

Teresa Di Vicenzo is the only woman ever to marry James Bond. Preferring to be called Tracy because Teresa was a saint, she remains one of only two women with whom Agent 007 has truly fallen in love.

> "Why do you persist in trying to **rescue me** Mr. Bond?"
>
> **Tracy Di Vicenzo**

Tracy was born in 1943 to an English mother and a Corsican bandit, Marc Ange Draco, who went on to lead the biggest crime syndicate in Europe, the Union Corse. Tracy's mother died when she was 12, and she became involved in numerous scandals until Draco cut off her allowance. She then secretly married an Italian count who died when he crashed his Maserati while driving with one of his mistresses.

At her very lowest point, Tracy attempts suicide, walking into the sea in Portugal. Bond saves her, but she soon flees. In the casino at Estoril, she recklessly gambles with money she does not have, and Bond volunteers to cover her losses. They meet in 007's suite, but Tracy remains in a very self-destructive mind frame. After a night of lovemaking, Tracy's suicidal mood passes. She meets

DERVAL, DOMINO

APPEARANCE
Thunderball (1965)
STATUS Alive; whereabouts unknown
CHARACTERISTICS Good swimmer, excellent dancer, lonely; seeking escape from a suffocating relationship
PLAYED BY Claudine Auger

Dominique Derval, the kept woman of Emilio Largo, becomes the sole link for James Bond to stop a nuclear extortion plot.

Domino, as her friends call her, grew up in France with her brother François, a Major with the *Armée de l'air* serving with NATO. Through him, Domino met Largo in Capri, and they began an affair. Despite a life of luxury, she finds the relationship empty. The only person to whom she feels connected is her brother.

Domino has been in Nassau for about three weeks when she meets 007 while snorkeling. Although attracted to him, she cannot act on her impulses, due to the watchful eye of Largo. When she spends time with Bond at the Café Martinique, she openly talks about her disenchantment.

Domino and Bond flirt during a few brief meetings and eventually,

while scuba diving, they make love underwater. On the beach afterward, Bond reveals that Largo killed her brother and stole two atomic weapons. She agrees to help Bond by taking a Geiger counter camera with her to the *Disco Volante,* Largo's yacht, to learn whether the missing bombs are aboard.

Largo catches Domino with the gadget and tortures her to find out what she knows, leaving her in a mild state of shock. Largo's chief scientist, Ladislav Kutze, nervously enters her cabin and unties her. Domino goes up to the bridge with a spear gun and shoots Largo in the back just as he prepares to kill Bond. Bond grabs her, and they leap into the sea before the speeding *Disco Volante* crashes and explodes.

In the novel *Thunderball,* Domino's surname is Vitali.

> "Promise me one thing. You will **kill Largo for me** whatever happens."
>
> **Domino to 007**

PAINFUL REVELATIONS *Bond explains to Domino that Largo killed her brother.*

DINK

APPEARANCE
Goldfinger (1964)
STATUS Alive; whereabouts unknown
CHARACTERISTICS Cheerful, obliging
PLAYED BY Margaret Nolan

Dink massages the kinks out of Bond's body while he is on brief leave in Miami after dismantling Mr. Ramirez's drug operations in Mexico. Bond summarily dismisses Dink, described in the script as "a sumptuous bunny girl," when Felix Leiter arrives for a chat.

Bond again at her father's birthday celebration. There, she discovers that her father has offered 007 information if he will spend time with her. Angry, Tracy nearly leaves, but Bond confirms his feelings for her are genuine. They remain together until Bond disappears on assignment to Switzerland to find Blofeld.

Tracy pries his location out of her father and rescues James from Irma Bunt and a host of SPECTRE killers. During a blizzard, Bond and Tracy take refuge in a barn, where Bond proposes marriage. They discuss potential residences once married: Acacia Avenue, Tunbridge Wells; Belgrave Square, London; Via Veneto, Rome; Paris; and Monaco. The next morning, Blofeld captures Tracy and holds her prisoner

WEDDING DAY *Tracy and Bond marry in a spectacular ceremony held in Draco's picturesque Portuguese estate.*

at his clinic, Piz Gloria, until her father and 007 arrive, rescue her, and destroy Blofeld's labs.

Bond returns to Portugal and buys Tracy an engagement ring. At their wedding, Draco offers Bond a dowry of £1 million, but 007 refuses. Leaving on their honeymoon, Tracy expresses her desire to have three boys and three girls. Bond tells Tracy, "We have all the time in the world." A Mercedes approaches with Blofeld at the wheel. From a rear window, Irma Bunt fires nine shots from an MP40 submachine gun. One bullet hits Tracy in the head, killing her instantly.

Tracy's death remains one of Bond's few unhealed wounds. In *For Your Eyes Only*, he visits Tracy's grave in England. On other occasions, Bond reacts with uncharacteristic sensitivity whenever anyone refers to his marriage.

In the Fleming novel, Tracy married Count Guilo di Vicenzo, who stole a large portion of her money. She also gave birth to a child who died of spinal meningitis. These factors explain Tracy's suicidal tendencies. Her death sends Bond into a self-destructive spiral.

TIME RUNS OUT *Tracy dies from a bullet fired by Irma Bunt. Sadly, Bond could not save her from his enemies.*

DUFOUR, CORINNE

APPEARANCE
Moonraker (1979)
STATUS Dead; killed by Drax's dogs
CHARACTERISTICS Top-notch pilot;
idealistic, romantic, good-hearted
PLAYED BY Corinne Clery

A helicopter pilot of French descent working for the Drax Corporation, Corinne Dufour reveres billionaire Hugo Drax, seeing him as an inspirational success story. She flies Bond from Los Angeles International Airport to the Drax Estate in the Mojave Desert. During the flight, she gives Bond an overview of the Drax Aerospace facilities where the Moonraker shuttle is constructed and Drax's château, brought to California stone-by-stone from France. She introduces 007 to Drax and then takes Bond to meet Dr. Holly Goodhead. Bond slips into Corinne's room as she's getting ready for bed and asks her to help him acquire information. She tells Bond that some secret projects at the facilities have been moved to other locations. After sleeping with 007, she finds him searching Drax's office. She inadvertently reveals the location of Drax's safe. Bond cracks the safe and photographs the documents inside while she watches. The next day, Drax fires her during a pheasant shoot on his estate. He then sends his Dobermans to kill her.

FEARING, PATRICIA

APPEARANCE
Thunderball (1965)
STATUS Living; whereabouts unknown
CHARACTERISTICS Good
masseuse; loves a touch of mink
PLAYED BY Molly Peters

Patricia Fearing is an osteopath at Shrublands health clinic. When she finds Bond passed out on a motorized traction table set at full throttle, she fears she will lose her job. Bond remains silent, at a price, and they adjourn to a nearby steam bath. Later that evening, she is enjoying a massage by Bond, when he suddenly leaves her to investigate the arrival of a body at the clinic.

FELICCA

APPEARANCE
The Spy Who Loved Me (1977)
STATUS Dead; shot by Sandor
CHARACTERISTICS Easily led
PLAYED BY Olga Bisera

Felicca meets Bond at the apartment of black market trader Aziz Fekkesh. She has been instructed to keep Bond occupied while Fekkesh arranges to sell a microfilm of shipping boss Stromberg's submarine tracking system to Major Anya Amasova. When she sees Sandor, Stromberg's henchman, preparing to shoot 007, she screams. Bond spins her around so that she takes the bullet meant for him and he chases after Sandor. The nature of her relationship to Fekkesh, Sandor, and Stromberg remains unknown.

Turkish Bath

STEAMED UP *Patricia Fearing has her hands full dealing with Bond at the Shrublands clinic.*

FIELDS, AGENT

APPEARANCE
Quantum of Solace (2008)
STATUS Dead; drowned in oil by
Dominic Greene's men
CHARACTERISTICS By-the-book,
until she meets Bond; resourceful
PLAYED BY Gemma Arterton

"My orders are to turn
you around and put you
on the first plane back to
London."

Agent Fields to 007

ENGLISH ROSE *Wearing a dress bought by Bond,
Fields joins him at the Greene Planet fundraising
party, where she incurs the rage of Dominic Greene.*

Agent Fields works for the British
Consulate in Bolivia. Meeting Bond
at La Paz El Alto Airport, she informs
him he is to be on the next plane to
London and that if he attempts to
flee, she will take him to the plane in
chains. She escorts Bond to an
undesirable hotel, insisting it
fits their cover of teachers on
sabbatical. Bond refuses to
stay there and checks them
into the five-star Andean
Grand Hotel. Won over by
Bond's charm and charisma,
she sleeps
with him.

Agent Fields and Bond
attend a Greene Planet
fundraiser together. When
Dominic Greene's minion
Elvis attempts to pursue
Bond and Camille, Fields
trips him up, sending him
headlong down a flight of
stone steps.

The next evening, Bond
discovers Fields's dead body
covered in black oil on his
hotel room bed. He tells M
that Greene's men murdered
Fields in this way as
"misdirection"—the oil the
US government believes they
will receive in exchange for ignoring
an upcoming Bolivian coup does not
exist.

Later, in an act of poetic justice,
Bond strands Greene in the Bolivian
desert with nothing to drink but a
can of motor oil.

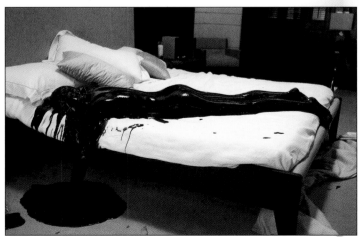

A BLACK DEATH *Dominic Greene arranges for Agent Fields to be drowned with
crude oil–an ironic reference to the US and UK governements' mistaken belief
that vast oil reserves lie beneath the Bolivian desert.*

GALORE, PUSSY

APPEARANCE
Goldfinger (1964)
STATUS Living on a private island
CHARACTERISTICS Ambitious, strong, uncompromising, self-assured; a superb pilot and expert at judo
PLAYED BY Honor Blackman

A born leader who holds men in contempt, Pussy Galore leads an all-female aerial acrobatic troupe—Pussy Galore's Flying Circus—that serves as cover for various illegal activities. Employed as Goldfinger's personal pilot, Galore plays a key role in his plot, Operation Grand Slam, to irradiate the gold supply at Fort Knox. The plan calls for her pilots to spray the entire Fort Knox area with Delta-9 nerve gas, allowing Goldfinger to plant his dirty bomb inside the depository. She also helps bring in the nuclear device to Fort Knox. Galore plans to use the cash that she gains for her part in Operation Grand Slam to buy an island in the Bahamas.

Galore flies 007 from Switzerland to Goldfinger's Kentucky estate. Although Bond remains a prisoner, Pussy briefly treats him as a free man for the benefit of watching CIA agent Felix Leiter. Bond tells her that Goldfinger plans to use her pilots not to spray knock-out gas over Fort Knox, as she had thought, but to

> "You can turn off the charm.
> I'm immune."
>
> **Pussy Galore to 007**

spray a lethal nerve gas. Felix Leiter later reports that Pussy Galore helped switch the nerve gas for a harmless substance, thereby saving thousands of lives and ruining the plot. Despite this good deed, Galore participates with Goldfinger in the hijacking of the President's plane with 007 aboard, before happily ending her adventure in Bond's arms.

In Ian Fleming's novel *Goldfinger*, Pussy Galore is American, not British, and she is the leader of a gang of lesbian cat burglars named The Cement Mixers. Hugely resentful of men, she nevertheless seduces Bond at the novel's end.

PUSSY GALORE AND HER FLYING CIRCUS *Dressed in black, Pussy Galore and her loyal pilots begin on the side of greed and self-interest but eventually see the error of their ways.*

GOODHEAD, DR. HOLLY

APPEARANCE
Moonraker (1979)
STATUS Living; whereabouts unknown
CHARACTERISTICS Secretive, clever, calm under pressure; a top-flight astronaut
PLAYED BY Lois Chiles

Fully-trained astronaut, CIA agent, and Vassar College graduate, Dr. Holly Goodhead works for the Drax Corporation, supposedly on loan from NASA. In reality, her job entails investigating billionaire Hugo Drax's suspicious activities for the CIA. Holly's skills as an astronaut allow her to travel into orbit with Bond and undermine Drax's plot to annihilate the Earth's entire population and repopulate the planet with his own squad of physically perfect humans.

Holly meets Bond after the disappearance of one of the Moonraker shuttles. She declines to share any of her concerns about Drax in California or when Bond confronts her about her CIA connection in Venice. Despite sleeping with Bond, she does not trust him until he saves her life on the Sugarloaf Mountain funicular railroad in Brazil.

Drax's thugs kidnap Holly and bring her to his space shuttle launch complex. She remains a prisoner until Jaws throws Bond into her holding quarters. The pair escapes and takes over a shuttle. They travel to Drax's secret space station where they discover the extent of Drax's plan. Holly and Bond then work together to destroy his operation. She pilots Drax's personal shuttle while he uses the craft's laser weapon to destroy Drax's satellite globes filled with deadly nerve gas. Holly ends up in Bond's arms, orbiting the Earth.

ZERO GRAVITY *At the end of the mission, Bond and Holly float in each other's arms.*

GOODNIGHT, MARY

APPEARANCE
The Man With The Golden Gun (1974)

STATUS Living; whereabouts unknown

CHARACTERISTICS Enthusiastic, brave; desperate to be taken seriously; often finds herself in over her head

PLAYED BY Britt Ekland

Staff intelligence officer Mary Goodnight has been in Hong Kong two years before 007 arrives to kill Scaramanga. She helps Bond locate Andrea Anders, Scaramanga's girlfriend, but fails to notify Lt. Hip of Bond's presence, an oversight that gives Scaramanga and his servant Nick Nack a chance to steal the invaluable Solex Agitator from its designer, Gibson. After this, Goodnight suffers a series of indignities. When Bond propositions her, she slips into his room, only to have Bond shove her into a closet when Andrea arrives. She has to keep hidden while the pair makes love.

Goodnight soldiers on but soon finds herself kidnapped by Scaramanga. On the villain's island, she awaits Bond's arrival.

During 007's and Scaramanga's duel, the technician Kra makes a crude pass at her. Goodnight hits him over the head with a spanner, sending him into the temperature-sensitive vats of Scaramanga's solar energy plant. After Bond kills Scaramanga, Mary helps him retrieve the Solex,

"My hard-to-get act didn't last very long, did it?"
Goodnight to 007

accidentally triggering a lethal solar ray. When the island explodes due to Kra's body in the cooling vats, she escapes with Bond in Scaramanga's junk. After a final battle with Nick Nack, she ends up where she has hoped to be all along, in 007's arms.

Goodnight appears in three Fleming novels: *On Her Majesty's Secret Service,* in which she replaces Bond's secretary, Loelia Ponsonby, *You Only Live Twice,* and *The Man With The Golden Gun.*

HITWOMAN *Goodnight teaches Kra not to turn his back in Scaramanga's solar plant.*

DINNER FOR TWO *Bond and Goodnight get better acquainted in Bangkok. She claims that becoming one of his passing fancies is not her style but her resolve does not last long.*

HAVELOCK, MELINA

APPEARANCE
For Your Eyes Only (1981)
STATUS Living; whereabouts unknown
CHARACTERISTICS Experienced marine archaeologist; expert crossbow shot and scuba diver; passionate, courageous, protective, independent
PLAYED BY Carole Bouquet

The daughter of Timothy and Iona Havelock, Melina is a half-Greek, half-English marine archaeologist, who, according to the script, "reflects her ancestry: warmth overlaid with reserve." Melina grew up a water gypsy on her father's yacht, the *Triana*, traveling wherever his archaeological work took the family, including the Greek Islands, North Africa, and Turkey. In the script, Melina reveals that she later went to boarding school in England and attended Scripps Institution of Oceanography in La Jolla, California, where she earned a PhD.

As Melina returns to the *Triana* via seaplane, she has no idea her smiling pilot is Cuban hitman Hector Gonzales. Soon after she has gone aboard, Gonzales flies over Corfu Harbour and machine-guns her mother and father.

Gonzales to kill her parents.

Bond informs Melina that her father was on a mission for British Intelligence to recover the ATAC transmitter, recently lost in the wreck of the *St. Georges* surveillance ship. Melina deciphers her father's notes written in a special shorthand and uses her family's submarine, the *Neptune*, to help 007 salvage the ATAC. Smuggler Aris Kristatos captures the pair, takes the ATAC, and then drags Bond and Melina behind his ship over a coral reef. Bond and Melina survive and learn Kristatos has taken the ATAC to the abandoned St. Cyril's Monastery.

> "I'm half Greek, and Greek women, like Elektra, always **avenge their loved ones.**"
>
> Melina to 007

Melina sets out to hunt her parents' killer. Through a detective agency, she tracks Gonzales to his Spanish villa and shoots him dead with her crossbow, inadvertently helping to free Bond from capture by Gonzales's men. She and Bond escape in her Citroen 2CV. That night, she confesses to Bond she will not rest until she discovers who paid

When Melina finally comes face to face with Kristatos, she tells Bond to step aside so that she can exact her revenge on her parents' killer. Before she can fire her crossbow, Kristatos's enemy Milos Columbo throws a knife into his back.

In Fleming's short story *For Your Eyes Only*, Melina's name is Judy. She tracks her parents's killers, Gonzales

and Von Hammerstein, to the Vermont woods where she fires a crossbow bolt into Von Hammerstein's back. Bond observes that she has the "vibrations of a wild animal" and nicknames her "Robina Hood."

FLYING VISIT *(far left) Melina with her marine archaeologist father Sir Timothy Havelock and mother Iona, shortly before a joyful family reunion turns to tragedy.*

READY TO FIRE *(center left) Melina fires her crossbow bolt into the chest of one of Gonzales's goons in the woods near the hitman's Spanish villa.*

FOR YOUR EYES ONLY *(top) At the end of the mission, Melina prepares for a moonlight swim with 007.*

IVANOVA, POLA

APPEARANCE
A View To A Kill (1985)
STATUS Living; whereabouts unknown
CHARACTERISTICS Clever, devious
PLAYED BY Fiona Fullerton

HOT TUB *Bond and Pola Ivanova do their best to relieve lingering East–West tensions.*

Pola Ivanova works as a KGB agent and was once ordered to seduce James Bond in London while she toured with the Bolshoi.

With the aid of a waterproof Walkman and a microphone on the end of a telescoping rod, Pola and fellow agent Klotkoff record Max Zorin's activities at his oil pumping station in San Francisco. Pola then meets 007 again, and they retire to the Nippon Relaxation Spa in Chinatown. Bond steals the tape of the bugged conversation, much to the consternation of Pola and KGB chief General Gogol.

JINX

APPEARANCE
Die Another Day (2002)
STATUS Living; still working for the good guys
CHARACTERISTICS Self-assured, independent, sexual, feisty
PLAYED BY Halle Berry

Nicknamed Jinx because she was born on Friday the 13th and because her relationships never last, the enigmatic NSA agent Giacinta Johnson teams up with James Bond to prevent Gustav Graves from using his Icarus satellite superweapon to turn North Korea into a new superpower.

In Los Organos, Cuba, Jinx discovers that escaped North Korean terrorist Zao is a secret patient at a clinic run by Dr. Alvarez, who specializes in DNA replacement therapy. Jinx also catches Bond's eye, emerging from the sea in her bikini and knife belt. Bond and Jinx recognize each other's predatory nature and seduce each other.

The next morning, Jinx assassinates Dr. Alvarez. She makes a back-up disk of the files on Alvarez's computer and programs a cell phone bomb to destroy the clinic. After failing to assassinate Zao, she performs an amazing 200-ft (61-m) backdive and escapes in a Sunseeker Superhawk 48 powerboat.

Jinx travels to Iceland to investigate Gustav Graves

KILLING AGENDA *Jinx infiltrates the clinic of geneticist Dr. Alvarez. After hearing him confess his evil practices, she shoots him dead.*

Jinx:
I'm so good.
007:
Especially when you're bad.

under the alias of Miss Swift of *Space and Technology* magazine and arrives at his Ice Palace in a 2003 Ford Thunderbird. She attends the unveiling of the Icarus satellite by Graves. Bond later rescues her from being burned to death by a diamond-cutting laser. 007 also saves her from drowning inside Graves's melting Ice Palace.

Jinx and 007 officially join forces to disable the Icarus satellite weapon. Entering North Korea on jet gliders known as switchblades, they parachute near an airfield. They sneak aboard an Antonov transport plane, from which Graves and a trio of North Korean generals plan to supervise Icarus's destruction of South Korea's defenses. After the plane depressurizes, Jinx flies the plane into the beam of the Icarus satellite, destroying the satellite's control mechanism. Jinx and double agent Miranda Frost battle to the death, with Jinx defeating the gold medal-winning fencer by slamming a broken-off sword into her heart.

After escaping the disintegrating plane, Jinx and Bond helicopter to a South Korean Buddhist temple, where they make love on a bed covered with Graves's diamonds.

" Jones, Christmas Jones. And don't make any jokes. I've heard them all. "

American nuclear physicist Dr. Christmas Jones works for the International Decommission Agency (IDA). She has a peace tattoo below her naval and speaks fluent Russian. Wearing a tank-top, shorts, and heavy duty boots, she uses a tactical fission HP Jornada 430SE palm-sized computer to acquire readouts on the makes of various nuclear devices.

Christmas meets Bond in Kazakhstan, where he poses as Russian atomic scientist Dr. Arkov. Christmas recognizes that Bond's credentials are forged and, in the confusion, anarchist terrorist Renard escapes with a nuclear weapon.

Christmas joins forces with Bond to find the weapon. They travel on an observation rig in a harrowing chase through an unused pipeline where it appears that a bomb has been placed in a "pig." At the last moment, Bond and Christmas realize that the pipeline explosion is just a diversion. Christmas helps 007 confront Baku-based casino and caviar factory owner Valentin Zukovsky to uncover Renard's and his accomplice, oil tycoon Elektra

IN THE DEEP END *Christmas Jones risks drowning to help 007 foil Renard's plot.*

King's, true plot. The pair plans to cause the meltdown of a Russian submarine's reactor by loading it with weapons-grade plutonium. This will destroy Istanbul, killing eight million people and giving Elektra's pipeline total control over oil supplies to the West.

Christmas eventually helps Bond prevent Renard from loading a plutonium rod into the submarine's reactor. After Renard's death, she and Bond escape just as the hydrogen gas ignites, blowing the submarine apart.

At the end of the adventure, Dr. Jones and 007 find themselves in each other's arms, ready to welcome in the new millennium.

JONES, DR. CHRISTMAS

APPEARANCE
The World Is Not Enough (1999)
STATUS Living; whereabouts unknown
CHARACTERISTICS Gifted scientist, confident of her skills in a male-dominated profession; brave under pressure
PLAYED BY Denise Richards

FIRST MEETING *Christmas and Bond must work together to survive when Renard steals a nuclear device.*

JONES, KIMBERLEY

APPEARANCE
A View To A Kill (1985)
STATUS Living; whereabouts unknown
CHARACTERISTICS Skillful submarine pilot; appreciates the finer things in life
PLAYED BY Mary Stavin

British agent and iceberg submarine pilot Kimberley Jones transports James Bond to and from the KGB's Siberian research center when he receives instruction to investigate the death of Agent 003. After completing his mission, Kimberley places the sub on automatic pilot, and the two plan to enjoy vodka, caviar, and each other during the five-day trip to Alaska.

LAMORA, LUPE

APPEARANCE
Licence To Kill (1989)
STATUS Living; whereabouts unknown
CHARACTERISTICS Discontented, mercenary, rueful
PLAYED BY Talisa Soto

> "You know, I love James so much."

Lupe to Pam Bouvier

The beautiful mistress of drug baron Franz Sanchez, Lupe Lamora realizes that James Bond is the one man who can help her break free from her destructive and very dangerous relationship. Accordingly, she helps Bond in his quest to bring down Sanchez's empire.

Lupe comes from an impoverished background, which it took her 15 years to escape. Franz Sanchez first saw her in a Miss Galaxy beauty contest and, struck by her beauty, rigged the competition so that she won. He then gave her a job in his Isthmus City casino, and she eventually became his mistress.

When Lupe embarks on an affair with Alvarez, Sanchez enters US territory and whips her with a stingray tail for her betrayal. During Bond's and DEA agent Felix Leiter's attempt to capture Sanchez, 007

meets Lupe and offers assistance to the beaten young woman, which she refuses.

Lupe encounters Bond again on board Milton Krest's drug smuggling ship, the *Wavekrest*, and later in Isthmus City, where she helps 007 to deceive Sanchez and infiltrate his organization. She also sleeps with Bond and states that she has deep feelings for him.

When Lupe reveals how she feels about 007 to CIA contract pilot and agent Pam Bouvier, she ignites Pam's jealous streak. After Bond kills Sanchez, Lupe again makes a play for 007's affections. Bond understands Lupe's complex love/hate relationship with men and turns down her invitation. Lupe quickly shifts her amorous attentions to the wealthy President of Isthmus City, Hector Lopez.

LIN, WAI

APPEARANCE
Tomorrow Never Dies (1997)
STATUS Living; on active duty
CHARACTERISTICS Martial arts expert; independent, intelligent
PLAYED BY Michelle Yeoh

Colonel Wai Lin, a top agent for the Chinese People's External Security Force, teams with Bond to stop a manufactured war from breaking out between Britain and China. Wai Lin remains among the most athletic of all the Bond women, displaying fighting skills beyond compare.

Described in the script as "a petite, stunningly beautiful Chinese woman," Wai Lin's investigation of media mogul Elliot Carver begins when her organization discovers stealth material is missing from one of the bases of General Chang, a key figure in the Chinese military. Wai Lin follows a lead to Carver's

BREAK-IN *Bond catches Wai Lin infiltrating Carver's headquarters. The two agents soon become partners.*

EASY RIDERS *Bond and Wai Lin escape Carver's men in Saigon on a BMW Cruiser R1200 motorbike.*

BICYCLE SHOP SHOWDOWN *Wai Lin uses her martial arts skills to defeat General Chang's men.*

headquarters in Hamburg, Germany. Believing that Chang and Carver might be building a stealth plane, she infiltrates the launch party of Carver's new satellite news network CMGN and poses as a representative of the New China News Agency. Carver suggests that she work in his Beijing bureau, but she reminds him that he doesn't have a bureau in Beijing; the Chinese have refused him broadcast rights.

> "I hate to disappoint you, but I don't even have a little red book."

Wai Lin to 007

Wai Lin tries to break into Carver's secret laboratory but discovers 007 has beaten her to it. As guards pursue Bond, Lin escapes with ease.

Wai Lin next encounters 007 diving in the sunken HMS *Devonshire* off the coast of Vietnam. They discover Carver has stolen a cruise missile from the ship. Captured by Carver's enforcer Stamper, Lin and Bond are flown to Carver's Saigon headquarters. There, she discovers the extent of Carver's plan to manipulate China and Britain into war and also confirms the participation of General Chang in the plot.

Handcuffed together, Wai Lin and Bond pull off a series of hairsbreadth escapes before she leaves Bond shackled to a pipe, telling him she "works alone." After Chang's men attack her, and Bond comes to her aid, 007 convinces her that preventing a war is also his goal. Wai Lin then learns that Carver and Chang have built a stealth ship, not a stealth plane.

Bond and Wai Lin locate, slip aboard, and plant limpet mines on Carver's stealth ship. When Stamper captures Wai Lin, Bond proves his loyalty by trying to bargain for her freedom. Bond sets off a grenade, blasting a hole in the ship's hull and allowing Lin to escape. During the ensuing battle, Carver attempts to launch his stolen British Tomahawk missile at Beijing.

DEFACING THE BUILDING
*In a nod to the classic 1926
Douglas Fairbanks film The
Black Pirate, Bond and Wai
Lin escape Carver's clutches
by tearing down a banner of
his face on the side of his
Saigon headquarters.*

Stamper recaptures Wai Lin and tries to stop Bond disabling the missile by threatening to kill her. Wai Lin tosses Bond detonators to cause the missile to self-destruct. Stamper then tries to drown her by lowering her into the water wrapped in a heavy chain, but Bond revives her with an underwater kiss of life. She ends her adventure in Bond's arms, amid the wreckage of Carver's ship.

LINDA

APPEARANCE
The Living Daylights (1987)
STATUS Living; whereabouts unknown
CHARACTERISTICS Wealthy, bored
PLAYED BY Kell Tyler

Linda, a single woman, finds life on the Mediterranean boring, full of "playboys and tennis pros." She hopes to find a real man. Within seconds of expressing this desire to her friend Margot, Bond parachutes onto her *Moonmaiden II* yacht. As 007 calls Exercise Control to tell them he will report on an attack on agents in one hour, Linda pours him a glass of champagne. Eyeing her and the drink, Bond delays his report time to two hours.

ADRIFT AT SEA *Linda hopes to meet a "real man." Moments later, 007 arrives via a smoldering parachute.*

LING

APPEARANCE
You Only Live Twice (1967)
STATUS Working undercover
CHARACTERISTICS Fun, but devious
PLAYED BY Tsai Chin

M's office arranges for Ling, a double agent, to aid in the fake murder of James Bond. Posing as Bond's lover in Hong Kong, Ling stages a betrayal, trapping Bond in a Murphy wall bed as two gunmen spray it with machine gun fire.

It is rumored Ling later married into a fortune, changed her name, and became a professional gambler of some repute.

LYND, VESPER

APPEARANCE
Casino Royale (2006)
STATUS Dead in Venice
CHARACTERISTICS Enigmatic,
conflicted, complicated
PLAYED BY Eva Green

> "Am I going to **have a problem** with you, Bond?"
>
> Vesper Lynd

Vesper Lynd both opens and shuts James Bond's heart. The internal torment she suffers and the pain she causes leave permanent scars on 007.

Lynd works for the Financial Action Task Force of Her Majesty's Treasury as an International Liaison Officer with experience with illicit banking practices. She supervises the British government's funds that finance Bond in a high-stakes poker tournament organized by Le Chiffre.

Bond speculates that she grew up an orphan. In a production draft of the script, Vesper reveals that her father killed her mother and then shot himself. When Bond meets Lynd, she wears an Algerian love knot necklace, a gift from her French-Algerian lover. At some point Vesper, comes to believe the terrorist network associated with Mr. White has kidnapped her lover. Should she fail to cooperate, she believes he will be killed.

Bond's arrogance initially angers Vesper, but she observes him closely enough to have a tuxedo hand tailored by eye. When Lynd witnesses Bond killing Ugandan warlord Obanno and his lieutenant, Bond's gentle sympathy for her shattered emotions draws her closer to him.

Even so, she denies him more Treasury funds to stay in the tournament when he over-plays his hand. After CIA agent Felix Leiter gives Bond funds to continue, Le Chiffre's girlfriend, Valenka, poisons him. Bond lapses into cardiac arrest, but Vesper saves him, reattaching a wire to his portable defibrillator and restarting his heart.

After Bond wins the poker game, Le Chiffre kidnaps Vesper, luring Bond into a trap in order to extort the tournament winnings. Vesper knows Bond will be brutally tortured, but she makes a deal with Mr. White to spare Bond's life in return for delivering the funds. Before she can transfer the funds to White's accomplice Gettler, Bond confesses his love for her and resigns from MI6.

In Venice, Bond uncovers Lynd's deception. Although he kills her enemies, Vesper cannot live with her actions. She locks herself in a submerged elevator and drowns. Bond closes himself off emotionally after her death, repressing his love for Vesper and transforming it into cold dedication to his work. Bond finds her betrayal bitter, telling M, "The bitch is dead."

Vesper does leave Bond an essential clue to help him trace the terrorist network—on her cell phone, she stores Mr. White's number.

In Ian Fleming's novel, Vesper

REST AND RECUPERATION *Vesper finds herself emotionally drawn to Bond during his recovery from the brutal torture inflicted by Le Chiffre.*

works for Section S, a part of the Secret Service devoted to the Soviet Union. Her lover, a Polish Free Fighter, has been in Soviet custody since the end of World War II, and she knows that if she fails to deliver key intelligence to her Soviet handlers, he will be murdered. After Bond's torture by Le Chiffre, she tries to forget her lover, but her burden of guilt for his inevitable death and Bond's suffering proves too great and she kills herself with an overdose of sleeping pills. Her death makes Bond vow to "go after the threat behind the spies, the threat that made them spy."

It is through his tragic affair with Vesper Lynd that James Bond finds the inner sense of purpose that drives him to rise to any challenge, to defeat any foe, to be the greatest secret agent the world has ever known.

MAGDA

APPEARANCE Octopussy (1983)
STATUS Living; whereabouts unknown
CHARACTERISTICS Extremely athletic, agile, enigmatic; performs sleight-of-hand magic tricks
PLAYED BY Kristina Wayborn

Magda is the associate of exiled Afghan prince Kamal Khan and also a member of Octopussy's circus troupe, where she performs magic tricks and juggles. She resides at Khan's Monsoon Palace and aids him, helping to deceive Octopussy and James Bond until she discovers that he planned for her to die in a nuclear explosion.

Magda helps Khan in his effort to re-purchase a Fabergé egg being sold at auction. When he learns the jeweled egg is a forgery, he instructs Magda to seduce Bond and take the original from him. During their lovemaking, Bond notices an octopus tattoo on Magda's rear, which he refers to as "my little Octopussy." After snatching the egg, she demonstrates her athletic ability by backflipping from Bond's hotel balcony and twirling to the ground using her sari.

Magda believes Khan only smuggles jewels from the Soviet Union. He does not reveal to her his plot to explode a nuclear weapon on a US Air Force Base in West Germany. She joins forces with Octopussy and 007 when

IN COSTUME *As well as being Octopussy's second in command, Magda also performs in Octopussy's Circus.*

she learns that Kamal left them to be killed in the explosion.

During a final assault on the Monsoon Palace by Octopussy's troupe, Magda leads the fight with stun grenades and weighted skirts. Using her acrobatic ability, she disables many better-armed guards. She is saved by Q when Kamal's men attack the troupe.

Magda: He suggests a trade. The egg for your life.
007: I'd heard the price of eggs was going up, but isn't that a little high?

MANUELA

APPEARANCE
Moonraker (1979)
STATUS Living; whereabouts unknown
CHARACTERISTICS Good with martinis and Rio geography
PLAYED BY Emily Bolton

Manuela works for Station VH in Rio de Janeiro, Brazil. She follows Bond from the airport to his hotel suite, where she shakes him a martini. After spending five romantic hours with Bond, she takes him into Rio during Carnival. The pair slips through the crowds to an import/export subsidiary of the Drax Corporation, Carlos and Wilmsberg, Inc., on Carioca Avenue. Bond, who is investigating millionaire Hugo Drax following the disappearance of a shuttle, finds a clue: a sticker for Drax Air Freight. Meanwhile Jaws, dressed in a carnival costume, attacks

Manuela. Bond arrives just in time to save her, and crowds carry Jaws away. Manuela tells 007 that Drax Air Freight operates out of San Pietro Airport and Bond takes her home.

WATCHING AND WAITING *At the Rio Carnival, Manuela anxiously awaits Bond's return from his investigation of a warehouse.*

MARIE

APPEARANCE
Diamonds Are Forever (1971)
STATUS Unknown
CHARACTERISTICS Seductive, surprisingly informative
PLAYED BY Denise Perrier

Marie resides at Ernst Stavro Blofeld's coastal compound. The nature of her relationship to Blofeld remains unexplained. She seems extremely happy to see the dashing Bond when he arrives at the compound from Cairo, Egypt. Her interest is short-lived. Bond immediately rips off Marie's bikini top, choking her with it until she finally reveals to him the whereabouts of Blofeld.

STRONG-ARM TACTICS *Bond wastes no time learning where Blofeld is hiding himself.*

133

MASTERSON, JILL

APPEARANCE
Goldfinger (1964)
STATUS Dead; by skin asphyxiation
CHARACTERISTICS Bored,
adventurous, fun-loving
PLAYED BY Shirley Eaton

When James Bond enters
Goldfinger's suite at Miami's
Fontainebleau Hotel, he discovers
Goldfinger's paid companion Jill
Masterson on the balcony with
binoculars. She is telling Goldfinger,
via radio, which cards are held by Mr.
Simmons in a game of gin rummy,
enabling Goldfinger to cheat.
When questioned by Bond, Jill
states that her relationship with
Goldfinger is purely professional.

Bond takes over the radio link
and commands Goldfinger to start
losing his ill-gotten gains.
Impressed, Jill accepts Bond's
invitation to dinner at his hotel
suite, seeing Bond as an escape
from a job she hates. Her
feelings of liberation
prove tragically short-lived.
Goldfinger's manservant
Oddjob knocks out Bond.
When he comes to, he finds
Jill dead, painted from head to
toe in gold leaf. Bond later

GOLDEN GIRL *In the
novel, Bond never sees Jill
painted gold. He hears
about Goldfinger's
murderous actions from
Jill's sister, Tilly.*

learns that she has died from skin
asphyxiation.

In the novel, Jill's last name is
Masterton. She does not die with
Bond, but Goldfinger kills her days
later. Fleming's rationale for Jill's
death has caused controversy. Some
claim there is no chance of Jill dying
by being painted gold. Others believe
that failing to leave a patch of skin
open on Jill's back could be fatal.

MASTERSON, TILLY

APPEARANCE
Goldfinger (1964)
STATUS Dead; broken neck
CHARACTERISTICS Vengeful, angry
PLAYED BY Tania Mallet

Tilly Masterson wants to kill Auric
Goldfinger for murdering her sister,
Jill. Bond meets Tilly on a Swiss
mountain road, when she takes a shot

> "I'm beginning
> to like you,
> Mr. Bond."
>
> Jill Masterson

at Goldfinger and nearly hits 007.
After a car chase, Bond shreds her
Mustang's tires with the wheel hubs
of his DB5. He spots her ArmaLite
AR-7 case, which she claims holds
her ice skates. Bond also realizes
that she has lied about her
name, which she claims to be
Tilly Soames.

That night, Bond finds
Tilly trying to stalk
Goldfinger at his factory.
When her rifle trips an
alarm wire, she admits
she is Jill's sister and
escapes with Bond.
Oddjob soon breaks
her neck with his
deadly, metal-rimmed,
dressage top hat.

In the novel, Tilly is a
lesbian with the last name
Masterton and survives until
near the end.

MILOVY, KARA

APPEARANCE
The Living Daylights (1987)
STATUS Alive; one of the world's virtuoso cellists
CHARACTERISTICS Talented, innocent, artistic, loyal, trusting
PLAYED BY Maryam d'Abo

Cellist Kara Milovy is the Czech lover of rogue KGB General Georgi Koskov. He sets her up as a sniper, instructing her to fire blank bullets at him to make his defection to the British appear genuine. Bond, sensing she doesn't know what she's doing, shoots the rifle from her hands.

When Koskov is snatched back,

TOBOGGAN RUN *Kara and Bond escape across the Czech border aboard her cello case.*

apparently by the KGB, Bond decides to investigate the mysterious sniper who, Moneypenny informs him, is a cellist on a scholarship to the Bratislava Conservatoire. Bond tracks Kara down and pretends to be Koskov's friend to win her trust and bring her out of Czechoslovakia to Austria.

Their romantic interlude in Vienna is cut short when Bond discovers that Kara's cello, a Stradivarius named The Lady Rose,

was purchased for her by arms dealer Brad Whitaker. Suspecting a link between Koskov and Whitaker, Bond takes Kara with him to Tangier, where Whitaker is based. Without Bond's knowledge, Kara telephones Whitaker's villa and discovers that "Georgi" is there. Now working with Koskov, she drugs Bond's martini. Just before he passes out, Bond tells her the truth: that he is not Koskov's friend but a British agent, and that Koskov has betrayed the Russians, the British, and Kara herself, setting her up to be killed.

Koskov kidnaps Bond, and Kara accompanies them to Afghanistan. Bond has convinced Kara of Koskov's treachery and she becomes a valuable ally, helping Bond escape from a Soviet airbase and joining a group of mujaheddin fighters to rescue Bond when he becomes trapped in Koskov's drug convoy.

At the end of the adventure, Kara gives a concert at the Schonbrunn Palace Theater in Vienna. After the concert, General Gogol of the Foreign Service grants her a visa so that she can travel from East to West whenever she desires.

> **"Whoever she was, I must have scared the living daylights out of her."**
> 007

CLASSICAL SUBTERFUGE
Kara Milovy plays Mozart's 40th Symphony in G minor shortly before posing as a KGB assassin aiding in the fake defection of her lover General Georgi Koskov.

O'TOOLE, PLENTY

APPEARANCE
Diamonds Are Forever (1971)
STATUS Dead, killed by assassins Wint and Kidd
CHARACTERISTICS Beautiful, unlucky
PLAYED BY Lana Wood

Plenty O'Toole works the casino floor finding wealthy men who will ply her with money and favors. She has consistently bad luck. When she meets Bond, he tips her $5000 of his winnings at craps. She asks if he wants to get a drink. In Bond's hotel suite at the Tropicana, Morton Slumber's thugs grab her and throw her, from several floors up, into the hotel pool. She survives but ends up dead in Tiffany Case's pool, her feet tied to a flagstone.

In the original script, Plenty returns from the hotel pool to Bond's suite and finds him with Tiffany. She locates Tiffany's address and goes to her house. Wint and Kidd mistake her for Tiffany and kill her.

Plenty: Hi, I'm Plenty.
007: But of course you are.
Plenty: Plenty O'Toole.
007: Named after your father, perhaps?

OCTOPUSSY

APPEARANCE
Octopussy (1983)
STATUS Living, whereabouts unknown
CHARACTERISTICS Leader, morally ambivalent, spiritual, athletic
PLAYED BY Maud Adams

Octopussy leads a modern incarnation of a secret order of female bandits and smugglers. Fabulously wealthy, she lives at The Floating Palace on Lake Pichola in Udaipur, India. This splendid palace is populated solely by women and is only accessible via her private barge. Partnered with exiled Afghan prince Kamal Khan in a $300 million jewelry smuggling operation, Octopussy runs a European circus that provides the perfect cover for this operation.

Octopussy's father, Major Dexter Smythe, committed a murder and stole a cache of North Korean gold many years ago. James Bond traveled to Sri Lanka to bring Smythe to justice, but after meeting Bond, Smythe chose to commit suicide before his final arrest. When Octopussy meets Bond, she thanks him for giving her father an honorable alternative to public disgrace. Her father, a leading authority on octopi, gave his daughter the pet name of Octopussy.

Octopussy first discovered she had a knack for smuggling when she finished selling off her father's gold. Contacts in Hong Kong offered her a commission to smuggle diamonds. She needed an organization so she revived the ancient octopus cult and chose as her symbol the poisonous blue-ringed octopus. She assembled her all-female team, led by tall blonde Gwendoline and short brunette Midge, from young women discovered all over Southeast Asia who were looking for a guru and spiritual discipline. Octopussy gives them a purpose, a sisterhood, and a way of life.

Octopussy meets Bond when he sneaks into her compound to find information about the death of 009. She tries to induce Bond to work for her, unaware that her partner Khan wants 007 dead. After an emotional confrontation, Octopussy sleeps with

ARMED TO THE HILT *Octopussy's circus performers also train in commando tactics.*

PAINTED SMILE *The circus is the perfect front for smuggling.*

TWO OF A KIND *Bond and Octopussy strike up an almost instant rapport, united by a love of intrigue, danger, and passion.*

REVENGE *Octopussy attacks Kamal for his treachery.*

Bond before thugs attack the pair in an attempt to kill 007. When Bond falls into the lake with one attacker and a crocodile joins the fray, Octopussy believes Bond has been killed.

Octopussy travels to Europe for a scheduled tour of her circus that will take her across the border from East to West Germany. She supervises the transfer of Soviet jewels from General Orlov onto her train for smuggling into the West. At a performance of her circus at a US Air Force Base in Feldstadt, the appearance of Bond, alive, stuns her. 007 reveals that Kamal has removed the smuggled jewels from her circus train and replaced them with an atomic bomb. Octopussy then provides vital help in disarming the bomb.

Later, with her troupe, Octopussy seeks revenge on Kamal Khan in India. She and her highly trained force of female guards attack Khan's Monsoon Palace, but Khan and his henchman Gobinda capture her and flee. Bond rescues her from Khan's Beech 18 plane. At the film's close, she finds herself in 007's arms as he recuperates on her barge.

In Fleming's short story, Major Dexter Smythe gives the pet name Octopussy to an octopus in Jamaica. The story recounts Bond confronting Smythe with his past crime, Bond's personal connection to the event, and Smythe's subsequent death and consumption by the octopus that so intrigued him.

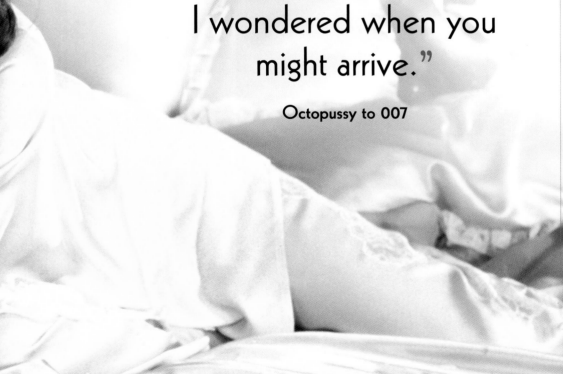

"Good evening.
I wondered when you
might arrive."

Octopussy to 007

PEACEFUL FOUNTAINS OF DESIRE

APPEARANCE
Die Another Day (2002)
STATUS Living; whereabouts unknown
CHARACTERISTICS Efficient, professional, competent
PLAYED BY Rachel Grant

Masseuse Peaceful Fountains of Desire is actually working for Chinese Intelligence agent Mr. Chang, who doubles as the concierge at the Rubyeon Hotel in Hong Kong. James Bond checks into the hotel, and Peaceful arrives at his room. When he finds a Llama Especial pistol stashed in Peaceful's garter, Bond throws an ashtray at a closet mirror, breaking the glass and revealing Mr. Chang and his team prepared to film Peaceful's "interrogation" of Bond.

ROMANOVA, TATIANA

APPEARANCE
From Russia With Love (1963)
STATUS Living; whereabouts unknown
CHARACTERISTICS
Loyal, innocent, graceful, passionate
PLAYED BY Daniela Bianchi

Corporal of State Security Tatiana Romanova plays a key role in a SPECTRE plot to kill 007. Tatiana—Tania to her friends—works in the cryptographic section of the Soviet consulate in Istanbul, Turkey. She formerly lived in Moscow, where she worked in the English decoding group in the KGB Central Index. She studied ballet in Leningrad (now St. Petersburg) but was dismissed when she grew an inch over the regulation height.

Tatiana meets with Rosa Klebb, believing Klebb works for SMERSH. Under threat of death, she agrees to Klebb's assignment "to give false information to the enemy." She contacts Istanbul head of Station T, Turkey, Kerim Bey, claiming she wishes to defect with a Lektor decoder, but only on the condition that James Bond escorts her and the decoder to England. She meets 007 in his hotel room, slipping into his bed wearing only a black choker and black stockings. Unknown to Tatiana and Bond, Klebb and a SPECTRE cameraman film their lovemaking.

Tatiana helps Bond obtain the Lektor and escapes with him aboard the Orient Express bound for Paris.

Tatiana is deeply conflicted about her emotions for Bond versus her fear of Klebb and loyalty to her country. When Bond confronts her about the murder of Kerim Bey on the train, she truthfully professes ignorance but refuses to reveal Klebb's plot. SPECTRE assassin Donald Grant subsequently drugs her while he dines with her and Bond. During a fatal confrontation, Grant reveals to 007 that Tatiana is a completely innocent pawn in SPECTRE's conspiracy.

After Grant's death, Bond escapes with Tatiana to Venice. Confronted by Rosa Klebb, Tatiana must decide where her true loyalties lie. As Klebb prepares to shoot Bond, Tatiana knocks the gun from her hand. She then shoots Klebb, choosing Bond's world rather than Soviet-style obedience. Her adventure ends on Venice's Grand Canal in 007's arms.

In the novel, Tatiana does not participate in Bond's final confrontation with Klebb, and her loyalties lie much more with Bond throughout the story.

THE INTERVIEW *Tatiana reports to Colonel Klebb, still thinking Klebb works for SMERSH.*
SECRET MEETING *Bond interrogates Tatiana on the Bosphorus about the Lektor decoder, using a tape recorder hidden inside a camera.*
ESCAPE *Tatiana and 007 flee Istanbul on the world's most romantic train, the Orient Express.*
THE CHOICE *Tatiana must decide between Mother Russia or Bond. She never learns that Klebb works for SPECTRE.*
THE SEDUCTRESS *(left) This classic scene where Bond meets Tatiana has been used by the Bond film producers to test actors for the role of 007.*

**Tatiana: I think my mouth is too big.
007: No, it's just the right size. For me, that is.**

RYDER, HONEY

APPEARANCE
Dr. No (1962)
STATUS Living; whereabouts unknown
CHARACTERISTICS Self-reliant, vulnerable, vengeful, passionate
PLAYED BY Ursula Andress

Honey Ryder stands as the archetypal Bond woman: strong, resilient, and beautiful. Searching Caribbean beaches for seashells, she becomes swept up in 007's mission to stop Dr. No "toppling" US rockets.

Before encountering James Bond, Honey traveled the world with her marine zoologist father. They arrived in the Caribbean to study seashells. When he visited Crab Key, he disappeared, and she never saw him again. Local authorities claimed that he must have drowned, but Honey believes Dr. No is responsible.

Honey meets Bond on Crab Key. Her iconic walk from the sea, clad in a white bikini, diver's belt, and knife, perfectly captures her radiant beauty and confidence.

Bond attracts Honey's attention by joining in as she sings a local calypso *Underneath The Mango Tree*. Later, Honey tells Bond that, after her father's death, she was raped by her landlord.

THE BIKINI *Ursula Andress and designer Tessa Welbourn could not find the right swimsuit for Honey, so they designed their own athletic-cut bikini.*

> **Honey Ryder:** What are you doing here? Looking for shells?
>
> **007:** No, I'm just looking.

Honey then relates how she took her revenge: by placing a deadly black widow spider beneath her landlord's mosquito net.

Honey's arrival on the island via sailboat triggers Dr. No's radar system; his guards capture Honey and Bond and kill Bond's Cayman Islander ally, Quarrel.

By visiting Crab Key, Bond and Honey have been exposed to radioactive waste from No's nuclear generator. They are cleansed before being taken to well-appointed rooms. Bond and Honey then pass out after drinking drugged coffee.

At dinner, Bond tells Dr. No that Honey has nothing to do with his mission, but No senses Bond's protective feelings for Honey and uses her to provoke 007. Dr. No's men manacle her in a chamber that slowly fills with water, but Bond rescues her. They escape in a boat seconds before Dr. No's nuclear reactor explodes, obliterating Crab Key. Honey ends up adrift in Bond's arms.

In the novel *Dr. No*, Fleming gives Honey the name Honeychile Rider and she has a broken nose. When Bond first sees her, she appears naked on the beach except for a belt and knife, resembling "Botticelli's Venus." Bond remembers Honeychile when he returns to Jamaica in the novel, *The Man With The Golden Gun*, noting that he had heard she had married a Philadelphia doctor and had two children. Her character appeared in later Bond novels.

SEVERINE

APPEARANCE
Skyfall (2012)
STATUS Dead; shot by Silva
CHARACTERISTICS Enigmatic,
frightened of Silva
PLAYED BY Bérénice Lim Marlohe

Severine, the long-time mistress of
cyber-criminal Silva meets a tragic
fate at his hands.

In a Shanghai hotel room, Severine
shows a stolen Modigliani painting,
"Woman with a Fan," to Silva's latest
target. The mercenary Patrice
assassinates the man, firing from an
adjacent building.

When Bond subsequently attacks
Patrice, Severine spots 007. She later
encounters him at Macau's Floating
Dragon Casino. Wearing a stunning
dress and, as Bond notes, a Beretta 70
strapped to her thigh, she has three
bodyguards who are controlling her,
not protecting her.

Severine appears confident, but
Bond senses that she is afraid. A tattoo
on her wrist tells him that she was
involved in the Macau sex trade. He
surmises that she was eventually
"rescued" by her current employer.
Daring to hope that Bond can free
her from her role as mistress to a man
she now hates, she tells Bond that if
he can defeat her bodyguards, he can

ON WATCH *From a vantage point on a
staircase at the Floating Dragon Casino,
Severine sees Bond arrive to cash in the
dead assassin Patrice's gambling chip.*

> " I know when a
> woman is afraid
> and pretending
> not to be."
>
> 007 to Severine

meet her on the yacht *Chimera*, due
to sail in an hour. Bond dispatches
the bodyguards and joins her on
board the yacht. In the morning, she
and Bond are captured by the crew
and taken to Silva's island base, a
virtually deserted, dead city.

After meeting and being
interrogated by Silva, Bond is taken
outside into a courtyard. Severine is
bound to a fallen statue. Silva places
a shot glass of 1962 Macallan Scotch
on her head and forces Bond to
engage in a William Tell-like
shooting challenge with antique
dueling pistols. Bond misses the glass
on purpose, convincing Silva that he
has lost his marksmanship skill. Silva,
having no further use for Severine,
cold-bloodedly shoots her dead.

SIMONOVA, NATALYA

APPEARANCE
GoldenEye (1995)
STATUS Living; whereabouts unknown
CHARACTERISTICS Excellent
computer programmer, loyal, resourceful
PLAYED BY Izabella Scorupco

Natalya Simonova was just a second-
level computer programmer for the
Russian military in Siberia until fate
conspired to make her a central
figure in a globehopping adventure
with James Bond.

At the Severnaya Space Weapons
Research Centre, which the rest of
the world believes is an abandoned
radar station, Natalya programs the
guidance systems of satellites. Her
co-worker, Boris Grishenko, proves
childishly irritating, but Natalya cares
for him, as the screenplay notes, like
a "pesky younger brother."

By a combination of quick
thinking and good luck, Natalya
survives a massacre at Severnaya
carried out by the Janus
organization's General Ourumov and
Xenia Onatopp and a detonation of
the Petya GoldenEye superweapon.
Natalya travels to St. Petersburg,
resolved to find out who was behind
the killings. However, as the only
witness and known survivor of the
massacre, Natalya is suspected by
Russian Intelligence and also
targeted by Janus. Fortunately, MI6
has dispatched Bond to find her, and
he saves her life several times.

Natalya discovers that Boris not
only survived the Severnaya
bloodbath, he actually aided the
killers. Using her considerable
computer skills, she traces Boris to
Cuba. Discovering that Boris has
joined a plot to detonate Mischa, the
second GoldenEye satellite, she
travels to Cuba with Bond, looking
for a satellite dish and control center
for the GoldenEye weapons system.

Natalya infiltrates Janus's secret
command center with Bond and
seizes the opportunity to reprogram
the guidance of Mischa. Boris
discovers her hacking and tries in
vain to break the code of her
password. He cannot, and Mischa
burns up in the atmosphere, foiling
Janus's plot to plunge Britain into
economic chaos. Natalya hijacks a
helicopter to rescue Bond after he
kills Janus's mastermind, traitorous
former MI6 agent Alec Trevelyan.

DESOLATION
*Natalya's
co-workers lie dead
in the Severnaya
station moments
before Petya's
detonation.*

JUBILATION
*Natalya and
James take a
moment after
wrecking Alec
Trevelyan's plot.*

SOLANGE *see page 128*

SOLITAIRE

APPEARANCE
Live And Let Die (1973)
STATUS **Living; whereabouts unknown**
CHARACTERISTICS **Clairvoyant; gifted reader of tarot pack; innocent of the ways of the world, sensitive, impressionable, courageous**
PLAYED BY **Jane Seymour**

The corrupt president of the Caribbean island of San Monique, Dr. Kananga, alias Harlem gangster Mr. Big, believes Solitaire has the power of the Obeah. She describes herself as the High Priestess, the wife to the Prince no longer of this world. She believes she is the spiritual bridge to the Secret Church where the present and the future can be seen through tarot cards. She lives in a guarded grand white house on a cliff above the Caribbean that no one dares enter except for Dr. Kananga. Her change of loyalties from Kananga to Bond is crucial to the collapse of Kananga's drug empire.

Solitaire's supposed powers exist only while she retains her virginity. Once compelled to earthly love, Solitaire believes the Gods will take away her gift. Her mother, Kananga claims, also had the power. Solitaire implies that Kananga killed her mother when he discovered she had taken a lover.

When Solitaire first meets Bond in Mr. Big's office, Bond selects the Lovers card from her tarot deck. The implications of this card and her attraction to 007 cause Solitaire to begin to doubt her relationship with Kananga. She sends Bond a tarot card warning him of CIA agent Rosie Carver's impending betrayal.

Bond later pays her a night time visit, using a tarot pack full of Lovers cards to help convince her to sleep with him. Bond and Solitaire escape from San Monique, but Kananga, furious at this perceived betrayal, kidnaps her and takes her back to his base to be sacrificed in a voodoo ritual. Bond heroically rescues her.

In the Ian Fleming novel, Solitaire's real name is Simone Latrelle. Mr. Big found her in a cabaret in Haiti doing a telepathic act. She escapes with Bond on a train to Florida. Mr. Big kidnaps her, taking her to Jamaica where he plans to kill her and Bond by dragging them over a coral reef.

"When he finds out I've lost my powers, **he'll kill me.**"

Solitaire to 007

IN THE CARDS *Solitaire ponders the dangerous consequences of losing her clairvoyant powers.*

SOLANGE

APPEARANCE
Casino Royale (2006)
STATUS Dead; killed by
Le Chiffre's men
CHARACTERISTICS Sad, lonely
PLAYED BY Caterina Murino

LONELY GIRL *Bond first sees Solange riding her horse along the beach in Nassau.*

STOLEN KISSES *Out of love with her boorish husband, Solange finds herself drawn to 007.*

Solange, wife of terrorist middleman Alex Dimitrios, inadvertently provides James Bond with information that allows him to stop a bomber destroying a Skyfleet prototype aircraft at Miami airport.

Solange lives a life of luxury with her husband. Nevertheless, she feels that she has wasted her chance of true happiness by getting involved with the wrong men. Aware that her husband is a bad man, she knows little about how he makes his money. She has long since become weary of his bad temper and coldness. When Bond emerges from the surf in Nassau, Solange watches, instantly attracted.

That evening, Solange arrives at a poker game where her husband plays against Bond. Losing, Dimitrios reacts coldly to his wife's affection. Bond soundly defeats her husband, even winning his car, a superb Aston Martin DB5. When Solange mistakenly gets into the Aston Martin, Bond invites her for a drink. Sensing a spark of humanity long absent from her life, she accepts, despite realizing that Bond may be using her to get closer to her

husband. Bond and Solange's passion is interrupted by a telephone call from Dimitrios, who tells Solange he is flying to Miami that night. Bond makes a quick exit to pursue him.

When the bomb plot goes awry, Le Chiffre tortures and kills Solange, leaving her body in a hammock.

In Fleming's story *007 in New York*, Bond hopes to meet a girlfriend

007: Can I ask you a personal question?
Solange: Now would seem an appropriate time.

named Solange who works in the old Abercrombie & Fitch. She was the inspiration for the name in *Casino Royale*, not the fanciful mention in the short story *From A View To A Kill*.

SUTTON, STACEY

APPEARANCE
A View To A Kill (1985)
STATUS Living; whereabouts unknown
CHARACTERISTICS Determined, skittish, emotional
PLAYED BY Tanya Roberts

Oil heiress Stacey Sutton becomes a vital ally to James Bond during his investigation of industrialist Max Zorin. Her knowledge of geology and mining uncover the nature of Zorin's Project Main Strike, a plot to cause a massive earthquake that will destroy Silicon Valley.

When Stacey's grandfather died, he left Sutton Oil to her father, who expected only child Stacey to take over the family business. In college, she studied geology. Zorin soon seized control of Sutton Oil in a rigged proxy fight. The resulting legal battles put a tremendous financial strain on Stacey, and she took a position as a geologist with the State of California to help pay her legal fees. She has managed to hold onto her family home outside San Francisco, although she has had to sell most of her furnishings. Her only real remaining possessions include a

Himalayan Persian cat named Pussy, three canaries, and a Ming vase with her grandfather's ashes inside.

Her government job gives her access to information that might expose Zorin's plans for Main Strike. Knowing this, Zorin offers to settle Stacey's lawsuit for $5 million in exchange for her shares in his company. She refuses this large payoff after Zorin's goons attack her in her own home.

Stacey braves a deadly fire at San Francisco City Hall, drives an out-of-control fire truck, climbs mine shafts, and hangs from the Golden Gate Bridge all in her effort to help Bond stop Zorin. After Zorin's death, she and 007 retire to her steamy shower.

"I'd sell everything and live in a tent before I give up."

Stacey to 007

SUZUKI, KISSY

APPEARANCE
You Only Live Twice (1967)
STATUS Living
CHARACTERISTICS Intrepid, good
with firearms, excellent swimmer
PLAYED BY Mie Hama

Kissy Suzuki serves as a local agent for Japanese Intelligence chief Tiger Tanaka on the island of Matsu where she works as an Ama diver. She possesses an adventurous spirit and appears willing to take on any challenge.

Kissy pretends to marry James Bond to give him cover for his investigation of captured US and Soviet spacecraft. Kissy offers a valuable clue to Bond and Tanaka

DEADLY SHOT *Suzuki fires a shot that saves Tanaka's life during the battle inside SPECTRE's volcano complex.*

when she explains that an Ama girl died in Ryuzaki, a cave on the mainland that served as an ancient vent for a nearby volcano. Kissy takes Bond to the cave the following morning, and they find it filled with lethal phosgene gas. Upon further examination, Bond and Kissy discover an apparent lake within the volcano's crater is only a canopy for the rocket base below. Kissy undertakes an arduous return journey to her village in order to alert Tanaka and his SIS ninjas.. Kissy avoids an attack by a SPECTRE helicopter as she swims from the mainland to the island. Returning with Tanaka, she ably participates in the assault on the rocket base, saving Tanaka's life at least once. When Blofeld sets off explosions that destroy the base, Kissy and Bond escape out of Ryuzaki cave. They find a raft and relax in each other's arms until

rescued by M's submarine.

Kissy Suzuki appears in the original Ian Fleming novel. At 17, she was cast as an Ama diving girl in a movie. Not liking Hollywood, she returned to her family on the island of Kuro and dives for awabi shells. Bond meets her when Tiger Tanaka asks him to kill Dr. Shatterhand (in reality, Blofeld). A local official arranges for Bond to live with the Suzuki family under the name of Taro Todoroki, a purported anthropologist. Kissy helps 007 get to Shatterhand's castle, rescues him when he falls, injured, into the sea, and takes him as her lover while he suffers from amnesia. Kissy becomes pregnant but never tells Bond. When Bond recognizes the word "Valdivostok" on a scrap of newsprint, Kissy helps him travel to the city and away from her forever.

TARO, MISS

APPEARANCE
Dr. No (1962)
STATUS Living; whereabouts unknown
CHARACTERISTICS Charming but devious
PLAYED BY Zena Marshall

Miss Taro is Dr. No's Eurasian henchwoman and spy at Government House in Jamaica, where she works as Pleydell-Smith's secretary. As part of a trap, she invites Bond to her house, and the Three Blind Mice assassins nearly kill him en route. Surprised when Bond turns up alive, she makes love to him, hoping to delay him so that Professor Dent, another Dr. No minion, can arrive to kill him. Bond has Taro arrested instead and then kills Dent.

"The demure, efficient–looking little secretary in the horn-rimmed glasses," is how Fleming describes Miss Taro in the novel *Dr. No*.

TRENCH, SYLVIA

APPEARANCE Dr. No (1962),
From Russia With Love (1963)
STATUS Living; whereabouts unknown
CHARACTERISTICS She knows what
she wants but not how to get it
PLAYED BY Eunice Gayson

Sylvia Trench is the first James Bond
woman. She plays a vital role in the
cinematic history of 007 by
introducing James Bond to audiences
in *Dr. No*. It is from her discerning
perspective that the world first sees
007 and hears him say, "Bond, James
Bond." Described in the script for
Dr. No as "willowy, exquisitely
gowned, with a classic, deceptively
cold beauty," Sylvia Trench battles
Bond over a game of Chemin de fer
at the Le Cercle casino at Les
Ambassadeurs in London. She loses
to Bond but finds him terribly
intriguing. She follows him from
the table when a Secret Service
representative calls Bond away.
Bond offers to take her golfing
and to dinner the next day.
Taking his card, she tells him
she will let him know in the
morning. She then travels to his
home and lets herself inside,
planning to spend the rest of the
night with him. Slipping into one of
Bond's pajama jackets, she practices
her putting. She greets 007 when he
arrives, and the pair spends a
passionate time together before he
flies to Jamaica.

Sylvia also appears in *From Russia
With Love*. As she shares a picnic
with Bond, he receives a phone call
from Miss Moneypenny to meet
with M, forcing Bond to cut their
picnic short.

THE GAME OF LOVE *Bond
discovers that Sylvia has
infiltrated his apartment
in* Dr. No.

PLEASURE BEFORE BUSINESS *Sylvia Trench
and Bond enjoy a riverside picnic in* From
Russia With Love.

> "Too bad you have
> to leave. Just as things
> were getting
> interesting again."

Sylvia Trench to 007

VIDA & ZORA

APPEARANCE
From Russia With Love (1963)
STATUS Both living, thanks to Bond
CHARACTERISTICS Jealous,
passionate; savage fighters when roused
PLAYED BY Aliza Gur (Vida),
Martine Beswick, credited as Martin
Beswick (Zora)

Zora and Vida love the same man—
the son of the gypsy chief Vavra.
Their rivalry must be settled the
gypsy way. They agree to fight
barehanded to the death. Vavra allows
Head of Station T Kerim Bey and
James Bond to witness the bitter
death match. Bulgarian assassin
Krilencu attacks the gypsy camp,
interrupting the battle. After the gun
battle, Bond asks that the fight be
stopped. Vavra agrees but adds that
Bond must decide who will marry
his son. The winner is never revealed.

VON SCHLAF, COUNTESS LISL

APPEARANCE
For Your Eyes Only (1981)
STATUS Dead; run over by Locque's
dune buggy
CHARACTERISTICS Expensive, regal
PLAYED BY Cassandra Harris

Countess Lisl Von Schlaf claims to be
a member of the Austrian nobility
but is in fact from Liverpool,
England. She is engaged in both a
business and personal relationship
with Greek smuggler Milos
Columbo. Bond notices her with
Columbo while he dines with
shipping magnate Aris Kristatos at
Columbo's casino. Kristatos describes
Lisl as an "expensive mistress… if she
bets, it's with other people's money."

Thanks to a concealed bug,
Columbo overhears Kristatos and
Bond's conversation and realizes that
Bond is a potentially dangerous spy.
He stages a furious argument with
Lisl; she leaves abruptly, and Bond,
seeing an opportunity to find out
more about Columbo, offers to drive
her home. Kristatos wants Bond to
investigate and hopefully kill
Columbo, so he offers to lend Bond
his own car and chauffeur.

Riding in the back of Kristatos's
Rolls-Royce, Bond claims to be a
writer researching a novel about
Greek smugglers. "Do you know
any?" he asks innocently.

When they arrive at Lisl's house,
she invites Bond in for champagne
and oysters. During a romantic
evening together, Lisl freely admits to
Bond that Columbo asked her to
find out more about him.

The following morning, Bond and
Lisl are strolling contentedly along
the beach near her house. Under
orders from Kristatos, Emile Locque
and Claus, driving dune buggies,
ambush them. Columbo's men then
arrive and kill Claus, but Bond
cannot prevent Locque from running
Lisl down, killing her.

Countess Lisl:
My nightie's slipping.
007: So is
your accent,
Countess.

WARMFLASH, DR. MOLLY

APPEARANCE
The World Is Not Enough (1999)
STATUS Living; whereabouts unknown
CHARACTERISTICS Expert practitioner;
excellent bedside manner for 007
PLAYED BY Serena Scott Thomas

Molly Warmflash is a striking MI6
doctor with a strong attraction to
Bond. He visits her when he has
been placed on the inactive roster for
a dislocated collar bone. Dr.
Warmflash warns Bond to stay out of
action but, after the two of them
spend an amorous afternoon together
at Castle Thane in Scotland, Dr.
Warmflash agrees to give 007 "a
clean bill of health." At an MI6
briefing, Bond, M, and others listen
as Dr. Warmflash uses a hologram to
explain the unusual effects of a bullet
fired by 009 into Renard's head.

SUPPORTING CAST

W ho are those we relegate to the Supporting Cast? They are station chiefs, spymasters, astronauts, organized crime kingpins, ingenious scientists, and experts of all kinds. They may be close colleagues of 007 or even would-be enemies. More often than not, they are individuals who choose to stand by Bond at just the right instant. For a moment, their lives are swept up in adventure. If they are lucky, they encounter the eye of the storm as it passes; if not, they sacrifice their lives for a noble cause. For a moment, they are part of the world of 007.

"00" SECTION

APPEARANCES
Thunderball (1965), Octopussy (1983), The Living Daylights (1987), GoldenEye (1995), The World Is Not Enough (1999)
STATUS Some living, many deceased; 00 agents tend to have short life spans
CHARACTERISTICS Utterly dedicated
PLAYED BY Andy Bradford (009, Octopussy), Glyn Baker (002, The Living Daylights), Frederick Warder (004, The Living Daylights), Sean Bean (006, GoldenEye)

The "00" section designates the most elite and trusted agents in British Intelligence. While James Bond holds the number 007, many of his contemporaries make appearances in his adventures.

In *Goldfinger* and *The Living Daylights*, M threatens to replace 007 with 008 unless Bond can remain detached in his missions. In *Thunderball*, every 00 agent in Europe attends a briefing on Operation Thunderball. In *The Man With The Golden Gun*, Bond and Moneypenny discuss Bill Fairbanks, the late 002, assassinated by Francisco Scaramanga in the arms of dancer Saida. A new 002 accompanies 004 and 007 on a training exercise o the Rock of Gibraltar in *The Living Daylights*, but an assassin eliminates 004. 009 dies in *Octopussy*, dressed as a clown carrying a forged Fabergé Egg. In *A View To A Kill*, Bond discovers 003's frozen body in Siberia, with a vital microchip in a locket. In *The World Is Not Enough*, a new 009 shoots terrorist Renard in the head. In *GoldenEye*, Alec Trevelyan, 006, is a traitor who uses his position to plot the ultimate betrayal of Great Britain. In Ian Fleming's novels, 007 shares an office with 008 and 0011.

The agents who populate this section's ranks are the UK's secret aristocracy, the Western World's silent saviors, the civil servants entrusted with matters of life and death, who carry the burden of a licence to kill.

BROTHERS IN ARMS 006 and 007 infiltrate the Arkangel Chemical Weapons Facility in the USSR, but only one of them is loyal to Queen and country.

PAINTBALLED 002 suffers the humiliation of the SAS catching him during a training mission on Gibraltar.

OPERATION THUNDERBALL Bond arrives fashionably late for a meeting to discuss the theft of two atomic bombs.

AKAKIEVICH, COLONEL

APPEARANCE
The World Is Not Enough (1999)
STATUS Dead; shot by Renard
CHARACTERISTICS Not overly bright
PLAYED BY Claude-Oliver Rudolph

Colonel Akakievich serves as a commanding officer in the army of the Commonwealth of Independent States (CIS). Working with the International Decommissioning Agency (IDA), he has overseen the decommissioning of four nuclear test facilities in the past year. When James Bond, posing as Dr. Arkov of the Russian Atomic Energy Department, arrives in Kazakhstan, Akakievich informs him that he greatly admires his research. He also informs Bond that IDA physicist Dr. Christmas Jones is "not interested in men. Take my word for it."

Bond descends into the underground nuclear test chamber and confronts Renard, who is posing as one of Arkov's men. Akakievich and Jones arrive soon after with a photo of the real Dr. Arkov, who is 63 years old. They declare Bond an imposter and forbid Renard and his men to leave with the nuclear bomb. Renard proceeds to shoot Akakievich and his men and steal the bomb.

DEATH OF A CLOWN A dying 009 gatecrashes an embassy gathering to leave a vital clue.

ASTRONAUTS

APPEARANCE
You Only Live Twice (1967)
STATUS Welcomed home as heroes
CHARACTERISTICS Well-trained, brave
PLAYED BY Paul Carson, Norman Jones, Laurence Herder, Richard Graydon, Bill Mitchell, George Roubicek

When *Bird 1* engulfs *Jupiter 16*, its doors clip the lifeline of Chris, an astronaut performing an EVA (extravehicular activity). Another one becomes a prisoner of SPECTRE. Later, Blofeld's plot snares two Soviet cosmonauts. When Bond invades Blofeld's base, he frees the three astronauts and saves two more.

AUBERGINE, ACHILLE

APPEARANCE
A View To A Kill (1985)
STATUS Dead; poisoned
CHARACTERISTICS Jocular, pompous bon viveur out of his depth
PLAYED BY Jean Rougerie

With his carefully groomed mustache, Achille Aubergine is a classic European gentleman detective in the tradition of Agatha Christie's Hercule Poirot. A friend of Sir Godfrey Tibbett with connections within the Sureté, Aubergine lunches with Bond at Le Jules Verne restaurant in the Eiffel Tower. Aubergine does not know the secret of Max Zorin's success but feels it is to be found at Zorin's stud farm estate outside Paris. May Day kills Aubergine when she whips a hook, dipped in poison and attached to a butterfly marionette, into his cheek.

STUNG BY A BUTTERFLY *French detective Aubergine suffers a fatal wound while dining at Le Jules Verne restaurant.*

BAINES

APPEARANCE
Live And Let Die (1973)
STATUS Dead; poisoned
CHARACTERISTICS Scared witless
PLAYED BY Dennis Edwards

British secret service agent Baines is captured soon after arriving on the Caribbean island of San Monique to investigate the activities of Dr. Kananga, the island's prime minister. Betrayed by double agent Rosie Carver, Baines becomes top billing at a voodoo ceremony featuring a human sacrifice. High Priest Dambala approaches Baines with a poisonous snake, which administers the fatal bite. The local authorities find the body and report the death, to Kananga's displeasure.

BEAM, GREGORY

APPEARANCE
Quantum Of Solace (2008)
STATUS Living; out of a job
CHARACTERISTICS Arrogant
PLAYED BY David Harbour

The CIA section chief of South America, Beam is happy working with villains for his country's sake. He forms a deal with villain Dominic Greene to ignore a political coup in Bolivia; in exchange, the new government will give the US the lease to any oil found in the country. Beam also agrees to have Bond, a thorn in Greene's side, killed, and orders Leiter, Bond's friend, to help, to test his loyalty. With Greene's death and no political coup, the CIA removes Beam from office, replacing him with agent Felix Leiter.

BELL, MRS.

APPEARANCE
Live And Let Die (1973)
STATUS Alive; no thanks to Bond
CHARACTERISTICS Nonplussed
PLAYED BY Ruth Kempf

A student with the Bleeker Flying School, Mrs. Bell endures a horrifying ground check with 007 at Lakeside Airport, New Orleans. Riding in a Cessna 140 and thinking Bond may be a substitute instructor, Mrs. Bell finds herself in a student pilot's nightmare. Bond proceeds to elude pursuers working for drug lord Dr. Kananga/Mr. Big. In the process, he destroys a small fleet of planes, shears the wings of the Cessna, and leaves Mrs. Bell dumbfounded.

BENSON, CAPT.

APPEARANCE
The Spy Who Loved Me (1977)
STATUS Living; whereabouts unknown
CHARACTERISTICS Confident, intelligent, conscientious staff officer
PLAYED BY George Baker

Captain Benson is commander at Faslane Naval Base when HMS *Ranger*, one of the Royal Navy's four Polaris submarines, goes missing. When James Bond and Q arrive for a meeting at Faslane, a map of the *Ranger's* course in Bond's possession shocks Benson. He realizes that the Soviets have technology that could enable them to track British submarines and sink them.

BENZ

APPEARANCE
From Russia With Love (1963)
STATUS Killed by Donald Grant
CHARACTERISTICS Watchful
PLAYED BY Peter Bayliss

Benz works for the Soviet Consulate in Istanbul under Koslovski, chief of security, often watching the airport and train stations. Benz spots Tatiana and Bond boarding the Orient Express and follows them, hoping to have Bond and Tatiana stopped at the border and recover the stolen Lektor decoder. Instead, Bond's ally Kerim Bey confronts Benz and jokingly refers to him as "Commissar." Tied up and gagged, Benz is forced to sit and listen to Kerim Bey recounting his colorful life story. Unfortunately SPECTRE assassin Donald Grant is also on board the train and kills both Kerim Bey and Benz.

BEY, KERIM

APPEARANCE
From Russia With Love (1963)
STATUS Dead; killed by Donald Grant
CHARACTERISTICS Robust, confident, dependable, sagacious
PLAYED BY Pedro Armendariz

Head of Station T in Istanbul, Turkey, Kerim Bey provides essential aid to Bond on his mission to recover a Lektor decoder. Bey becomes a loyal friend and trusted companion of 007.

Bey worked as a strongman in a circus act in his youth. In Fleming's novel, he is named Darko Kerim, and the circus act enables him to spy on Soviets when traveling across the border. Kerim Bey employs his sons as agents in key positions. As in the novel, Bey appears to "consume a large quantity of women" and to be "greedy for life." His instincts, understanding, and attitude to his work greatly impress Bond.

Bey believes that the Soviets are luring Bond into a trap. Shortly after Bond arrives in Istanbul, a limpet mine explodes near Bey's desk. Bey takes Bond to a gypsy camp in order to escape any further attempts on his life. However, the Soviet-controlled agent Krilencu raids the encampment with a team of

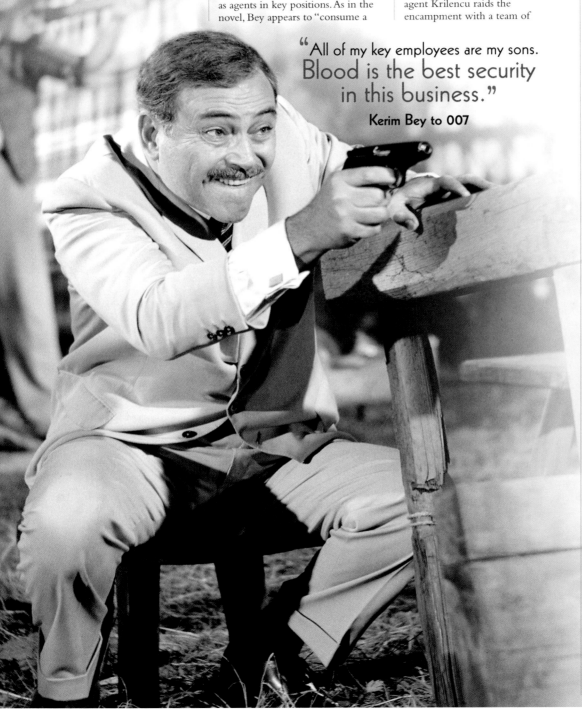

"All of my key employees are my sons. Blood is the best security in this business."
Kerim Bey to 007

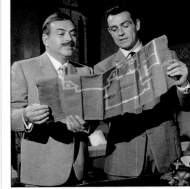

PLAN OF ATTACK *Kerim Bey and Bond look over a copy of the original architect's blueprints of the Soviet Consulate in Istanbul.*

Bulgarians. Bey, with Bond's help, later assassinates Krilencu. Kerim Bey helps Bond carry out an attack on the Soviet consulate. While on the Orient Express, Rosa Klebb's henchman Donald "Red" Grant kills him.

BORCHOI

APPEARANCE
Octopussy (1983)
STATUS Living; whereabouts unknown
CHARACTERISTICS No-nonsense, influential art expert
PLAYED BY Gabor Vernon

CHEAP IMITATION *Art expert Borchoi recognizes that the real Romanoff Star has been stolen and replaced by a fake.*

Comrade Borchoi serves as a curator for Leningrad's Hermitage Museum, in the Soviet Union. When General Gogol, head of the KGB, becomes suspicious of General Orlov's activities within the Kremlin Art Repository, he brings Borchoi to its vaults to confront Lenkin, the curator of the Kremlin collection. Borchoi picks up the Romanoff Star and examines it with a jeweler's magnifier. When he recognizes that it is actually a fake, Borchoi drops it on the floor and crushes it to pieces with his shoe.

BRAY, SIR HILARY

APPEARANCE On Her Majesty's
Secret Service (1969)
STATUS Living; whereabouts unknown
CHARACTERISTICS
By-the-book, stuffy
PLAYED BY George Baker

Genealogist Sir Hilary Bray works at
Britain's Royal College of Arms.
Ernst Stavro Blofeld asks Sir Hilary
to establish his title, Count Balthazar
de Bleauchamp. This gives Bond the
chance to visit Blofeld disguised as
Bray. Sir Hilary agrees to Bond's
deception as the matter is of
national importance. The real Sir
Hilary then loses himself among
the churches of Brittany, where
he plans to do several brass
rubbings. He informs 007 that
the real de Bleauchamps are
without earlobes and that the
family tombs are located in the
Augsburg Cathedral in southern
Germany, although Blofeld later
claims the tombs are located in
the St. Anna Kirche.

BRINK, JACOBA

APPEARANCE
For Your Eyes Only (1981)
STATUS Living; whereabouts unknown
CHARACTERISTICS Demanding,
overprotective, motherly
PLAYED BY Jill Bennett

Jacoba Brink, "once a world class
skater herself," is the strict,
overprotective ice-skating coach of
Olympic hopeful Bibi Dahl. She
clearly does not approve of her
pupil's infatuation with men,
especially Bond. When Bibi lashes
out at Kristatos for
being unable to
practice at St. Cyril's
Monastery, he accuses
Brink of poisoning her
against him. The two
women decide to leave
him and find a new
sponsor. As Brink tries
to engineer their
departure, she finds
Bond and his team
plotting their attack
and leads them to
Kristatos.

BUKHARIN, GENERAL

APPEARANCE
Tomorrow Never Dies (1997)
STATUS Living; whereabouts unknown
CHARACTERISTICS Diplomatic,
hesitant, soft-spoken
PLAYED BY Terence Rigby

Russian General Bukharin works
with British Admiral Roebuck in the
Ministry of Defence Situation Room
to identify fanatics at a terrorist
bazaar on the Khyber Pass.
Unfortunately, they discover that the
terrorists already have Soviet SB-5

TOP BRASS General Bukharin works closely
with the irascible Admiral Roebuck.

nuclear torpedoes, prompting
Roebuck to bark at Bukharin, "Can't
you people keep anything locked up?"

THE BUTTERFLY
EFFECT The
Butterfly Girl
prepares for her
butterfly
marionette act.

BUTTERFLY GIRL

APPEARANCE
A View To A Kill (1985)
STATUS Living; whereabouts unknown
CHARACTERISTICS Beautiful,
talented whistler
PLAYED BY Carole Ashby

As Bond lunches with the detective
Aubergine at Le Jules Verne restaurant
in the Eiffel Tower, the cabaret act
"Dominique et ses Papillons" begins.
The Butterfly Girl whistles a tune
while a hooded figure uses a fishing
pole to animate butterfly marionettes
from the girl's hands. Assassin May
Day knocks out the hooded figure
and uses the fishing pole to embed a
poisoned hook attached to a
butterfly into Aubergine's cheek.

CAMPBELL

APPEARANCE On Her Majesty's
Secret Service (1969)
STATUS Frozen to death
CHARACTERISTICS Keen, foolhardy
PLAYED BY Bernard Horsfall

British Secret Service agent
Campbell works in Switzerland and
tries to aid 007 on Operation
Bedlam without much success.

Campbell first helps Bond by
supervising a construction crane and
basket to deliver a safecracking
device and copy machine to Bond at
Gebrüder Gumbold's Bern offices.

He later tries to take the cable car
to The Bleuchamp Institute for
Allergy Research atop Piz Gloria to
assist Bond, but Blofeld's henchman
Grunther tells him it is private
property. A determined Campbell
ignores him and climbs to Piz Gloria.

However, Blofeld's men capture
him. Blofeld tortures Campbell,
forcing the agent to reveal enough
information to unmask his and
Bond's true identities. This leads to
Bond's capture. Campbell meets his
end when Blofeld hangs him upside
down by a rope from an ice wall,
making his death look like a
climbing accident.

CAPLAN, PAULA

APPEARANCE Thunderball (1965)
STATUS Dead; suicide
CHARACTERISTICS Wry, knowing
PLAYED BY Martine Beswick

British Secret Service agent Paula Caplan aids Bond on his mission to recover two missing nuclear weapons by helping him make contact with Domino Derval, mistress of the mysterious Emilio Largo. Paula is later kidnapped by Largo's henchmen and she takes cyanide rather than give in to torture. Paula's full name does not appear in drafts of the shooting scripts. In the release script, her last name is spelled Kaplan.

CARTER

APPEARANCE Casino Royale (2006)
STATUS Dead; bitten by a cobra
CHARACTERISTICS Cannot play it cool
PLAYED BY Joseph Millson

Carter, Bond's Madagascar colleague, keeps bomb-builder Mollaka under surveillance in a crowd while he watches a cobra/mongoose fight.

Carter tries to talk with Bond, but his constant touching of his earpiece tips off Mollaka, sending him running. Carter gives chase, trips, accidentally fires his gun in the air, and falls headlong into the bottom of the pit where the cobra and mongoose fight.

CARTER, COMMANDER

APPEARANCE
The Spy Who Loved Me (1977)
STATUS Living; whereabouts unknown
CHARACTERISTICS Tough worker
PLAYED BY Shane Rimmer

Commander Carter leads the USS Wayne's attack on the Liparus supertanker owned by shipping magnate Karl Stromberg. When the Liparus captures his submarine, Carter and his crew, including Bond, surrender. Freed by 007, the Wayne's crew tries to stop Stromberg's plot to start a nuclear war. Carter helps 007 to blast open the operations room. When explosions wrack the ship, Carter uses the Wayne's torpedoes to destroy the Liparus's bows and reach safety. Carter then receives orders from the UN Security Council to destroy Stromberg's base Atlantis.

CARVER'S PR

APPEARANCE
Tomorrow Never Dies (1997)
STATUS Living; whereabouts unknown
CHARACTERISTICS Good at her job, but not good enough for Carver
PLAYED BY Daphne Deckers

Media mogul Elliot Carver's PR introduces Bond to Carver as a new banker at a party to launch his satellite network. When 007 later shuts down the power to the building, cutting Carver off in the middle of his speech, Carver angrily blames his PR for the incident and fires her.

CASINO ROYALE PLAYERS

APPEARANCE
Casino Royale (2006)
STATUS Living; whereabouts unknown
CHARACTERISTICS Mysterious, very big spenders
PLAYED BY Tsai Chin (Madame Wu), Lazar Ristovski (Kaminovski), Urbano Barberini (Tomelli), Veruschka (Gräfin von Wallenstein), Tom So (Fukutu), Ade (Infante), Charlie Levi Leroy (Gallardo), Andreas Daniel (Dealer), Carlos Leal (Tournament Director)

In addition to Bond, Le Chiffre, and CIA agent Felix Leiter, these seven characters make up the participants needed for a high stakes poker game set up by Le Chiffre at the Casino Royale in Montenegro. The players buy into the game for $10 million. If they lose that amount, they may stake an additional $5 million each. This makes the total possible stake in the winner-takes-all tournament a staggering $150 million. Very little is known about these international casino players. Madame Wu is a Chinese woman who has played poker with Le Chiffre in the past. Kaminovski is an extremely wealthy Russian. Tomelli runs a media empire in Italy. Gräfin von Wallenstein is a German countess. The gentleman with the long, silver hair in a ponytail, Fukutu, is a computer software mogul in Japan. Infante is a larger-than-life exiled African dictator. Gallardo is an Argentinean billionaire.

Tomelli, Infante, and Felix Leiter are all impressed by the complexity of Bond's dry martini and, to Le Chiffre's irritation, order an identical one for themselves.

Bond eventually beats Le Chiffre and wins the jackpot. Generous to a fault, Bond leaves the highly efficient dealer a large $500,000 tip.

CHA & NARA

APPEARANCE
The Man With The Golden Gun
(1974)
STATUS Living; whereabouts unknown
CHARACTERISTICS Inconspicuous,
dangerous; superb martial artists
PLAYED BY Joie Pacharintraporn
(Cha), Cheung Chuen Nam aka Yuen
Qiu (Nara)

At first, the two nieces of Hong Kong detective Lieutenant Hip come across as giggling schoolgirls. In reality, these daughters of a karate school owner are tremendously skilled fighters who eagerly demonstrate their talents. When Hip arrives with them hoping to rescue 007, they flatten a squad of millionaire Hai Fat's martial arts students with their karate moves.

CHANG, MR.

APPEARANCE
Die Another Day (2002)
STATUS Living; whereabouts unknown
CHARACTERISTICS Sophisticated,
intelligent, well-groomed
PLAYED BY Ho Yi

The manager of Hong Kong's Rubyeon Royale Hotel, Mr. Chang also works for Chinese Intelligence. He knows Bond well and opens the Presidential Suite for 007 when he arrives unshaven and dirty. Bond asks Chang to get him into North Korea so he can kill the terrorist Zao, who has just murdered three Chinese agents. Chang tells Bond that Zao is in Havana, Cuba. He gives Bond a plane ticket and passport and asks him to say "goodbye" to Zao from the Chinese.

"Hong Kong's our turf now..."

Mr. Chang to 007

CHARLIE

APPEARANCE
Live And Let Die (1973)
STATUS Dead; killed by a poison dart
CHARACTERISTICS Loyal chauffeur
PLAYED BY Joie Chitwood

Charlie works for the CIA. Via a baggage tag that matches Charlie's license plate, Charlie collects Bond at JFK Airport. On FDR Drive, a white Corvorado fires a tiny metal dart into Charlie's temple. The dart kills Charlie, but not before triggering his right foot to stomp the accelerator, trapping Bond in Charlie's out-of-control car.

CHE CHE

APPEARANCE On Her Majesty's
Secret Service (1969)
STATUS Living; whereabouts unknown
CHARACTERISTICS Friend and foe
PLAYED BY Irvin Allen

Crimelord Marc Ange Draco's henchman Che Che engages Bond in a brutal fight in the room of Draco's daughter, Tracy di Vicenzo, at the Hotel Estoril in Portugal. Bond knocks out Che Che during the encounter. Undaunted, he returns to spy on 007 and, next morning, presses a knife into Bond's ribs and escorts him to his boss. Che Che later joins the assault on Piz Gloria, killing several of Blofeld's men with a flame-thrower. He also attends Bond and Tracy's wedding.

CLIVE, MAJOR

APPEARANCE
Octopussy (1983)
STATUS Living; whereabouts unknown
CHARACTERISTICS Trusting and
gullible; an over-eager gambler
PLAYED BY Stuart Saunders

A retired British army officer, Major Clive loses 220,000 rupees to exiled Afghan prince Kamal Khan playing backgammon at the Shiv Niwas Palace Hotel casino in India. His loss comes as no surprise as Khan plays with loaded dice that reveal a winning double six when needed. Clive refuses Kamal's offer to increase the stakes to 100,000 rupees, and Bond takes his place at the table.

COLTHORPE

APPEARANCE
The Man With The Golden Gun (1974)
STATUS Living; whereabouts unknown
CHARACTERISTICS Has an
excellent eye for detail
PLAYED BY James Cossins

Armaments expert Colthorpe works with Q as a ballistics specialist. He examines the golden dum-dum bullet that killed 002, which Bond has retrieved from Beirut belly-dancer Saida. Examining the bullet's nickel content, Colthorpe and Q determine that it was cast by the Portuguese gun-maker Lazar, who lives in Macau. Bond sets off to find Lazar and discover where to find the man who killed 002—Francisco Scaramanga.

COLUMBO, MILOS

APPEARANCE
For Your Eyes Only (1981)
STATUS Living; whereabouts unknown
CHARACTERISTICS Possesses a zest
for life, well-groomed, ruggedly
handsome, pistachio nut lover
PLAYED BY Topol

Greek Milos Columbo smuggles gold, diamonds, cigarettes, and pistachio nuts using a fleet of intercoastal freighters in the Aegean Sea. He owns shares in the Achillion Casino in Gastouri, outside of Corfu, and is known as "The Dove" among members of the Greek underworld.

Smuggler Aris Kristatos fought with Columbo in World War II against the Nazis and Communists, but was, in fact, a double agent. When Columbo learned the truth, it resulted in a blood feud between the two. Hoping Bond will kill Columbo for him, Kristatos leads Bond to believe that it is Columbo who is involved in white slavery, heroin

UNITED FRONT *Columbo and his men, Santos, Nikos, and Karageorge watch with Melina as 007 climbs the Meteora mountain.*

> ## "You have
> what the Greeks call
> *thrassos*—guts."
> ### Columbo to 007

smuggling, contract murder, and the salvaging of the British spy ship, the *St. Georges*, to retrieve the vital ATAC transmitter.

Columbo asks his mistress, Countess Lisl Von Schlaf, to discover more about Bond, but after she spends the night with 007, hitmen working for Kristatos kill her on the beach. Columbo captures Bond and earns his trust by returning his Walther PPK. Columbo takes Bond to a warehouse in Albania where Kristatos refines heroin before shipping it to England, and they engage in a gun battle with Kristatos's men.

Armed with a clue that Kristatos has taken the ATAC to St. Cyril's Monastery, Bond contacts Columbo as he is in great need of help. There are 439 St. Cyril's that exist in

Greece, but Columbo knows which one Kristatos is using as a base. With his men and Melina Havelock, daughter of marine archaeologist Sir Timothy Havelock, Columbo helps 007 infiltrate the monastery. The feud between Columbo and Kristatos ends when Columbo throws a knife into Kristatos's back.

Wounded from his battle with Kristatos, Columbo appears to

ATAC ATTACK *Columbo and Kristatos battle to the death over the ATAC transmitter.*

become the new sponsor of Kristatos's protégée Bibi Dahl, an Olympic ice-skating hopeful.

In Fleming's short story *Risico*, the character's name is Enrico Colombo and the name of his ship is the *Colombina*.

CORINNE

APPEARANCE
Quantum Of Solace (2008)
STATUS Living; whereabouts unknown
CHARACTERISTICS Trusting
PLAYED BY Stana Katic

Corinne Veneau is a Canadian Intelligence officer and the girlfriend of Yusef, a Quantum agent. Entering Yusef's apartment in Kazan, Russia, she and Yusef are confronted by Bond. He explains to Corinne that Yusef's love for her is a ruse, that his life will apparently soon be in danger, and that she will be forced to hand over secrets to save him. Bond advises Corinne to contact her superiors and tell them that their security seals have a leak. Corinne quits the apartment, leaving Bond to confront Yusef and discover the truth about Vesper.

DAWES

APPEARANCE
Live And Let Die (1973)
STATUS Dead
CHARACTERISTICS Good listener
PLAYED BY James Drake

Dawes becomes one of three British agents killed within 24 hours under the orders of dictator Dr. Kananga, prompting M to send Bond to investigate. Dawes, representing the United Kingdom, watches Dr. Kananga at the UN. While listening to a procedural speech from the Hungarian delegate, an unknown assailant removes the translation audio feed, replacing it with a plunger device that sends a devastatingly painful signal to Dawes through his earpiece. Within seconds, Dawes falls over dead.

DAY, COMMANDER

APPEARANCE
Tomorrow Never Dies (1997)
STATUS Dead; drowned
CHARACTERISTICS Efficient, cautious
PLAYED BY Christopher Bowen

Commander Richard Day is captain of the HMS *Devonshire* in the South China Sea. When two Chinese MiGs fly past, the pilots state that the *Devonshire* is in Chinese territorial waters. Day insists that his ship is in international waters and that his crew will defend themselves if attacked. Day believes the Chinese pilots have launched an aerial torpedo to sink the *Devonshire* and orders his crew to abandon ship.

DOLLY

APPEARANCE
Moonraker (1979)
STATUS Living; whereabouts unknown
CHARACTERISTICS Love-struck
PLAYED BY Blanche Ravalec

Dolly helps rescue Jaws at Sugarloaf Mountain in Rio de Janeiro, Brazil, when his cable car crashes into the tramway station. She falls in love with Jaws, accompanies him into space, and softens his cold-as-steel heart. When billionaire Hugo Drax explains his plan to repopulate Earth with physically perfect specimens, Dolly questions how she and Jaws would fit into this plan. She and Jaws help 007 escape from Drax's space station, and the pair enjoys champagne before space shuttle captain Colonel Scott rescues them.

DOWAR, CLAIR, MP

APPEARANCE Skyfall (2012)
STATUS Living
CHARACTERISTICS Firm; accusatory
PLAYED BY Helen McCrory

Clair Dowar MP oversees an official inquiry into breaches of national security to which M is summoned. Dowar pours scorn on M's handling of recent security breaches and the loss of operatives "for which you are almost single-handedly responsible." Intelligence and Security Committee Chairman Gareth Mallory interrupts Dowar and suggests that M should be allowed to defend herself. When the cyber-terrorist Silva bursts into the chamber and attempts to murder M, Dowar dives for cover. Amidst the ensuing chaotic gun battle, Eve Moneypenny manages to hurry Dowar and other dignitaries to safety.

DRACO, MARC ANGE

APPEARANCE On Her Majesty's Secret Service (1969)
STATUS Living; whereabouts unknown
CHARACTERISTICS Exudes strength, charm, animal magnetism, and authority, but also menace
PLAYED BY Gabriele Ferzetti

Corsican Marc Ange Draco is the head of the Union Corse, the biggest crime syndicate in Europe. He also briefly holds the title of Bond's father-in-law. His legitimate business fronts include construction, electrical supplies, and numerous agricultural holdings. Born in Corsica, his patriotic drink of choice is Corsican brandy.

Draco was a bandit hiding in the mountains when he met a romantic English girl. The two fell in love, married, and had a child, Teresa (Tracy), in 1943. Twelve years later,

PROUD FATHER *(above) Draco never suspected the tragic price his daughter would pay for marrying 007.*

Draco's wife died. By then, Draco had been elected capu or "chief" of the Union Corse.

Never giving his daughter a proper home or supervision, Draco watched Tracy immerse herself in one scandal after another to spite him. Although Draco cut off Tracy's allowance, he instructed his men to follow her wherever she traveled and make sure she was safe.

Bond rescues Tracy from a suicide attempt and then brutally defeats Draco's men. Draco believes he has at last found the perfect man for his daughter and offers 007 £1 million on the day he marries her. Bond refuses but agrees to continue seeing Tracy in exchange for information regarding his archenemy Blofeld. Tracy sees through her father's motives and tells him to give Bond the information he wants or he will never see her again. Left with no alternative, Draco reveals to 007 that Blofeld's contact is Swiss lawyer

> ## "On the day you marry her, I will give you a personal dowry of one million pounds. In gold."
>
> ### Draco to 007

Gebrüder Gumbold. However, Draco's wishes are fulfilled, as Bond and Tracy slowly fall in love.

Later, when Blofeld kidnaps Tracy, and holds her hostage at his alpine base Piz Gloria, Bond enlists Draco's help to mount a helicopter attack on Blofeld's lair and rescue her.

At Bond and Tracy's wedding, Draco presents Bond with a £1 million dowry for marrying his daughter, but 007 politely refuses the money. Tragically, Bond and Tracy's happiness does not last. Leaving on honeymoon, Draco's beloved daughter is gunned down by Blofeld's henchwoman, Irma Bunt.

TOUGH LOVE *(above) Draco tries to convince Tracy that 007 doesn't need her help.*

FOND FAREWELL *(right) Tracy tells her father she will obey her husband just as she has obeyed him.*

DUFF, SUPT.

APPEARANCE
Dr. No (1962)
STATUS Living; whereabouts unknown
CHARACTERISTICS Reliable, knowledgeable; a great help to 007
PLAYED BY William Foster-Davis

Superintendent Duff, the Jamaican Police Commissioner, aids James Bond and Government House in the investigation into the disappearance of British Secret Service representative John Strangways and his secretary, Mary. Duff reports that the car a chauffeur named Mr. Jones used to pick up Bond at Palisadoes Airport was stolen and reveals that Mr. Jones does not hail from Kingston. Bond hands Duff a photograph of Strangways and Quarrel, a fisherman whom Bond noticed tailing him from the airport, and asks Duff to investigate him. 007 also requests a car from Duff when he has the traitorous Miss Taro arrested.

FALCO

APPEARANCE
Die Another Day (2002)
STATUS Living; whereabouts unknown
CHARACTERISTICS Wry, cynical; initially sceptical of MI6's efficiency
PLAYED BY Michael Madsen

Damian Falco is the hard-bitten chief of the National Security Agency (NSA) and the boss of NSA agent Jinx. He does not trust Bond and has mixed feelings about joining forces with the British to stop billionaire Gustav Graves from destroying the Korean Demilitarized Zone so that North Korea can invade the South.

> "Put your house in order, or we're gonna do it for you."
>
> Falco to M

He believes the Americans can handle the situation on their own.

When Falco becomes aware of information leaking from North Korea, he believes 007, who the North Koreans hold captive, to be the source. Falco subsequently engineers and supervises a prisoner exchange.

Falco then encourages M to imprison Bond on a British warship in Hong Kong Harbor. Later, at NSA headquarters, an angry Falco implies to M over a video link that she intentionally let 007 escape, enabling Bond to destroy the Alvarez clinic in Los Organos. Falco fails to mention that his agent Jinx played a part in the clinic's destruction.

Falco reluctantly agrees to send Jinx into North Korea with Bond to stop Graves. He has no intention of leaving this situation solely in the hands of MI6.

When Bond kills Graves and stops the destruction of the DMZ, Falco refuses to admit that he was wrong about 007, allowing M to simply smile at what her best agent just accomplished.

FIREWORKS *In the US Command Bunker in the DMZ, Falco tells 007, M, and Jinx that Defcon Two has been declared.*

FALLON

APPEARANCE Licence To Kill (1989)
STATUS Killed by tank blast
CHARACTERISTICS No-nonsense, businesslike, disciplined
PLAYED BY Christopher Neame

Fallon is MI6's man in Isthmus City, whom M orders to bring Bond back to London at any cost. Fallon arrives at the safe house belonging to Hong Kong narcotics agents Kwang and Loti, who have just prevented Bond from assassinating Sanchez. Fallon prepares to drug Bond and ship him home, when Heller, Sanchez's head of security, fires a tank shell at the house, killing Fallon instantly.

FANNING, JIM

APPEARANCE Octopussy (1983)
STATUS Living; whereabouts unknown
CHARACTERISTICS Fussy art expert
PLAYED BY Douglas Wilmer

British Secret Service art expert Jim Fanning accompanies Bond to Sotheby's auction house in London to help spot the seller of a rare Fabergé Egg. Fanning predicts that the egg will fetch between £250,000 and £300,000. When exiled Afghan prince Kamal Khan and 007 become embroiled in a bidding war, which reaches £500,000, Fanning nearly faints.

FARREL, ADMIRAL

APPEARANCE GoldenEye (1995)
STATUS Dead; crushed
CHARACTERISTICS Easily seduced
PLAYED BY Billy J. Mitchell

Canadian Navy Admiral Chuck Farrel has no clue that his betrayal of his country serves a Janus plot to steal a new Tiger helicopter. When he takes on Xenia Onatopp, a member of Janus, as a lover, he does virtually everything he can to please her, including buying her an expensive black-market Ferrari. During a night of lovemaking, Xenia suddenly crushes Farrel's rib cage with her thighs. His ID allows Alec Trevelyan to slip aboard the French warship and gain access to the Tiger.

FEKKESH, AZIZ

APPEARANCE The Spy Who Loved Me (1977)
STATUS Dead; killed by Jaws
CHARACTERISTICS Furtive, nervous; realizes too late that he is in mortal peril
PLAYED BY Nadim Sawalha

Egyptian middleman Aziz Fekkesh tries to negotiate the sale of plans for Karl Stromberg's submarine tracking system. Fekkesh fails to meet Bond for an appointment in Cairo. At the Pyramids of Giza Son et Lumière show, Fekkesh sees Jaws and tries to run for safety. Bond follows the chase into an ancient tomb. Inside, Jaws kills Fekkesh with a fatal bite before Bond can reach them. After Jaws escapes, 007 finds Fekkesh's appointment book, which leads him to businessman Max Kalba.

FERRARA, LUIGI

APPEARANCE For Your Eyes Only (1981)
STATUS Dead; neck sliced
CHARACTERISTICS Charming, enthusiastic, suspicious
PLAYED BY John Moreno

Luigi Ferrara works as MI6's young agent in the northern town of Cortina in Italy. On the steamed mirror in his hotel bathroom, Bond receives a message to meet this Italian contact at the peak of the Tofana ski lift at 10 a.m.

Ferrara introduces Bond to shipping magnate Aris Kristatos and later informs 007 that his office in Milan might be able to help with information on Milos Columbo, the arch rival of Kristatos. Locque, a hitman working for Kristatos, murders Ferrara by slicing his throat. Bond avenges his death by kicking Locque's crashed Mercedes, with Locque inside, off a cliff.

APPOINTMENT IN CORTINA Luigi Ferrara meets with James Bond to discuss Operation Undertow.

FOREIGN SECRETARY

APPEARANCE Quantum Of Solace (2008)
STATUS Living
CHARACTERISTICS Patronising, world-weary, a seasoned politician
PLAYED BY Tim Pigott-Smith

When the British Foreign Secretary informs M that England's interests are now aligned with Dominic Greene's regarding the oil in Bolivia, M insists that Greene is a "major player" in a dangerous organization. He interrupts her, adding that foreign policy cannot be based on hunches and innuendo. With the

world fast running out of oil if "we (i.e. the British government) did not "do business with villains, we'd have almost no one to trade with… Right or wrong doesn't come into it. We're acting out of necessity."

The Foreign Secretary concludes the interview by darkly advising M to pull in Bond before the Americans "put him down."

FRAZIER, PROFESSOR

APPEARANCE The Man With The Golden Gun (1974)
STATUS Living
CHARACTERISTICS Thrilled at the prospect of discovery
PLAYED BY Gerald James

SECRET MEETING Prof. Frazier (fourth on the right) meets Bond and Lt. Hip aboard the partially sunken Queen Elizabeth.

A solar energy expert retained by British Intelligence to work on bringing the defected scientist Gibson back to the British side, Professor Frazier becomes excited when he discovers Gibson brought the Solex Agitator, a device that turns the sun's power into electricity, to a meeting with Lt. Hip. When Bond and Lt. Hip tell him that the Solex was not found on Gibson after he was assassinated by Scaramanga, Professor Frazier appears crestfallen.

GIBSON

APPEARANCE
The Man With The Golden Gun (1974)

STATUS Dead; shot by Scaramanga

CHARACTERISTICS Mercenary, brilliant

PLAYED BY Gordon Everett

ONE FOR THE ROAD *Gibson orders a last drink at the Bottoms Up bar.*

British solar energy expert Gibson goes underground to work for Hai Fat, a Thai multi-millionaire. Gibson offers to re-defect to the British, but Scaramanga shoots him before he can turn over the Solex Agitator, a device that turns the sun's power into electricity.

GOGOL, GENERAL

APPEARANCES
The Spy Who Loved Me (1977), Moonraker (1979), For Your Eyes Only (1981), Octopussy (1983), A View To A Kill (1985), The Living Daylights (1987)

STATUS Living; retired

CHARACTERISTICS Détente-conscious; experienced in the ways of the world; something of a bon viveur

PLAYED BY Walter Gotell

General Anatol Gogol, the head of the KGB, crosses paths with Bond and British Intelligence on six assignments. Little is known about his personal life, but he enjoys a close relationship with his secretary, Miss Rublevich.

In *The Spy Who Loved Me*, Gogol and M team their top agents, 007 and Agent XXX, in an effort to discover the third party behind the disappearance of both nations' nuclear missile-equipped submarines. *Moonraker* finds Gogol in Moscow, assuring Colonel Scott of NASA that he will give the US 12 hours to determine the origins of billionaire Hugo Drax's space station before the

"How can I sleep?
Nothing but problems."

General Gogol

Soviets attack. In *For Your Eyes Only*, Gogol vies with the British as he prepares to purchase the ATAC transmitter from the evil Aris Kristatos. 007 destroys the ATAC and informs Gogol "That's détente, Comrade, you don't have it, I don't have it." Gogol takes Bond's advice to heart, because in *Octopussy*, the KGB chief opposes Russian General Orlov and his desire to launch war against the West. *A View To A Kill* sees Gogol trying to keep rogue KGB agent Max Zorin under control. He even awards Bond the Order of Lenin when 007 stops Zorin from destroying Silicon Valley. In his final appearance, in *The Living Daylights*, Gogol receives a promotion to the Foreign Service.

A MESSAGE FROM THE KGB
General Gogol informs General Orlov that he is a disgrace to the Soviet Union.

GRANT'S MASSEUSE

APPEARANCE
From Russia With Love (1963)
STATUS Unknown
CHARACTERISTICS Tactile
PLAYED BY Jan Williams

The silent blonde who massages SPECTRE hitman Donald Grant is described in more detail in Ian Fleming's novel. She has been Grant's masseuse for two years, but his perfect physique and malevolent essence repulse her. She is sometimes mysteriously told her services are not needed for a week or two. She has seen small wounds on Grant, but she knows nothing of his work and does not ever plan to ask.

GRAY, FREDERICK

APPEARANCE The Spy Who Loved Me (1977), Moonraker (1979), For Your Eyes Only (1981), Octopussy (1983), A View To A Kill (1985), The Living Daylights (1987)
STATUS Living; whereabouts unknown
CHARACTERISTICS Nonplussed and irritated by changes in his routine
PLAYED BY Geoffrey Keen

Sir Frederick Gray, the Minister of Defence, instructs Bond on the vital military and political factors for six of his missions. He plays a key role in 007's world, serving as the principle link between the Prime Minister and British Intelligence.

In *The Spy Who Loved Me*, Gray meets Bond at Faslane Naval Base in Scotland. *Moonraker* finds Gray furious with 007 for accusing billionaire Hugo Drax of illegal activities. When M is on leave in *For Your Eyes Only*, Gray briefs Bond on Operation Undertow. For *Octopussy*, Gray returns the stolen Romanoff Star to KGB chief General Gogol. *A View To A Kill* finds Gray concerned about the political implications of investigating the activities of industrialist Max Zorin.

Gray's final appearance in *The Living Daylights* sees the minister upset that the KGB has snatched back General Koskov only hours after he defected to the West.

GREENWALT, DR.

APPEARANCE
Tomorrow Never Dies (1997)
STATUS Living; whereabouts unknown
CHARACTERISTICS Nervous, cautious, well-educated
PLAYED BY Colin Stinton

Dr. Dave Greenwalt is the US Air Force GPS (Global Positioning Satellite) expert. Bond arrives at the US Air Force base in Okinawa, Japan, to meet with Greenwalt and CIA contact Jack Wade. 007 brings the GPS encoder he stole from Henry Gupta's laboratory in Hamburg. Attaching the encoder to his GPS calibration unit, Greenwalt is able to determine the actual location where HMS *Devonshire* sank.

GUMBOLD, GEBRUDER

APPEARANCE
On Her Majesty's Secret Service (1969)
STATUS Living; whereabouts unknown
CHARACTERISTICS Stern, precise
PLAYED BY James Bree

Gebrüder Gumbold, a lawyer based in Bern, Switzerland, represents the interests of SPECTRE chief Blofeld. Blofeld wants the College of Arms in London to verify his lineage as Count Balthazar de Bleauchamp and uses Gumbold to make the necessary contacts with Sir Hilary Bray of the College of Arms.

Criminal mastermind Marc Ange Draco informs 007 of Gumbold's connection to Blofeld. Bond breaks into the lawyer's office during Gumbold's lunch hour to crack his safe and photocopy the College of Arms letters. He exits the office just as Gumbold returns.

HALL, DR.

APPEARANCE
Skyfall (2012)
STATUS Alive
CHARACTERISTICS Unemotional and impassive; by the book
PLAYED BY Nicholas Woodeson

Doctor Hall is an MI6 psychoanalyst who engages James Bond in a word

association test when 007 returns to MI6 after being absent, believed dead, for three months. One noted exchange occurs when Bond replies "bitch" to Hall's "M." When Hall mentions "Skyfall," however, Bond replies "Done," and exits the room. Hall subsequently fails Bond for his psychological evaluation, claiming, "alcohol and substance addiction indicated, and pathological rejection of authority based on unresolved childhood trauma."

HAMILTON

APPEARANCE
Live And Let Die (1973)
STATUS Dead; assassinated while watching his own funeral
CHARACTERISTICS Unwisely curious
PLAYED BY Robert Dix

Hamilton is the second of three British agents killed by dictator Dr. Kananga's minions. On loan to American Intelligence, Hamilton watches the Fillet of Soul restaurant on Docker Street in New Orleans. He sees a jazz funeral pass and asks another observer, "Whose funeral is it?" He gets a surprising answer: "Yours." The man jabs a switchblade between Hamilton's ribs, and his dead body falls to the street. The pallbearers place a bottomless coffin over his body. When they lift the coffin, Hamilton remains inside and the mourners break into a celebratory jazz dance.

HARGREAVES, ADMIRAL

APPEARANCE
The Spy Who Loved Me (1977)
STATUS Living; whereabouts unknown
CHARACTERISTICS Decisive leader
PLAYED BY Robert Brown

Admiral Hargreaves serves as Flag Officer of Submarines for the Royal Navy. He retains the ultimate responsibility for the four Polaris R-class submarines headquartered at Faslane Naval Base in Scotland. He is one of three individuals allowed to know the pre-arranged courses of the submarine fleet.

When Hargreaves meets Bond, he mentions HMS *Ark Royal* to 007, referencing Bond's service on the legendary World War II aircraft carrier sunk by a U-boat off Gibraltar. Hargreaves listens to the

Minister of Defence reveal how an enemy located HMS *Ranger* using a new submarine tracking system. Hargreaves acknowledges that such a system could undermine Western defense strategies.

After the submarine crisis, Hargreaves continued his career in public service, ultimately serving in other highly sensitive positions.

HAVELOCK, TIMOTHY & IONA

APPEARANCE
For Your Eyes Only (1981)
STATUS Dead; both murdered in cold blood
CHARACTERISTICS Attentive, patriotic
PLAYED BY Jack Hedley and Toby Robins

Marine archaeologists Timothy and Iona Havelock have traveled all over the world on their ship, the *Triana*, searching for relics in their Neptune 2-man sub. Proud parents of Melina, they currently work for British Intelligence on a mission to find the *St. Georges*, a missing British spy ship. Sir Timothy records his findings in a daily log written in a special kind of shorthand, which only Melina can decipher. Before Timothy can deliver his report to British Intelligence, Cuban hitman Hector Gonzales guns down him and Iona.

In Ian Fleming's short story *For Your Eyes Only*, Major Gonzales, who works for a man named Von Hammerstein, guns down Colonel Timothy Havelock and his wife. Gonzales kills them after they refuse to sell their 20,000 acres of Jamaican plantation land, which has been in the family for three centuries. M, who is best friends with the Havelocks and was best man at their wedding ceremony in Malta in 1925, asks James Bond to avenge their deaths.

WELCOME HOME, MELINA, MY DARLING
Timothy and Iona Havelock enjoy a happy reunion with their daughter Melina before tragedy strikes.

HAWKER

APPEARANCE
Goldfinger (1964)
STATUS Living; whereabouts unknown
CHARACTERISTICS Loyal caddy
PLAYED BY Gerry Duggan

Hawker caddies for Bond during his golf match with Goldfinger, watching admiringly as 007 outfoxes his cheating opponent. When Goldfinger loses his ball, Hawker suspects Oddjob is lying about finding it, and he is; Bond is standing on the real ball. Later, Hawker watches as 007 replaces Goldfinger's Slazenger 1 ball with a Slazenger 7. Goldfinger plays the wrong ball on the last hole and loses the match.

HAWKINS

APPEARANCE
Licence To Kill (1989)
STATUS Living; whereabouts unknown
CHARACTERISTICS By-the-book, athletic, hard-edged
PLAYED BY Grand L. Bush

IN OVER YOUR HEAD *Hawkins advises Bond to lay off the Sanchez case.*

DEA agent Hawkins, along with Agent Mullens, stops fellow agent Felix Leiter on Key West's Seven Mile Bridge and informs him that drug lord Franz Sanchez is in the Bahamas.
When Bond pursues his vengeance mission against Sanchez for the maiming of Leiter, Hawkins reminds 007 that he is out of his jurisdiction and in way over his head. Hawkins later leads Bond to the Hemingway House where M revokes Bond's licence to kill.

HENDERSON, DIKKO

APPEARANCE
You Only Live Twice (1967)
STATUS Dead; stabbed in the back
CHARACTERISTICS Guarded; never fully adopted Japanese culture
PLAYED BY Charles Gray

Dikko Henderson moved to Japan just before World War II, and lost his right leg in Singapore in 1942. He loves the Orient and works for MI6 as a station chief, although he expresses doubts about ever fully embracing the culture. Henderson maintains a close

> "Oh that's stirred not shaken.
> That was right, wasn't it?"
> ### Henderson to Bond

relationship with the Japanese SIS and has Japanese agent Aki meet 007 for him. Although Henderson gives Bond a martini "stirred, not shaken," 007 is too polite to correct him. Henderson believes a mysterious rocket capturing US spacecraft is being launched from Japan, and that a Japanese industrial concern is involved. Bond never finds out more because Henderson receives a knife in his back. It is rumored that a few years after Henderson's death, Blofeld used him as a model for his surgically-created looks.

HERGERSHEIMER, KLAUS

APPEARANCE
Diamonds Are Forever (1971)
STATUS Unknown
CHARACTERISTICS Friendly, conscientious, innocent
PLAYED BY Ed Bishop

Former NASA employee Klaus Hergersheimer works for WW Techtronics, a division of Whyte Enterprises, Inc. As a member of G Section for three years, he has the thankless duty of checking radiation shields for replacement. While making rounds in Section 5, Klaus finds Bond without a shield. Hergersheimer gives one to Bond but later discovers that 007 impersonated him while infiltrating Professor Dr. Metz's lab.

HIP, LT.

APPEARANCE The Man With The Golden Gun (1974)
STATUS Living
CHARACTERISTICS Good martial artist
PLAYED BY Soon-Taik Oh

British Secret Service contact in Hong Kong and a Lieutenant in the Hong Kong police force, Hip works to secure the re-defection of solar energy expert Gibson. Hip travels with Bond to Bangkok to investigate Hai Fat's connection to Gibson and Scaramanga. He shuttles Bond to Hai Fat's house and helps rescue Bond at Hai Fat's martial arts school. Hip collects the Solex from Bond and delivers it to Mary Goodnight. Shortly after he realizes she has been kidnapped, he disappears.

HOME SECRETARY

APPEARANCE Thunderball (1965)
STATUS Unknown
CHARACTERISTICS Extremely traditional, generally irritated
PLAYED BY Roland Culver

The Home Secretary represents the Prime Minister during Operation Thunderball. He has to decide if Britain should pay a ransom of £100,000,000 to recover two atomic bombs hijacked by SPECTRE. His fatalistic attitude places little faith in the work of 007. He orders his assistant Kenniston to secure $280,000,000 worth of flawless blue-white diamonds, which will be dropped in the Mergui Archipelago off the coast of Burma.

HOODS CONVENTION

APPEARANCE Goldfinger (1964)
STATUS Dead; gassed
CHARACTERISTICS Greedy, suspicious
PLAYED BY Bill Nagy (Mr. Midnight), Hal Galili (Mr. Strap), Roland Brand, Bill Brandon, Norman Chaucer, Bill Edwards, Laurence Herder, William Hurndell, John Maxim, John McCarthy, Lenny Rabin (other gangsters)

Goldfinger enlists top US crime figures to smuggle materials for Operation Grand Slam. The hoods are each to be paid $1 million in gold. Goldfinger offers them $10 million each in gold from Fort Knox if they help him rob it. All but Mr. Solo agree. Goldfinger decides to cover his tracks and orders Kisch to eliminate the group with nerve gas.

A BED FOR THE NIGHT *007 considers an offer of hospitality from Sheik Hosein.*

HOSEIN, SHEIK

APPEARANCE
The Spy Who Loved Me (1977)
STATUS Living; whereabouts unknown
CHARACTERISTICS A gracious host who appreciates the treasures of Egypt
PLAYED BY Edward de Souza

A friend from Bond's student days at Cambridge University, Sheik Hosein lives the life of a hedonistic bedouin in the Egyptian desert, but he also has ties to the British Secret Service. Hosein helps 007 locate the men behind the sale of megalomaniac Karl Stromberg's submarine tracking system technology. He advises Bond to get in touch with the Egyptian Aziz Fekkesh and then businessman Max Kalba. After a member of Hosein's harem of beautiful wives suggestively presents 007 with a rose, Bond agrees to stay for the night at Sheik Hosein's camp.

> "Well, what can I offer you?
> Sheep's eyes? Dates?
> Vodka Martini?"
>
> **Sheik Hosein to 007**

HOTEL RECEPTIONIST

APPEARANCE
From Russia With Love (1963)
STATUS Living; whereabouts unknown
CHARACTERISTICS Nervous
PLAYED BY Arlette Dobson

SPECTRE bribes the Istanbul hotel staff to guide James Bond to a bugged room. When Bond objects to the arrangements, the hotel receptionist then offers 007 the Bridal Suite. Behind the suite's two-way mirrored wall, SPECTRE member Rosa Klebb films Bond's first meeting with Tatiana Romanova, a supposed defector from Soviet Intelligence.

IRINA

APPEARANCE
GoldenEye (1995)
STATUS Living; whereabouts unknown
CHARACTERISTICS Gorgeous; limited singing skills
PLAYED BY Minnie Driver

Irina, the mistress of Russian Mafia head Valentin Zukovsky, works as a country music singer in his club in St. Petersburg, Russia, performing with three backup singers. She is beautiful, but profoundly untalented—Bond compares her singing to strangling a cat. Irina finds it insulting when Zukovsky asks her to cut short her rehearsal of Tammy Wynette's "Stand By Your Man," and she storms off the stage.

> "Who's strangling the cat?"
>
> **007 on Irina's singing**

SOUGHT-AFTER ITEM *Kalba shows Bond and Anya the microfilm cartridge containing the blueprints of Stromberg's submarine tracking system.*

KALBA, MAX

APPEARANCE
The Spy Who Loved Me (1977)
STATUS Dead; killed by Jaws
CHARACTERISTICS Cool, calm, collected; experienced black-marketeer
PLAYED BY Vernon Dobtcheff

Owner of the Mujaba Club in Cairo, Egypt, Max Kalba receives the microfilm of megalomaniac Karl Stromberg's submarine tracking system from Stromberg's secretary via his underground network. Through middleman Aziz Fekkesh, Kalba offers to sell the microfilm to the Soviets or the British, whoever offers the highest bid. After Stromberg's enforcer, Jaws, kills Fekkesh, Kalba meets with KGB agent Anya Amasova and 007. Before a deal can be made, Jaws lures Kalba to a secluded phone booth, takes the microfilm and fatally bites him.

In an early script draft, Kalba and Bond engage in a duel over a game of backgammon. 007 wins, but Jaws kills Kalba before he can pay Bond.

KELLY, ADMIRAL

APPEARANCE
Tomorrow Never Dies (1997)
STATUS Living; whereabouts unknown
CHARACTERISTICS Member of the Royal Navy, professional, focused
PLAYED BY Michael Byrne

As captain of the HMS *Bedford*, Admiral Kelly prepares the Pacific fleet of the Royal Navy for war

against the Chinese, unaware that media mogul Elliot Carver has been pitting the two powers against each other. After James Bond causes an explosion that makes Carver's stealth ship visible to radar, Admiral Kelly orders his crew to destroy Carver's damaged vessel.

KERIM BEY'S GIRLFRIEND

APPEARANCE
From Russia With Love (1963)
STATUS Unknown
CHARACTERISTICS Bored, seductive
PLAYED BY Nadja Regin

Kerim Bey's girlfriend enjoys the intrigue of liaising in the Istanbul office of the British Secret Service. She inadvertently saves Bey's life by inducing him to join her on the settee before a limpet mine explodes near his desk. After the shock of nearly being killed, she moved to Central America and studied dance.

ALL WORK AND NO PLAY *(below) Kerim Bey's girlfriend suggests to the preoccupied Head of Station T that there might be more to life than espionage.*

KINCADE

APPEARANCE
Skyfall (2012)
STATUS Living
CHARACTERISTICS Kindly,
protective, loyal
PLAYED BY Albert Finney

Kincade, the gamekeeper for the
Skyfall estate since James Bond was a
boy, plays a crucial part in Bond and
M's battle against the vengeful
cyber-terrorist Silva.

Bond and M encounter Kincade
when they seek refuge at Skyfall
Lodge in the Scottish Highlands.
Mishearing, Kincade calls M
"Emma." Kincade informs Bond
that Skyfall was sold after he was
presumed dead. In addition, the

007: Some men are
coming to kill us.
But we're going to
kill them first.
Kincade: Then we'd
better get ready.

entire gun collection, except for Bond's father Andrew's old hunting rifle, was sold to an Idaho collector. Bond tells Kincade that they are about to be attacked and Kincade helps Bond and M board up Skyfall's windows and prepare booby-traps. The gamekeeper notices Bond practicing with his father's hunting rifle out on the moor and is impressed when Bond hits some tea cups with remarkable accuracy.

Kincade shows M Skyfall's priest hole tunnel leading under the moor. It was there that young James Bond hid for two days after being told that his parents had died in a climbing accident. Kincade tells M that when James eventually emerged he was a boy no longer.

When Silva's men attack Skyfall, two of them shoot at Kincade's mirrored reflection, enabling Kincade to blast them with his 12-gauge double-barreled sawed-off shotgun. He dryly remarks, "Welcome to Scotland." Bond later saves Kincade's life when he cannot reload his shotgun fast enough.

UP FOR THE FIGHT *(right) "Are you ready?" asks Bond as Silva's men approach. "I was ready before you were born, son," answers Kincade.*

As the battle intensifies, Kincade guides M through the escape tunnel, across the moor, to a chapel on the estate. There, Silva orders Kincade to retreat as he confronts M. After Bond kills Silva and M dies in Bond's arms, Kincade respectfully places his hat across his chest.

"What did you say you did for a living?"

Kincade to 007

PATERNAL EYE *(right) Years ago, Kincade had taught the young James to shoot. Bond showed him that his marksmanship had greatly improved.*

M'S GUARDIAN *(below) Kincade leads a wounded M away from Skyfall, now in flames, in order to take refuge in a chapel on the estate.*

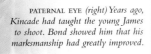

KING, SIR ROBERT

APPEARANCE
The World Is Not Enough (1999)
STATUS Dead; blown up in MI6 headquarters
CHARACTERISTICS Man of integrity
PLAYED BY David Calder

Sir Robert King is the father of Elektra King. After reading law at Oxford University with M, Sir Robert married into the Vavra family, renaming their oil empire King Industries. When terrorist Renard kidnaps Elektra, Robert consults M, now head of MI6, who advises him not to pay the ransom.

Sir Robert ultimately becomes the victim of patricide. Elektra plots to kill him to take revenge for

refusing to pay her ransom and also to seize what she believes to be her family's stolen heritage of Central Asian oil reserves. Elektra works with Renard to have her father obliterate himself with stacks of specially treated £50 notes. Sir Robert dies inside MI6 headquarters.

"Be careful, M. I might try to steal him from you."

King on 007

OIL KING *(below) Sir Robert's wealth and MI6 connections make him a target for the terrorist Renard.*

KLOTKOFF

APPEARANCE
A View To A Kill (1985)
STATUS Dead; chopped into fish bait
CHARACTERISTICS Loyal, dutiful
PLAYED BY Bogdan Kominowski

KGB agent Klotkoff joins General Gogol when he reprimands tycoon Max Zorin for "assassinating" 007. Klotkoff calls Zorin "a physiological freak," prompting Zorin's lover May Day to lift Klotkoff into the air and hurl him to the ground.

At Zorin's oil pumping station, Klotkoff and agent Pola Ivanova record Zorin discussing plans to destroy Silicon Valley. They then try to detonate a mine at the station. Pola escapes, but Zorin orders Klotkoff be thrown into the intake pipe rotors.

KWANG

APPEARANCE
Licence To Kill (1989)
STATUS Dead; committed suicide
CHARACTERISTICS Decisive, driven
PLAYED BY Cary-Hiroyuki Tagawa

Disguised as an Asian drug lord, Kwang, like his partner, Loti, is a Hong Kong narcotics agent who has spent years trying to infiltrate drug lord Franz Sanchez's operations. When Bond tries to kill Sanchez, Kwang's ninja team attacks. They take Bond to their safe house for questioning, but then Heller, Sanchez's security chief, attacks the house. Kwang commits suicide by biting into a cyanide tablet rather than face Sanchez's wrath.

LAZAR

APPEARANCE
The Man With The Golden Gun (1974)
STATUS Living
CHARACTERISTICS Skilled craftsman
PLAYED BY Marne Maitland

A Portuguese weapons maker based in Macau, Lazar makes customized bullets for assassin Francisco Scaramanga, and it is likely that he made Scaramanga's unique component golden gun for him. Lazar prides himself on custom, hand-crafted work. When Bond meets Lazar, 007 turns a gun on the weapons maker. Lazar agrees to let Bond trace the delivery of the golden bullets to Scaramanga at the Casino de Macau.

LEBANESE GANGSTERS

APPEARANCE
The Man With The Golden Gun (1974)
STATUS Living
CHARACTERISTICS Ill-tempered
PLAYED BY George Silver (owner), Terry Plummer (Rahman), Rocky Taylor (Hammud)

BUILT FOR TROUBLE *James Bond must face off with this trio in order to retrieve the golden bullet that killed agent 002.*

When Bond attempts to steal a golden bullet held as a lucky charm in the navel of a belly dancer called Saida, the Lebanese nightclub owner and his two bouncers, Rahman and Hammud, attack. Bond fights back, at one point using a can of Fabergé Brut to sting the eyes of one of his adversaries.

KRUG, MR.

APPEARANCE
Die Another Day (2002)
STATUS Living; whereabouts unknown
CHARACTERISTICS Burly, hostile
PLAYED BY Ian Pirie

Mr. Krug is a South African criminal staying in Room 42 of the Gran Blanco Hotel in Los Organos off the Cuban coast. Here he waits with other criminals to be taken to the clinic of gene therapy specialist Dr. Alvarez, where he will acquire a new identity. Bond knocks Krug unconscious and then uses his admittance papers to gain access to the clinic.

LA PORTE, MADEMOISELLE

APPEARANCE Thunderball (1965)
STATUS Unknown
CHARACTERISTICS Efficient, exotic
PLAYED BY Maryse Guy Mitsouko

When Bond attends the funeral of SPECTRE No. 6, Colonel Jacques Boitier, he brings the beautiful Mademoiselle La Porte as his escort. La Porte works for the British Secret Service's French station. It transpires that Boitier is actually alive and is posing as his own widow at his supposed funeral. La Porte helps Bond escape from a trio of SPECTRE gunmen after Bond kills Boitier at his chateau.

LEE, CHUCK

APPEARANCE
A View To A Kill (1985)
STATUS Dead; strangled by May Day
CHARACTERISTICS Youthful, keen
PLAYED BY David Yip

Chuck Lee is a young Chinese-American CIA agent who poses as a Fisherman's Wharf seafood vendor and gives Bond information regarding tycoon Max Zorin's employee Bob Conley and ex-Nazi Dr. Mortner. He also introduces 007 to fisherman O'Rourke, who tells Bond that Zorin's oil pumping station ruined an excellent crab patch.

May Day later strangles Chuck Lee in his truck outside geologist Stacey Sutton's home. San Francisco police recover his body in Chinatown.

Bond producers had planned to bring CIA agent Felix Leiter back as 007's contact in San Francisco. But with Chinatown such a key part of the city, they chose to make this character a Chinese-American CIA agent instead.

LEILA

APPEARANCE
From Russia With Love (1963)
STATUS Living; whereabouts unknown
CHARACTERISTICS Fit, superb dancer
PLAYED BY Lisa (Leila) Guiraut

At a gypsy camp in Istanbul, Turkey, Bond and head of Station T, Kerim Bey, are treated to a belly dance by a beautiful and talented woman who takes a great deal of interest in 007.

LEITER, DELLA

APPEARANCE
Licence To Kill (1989)
STATUS Dead; stabbed in the chest
CHARACTERISTICS Bubbly, beautiful
PLAYED BY Priscilla Barnes

Vivacious Della Churchill marries 007's close friend, DEA agent Felix Leiter, in a wedding ceremony in Key West, Florida. Her disapproving elderly uncle believes the marriage is a mistake. After the wedding, Bond travels to the airport to catch his Istanbul flight. On hearing that drug lord Sanchez has escaped custody, 007 returns to Leiter's house to find that Sanchez's henchmen have murdered Della and maimed Felix.

WELCOME TO THE GYPSY LIFE
Leila lets 007 in on her belly dancing secrets.

LEITER, FELIX

APPEARANCES Dr. No (1962), Goldfinger (1964), Thunderball (1965), Diamonds Are Forever (1971), Live And Let Die (1973), The Living Daylights (1987), Licence To Kill (1989), Casino Royale (2006), Quantum Of Solace (2008)

STATUS Living; whereabouts unknown

CHARACTERISTICS Reliable aide and friend to Bond

PLAYED BY Jack Lord (Dr. No), Cec Linder (Goldfinger), Rik Van Nutter (Thunderball), Norman Burton (Diamonds Are Forever), David Hedison (Live And Let Die, Licence To Kill), John Terry (The Living Daylights), Jeffrey Wright (Casino Royale, Quantum Of Solace)

CIA CONTACT *Felix Leiter in* **Dr. No.**

Felix Leiter is Bond's Texas-born CIA ally and close friend in six Fleming novels and eight 007 films. Fleming gives his age as 35 in *Casino Royale*. The description of him in that novel reads: "A mop of straw-coloured hair lent his face a boyish look which closer examination contradicted."

An ex-member of the US Marine Corps, jazz-lover Leiter joins the CIA and comes to Bond's rescue at the casino at Royale-les-Eaux in northern France.

In the novel *Live And Let Die*, Leiter's friendship with Bond develops as the two barhop in Harlem and enjoy good meals together. Leiter loses his right arm and leg to a shark, courtesy of gangster Mr. Big's thugs. Bond finds his friend's body wrapped in a white sheet with a note attached to his chest, which reads: "He disagreed with something that ate him." This same scenario would be used by the filmmakers not for the film *Live and Let Die*, but as a key plot device for *Licence To Kill*, when drug baron Franz Sanchez feeds DEA agent Leiter to the sharks.

After being discharged by the CIA for his handicap, Leiter joins Pinkerton's Detective Agency and helps Bond in the novels *Diamonds Are Forever* and *Goldfinger*. CIA chief Allen Dulles calls Leiter back into CIA duty in the novel *Thunderball*, because he knows how well Bond and Leiter work together. Leiter arrives in Jamaica in the novel *The Man With The Golden Gun* and injures Scaramanga, paving the way for 007 to terminate the assassin.

In the films, Leiter first meets Bond at Kingston Harbour in *Dr. No*. He helps 007 discover more information about Dr. No's operation at Crab Key and arrives with his marines at the end to rescue Bond and Honey Ryder. In *Goldfinger*, Leiter briefs Bond on Auric Goldfinger at the Fontainebleau Hotel in Miami, Florida. Later, with his colleague Johnny, Leiter keeps a sharp watch on Bond's activities in Kentucky. Once Bond prevents Operation Grand Slam, Leiter escorts 007 to a plane waiting to fly him to Washington, D.C., so that the US

ON THE CASE *In Goldfinger, Leiter tells M 007 has landed.*

FAITHFUL FRIEND *In the Bahamas, Leiter keeps his eye on James Bond in* **Thunderball.**

BON VOYAGE *Leiter (on right) and Willard Whyte bid Bond and Tiffany farewell in* Diamonds Are Forever.

President can thank Bond personally. In *Thunderball*, Leiter flies around the islands of the Bahamas as 007 tries to locate two stolen nuclear weapons. In *Diamonds Are Forever*, Leiter provides

Morocco. Leiter instructs his two assistants, Ava and Liz, to bring 007 to the CIA's yacht after Bond fakes the assassination of KGB head General Pushkin. Leiter works for the DEA in Key West, Florida, at the time of the events of *Licence To Kill*.

In *Casino Royale*, Bond and Leiter meet for the first time at the casino in Montenegro. Leiter gives Bond $5 million to buy back into the Texas Hold 'Em poker game after Treasury officer Vesper Lynd refuses 007 further funds. In return, the CIA will get to apprehend Le Chiffre once 007 has cleaned him out.

DEA AGENT *Leiter hunts Sanchez on his wedding day.*

TEAM PLAYER *Leiter, partnered with his assistants Ava and Liz, reunites with Bond in Tangier, Morocco, to hunt arms dealer Brad Whitaker in* The Living Daylights.

ample assistance to Bond in Las Vegas and leads a helicopter raid on Blofeld's oil rig off the coast of Baja California, Mexico. *Live And Let Die* sees Leiter assisting 007 in New York City, New Orleans, and the island of San Monique as Bond investigates the activities of Dr. Kananga/Mr. Big. Leiter returns to the series in *The Living Daylights* keeping a sharp eye on American arms dealer Brad Whitaker's activities in Tangier,

In *Quantum of Solace*, Leiter works under CIA South American Section Chief Gregory Beam. Leiter criticizes the CIA's involvement with Dominic Greene. In La Paz, Bolivia, Beam involves Leiter in a trap to kill Bond, but Leiter tips Bond off and informs him that General Medrano cannot take over the Bolivian government until Greene bribes the Colonel of Police. M later tells Bond that Leiter has replaced Beam.

DRINKING BUDDIES *In a bar in downtown La Paz, Leiter tells Bond that General Medrano will pay off the army and police at the Perla de las Dunas hotel.*

LENKIN

APPEARANCE
Octopussy (1983)
STATUS Arrested
CHARACTERISTICS Nervous, extremely jittery art forger
PLAYED BY Peter Porteous

FABERGÉ FAKE *Lenkin worries that an inventory will reveal his and General Orlov's art forgery plot.*

Lenkin is a brilliant forger of Russian jewelry in league with Soviet General Orlov to replace the treasures in the Kremlin Art Repository with near perfect forgeries. Lenkin begs Orlov to retrieve an original Fabergé Egg stolen in transit by agent 009. An unscheduled inventory of the repository will take place in two days time, and Lenkin desperately needs the egg to guarantee that their forgery scheme will not be revealed.

Later, KGB head General Gogol becomes suspicious of General Orlov's activities within the Repository. Gogol brings in Hermitage Museum curator Borchoi to the Repository's vaults. Borchoi determines that the treasures are indeed fakes, leading KGB agents to arrest Lenkin.

LOPEZ, HECTOR

APPEARANCE
Licence To Kill (1989)
STATUS Living; whereabouts unknown
CHARACTERISTICS Adaptable, looks good in a uniform
PLAYED BY Pedro Armendáriz Jr.

Signs and banners around Isthmus City give the impression that Hector Lopez is a popular and effective president. However, he is merely a puppet ruler, completely under the control of drug lord Franz Sanchez, who reminds Hector that "you're only president for life."

After Sanchez is killed by James

Bond, Lopez's reign of power could be in doubt. Instead, Lopez manages to avoid both political upheaval at home and condemnation abroad and remains in power. What is more, he now boasts a trophy girlfriend: the beautiful Lupe Lamora, formerly Sanchez's mistress.

LOTI

APPEARANCE
Licence To Kill (1989)
STATUS Dead; shot by Heller
CHARACTERISTICS Purposeful, strong-willed, unflinching
PLAYED BY Diana Lee-Hsu

Loti is partnered with fellow Hong Kong narcotic agent Kwang who, posing as an Asian drug lord, conducts business with Franz Sanchez in Isthmus City. Loti, specially trained in ninja fighting techniques, attacks Bond when he attempts to assassinate Sanchez.

Loti and Kwang capture Bond and take him to their safe house outside of the city. They fear that Bond's attempt to kill Sanchez will ruin their infiltration of the drug lord's operation. After a force led by Heller, Sanchez's chief of security, destroys part of the house, Heller himself bursts in and shoots Loti dead.

M

APPEARANCE/PLAYED BY

Dr. No (1962), From Russia With Love (1963), Goldfinger (1964), Thunderball (1965), You Only Live Twice (1967), On Her Majesty's Secret Service (1969), Diamonds Are Forever (1971), Live And Let Die (1973), The Man With The Golden Gun (1974), The Spy Who Loved Me (1977), Moonraker (1979) (Bernard Lee); Octopussy (1983), A View To A Kill (1985), The Living Daylights (1987), Licence To Kill (1989) (Robert Brown); GoldenEye (1995), Tomorrow Never Dies (1997), The World Is Not Enough (1999), Die Another Day (2002), Casino Royale (2006), Quantum Of Solace (2008) (Judi Dench)

STATUS Living; MI6 headquarters

CHARACTERISTICS Tough, decisive, disapproving, authoritative

M serves as the head of the British Secret Service, known alternately in the films as MI7 and MI6. M sends James Bond on missions from his wood-paneled London office. M stands as the bulwark of the British establishment, a Churchillian figurehead of England's glorious past and continued importance on the world stage.

> "If you carry a 00 number, it means you're **licenced to kill.** Not get killed."
>
> **M to Bond**

Ian Fleming created a stern, almost parental relationship between M and 007 that continues in the films. M recognizes Bond's unique skills and innate talent but barely tolerates his often-unorthodox methods and

NEW CHIEF M (Robert Brown) hands 007 his assignment for Operation Trove in Octopussy.

hedonistic lifestyle.

Fleming gave M's real name as Vice-Admiral (ret.) Sir Miles Messervy KCMG in his final novel The Man With The Golden Gun. M runs the secret service with naval efficiency, expecting his staff and agents to be available whenever duty calls. His gruff exterior and solid sense of judgment inspire unyielding loyalty from those who work for him, particularly his top agent, 007.

M's final naval appointment was to the battlecruiser HMS Repulse, sunk by Japanese torpedoes on December 10 1941. He keeps the ship's bell as the doorbell of his home. M resides in a small Regency manor-house on the edge of Windsor Forest called Quarterdeck.

M's hobby is painting watercolors of England's wild orchids (in the films his hobby is lepidoptery—the study of butterflies and moths). He smokes a pipe and keeps his tobacco in a jar made from an old navy shell. M is a member of two gentleman's clubs: the Seniors, a club for ex-Navy, and Blades. Fleming's M remains a lifelong bachelor.

The character of M was inspired by several figures from Fleming's past. At the top of the list is Rear Admiral John H. Godfrey, Fleming's commanding officer in Naval Intelligence during World War II. Fleming acquired the idea for the letter M from Sir Mansfield Smith-Cumming, who, as head of the Secret Service, signed documents with the letter "C," a tradition continued by his replacements. Long before

Fleming himself became involved in intelligence work, he addressed letters to his mother Eve with the letter "M."

For Bond's first 11 screen missions, M comes very close to Fleming's version of the character. In the film Dr. No, it appears that M may be relatively new to his position because he informs 007 that since he became "head of MI7, there's been a 40 per cent drop in 00 operative casualties, and I want it to stay that way."

M does not feature in the film For Your Eyes Only, and a new M gives 007 his assignment in Octopussy. This M appears to be Admiral Hargreaves, who a few years earlier served as flag officer of submarines for the Royal Navy. He exhibits mild contempt for 007's reputation and personality and revokes Bond's "licence to kill" in the subsequent eponymous film.

AUTHORITY FIGURE A similar portrait of M (Bernard Lee) hangs in the MI6 Remote Operations Centre at Castle Thane in Scotland.

By *GoldenEye*, a new, female M takes charge of MI6. She views Bond as a "sexist, misogynist dinosaur, a relic of the Cold War," but like her predecessors, she sees a use for Bond and his methods.

This M read law at Oxford and has children. She needles Bond about his womanizing reputation. Bond's friend, senior analyst Bill Tanner, refers to her as "the evil Queen of numbers" for her reliance on statistical analysis.

In *Casino Royale*, M presides over Bond's initiation as an "00" agent, a narrative shift that relaunches both Bond and M in the 21st century. This M appears to be a veteran administrator of MI6 who dates back to the era of the Cold War and claims to miss the autonomy she formerly enjoyed. She lives in a modern secure flat accessed by a private elevator and has a husband. M acts as a guiding force in Bond's painful transformation from a skilled agent who sometimes fails to see the bigger picture to a hardened operative whose actions are guided by larger objectives.

In *Quantum of Solace,* M is concerned about Bond's mental state after Vesper's betrayal. Angered by his killing of suspects Mitchell and Slate, as well as Guy Haines's bodyguard (a member of Special Branch), she tries to control Bond's activities by cancelling his credit cards and placing an alert on all his passports. After the deaths of René Mathis and Agent Fields, she removes Bond from active duty, but he escapes MI6 custody. Later, M feigns surprise that Bond spares Yusef Kabira's life. His emotions now in check, Bond walks away, ready to be the professional she expects.

In the novel *Dr. No*, Bond sees M after convalescing in hospital and Fleming notes: "M was the symbol of normality he had longed for." M does represent a hoped-for normality. In a world filled with wars and upheavals, we all hope somewhere a sensible, reliable figure sits behind a desk addressing the outrages of the day with an even hand and watching over the great game of global espionage with clear gray eyes.

KIDNAPPED *M (Judi Dench) finds herself in deadly peril when Elektra King imprisons her in* The World Is Not Enough.

NO REGRETS *"Bond, I need you back," says M at the conclusion of A Quantum Of Solace. "I never left," Bond replies.*

"**I have to know I can trust you and that you know who to trust.**"

M to Bond

M (continued)

In *Skyfall*, M finds herself in political hot water when a hard drive containing the names of virtually every NATO agent secretly embedded in global terrorist organizations falls into enemy hands in Istanbul. She instructs MI6 agent Eve Moneypenny to take a high-risk shot while Bond is grappling with the enemy agent who has stolen the list. Eve accidentally hits Bond, the enemy agent escapes, and Bond is presumed killed.

Professional to the core, M hides her feelings at the loss of her top agent. She later writes Bond's obituary, describing 007 as "an exemplar of British fortitude."

Following the national security breach, M is summoned to meet the new Intelligence and Security Committee Chairman Gareth Mallory, who informs her that she will "voluntarily retire" in two months' time. To make matters worse, M later witnesses a cyber-terrorist attack on MI6 headquarters that results in eight members of staff losing their lives.

Unknown to M, Bond survived Moneypenny's shot and has been hiding out in a Turkish seaside town. When he hears news of the attack on MI6, he shows up at M's London apartment. He is furious that M did not

ENDGAME *(above)* Silva holds a gun to M's head before begging her to end both their lives with a single bullet.

allow him to finish the job and secure the list. She tells him it was a judgment call: lose him or all the other agents on the list. Refusing to apologise, she is nevertheless gratified that Bond has returned to aid MI6 in its hour of need.

However, he will have to be declared fit for active service. Bond fails physical, shooting, and psychological tests, but M conceals this from Bond and Mallory. She sends Bond to Shanghai to pursue the agent that stole the list, now identified as Patrice. Meanwhile, the first five MI6 agents' real identities are posted on the

BACK IN TIME
After escaping from London in Bond's Aston Martin DB5, Bond and M arrive at Skyfall, the Scottish estate where Bond grew up.

"**Regret is unprofessional.**"
M

web, resulting in three agents' deaths. This appalling event places M under further pressure.

Bond's mission results in the capture of cyber-terrorist Silva. After confronting Silva, M reveals to Bond that when she ran Station H, Hong Kong, Silva, born Tiago Rodriguez, was one of her most brilliant agents. When she learned he was hacking the Chinese and jeopardizing the handover of Hong Kong from British to Chinese rule, she traded him to the Chinese in exchange for six agents and a peaceful transition. Since learning of her betrayal, Silva has longed to get his revenge.

At a Board of Inquiry in Whitehall, M is harangued by Clair Dowar MP, who accuses her department of being obsolete. M argues that the espionage world must now do battle in the shadows. She then quotes from Alfred, Lord Tennyson's poem *Ulysses*, (a favorite of her late husband's), stressing British fortitude in the face of inevitable decline.

Meanwhile, Silva has escaped from an MI6 high-security cell. He bursts into the inquiry chamber, gun blazing. Mallory saves M's life by taking a bullet in the shoulder, and Bond arrives to whisk M away to the temporary safety of his childhood home, Skyfall, in Scotland. There, M helps Bond and Skyfall's gamekeeper Kincade prepare booby traps for Silva's inevitable attack. M apologizes to Bond for recent errors of judgment, to which he replies that she was only doing her job.

During Silva's attack on Skyfall, M fires Bond's Walther PPK at one of Silva's men, but misses and is wounded. Taking refuge in a nearby chapel, she is attacked by Silva. Bond kills Silva and cradles M in his arms. As M dies she tells him, "At least I got one thing right"—referring to her successful shaping of Bond as MI6's top agent.

Following her tragic death, M is awarded the GCMG (Dame Grand Cross) with highest honors. In her will, she bequeaths Bond her Royal Doulton British bulldog, complete with Union Jack emblem, that always rested on her desk. An inscription on the box reads: "From the estate of Olivia Mansfield, bequeathed to James Bond." At the end of *Skyfall*, Gareth Mallory assumes the role of M as the new head of MI6.

MALLORY, GARETH

APPEARANCE
Skyfall (2012)
STATUS Living; running MI6
CHARACTERISTICS More to him than meets the eye; authoritative; a good shot
PLAYED BY Ralph Fiennes

Gareth Mallory, the new Chairman of the Intelligence and Security Committee regulating MI6, oversees the transition between M's "voluntary retirement" and her unnamed successor's arrival. He is initially skeptical about Bond's capability for field work and suggests Bond take retirement.

Impeccably tailored, trim, and controlled, Mallory was once an SAS Lieutenant Colonel in the Hereford Regiment in Northern Ireland, where he spent three months in IRA custody. He views M's philosophy of doing battle in the shadows as old-fashioned and criticizes her for being sentimental about Bond. Believing 007 is past his prime, he sends field agent Eve Moneypenny to Macau to aid him.

During M's Board of Inquiry, when M is being chastised by Clair Dowar MP for losing the list of NATO agents, Mallory shows a more supportive side to his character. He interrupts Dowar and suggests M should be allowed to have her say. M's persuasive argument that conducting battle in the shadows is the only way to fight the opaque enemies of today registers with him.

When cyber-terrorist Silva barges in to kill M, Mallory takes a bullet in the shoulder, saving her life. He then

BRAVE NEW WORLD *(above) Established in his wood-paneled office, Mallory gives Bond a new top-secret mission.*

grabs a fallen police officer's Glock 17 and engages in a gun battle to ward off Silva.

Mallory supports Q and Chief of Staff Bill Tanner as, acting unofficially, they place a digital trail of clues to ensure that Silva will follow Bond and M to Skyfall. Following M's tragic death, her successor is finally named. The new M is none other than Gareth Mallory.

Mallory: So 007... lots to be done. Are you ready to get back to work?
Bond:
With pleasure, M, with pleasure...

MARY

APPEARANCE
Dr. No (1962)
STATUS Dead; brutally shot
CHARACTERISTICS Loyal, efficient
PLAYED BY Dolores Keator

Mary Prescott works as Commander Strangways's secretary in Kingston, Jamaica. After Dr. No's Three Blind Mice assassins eliminate Strangways, they target Mary, who prepares to contact London using an ultra-shortwave radio hidden in a bookcase. The Three Blind Mice fire bullets into Mary's chest, killing her instantly.

In Fleming's novel, her name is Mary Trueblood.

"Being dead doesn't mean one can't still be helpful."

Mathis to 007

MATHIS

APPEARANCE
Casino Royale (2006), Quantum Of Solace (2008)
STATUS Dies in Bond's arms
CHARACTERISTICS Charming and confident; a man of the world
PLAYED BY Giancarlo Giannini

In *Casino Royale*, René Mathis is 007's contact in Montenegro. Unable to outbid international criminal Le Chiffre for the Chief of Police's services, Mathis arranges for the Chief's arrest.

Mathis gives Bond a bugging device that Bond slips into Le Chiffre's inhaler. Mathis also knows the rules of Texas Hold 'Em poker well enough to explain the game to Treasury official Vesper Lynd.

When Bond tries to rescue the kidnapped Vesper, Le Chiffre captures him and remarks, "your friend Mathis is really my friend Mathis." This is a lie told to conceal that Vesper is the real traitor. After Bond survives Le Chiffre's torture, his suspicions intensify when Mathis tries to extract information from him as he recovers. Two MI6 agents taser Mathis and drag him away. After Vesper's betrayal, M suggests to Bond that Vesper's actions cleared Mathis of suspicion. Bond tells M to keep "sweating him."

After much interrogation, MI6 clears Mathis, purchasing him a villa in Talamone, Italy, which he shares with a lady friend named Gemma. When Bond arrives and inquires about Bolivia, Mathis reveals he was stationed in South America for seven years.

In La Paz, Mathis contacts an old friend, Carlos, Bolivian National Police Force Colonel. Mathis is unaware, however, that Carlos is in league with Dominic Greene and General Medrano plot to take over the Bolivian government. Two of Carlos's officers shoot Mathis, intending to pin the murder on Bond, but Bond dispatches the officers. As he dies, Mathis

LAST MOMENTS *Bond cradles the dying Mathis in his arms.*

begs Bond to forgive Vesper— "She gave everything for you"—and also to forgive himself. Determined to suppress his grief at Mathis's death so as not to compromise his mission, Bond deposits his friend's body in a dumpster and takes money from his wallet. "He wouldn't care," Bond explains to Camille.

Mathis appears in two Fleming novels: *Casino Royale* and *From Russia With Love*.

MAX

APPEARANCE
For Your Eyes Only (1981),
The Living Daylights (1987)
STATUS Living; whereabouts unknown
CHARACTERISTICS Talkative, good
listener, retentive memory
PLAYED BY Krone; voice: Jack Hedley

A Blue and Gold Macaw owned by
marine archaeologist Sir Timothy
Havelock and his wife, Iona, Max
provides vital information to Bond
during Operation Undertow. When
Max hears 007 mention the "ATAC,"
he repeats the phrase he heard from
Soviet agent Aris Kristatos, "ATAC
to St. Cyril's," giving Bond a lead on
where to find Kristatos.

MI6 later adopts Max and he
appears in the Blayden safe house in
The Living Daylights.

PRETTY POLLY *Max loves pistachio nuts,
enjoys playing, and has excellent recall.*

MEI-LEI

APPEARANCE
Goldfinger (1964)
STATUS Living; whereabouts unknown
CHARACTERISTICS Highly attentive,
always on hand to help
PLAYED BY Mai Ling

Mei-Lei is the stewardess on
Goldfinger's personal Lockheed
JetStar. When pilot Pussy Galore flies
Bond, who has been abducted, into
Friendship Airport, Baltimore,
Mei-Lei makes 007 a martini—
shaken, not stirred. Pussy tells Mei-Lei
to keep an eye on Bond while he
changes his clothes, and she spies on
him in the airplane lavatory. She
reportedly moved to Japan after the
collapse of Operation Grand Slam.

MENDEL

APPEARANCE
Casino Royale (2006)
STATUS Living; whereabouts unknown
CHARACTERISTICS Business-focused
PLAYED BY Ludger Pistor

A jovial Swiss banker representing
the Basel Bank, Mendel oversees the
transfer of all funds during the poker
game at Casino Royale. He arrives
with a briefcase computer at the
clinic where Bond recovers so that
Treasury officer Vesper Lynd can
transfer Bond's winnings to the
government. M later contacts 007 to
ask why the Treasury hasn't received
the money. Bond calls Mendel, only
to learn that someone is withdrawing
the funds. As Bond suspects, it is
Vesper Lynd.

MIKLOS, ROSIKA

APPEARANCE
The Living Daylights (1987)
STATUS Living; whereabouts unknown
CHARACTERISTICS Resourceful
PLAYED BY Julie T. Wallace

A Trans-Siberian pipeline worker
based in Bratislava, Czechoslovakia,
Rosika Miklos has assisted British
Intelligence in the past. She helps
Bond with KGB General Koskov's
defection to the West. Rosika
distracts the pipeline supervisor's
attention with her ample cleavage
while the control panel signals
numerous alerts as a scouring plug,
or "pig," shoots through the line with
Koskov inside.

MINISTER OF DEFENCE

APPEARANCE
Tomorrow Never Dies (1997)
STATUS Living; based in London
CHARACTERISTICS Hears both
sides before reaching a decision
PLAYED BY Julian Fellowes

During the early hours of the South
China Sea crisis, the Minister of
Defence referees a tense debate between
warmongering Admiral Roebuck and
the more cautious M. He solves the
dispute by giving M 48 hours to
investigate the sinking of HMS
Devonshire before Roebuck sends the
British fleet into striking distance of
the Chinese Air Force.

MISHKIN, DIMITRI

APPEARANCE GoldenEye (1995)
STATUS Dead; killed by Ourumov
CHARACTERISTICS Intelligent,
formidable, speaks his mind
PLAYED BY Tchéky Karyo

Defence Minister Dimitri Mishkin
supervises the meeting where General
Ourumov claims Siberian separatists
detonated the GoldenEye and
conducted the massacre at Severnaya.
Mishkin considers this presumptuous.

He later interrogates Natalya
Simonova and Bond and discovers
Ourumov's connection to the
GoldenEye detonation. Ourumov
interrupts the interrogation and kills
the defenseless minister.

MONEYPENNY, MISS

APPEARANCE/PLAYED BY

Dr. No (1962), From Russia With Love (1963), Goldfinger (1964), Thunderball (1965), You Only Live Twice (1967), On Her Majesty's Secret Service (1969), Diamonds Are Forever (1971), Live And Let Die (1973), The Man With The Golden Gun (1974), The Spy Who Loved Me (1977), Moonraker (1979), For Your Eyes Only (1981), Octopussy (1983), A View To A Kill (1985) (Lois Maxwell); The Living Daylights (1987), Licence To Kill (1989) (Caroline Bliss); GoldenEye (1995), Tomorrow Never Dies (1997), The World Is Not Enough (1999), Die Another Day (2002) (Samantha Bond)

STATUS Living

CHARACTERISTICS Highly efficient, tolerant, loyal, good sense of humor

Miss Moneypenny is the long-serving secretary to James Bond's boss, M. Ian Fleming sums up her character in the novel *Thunderball*, when he reveals that she "often dreamed hopelessly about Bond," but never acted on her feelings. Details Fleming reveals about her are that she has warm lips, doesn't smoke, owns a poodle, and started her career in the Cipher Department.

Moneypenny is not an especially memorable character in the novels—in fact, Fleming gives the secretaries Loelia Ponsonby and later Mary Goodnight more prominence. In the films, Moneypenny often has an important role to play. Her welcoming, easy-going flirtatiousness helps to establish Bond's irresistibility to women and contrasts well with the femme fatales and pliable heroines Bond encounters on his missions. In addition, Moneypenny often delivers important plot exposition.

When Ian Fleming first met Moneypenny actress Lois Maxwell, he said to her, "When I wrote Miss Moneypenny, I envisaged a tall, elegant woman with the most kissable lips in the world, and you, my dear, are the epitome of that dream of mine." Fleming based the character on two particular women— "Paddy" Bennett, who worked with him in Naval Intelligence, and Miss Pettigrew, private secretary to SIS chief

007: What gives?

Moneypenny:
Me, given an ounce of encouragement.

BOND BADINAGE *The verbal jousts between Moneypenny (Lois Maxwell) and 007 were a highlight of many movies, including* On Her Majesty's Secret Service *(left) and* The Man With The Golden Gun *(right).*

Stewart Menzies. In the first draft of *Casino Royale*, Fleming gave her the name of Miss Pettavel or "Petty," but he changed it during revisions, adopting the name Moneypenny from his brother Peter's incomplete novel, *The Sett*. Moneypenny's first name is never revealed in the novels or films, although sometimes Bond nicknames her "Penny."

Moneypenny's relationship with 007 has varied from film to film. In *Dr. No* and *From Russia With Love*,

Moneypenny flirts with Bond, but there is nothing hopeless in her attitude. In *Goldfinger*, Moneypenny actively attempts to interest Bond in a relationship, making wistful comments about marriage, a theme repeated when *Goldfinger's* director, Guy Hamilton, returns to the series with *Diamonds Are Forever*. While in *You Only Live Twice*, Bond is nothing short of dismissive when Moneypenny urges him to say, "I love you" to her (a recognition code, as it turns out). In *On Her Majesty's Secret Service*, there is genuine emotion between the two. She rewrites Bond's letter of resignation and, at 007's wedding, Bond and Moneypenny share a look that conveys both tenderness and admiration.

In *Live And Let Die*, a sisterly Moneypenny helps to hide Bond's latest paramour to prevent M discovering her. This marks the

> ## "Moneypenny, what would I do without you?"
> **007**

When Timothy Dalton took over as Bond, and Caroline Bliss became Moneypenny, the character found herself with a hair bun, a pencil behind the ear, librarian glasses, and a hopeless crush on 007. With Pierce Brosnan's introduction in *GoldenEye*, Samantha Bond's Moneypenny returned the character to that of Bond's sexual equal, willing to flirt as much on her terms as on his. In *Tomorrow Never Dies*, she teases 007 about him being asked to "pump" a former girlfriend "for information;" however, in *The World Is Not Enough*, she is dropping hints about marriage. In *Die Another Day*, Moneypenny finally manages to be alone with Bond, but only in virtual reality.

Moneypenny's entire character has been predicated on the premise of unrequited desire. Any relationship she may have with Bond can only be imagined by her as she sees Bond

OTHERWISE ENGAGED
Bond is intrigued to learn that a gentleman has taken Moneypenny (Samantha Bond) to the theater in GoldenEye.

UP CLOSE BUT IMPERSONAL *Moneypenny finally gets a chance to live out her fantasy of a wild romantic fling with Bond, but only courtesy of Q's latest virtual reality gadget.*

point where Moneypenny's relationship with Bond changes, and the flirting temporarily stops. In *Octopussy*, Moneypenny has a younger assistant, Penelope Smallbone.

sweeping in and out on his adventures. She is, in many ways, a representative of the audience—an ordinary person, intrigued and seduced by the elegant secret agent whom she only occasionally encounters.

MONEYPENNY (continued)

Miss Moneypenny is reintroduced into the Bond film series in *Skyfall* as a field agent named Eve.

Eve first aids Bond in Istanbul by driving a Land Rover Defender to pursue the mercenary Patrice, who has stolen a top-secret MI6 hard drive. Eve and Bond are soon separated, and Eve navigates Istanbul with the help of Chief of Staff Bill Tanner, stationed at MI6 headquarters in London. The breakneck chase leads Eve, Patrice, and Bond to an Istanbul bridge. Patrice and Bond vault off the bridge, landing atop a speeding train; Eve drives the Land Rover alongside the train, aiding Bond by informing him of Patrice's actions and alerting M to Bond's status. Eve eventually runs out of road. Armed with an M16 A4 assault rifle, she alerts MI6 that the train, on which Bond is fighting Patrice, is about to enter a tunnel. To prevent Patrice escaping with the hard drive, M orders Eve to "take the shot," even though Eve points out that she cannot guarantee that she'll hit Patrice and miss Bond. M orders her to fire regardless. Eve's shot accidentally hits Bond. He plummets into a river and Patrice gets away.

IN THE FIELD
Eve abandons her Land Rover to pursue enemy operative Patrice in Istanbul.

> **Bond:** In your defense, a moving target is much harder to hit.
>
> **Moneypenny:** Then you better keep moving.

Eve is temporarily suspended for "killing" 007. When Bond returns to London alive three months later, she informs Bond that she is now assisting the Intelligence and Security Committee Chairman Gareth Mallory during the transition period between M's "voluntary retirement" and her unnamed successor's arrival.

Eve next arrives in Macau to aid Bond at Mallory's request. They flirt with one another and she shaves 007.

At the Floating Dragon Casino, Eve serves as Bond's back-up and saves his life by knocking one of Severine's bodyguards unconscious as he is about to fire a Steyr M9-A1 handgun at Bond.

Eve is present at M's Board of Inquiry hearing in London. Silva bursts in to murder M, but Bond arrives, kicking a Glock 17 to Eve, who assists in the ensuing gun battle. She also aids the escape of government officials, including Clair Dowar, MP.

After M's funeral, Eve presents Bond with a Royal Doulton British Bulldog that M bequeathed him in her will. She informs 007 that she's not returning to the field, having elected to take a desk job as assistant to the new M—Gareth Mallory.

Eve finally reveals her surname to Bond. Her name is Eve Moneypenny, and she predicts that they will share one or two more "close shaves" in the future.

MACAO MEETING *(opposite) Eve shows up in Macau to assist Bond and soon experiences the first of their close shaves.*

M's BEQUEST *(left) Eve presents Bond with a box containing M's china bulldog. "Maybe it was her way of telling you to take a desk job." "Just the opposite," replies Bond.*

A NEW ROLE *(below) As the new M's assistant, Eve formally introduces herself to Bond as Eve Moneypenny.*

MUNGER, SIR DONALD

APPEARANCE
Diamonds Are Forever (1971)
STATUS Unknown
CHARACTERISTICS Business-minded
PLAYED BY Laurence Naismith

Sir Donald Munger serves as chairman of the Diamond Syndicate, which controls most of the legal diamond trading in the world. Sir Donald raises concerns with the Prime Minister regarding the increase in smuggling from South African mines, urging the British Secret Service to become involved.

NEVADA SHERIFF

APPEARANCE
Diamonds Are Forever (1971)
STATUS Unknown
CHARACTERISTICS Out of his depth
PLAYED BY Leroy Hollis

WW Techtronics security contacts the Clark County, Nevada Sheriff's office after Bond steals a moonbuggy. The Sheriff and numerous Las Vegas police cars pursue Bond as he drives them in circles in a Mustang Mach 1. After numerous crashes, the Sheriff finds he has the only remaining drivable car. He tries to follow Bond when the Mustang tilts onto two wheels to drive through a narrow ally, but the Sheriff merely flips his car over. He later transfers to the Louisiana State Police.

NIKOLI, CAPT.

APPEARANCE
The World Is Not Enough (1999)
STATUS Dead; poisoned
CHARACTERISTICS Too trusting
PLAYED BY Justus Von Dohnanyi

Nikoli, casino and caviar factory owner Valentin Zukovsky's nephew, is captain of a nuclear submarine in the Russian Navy. Billionaire heiress Elektra King pays Valentin $1 million to have Nikoli smuggle Russian machinery to Maiden's Tower in the Bosphoros. Ex-KGB assassin Renard poisons Nikoli and his crew, hides stolen plutonium in the submarine's reactor, and pilots it into Istanbul.

OLYMPE

APPEARANCE On Her Majesty's Secret Service (1969)
STATUS Living; whereabouts unknown
CHARACTERISTICS Skilled at chess
PLAYED BY Virginia North

Olympe is the secretary, lover, and chess opponent of Marc Ange Draco, head of the Union Corse. She is aware of most of his dealings, including trying to make Bond marry his daughter, Tracy. At Draco's birthday party, Olympe hints to Tracy that Draco is arranging something. Olympe's verbal slip causes Tracy to confront Draco and demand he give 007 information about Blofeld without obligation.

PEPPER, SHERIFF J. W.

APPEARANCE
Live And Let Die (1973), The Man With The Golden Gun (1974)
STATUS Living
CHARACTERISTICS Overbearing; uncouth
PLAYED BY Clifton James

Sheriff J. W. Pepper spends his afternoons ticketing speeders and taking care of local problems, like shooting Mrs. Pearson's rabid dog. When he catches Harlem gangster Mr. Big's henchman Adam in his car trying to cut off Bond's escape in a boat, Pepper relishes arresting a black man a little too much.

Pepper is unprepared for the arrival of Bond and the boats giving chase. Bond leaps his craft over Pepper's head and another boat crashes into Pepper's car. A third boat sails overhead, letting Adam escape. Pepper commandeers a State Trooper car, coordinates law enforcement efforts, and yells and screams at everyone to no avail. He enlists his brother-in-law Billy Bob, but Adam steals Billy Bob's jet boat.

When Pepper catches up with Bond, he discovers that he is a British secret agent working with the cooperation of the CIA. Stunned at the destruction left by Bond, he asks, "A secret agent? On whose side?"

Bond meets Pepper again while chasing Francisco Scaramanga in Bangkok. Pepper first sees Bond when he tours with his wife, Maybelle. Later, while car shopping, Pepper finds himself in a stolen AMC Hornet with Bond. He is an enthusiastic passenger when Bond spiral-jumps across a canal attempting to catch Scaramanga. Unfortunately, Bond fails to catch the assassin, and the Thai police arrest Pepper.

> "What are you? **Some kinda doomsday machine, boy?**"
> Sheriff Pepper to 007

A RELAXING HOLIDAY J.W. and Maybelle Pepper (Jay Sidow) sail through the Bangkok klongs.

PERLA DE LAS DUNAS RECEPTIONIST

APPEARANCE
Quantum Of Solace (2008)
STATUS Unknown
CHARACTERISTICS Vulnerable
PLAYED BY Oona Chaplin

The receptionist's screams as General Medrano attempts to assault her rekindle painful childhood memories for Camille of Medrano strangling her mother and sister. Camille kills Medrano's lieutenant and guard and attacks Medrano, knocking the receptionist out of the way. It is unknown whether the receptionist survives when the hotel explodes.

PINDER

APPEARANCE
Thunderball (1965)
STATUS Living; whereabouts unknown
CHARACTERISTICS Businesslike, calm
PLAYED BY Earl Cameron

TEAM PLAYER *Bond and Paula meet Bahamian contact Pinder on the Nassau streets.*

Pinder, a native Bahamian, works for the British Secret Service in Nassau. He provides a location headquarters for Bond in the basement of his shop, which sells boating supplies. He coordinates with local officials, such as the governor, to provide Bond with the material and logistical support he needs.

PLEYDELL-SMITH

APPEARANCE
Dr. No (1962)
STATUS Living; whereabouts unknown
CHARACTERISTICS Likes bridge and pipe smoking
PLAYED BY Louis Blaazer

The Principal Secretary at Government House in Kingston, Pleydell-Smith offers assistance to 007. Unfortunately for him, his secretary, Miss Taro, works as a Dr. No minion who leaks vital information from his office.

At the end of the novel, Pleydell-Smith's wife, Betty, agrees to take Honey Rider, a beautiful Jamaican shell diver, under her wing and perhaps help her acquire a job at the Jamaica Institute.

PRIME MINISTER

APPEARANCE
For Your Eyes Only (1981)
STATUS Living
CHARACTERISTICS World leader
PLAYED BY Janet Brown

Newly-elected Prime Minister Margaret Thatcher calls 007 to congratulate him on completing Operation Undertow. The call is placed to Bond's speaker Seiko watch on the *Triana*, where Bond and marine biologist Melina Havelock prepare for a moonlight swim. Bond leaves his watch next to Melina's talkative macaw, Max, who tells the Prime Minister to "give us a kiss." Thatcher blushes at "Bond's" flirtations.

PUSHKIN, GENERAL LEONID

APPEARANCE
The Living Daylights (1987)
STATUS Living; whereabouts unknown
CHARACTERISTICS Capable, tough
PLAYED BY John Rhys-Davies

When General Gogol departs as the head of the KGB to become head of the Foreign Service, Pushkin takes over his role. What Pushkin doesn't count on is KGB General Georgi Koskov, who defects to the West and informs the British that Pushkin has begun operation *smiert spionam* to eliminate western agents.

M orders 007 to kill Pushkin, but Bond, who knows that the KGB head is "tough and resourceful," confronts him at the Hotel Ile De France in Tangier, Morocco. Pushkin convinces Bond of his innocence, and they plan to turn the tables on Koskov and his ally Whitaker. Bond fakes Pushkin's death and foils

KGB CALLING *Pushkin arrives to take Kara Milovy in for questioning.*

Koskov's plan in Afghanistan. Pushkin later arrives at Whitaker's estate, arrests Koskov, and orders him sent back to Moscow.

PUSS-FELLER

APPEARANCE
Dr. No (1962)
STATUS Living; whereabouts unknown
CHARACTERISTICS Well-built, immaculate, affable
PLAYED BY Lester Prendergast

Puss-Feller owns a restaurant-nightclub on Kingston Harbour, Jamaica, where performers such as Byron Lee and The Dragoneers sing local hits like "Jump Up Jamaica." According to Bond's guide, Quarrel, Puss-Feller "wrestles alligators." In Fleming's novel, he acquires his name from wrestling an octopus and escaping with his life.

COLD LOOK *Puss-Feller is hostile to Bond, until put wise by the CIA's Felix Leiter.*

Q

APPEARANCE/PLAYED BY
Dr. No (1962) (Peter Burton); From Russia With Love (1963), Goldfinger (1964), Thunderball (1965), You Only Live Twice (1967), On Her Majesty's Secret Service (1969), Diamonds Are Forever (1971), The Man With The Golden Gun (1974), The Spy Who Loved Me (1977), Moonraker (1979), For Your Eyes Only (1981), Octopussy (1983), A View To A Kill (1985), The Living Daylights (1987), Licence To Kill (1989), GoldenEye (1995), Tomorrow Never Dies (1997), The World Is Not Enough (1999) (Desmond Llewelyn); Die Another Day (2002) (John Cleese)

STATUS Living; spends most of his time at MI6 headquarters

CHARACTERISTICS An endlessly inventive scientific genius

Q runs that rarified section of British Intelligence that transforms the ordinary into the lethal, the pedestrian into the remarkable, and the insignificant into the life-saving. Q, also known as Major Boothroyd, stands as proof of the superiority of British ingenuity and craftsmanship. His initial stands for Quartermaster, but Q's duties reach far beyond merely dispensing gear. Q Branch runs a full research and development operation of monumental scale.

Q's origins can be traced to World War II, where Ian Fleming often had to liaise with the office of Charles Frasier-Smith who provided inventive ways to conceal maps, compasses and guns to those moving behind enemy lines. Fleming mentions Q briefly in the novel Casino Royale, with M instructing Bond, "Talk to Q about rooms and trains, and any equipment you want."

The cinematic character's origins begin with the novel Dr. No, where Fleming introduces the Armourer, aka Major Boothroyd. Fleming based the Major on Glasgow gun expert Geoffrey Boothroyd who

HIDDEN TREASURES Q (Desmond Llewelyn) gives Bond, Anya Amasova, General Gogol, and M a tour of his Egyptian facilities in The Spy Who Loved Me.

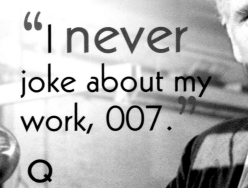

" I never joke about my work, 007. "

Q

wrote the author to complain about Bond's use of a Beretta .25, which he termed "a lady's gun." The filmmakers reproduce this scene in the first Bond film. With *From Russia With Love*, the filmmakers wished to echo the scene from *Dr. No* where 007 receives equipment in M's office before leaving on his mission. In that novel, Bond uses a

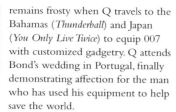

HANDY LUGGAGE *Q's suitcase is filled with gadgets to assist Bond in Isthmus City in* Licence To Kill.

trick briefcase, and the filmmakers asked Richard Maibaum to script a scene where Major Boothroyd presents this to 007. When actor Peter Burton proved unavailable, Desmond Llewelyn stepped into the role, which was re-christened Q in the dialogue (but not the credits). Only KGB agent Anya Amasova refers to Q as Major Boothroyd in the films.

In *Goldfinger*, Q's irritation with 007 for destroying his equipment is clear. He displays his satisfaction with his ever-more lethal inventions. Bond treats him as a slightly dotty genius. The relationship between the pair

GONE FISHING *Q manages to fit in a spot of relaxation while waiting for Bond in* Octopussy.

GADGET CENTRAL *Q (John Cleese) shows 007 the room where he stores relics from past missions in* Die Another Day.

remains frosty when Q travels to the Bahamas (*Thunderball*) and Japan (*You Only Live Twice*) to equip 007 with customized gadgetry. Q attends Bond's wedding in Portugal, finally demonstrating affection for the man who has used his equipment to help save the world.

As the scope of Bond's adventures widened, so did the scope of Q's operation. Q Branch research labs servicing agents in Egypt, Brazil, and India hum with activity. Q's affection for 007 grows to the point that, in *Licence To Kill*, he travels to Isthmus City with a bag of gadgets to aid Bond on a private mission of vengeance.

Major Boothroyd retired in 1999, turning his department and title over to an assistant Bond dubbed R. The new Q proves to be just as effective in developing cutting-edge gadgetry and even more effective at topping Bond's quips with withering observations.

Q does not appear in *Casino Royale*, only the second film not to have any character called Q or Major Boothroyd.

Whenever James Bond enters Q's MI6 laboratory, he always finds the ingenious inventor and his technicians hard at work experimenting with new and intriguing gadget prototypes. Below is just a small sample of the many technical wonders Q has devised over the years which have yet to be put to deadly purpose "in the field."

BLAST OFF! *Q's leg cast conceals a rocket launcher.*

DON'T LOSE YOUR HEAD *Q's technician demonstrates exploding bolos in MI6's monastery headquarters.*

AN EAR FOR MUSIC *Q always has his finger on the pulse of contemporary culture, as demonstrated by this ghetto-blaster rocket launcher.*

SLEEPING SOMBRERO *A gaucho taking a siesta splits in two, revealing a firing gun.*

PIPE DOWN *In Castle Thane, Q's technician fires bagpipes that house a machine gun and a flamethrower.*

SMASHING, Q! *Q's assistant Smithers demonstrates how his fake plaster cast can take out the enemy.*

Q (continued)

Skyfall reintroduces Q as a slender young man in his twenties. Q first meets 007 in the Sackler Room of London's National Portrait Gallery. After observing J. M. W. Turner's famous 1839 painting, *The Fighting Temeraire*, which shows the grand old warship being hauled to scrap "due to the inevitability of time," Q introduces himself to Bond as MI6's new quartermaster. Bond initially expresses disbelief. "You must be joking… you still have spots."

Acknowledging that the young technological genius and the experienced field agent both have a place in the intelligence world, Bond addresses him as Q for the first time. Q presents 007 with his ticket to Shanghai as well as a Walther PPK, customized so that only he can fire it, and a radio transmitter. Bond makes reference to the simplicity of the weapons, and Q responds that his department no longer makes such devices as exploding pens.

ART APPRECIATION *When Q sits down next to Bond in the National Gallery, Bond has no idea who this young man is. However, after some verbal sparring, they part on terms of mutual respect. "Brave new world," Bond wryly remarks.*

GOING UNDERGOUND *Hoping to discover Silva's plans from his computer, Q, with Bond's help, discovers a map of subterranean London.*

Later, when Bond has captured cyber-terrorist Silva and incarcerated him in MI6's temporary headquarters in London's catacombs, Q connects Silva's laptop to MI6's computer network in an attempt to decrypt the information on it.

Data from Silva's laptop soon corrupts MI6's computer systems, releasing Silva from his cell. On a three-dimensional map of London's subterranean tunnel network, Q

> Q: Age is no guarantee of efficiency.
> Bond: And youth is no guarantee of innovation.

tracks Silva with Bond in pursuit. Bond rescues M from Silva's attack at the Board of Inquiry and asks Q to leave an electronic trail for Silva to follow as they head to Bond's childhood home, Skyfall, in Scotland. Q knows that he has to make this "breadcrumb trail"

BREADCRUMB TRAIL As Chief of Staff Tanner looks on, Q creates a cunning series of clues for Silva, ensuring that he tracks M to Scotland.

convincing so that Silva doesn't smell a rat. Intelligence and Security Committee Chairman Gareth Mallory discovers Q explaining the plan to Chief of Staff Tanner and surprises them both by offering his support.

The new Q has one important thing in common with former MI6 quartermasters: he expects James Bond to return his equipment in one piece.

QUARREL

APPEARANCE
Dr. No (1962)
STATUS Dead; torched
CHARACTERISTICS Excellent seaman, good navigator
PLAYED BY John Kitzmuller

Cayman Islander Quarrel, the most expensive charter fisherman in Kingston, Jamaica, provides vital help to 007 during his mission to investigate the murder of British secret service representative Strangways.

Quarrel works with Strangways to gather rock samples from nearby islands, including Crab Key, although Quarrel dislikes traveling there. Friends who visited never returned. Quarrel believes the local legend that a fire-breathing dragon roams Crab Key's swamps.

After the murder of Strangways, Quarrel meets CIA agent Felix Leiter, and the pair attempts to tail James Bond when he arrives in Jamaica. Soon, Quarrel, Leiter, and Quarrel's friend Puss-Feller learn 007's true identity, and they all join forces. Quarrel even offers to break the arm of a photographer who snaps a photo of 007. Discovering the rocks from Crab Key are radioactive, Bond requests that Quarrel take him to the island. Quarrel drinks heavily from a jug of rum during the journey and, after the pair link up with Honey Ryder, Quarrel is nervous about heading into the island's swamps. There he confronts the "dragon," a swamp vehicle equipped with a flame thrower, which burns him to death.

Quarrel appears in the Fleming novels Live And Let Die and Dr. No.

QUARREL JR.

APPEARANCE
Live And Let Die (1973)
STATUS Living
CHARACTERISTICS Even-tempered, reliable, loyal
PLAYED BY Roy Stewart

Quarrel Jr., the son of Bond's Cayman Islander boatman in Dr. No, aids 007 in gaining access to remote parts of the island of San Monique during his investigation into the murders of three British agents.

Bond has known Quarrel Jr. for years, referring to him as "the man who shares my hairbrush." Quarrel adopts the façade of a lazy fisherman but works as a liaison agent for 007. He maintains communications gear and weapons behind a hidden door on his boat. Quarrel reveals the location of Solitaire's house to Bond

007's CARIBBEAN CONTACT Quarrel Jr. aboard his fishing boat.

and aids in 007's nighttime hang-glider incursions into Dr. Kananga's territory. He waits for Bond at a dock when 007 escapes with Solitaire, taking the pair to Santa Mina so they can catch a flight to New Orleans. When Bond and Leiter return to San Monique, Quarrel Jr. preps 007's shark gun and scuba gear, helps him get ashore to save Solitaire, and plants the incendiary bombs that destroy Kananga's poppies. He harbors no superstitions, urging Bond to shoot Baron Samedi, the voodoo god of cemeteries, "right between the eyes." Quarrel Jr.'s father performs a similar role in Bond's mission in the Ian Fleming novel.

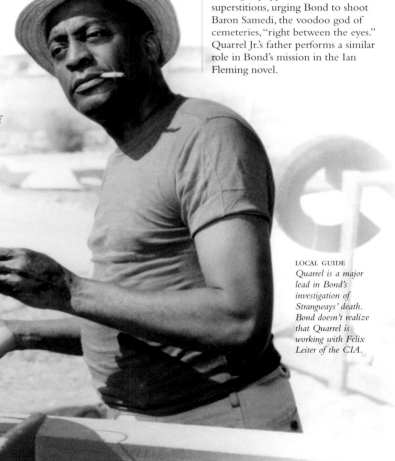

LOCAL GUIDE Quarrel is a major lead in Bond's investigation of Strangways' death. Bond doesn't realize that Quarrel is working with Felix Leiter of the CIA.

RAOUL

APPEARANCE
Die Another Day (2002)
STATUS Living; residing in Havana
CHARACTERISTICS Loves his
country and will never betray it
PLAYED BY Emilio Echevarria

Raoul is a British sleeper agent in Havana, Cuba, whom Bond "rudely awakens" after thirty years when he arrives at his cigar factory. He tells Raoul's assistant that he's there "to pick up some delectados." The delectado cigar, thanks to the slow-burning Volado tobacco, never burns out, just like a sleeper.

Raoul provides Bond with vital information regarding North Korean terrorist Zao, who has traveled to Dr. Alvarez's gene therapy clinic on the island of Los Organos. Raoul loans Bond "a fast car"—a 1957 Ford Fairlane—to travel there as well as a book entitled *Birds Of The West Indies* and a pair of binoculars to help him with his cover as an ornithologist. Later, Raoul determines that a diamond from Zao's bullet pendant is chemically identical to African conflict diamonds. He helps Bond identify the diamond as belonging to Gustav Graves.

ROBINSON

APPEARANCE
Tomorrow Never Dies (1997),
The World Is Not Enough (1999),
Die Another Day (2002)
STATUS Living;
whereabouts unknown
CHARACTERISTICS Statuesque, loyal
PLAYED BY Colin Salmon

Charles Robinson works as a Chief of Staff for M and is never far from her side.

In *Tomorrow Never Dies,* it is Robinson, from his post in the MI6 situation room, who communicates with 007 while Bond is on an anti-terrorism mission in the Khyber Pass. Robinson later informs Bond of media mogul Elliot Carver's background as M's limousine races through the London streets.

Robinson returns in *The World Is Not Enough,* where he briefs 007 and other MI6 agents at Castle Thane regarding the terrorist bombing at London's MI6 headquarters. He later escorts M to Elektra King's pipeline station in Baku when King requests her protection.

In *Die Another Day,* Robinson plays a key role in Bond's virtual reality shooting gallery exercise through the corridors of MI6. As Robinson and Bond enter M's office, unidentified enemy agents shoot Robinson dead. Thankfully, it's only a simulation. He is later present at a US Command Bunker in South Korea where he briefs 007 and Jinx on the staged coup in North Korea.

UNDER PRESSURE *Robinson and M in the situation room in* Tomorrow Never Dies. *Robinson relays vital information as Bond infiltrates a terrorist arms deal in Afghanistan.*

RODNEY

APPEARANCE The Man With The
Golden Gun (1974)
STATUS Dead; shot in the head with
a golden bullet
CHARACTERISTICS A gruff old-style
gangster out of his element
PLAYED BY Marc Lawrence

Rodney, a hood from Las Vegas, comes to a private island off the south-eastern coast of China at the behest of Nick Nack. He hopes to kill the legendary assassin Francisco Scaramanga for a fee. Rodney finds himself a live pawn in a training exercise for Scaramanga, the million-dollar-a-shot killer. When Rodney's first shot misses Scaramanga, Rodney becomes lost inside Scaramanga's fun house-like maze, designed to confuse and unnerve. As Rodney pursues Scaramanga, Nick Nack teases his

boss, further confirming for Rodney the uneasy feeling that his grim fate is sealed. Scaramanga kills Rodney with a single shot to the head, using his custom component golden gun.

ROEBUCK, ADMIRAL

APPEARANCE
Tomorrow Never Dies (1997)
STATUS Living; whereabouts unknown
CHARACTERISTICS Not a fan of the
spy business
PLAYED BY Geoffrey Palmer

> " Thank you, M. We've seen enough. This is now a military operation."
> **Admiral Roebuck**

Admiral Roebuck engages in a heated argument with M over firing a Tomahawk missile from HMS *Chester* into the Khyber Pass, taking out half of the world's terrorists at an arms swap-meet. Although M wishes to give 007 more time to investigate, the overeager Roebuck orders the missile to be launched. His impatience nearly leads to disaster. Two nuclear torpedoes are among the arms on offer, and tragedy is only averted when Bond removes them before the missile strikes.

Later, Admiral Roebuck recklessly wants to declare war against China after the sinking of HMS *Devonshire.* M, however, once again prefers to err on the side of caution and asks the Minister of Defence for permission to investigate. Roebuck and M lock horns, with Roebuck barking at M: "Sometimes I don't think you have the balls for this job." M wittily retorts: "Perhaps. But the advantage is I don't have to think with them all the time."

RONSON

APPEARANCE
Skyfall (2012)
STATUS Dead; shot by Patrice
CHARACTERISTICS Unkown
PLAYED BY Bill Buckhurst

In a safe house in Istanbul, MI6 agent Ronson and two other operatives safeguard an invaluable computer hard drive containing a list of NATO agents secretly embedded in global terrorist organizations. Assassin-for-hire Patrice kills the two operatives, critically wounds Ronson, and steals the hard drive. Bond soon arrives and, via a radio link with M, reports that Ronson needs urgent medical attention and that the hard drive is missing. Bond then attempts to staunch the flow of blood from Ronson's wound, but M orders 007 to hunt down whoever has stolen the hard drive. Ronson, too badly injured to speak, watches as Bond reluctantly leaves to pursue Patrice.

FADING FAST *Realizing the seriousness of the theft of the hard drive, M orders Bond to leave Ronson and pursue Patrice. Ronson dies before medical help can arrive.*

RUBAVITCH

APPEARANCE
The Living Daylights (1987)
STATUS Living; whereabouts unknown
CHARACTERISTICS Elegant, discreet, dedicated
PLAYED BY Virginia Hey

Rubavitch is the beautiful mistress of KGB chief General Leonid Pushkin, whom she accompanies to the North African Trade Convention in Tangier, Morocco. She is present in the room as Bond confronts Pushkin about the KGB plot *smiert spionam* (Death to Spies). When Pushkin alerts his bodyguard that he is in trouble, Bond partially disrobes Rubavitch, distracting the guard long enough to knock him unconscious. When Leonid seemingly dies, Rubavitch displays enormous grief but is then relieved to find he's alive and well.

RUBLEVITCH

APPEARANCES
The Spy Who Loved Me (1977), For Your Eyes Only (1981), Octopussy (1983)
STATUS Living in a free world
CHARACTERISTICS Dedicated to her boss
PLAYED BY Eva Rueber-Staier

Rublevitch is the secretary to General Gogol in Moscow. In *The Spy Who Loved Me*, their relationship is strictly business. However, in *For Your Eyes Only*, she sits on the edge of his desk and he kisses her hand, showing their relationship has deepened. In *Octopussy*, Gogol admires Rublevitch's striking figure in the Moscow War Room as she walks past to deliver a message to General Orlov.

SADRUDDIN

APPEARANCE
Octopussy (1983)
STATUS Living; whereabouts unknown
CHARACTERISTICS Pleasant, friendly
PLAYED BY Albert Moses

This senior Indian gentleman runs the Station I, India office of MI6. Vijay, his main assistant, becomes 007's principal aide in Udaipur, India. Sadruddin books 007 into the Shiv Niwas Palace Hotel. He later provides Bond with the little information that is available on the mysterious woman Octopussy.
In early drafts, Sadruddin played a more central role in Bond's investigation, but the character of Vijay took over many of the field duties.

SAIDA

APPEARANCE The Man With The Golden Gun (1974)

STATUS Living

CHARACTERISTICS Skilled dancer

PLAYED BY Carmen Sautoy

The key to finding Scaramanga lies in Beirut belly dancer Saida's navel. In 1969, Saida was making love to agent 002 when he was shot. She later obtained the distinctive golden bullet and placed this "lucky charm" in her navel. Bond removes the bullet with his teeth just as gangsters hit him, causing him to swallow it.

SAUNDERS

APPEARANCE

The Living Daylights (1987)

STATUS Dead; killed by Necros

CHARACTERISTICS Diligent

PLAYED BY Thomas Wheatley

Head of Section V, Vienna, Saunders is furious when Bond refuses to kill Kara Milovy, KGB General Koskov's sniper. However, he comes to appreciate Bond's methods and supplies information about Koskov and arms dealer Brad Whitaker. Saunders is killed by a booby-trap set by Whitaker's henchman Necros. Bond finds a balloon inscribed with the Russian words *smiert spionam* ("death to spies") near his body.

SCOTT, COLONEL

APPEARANCE

Moonraker (1979)

STATUS Living; whereabouts unknown

CHARACTERISTICS Excellent soldier

PLAYED BY Michael Marshall

When Bond alerts NASA to the presence of a huge space station orbiting earth, the US launches a contingent of Space Marines to attack, led by Colonel Scott. A no-nonsense soldier, Scott leads his men into a battle in space, fighting aerospace magnate Hugo Drax's troops with laser weapons. Despite heavy losses, Scott manages to get his men on board the space station. Their assault causes so much damage that the station begins to disintegrate. Scott retreats with his men, and later rescues Jaws and his girlfriend, Dolly, as they float in space.

SFPD CAPTAIN

APPEARANCE

A View To A Kill (1985)

STATUS Living; whereabouts unknown

CHARACTERISTICS Blustering

PLAYED BY Joe Flood

San Francisco's Police Captain arrests Bond for the murders of corrupt bureaucrat W. G. Howe and CIA agent Chuck Lee, but Bond escapes in a fire truck with geologist Stacey Sutton. The captain and his men give chase, but Bond evades capture. Later, the captain is so shocked to see Bond hanging from an airship that he crashes his new police car.

SHAH, KAMRAN

APPEARANCE

The Living Daylights (1987)

STATUS Living; whereabouts unknown

CHARACTERISTICS Charming, well-spoken, dedicated to his cause

PLAYED BY Art Malik

Kamran Shah is an Oxford-educated mujaheddin rebel who is Deputy Commander of the Eastern District in Afghanistan during the Soviet-Afghan War.

Soviet troops capture Shah as he reconnoiters Colonel Feyador's airbase in preparation for a raid. The base's jailer informs Shah that he will be executed the following day. Thankfully, Bond rescues Shah, and he takes Bond and his companion, Kara Milovy, to his headquarters.

The next morning, Shah allows Bond and Kara to ride with him as he escorts Afghan drug dealers the Snow Leopard Brotherhood to an opium-for-diamonds trade with General Koskov. Shah doesn't realize until almost too late that Koskov plans to purchase American high-tech weapons and use them against the mujaheddin. Shah helps Bond obtain an explosive device and a timer and raids Colonel Feyador's airbase, killing Feyador in the process. As Shah and his men, on horseback, flee a convoy of Soviet armored vehicles, Bond drops a bomb from a cargo plane. The explosion destroys the convoy as they cross a bridge, to the great relief of Shah and his men. Bond then destroys the aircraft, which is loaded with Koskov's opium.

Unfortunately, Kamran Shah and his men arrive too late to witness Kara's triumphant cello concert in Vienna because, laden with weapons, they have had "trouble at the airport."

Kara: James is trapped. You must help him!
Shah: He'll have to take his chances.
Kara: You can't leave him. You owe him your life!

SHARKY

APPEARANCE
Licence To Kill (1989)
STATUS Dead
CHARACTERISTICS Kind-hearted,
courageous, and loyal to his friends
PLAYED BY Frank McRae

Based in Key West, Florida, Sharky is a fisherman friend of DEA agent Felix Leiter. He presents Felix and his new bride, Della, with a box of hand-tied fishing lures as a wedding present. He later refuses to believe police detective Rasmussen's claim that a chainsaw removed his good

friend Leiter's left leg below the knee, informing Bond that the culprit was a shark.

Sharky helps Bond raid drug smuggler Milton Krest's marine warehouse in Key West and helps Bond to get the better of corrupt DEA agent Ed Killifer. He pilots his boat, the *Pa Ja Ma*, off the Cay Sol Bank, Bahamas, to enable Bond to get as close as possible to Krest's ship, the *Wavekrest*. However, while Bond sneaks aboard, two of Krest's henchmen, Clive and Oliver, kill Sharky and hang him over the stern of his boat suspended between two dead sharks.

LAUGHING OFF MURDER *The cruel death of Sharky underlines the viciousness of Milton Krest's smuggling racket.*

SIERRA

APPEARANCE
Goldfinger (1964)
STATUS Living; whereabouts unknown
CHARACTERISTICS Suspiciously still
while everyone panics
PLAYED BY Raymond Young

Sierra is James Bond's contact in Mexico. He meets 007 at the El Scorpio bar and congratulates Bond on destroying drug baron Mr. Ramirez's heroin lab. Sierra recommends that Bond should not return to his hotel as Ramirez's men will be watching it. He suggests that 007 leave on a plane to Miami, Florida within the hour. Bond informs him that he will be on the flight, but only after he has taken care of some unfinished business.

SIMMONS, MR.

APPEARANCE Goldfinger (1964)
STATUS Living; whereabouts unknown
CHARACTERISTICS Gullible
PLAYED BY Austin Willis

Mr. Simmons plays gin rummy with Goldfinger for one week on the pool deck of the Fontainebleau Hotel for stakes as high as $5 per point. Unaware Goldfinger is cheating, Simmons continues to lose, racking up losses of $10,000. Bond quickly deduces Goldfinger's method of cheating and convinces Goldfinger to lose $15,000 back to Simmons.

In the Fleming novel, Goldfinger cheats Mr. Du Pont at canasta. Du Pont, who knew Bond from Casino Royale, asks 007 to figure out how.

SMALLBONE, PENELOPE

APPEARANCE Octopussy (1983)
STATUS Living; working somewhere in
the MI6 secretarial pool
CHARACTERISTICS Former potential
replacement for Miss Moneypenny
PLAYED BY Michaela Clavell

Penelope Smallbone is Miss Moneypenny's assistant and the second assistant to M. Moneypenny, who claims to have described Bond to Smallbone in "nauseating detail," assures Smallbone that a bouquet of flowers is all she will ever receive from Bond. Smallbone is never seen again; presumably she transferred to another MI6 department.

SMITHERS, COLONEL

APPEARANCE Goldfinger (1964)
STATUS Living; whereabouts unknown
CHARACTERISTICS Influential figure
PLAYED BY Richard Vernon

Colonel Smithers is head of the Bank of England. Smithers suspects Goldfinger is smuggling large quantities of gold out of Britain and wants the British Secret Service to investigate. To use as bait to catch Goldfinger, Smithers loans Bond a gold ingot worth £5,000 from a Nazi hoard at the bottom of Lake Toplitz Salzkammergut, Austria. Smithers also gives Bond the opportunity to display his knowledge of brandy, to M's irritation.

SNOW LEOPARD BROTHERHOOD

APPEARANCE
The Living Daylights (1987)
STATUS Living; whereabouts unknown
CHARACTERISTICS Tough traders
PLAYED BY Tony Cyrus (Chief)

The Snow Leopard Brotherhood is the biggest group of opium traders in the Golden Crescent, a mountainous area in Asia. The chief trades opium for diamonds with Soviet General Koskov and arms dealer Brad Whitaker. It is the chief's biggest deal since the Soviet invasion. According to Bond, his opium is "worth half a billion dollars on the streets of New York."

STRANGWAYS, JOHN

APPEARANCE Dr. No (1962)

STATUS Dead; murdered by the Three Blind Mice

CHARACTERISTICS Likes fishing and bridge; his routines are too easy to follow

PLAYED BY Timothy Moxon

Commander John Strangways is "the chief Secret Service agent for the Caribbean." Three men, disguised as blind beggars, gun down Strangways as he leaves The Queen's Club in Kingston. They then kill his secretary, Mary, and dispose of the bodies. Their disappearances lead Bond to Jamaica to investigate.

Strangways appears in the Ian Fleming novels *Live And Let Die* and *Dr. No.* He is described as a "tall lean man with a black patch over the right eye..." He drives a Sunbeam Alpine in the novels, which is the car Bond drives to Miss Taro's house in the film.

STREET URCHIN

APPEARANCE
The Man With The Golden Gun (1974)

STATUS Unknown

CHARACTERISTICS Industrious and persistent

PLAYED BY Unknown

A street urchin, or more exactly a klong urchin, pesters tourists by selling carved wooden elephants on the canals of Bangkok. Bond, pursued by Chula and other martial arts students, finds the longtail boat he has stolen slowing to a crawl.

When the urchin pulls himself aboard, Bond offers him 20,000 baht to make his engine run faster. The urchin simply opens the fuel line and awaits his riches. Bond does not pay, but instead shoves the annoying child overboard into the klong as he speeds away.

STROMBERG'S ASSISTANT

APPEARANCE
The Spy Who Loved Me (1977)

STATUS Dead; eaten by a shark

CHARACTERISTICS Thankfully willing to betray her psychopathic boss

PLAYED BY Marilyn Galsworthy

The personal assistant of megalomaniac Karl Stromberg tries to sell the submarine tracking system developed by Dr. Bechmann and Professor Markovitz to a world power behind her boss's back. Stromberg announces his knowledge of the plot but pretends to be unaware of his assistant's involvement. While she stands in his elevator, he pushes a button that drops her into a tank, where a shark eats her.

QUICK SALE *A boy tries to sell Bond a carved elephant, but 007 has no time to lose.*

STRUTTER, HAROLD

APPEARANCE
Live And Let Die (1973)

STATUS Dead; laid to rest in New Orleans

CHARACTERISTICS Investigative mind

PLAYED BY Lon Satton

CIA agent Harold Strutter meets James Bond in New York. Strutter follows 007 to Harlem, then locates him in a back alley behind a Fillet of Soul restaurant. He explains that the gangster Mr. Big tracked Bond's movements, and only Big can pull together that kind of "black muscle in this town." Strutter travels to New Orleans to keep a close watch on the Fillet of Soul restaurant in the French Quarter, but suffers the same fate as British agent Hamilton when a faux jazz funeral passes by and becomes his own.

TALBOT, CMDR.

APPEARANCE
The Spy Who Loved Me (1977)

STATUS Dead

CHARACTERISTICS Ready for combat

PLAYED BY Bryan Marshall

Commander Talbot captains the HMS *Ranger*, one of Britain's four nuclear submarines. When the submarine encounters a strange phenomenon underwater, Talbot surfaces and cannot believe what he sees: a supertanker's bow open and ready to swallow his craft. Talbot remains a prisoner until James Bond frees him. He leads a raid on the ship's armory, providing weapons to the British, Soviet, and US sailors. A *Liparus* crew member kills him with a hand grenade during the resultant battle.

TANAKA, TIGER

APPEARANCE
You Only Live Twice (1967)
STATUS A closely-guarded secret
CHARACTERISTICS Professional,
friendly; a skilled ninja
PLAYED BY Tetsuro Tamba

Tiger Tanaka serves as head of the Japanese SIS and provides vital support to James Bond on his mission to stop spacecraft from disappearing in orbit and prevent World War III.

Tiger has 007 delivered to his office via a hidden chute beneath a subway tunnel in Tokyo. Tanaka works closely with Bond to uncover Ernst Stavro Blofeld's plot to abduct US and Soviet spacecraft, offering Bond intelligence analysis of materials obtained from Mr. Osato's safe, the services of one of his top female agents, Aki, as well as material and logistical support on his mission. He trains Bond as a modern ninja and outfits him with weapons and gear. When 007 goes undercover as a Japanese fisherman, Tanaka arranges a fake marriage with his local agent Kissy Suzuki on an island of Ama fishermen and pearl divers. He poses as a local peasant farmer, bringing his ninja fighters to the area to support 007. When Kissy returns to the Ama village to report that Bond found a secret rocket base inside a mainland volcano, Tanaka leads the ninja attack on Blofeld's headquarters and skillfully fights the SPECTRE guards and technicians during the assault.

Tanaka reveals little of his past in the film, but Ian Fleming's novel fills many gaps. Tanaka studied at Trinity College, Oxford before World War II, gaining a first in Philosophy, Politics and Economics. He worked as a spy for Japan, serving as an assistant naval attaché for the London embassy. During World War II, he worked as personal aide to Admiral Ohnishi, the founder of the official Kamikaze Corps, which Tanaka joined before the war ended.

TANNER

APPEARANCES The Man With The Golden Gun (1974), For Your Eyes Only (1981), GoldenEye (1995), The World Is Not Enough (1999), Quantum Of Solace (2008), Skyfall (2012)
STATUS Living; MI6 headquarters
CHARACTERISTICS Loyal, efficient
PLAYED BY Michael Goodliffe (The Man With The Golden Gun), James Villiers (For Your Eyes Only), Michael Kitchen (GoldenEye, The World Is Not Enough), Rory Kinnear (Quantum Of Solace, Skyfall)

MI6 STALWART *Tanner (Michael Kitchen, top) is informed of events in Severnaya in* GoldenEye; *Tanner (Rory Kinnear, above) helps direct the chase to capture Patrice in Istanbul from M's London office in* Skyfall.

SECOND IN COMMAND *Tanner (James Villiers) deputizes for M during Operation Undertow in* For Your Eyes Only.

Bill Tanner first appears briefly in *The Man With The Golden Gun* as the Chief of Staff, listening to Bond discuss Scaramanga's background.

He next surfaces in *For Your Eyes Only* when M is on leave, to give 007 his Operation Undertow assignment. He suggests 007 use Q's Identigraph to identify who paid off the assassin Gonzales.

The Tanner in *GoldenEye* and *The World Is Not Enough* is an MI6 senior analyst. He calls M "the evil Queen of numbers" and agrees with 007's instinctual approach. In *The World Is Not Enough*, Tanner advises

M not to travel to Azerbaijan at Elektra King's request, but he fails to convince her.

Tanner in *Quantum of Solace* is M's right-hand man. He plays by-the-book, leading M to explain that things aren't always what they seem.

In *Skyfall*, Tanner helps M and Bond identify Patrice, protects M during Silva's attack on the Board of Inquiry, and assists Q in leaving a digital "breadcrumb trail" for Silva to follow.

RIGHT-HAND MAN *Tanner (below) with M at the Board of Inquiry.*

TIBBETT, SIR GODFREY

APPEARANCE
A View To A Kill (1985)
STATUS Dead; strangled by May Day
CHARACTERISTICS Well-groomed, gentlemanly, long-suffering
PLAYED BY Patrick Macnee

Described as a "dapper trainer" in the script, Sir Godfrey Tibbett is a refined Englishman who works with MI6 to uncover the mystery of tycoon Max Zorin's winning racehorses. Bond poses as a wealthy English sportsman named St. John-Smythe at Zorin's annual thoroughbred racehorse sale, and Tibbett poses as his valet and chauffeur. Bond relishes ordering Tibbett about as part of their cover. They learn that Zorin's breeding consultant, Dr. Mortner, has injected steroids into the racehorses. When the pair's real identities are discovered, Tibbett is strangled by Zorin's lover, May Day.

> **Tibbett:** Do we have to keep this up when we're alone?
> **007:** A successful cover becomes almost second nature.

SUPER DRUG *Sir Godfrey Tibbett and Bond uncover Zorin's horse-doping plot.*

TRAIN CONDUCTOR

APPEARANCE
From Russia With Love (1963)
STATUS Unknown
CHARACTERISTICS Efficient, bribable
PLAYED BY George Pastell

The conductor on the Orient Express becomes an unwitting pawn in SPECTRE's game of murder and betrayal with the British and the Soviets. He has the grim duty of telling Bond of the death of his ally Kerim Bey, the head of Station T, Turkey. The conductor believes that Bey and Benz, the Soviet security man, killed each other. Bond requests that the conductor keep the deaths quiet until the train reaches Trieste, sealing the deal with a healthy bribe and the promise of more money from Bey's "influential friends."

MURDER ON THE ORIENT EXPRESS
The train conductor shows 007 the dead bodies of Kerim Bey and Benz—killed by SPECTRE assassin Donald Grant.

TYNAN, DR.

APPEARANCE
Diamonds Are Forever (1971)
STATUS Dead; killed by Wint and Kidd
CHARACTERISTICS Skilled at dental extractions
PLAYED BY Henry Rowland

An American dentist working at a Diamond Syndicate mine in South Africa, Dr. Tynan works as part of the mine's social services structure. Tynan makes contact with the miners, persuading them to bring him choice stones hidden in their mouths for cash payments. Tynan rides his motorcycle to a remote desert location for his regular appointments with Joe, a helicopter pilot who takes the diamonds to smuggler Mrs. Whistler. Tynan ultimately meets assassins Mr. Wint and Mr. Kidd who inform him Joe couldn't make the appointment. They then kill him with a scorpion, telling Joe that Tynan was "bitten by the bug."

STING IN THE TAIL *Dr. Tynan falls for Mr. Kidd's toothache ruse, leading to his death.*

UNNAMED FOREIGN AGENT

APPEARANCE Thirteen Bond films
to date
STATUS Living, whereabouts unknown
CHARACTERISTICS Chameleon-like;
loves disguises
PLAYED BY Michael G. Wilson

This mysterious foreign agent
fleetingly appears in several of Bond's
assignments, always under a different
identity. He first appears in *Goldfinger*
as a tall Korean guard. In *Moonraker*,
he walks past the Venini Glass
Factory in Venice and later appears as
a NASA control room technician.
For Your Eyes Only sees the agent
disguised as a Greek Orthodox priest,
possibly shadowing a meeting
between Bond and Q. *Octopussy* finds
him on a boat in India acting as
though he is an American tourist.
This foreign agent heads to the opera
in Vienna in *The Living Daylights*,
shadowing British operative
Saunders. In *GoldenEye*, the agent
appears to be a member of the

ORTHODOX
AGENT *The
Unnamed
Foreign Agent
appears as a
priest officiating
at a wedding
in* For Your
Eyes Only.

Russian Defense Council, leading
many to believe him to be a Russian
agent. The agent then masquerades as
an Elliot Carver media executive
named Tom Wallace in Tomorrow
Never Dies. In *The World Is Not
Enough*, he appears as an employee in
Zukovsky's Baku casino. He turns up
twice in *Die Another Day*—first
leaning against a car as Bond passes
him on the streets of Havana, then
as US General Chandler in a
command bunker in South Korea.
In *Casino Royale*, he is in disguise
again—this time as the corrupt Chief
of Police in Montenegro.

BIG TOP THRILLS
*The US General
(left) and his aide
(right) get a big
bang out of
Octopussy's Circus.
Kamal Khan
(center) prepares to
leave the big top
before an atomic
bomb explodes.*

US GENERAL

APPEARANCE
Octopussy (1983)
STATUS Living; whereabouts unknown
CHARACTERISTICS Extremely
focused on his job
PLAYED BY Bruce Boa

Octopussy invites the general in
command of the US Air Force Base
in Feldstadt, West Germany and his
aide as her personal guests to a
performance of her circus. When
James Bond breaks into the heavily
guarded tent disguised as a circus
clown, he makes his way to
Octopussy and informs the base
commander that there is a bomb in
the cannon. The general's aide tells
his boss that Bond is either drunk or
crazy. However, when Octopussy
blasts the lock off the cannon,
revealing the detonator, the general
orders his men to release Bond so he
can disarm the device.

VAVRA

APPEARANCE
From Russia With Love (1963)
STATUS Unknown
CHARACTERISTICS Friendly, earthy
PLAYED BY Francis de Wolff

Vavra and his rough-living gypsy
tribe are used for dirty work by the
head of Station T, Kerim Bey. The
gypsies consider Bey to be a close
family friend. They take in Kerim
and Bond when they are trying to
avoid Soviet agents. Bond and Kerim
arrive at the camp and witness a
fierce fight taking place between
gypsy women Vida and Zora over
the affections of one of Vavra's sons.
When Bulgarian assassin Krilencu
and his men attack the camp, Bond
saves Vavra's life. In return, Vavra calls
007 an honorary son. The head of
the gypsy tribe relents to Bond's
request to call off the fight between
Vida and Zora.

VENZ

APPEARANCE
A View To A Kill (1985)
STATUS Living; whereabouts unknown
CHARACTERISTICS Protective, loyal
PLAYED BY Dolph Lundgren

Venz and fellow KGB agent
Klotkoff accompany General Gogol
to meet errant agent Max Zorin
at his racetrack. When May Day,
Zorin's lover, lifts Klotkoff into the
air and then throws him to the
ground, Venz checks on his
colleague's condition.

VERITY

APPEARANCE
Die Another Day (2002)
STATUS Living; whereabouts unknown
CHARACTERISTICS Defensive,
possessive, ever watchful
PLAYED BY Madonna

Double agent Miranda Frost shares a
close, protective relationship with
Verity, her fencing instructor. It is
mildly implied that Verity may be
attracted to Miranda, and she
certainly comes to Frost's defense
when Bond reminds her that
Miranda won the gold medal at the
2000 Olympic Games in Sydney,
Australia by default. After giving 007
a fencing tip, she introduces him to
Miranda's fencing partner, billionaire
Gustav Graves. Verity declines to
wager on a fencing match between
these two men.

Gustav Graves: Care
to place a bet Verity?

Verity: No thanks,
I don't like
cock fights.

VIJAY

APPEARANCE Octopussy (1983)
STATUS Dead; killed by thugs
CHARACTERISTICS Resourceful, loyal
PLAYED BY Vijay Amritraj

Vijay works for Sadruddin, head of Section I, India and is Bond's main contact while 007 investigates Operation Trove. Vijay first meets Bond dressed as a snake charmer. He plays "The James Bond Theme" on a pungi to a cobra as 007 walks past. Vijay prefers his more usual cover, as part-time tennis pro at exiled Afghan prince Kamal Khan's club.

Vijay displays his tennis skills during a chase in a tuk-tuk taxi through the streets of Udaipur, making an overhand smash right onto a thug's head. Later, disguised as a fisherman, he keeps watch on jewel smuggler Octopussy's Floating Palace while 007 is in residence. During Vijay's watch, Khan's henchman Gobinda and Mufti's thugs attack and fatally wound him with a yo-yo buzz saw. Q finds Vijay before he dies. Vijay tells him, "It was Kamal's men."

VILLIERS

APPEARANCE Casino Royale (2006)
STATUS Living; whereabouts unknown
CHARACTERISTICS Young, keen
PLAYED BY Tobias Menzies

Villiers, M's aide, keeps his boss informed at all hours. He endures her temper, when she faces a Parliamentary inquiry after MI6's new 00 James Bond shoots a bomb maker in a foreign embassy. Villiers reports to M that 007 is using her password to conduct research in MI6's database. He also provides key research into the target of a terrorist bombing in Miami.

WADE, JACK

APPEARANCE
GoldenEye (1995),
Tomorrow Never Dies (1997)
STATUS Living; retired
CHARACTERISTICS Jocular, feels like he's seen it all; amateur botanist
PLAYED BY Joe Don Baker

CIA agent Jack Wade provides indispensable help to Bond during two of his post-Cold War missions. Wade dislikes formality and has a cheerfully cynical view of his job. Married at least three times, he sports a rose tattooed on his hip with the name "Muffy," in honor of his third wife. A veteran of the Vietnam War, Wade developed a keen interest in gardening by accident while in Cambodia. He created explosives using plant fertilizer and diesel fuel and then realized that the mixture made excellent compost.

When Wade meets Bond in St. Petersburg, Russia during *GoldenEye*, he drives a decidedly unpretentious Moskvich automobile and initially finds Bond's manner irksome, calling him a "stiff-assed Brit." Wade soon takes a liking to 007 and comes to respect Bond's spycraft. Wade gives Bond important information concerning Russian Mafia boss Valentin Zukovsky that allows 007 to track down Alec Trevelyan, formerly Agent 006 of MI6.

Wade later meets Bond in the Caribbean, giving him and computer programmer Natalya Simonova a Cessna 172 and cover from the CIA to fly into Cuban airspace so that they can locate a satellite dish that will be used to detonate the second GoldenEye satellite. Wade tells Bond to get on the radio if he needs help, and he will send in the Marines. At the end of *GoldenEye*, Wade arrives

CIA ALLY Jack Wade helps Bond investigate the sinking of HMS Devonshire.

with his promised commando force to rescue 007.

In *Tomorrow Never Dies*, Bond meets Wade in Okinawa, Japan, while investigating the sinking of HMS *Devonshire*. They discover that the GPS encoder Bond took from media mogul Elliot Carver's office could have sent the frigate off course, launching a military confrontation between Britain and China.

WHISTLER, MRS.

APPEARANCE
Diamonds Are Forever (1971)
STATUS Dead; drowned
CHARACTERISTICS Kindhearted, but with a dishonest streak
PLAYED BY Margaret Lacey

BY THE BOOK Mrs. Whistler leaves her young class to greet her colleagues in the diamond-smuggling racket, Mr. Wint and Mr. Kidd.

Mrs. Whistler is a missionary teacher in South Africa, financing her school by smuggling diamonds. When she meets the killers Mr. Wint and Mr. Kidd, she says she is happy to see them again, implying they have had a role in her smuggling activities. Her desire to have photographs of the Amsterdam canals sent to the children at her school is sadistically fulfilled. Wint and Kidd drown Mrs. Whistler, and Kidd snaps pictures as police pull her body from the Amster.

WHYTE, WILLARD

APPEARANCE
Diamonds Are Forever (1971)
STATUS Living; whereabouts unknown
CHARACTERISTICS Eccentric, reclusive, but energetic when roused to action
PLAYED BY Jimmy Dean

Billionaire Willard Whyte has a vast business empire that includes an aerospace complex, hotels, casinos, cruise ships, and oil wells. Whyte has become a notorious recluse, ensconced in the penthouse of his Las Vegas hotel, The Whyte House. He controls his empire through a few trusted subordinates, such as Tom at WW Techtronics and Bert Saxby. Bond's archenemy Ernst Stavro Blofeld convinces Saxby to betray Whyte, and together they kidnap him. They then seize Whyte's empire and use its resources to finance the building of a massive laser satellite powerful enough to blow up intercontinental ballistic missiles in their silos. Whyte becomes a prisoner in his own summer home, ten miles outside of Las Vegas. Gymnasts extraordinaire Bambi and Thumper guard the billionaire.

Bond rescues Whyte, but not before Blofeld, using a voice simulator to impersonate Whyte, successfully launches his deadly space weapon, destroying nuclear installations in the Soviet Union, the US, and China. Whyte reclaims control of his empire and helps 007 discover and destroy Blofeld's command center, situated in an oil rig off the coast of the Baja peninsula, Mexico.

ZUKOVSKY, VALENTIN

APPEARANCE GoldenEye (1995),
The World Is Not Enough (1999)
STATUS Dead; shot by Elektra King
CHARACTERISTICS Roguish but
dangerous head of the Russian Mafia
PLAYED BY Robbie Coltrane

Ex-KGB operative Valentin
Dimitrovich Zukovsky runs the only
major competition to the Janus
crime syndicate in Russia, selling
arms and engaging in numerous
other extra-legal business ventures.
During the Cold War, James Bond
shot Zukovsky in the right knee and
stole his car and his girlfriend. Years
later, this not unnaturally proves a
barrier to approaching Zukovsky for
information on Janus, the alias of
Alec Trevelyan.

Zukovsky operates out of building
23 in a warehouse district of St.
Petersburg. According to Jack Wade
and Zukovsky himself, Valentin has
no compunction about killing
uninvited guests. Zukovsky maintains
a vast knowledge of firearms. He can
tell Bond's Walther PPK merely from
the sound of it cocking. He enjoys
mocking Bond but demonstrates a
flash of temper. Bond eventually
negotiates a tenuous peace. Neither
man likes the other, but they soon
realize they occasionally share the
same goals. In exchange for a rigged
sale of C4 explosives where
Zukovsky will be allowed to pocket
a large profit, Zukovsky tells 007 all
he knows about Janus and arranges
an introduction.

A few years later, Valentin moves to
Baku and claims to have become a
legitimate businessman, opening his
own casino and caviar factory. He
still has a few shady dealings in the
works, including one transaction
with oil heiress Elektra King.

He smuggles Russian equipment and
supplies for her, using his nephew
Nikoli and a Russian navy
submarine.

When Valentin realizes that Elektra
and her lover Renard have killed
Nikoli, he becomes furious. Elektra
shoots him before he can take action.
Zukovsky's final act before he dies is
to fire his silver-handled walking
stick, which conceals a rifle, at a
wrist restraint, freeing 007 from
Elektra's torture chair. In an ironic
twist, the walking stick Valentin uses
as a result of Bond's bullet to his
knee saves 007's life.

A REUNION WITH 007
"Walther PPK. 7.65mm,"
says Valentin Zukovsky.
"Only three men I know
use such a gun. I believe
I've killed two of them."

ONE GIRL IS NOT ENOUGH *Zukovsky with his*
two girlfriends, Nina and Verushka.

> **"**I'm looking for a
> submarine. It's big and
> black and the driver's
> **a very good**
> **friend of mine."**
>
> Zukovsky to Elektra King

VEHICLES

When Ian Fleming lovingly described James Bond's battleship-gray 4½-litre Bentley with the Amherst Villiers supercharger in *Casino Royale*, he tapped into the world's growing love of powerful machines. James Bond was the first hero of the Jet Age, and the novels and films offer a wonderful catalog of the most elegant, interesting, and deadly modes of transport ever conceived. The vehicles in the world of 007 speak to our love of the speed, power, and romance of travel. They transport us into a world where every ticket is first class, every journey is an adventure. They offer so much more than a gadget-laden Aston Martin or a submersible Lotus Esprit. They are a catalog of our aspirations, a reminder that life is a journey and the way we choose to move through it says more about us than the kind of car we drive. Anyone can look good behind the wheel of an Aston Martin DBS. When life hands you a Citroën 2CV or a Routemaster bus, can you still steer through the obstacles you face without breaking sweat? As you look through these pages at the amazing and the ordinary, remember, as Fleming noted in You Only Live Twice, "It is better to travel hopefully than to arrive."

ACROSTAR "BEDE" JET

APPEARANCE
Octopussy (1983)
FLOWN BY James Bond

EVASIVE ACTION *007 flies his Acrostar through the enemy's hangar to escape a missile.*

To escape troops in an unidentified Latin American country, Bond employs a jet small enough to fit inside a horse trailer. Jim Bede invented this remarkable aircraft, and a number were specially modified as Acrostars, one of which was obtained by Q Branch. The BD-5J "Acrostar" Microjet is just 12-ft (3.6-m) long, with a wingspan of only 13 ft (3.9 m). It is powered by a single TRS-18 microturbo jet engine, giving a top speed of 320 mph (514.9 kph).

Impersonating an officer named Colonel Toro, Bond is on a mission to sabotage a spy plane. Unmasked and captured, 007 manages to escape his guards. He leaps onto a Range Rover convertible pulling what looks like a horse trailer. In fact, the trailer contains the Acrostar. Bond jumps into the cockpit as trucks and motorcyclists roar toward him. The jet's folding wings descend, and Bond speeds toward the vehicles, taking off just over his pursuers' heads.

Troops fire a Rapier surface-to-air missile at the Acrostar and Bond tries to evade it through a series of ravines and mesas, to no avail. In an inspired maneuver, he then flies straight into the airplane hangar housing the spy plane. Colonel Toro's men race to close the doors at the far end, but Bond's plane zooms through the ever-diminishing gap. The pursuing missile smashes into the shut doors, obliterating the hangar in a massive explosion.

Bond flies off, but soon notices that the jet's fuel gauge is registering almost empty. Bond promptly lands on a country road, pulls into a petrol station, and nonchalantly asks the astonished attendant to "Fill her up."

GETAWAY PLANE *Enemy soldiers flee in panic as Bond's Acrostar roars over their heads.*

AEROSPATIALE/EUROCOPTER HELICOPTERS

APPEARANCES
You Only Live Twice (1967), Octopussy (1983), A View To A Kill (1985), Licence To Kill (1989), GoldenEye (1995), Tomorrow Never Dies (1997), The World Is Not Enough (1999), Die Another Day (2002)
USED BY James Bond, General Gogol, General Orlov, Stacey Sutton, Franz Sanchez, Dario, Heller, Xenia Onatopp, Natalya Simonova, Elliot Carver's men, Elektra King, M, Mr. Van Bierk

James Bond, his colleagues, and his enemies have often been transported to and from important locations in various French-built Aerospatiale helicopters.

In *You Only Live Twice*, an Aerospatiale Alouette 316B transports 007 to Japanese secret service chief Tiger Tanaka's ninja-training school in Japan.

In *Octopussy*, during Operation Trove, Bond takes an Aerospatiale SA-316 Alouette III to Udaipur, India. An Aerospatiale SA-365C Dauphin flies Soviet General Orlov to Kamal Khan's Monsoon Palace to finalize their plans to explode an atomic bomb on the US Air Force Base in Feldstadt, West Germany. KGB General Gogol also takes a 365 to the East/West German border to arrest Orlov for stealing jewelry from the Kremlin Art Repository.

A View To A Kill features state geologist Stacey Sutton arriving at businessman Max Zorin's French chateau in an Aerospatiale AS 355 Ecuruil 2 helicopter.

During the events of *Licence To Kill*, 007 arrives in Key West for the wedding of his good friend, DEA agent Felix Leiter. Bond, Leiter, and the DEA take control of a US Coast Guard HH-65A Dauphin when they learn that drug lord Franz Sanchez has arrived in US airspace. Leiter hoists Bond down on the rescue winch, and 007 lassoes the tail end of Sanchez's stolen Cessna 172 monoplane in mid-air, capturing the drug baron. Later in the film, Sanchez and his men Dario and Heller take an Aerospatiale 350B A-Star to the Olympatec Meditation Institute that houses Sanchez's cocaine laboratories.

DIAMOND DELIVERY *Van Bierk's helicopter lands at Moon's base in* Die Another Day.

In 1992, Aerospatiale and Deutsche Aerospace merged to form the Eurocopter Group. All Aerospatiale helicopters were henceforth known as Eurocopters.

In *GoldenEye*, after Bond's plane crashes in the Cuban jungle, Janus member Xenia Onatopp slides down a rope from a Eurocopter 355 Twin Star and tries to squeeze 007 to death between her thighs. Bond fires

death between her thighs. Bond fires the machine gun attached to her belt at the Twin Star, bringing it to a violent explosion. As the Twin Star crashes, the rope holding Onatopp quickly wedges her against a tree, squeezing her to death. Later in the film, computer programmer Natalya Simonova hijacks another 355 Twin Star to rescue 007. Bond leaps from the satellite antenna to the skids of the helicopter as it flies to safety.

In *Tomorrow Never Dies*, a Eurocopter Panther AS 565 Attack helicopter is observed by MI6 as one of the weapons for sale at a terrorist supermarket on the Khyber Pass. Another Eurocopter—an EC-135—remains in the background as Q gives Bond his new remote-controlled BMW 750iL at Hamburg Airport. In Saigon, media mogul Elliot Carver's men point the nose of a Eurocopter 350B A-Star to the ground and try to use the rotary blades to chop up Bond and Chinese agent Wai Lin as they speed through the streets on a stylish BMW R1200 motorbike.

The World Is Not Enough features a Eurocopter AS-365N Dauphin that pauses above the Caucasus Mountains to allow Bond and oil heiress Elektra King to jump from the helicopter onto the snow and ski to the pipeline. A Eurocopter EC-135 later flies M to Elektra's Azerbaijan oil pipeline station.

Die Another Day uses a very similar helicopter to an Aerospatiale SA 330 Puma, the Mil Mi-8 helicopter. Taking on the identity of diamond smuggler Mr. Van Bierk, Bond uses Van Bierk's helicopter to fly into Colonel Moon's base by the DMZ. When Moon learns Bond's true identity, he destroys the Mil Mi-8 with a tank-buster gun.

See also Eurocopter Tree-cutter; Tiger Helicopter

MARKET MAYHEM *(below) Carver's helicopter pursues Bond and Wai Lin through the streets of Saigon in* Tomorrow Never Dies.

JUMP OFF
Natalya Simonova arrives to rescue Bond in GoldenEye.

FIREBALL *(below)*
Bond's adroit use of a washing line brings down Carver's chopper.

AMC HORNET

APPEARANCE
The Man With The Golden Gun (1974)
USED BY James Bond, Sheriff Pepper

James Bond puts a 1974 AMC Hornet X Hatchback to the test in a chase with master assassin Francisco Scaramanga.

After the kidnapping of staff intelligence officer Mary Goodnight outside a kick-boxing arena, Bond spies Scaramanga's AMC Matador. Goodnight then informs him by walkie-talkie that she is trapped inside the trunk and has the prized Solex Agitator with her. Bond enters a car dealership and slips into a Hornet Hatchback only to discover he has a passenger along for the ride—Sheriff J. W. Pepper. Bond crashes the car through the showroom window and onto the Bangkok streets, weaving in and out of traffic at breakneck speed and even pulling a 180° reverse-to-forward maneuver.

Bond follows Pepper's advice on a turn by a klong and ends up on the opposite bank from Scaramanga, Goodnight, and the Solex. Spying a collapsed bridge, Bond accelerates to a speed between 39 and 41 mph (63–66 kph) and, using the remains of the bridge as a ramp, sends the Hornet rocketing into space. The

AIRSHIP

APPEARANCE
A View To A Kill (1985)
USED BY Max Zorin, May Day, Scarpine, Dr. Mortner

PUMPED UP *A Portakabin's roof folds back, and Zorin's airship rapidly inflates.*

Max Zorin owns two airships that play a role in his plan to destroy Silicon Valley. His larger airship, the Zorin Industries Skyship 6000, features a high-tech boardroom where he conducts a meeting with his cartel about seizing control of the microchip market. The airship also features collapsible stairs, which come in handy when a Taiwanese tycoon opts out of the plan. Zorin's lover, May Day, escorts the tycoon from the meeting to the stairs and, with the push of a button, sends him hurtling out of the ship.

Zorin also has a smaller airship, designated G–BIHN, hidden inside a Portakabin at his Main Strike mine. When Zorin, Nazi experimenter Dr. Carl Mortner, and henchman Scarpine depart the mine in the G–BIHN airship before setting off an explosion they believe will trigger a devastating earthquake, Zorin kidnaps geologist Stacey Sutton. Bond grabs onto a mooring rope, leading Zorin to attempt to knock

THE BALLOON BURSTS *Dr. Mortner's attempt to kill Bond and Stacey ends when he drops a lit bundle of dynamite and blows up himself and Zorin's airship.*

Bond loose in various ways. When Zorin tries to use the Golden Gate Bridge to force Bond free, 007 secures the mooring rope to one of the bridge's cables. Dr. Mortner destroys the airship when he inadvertently drops lit dynamite into the cabin.

"This'll hurt him more than me!"

Zorin to Scarpine, as Bond hangs from the airship's mooring rope

ALONG FOR THE RIDE *Bond seizes one of the airship's mooring ropes, determined to save Stacey Sutton from Max Zorin's clutches.*

weight of the Hornet, including passengers, is between 3,214 and 3,228 lb (1,458–1,464 kg); the ramps sit between 51.9 and 52.09 ft (15.82–15.88 m) apart. Turning over once in mid air, the car lands precisely on the remains of the bridge on the opposite bank. Bond and Pepper then continue their pursuit of Scaramanga.

Unfortunately, despite this spectacular maneuver, Bond fails to catch Scaramanga who transforms his AMC Matador into a plane.

AMC MATADOR

APPEARANCE
The Man With The Golden Gun (1974)
USED BY Scaramanga, Nick Nack

As staff intelligence officer Mary Goodnight places a listening device in the trunk of Francisco Scaramanga's 1974 AMC Matador X Coupé, the master assassin shoves her inside and drives off. Bond steals an AMC Hornet and gives chase until

Scaramanga pulls into a hangar. Behind closed doors, Scaramanga converts the Matador into an airplane with a jet engine and wing attachment that locks onto the car. An airplane instrument panel flips down in the car's dashboard.

Delayed by the Bangkok police, Bond watches Scaramanga's car plane take to the skies. The AMC Matador is later found abandoned about 200 miles (322 km) west of Bangkok.

ANTONOV

APPEARANCE
Die Another Day (2002)
USED BY Gustav Graves, North Korean Generals, Jinx

The Russian Antonov An-124, one of the largest fleet aircraft in existence, serves as the flying headquarters of Gustav Graves/ Colonel Moon as he directs the Icarus satellite's destruction of the South Korean defense lines along the De-Militarized Zone. Infiltrated by James Bond and Jinx, the plane depressurizes and flies into the blazing heat from the Icarus space mirror. As Icarus destroys the Antonov, James Bond and Jinx battle Graves and Miranda Frost to the death and escape via a Notar MD-600 helicopter from the cargo bay of the plane. They freefall in the helicopter as the plane explodes.

ASTON MARTIN DB5

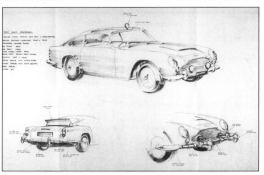

TOP GEAR *The Bond DB5 in full bloom illustrates the wealth of gadgets installed by Q Branch.*

ORIGINAL DESIGNS *Ken Adam's sketches show a top-mounted search light, a flip-up bullet screen, and tire knives built into front and rear bumpers.*

APPEARANCES Goldfinger (1964), Thunderball (1965), GoldenEye (1995), Tomorrow Never Dies (1997), The World Is Not Enough (1999), Casino Royale (2006), Skyfall (2012)

DRIVEN BY James Bond, Alex Dimitrios

The most well-known and sought-after Aston Martin ever made, the DB5 had a production run of only 1,023 cars and was produced between 1963 and 1965. No car is more closely identified with 007. The DB5's essential Britishness, bespoke craftsmanship, sleek, classic styling, made it a perfect fit for James Bond.

In the novel *Goldfinger*, Bond chooses an Aston Martin DB Mk III from the Service motor pool (Fleming refers to the car simply as a "DB III"—the Aston Martin DB3

ARMREST OPTIONS *These switches control the DB5's formidable defense mechanisms, which include fixed front-firing machine guns.*

was purely a racing model retired two years before *Goldfinger* was written. The Mark III was introduced in 1957, the year before Fleming wrote *Goldfinger*). The battleship-grey car serves as part of Bond's cover as "a well-to-do, rather adventurous young man with a taste for the good, the fast things of life." The car's extras

THE FINER THINGS *Alex Dimitrios may have no morals, but he has exquisite taste in cars and women, as 007 soon discovers on Paradise Island in* Casino Royale.

included "switches to alter the type and color of Bond's front and rear lights if he was following or being followed at night, reinforced steel bumpers fore and aft in case he needed to ram, a long-barreled Colt .45 in a trick compartment under the drivers seat, a radio pick-up tuned to receive an apparatus called the Homer, and plenty of concealed space that would fox most customs men."

When Bond enters Q's lab in the film *Goldfinger*, Q tells 007 his Bentley has had its day and shows him a new Silver Birch Aston Martin DB5. The car's gadgetry not only offered Bond protection and weaponry, but it also subtly mocked

PRE-GPS *Q's onboard moving map system predated in-car analog systems by 19 years and commercial GPS systems by 30 years.*

"*Ejector seat? You're joking!*"

Bond to Q

a growing concern over automobile safety at the time.

Bond uses the car's tracking system to follow Goldfinger's Rolls Royce Phantom III to Switzerland. He later engages the tire scythe to disable Tilly Masterson's car to discover why she fired a shot at him. When Bond and Tilly attempt to escape from the Auric Enterprises compound, Bond uses the car's smoke screen and oil slick functions. Trapped in a dead end, Bond protects himself with the rear bulletproof screen. Once captured, Bond fires the guard riding with him out of the roof with the ejector seat. The bulletproof windscreen comes in handy when the elderly gatekeeper

DON'T TOUCH IT! *Pushing this red button causes part of the roof to blow away and activates the passenger ejector seat.*

sprays the car with machine-gun fire. Bond soon employs the front wing machine guns and the extending front bumpers while trying to escape the plant—without success. He ends up playing chicken not with another car but his own reflection in a mirror and crashes into a wall.

Bond's DB5 has been recovered and repaired by *Thunderball*. Bond uses it to escape SPECTRE gunmen, washing them down with high-pressure water jets. Later, Bond drives the car on his return from his visit to the Shrublands health clinic, and Count Lippe pursues him in a black Ford Skyliner. Before Bond can engage any gadgets, Fiona Volpe fires a rocket from her BSA Lightning motorbike that destroys the Skyliner.

The DB5 does not return for 30 years, when it serves as 007's personal car in *GoldenEye*. Bond engages in a playful but dangerous chase with Xenia Onatopp on the road to Monte Carlo, while being evaluated by Caroline of MI6. This car's special equipment includes a cooler for a bottle of 1988 Bollinger and a digital color fax printer/communicator built into the CD player.

Bond uses his DB5 to visit Professor Inga Bergstrom at Oxford in *Tomorrow Never Dies*. It saves 007 valuable time when he must return to London in a hurry. The DB5 in *The World Is Not Enough* can be seen on the satellite image provided by R at the film's end.

Casino Royale tells the story of how Bond acquired the DB5. At the One and Only Club, Bond discovers the identity of Alex Dimitrios, thanks to his left-hand

drive 1964 Silver Birch Aston Martin. Bond later wins the car in a poker game with Dimitrios.

The DB5 in *Skyfall* is right-hand drive with the licence plate BMT 216A, as in *Goldfinger*. In *Skyfall*, Bond rescues M from Silva's assassination attempt at the board of enquiry and takes her to a lockup where he stores his Silver Birch Aston Martin DB5. Bond then whisks M away to his Scottish childhood home, Skyfall Lodge. During their journey to Scotland, M complains about the uncomfortable ride and Bond jokingly threatens to employ the vehicle's passenger ejector seat.

When Silva's men approach Skyfall, Bond uses the car's front-firing machine guns to take out several of them. Later, Silva orders his helicopter gunner to destroy the DB5 to draw Bond out of the house. The explosive gunfire destroys the vintage vehicle.

Goldfinger DB5 modifications (BMT 216A):
• Extending front and rear ramming bumpers
• Secret drawer (not seen) under driver's seat holding a 7.63 mm Mauser, silencer, Armalite rifle, telescopic sight, throwing knife, hand grenade
• Radio telephone (not seen) in compartment in driver's door
• Homer receiver: range 150 miles (241 km), works via radar scanner in racing mirror (not seen)
• Homer "moving map" display behind dashboard radio speaker grill.
• Bulletproof windscreen and windows
• Revolving number plates, valid all countries (or at least UK, Switzerland, and France)
• Caltrop dispenser behind driver's rear light cluster (not seen)
• Tire knife mechanically extends from passenger-side rear wheel hub
• Smoke screen, fired from exhaust pipe
• Oil slick dispenser behind passenger rear light cluster
• Retractable bulletproof screen in rear
• Front wing machine guns behind left and right indicator lights
• Passenger ejector seat, engaged and fired by pressing red button in gear lever knob

Thunderball modifications:
• High-pressure water cannons

GoldenEye modifications (BMT 214A):
• Champagne cooler in center armrest
• Digital color fax printer/communicator CD unit

GETAWAY VEHICLE *Bond prepares to spirit M away to Skyfall in his beloved Aston Martin.*

AN EXPLOSIVE ENDING *(right) Hunting M and Bond at Skyfall, Silva orders the DB5 to be destroyed.*

CLASSICS *(below) James Bond looks out at the golf course beside the Aston Martin DB5 in Goldfinger. The relationship between Bond and the DB5 has lasted more than 40 years.*

ASTON MARTIN DBS

On Her Majesty's Secret Service (1969), Diamonds Are Forever (1971), Casino Royale (2006), Quantum Of Solace (2008)

USED BY James Bond, Tracy di Vicenzo

The Aston Martin DBS, originally produced from 1967 to 1972, features in *On Her Majesty's Secret Service* and *Diamonds Are Forever*. A new version of the DBS, based on the DB9 model, awaits 007 when he arrives in Montenegro for the high-stakes poker game at the Hotel Splendide in *Casino Royale*.

In *On Her Majesty's Secret Service*, Bond, driving a silver DBS, pursues a suicidal Tracy Di Vicenzo in her red Mercury Cougar. Finding her car abandoned on a Portuguese coastal road, Bond opens the glove compartment to reveal a sniper rifle with a telescopic sight. Bond uses the sight to spy on Tracy as she enters the water, intent on drowning herself. 007 speeds the DBS across the dunes to rescue her. At the end of the film, Bond and Tracy leave on their honeymoon in the DBS. When Bond stops on a mountain road to remove the wedding flowers from the car, Ernst Stavro Blofeld drives past in a Mercedes. Irma Bunt in the back seat fires a machine gun at the DBS, killing Tracy.

The DBS appears only briefly in *Diamonds Are Forever*, in the background of Q's workshop.

In *Casino Royale*, 007 discovers that the glove compartment of his new Aston Martin DBS contains a Walther P99 with silencer, a Medipac, and several combipens.

When Valenka poisons Bond, he stumbles to the DBS and, with Vesper Lynd's timely intervention, uses the Medipac to counteract the digitalis in his system. Bond later uses the DBS to pursue Le Chiffre and his men when they kidnap Vesper. When he sees Vesper tied up in the middle of the road, he swerves the speeding DBS, launching the car into seven barrel rolls before finally crashing.

In *Quantum Of Solace*, Bond is driving his spotless Aston Martin DBS near Lake Garda, Italy when assassins in two pursuing Alfa Romeo 159s attempt to machine-gun him off the road. The first Alfa smashed head-on into a truck. Bond then detours through a marble quarry and, when the other Alfa swerves to dodge a bulldozer, fires his Heckler & Koch, sending the car barreling down a cliff. Bond drives into the peaceful narrow streets of Siena's medieval center, his DBS now battered, covered in dust, and missing a door. The doors to an MI6 safe house swing open and Bond drives down a passageway and stops. He gets out, walks round to the back of the car, and opens the trunk. Inside is Mr. White. "Time to get out," says Bond, grimly.

THE RIGHT CAR *MI6 presents Bond with a top-of-the-range Aston Martin DBS to support his cover as a top professional poker player in* Casino Royale.

OVER AND OUT *Bond spins the wheel to avoid Vesper's body and sends his DBS somersaulting across the road.*

DUST AND DANGER *Quantum assassins pursue Bond's DBS through a marble quarry near Siena, Italy.*

ASTON MARTIN V8

APPEARANCE
The Living Daylights (1987)
USED BY James Bond, Kara Milovy

Bond uses his gray Aston Martin V8 Volante to escape with cellist Kara Milovy through the Czech mountains. As the police try to stop them crossing the border to Austria, 007 uses various gadgets to evade them. These include a police band scanner radio, ice tires, retractable outriggers for use on snow and ice, and a jet engine booster rocket, which is concealed behind the rear licence plate. Bond also uses laser beams built into the front hubcaps to cut the chassis off a police car. A heads-up display on the windshield targets a pair of heat-seeking missiles hidden behind the fog lights that 007 uses to destroy roadblocks. The car also boasts a self-destruct system.

SMOOTH AS ICE *(left) The winterized V8 races across a frozen lake near the Czech—Austrian border.*

EXPLOSIVE ACCELERATION *(below) The V8 exits a boathouse just before a shell blasts it to matchwood.*

ASTON MARTIN VANQUISH

APPEARANCE
Die Another Day (2002)
USED BY James Bond

Bond drives the Aston Martin Vanquish V12 with Tungsten Silver coachwork and charcoal leather interior on his mission in Iceland. Q presents 007 with the brand new Vanquish at MI6's secret London Underground station headquarters, and the car's most remarkable feature is its adaptive camouflage. Cameras on all sides of the car record images which are then displayed onto a light-emitting polymer skin on the opposite side, giving the illusion of transparency—but only if viewed from the appropriate angles and in the proper environment. The car also houses a remarkable array of weaponry, including a thermal imaging mechanism concealed within the car's CD player, heat-seeking missiles housed behind the grille, two machine-fired 12-gauge target-seeking shotguns hidden in the car hood, tire spikes for ice driving, and an ejector seat capable of blasting the passenger seat out with enough force to flip the Vanquish 180°—a feature Bond discovers during his mission. Additionally, the bodywork, windscreens, and windows are all bulletproof.

Bond uses the Vanquish to great advantage during his investigation of billionaire diamond tycoon Gustav Graves/Colonel Moon. The camouflage fails under a fusillade from a Jaguar XKR driven by Graves's henchman Zao, but the Vanquish manages to out-maneuver the XKR on a frozen lagoon. The Vanquish's thermal imaging system locates Jinx inside the melting Ice Palace. The car also carries Bond and Jinx to a hot spring, where 007 revives the NSA agent.

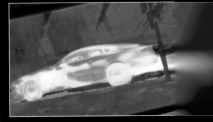

HOT ROD *A heat-seeking targeting system reveals the Vanquish; its adaptive camouflage makes it invisible to the naked eye.*

SNOW TIRES *Bond uses these ice spikes to literally climb a wall.*

FIRE AND ICE *Four heat-seeking missiles are concealed in the Vanquish's grille.*

READY FOR BATTLE *Two mighty vehicles face off on a frozen lake in* **Die Another Day***: Bond's Aston Martin Vanquish and Zao's Jaguar XKR*

AUDI CARS

APPEARANCES
The Living Daylights (1987),
Skyfall (2012)
USED BY Bond, Saunders, Patrice

In *The Living Daylights*, Bond uses an Audi 200 Quattro belonging to Saunders, head of Section V, Vienna, to smuggle Soviet General Georgi Koskov from communist Czechoslovakia into Austria. Installing Koskov in the front passenger seat, Bond drives to the Trans-Siberian Pipeline and sends Koskov through the pipe to freedom. Bond later collects Saunders in the Audi, and they also cross the border.

In *Skyfall*, assassin-for-hire Patrice drives an Audi A5 B8 in Istanbul after stealing a vital computer hard drive. He is pursued by Bond and Eve in a Land Rover. In Eminonu Square marketplace, Bond causes the Land Rover to smack into the Audi and it crashes.

BANGKOK LONGTAIL

APPEARANCE
The Man With The Golden Gun (1974)
USED BY James Bond, Chula and kickboxing school students

Bond escapes from Hai Fat's kickboxing school and star pupil Chula by leaping into a longtail boat. Powered by car engines and propellers, the boats are a common sight in Bangkok's floating market. In the resulting chase, Bond slices Chula's boat in half before cruising down the klong.

BATH-O-SUB

APPEARANCE
Diamonds Are Forever (1971)
USED BY Ernst Stavro Blofeld

Blofeld has a one-man submarine, known as a bath-o-sub, in case he needs to make a quick escape from his satellite control center on an oil rig off the coast of Mexico. When 007 releases a weather balloon on the oil rig, US government helicopters launch an attack. As the attack becomes more fierce, Blofeld orders his sub to be prepared. Bond takes over the crane lowering the sub into the ocean. He then uses the bath-o-sub, with Blofeld in it, as a wrecking ball to destroy the computers and thus prevent the satellite from blasting Washington DC.

BEDFORD, HMS

APPEARANCE
Tomorrow Never Dies (1997)
USED BY The Royal Navy

As tensions rise to a boiling point with China, the British fleet prepares for war in the South China Sea under its flagship HMS *Bedford*, commanded by Admiral Kelly. When James Bond triggers an explosion aboard press baron Elliot Carver's stealth ship, the *Bedford* sees the craft on its radar. HMS *Bedford* pursues the stealth ship and attempts to blow it out of the water. After Carver's stealth ship explodes, HMS *Bedford* searches for Bond and his ally Wai Lin of the Chinese People's External Security Force. Safe amid the wreckage, Bond and Wai Lin decide to remain "under cover" a little longer.

BEECH 18

APPEARANCE
Octopussy (1983)
USED BY Kamal Khan, Gobinda

AERIAL DUEL *Gobinda prepares to battle Bond in midair on Khan's Beech 18.*

Kamal Khan uses his personal Beech 18, a twin-engine, low-wing, conventional-gear aircraft, to escape justice with counterfeit currency plates. Bond leaps from horseback onto the tail during take off to rescue Khan's hostage Octopussy. When Bond climbs out on a wing and pulls out engine wires, Khan sends his henchman Gobinda to kill him. Bond uses the plane's aerial to swat Gobinda off the plane. He then kicks at the ailerons, and Kamal struggles with the controls as the Beech 18 loses altitude. 007 crawls into the cabin, grabs Octopussy, and jumps out as the plane skids toward the edge of a cliff. Bond and Octopussy survive, but the Beech 18 crashes and explodes, killing Khan instantly.

BELL HELICOPTERS

APPEARANCES
Thunderball (1965), You Only Live Twice (1967), On Her Majesty's Secret Service (1969), Diamonds Are Forever (1971), Live And Let Die (1973), The Spy Who Loved Me (1977), Moonraker (1979), For Your Eyes Only (1981), Quantum Of Solace (2008)
USED BY Bond, Felix Leiter, CIA, Irma Bunt, Draco's men, Willard Whyte, Kananga's men, Dr. Bechmann, Prof. Markovitz, Naomi, Corinne Dufour, Blofeld, General Koskov, Necros

Bell helicopters have proved useful to 007 in foiling several plots. Equally, many megalomaniacs have used Bell helicopters to try to stop Bond.

During Operation Thunderball, CIA agent Felix Leiter flies Bond in a Bell 47J helicopter on a search for the

AIR TAXI *A Bell carries Bond to Blofeld's clinic in* On Her Majesty's Secret Service.

scuttled Vulcan bomber.

In *You Only Live Twice*, as 007 circles Japanese volcanoes in the Little Nellie gyrocopter, four black Kawasaki/Bell 47G-3 helicopters attack with high-powered machine guns. Bond destroys all of them with Little Nellie's arsenal of weapons.

In *On Her Majesty's Secret Service*, Blofeld's henchman Irma Bunt flies with Bond to Piz Gloria in a Bell 206 JetRanger. Later, Bond returns with Draco's men in three Bell 204 Hueys with fake Red Cross markings to attack Blofeld's hideout.

Diamonds Are Forever features millionaire Willard Whyte and Felix Leiter leading an attack on Blofeld's oil rig headquarters in a Bell 206B helicopter. Two UH-1H Hueys and three OH-6A Cayuses participate in the attack as well.

Live And Let Die features a Bell 206 JetRanger belonging to Dr. Kananga that tries to machine-gun Bond and Solitaire in Kananga's poppy fields.

The Spy Who Loved Me presents two enemy Bell 206 JetRangers,

both owned by aquatic-obsessed Karl Stromberg. He destroys one carrying Dr. Bechmann and Prof. Markowitz after they have successfully developed the submarine tracking system for him. Later, Stromberg's pilot Naomi tries to eliminate Bond and Soviet agent Anya Amasova with high-powered machine guns attached to her Bell helicopter. Bond destroys the JetRanger with a missile fired from his Lotus submersible.

Bell 206 JetRangers are also used by the villain of *Moonraker*, Hugo Drax. Drax's assistant, Corinne Dufour, flies 007 in one from LA airport to Drax's estate in the California desert.

In *For Your Eyes Only*, a wheelchair-bound man resembling Blofeld tampers with an MI6 Augusta/Bell 206B helicopter (with Universal Exports painted on the side). Using a high-voltage line off the craft's generator, the man sends a deadly shock to the pilot, then takes the lone passenger—Bond—for a wild ride. Bond slips into the cockpit, disconnects the remote control, impales the man's wheelchair on one of the skids, and drops the mastermind down a chimney.

In *The Living Daylights*, General Koskov and the assassin Necros utilize a Bell UH-1H Huey disguised with Red Cross markings to fake Koskov's own kidnapping.

In *Quantum of Solace*, a Bell UH-1H Huey attacks Bond and Camille while they are investigating Dominic Greene's Tierra Project in Bolivia.

DIVING FOR COVER *Naomi's Bell 206 JetRanger drives Bond and Anya Amasova into the sea in* The Spy Who Loved Me.

BENTLEY MK IV

APPEARANCE
From Russia With Love (1963)
DRIVEN BY James Bond

James Bond's personal Mark IV drophead coupé (circa 1936) Derby Green Bentley can be seen briefly as Bond answers a call from Miss Moneypenny on the car's MTS radio telephone, which had recently been introduced in Britain. Bond also has a "cricket," an early form of a pager that informs him when he has a call.

In the Fleming novels, Bond owns a series of Bentleys. He first owns a 1930 4-cylinder 4 ½-liter Bentley convertible, which is destroyed during a car chase. Bond replaces that car with a 1953 Bentley Mark VI convertible with an open touring body. He later purchases a wrecked Bentley Continental that he has specially modified.

BIRD 1

APPEARANCE
You Only Live Twice (1967)
USED BY Blofeld, SPECTRE astronauts

Blofeld utilizes a two-stage rocket to capture US and Soviet spacecraft. A two-man craft with a large cargo bay, *Bird 1* is unique for its era, because it has a fully reusable main capsule. *Bird 1*'s ability to land on four deployable legs as the craft nears touchdown also stands as a remarkable engineering achievement. The craft features a precision internal gyroscopic guidance system and retro-rockets which allow for vertical touchdown with safety and accuracy that has yet to be duplicated in manned spaceflight. *Bird 1* launches from Blofeld's rocket base headquarters in Japan, concealed inside a dormant volcano. 007 blows up *Bird 1* in orbit by unlocking and pressing the destructor button. Blofeld himself wipes out the ground-control technology when he sets off a series of explosions.

BMW 750IL

APPEARANCE
Tomorrow Never Dies (1997)
DRIVEN BY **James Bond**

James Bond's specially equipped BMW 750iL proves its worth when 007 visits Hamburg, Germany. Bond collects the car at the airport from Q, who poses as an Avis Rent-A-Car agent. Bond uses the traditional car as part of his cover as a banker. He makes a quick escape in the BMW from Elliot Carver's media complex. Later, Elliot Carver's men unsuccessfully attempt to break into the sedan on the fourth floor of the six-story car park to retrieve a GPS encoding device. The device remains hidden in the car's glove compartment, which doubles as a safe and carries a spare Walther PPK. Owing to the car's top-level security system, attempts to smash its windshields with sledgehammers and tire irons prove fruitless. The electrified door handles further prevent entry to the would-be thieves.

The 750iL can be driven by remote, using the touch pad on 007's specially modified Ericsson mobile phone. Two taps cause the car's ignition to roar to life. A press of a button on the touch pad emits tear gas from the car. The touch pad allows Bond to drive the BMW from the backseat, where a German female voice warns him of potential driving

hazards. Bond remotely drives the 750iL to the first floor of the car park and then back to the fifth floor in attempts to escape from Carver's men.

The 750iL's top secret gadgetry includes twelve rockets hidden in the sunroof, caltrops spilling from the back bumper, re-inflatable tires, and a cable-cutting device that extends from the BMW's hood badge. On the fifth floor, Bond removes the GPS encoder from the glove compartment and leaps from the BMW as he sends the sedan flying off the roof of the garage straight into an Avis Rent-A-Car.

> "If you'd just sign here, Mr. Bond. It's the insurance damage waiver for your **beautiful new car.**"
>
> **Q to 007**

BMW Z3

APPEARANCE
GoldenEye (1995)
DRIVEN BY James Bond, Jack Wade

James Bond's blue BMW Z3 may be a small car, but Q assures Bond it's packed with all the usual refinements. With agile five forward gears, all points radar, a self-destruct system, and a parachute that fires out the back, it seems well-suited to any situation. Q is particularly proud of the Stinger missiles behind the headlights. It can also accelerate from 0 to 60 mph (96.6 kph) in 8.5 seconds with a top speed of 130 mph (209.2 kph).

While none of the more aggressive additions plays a role in Bond's mission, 007 does use the radar in the Caribbean. The screen pops up between the front seats to alert him of CIA contact Jack Wade's approaching Cessna 172. Wade temporarily trades Bond the Cessna for the Z3, with Bond admonishing him not to push any of the buttons. He looks mildly worried when Wade responds that he's just going to go "bombing around" in it.

BMW Z8

APPEARANCE
The World Is Not Enough (1999)
DRIVEN BY James Bond

Q provides Bond with a customized BMW Z8 for his mission to Baku to protect oil heiress Elektra King. The "fully loaded" car with the very latest in interceptive countermeasures, titanium armor, multitasking heads-up display, and the all-important six beverage cup holders, has enough firepower to blast a helicopter from the skies. Bond sacrifices the Z8 during his mission to Baku in order to save his own life.

At a caviar factory by the Caspian Sea, Bond and nuclear

physicist Dr. Christmas Jones question caviar factory owner Valentin Zukovsky about King when her Eurocopter AS-355F1 Ecureuil II "Twin Squirrel" helicopters, equipped with five-blade tree-cutting rigs, suddenly raid the factory. Bond uses his key fob to remotely drive his BMW toward him. Inside,

Bond activates a target-locking missile launcher concealed behind the car's exterior air vent by pressing buttons on the center of the steering column next to the BMW badge. Bond destroys one helicopter but has to evacuate the Z8 as another slices the car in half. Bond comments, "Q's not going to like this."

NIGHT RAID *(above left) King's tree-cutter copters hone in on Bond's Z8.*

SLICED *(above) Tree-cutting saws rip Bond's Z8 in half during the factory attack.*

BMW R1200

APPEARANCE
Tomorrow Never Dies (1997)
USED BY James Bond, Wai Lin

Carver's Eurocopter 350B A-Star helicopter pursues Bond and Wai Lin with its co-pilot firing a machine gun at them. Mounted on a BMW R1200 motorbike, they speed along streets, walkways, and rooftops, jumping from one building to another to escape a hail of bullets. When the chopper traps Bond and Wai Lin in a courtyard, they grab a washing line and lay the R1200 on its side, sliding just beneath the rotors. Bond slings the line into the helicopter's tail rotors, causing it to crash and explode.

THE HIGH WAY *(right) 007 and Wai Lin leap over rooftops to evade Carver's helicopter.*

EVASIVE ACTION *Seemingly trapped in a cul-de-sac by Carver's helicopter, Bond and Wai Lin skid beneath its whirling blades.*

BOBSLED

APPEARANCE On Her Majesty's Secret Service (1969)
USED BY James Bond, Blofeld

Following the defeat of his guards by a force led by Bond and his ally Marc Ange Draco, Ernst Stavro Blofeld escapes from Piz Gloria, his mountaintop base, in a two-man racing bobsled. Bond, in another bobsled, pursues Blofeld down the mountain. Blofeld attempts to kill Bond with a grenade but only ends up blasting him across a hairpin turn, where 007 leaps onto Blofeld's sled. The two men battle on the sled until Blofeld pins Bond down. As Blofeld pummels Bond, a low-hanging branch sweeps the master criminal off the bobsled, breaking his neck.

BOMB SLED

APPEARANCE
Thunderball (1965)
USED BY SPECTRE frogmen, Emilio Largo

To transport two NATO atomic weapons, SPECTRE commissions a motorized underwater bomb sled. The sled is used to extract weapons from a hijacked Vulcan bomber. The bright orange sled is easily identifiable from the air, helping the US aquaparas to locate the craft. The sled is equipped with headlamps for night work and six forward-firing CO2 spearguns for defense.

BONDOLA

APPEARANCE
Moonraker (1979)
DRIVEN BY James Bond

When a knife-thrower kills Bond's gondolier, Franco, Bond opens a hidden control panel on the left side of his gondola. He engages the throttle, and a propeller underneath the boat sends it speeding down the Venetian canals. Approaching St. Mark's Square, Bond unveils another control panel from the right side of the boat and pushes buttons that inflate a skirt underneath, turning the gondola into a hovercraft. He cruises through the square, using a steering wheel that emerges from the footrest. Tourists cannot believe what they see; even a pigeon does a double-take. Bond reenters the water and punts the boat like a normal gondola for a nighttime surveillance of billionaire Hugo Drax's secret nerve gas laboratory.

BSA A65L LIGHTNING

APPEARANCE
Thunderball (1965)
DRIVEN BY Fiona Volpe

The BSA A65L Lightning 650cc is one of the finest British motorcycles ever built. Manufactured by the Birmingham Small Arms Company, the twin cylinder 1965 Lightning hit the roads in late 1964, just in time for SPECTRE member Fiona Volpe to purchase one and outfit it with four front-firing rockets. Volpe uses the Lightning to eliminate fellow SPECTRE member Count Lippe, whom Blofeld feels has endangered the NATO project. While Lippe pursues 007's Aston Martin DB5 in a Ford Skyliner, Volpe drives the BSA close behind. She fires the rockets, which appear to skew wildly, but manage to hit their mark and blow up the rear portion of the car. As Lippe careens off the road, the gas tank ignites. Volpe takes the BSA to a nearby lake and disposes of it.

CABLE CAR

APPEARANCES
On Her Majesty's Secret Service (1969), Moonraker (1979)
USED BY James Bond, Grunther, Irma Bunt, Blofeld's Angels of Death, Holly Goodhead, Jaws

James Bond twice faces danger in connection with cable cars.

In *On Her Majesty's Secret Service*, he attempts to escape Blofeld's Piz Gloria base by going hand-over-hand down the guide cable from the cable car's wheelhouse. When a gondola ascends to Piz Gloria, Bond almost loses his hands as the guide-wheels roll over the cable.

In *Moonraker*, Bond and astronaut Dr. Holly Goodhead board an aerial tramway to descend Sugar Loaf Mountain. Jaws stops the cable car wheel and shears the tow-cable with his

JAW-DROPPING *Bond and Jaws grapple on top of a cable car in Moonraker.*

BLAME IT ON RIO *(below right) Bond and Holly climb atop the aerial tramway car at Sugar Loaf Mountain.*

teeth, causing the safety brake on the guide wheels to engage. Jaws then rides another car up to meet the pair. He leaps onto their car, but 007 and Goodhead escape by sliding down the guide cable on a chain. Jaws signals a helper to disengage the car's brake hoping to run Bond and Holly down; instead, he crashes into the station. Emerging from the wreckage, Jaws meets and falls in love with his soulmate Dolly.

WILD ONE *A leatherclad Fiona Volpe revs her lethal BSA Lightninag.*

CAGIVA MOTORCYCLE

APPEARANCE
GoldenEye (1995)
DRIVEN BY James Bond, Soviet soldiers

As Bond pursues a plane taxiing away from a Soviet chemical weapons facility, two soldiers on Mera Cagiva 600 W 16 bikes give chase. Bond climbs onto the plane, struggles with the pilot, and shoots one soldier off his bike. Bond and the pilot roll out of the plane, and the second soldier's bike hits the pilot. Bond retrieves the bike and races after the plane, driving it over a cliff and diving off into a freefall.

CAPTURED TRAWLER

APPEARANCE
Tomorrow Never Dies (1997)
USED BY Wai Lin, Elliot Carver's men

Wai Lin hires a trawler to take her into Vietnamese waters, where HMS *Devonshire* sank. Upon reaching the surface with Bond—who parachuted into the sea on the same quest—Wai Lin indicates for the trawler to collect them. But Carver's enforcer, Stamper, fires a speargun harpoon into the helmsman's chest, and he and his men take control of the ship and capture Wai Lin and Bond.

CESSNA 140

APPEARANCE
Live And Let Die (1973)
USED BY James Bond, Mrs. Bell

The Cessna 140 N77029, used as a training plane by The Bleeker Flying School, makes a handy escape craft for Bond when Dr. Kananga/Mr. Big's minions try to capture him and take him for a "skydive" at Lakeside Airport in New Orleans. To the great relief of Mrs. Bell, the student pilot inside, Bond never actually takes the plane into the air. As Kananga's henchmen give chase, Bond drives the plane around the airfield and through the hangar, ripping the wings off in the process.

CESSNA 185 SEAPLANE

APPEARANCE
Licence To Kill (1989)
FLOWN BY Sanchez's pilot, James Bond

Off the coast of Key West, a Cessna 185 seaplane lands near the *Wavekrest*, Milton Krest's research ship and distribution base for Franz Sanchez's drug operation. The *Sentinel*, a remote-controlled submersible, delivers $5 million from the *Wavekrest* to the Cessna pilots in exchange for cocaine. Underwater, Bond destroys the drug shipment in the *Sentinel* and fires the harpoon of a CO_2 speargun into the pontoon of the seaplane. He barefoot skis behind the Cessna as it taxis, takes over the plane, disposes of the pilots, and flies away with Sanchez's drug money.

CHESTER, HMS

APPEARANCE
Tomorrow Never Dies (1997)
USED BY The Royal Navy

Admiral Roebuck orders the Royal Navy frigate HMS *Chester* to launch a missile strike into a terrorist arms bazaar. When Roebuck and MI6 learn that an L39 Albatross jet at the bazaar carries Soviet SB-5 nuclear torpedoes, Roebuck orders the *Chester* to abort the missile. The missile, however, is too far away to destroy.

CHEVROLET DELIVERY TRUCK

APPEARANCE
From Russia With Love (1963)
DRIVEN BY Rhoda, James Bond

This Chevrolet C30 1961 flatbed delivery truck plays an important role in SPECTRE's plot to steal the Lektor and humiliate James Bond. Driver Rhoda parks the truck across the Orient Express's track as though he has engine trouble in order to pick up assassin Donald "Red" Grant. Instead, Bond steals the truck and kidnaps Rhoda. In the truck, Bond dodges hand grenades from a SPECTRE helicopter and, after downing the chopper, forces Rhoda to guide him to SPECTRE's escape boat.

CHIMERA

APPEARANCE
Skyfall (2012)
OWNED BY Silva

The *Chimera* is a 56-meter yacht owned by Silva. After their encounter at the Floating Dragon Casino, Severine and Bond arrange to meet on board the yacht, but Silva's men hold them at gunpoint as the boat carries them to Silva's island base.

CITROËN 2CV

APPEARANCE
For Your Eyes Only (1981)
DRIVEN BY James Bond, Melina Havelock

Bond tests the limits of his driving skills on narrow, twisting Spanish backroads when he is forced to escape in Melina Havelock's Citroën 2CV as Hector Gonzales's henchmen pursue him in far more powerful Peugeot 504 sedans.

Created in 1939, the low-powered, low-cost 2CV became Citroën's version of a "people's car." It is the antithesis of Bond's hand-built British sports cars.

After James Bond's white Lotus Esprit Turbo self-destructs when Gonzalez's men try to attack it, Bond jumps into the passenger seat of marine archaeologist Melina Havelock's yellow 2CV. Two Peugeot 504 sedans give chase through the countryside. In a small town, the 2CV overturns, allowing 007 to take the wheel from Melina. Bond uses the 2CV's remarkable maneuverability and durability to turn the tables on his pursuers in spectacular style.

"I love a drive in the country, don't you?
Hold tight!"

007 to Melina

CROCODILE MINI-SUBMARINE

APPEARANCE
Octopussy (1983)
DRIVEN BY **James Bond**

James Bond uses a crocodile mini-submarine built by Q to inconspicuously approach the heavily guarded floating palace belonging to jewel smuggler Octopussy.

Later, when Bond and one of Mufti's thugs crash into the quay, Bond pretends to be eaten by the crocodile, much to the distress of Octopussy. He actually escapes in the crocodile submarine and reports back to Q.

DEVONSHIRE, HMS

APPEARANCE
Tomorrow Never Dies (1997)
USED BY **The Royal Navy**

The British frigate HMS *Devonshire* becomes a pawn in Elliot Carver's plot to foment a war between China and Britain. Carver uses one of his satellites to beam a false GPS signal to the *Devonshire*. When the Chinese military accuses the *Devonshire* of being in their waters, the *Devonshire*'s captain, Commander Day, argues the ship is in international waters, In fact, it has been guided into Vietnamese waters. Secure in Carver's invisible-to-radar stealth ship, Stamper creates an international incident by sinking the *Devonshire* with the Sea Vac drill and shooting down a Chinese MiG fighter with a missile. Stamper then machine-guns the *Devonshire*'s 17 survivors while the stealth ship's crew

DOOMED *Sailors aboard the* **Devonshire** *fight for their lives as the sea pours through the gaping hole made by Carver's Sea Vac drill.*

salvage one of its Tomahawk missiles. Bond and Wai Lin later locate the wreck and discover that a missile is missing. During their search, the *Devonshire* slips off the edge of a shelf and plunges into an abyss.

DISCO VOLANTE

APPEARANCE
Thunderball (1965)
USED BY Emilio Largo, SPECTRE

Emilio Largo purchased an early Rodriguez hydrofoil that he has customized with two Pratt & Whitney J12 jet engines to assist and supplant the onboard diesel. He has an outer shell, or cocoon, designed and built to give the appearance of a staid motor yacht. Behind the foils, Largo installs an underwater hatch. In the rear, he adds a smoke pot to create a smoke screen. On the cocoon, Largo mounts a front-facing WWII-era anti-aircraft gun. He also installs placements for two smaller machine guns. Christening the motor vessel *Disco Volante* ("flying saucer" in English), Largo registers the craft in Panama. With the cocoon attached,

BREAKING AWAY *Under fire by the US Navy and the US Coast Guard, the Disco Volante jettisons its cocoon, revealing itself to be a powerful hydrofoil.*

UP TO NO GOOD *A hatch in the bottom of the* Disco Volante*'s hull enables Largo and his men to come and go unseen.*

the *Disco* can move at nearly 20 knots owing to the light catamaran design of the outer shell. Without the cocoon, the *Disco* can travel at 70 knots on her foil with her two rear jet engines at full thrust, a speed that enables the *Disco* to outrun virtually any pursuing waterborne craft. The hydrofoil portion weighs 20 tons (18.1 tonnes) and measures 65 ft (19.8 m) in length. The disguise allows Largo to secretly crew the vessel through the underwater hatch, collect and move the atomic weapons, and shed the cocoon for maneuverability and speed, if necessary.

The *Disco Volante* disintegrates in an explosion in Biscayne National Park while fleeing from the Royal Navy and US Coast Guard. All hands are lost except for Largo's mistress, Domino Derval, nuclear physicist Latislav Kutze, and uninvited passenger James Bond.

DOUGLAS DC-3

APPEARANCE
Quantum Of Solace (2008)
USED BY James Bond, Camille

Manufactured by the Douglas Aircraft Company, the DC-3 is an American fixed-wing, propeller-driven aircraft, primarily used today as a cargo plane.

When Bond wants to investigate Dominic Greene's Tierra Project, he trades a Range Rover for a DC-3 at a Bolivian desert airfield. Bond observes to Camille that the DC-3's owner will profit greatly when he "sells them out." This is just what happens; they are soon menaced by a sleek SIAI-Marchetti SF.260 TP fighter, which strafes the DC-3 with machine-gun fire, setting one of the plane's engines on fire.

Bond takes evasive action, flying

MOMENT OF CALM *Thrown together by their enmity for Dominic Greene, Bond and Camille are only in the air a few minutes before they are attacked.*

the clumsy plane through a desert canyon. He tries to blind the Marchetti pilot with the smoke billowing from his engine and manages to persuade him to fly beneath him. When the pilot does so, he crests a saddleback ridge, clips a wing, and crashes.

A Bell helicopter then fires at the DC-3. Bond forces the crippled aircraft into a vertiginous climb, forcing it to stall. He and Camille freefall from the plane into a desert sinkhole. Camille's parachute breaks their fall as the DC-3 explodes above them.

DRAGON TANK

APPEARANCE
Dr. No (1962)
USED BY Dr. No's men

Dr. No uses a swamp vehicle painted like a dragon and outfitted with a flame thrower to frighten away visitors to Crab Key. Both Honey Ryder and Quarrel know of the "dragon" and fear it. When Bond, Honey and Quarrel enter the island's swamplands, the dragon tank hunts them down. The dragon's flame-thrower burns Quarrel to death, and Dr. No's men capture Bond and Honey.

In the novel, the dragon tank incinerates two wardens from the Audubon Society who live on Crab Key to monitor a population of roseate spoonbills. This initiates 007's battle with Dr. No.

ESCAPE POD

APPEARANCE
The Spy Who Loved Me (1977)
USED BY James Bond, Anya Amasova

When the USS *Wayne* torpedoes shipping magnate Karl Stromberg's *Atlantis* base, Bond and Soviet agent Anya Amasova flee in a handy escape pod. The pod, which rises to the ocean surface and emits a radio signal that allows it to be discovered, is equipped with a round bed and stocked with books, magazines, and spirits. Pressing a switch causes curtains to drape over the observation window.

CURTAIN CALL *Bond and Anya demonstrate a new era of Western–Soviet cooperation inside Stromberg's escape pod.*

PICKED UP *M, Q, Sir Frederick Gray, and KGB chief Gogol inspect Stromberg's pod.*

EUROCOPTER TREE-CUTTER

APPEARANCE
The World Is Not Enough (1999)
USED BY Elektra King's men

King Industries uses Eurocopter AS-355F1 Ecureuil II "Twin Squirrel" helicopters fitted with five giant vertically-suspended buzz saws to remove trees in the path of the future King oil pipeline. When Elektra King discovers Bond is alive at Valentin Zukovsky's caviar factory, she orders two tree-cutting choppers to eradicate Bond, Zukovsky, and Christmas Jones. As one of the helicopter's saws slices through buildings, Bond reaches his BMW Z8 and destroys the other one with a target-locking missile. The first chopper sneaks up behind, slices through the BMW, and chases Bond along a wooden walkway. Zukovsky and Christmas attempt to escape the deadly buzz saws by jumping into Zukovsky's Rolls-Royce and reversing along a walkway. The chopper slices the walkway to pieces, causing the Rolls to fall into the sea. Bond then opens a rusted gas jet, waits for the chopper to hover over it, and fires a flare gun at the gas. The resulting fireball sends the chopper's saws flying out of control and Zukovsky tumbling into a caviar pit.

See also Aerospatiale Helicopters

SLICED APART
The whirling blades of the tree-cutter zero in on 007's BMW.

FAIREY HUNTRESS SPEEDBOAT

APPEARANCE
From Russia With Love (1963)
DRIVEN BY James Bond, Morzeny, SPECTRE operatives

James Bond steals the Fairey Huntress speedboat on the Dalmatian Coast and uses it to escape with Soviet cipher clerk Tatiana Romanova and the Lektor decoder. The 23-ft (7-m) speedboat is confronted by SPECTRE's two Huntsmans and two Huntresses. While these boats have grenade launchers and machine-gunners, Bond's Huntress has a custom-made fuel drum rack. When bullets hit the drums, Bond releases them into the water and appears to surrender. Instead, he ignites the fuel slick with a flare which catches the SPECTRE boats on fire.

WATER RACE *Morzeny shouts orders to his fellow SPECTRE attackers in his Fairey Huntsman.*

FERRARI F355 GTS

APPEARANCE
GoldenEye (1995)

DRIVEN BY Xenia Onatopp, Admiral
Chuck Farrel

Xenia Onatopp, in a Ferrari Spider
F355 GTS sports car with fake
French registration plates,
engages Bond, in his Aston
Martin DB5, in a high-speed
game of cat-and-mouse along
the mountain roads of Monaco.
After a hair-raising chase,
which makes Bond's passenger,
MI6 psychotherapist Caroline,
gasp with terror, Bond allows
the Ferrari to speed ahead. He
pulls over to the side of the
road overlooking Monte
Carlo., and he and Caroline
enjoy a refreshing bottle of
Bollinger.

Later, Bond observes the
Ferrari—owned by Admiral
Chuck Farrel—outside the
Monte Carlo casino. From the
outdoor Fort Antoine Theatre,
Bond watches Farrel and
Onatopp drive in it to the
quayside where the yacht
Manticore is berthed.

HOT PURSUIT *Xenia's Ferrari F355 speeds past cyclists on a training ride. Bond's Aston Martin DB5 follows.*

DUST DEVIL *Capable of 0 to 60 mph in just 4.7 seconds, the red Ferrari had the edge on Bond's vintage Aston Martin.*

FIRE TRUCK

APPEARANCE
A View To A Kill (1985)
USED BY James Bond,
Stacey Sutton

Bond and Stacey Sutton escape a flaming San Francisco City Hall by stealing a Tiller fire truck with an unlocked mid-mount ladder. The San Francisco police give chase, and when Bond attempts to lock down the rear ladder assembly, he finds himself swinging dangerously over busy city streets. After leaping a drawbridge, Bond and Stacey escape and use the Tiller as cover to steal a truck heading into Zorin's Main Strike Mine.

FORD MUSTANG

APPEARANCES
Goldfinger (1964), Thunderball (1965), Diamonds Are Forever (1971)
DRIVEN BY Tilly Masterson, Fiona Volpe, Tiffany Case, James Bond

The Ford Mustang was a legendary success in the 1960s, being unveiled on all three major American television networks on April 19, 1964. It proved to be the perfect mass-production counterpart to Bond's Aston Martin; over one million 1964 1/2 Mustangs were sold in comparison to 1023 hand-built DB5s. Tilly Masterson drives a 1964

TOO CLOSE FOR COMFORT *Bond glimpses Tilly Masterson in his rear-view mirror in* Goldfinger.

1/2 cream Mustang convertible. Unfortunately, her attempt to shoot Goldfinger while Bond happens to be in the way results in him using the tire knives in his DB5's wheel hubs to blow out her Mustang's port side tires and rip through its body and door panels.

In *Thunderball*, SPECTRE enforcer Fiona Volpe drives a 1965 powder-blue Mustang convertible with a white top in Nassau. After reconnoitering Emilio Largo's yacht, Bond hitches a ride with her to the Coral Harbour hotel.

In *Diamonds Are Forever*, Tiffany Case drives a red Mustang Mach 1 "Fastback." Tiffany and Bond use the car to escape from guards at WW Techtronics in the Nevada desert and to elude the Las Vegas police and Clark County Sheriff during a spectacular chase in downtown Las Vegas. Bond puts the strength of the car's axels and its balance to the test when he drives it through a narrow alley on two wheels. The Sheriff attempts to follow but, lacking Bond's expertise behind the wheel, turns his police cruiser over.

FORD SKYLINER

APPEARANCE
Thunderball (1965)
DRIVEN BY Count Lippe

WHEELS ON FIRE *While pursuing Bond, Count Lippe's Ford Skyliner receives a direct hit from Fiona Volpe's motorbike.*

The 1957 Ford Fairlane 500 Skyliner, with its distinctive and celebrated retractable hardtop roof, provides a fiery end for SPECTRE operative Count Lippe when he decides to kill James Bond on a British motorway.

Lippe's Skyliner is in perfect working order when, in a fit of vengeance, he pursues Bond, firing a handgun at Bond's Aston Martin DB5. Bond prepares to defend himself by unleashing the furies of his car's arsenal, but he never gets the chance. Unknown to Lippe, his inefficiency has incurred the wrath of Ernst Stavro Blofeld, SPECTRE No. 1. He orders head executioner Fiona Volpe to extract the price of failure. Riding a BSA A65L Lightning 650cc motorcycle, Fiona Volpe fires rockets into the rear of Lippe's car. The explosion ignites the hydraulic system and eventually the gas tank, killing Lippe and destroying the car.

FORD THUNDERBIRD

APPEARANCES
Goldfinger (1964), Thunderball (1965), Diamonds Are Forever (1971), A View To A Kill (1985), Die Another Day (2002)
USED BY Felix Leiter, Johnny, Emilio Largo, Wint & Kidd, Gen. Gogol, Jinx

TOP GEAR *Posing as Miss Swift from* Space & Technology *magazine, Jinx arrrives in style at Gustav Graves's Ice Palace.*

Five Ford Thunderbirds have been used by Bond's colleagues and enemies. In *Goldfinger*, Felix Leiter and CIA colleague Johnny drive a 1964 white Ford Thunderbird in Kentucky while investigating Goldfinger's activities. *Thunderball* features Emilio Largo driving a 1965 white Ford Thunderbird in Paris. In *Diamonds Are Forever*, assassins Wint and Kidd drive an unconscious Bond in a 1971 Ford Thunderbird through a tunnel from the Whyte House Hotel to the Nevada desert. *A View To A Kill* features KGB General Gogol driving a 1983 Ford Thunderbird in San Francisco while tailing Bond and his agent Pola Ivanova to a spa. *Die Another Day* showcases Jinx arriving in Iceland in a sporty 2003 coral Thunderbird.

GLASTRON SPEEDBOATS

APPEARANCES
Live And Let Die (1973), Moonraker (1979), A View To A Kill (1985)
USED BY James Bond, Adam, Kananga's thugs, Drax's minions, Jaws, May Day, Max Zorin

In *Live And Let Die*, James Bond escapes from Kananga's crocodile farm in a Glastron GT-150 and heads for the Irish Bayou in the Louisiana swamps. His pursuers drive the V-162 Futura, the V-145 Fireflite, the V-156 Sportster, and a V-184 Crestflite. The Sportster is the first casualty, crashing into a tree. When Bond finds his stretch of bayou leads to a causeway, he sends his GT-150 up an embankment, sailing over Sheriff J. W. Pepper's car and into the water on the other side. The pursuer in the Futura slams into the Sheriff's vehicle. Fuel spilling out of his engine due to a bullet hole from Pepper's gun, Bond ditches the GT-150 and steals a Glastron CV-19 from Deke Rodgers. The pursuers in the Firelite manage to get themselves stuck in the pool at Deke's home. Adam soon steals an even faster Glastron CV-21 jet boat from Louisiana wildlife ranger Billy Bob, Sheriff Pepper's brother-in-law.

Bond, the CV-21, and the Crestflight crash through a wedding ceremony, where the Crestflight ends up stuck in the catering tent. Bond leads Adam to Haley's Landing, douses him with gasoline, and then sends the CV-21 into a cargo ship where it spectacularly explodes.

While pursuing Sir Hugo Drax across the globe in *Moonraker*, 007 encounters Glastron boats driven by Drax's assassins in Venice. Bond himself takes a heavily customized silver flake Glastron/Carlson CV-23HT, specially outfitted with an array of gadgets from Q Branch, on a voyage up the River Tiparapé in Brazil. When Jaws and Drax's minions give pursuit in three SSV-189 boats armed with grenade launchers, Bond employs Q's defensive armaments, including a bulletproof shield, six mines ejected from the stern, a rear-launched torpedo hidden beneath the rear light fixture, and a roof-top hang glider. After Bond uses the hang glider to escape, the boat is destroyed when it tumbles down a massive waterfall.

In Paris, Max Zorin orchestrates the assassination of Achille Aubergine in *A View To A Kill* and collects May Day in a Glastron CVX-18 Intimidator.

LOW-FLYING BOAT *Sheriff Pepper is distracted from arresting Mr. Big's henchman Adam by 007's speedboat acrobatics.*

HERCULES C-130

APPEARANCE
The Living Daylights (1987)
USED BY **M, 002, 004, James Bond**

The Hercules C-130, one of the most common cargo planes in the world, serves as M's mobile headquarters as he briefs agents 002, 004, and 007 on war games with the SAS on the Rock of Gibraltar. The three double-0s skydive out of the open cargo bay and parachute onto the rock. M, who has allowed a desk to be loaded into the cargo bay, chases after his papers, which blow around in the wind.

ON MANEUVERS *Three MI6 agents, including 007, parachute from the Hercules to commence a training exercise.*

HILLER UH-12

APPEARANCES
From Russia With Love (1963), Goldfinger (1964)
USED BY **SPECTRE, Pussy Galore, Goldfinger**

SPECTRE uses the versatile Hiller UH-12C helicopter in *From Russia With Love*. The extremely stable, easy-to-fly craft is seen on SPECTRE Island bringing SPECTRE No. 3 Rosa Klebb to meet master assassin Donald "Red" Grant. Later, Bond encounters the helicopter when it begins chasing him and Tatiana as they make their escape from the Orient Express. Despite its safety record, the Hiller UH-12C cannot withstand the grenade explosion in the cockpit caused by the co-pilot.

In *Goldfinger*, Pussy Galore pilots a white Hiller UH-12E4 to Fort Knox. She transports Goldfinger, his associate Mr. Ling, and the atomic device Goldfinger plans to use to irradiate Fort Knox.

WANTED MAN *A SPECTRE Hiller helicopter hunts Bond in* From Russia With Love.

HONDA 3-WHEELER

APPEARANCE
Diamonds Are Forever (1971)
USED BY **WW Techtronics Guards, James Bond**

When 007 steals the WW Techtronics Moonbuggy, three guards give chase on Honda US 90 ATC 3-Wheelers. These vehicles can ride on most terrain and have greater stability than traditional motorcycles. Bond steals one from a Techtronics guard and uses it to reach smuggler Tiffany Case. The ATC uses a 90cc engine and drives on 22-in (55.8-cm) tires that are inflated with very low pressure. The machine can climb a gradient as steep as 35°.

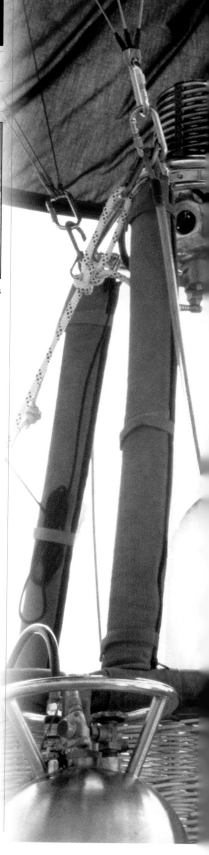

UNDER THE GUN
To escape capture by Bond, the Cigar Girl hijacks a hot-air balloon.

HOT AIR BALLOON

APPEARANCES
Octopussy (1983),
The World Is Not Enough (1999)
USED BY Q, James Bond, Cigar Girl

Bond rarely uses hot air balloons for transportation, but he does fly with Q in one that is decorated with a Union Jack in *Octopussy*. The pair use the balloon as they try to stop exiled Afghan prince Kamal Khan fleeing his Monsoon Palace. Television cameras attached to the balloon's structure allow for aerial surveillance of the palace.

In *The World Is Not Enough*, an assassin known as the Cigar Girl steals a hot air balloon to escape from 007. Bond leaps from a speeding boat onto one of the balloon's tethers. When the Cigar Girl commits suicide by blowing up the balloon's gas tanks, 007 has no choice but to let go of the tether and fall onto the Millennium Dome, painfully dislocating his collarbone.

ICEBERG SUBMARINE

APPEARANCE
A View To A Kill (1985)
USED BY James Bond

Following a dramatic ski chase, James Bond escapes Siberia in a submarine disguised as an iceberg. The iceberg has a Union Jack design on the inside of its hatch. Pilot and MI6 agent Kimberley Jones seems more than willing to enjoy vodka, caviar, and spending time with 007 during the five-day voyage to Alaska while the autopilot does the difficult work.

ICE DRAGSTER

APPEARANCE
Die Another Day (2002)
USED BY Gustav Graves,
James Bond

Billionaire Gustav Graves enjoys racing his ice dragster to speeds of 324 mph (521.4 kph). To bring the ice jet to a stop, a parachute and grappling anchor emerge from the rear. Bond later steals the ice dragster to escape the heat beam of the Icarus satellite. Trapped on the face of a glacier, he uses the dragster's rear hatch and parachute to parasurf a tidal wave created as the heat beam destroys the glacier face.

LIVING THE DREAM *A braking parachute billows behind the dragster developed and raced in Iceland by diamond tycoon Gustav Graves.*

JAGUAR XKR

APPEARANCE
Die Another Day (2002)
DRIVEN BY Zao

In Iceland, Zao drives a gadget-laden 400-h.p. Jaguar XKR that rivals the most impressive vehicles from Q Branch. When Bond tries to use the adaptive camouflage on his Aston Martin Vanquish, Zao turns on a thermal imaging screen, giving him a perfect view. Zao hits a switch, and a Gatling gun rises and fires. The hail of bullets cause the Vanquish's adaptive camouflage to fail, rendering it visible. As Bond chases Bond over a frozen lake, Zao employs his battery of 18 heat-seeking missiles concealed behind the XKR's grille. Zao presses a button, revealing a rocket launcher. He fires at the Vanquish, overturning it. Another rocket barely misses as Bond uses his ejector-seat to right the car. Zao then launches a barrage of mortar bombs, which Bond

SHOOTING ON SIGHT *Zao targets Bond's Aston Martin with his XKR's Gatling gun.*

destroys with the Vanquish's target-seeking shotguns. Zao eventually corners Bond inside the melting Ice Palace and prepares to destroy the Vanquish with a battering ram protruding from his XKR's grille. The Vanquish's camouflage system corrects itself, the car seems to vanish, and Zao and his XKR fall into a lake of freezing water.

RACING DEMONS *Bond shunts Zao's XKR during their battle on the ice.*

JUNK

APPEARANCES
The Man With The Golden Gun (1974), Tomorrow Never Dies (1997)
USED BY Scaramanaga, James Bond, Nick Nack, Andrea Anders, Mary Goodnight, Wai Lin

In *The Man With The Golden Gun*, Scaramanga's diesel-powered junk survives the destruction of his island and allows Bond and staff intelligence officer Mary Goodnight to escape. When henchman Nick Nack interrupts the couple's lovemaking, Bond cages him in the crow's nest.

In *Tomorrow Never Dies*, Bond and Chinese agent Wai Lin hire a similar junk in Hao Long Bay to search for media mogul Elliot Carver's ship.

TOOLING UP *Aboard a rented junk, Bond and Wai Lin prepare to attack Carver's ship.*

JUPITER 16

APPEARANCE
You Only Live Twice (1967)
USED BY NASA

The US two-man spacecraft *Jupiter 16* becomes the first captured by Blofeld's *Bird 1* intruder rocket. While on an extended mission to practice EVAs (extravehicular activities) and conduct experiments, astronaut Chris exits the capsule using a maneuvering unit. Calls from Houston and Hawaii for Chris to re-enter the *Jupiter* capsule come far too late. *Bird 1*'s nose cone opens and swallows the capsule, snaps the astronaut's oxygen tether, and leaves Chris floating in orbit.

The *Jupiter* capsule mirrors the *Gemini* spacecraft used by NASA in 1965–66. The craft is called *Gemini* in the script, but filmmakers changed it to *Jupiter* because the *Gemini* program ended during the film's production.

KAWASAKI 900

APPEARANCE
The Spy Who Loved Me (1977)
DRIVEN BY Stromberg assassin

Leaving *Atlantis*, the marine research laboratory in Sardinia belonging to shipping tycoon Karl Stromberg, Bond and KGB agent Anya Amasova are pursued by an assassin riding a Kawasaki 900 motorcycle with sidecar. The sidecar is, in fact, a rocket that can be launched simply by pressing a button located on the motorcycle's handlebar. Driving his Lotus Esprit, Bond is able to maneuver between two lorries out of the path of the rocket, which ultimately destroys the trailer of a Sardadream mattress truck. The motorcyclist, blinded by the resulting cloud of feathers, goes careening off the road.

KAWASAKI-VERTOL KV107

APPEARANCE
You Only Live Twice (1967)
FLOWN BY Japanese SIS

The Japanese SIS uses a tandem-rotor Kawasaki-Vertol KV107-11, capable of lifting over 22,000 lb (10,000 kg), to handle disruptive automobiles on the roads. When gunmen in a Toyota Crown S40 chase Bond and Aki in her Toyota 2000GT, the pair radios Tiger Tanaka. Aki asks Tiger for the "usual reception." The KV107-11 flies in, sets an industrial magnet on the roof of the Crown and flies off with the Toyota. The helicopter drops the pursuer's car in Tokyo Bay, despite the obvious disadvantage of not being able to question the occupants.

MAGNETIZED *Tanaka's Kawasaki uses a magnet to snatch up a car full of enemy agents on Bond and Aki's tail.*

KENWORTH TRUCKS

APPEARANCE
Licence To Kill (1989)
USED BY James Bond, Franz Sanchez, Sanchez's men, Pam Bouvier

Drug lord Franz Sanchez's team uses four Kenworth W900B tanker trucks to transport cocaine shipments. After setting Sanchez's lab on fire, Bond works with CIA contract pilot and agent Pam Bouvier to destroy the shipment. Bond jumps from a Piper crop-duster atop one tanker trailer. He takes control of the W900B, then shows his expert driving skills by tipping the truck and tanker up on its side wheels, allowing a Stinger missile to pass below. He also performs a wheelie on the tankerless truck to drive it through a wall of fire. Bond proceeds to destroy each of the tanker trailers. He forces one into a cliff face, where a Stinger missile strikes it. He takes out another two by releasing a tanker down a mountain where it crashes into another trailer being pulled below. Another wrecks when Sanchez cuts the hydraulic brake line as he tries to kill 007. Bond sets Sanchez on fire, and he stumbles into the wreckage. As Sanchez immolates, the tanker and truck explode. Bond uses the sole surviving W900B cab to ride to freedom with Pam.

FIREBALL Bond sends a tanker trailer down a slope and hits the lead truck in Sanchez's convoy.

L39 ALBATROSS

APPEARANCE
Tomorrow Never Dies (1997)
USED BY James Bond, unknown pilot

If a cruise missile hits the Soviet SB-5 nuclear torpedoes hanging from an L39 Albatross jet at a terrorist arms bazaar, mass destruction will result. Bond jumps into the cockpit of the Albatross, knocks out the co-pilot, and uses the jet's machine guns to wreak havoc. Bond takes off just before the missile hits. As he emerges from the fireball, so does a second Albatross with cannons blazing. The co-pilot in Bond's aircraft then revives and tries to garrote 007. With the second Albatross positioned overhead, Bond fires the rear-seat ejector. This sends the co-pilot smashing into the second Albatross, causing an explosion. "Backseat driver," Bond quips.

LAND ROVER

APPEARANCE
The Living Daylights (1987)
USED BY Imposter agent, James Bond

An imposter agent eliminates 004 in an exercise on the Rock of Gibraltar and escapes in a stolen Series III MOD Land Rover. Bond leaps onto the roof. The Land Rover smashes through a barrier and a soldier fires, hitting the gas tank; flames lick around explosives packed in the back. Bond grapples with the driver as the Land Rover crashes over a cliff. As the vehicle plummets toward the sea, Bond releases his reserve parachute, bailing out as the Land Rover explodes.

LINCOLN CONTINENTAL

APPEARANCES
Goldfinger (1964), Thunderball (1965)
USED BY Oddjob, Mr. Solo,
James Bond

Goldfinger offers a luxurious 1964 Continental to gangster Mr. Solo after he refuses to take part in Operation Grand Slam. Oddjob drives Solo to a secluded spot, shoots him dead, then takes the car to a scrapyard where it is crushed and loaded into a waiting 1964 Ford Falcon Ranchero.

In Thunderball, Bond briefly drives a 1965 Continental convertible in the Bahamas when visiting the home of SPECTRE's Emilio Largo.

TAKEN FOR A RIDE Oddjob pretends to drive Mr. Solo to the airport in Goldfinger.

LIPARUS

APPEARANCE
The Spy Who Loved Me (1977)
USED BY Karl Stromberg and his men

Shipping tycoon Karl Stromberg's Liparus stands as a marvel of naval engineering. Designed to look like a supertanker—at over one million tons, it would be one of the largest ever built—the ship is, in fact, a floating submarine pen and command center. Stromberg builds the ship to take advantage of his submarine tracking technology and also to capture nuclear submarines.

Built in secret and manned by a loyal private navy, the Liparus has remained at sea for nine months. Stromberg uses the ship to kidnap both British and Soviet nuclear submarines (HMS Ranger and Potemkin, respectively). Armed with atomic weapons, Stromberg hopes to launch a nuclear war that will force civilization to rebuild beneath the sea. He later seizes the USS Wayne

> "Now where the hell is she? By God, she's right behind us. Impossible."
>
> ### Commander Carter

with 007 aboard. The ship contains prisoner bays, a maglev monorail, and a substantial armory.

Bond ultimately initiates a battle to destroy the Liparus. Bond, Commander Carter, and the surviving crew members manage to climb back aboard the Wayne. They launch a torpedo to blast their way out of Stromberg's Liparus just before the ship meets its end at the bottom of the ocean.

PENNED IN The Liparus houses the most sophisticated floating submarine command center ever built. The ship ends up where Stromberg hoped all humanity would—the ocean floor.

LITTLE NELLIE

APPEARANCE
You Only Live Twice (1967)
FLOWN BY James Bond

James Bond uses the Wallis autogyro, no. G-ARZ B, for surveillance work in Japan while attempting to locate Blofeld's rocket base hidden on the southern islands. Operated under the code name Little Nellie, she proves to be a one-man air force, capable of defending herself and destroying a whole fleet of enemy aircraft.

Unlike a helicopter, only the Wallis autogyro's rear engine provides power during flight. Once airborne the top rotor freely spins by the force of air, creating an airfoil. Designed by Wing Commander Ken Wallis, the autogyro offers the advantages of precise handling, safe operation, high ground speed, and high altitude operation. The design also allows for safe descent should the engine fail in flight.

> Tanaka: A toy helicopter?
>
> Q: No, it's certainly not a toy. You'll see.

Q Branch modifies the craft, outfitting it with an array of weapons and breaking it down so that it can fit into four alligator leather trunks. The weapons include two fixed machine-guns firing incendiary and high-explosive bullets harmonized for targets 100 yd (91.4 m) ahead, two forward-firing rocket launchers with seven rockets each, two heat-seeking air-to-air missiles, two rear-firing flame guns with a range of 80 yd (73 m) paired with smoke ejectors, and small high-explosive aerial mines. It also boasts radio communications and a helmet-mounted cine-camera triggered by using any of the forward-firing weapons. Bond uses these weapons as he battles four SPECTRE helicopters over the rocket base, destroying them one by one.

PORTABLE POWER *Q's technicians set to work assembling Little Nellie from parts supplied in four large alligator leather trunks.*

LOCKHEED JETSTAR PLANE

APPEARANCE
Goldfinger (1964)
FLOWN BY **Pussy Galore, Sydney**

Sold commercially starting in 1961, the Lockheed JetStar was the first and most luxurious private jet available for many years. Goldfinger's JetStar, piloted by Pussy Galore and copilot Sydney, comes with swivel seats, a wet bar, and a well-sized powder room. Goldfinger has installed two peepholes into the powder room and a two-way mirror on the medicine cabinet to keep his eye on passengers. He uses the plane to fly 007 from Switzerland to America, where it lands in Baltimore and travels on to Bluegrass Field in Lexington, Kentucky. The four-engine jet can achieve Mach 8, cruise at 41,000 ft (12,497 m), and travel over 2,000 miles (3,219 km) before refueling.

AIR FORCE 007 *Bond engages Little Nellie's rear-firing flame gun during his battle with SPECTRE helicopters in Japan.*

LOCKHEED US VC-140B

APPEARANCE

Goldfinger (1964)

USED BY Pussy Galore, Goldfinger, James Bond

The aircraft sent to collect James Bond after he has helped foil Goldfinger's mission to irradiate the US Treasury Bullion Depository is a Lockheed US VC-140B, the military VIP version of the JetStar, often used to fly the US President. This proves lucky for Goldfinger, as his pilot, Pussy Galore, flies Goldfinger's own JetStar. Goldfinger, dressed as a US Army General, kidnaps the crew and, with Galore, takes over the plane. When confronting Bond, Goldfinger discharges his gold-plated Colt .45, blowing out a window. As a result, Goldfinger finds himself sucked out of the cabin. The JetStar crashes, but 007 and Galore parachute to safety.

LOTUS ESPRIT

APPEARANCE

The Spy Who Loved Me (1977)

USED BY James Bond, Anya Amasova

The modified Lotus Esprit S1 stands as one of the greatest cars ever built. Despite its size—165 in (419 cm) long, 73 in (185.4 cm) wide, and 44 in (111.7 cm) from ground to rooftop—Q modifies the Lotus to carry an arsenal of weapons and a full underwater conversion system, allowing the vehicle to operate as a submarine. All of this gadgetry exists on the car without sacrificing the Esprit's performance.

James Bond drives the Lotus in Sardinia during his joint mission with Major Anya Amasova of the KGB to investigate shipping tycoon Karl Stromberg. Although Q Branch designed and built the Lotus under strict security, Amasova stole the plans two years before her adventure with Bond. When Stromberg's assassins chase the pair, Bond employs a cement sprayer concealed under the rear license plate to blot out a pursuing car's windscreen.

Bond drives it into the sea to avoid a helicopter gunship and rapidly converts the Lotus into a submarine: the tires fold inside the car's body, rudders and fins emerge from the sides, rear screws and propellers deploy from the back bumper, louvers descend over the windows to cut surface glare, and a periscope rises from the car's roof. A video screen allows 007 a view behind the Lotus and digital readouts replace the analog dashboard. A targeting screen on the center console allows Bond to aim and fire a sea-to-air missile using the car's gearshift. Front-mounted torpedoes fire from controls on the steering wheel. The light switch initiates an ink cloud from the car's rear, and the hazard switch releases a mine from underneath. The Lotus is damaged during an underwater battle with Stromberg's men, but 007 reconverts it to a land car in the water and drives it up onto a beach.

BACK ON LAND *The Lotus converts back to normal car mode as it emerges from the waves.*

LOTUS ESPRIT TURBO

APPEARANCE
For Your Eyes Only (1981)
DRIVEN BY James Bond

Bond's white Lotus Esprit Turbo can achieve 0 to 150 mph (241.4 kph) in just 15 seconds. Bond doesn't get a chance to exploit the car's speed or use any of its gadgets. As Bond and Melina run to the car to escape a posse of gunmen, they see a thug smashing one of its windows. This triggers the self-destruct system, and the Lotus explodes.

Bond later drives a red Turbo in Cortina, Italy. He discovers the body of agent Ferrara in the car.

SELF-DESTRUCTIVE *A gunman inadvisedly attacks 007's Lotus.*

MAGLEV TRAIN

APPEARANCE
The Spy Who Loved Me (1977)
USED BY Karl Stromberg and his men, Anya Amasova, James Bond

A maglev (magnetic levitation) monorail train runs around the perimeter of the submarine pen inside Karl Stromberg's ship, the *Liparus*. Stromberg's maglev car shoots out of a hole in the side of the *Liparus*. The hull separates to reveal a motorboat, which Stromberg uses to take agent Anya Amasova to his *Atlantis* base. After escaping Stromberg's men, 007 forces the driver of a maglev car to take him to the prisoners' quarters, where 007 releases the captured sub crew.

M1 SUB

APPEARANCE
You Only Live Twice (1967)
USED BY M, Moneypenny, James Bond, Kissy Suzuki

M maintains a diesel-electric submarine for use by the British Secret Service. After the staging of Bond's death, 007's shrouded body is brought to the submarine. M briefs Bond on his upcoming mission in his office on the sub. When 007 finds himself adrift at sea with Japanese secret agent Kissy Suzuki at the end of the movie, HMS *M1* surfaces beneath the lifeboat, and M orders Moneypenny to tell Bond to come below and report.

MANTIS

APPEARANCE
For Your Eyes Only (1981)
USED BY Mantis Man

The Osel "Mantis" One-Man Atmospheric Submersible, capable of working at depths of 1900 ft (579 m), attacks the *Neptune* submarine, with Bond and marine archaeologist Melina Havelock inside it, off the Albanian coast.

The Mantis arms have pincers and a destructive revolving drill with which it attacks the *Neptune*. Bond overpowers the Mantis, forcing it into a hole in the hull of the *St. Georges* wreck, where it remains.

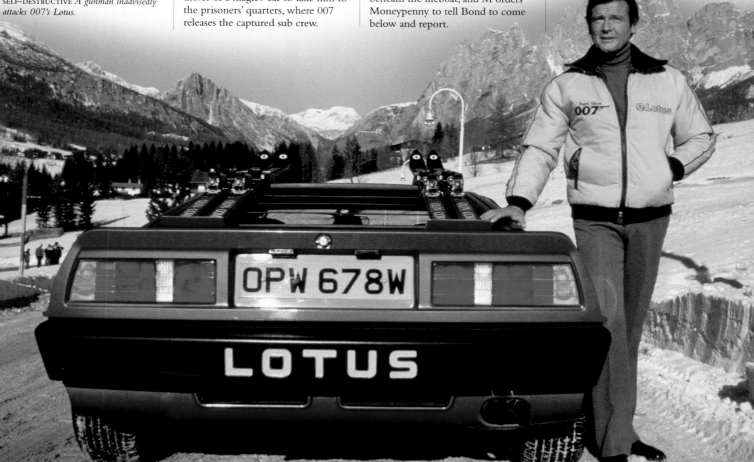

MERCURY COUGAR

APPEARANCE On Her Majesty's Secret Service (1969)

USED BY Tracy Di Vicenzo, James Bond

James Bond first meets Tracy Di Vicenzo as she speeds along a Portuguese coastal road past his Aston Martin DBS in a red Mercury Cougar convertible. Bond soon finds the Cougar deserted on Guincho Beach. After Bond rescues Tracy from drowning and fends off Draco's men, she abandons him and speeds off in her Cougar. Later that day, he spots the distinctive car parked outside the Palacio Estoril Hotel and decides to renew acquaintance with Tracy.

When 007 later finds himself pursued by Irma Bunt and Blofeld's men in the village of Grindenwald, Switzerland, Tracy comes to the rescue, and her Mercury Cougar becomes the perfect escape vehicle. As Bunt and her men give chase in a black Mercedes, Tracy joins a stock car race. The adventurous Tracy holds her own with the professional stock car drivers and puts the Cougar through its paces, knocking several cars out of the way, including the black Mercedes, which flips over and explodes. Tracy and Bond then brave a blizzard and conceal the Cougar inside a barn. That night, Bond proposes marriage to Tracy. The car is abandoned in the barn and apparently never recovered.

MEYERS 200A

APPEARANCE
You Only Live Twice (1967)

FLOWN BY Helga Brandt, James Bond

Helga Brandt tries to kill 007 in a Meyers 200A, the 1966 speed record-holder for single-engine planes. Brandt, suspiciously wearing a parachute, drops a lipstick flare and triggers the rear arm rest side table to slide over Bond's arms. After Brandt bails out, Bond works a hand free, karate chops the plank, and pilots the aircraft to a no-gear crash landing before it explodes.

MONORAIL

APPEARANCE
You Only Live Twice (1967),
Live And Let Die (1973)

USED BY Ernst Stavro Blofeld,
James Bond, Solitaire

Monorail systems have featured in a number of Bond's adventures because they are often ideal transportation solutions for villains with massive headquarters.

In *You Only Live Twice*, an elaborate monorail network services Blofeld's volcano rocket base in Japan. The system features three types of electric monorail carriages—a small, domed carriage for moving people, a larger, open-topped carriage for moving equipment and supplies, and a similar open-topped carriage for moving groups of people. Bond secretes himself in one of the cargo carriages and finds himself in the astronaut quarters near the cells where Blofeld holds the US and Soviet astronauts captured by *Bird 1*. When 007 dons a spacesuit in the hope of flying in *Bird 1*, he travels to the launch pad on the monorail. Later, Blofeld attempts to shoot Bond from a small domed carriage on the monorail, but Tiger Tanaka, who is part of the invading ninja force, foils the plan by hurling a throwing star into Blofeld's wrist. Blofeld engages the engine and speeds away. After bandaging his hand, Blofeld reappears in the monorail carriage to set off a series of explosions and utterly destroy his already doomed rocket base.

In *Live And Let Die*, Dr. Kananga, aka Mr. Big, maintains an underground monorail as a potential escape route from his underground lair. Bond and Solitaire use it to escape after killing Kananga.

MOONBUGGY

APPEARANCE
Diamonds Are Forever (1971)
DRIVEN BY WW Techtronics Guards,
James Bond

The WW Techtronics moonbuggy receives quite a workout from 007 in the Nevada desert. When Professor Dr. Metz alerts security to an intruder, James Bond must figure out a way to escape the top secret facility.

Bond takes the moonbuggy, bursts through the wall, crashes through a security gate, and speeds into the desert. Able to attain speeds of up to 80 mph (129 kph) on tarmac, with a design based on a Corvair and steering from an Austin Healey Sprite, the craft easily outmaneuvers a pursuing security car. The moonbuggy has a harder time outrunning three Honda ATCs. Bond abandons the moonbuggy, kicks a WW Techtronics guard off an ATC, and rides to rendezvous with Tiffany Case.

In real life, the WW Techtronics moonbuggy never traveled to the moon, being rejected for the smaller and lighter, but less speedy and maneuverable, LRV (Lunar Roving Vehicle), which was built by Boeing and Delco.

MOONRAKER SPACE SHUTTLE

APPEARANCE
Moonraker (1979)
FLOWN BY Hugo Drax, James
Bond, Dr. Holly Goodhead

The Moonraker space shuttle can be launched into space by a rocket, orbit the earth, and reenter the atmosphere to land like a conventional aircraft. The shuttle is made at a facility owned by billionaire Hugo Drax in the California desert outside of Los Angeles. A number of Drax subsidiaries throughout the world produce components for the shuttle.

After one of his shuttles develops a fault during assembly, Drax's men steal a replacement as it is being flown to the British government piggybacked on a Boeing 747. Drax cannot afford to be one space shuttle down as he needs six shuttles to carry out his plan of global destruction and repopulation.

Investigating the missing space shuttle, Bond arrives at Drax's hidden South American launch facility in time to see the shuttle launch. Bond and CIA agent Dr. Holly Goodhead are taken into captivity, but the pair manages to escape and take over Moonraker 6. Holly pilots the shuttle on a pre-arranged flight program to Drax's secret space station.

Later, Bond and Holly use Drax's personal shuttle, Moonraker 5, to chase and destroy globes of lethal nerve gas that Drax has launched in order to wipe out Earth's population. With their mission accomplished, Bond and Holly make love in the shuttle's zero-gravity cargo bay.

COUNTDOWN *A Moonraker space shuttle prepares to launch from Drax's base in the Brazilian jungle.*

NEPTUNE

APPEARANCE
For Your Eyes Only (1981)
USED BY James Bond,
Melina Havelock

The *Neptune* 2-Man Lock-out submersible, measuring 23 ft (7 m) by 8 ft (2.4 m), belongs to marine archaeologist Timothy Havelock. His daughter Melina and James Bond use it to locate the sunken British spy ship the *St. Georges* off the Albanian coast. After retrieving the valuable ATAC transmitter from the ship, a Mantis one-man sub attacks the *Neptune*, but Bond and Melina use the *Neptune*'s more powerful engines to win the clash.

NING-PO

APPEARANCE
You Only Live Twice (1967)
USED BY Ernst Stavro Blofeld,
Helga Brandt

Bond discovers that Blofeld is using the *Ning-Po* to transport liquid oxygen—a key component of rocket fuel—to his secret base. When SPECTRE agents capture 007, they bring him aboard the *Ning-Po* to be interrogated by Helga Brandt.

Blofeld apparently named the ship after a notorious pirate ship of the Far East, which stood as a floating museum in Catalina Harbour for many years.

NOTAR MD-600N

APPEARANCES
Die Another Day (2002), Casino Royale (2006)
USED BY James Bond, Jinx, Villiers

As the Antonov flying command center disintegrates in *Die Another Day*, 007 and Jinx jump into a Notar MD-600N helicopter in the cargo hold. The chopper plunges backward off the ramp as the Antonov explodes. Bond frantically flicks switches trying to start the engine. 100 ft (30 m) from the ground, the engine kicks in, and Bond and Jinx fly the MD-600N to a Buddhist temple on the South Korean coast, where they make love amidst diamonds.

Bond also flies in a Notar MD-600N in *Casino Royale* as Villiers accompanies him from Miami to the estate of Alex Dimitrios.

OCTOPUSSY'S BARGE

APPEARANCE
Octopussy (1983)
USED BY Octopussy, Kamal Khan, James Bond, Magda

This lake barge, crewed by women, is the only legitimate means of accessing and leaving jewel smuggler Octopussy's heavily guarded palace in Udaipur, India. Afghan prince Kamal Khan visits Octopussy by traveling in this craft.

The crew rows to the command of an unidentified voice that instructs them with the words, "In, Out, In, Out." A flag depicting an octopus flies from the barge's mast. At the end of Operation Trove, Bond and Octopussy enjoy a romantic getaway on her barge.

OCTOPUSSY'S CIRCUS TRAIN

APPEARANCE
Octopussy (1983)
USED BY Octopussy, Octopussy's girls, Kamal Khan, General Orlov, Gobinda

Afghan prince Kamal Khan hide the bomb aboard the train in East Germany, knowing that the train will only receive a cursory look from

Jewelry smuggler Octopussy owns an S-class steam train, designated DR No 62 015. She uses it to transport her circus around Europe and to smuggle jewelry from East to West.

The train's smuggling activities are a perfect cover for Soviet General Orlov's plot to detonate an atomic weapon at Feldstadt Air Force Base in West Germany. Using the secret smuggling compartment in a prop circus cannon, Orlov and exiled guards at the West German border. Bond, upon discovering the bomb is on the train, steals General Orlov's Mercedes and gives chase. Bond leaps onto the train in an attempt to warn Octopussy that she is being used for an act of nuclear sabotage. He does not get the chance. Attacked by Gobinda and later Grischka, Bond tumbles from the train, which arrives as scheduled at Feldstadt with its deadly cargo.

ORIENT EXPRESS

APPEARANCE
From Russia With Love (1963)
USED BY Bond, Tatiana Romanova,
Kerim Bey, Donald Grant, Benz

The Orient Express remains the most famous train in the world. James Bond uses it as his escape route from Turkey to Italy with cipher clerk Tatiana Romanova and the Lektor cipher machine. Head of Station T Kerim Bey, Soviet security man Benz, and SPECTRE assassin Donald Grant all die inside its legendary carriages.

Bond uses the Orient Express because he can slip off it to smuggle the Lektor across the Yugoslavia/Italy border. SPECTRE No. 5 Kronsteen anticipates this plan, and thus Grant awaits Bond and Tatiana when they board, leading to a brutal confrontation in Bond's sleeper car.

The real train, founded in 1883, classically ran the Paris—Venice—Istanbul route. In February 1950, American Naval Attaché Captain Eugene Karpe died when pushed from the train after the exposure of his American spy ring. Karpe's murder inspired Ian Fleming to write *From Russia With Love*.

OSPREY HOVERCRAFT

APPEARANCE
Die Another Day (2002)
USED BY James Bond

Colonel Moon's hovercraft, equipped with RPGs, flame throwers, automatic weapons, gas masks, and enough ammunition for a small war, have been especially constructed to float over one million landmines in the Demilitarized Zone (DMZ) between North and South Korea. As Moon enters the DMZ on his hovercraft mothership (actually a Griffin 2000TD model), a captured James Bond detonates a bomb in the diamond-filled briefcase using his Omega watch. Chaos ensues when 007 commandeers an Osprey hovercraft, fires rockets at Moon's headquarters building and his car collection from holes in the hovercraft's sides, and then pursues Moon in the DMZ. Moon uses his tank buster gun to detonate mines near Bond and then attempts to stop him by using automatic weapons and a flame thrower. Bond eventually boards the mothership and presses the accelerator, causing Moon to be thrown against a massive caged propeller. The mothership crashes through a temple, but 007 saves himself by grabbing onto a bell, leaving Moon and the hovercraft to tumble down a waterfall.

ONE-MAN ARMY *Bond creates havoc in Moon's base aboard an Osprey hovercraft.*

DANGER IN THE AIR *Parahawks hunt Bond and Elektra in the Caucasus Mountains.*

PARAHAWK

APPEARANCE
The World Is Not Enough (1999)
USED BY Renard's men

Parahawks are ultralight vehicles and hybrid snowmobiles that use parachutes instead of fixed wings.

While Elektra King shows Bond her family's future oil pipeline, four parahawks speed toward them. These are the property of the Russian Atomic Anti-Terrorist Unit and have been loaned to the terrorist Renard by Dr. Arkov. Bond orders Elektra to ski for a gully while he leads the parahawks into the trees. One parahawk's chute becomes entangled, destroying it. Two others land and turn into snowmobiles, their drivers firing machine guns. The remaining airborne parahawk drops a grenade at Bond but destroys a snowmobile instead. 007 then causes one to ski off a precipice; this parahawk deploys its reserve parachute and flies away. Bond destroys the two remaining parahawks by stabbing one parahawk's chute with his ski. Bond and Elektra look on as the parahawks crash into each other.

PILATUS TURBO-PORTER

APPEARANCE
GoldenEye (1995)
FLOWN BY James Bond

As Bond enters a Soviet Union mountain dam facility, a Pilatus PC-6/B2-H4 Turbo-Porter flies overhead. When Bond later escapes from the Arkangel Chemical Weapons Facility beneath the dam, the Pilatus rolls down the runway. Bond attempts to catch and hijack the plane. Although he pulls the pilot from the cockpit, the plane sails off the runway without Bond.

Knowing the slow dive-speed of the Pilatus, Bond seizes a Cagiva motorbike and drives off the cliff-face end of the runway as part of a desperate plan. Bond tucks himself into a speed-dive position, knowing that his terminal velocity is higher than that of the Porter. After precious seconds tick past, Bond catches the pilotless plane in mid-dive and pulls the exceptionally aerodynamically stable craft into level flight, moments before the plane would have crashed into the ground. Bond flies the plane to freedom as the chemical facility explodes below.

PIPER CHEROKEE

APPEARANCE
Goldfinger (1964)
USED BY Pussy Galore's Flying Circus

Pussy Galore's all-female flying circus uses Piper PA-28 Cherokees with varying engine sizes ranging from 140 hp to 235 hp. The pilots perform precision acrobatic maneuvers as part of Pussy Galore's Flying Circus, a traveling aerial show. The Cherokees play a key role in Goldfinger's plot to irradiate the gold in Fort Knox. They are intended to spray the area with the deadly Delta-9 nerve gas.

PIPER PA-18 SUPER CUB

APPEARANCE
Licence To Kill (1989)
FLOWN BY Pam Bouvier

Pam Bouvier steals a Piper PA-18 Super Cub crop-duster to aid Bond. She flies Bond over one of Sanchez's drug-laden tanker trucks, enabling Bond to leap onto it. She then dusts Sanchez's men with insecticide. Sanchez fires a Stinger missile at the Piper, destroying its tail, but Pam manages to crash-land the plane safely in the rocky terrain.

Q BOAT

APPEARANCE
The World Is Not Enough (1999)
DRIVEN BY James Bond

James Bond pilots a one-man aquatic jet craft custom-built by Bentz Boats with modifications by Q Branch. 007 commandeers the craft when an explosion damages MI6 HQ. He uses the Q Boat to chase the Cigar Girl, Renard's terrorist accomplice, in her Sunseeker Superhawk 34 speedboat by leaping from a concealed torpedo ramp into the River Thames. Bond activates the boat's twin rear jet thrusters to catch up with and pass the Sunseeker.

The Q Boat's maneuverability allows it to turn 180° on a dime. Its stability and balance allow it to land on its hull after bounding over waves. When Bond slams the boat into the rear of the Sunseeker, sending it into a spiral, the Q Boat lands hull down. He employs the dive function, which briefly noses the bow underwater arcing the boat two to three ft (0.6–0.9 m) beneath the surface.

The boat's GPS auto-mapping system presents Bond an alternate route to catch his quarry when needed. The metal hull easily withstands bounding over a canal slipway, through the London Canoe Club boathouse, and the friction of grinding against pavement when Bond takes the Q Boat overland near Blackwall Basin on the Isle of Dogs. Bond fires the craft's two cannon-launched acoustic homing torpedoes. He damages the boat when he again ramps off the Sunseeker leaping onto a hot-air balloon tether.

The Q Boat makes an appearance in Q's lab at Castle Thane, MI6's remote operations center, where the damaged craft awaits repair. Q facetiously claims he will use the craft as a fishing boat during retirement.

RANGER, HMS

APPEARANCE
The Spy Who Loved Me (1977)
USED BY The Royal Navy, Karl
Stromberg and his crew

HMS *Ranger* is a Resolution-class
Royal Navy submarine that carries
sixteen Polaris nuclear missiles.
While traveling at a depth of 500 ft
(152.4 m), a loss of power forces the
Ranger to surface. The submarine
seems to vanish without a trace.
Bond eventually discovers it, along
with the *Potemkin*, a missing Soviet
sub, in the bow of shipping tycoon
Karl Stromberg's *Liparus*. Stromberg
sends the *Ranger* and *Potemkin* out to
fire their nuclear missiles and begin
World War III, but Bond and
Commander Carter send new target
coordinates to the subs, causing them
to destroy each other.

RED CROSS HELICOPTERS

APPEARANCE
On Her Majesty's Secret Service (1969),
The Living Daylights (1987)
USED BY Draco and his men, James
Bond, Necros, General Koskov

Although international humanitarian
laws govern the use of Red Cross/
Red Crescent emblems, twice
helicopters bearing false Red Cross
markings have found their way into
Bond's adventures. In *On Her Majesty's
Secret Service*, Marc Ange Draco and
Bond lead an attack on Piz Gloria in
three faux Red Cross Bell 204
Hueys. In *The Living Daylights*, the
tables turn when KGB General
Koskov fakes his own kidnapping
with a Bell UH-1H Huey painted
with Red Cross markings.

RENAULT 11 TXE TAXI

APPEARANCE
A View To A Kill (1985)
DRIVEN BY James Bond

After May Day, henchman and lover
of businessman Max Zorin, kills
French detective Achille Aubergine
and parachutes from the top of the
Eiffel Tower, James Bond steals a
1984 front-wheel drive Renault 11
TXE taxi in order to intercept her.
In his attempts to catch May Day,
he proceeds to destroy the vehicle
bit by bit.

Bond expertly spins the taxi down
a flight of steps to the Seine quayside,
dramatically leaps off a boat ramp,
and drives over the top of a tour bus.
The taxi then gets whittled down.
Bond slices the top off with a metal
gate arm, then, failing to avoid
another car, the rear end gets sheared
off in a collision.

Bond abandons the taxi on the
Pont Alexandre III Bridge, failing to
catch May Day and leaving the
vehicle half the car it was.

RIO AMBULANCE

APPEARANCE
Moonraker (1979)
DRIVEN BY Hugo Drax's henchmen

After escaping from Jaws on Sugar
Loaf Mountain, Bond and CIA agent
Dr. Holly Goodhead are knocked
out and subdued on gurneys inside a
speeding ambulance. Holly attracts
the attention of the attendant, whom
Bond temporarily unnerves with a
blast from a fire extinguisher. In the
ensuing struggle, Bond and the
attendant roll out the back of the
vehicle on a gurney, leaving the
ambulance to speed away with
Holly held captive.

ALL FRONT *(left) Bond
remains cool, calm, and
collected behind the wheel
of the sawn-off taxi.*

STAIR CRAZY *(below)
A few moments earlier,
Bond demonstrates the
maneuverability of the
Renault 11 TXE.*

BIG GAME FISHING *Bond blasts
through the Thames in the Q
Boat, hunting the assassin
known as the Cigar Girl.*

ROLLS-ROYCE

KEY APPEARANCES
Goldfinger (1964), On Her Majesty's Secret Service (1969), Octopussy (1983), A View To A Kill (1985), The World Is Not Enough (1999)

USED BY Auric Goldfinger, Marc Ange Draco, Kamal Khan, James Bond, Valentin Zukovsky, and others

SMOOTH RIDE *Kamal Khan arrives at his Monsoon Palace in his Rolls-Royce Phantom III in* Octopussy.

HIGH ROLLER *In* The World Is Not Enough, *Valentin Zukovsky owns a white Silver Shadow which his bodyguard, The Bull, drives.*

FOUL PLAY *007 finds May Day instead of Tibbett at the wheel in* A View To A Kill.

The Rolls-Royce is one of the most elegant and luxurious of all cars and a key vehicle in the world of James Bond, appearing briefly or prominently in numerous films.

In *Goldfinger*, Bond attaches a homing device to the trunk of Auric Goldfinger's 1937 Rolls-Royce Phantom III, allowing Bond to use his Aston Martin DB5's tracking system to follow Goldfinger from England to Switzerland. Bond soon discovers how Goldfinger transports his gold overseas: the bodywork of his Rolls is 24-karat gold.

In *On Her Majesty's Secret Service*, Che Che and Raphael escort Bond to crime boss Marc Ange Draco's Portuguese seaside headquarters in Draco's Rolls-Royce Mulliner Park Ward Drophead Coupé. The same Rolls later drops Bond off at Gebrüder Gumbold's office in Bern, Switzerland, and Tracy di Vicenzo then confides to her father that she is in love with Bond.

In *A View To A Kill,* Sir Godfrey Tibbett acts the role of Bond's chauffeur as he drives Bond, under the guise of James St. John Smythe, to Zorin's French chateau in a 1962 Rolls-Royce Silver Cloud II. May Day kills Tibbett in the car. Later, Zorin, May Day, and Scarpine try to drown Bond inside the car. He survives by breathing air from the tires.

Rolls-Royce makes the ultimate status statement, even for less-than-savory types. In *Octopussy*, Kamal Khan drives a Phantom III in India. In *The World Is Not Enough*, Valentin Zukovsky owns a white Silver Shadow to travel in style in Azerbaijan.

ROUTEMASTER BUS

APPEARANCE
Live And Let Die (1973)

DRIVEN BY James Bond

A double-decker Routemaster bus helps 007 escape the San Monique police. Bond spins the bus 180°, sending police motorcycles flying. He then swerves, forcing a police car off the road. Even when it appears 007 has made an error by turning down a road with a low bridge, he defeats his pursuers by driving under the bridge and shearing the top deck off, allowing him to get away.

GOLDEN ROLLS *Under surveillance by 007, Goldfinger motors through the Swiss countryside en route to his factory.*

ST. GEORGES

APPEARANCE
For Your Eyes Only (1981)
USED BY British Intelligence

An innocent-looking fishing trawler, the *St. Georges* is really a British electronic surveillance ship which, upon capturing an old World War II contact mine in its nets, explodes and sinks off the Albanian coast. Inside the ship's false freezer is an array of surveillance equipment as well as the ATAC, which uses a low frequency coded transmitter to order British submarines to launch ballistic missiles. The person behind the sinking is smuggler Aris Kristatos. He arranges for the mine to be caught in the trawler's fishing nets, so that he can salvage the ATAC for the Soviets.

SANTA MAVRA

APPEARANCE
For Your Eyes Only (1981)
USED BY Aris Kristatos

Businessman Aris Kristatos uses his motor yacht, *Santa Mavra,* to hunt for the ATAC. After Bond and marine archeologist Melina Havelock recover the ATAC, Kristatos uses the *Santa Mavra* to drag the pair behind a paravane over coral reefs. While the ship turns, Bond wraps the rope around a coralhead. The tension against the *Santa Mavra* snaps the rope, sends the paravane sailing out of the water, and knocks a crew member into the sea. Believing his helmsman Kurt has run over Bond and Melina, Kristatos escapes with the ATAC.

SPY SHIP *A few fishermen on deck preserve the illusion that the* St. Georges *is a humble trawler, instead of a surveillance ship full of state-of-the-art equipment.*

SEABEE SEAPLANE

APPEARANCE
The Man With The Golden Gun (1974)
FLOWN BY James Bond

James Bond uses the Republic RC-3 Seabee seaplane to fly from Hong Kong to arch assassin Scaramanga's private island in Red Chinese waters. Staff intelligence officer Mary Goodnight has a tracking beacon, which Bond uses to guide his way. Bond flies so low that he scrapes the tops of trees in an attempt to avoid detection by radar. Chinese military spotters spot the plane despite his efforts and notify Scaramanga of Bond's arrival.

Soon after Bond, in the Seabee, touches down on the water and glides up onto the beach, Scaramanga destroys the plane using his powerful solar cannon.

PIRATE SHIP *The* Santa Mavra *cuts through the Ionian Sea with her illicit ATAC cargo.*

SEAPLANE, GONZALES'S

APPEARANCE
For Your Eyes Only (1981)
FLOWN BY Hector Gonzales

Cuban hitman Hector Gonzales masquerades as a Kerkyra Charter Service pilot and flies marine archaeologist Melina Havelock from Athens to Corfu in a Cessna U206G Stationair Amphibian seaplane. After he has dropped her off in Corfu Harbour at her parents's ship, the *Triana,* he circles around and fires 3,000 rounds per minute of high-velocity 222 bullets from a concealed gun that he has outfitted under the hull of the plane. Melina's parents,

Timothy and Iona, die instantly. Melina, having gone below deck, races to her parents's bodies. She stares at the seaplane speeding away and vows revenge.

SENTINEL SUBMERSIBLE

APPEARANCE
Licence To Kill (1989)
USED BY Milton Krest

The *Sentinel* is a remote-controlled exploratory submersible used by Milton Krest, the business partner of drug lord Franz Sanchez. The *Sentinel* transports cocaine and cash in its watertight storage container between the well area of Krest's ship, the *Wavekrest,* and a Cessna 185 seaplane operated by Sanchez's pilots. The *Sentinel,* 4 ft (1.2 m) long and 3 ft (0.9 m) wide, has a guidance system, a searchlight, and a built-in video camera, all of which are powered by an umbilical lifeline leading back to the *Wavekrest.* Atop the *Sentinel* are a periscope and the storage container.

Underwater, Bond opens the storage container, takes out a knife, and destroys the entire cocaine shipment. When Krest sees Bond on the surveillance screen ruining the shipment, he orders his men to bring the *Sentinel* to the surface. Bond then uses the knife to destroy the built-in video camera.

SHARK HUNTER

APPEARANCES
The Spy Who Loved Me (1977),
Licence To Kill (1989)
USED BY Karl Stromberg's men,
Milton Krest's men

The Shark Hunter two-man
submersible is a "wet" submarine that
fills with water as it submerges,
requiring scuba-diving gear to be
worn by the occupants.

In *The Spy Who Loved Me*, shipping
magnate Karl Stromberg's men
emerge in one from the underwater
access tubes of his research laboratory
Atlantis. They fire missiles at Bond
and KGB agent Anya Amasova who
are in the Lotus Esprit submersible.
Bond ejects a cloud of black smoke
from the Lotus, and Anya launches a
mine on the seabed that destroys
the craft.

In *Licence To Kill*, henchman Milton
Krest owns a Shark Hunter. It helps
drug lord Franz Sanchez escape from
US custody. Krest also uses the sub
to transport his men from a tunnel
underneath his Ocean Exotica
warehouse to his ship, the *Wavekrest*.

SHERPA VAN

APPEARANCE
The Spy Who Loved Me (1977)
USED BY Jaws, Anya Amasova,
James Bond

Jaws employs Egyptian Postal
Telephone Service van no. 7124 in
his attempt to recover microfilm
blueprints of shipping tycoon Karl
Stromberg's submarine tracking
system. Bond follows Jaws and slips
into the cargo hold of the Leyland
Sherpa 240 van, where he is soon
joined by Soviet agent Anya
Amasova. A microphone planted in
the rear and a speaker in the cab
allow Jaws to listen in on the
conversation between Bond and
Amasova as he drives them to an
ancient Egyptian temple. When the
pair recovers the microfilm, they
attempt to escape in the van, which
Jaws proceeds to rip and dent. The
stress of the attack on the vehicle
soon leads to the blowing of the
cylinder head gasket, rendering the
van useless.

SKYFLEET S570

APPEARANCE
Casino Royale (2006)
USED BY Unknown

Terrorist banker Le Chiffre targets
the Skyfleet S570 prototype at
Miami International Airport. Le

Chiffre believes he can destroy the
Skyfleet S570, the world's largest
passenger aircraft, at the introduction
ceremony and cause Skyfleet stock to
plummet. Le Chiffre, through buying
"put options," will make tens of
millions as a result. He hires Alex
Dimitrios to find him
a saboteur to blow up
the plane. Dimitrios
employs Carlos, who
attempts to drive a
fuel tanker into the
plane. Bond stops
the truck and
causes Carlos to
obliterate himself.

SNOWMOBILES

APPEARANCES
A View To A Kill (1985),
Die Another Day (2002)
DRIVEN BY Siberian Research Centre
Officers, Gustav Graves's men

In *A View To A Kill*, Siberian
Research Centre guards use Polaris
Indy 600 snowmobiles to pursue
Bond. Bond hijacks a Polaris, but a
Soviet helicopter blasts it to bits.
Bond recovers a broken runner to
use as a snowboard. In *Die Another
Day*, guards in Iceland ride
Bombardier Ski-Doo MX ZREV

MOVING TARGET *Graves's guards try to get
Bond in their sights.*

snowmobiles. Bond clotheslines one
guard off a Ski-Doo. Another hits
Bond's "invisible" Vanquish. Bond
returns the favor by plowing through
two Ski-Doos with the Vanquish.

SOVIET ARMY UAZ-469

APPEARANCE
The Living Daylights (1987)
USED BY James Bond, Kara Milovy

Cellist Kara Milovy steals the basic Soviet army transport, a UAZ-469, during a mujaheddin raid on a Soviet airbase. Kara drives the UAZ up a cargo ramp into a Soviet transport plane piloted by 007, locking the vehicle in a specially built cargo sled. When the plane runs out of fuel, Bond and Kara jump in the UAZ and deploy the cargo sled parachute before the plane crashes. The UAZ survives the impact, and Bond and Kara drive away toward dinner in Karachi.

SPIRIT 54 YACHT

APPEARANCE
Casino Royale (2006)
USED BY James Bond, Vesper Lynd

To celebrate their newfound love, and forget the brutal mission that flung them together, Bond and Vesper Lynd embark on an idyllic Mediterranean voyage in a Spirit 54 yacht. So assured is Bond of his new life with Vesper, he even sends a resignation email to M. However, Bond and Vesper's bliss is shortlived; sailing down the Grand Canal, Vesper spots Gettler, and realizes she cannot escape her past.

After Vesper's tragic suicide, Bond remains on the yacht mourning the death of his dream to "float round the world" with her. A call from M informing him of Vesper's past and her deal to save his life jerks him back to reality, and he discovers that Vesper left him a vital clue on her cell phone.

STEALTH SHIP

APPEARANCE
Tomorrow Never Dies (1997)
USED BY Elliot Carver and henchmen

Media mogul Elliot Carver's stealth ship is vital to his plot to initiate a war between the UK and China. The craft, built with Chinese military materials on a catamaran design, produces very little wake disturbance. Its ultra-quiet all-electric engines powered by two 35-megawatt generators provide no acoustic (above water) or hydroacoustic (below surface) signature. The bow design minimizes pressure-wave propagation, another method of detecting a ship at sea. The angled radar-absorbing surface covers a carbon-fiber hull. The ship is virtually impossible to detect except with the naked eye. Carver bases the craft in Hao Long Bay off the Vietnamese coast. It lays in wait for the British frigate HMS *Devonshire* to

STEALTH SCIENCE *The bridge of Carver's stealth ship glitters with technology.*

sail off course, initiating a confrontation with the Chinese. The stealth ship launches a missile that shoots down a Chinese MiG jet and launches the Sea Vac drill that sinks the *Devonshire*. The ship serves as a platform to recover a missile from the *Devonshire*, which Carver later attempts to launch at Beijing. Bond blows a hole in the side of the stealth ship with a grenade, allowing the HMS *Bedford* to spot and shell the craft, blasting it to bits.

CLIFFHANGER
On the way to a rendezvous with Miss Taro, Bond is menaced by the Three Blind Mice assassins in their black hearse.

SUNBEAM ALPINE

APPEARANCE
Dr. No (1962)
DRIVEN BY James Bond

In Kingston, James Bond rents a marine blue Sunbeam Alpine Series II Sports Tourer convertible and drives it to secretary Miss Taro's house in Jamaica's Blue Mountains. A hearse carrying Dr. No's Three Blind Mice assassins accelerates behind Bond, attempting to run his Sunbeam off the cliffside road. Bond spots an angledozer ahead doing road repairs. He drives the Sunbeam under the angledozer's shovel-arm, which spans the road. Too high to follow, the hearse veers off the road and crashes in flames.

In the Fleming novel, Commander Strangways drives a Sunbeam Alpine.

SUNSEEKER MOTORBOATS

APPEARANCES
The World Is Not Enough (1999), Die Another Day (2002), Casino Royale (2006) Quantum of Solace (2008)
USED BY Cigar Girl, Renard, Jinx, Le Chiffre, General Medrano, Bond

In *The World Is Not Enough*, the Cigar Girl, positioned on a Sunseeker Superhawk 34 speedboat on the River Thames, uses a Heckler & Koch G36 rifle to fire at Bond as he stands amid the rubble following a bomb blast at MI6. Bond pursues her in a prototype Q boat. Cigar Girl beaches her Sunseeker and escapes in a hot-air balloon tethered near the Millennium Dome. Terrorist Renard later arrives at Maiden's Tower in Istanbul in a Sunseeker Manhattan 50 Flybridge motoryacht. This yacht also brings a captured Bond and nuclear physicist Christmas Jones to Maiden's Tower.

In *Die Another Day*, after backdiving off a cliff at Dr. Alvarez's clinic, NSA agent Jinx speeds away in a Sunseeker 48 speedboat.

In *Casino Royale*, Le Chiffre plays poker aboard his Sunseeker Predator 108. The yacht also serves as the meeting place where Alex Dimitrios informs him that the terrorist Carlos will replace Mollaka in the plot to destroy the Skyfleet S570.

In *Quantum of Solace*, Medrano escorts Camille in a Sunseeker Superhawk 43 from Kings Quay, Port-Au-Prince to an M4 Superyacht. Bond crashes his boat into the 43 and rescues her. Later, Bond journeys to Mathis's villa in Talamone, Italy, in a Sunseeker Sovereign 17.

READY TO RUMBLE
At the controls of a T-80 tank, Bond is an unstoppable force.

SWITCHBLADE GLIDERS

APPEARANCE
Die Another Day (2002)
FLOWN BY James Bond, Jinx

To evade North Korean radar, Bond and Jinx bail out of the back of a US Air Force Chinook helicopter riding personal jet gliders, known as switchblades. The switchblade gliders are invisible to radar and are based on the PHASST glider (Programmable High Altitude Single Soldier Transport). Electrically powered retractable wings control the gliders's acceleration and trajectory. During the descent, Bond and Jinx jettison their switchblades and parachute down to land safely in North Korea.

T-55 TANK

APPEARANCE
GoldenEye (1995)
DRIVEN BY James Bond

James Bond commandeers a Soviet T-55 tank in an attempt to rescue computer programmer Natalya Simonova from General Ourmov, who has driven off in his car taking Natalya with him. The 46-ton vehicle chases after Ourmov,

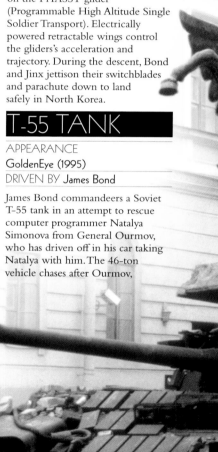

destroying a swath of historic St. Petersburg in the process. The tank crashes through a wall, plows through a narrow alley, squashes military jeeps and police cars, smashes through a truck, and knocks the plinth from beneath a statue of Tzar Nicholas sitting astride a winged horse.

When Ourmov takes Natalya aboard Alec Trevelyan's armored ICBM train, Bond rolls the tank down the railroad tracks in the train's path. He fires a shell and jumps out of the tank before the train smashes into it.

TANAKA'S TRAIN

APPEARANCE
You Only Live Twice (1967)
USED BY Tiger Tanaka

Tiger Tanaka, head of the Japanese Secret Intelligence Service, uses a private train to travel on the Tokyo subway system and possibly other rail lines. He tells Bond that it would be unwise, considering his position, to travel in the streets of Tokyo. The modern train includes servants, a well-stocked liquor cabinet, a

high-tech communications center, and precision optics for reading and projecting microdot information.

TEXRON TANKER

APPEARANCE
Casino Royale (2006)
DRIVEN BY Carlos, James Bond

Acting on the instructions of Dimitrios, a saboteur named Carlos uses a Texron fuel truck in an attempt to destroy the Skyfleet S570 prototype plane during its unveiling at Miami International Airport. Carlos attaches a key fob detonator to the fuel truck's undercarriage, intending to turn the truck's loaded fuel tank into a massive bomb. The truck's weight and ability to reach high speeds as well as the wide tarmac at MIA make the Texron vehicle nearly impossible to stop. When Bond leaps on top of the tanker, Carlos tries to dislodge him by swerving sharply and sideswiping a tow tug. Bond manages to climb back aboard and stay on the tanker as it smashes through a luggage flatbed and an articulated bus. The fuel truck continues on despite having numerous tires shot out, the brake line severed, and the tank itself punctured by machine gun fire. It also slams into police cars and smashes through a police SUV barricade. It is only when Bond manages to overcome Carlos and gain full control of the wheel that he can turn the truck into a controlled skid that brings it to a halt, just inches from the Skyfleet S570.

TIGER ATTACK *Ourmov and Onatopp arrive at the Severnya Space Weapons Control Centre. The Tiger's ability to withstand EMP makes it a vital component in their plot.*

TIGER HELICOPTER

APPEARANCE
GoldenEye (1995)
USED BY Xenia Onatopp, Alec Trevelyan, General Ourumov

Bond first notices the Tiger helicopter aboard the French-built stealth ship *La Fayette*, when he spies on Admiral Chuck Farrel and Janus member Xenia Onatopp in Monaco.

The 170 knots helicopter, the first working prototype and Europe's answer to the electronic battlefield, not only uses stealth technology, but it is also the only helicopter to be hardened against all forms of electronic interference, radio jamming, and electromagnetic radiation.

Onatopp and ex-MI6 agent Trevelyan steal the helicopter from the deck of the *La Fayette*, having attacked and killed the pilots. Later, General Ourmov and Onatopp take the Tiger helicopter to the Space Weapons Control Centre in Severnaya, Russia. When they set off the GoldenEye satellite weapon Petya, the Russian MiG-29 jet fighters fail in the resulting electromagnetic pulse; the Tiger remains unaffected.

At MI6 headquarters, Bond, MI6's Senior Analyst Bill Tanner, and M view the heat radiation image of the Tiger at Severnaya, which spurs Bond to travel to Russia to investigate the missing helicopter. He soon sees the Tiger in the statue graveyard where Alec Trevelyan reveals that he turned traitor and has become the head of the Janus crime syndicate.

Shot with a knockout dart, Bond awakens bound and trapped inside the helicopter. Behind him sits computer programmer Natalya Simonova who screams for Bond to save them. The helicopter fires missiles that target the craft itself, but Bond headbutts the ejector seat button, sending the crew compartment—with Bond and Natalya in it—rocketing skyward moments before the Tiger explodes.

TOW SLED

APPEARANCE
Thunderball (1965)
DRIVEN BY SPECTRE frogmen, James Bond, Largo

SPECTRE uses underwater motorized tow sleds during its NATO project. The sleds allow the SPECTRE frogmen to cover more distance quickly. Additionally, they can help position cumbersome items underwater, such as the camouflage used to cover the hijacked Vulcan bomber. They also serve as an escort for the bomb sled, with two fixed underwater CO_2 spearguns that can be fired from the pilot's handles.

TOYOTA 2000 GT

APPEARANCE
You Only Live Twice (1967)
DRIVEN BY Aki

Japanese Agent 294 Aki drives a white Toyota 2000 GT with a closed-circuit telecommunications system built into the rear seat as her company car. The 2000 GT marked Toyota's entrance into the sports car market, but the company only produced 341 models, and no convertibles were ever sold to the public. Aki uses the car to take Bond to meet his contact Dikko Henderson, to twice rescue Bond outside of Osato Industries headquarters, to lead SPECTRE gunmen on a chase out of Tokyo, and to travel to Kobe to investigate the *Ning-Po*.

TRANSPORT ALLIANZ C-160

APPEARANCE
Tomorrow Never Dies (1997)
USED BY James Bond, Jack Wade

At a US Air Force Base in the South China Sea, Bond enlists the help of CIA agent Jack Wade to plan a High Altitude, Low Opening (HALO) jump to locate the HMS *Devonshire*.

Bond leaps from a Transport Allianz C-160 plane at 29,000 ft (8,839 m), freefalls for 5 miles (8 km) at 200 mph (321.8 kph), and then pops his chute 200 ft (60.9 m) below the Chinese and Vietnamese radars.

TREVELYAN'S TRAIN

APPEARANCE
GoldenEye (1995)
USED BY Alec Trevelyan, General Ourumov, Xenia Onatopp

After the fall of the Soviet Union, Russia dismantled much of its nuclear deterrent. This included retiring the trains designed to move the USSR's intercontinental ballistic missiles (ICBMs) from location to location.

After the retirement of one such train, ex-MI6 agent Alec Trevelyan takes it over. He knows its armor plating will provide good security and that the mobility of the train will make locating him difficult. Bond derails the train by positioning a T-80BV tank in its path. Trevelyan traps 007 and computer programmer Natalya Simonova inside and booby traps the train to explode. Bond and Natalya escape, using the onboard computer to discover that Trevelyan plans to travel to Cuba.

TRIANA

APPEARANCE
For Your Eyes Only (1981)
USED BY Melina Havelock, Timothy Havelock, Iona Havelock, James Bond

Marine archaeologist Sir Timothy Havelock owns the research vessel *Triana*. Its legitimate research is the perfect cover for British Intelligence to recover the ATAC, a submarine communications device. Cuban hitman Gonzales murders Sir Timothy and his wife, Iona, on the vessel. Melina Havelock, the couple's daughter, witnesses the killings and vows revenge. Melina and Bond recover the ATAC using the *Triana* as a base, and smuggler Aris Kristatos keelhauls them from its bow. After the death of Kristatos, Bond and Melina return to the *Triana*.

TUK-TUK TAXI

APPEARANCE
Octopussy (1983)
USED BY James Bond, Vijay, Gobinda

Vijay, Bond's contact in India, drives Bond in a tuk-tuk three wheeler taxi through the Udaipur streets. Kamal Khan's henchman Gobinda and his driver give chase in another tuk-tuk. A jeep bursts onto the scene, and a goon leaps onto Bond's tuk-tuk, plunging a knife into 007's heart. Bond is unaffected as the knife sticks in a wad of cash in his suit. Bond punches the man, and Vijay uses a tennis racket to battle Gobinda's other goons. Gobinda fires a blunderbuss at 007, but Bond manages to jump out of the taxi before the shot hits him. Bond later reunites with Vijay in the tuk-tuk. They escape Gobinda and his men by driving through a cinema poster that hides the entrance to the offices of Station I.

US ARMY AMBULANCE

APPEARANCE
Goldfinger (1964)
USED BY Kisch, Goldfinger

An ambulance plays a key role in Goldfinger's faux convoy of US Army vehicles that blast their way into the grounds of the US Treasury Bullion Depository at Fort Knox as part of Operation Grand Slam. The ambulance is, in reality, a mobile platform for Goldfinger's powerful industrial laser, housing a hinged roof, a hydraulic lift, and a remarkably resilient electric battery array to power the laser.

VULCAN BOMBER

APPEARANCE
Thunderball (1965)
HIJACKED BY SPECTRE

The Vulcan bomber served as the key nuclear deterrent aircraft of the UK from the early 1950s to the mid-1980s. Hard to track on radar, the Vulcan was very effective in the era of subsonic bombers. SPECTRE's hijacking of NATO flight 759 sparks Operation Thunderball, the British secret service's effort to retrieve the two atomic weapons on board. SPECTRE hires Angelo Palazzi to impersonate Major François Derval, take control of the craft, kill the crew, and fly the Vulcan to the Golden Grotto near Nassau, Bahamas. Palazzi ditches the Vulcan in the ocean, but SPECTRE's Emilio Largo kills him. After removing the bombs, Largo's crew camouflages the plane. Bond locates it only hours before the first bomb is to be detonated.

WAVEKREST

APPEARANCE
Licence To Kill (1989)
USED BY Milton Krest

The *Wavekrest* is a marine research vessel owned by Milton Krest, who uses it to transport drugs for Franz Sanchez. Off the coast of Key West, Bond sneaks aboard the *Wavekrest*, destroys a cocaine shipment, and steals $5 million in drug money. Later, CIA contract pilot and agent Pam Bouvier disguises herself as the Isthmus City harbor pilot and crashes the *Wavekrest* through the dock to convince Sanchez that Krest wants him dead.

WAYNE, USS

APPEARANCE
The Spy Who Loved Me (1977)
USED BY James Bond, Anya Amasova, Commander Carter

Shortly after Bond and Soviet agent Anya Amasova board the USS *Wayne*, the submarine has to surface because of an electrical failure. The *Liparus* swallows it, and shipping tycoon Karl Stromberg orders Commander Carter and his crew to evacuate or face death. When Bond and the crews of the American, British, and Soviet subs defeat Stromberg's army, they file back into the USS *Wayne*. Carter orders a torpedo to smash open the tanker's bow doors. The *Wayne* slides out of the sub pen as the ship explodes and sinks. The *Wayne* then proceeds to destroy Stromberg's base *Atlantis* under Pentagon orders.

WETBIKE

APPEARANCE
The Spy Who Loved Me (1977)
USED BY James Bond

Q sends an aquatic vehicle known as a Wetbike to the USS *Wayne* for Bond's use. Q obtained the first engineering prototype, which Bond uses to travel to the ocean laboratory *Atlantis* to rescue KGB agent Anya Amasova. With a 50 horsepower Suzuki engine, the Wetbike's fixed nozzle outputs 500 lb (22.6 kg) of thrust, allowing it to safely transport Bond to *Atlantis*. When the USS *Wayne* attacks *Atlantis*, the torpedoes destroy the Wetbike.

ZAPOROZHETS 965

APPEARANCE
GoldenEye (1995)
USED BY Jack Wade, James Bond

In St. Petersburg, Russia, James Bond's roguish CIA contact Jack Wade drives a little blue Zaporozhets 965 which, he proclaims, "hasn't let me down yet." The car breaks down in St. Petersburg Square, but Wade quickly gets it going again with the aid of a wrench, a screwdriver, and a whack from a sledgehammer. He then drives Bond to the nightclub headquarters of arms dealer Valentin Zukovsky.

WEAPONS & EQUIPMENT

King Arthur had Merlin. James Bond has Q. With Major Boothroyd, 007 does not need magic spells to accomplish a mission. Bond is a hero created to embrace the power of technology. When the 007 films appeared in the 1960s, Bond spoke to the optimist in us who yearned to master technology, and who dreamed of GPS navigation systems and mobile phones. Bond understands that technology can destroy or liberate us. When the world was still wondering if a radium watch dial would slowly kill the wearer, Bond sported watches concealing Geiger counters, detonators, buzz-saws, and bullet-deflecting magnets. Bond relishes the danger of the modern age and harnesses it with confidence and style. He knows that in today's complex times, appearances can be deceiving. In Bond's world, a camera can be a tape recorder, and a tape recorder can be a book. A cigarette can kill your enemy in seconds. A mobile phone can drive your car. A hat may break your neck. On the following pages are the remarkable weapons and gadgets of James Bond's trade. Yet each one is simply a tool, to be applauded in the hands of the hero and feared when not. With 007, man is always the master; the gadget is the servant.

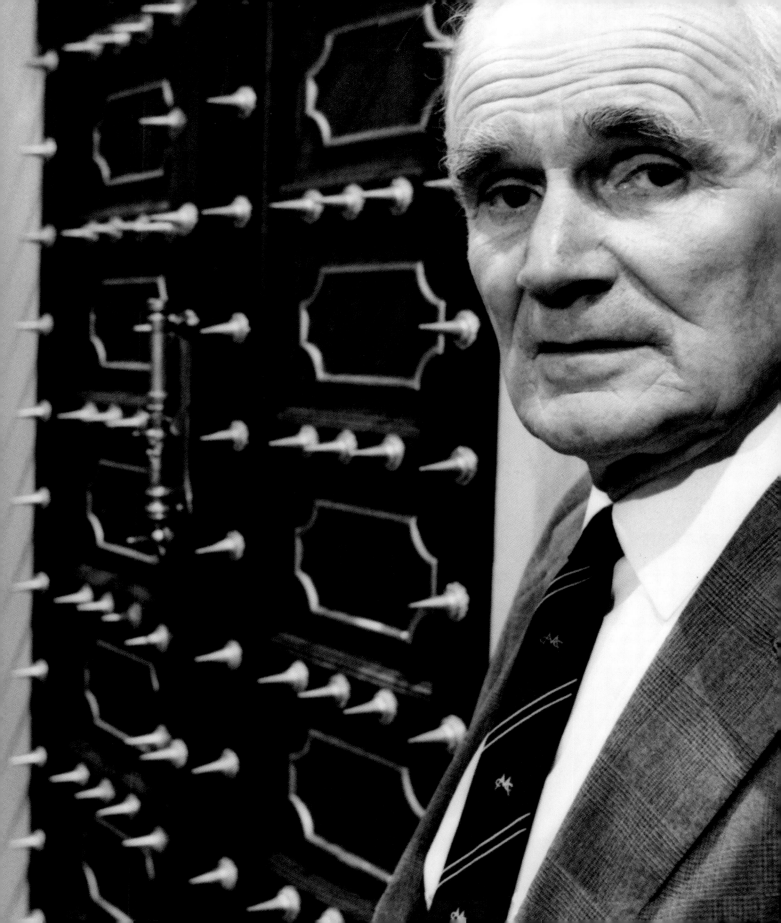

AEROSOL CAN

APPEARANCE
Live And Let Die (1973)
USED BY James Bond

When James Bond finds a snake in his bathroom at his hotel in San Monique, he uses a regular can of spray aftershave and his cigar to create a makeshift flame thrower. The highly-flammable propellant ignites and incinerates the serpent. In actual fact, Bond needn't have bothered—the snake was a desert kingsnake which is neither poisonous nor aggressive. CIA agent Rosie Carver receives quite a shock when she goes into the bathroom and sees the toasted reptile.

ANDERSON WHEELER 500 NE DOUBLE RIFLE

APPEARANCE Skyfall (2012)
USED BY James Bond

James Bond's father Andrew Bond's old hunting rifle, an Anderson Wheeler 500 Nitro Express Double Rifle, is the one weapon not sold to an Idaho collector in the Skyfall estate sale after Bond is presumed dead. It is retained by Skyfall gamekeeper Kincade, who proudly gives it to Bond when he arrives at the lodge with M. When Silva's men attack, Bond eliminates several of them with the Aston Martin DB5's machine guns, then takes out even more with the double rifle. Having run out of ammunition, he discards the heirloom.

ASAT MISSILE

APPEARANCE
Die Another Day (2002)
USED BY US Navy

When the Soviet Union developed a "killer satellite" in the 1970s to topple satellites, the US responded with the ASAT (Anti-Satellite Missile), designed to attack satellites in low Earth orbit.

Gustav Graves plans to use his Icarus satellite to destroy the DMZ, enabling North Korea to invade South Korea. A US warship launches an ASAT missile at Icarus, but the satellite's sun-fueled beam destroys it.

ASSAULT RIFLE

APPEARANCE
The Living Daylights (1987)
USED BY Brad Whitaker

Brad Whitaker's assault rifle is a Colt Commando Model M733 with ballistic face shield. When Bond fires the eight bullets of his Walther PPK harmlessly against the bulletproof shield, Whitaker fires a burst of 80 rounds, obliterating his military museum in a vain attempt to eliminate Bond.

ATAC

APPEARANCE
For Your Eyes Only (1981)
USED BY British Navy

The ATAC is a secretive Automatic Targeting Attack Communicator utilized by the St. Georges, a British electronic surveillance spy ship. It uses an ultra-low frequency coded transmitter to order British submarines to launch ballistic missiles.

When a contact mine becomes trapped in the St. Georges's nets, the ship explodes, and the ATAC is lost in the Ionian Sea off the Albanian coast. Both the Soviets and the British want this valuable device.

Bond and marine archaeologist Melina Havelock use the Neptune submersible to locate the St. Georges and retrieve the ATAC. When they surface, smuggler Aris Kristatos takes the ATAC, planning to deliver it to the KGB's General Gogol at St. Cyril's Monastery. Bond infiltrates the monastery and shatters the ATAC in front of Gogol. Bond's reason for destroying the device is détente-minded—if the British don't have it, the Soviets don't have it either.

ATOMIC DEVICES

APPEARANCES
Goldfinger (1964), Thunderball (1965), The Spy Who Loved Me (1977), Octopussy (1983), The World Is Not Enough (1999)
USED BY Goldfinger, Mr. Ling, Kisch, Emilio Largo, Ladislav Kutze, Karl Stromberg, James Bond, Kamal Khan, General Orlov, Renard, Elektra King

Nothing says you have arrived among the most elite of the world's megalomaniacs like possessing your own atomic device.

Goldfinger receives a "dirty bomb" from the Chinese government in order to perpetrate economic chaos in the West. The device is designed to spread maximum lethal radiation with minimal explosive power. A CIA atomic specialist disarms the weapon with only seconds to spare.

In Thunderball, SPECTRE briefly becomes a nuclear power when a freelancer working for them— Angelo Palazzi—hijacks NATO flight 759, armed with two atomic weapons, MoS-type, as part of a plot hatched by Emilio Largo. When an attempt to place one of the bombs in Biscayne Bay, Miami, goes awry, US aquaparas seize one bomb. Nuclear specialist Ladislav Kutze throws the arming device for the second bomb into the sea when Largo attempts to escape with it aboard the Disco Volante. The bomb is destroyed when the Disco Volante crashes into a small coral island in Biscayne National Park.

The Spy Who Loved Me sees shipping magnate Karl Stromberg obtaining a host of sea-launched ballistic missiles (SLBMs) by building a submarine tracking system, a disabling beam, and a supertanker to swallow the craft. Bond uses one of the detonators to blow open the security shutters protecting the Liparus's control room. Although 007 cannot stop Stromberg's crews from launching the

SLBMs, he does order them to target each other, resulting in their mutual destruction.

Rogue Soviet General Orlov hijacks one of his country's weapons to stage an accident on a NATO airbase in Germany in *Octopussy*. Bond, dressed as a circus clown, extracts the detonator in time.

In *The World Is Not Enough*, Elektra King and her lover Renard hatch a plot to steal a nuclear weapon from a decommissioning site in the former Soviet Union. They plan to use part of the plutonium to make it appear that King's oil pipeline has been sabotaged and use the other part to force the nuclear reactor in a Russian submarine to explode, irradiating Istanbul. Bond stops the plot by shooting King and impaling Renard with a plutonium reactor rod.

ATTACHÉ CASE

APPEARANCES
From Russia With Love (1963), Goldfinger (1964)
USED BY **James Bond, British Agent from Station Y**

The black leather attaché case that Q presents to Bond in *From Russia With Love* is the first of Bond's lethal exotic gadgets.

The case contains forty rounds of .25-caliber ammunition in tubes hidden beneath two of the feet studs. Built into the lower section of the top is a flat throwing knife, released by a button concealed beneath the right latch. Inside the case is an ArmaLite AR-7 folding sniper's rifle, which has been modified from the standard .22 survival model and contains an infrared telescopic scope. In the base of the case are fifty gold sovereigns. A tear-gas cartridge disguised as a tin of talcum powder attaches magnetically to the top of the case. The latches must be turned horizontally before opening or the cartridge will explode.

Bond takes the case on his mission to Istanbul. Head of Station T, Kerim Bey uses the AR-7 when he kills assassin Krilencu. Later, 007 uses the gun to wound the copilot of a SPECTRE helicopter. Bond offers the gold sovereigns from his case to Grant as a bribe for a cigarette. He tricks Grant into opening an identical case he stole from a murdered contact from Station Y, and the explosion of the tear-gas cartridge briefly overcomes Grant. During the resulting fight, 007 extracts the throwing knife from one

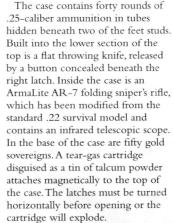

case and stabs Grant's shoulder, allowing him to gain the upper hand.

The case appears in *Goldfinger*, but Bond does not use it. When flying to the US, stewardess Mei Lei informs him that it was damaged when examined.

The attaché case in the novel *From Russia With Love* includes a cyanide death-pill for Bond to take if captured. 007 washes this pill down the lavatory, a point referenced in the film *Die Another Day*.

AVALANCHE-RESCUE RECEIVER

APPEARANCE
A View To A Kill (1985)
USED BY **James Bond**

In Siberia, James Bond uses a handheld avalanche-rescue receiver in a weatherproof yellow plastic casing to locate the frozen body of

MI6 agent 003. On finding the body, Bond locates a chip hidden inside a locket around 003's neck. The chip, which proves to be impervious to an electromagnetic pulse, launches Bond's investigation into the activities of business tycoon Max Zorin.

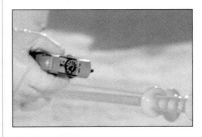

BATTLESUIT

APPEARANCE
Die Another Day (2002)
USED BY **Gustav Graves**

Gustav Graves wears a high-tech battlesuit that controls his Icarus satellite during his attempt to destroy South Korean defenses from his flying command center. Designed by top scientist Vlad, the body armor-styled suit covers Graves's chest and arms. The wrist buttons of the suit control the Icarus satellite, a visor displays the coordinates of the Icarus, and a chest button emits 100,000 volts of electricity. Graves uses this feature to murder his father, General Moon, and in his ensuing battle with Bond he is electrocuted.

COUNTDOWN *Bond desperately tries to disable Goldfinger's atomic device.*

DEATH BRINGER *Encased in his battlesuit, Graves prepares to wreak havoc on South Korea with his Icarus superweapon.*

BELL-TEXTRON JET PACK

APPEARANCES
Thunderball (1965),
Die Another Day (2002)
USED BY James Bond

While Q Branch has often modified equipment and vehicles from other manufacturers, in the case of the Jet Pack, the British Secret Service merely purchased a pre-existing piece of technology. The US Army issued a contract to Bell Aerospace in 1959 to develop a Rocket Belt. Shortly after, Bell unveiled the 21-second flying machine, but the Army deemed it too dangerous for use in the field. Q did not agree, realizing it could be a perfect device for an agent to employ in certain circumstances.

In *Thunderball*, Bond uses the Jet Pack to escape from SPECTRE gunmen at the chateau of SPECTRE's Jacques Boitier in France.

Years later, Bond sees the Jet Pack in a storeroom for Q Branch in an abandoned London Underground facility used by MI6. The Jet Pack in *Die Another Day* appears to be modified because Bond flips on the thrust, something he was unlikely to do with the original as the exhaust consisted of exceedingly hot steam.

BERETTA AUTOMATIC

APPEARANCES
Dr. No (1962), Licence To Kill (1989), Tomorrow Never Dies (1997), Die Another Day (2002)
USED BY Bond, Fiona Volpe, Andrea Anders, Anya Amasova, Octopussy, Pam Bouvier, Jinx

James Bond uses a .25 Beretta Automatic in six Ian Fleming novels. In *Dr. No*, M insists the gun be replaced.

In the film *Dr. No*, Bond notes that the Beretta has been his sidearm for ten years, despite warnings from M that it was unsuitable. After it jams on a job, Bond spends six months in hospital, and M orders 007 to stop using the Beretta.

Fiona Volpe in *Thunderball*, Andrea Anders in *The Man With The Golden Gun*, Anya Amasova in *The Spy Who Loved Me*, Octopussy, and Pam

"I've used a Beretta for ten years, and I've **never missed** with it yet."

Bond to M

GARTER GUN *Pam Bouvier shows Bond where she keeps her Beretta.*

Bouvier in *Licence To Kill* all carry a Beretta 950, a .25 automatic known as the Jetfire.

NSA agent Jinx uses a Beretta Cheetah to kill Dr. Alvarez and pursue Zao in *Die Another Day*. She later uses the Cheetah aboard Gustav Graves's Antonov. She also uses a Beretta Tomcat when investigating Graves's diamond mine in Iceland.

When Bond encounters Severine at Macao's Floating Dragon Casino in *Skyfall*, he observes that she has a Beretta 70 strapped to her thigh.

BINOCULAR/ MONOCULAR CAMERA

APPEARANCES
For Your Eyes Only (1981), GoldenEye (1995)

USED BY James Bond

In *For Your Eyes Only*, Bond spies on henchman Emile Locque paying off hitman Hector Gonzales in Spain using a Tasco binocular camera which combines 7 x 20 mm binoculars with a 110-format camera. Thugs destroy the film when they capture 007.

In *GoldenEye*, Bond uses a more advanced item in the form of a digital monocular to spy on Janus member Xenia Onatopp and Admiral Chuck Farrel in Monaco. With the push of a button, the monocular digitally transmits an image to MI6 for identification.

BOMBE SURPRISE

APPEARANCE
Diamonds Are Forever (1971)

USED BY Wint & Kidd, James Bond

Assassins Mr. Wint and Mr. Kidd attempt to kill Bond with a bomb inside a faux cake. Aboard an ocean liner, Wint and Kidd present Bond and smuggler Tiffany Case with a sumptuous meal, supposedly courtesy of billionaire Willard Whyte. When Bond confronts Wint, who poses as a sommelier, about his lack of knowledge of wines, a fight ensues. Case hurls the bombe dessert at Wint. She misses but reveals the bomb when the dessert hits the floor. 007 attaches the bomb to Wint's coattails and tosses him overboard. Wint explodes before hitting the water.

BOOK/TAPE RECORDER

APPEARANCE
Thunderball (1965)

USED BY James Bond

This sound-activated tape recorder is secreted inside a hollowed-out Nassau directory. Bond uses it to listen for intruders in his Coral Harbour hotel room in Nassau, Bahamas. When he plays the tape, he hears Quist, one of Emilio Largo's men, enter the room and hide in the bathroom. This allows Bond to scald Quist in the shower before the thug can shoot him. Bond knocks Quist senseless and sends him back to his "friends" with the words, "Tell them, the little fish I throw back into the sea."

BOUNDING MINES

APPEARANCE
Die Another Day (2002)

USED BY James Bond

Bounding mines are anti-personnel mines that are normally buried, and, when activated by pressure or a tripwire, burst 3–4 ft (0.9–1.2 m) in the air, causing severe injuries to a person's head and chest.

When James Bond and North Korean Colonel Moon engage in a chase on hovercrafts in the DMZ, Bond is pursued down a side road by one of Moon's men. Bond sees that this road is covered in bounding mines and detonates two of them with a machine gun. The flying shrapnel causes the North Korean hovercraft driver to crash into a tree.

BREITLING DIVER'S WATCH

APPEARANCE
Thunderball (1965)

USED BY James Bond

Following his arrival in the Bahamas on Operation Thunderball, Q gives Bond a modified Breitling Top Time chronograph with a built-in Geiger counter. The second hand measures radiation, allowing Bond to unobtrusively check if he is in the vicinity of the hijacked atomic weapons being ransomed by Emilio Largo and SPECTRE.

During the mission, Bond appears to find the watch uncomfortable, for he frequently wears his Rolex Submariner instead.

GETTING WARMER *Bond gets a radioactive reading on his Breitling watch.*

BRIEFCASE BOMB COMPARTMENT

APPEARANCE
Octopussy (1983)
USED BY James Bond

This briefcase contains a hidden compartment with a magnetic thermite explosive device. On a mission to destroy a spy plane, Bond infiltrates a Latin American airbase disguised as Colonel Luis Toro. He knocks out a technician, opens the briefcase, and places the explosive device against the inside of the spy plane's fuselage. The real Colonel Toro foils his efforts and takes possession of the explosive.

BROOM RADIO

APPEARANCE
Licence To Kill (1989)
USED BY Q

CLEAN SWEEP *Disguised as a humble gardener, Q utilizes his broom radio.*

This multi-band, low-frequency, high-level encryption walkie-talkie unit comes built into a standard broom. The unit scans channels for traffic and encrypts in sync with the capabilities of a designated receiver.

Disguised as a gardener, Q uses one outside drug lord Franz Sanchez's mansion to communicate with CIA contract pilot and agent Pam Bouvier. After making contact, he tosses the broom into the bushes.

BUG DETECTOR

APPEARANCES
From Russia With Love (1963),
Live And Let Die (1973)
USED BY James Bond

When James Bond checks into a hotel room on a mission, he finds it prudent to sweep the room for listening devices.

In *From Russia With Love*, Bond uses a device to check the voltage on the telephone line, which shows it is being monitored.

In *Live And Let Die*, Bond has a gadget inside his toiletries kit that reveals the location of listening devices.

CASSETTE TAPE

APPEARANCE
Diamonds Are Forever (1971)
USED BY Ernst Stavro Blofeld, Prof.
Dr. Metz, James Bond, Tiffany Case

Prof. Dr. Metz uses a cassette control tape labeled "World's Greatest Marches" to guide Ernst Stavro Blofeld's satellite weapon. Bond first sees the cassette in Metz's lab and later spies the tape in Willard Whyte's penthouse when he meets Blofeld. Bond brings a hidden copy of the music cassette to Blofeld's oil rig command center in his suit lining. Guards find it, but Blofeld unwittingly allows 007 to switch the music tape for the control tape. Bond passes the control tape to Tiffany Case, who believes it is the music cassette, and she switches the tape in the machine. When she finds out this cassette is the control tape, she tries to swap the tapes again, but Blofeld catches her.

CELLO CASE

APPEARANCE
The Living Daylights (1987)
USED BY James Bond, Kara Milovy

This impact-resistant, felt-lined fiberglass cello case, equipped with watertight seals and stainless steel locking latches, seats two people comfortably.

Always ready to use available tools, Bond commandeers cellist Kara Milovy's cello case to use as a sled to traverse the Czechoslovakia—Austria border. Without a car, Milovy and 007 ride in the open cello case across the snow, evading bullets. Bond, holding the priceless Stradivarius cello, uses the tailpiece spike to steer. When they reach the border gate, Bond tosses the cello in the air and catches it on the other side. He and Kara tell the guards they have nothing to declare but a cello.

CENTRIFUGE TRAINER

APPEARANCE
Moonraker (1979)
USED BY James Bond

BUCKLE UP *Bond straps himself into the centrifuge and Dr. Holly Goodhead attaches a wire to his chest to monitor heart rate.*

The centrifuge trainer at Hugo Drax's Moonraker facility in California simulates the gravity force an astronaut feels when shot into space. An instructor in an observation booth controls the speed and monitors the subject's vital signs. The capsule seats one and spins on an extended gimbal arm. Restraints are not used to keep the subject seated; the force of the centrifuge accomplishes that. Instead, the restraints keep the subject from knocking themselves out with their hands and arms. The centrifuge can reach a speed of 20 g's (20 times the force of gravity), but pressure on the body and internal organs would be fatal. Take-off pressure of a vertical lift-off exerts three g's; according to Dr. Goodhead, most people pass out at seven. A "chicken switch" kills the power when the subject releases his finger from the button. Goodhead challenges 007 to take a spin. Chang tells Dr. Goodhead that Drax wishes her to call, then he hijacks Bond's session in the centrifuge, disabling the chicken switch. Chang slowly increases the rpms toward seven g's. Bond releases the chicken switch only to find that it does not work. Chang gleefully raises the speed even higher. When the centrifuge surpasses 7 g's, Bond realizes the chicken switch has been disabled. When the pressure reaches 13 g's, Bond, on the verge of passing out, fires his wrist dart gun to disable the centrifuge.

FEELING THE FORCE *Bond begins to suspect that something is wrong with the centrifuge— Hugo Drax's henchman, Chang, has taken over in the control room.*

CHAKRA TORTURE KIT

APPEARANCE
Tomorrow Never Dies (1997)
USED BY Stamper, Dr. Kaufman

In Saigon, media baron Elliot Carver plans to have henchman Stamper torture Bond with his "toys," vicious-looking tools used in the ancient art of Chakra torture. According to Eastern philosophy, the body has seven Chakra points or energy centers. The Chakra tools probe a person's organs, inflicting the maximum amount of pain while keeping the victim alive for as long as possible.

Stamper was taught by the late Dr. Kaufman, whose record for keeping a victim alive was fifty-two hours. Stamper hopes to break the record, but before he can try, Bond and spy Wai Lin escape.

CHEQUE COPIER

APPEARANCE
A View To A Kill (1985)
USED BY James Bond

This Louis Vuitton cheque book is actually a device similar to a credit card flatbed imprinter, which allows the user to make an imprint of a previously written check. Bond employs this device to take a rapid copy of a check the mysterious industrialist Max Zorin has just written to Stacey Sutton in the study at his French chateau. The check is made out to Sutton for $5 million and dated May 3, 1985.

CIA STANDARD ISSUE EQUIPMENT

APPEARANCE
Moonraker (1979)
USED BY Dr. Holly Goodhead, James Bond

Suspicious of astronaut Dr. Holly Goodhead, James Bond breaks into her room at the Hotel Danieli in Venice. There Bond finds an array of CIA gadgetry, including a gold pen that contains a poison hypodermic needle (which he steals and later uses to kill Hugo Drax's python); a diary that fires a dart; a Christian Dior atomizer that shoots flames; and a handbag with a radio receiver and aerial. Bond realizes these items are all standard CIA equipment and deduces that the CIA has sent Goodhead to monitor Drax's activities.

IN THE BAG *The CIA fits Dr. Holly Goodhead's handbag with a radio receiver and a range of cunningly disguised gadgets.*

CIGARETTE CASE REMOTE CONTROL

APPEARANCE
Thunderball (1965)
USED BY Emilio Largo

SPECTRE's Emilio Largo possesses a remote control unit to enter the SPECTRE boardroom in Paris. The device, inside an ordinary-looking cigarette case, has one red button and one black. The black button slides back a large wooden cabinet. Pressing the red button opens a metal door behind the cabinet that leads to the boardroom.

CIGARETTE CASE SAFECRACKING UNIT

APPEARANCE
Moonraker (1979)
USED BY James Bond

When James Bond cracks into billionaire Hugo Drax's safe to find the blueprints for the Moonraker shuttle, he uses a safecracking unit disguised as a cigarette case. A panel in the case slides away to reveal an x-ray screen that shows the safe's tumblers and a digital readout that reveals the combination of the safe.

CIGARETTE LIGHTERS

APPEARANCES
The Spy Who Loved Me (1977),
Licence To Kill (1989)
USED BY James Bond

Non-gadget lighters play a key role in two 007 films.

In *The Spy Who Loved Me*, Major Anya Amasova learns 007 purchased his lighter in Berngarten, Austria, and she realizes Bond killed her lover. She vows to kill Bond when the mission ends. Bond must convince Anya to put the past behind her.

In *Licence To Kill*, newlyweds Felix and Della Leiter present Bond with an inscribed lighter. When drug lord Franz Sanchez kills Della and maims Felix, Bond takes his revenge by igniting a gasoline-soaked Sanchez.

CIGARETTE PACKAGE DETONATOR

APPEARANCE
Licence To Kill (1989)
USED BY James Bond

Although cigarettes always come with a health warning, Q Branch guarantees this package to do harm when used as directed.

Bond squeezes "Dentonite toothpaste" plastic explosive along the ledge of Sanchez's office in order to blast through two inches of armored glass. He places a fake cigarette blasting cap from the detonator package in the explosive paste.

The rest of the package works as an encrypted radio receiver, accepting only Bond's detonation signal. From a roof across a street, Bond sets off

the blast, but before he can shoot, Hong Kong narcotics officers attack him. Later, in part because of the detonation, Bond convinces Sanchez that he needs protection.

CODE-CRACKING DEVICE

APPEARANCE
GoldenEye (1995)
USED BY James Bond, Alec Trevelyan

Breaking into the Arkangel Chemical Weapons Facility, MI6 agents James Bond and Alec Trevelyan use an electronic code-cracking device that slides into a card reader slot and is activated by punching a number sequence on a keypad. The number Trevelyan enters when he inserts the device to relock the door is incorrect, setting off an alarm that alerts the guards.

COFFIN BODY COLLECTOR

APPEARANCE
Live And Let Die (1973)
USED BY New Orleans Mourners

Crime boss Mr. Big/Dr. Kananga has a macabre way of disposing of the bodies of those who try to spy on his New Orleans operation. The victim watches as a funeral procession passes. An assassin stabs the distracted victim. He falls to the street, whereupon the pallbearers set the empty coffin over him. A trio of claw mechanisms inside grabs and lifts the body. Two panels from the sides then slide over the open bottom.

CODE-CRACKER *Bond's mission to infiltrate the Arkangel Chemical Weapons Facility goes smoothly—until his partner Alec betrays him.*

COMMANDO KIT

APPEARANCE
Goldfinger (1964), Thunderball (1965), You Only Live Twice (1967), Live and Let Die (1973), A View To A Kill (1985), The Living Daylights (1987), GoldenEye (1995), Tomorrow Never Dies (1997), Die Another Day (2002)
USED BY James Bond

James Bond uses commando outfits to camouflage himself during dangerous insertion operations.
Commando black clothing, similar to the type worn by cat burglars, holds the obvious disadvantage of immediate incrimination if one is caught. Bond first wears a special waterproof suit in *Goldfinger*, then standard black while entering Largo's compound in *Thunderball*, and gray for his ninja outfit in *You Only Live Twice*. Bond returns to black with a tan leather holster in *Live And Let Die*. In *A View To A Kill*, Bond quickly removes his commando outfit to bed May Day. In *The Living Daylights*, 007 parachutes onto Gibraltar in commando blacks. In *GoldenEye*, 007 joins 006 on a commando raid on a nerve gas plant. *Tomorrow Never Dies* features a commando attack on media baron Elliot Carver's stealth ship. In *Die Another Day*, 007 wears two commando outfits—during his raid of the Graves diamond mine facility and his insertion into North Korea with NSA agent Jinx.

COMMANDO KNIFE BEACON

APPEARANCE
Die Another Day (2002)
USED BY James Bond

On the Pukch'ong Coast in North Korea, one of Bond's South Korean colleagues cuts the power cable to a radar dish. Bond removes a combat knife from his surfboard saboteur kit and sticks it in the ground. The knife's handle splits open to form a radio beacon dish. It emits a signal that replaces the radar dish's signal and recalibrates the approaching Mil Mi-8 helicopter's flight plan. The occupants believe they are landing at Colonel Moon's North Korean compound; they are actually landing in a forest where 007 and his colleagues capture diamond trader Mr. Van Bierk. Bond assumes Van Bierk's identity and uses the Mil Mi-8 to fly to Moon's compound.

COMPACT COMMUNICATOR

APPEARANCE On Her Majesty's Secret Service (1969)
USED BY Blofeld's Angels of Death

Upon opening this compact, a short-wave radio antennae emerges from the lid, allowing Blofeld to communicate with his Angels of Death around the world. Each night at midnight, the Angels must be alone so they can switch on the receiver and listen for Blofeld's voice. He will then tell them how to use their atomizers, which contain the deadly warfare agent Virus Omega. Fortunately, Bond and Marc Ange Draco destroy Piz Gloria, Blofeld's communications center.

COMPUTER MIRROR CAMERA

APPEARANCE
A View To A Kill (1985)
USED BY Max Zorin

This face-matching visual index computer system consists of a video camera, frame-grabbing software, and connection to a mainframe with contour-matching 3-D extrapolation software, which compares facial features to a large visual database.
Businessman Max Zorin uses this system when pretending to access The Progeny Index, the thoroughbred bloodline database, to find the perfect horse for his guest James St. John Smythe. In actuality, using a camera behind a wall mirror, Zorin accesses the mainframe to identify St. John Smythe as James Bond.

CROSSBOW

APPEARANCE
For Your Eyes Only (1981)
USED BY Melina Havelock

A crossbow is Melina Havelock's weapon of choice as she seeks revenge for her parents's murder. She "perforates" their killer Hector Gonzales at his Spanish villa and later hunts Aris Kristatos, who employed Gonzales. Before she can shoot Kristatos, Bond's ally Columbo hurls a knife into the villain's back.

CYANIDE CIGARETTE

APPEARANCE
Dr. No (1962)
USED BY **Mr. Jones**

After arriving in Jamaica, Bond discovers that the supposed Government House chauffeur Mr. Jones works for the opposition. Bond demands that Jones reveal the identity of his employer. Instead, Jones bites into a cigarette that contains a vial of cyanide and dies quickly. Pleydell-Smith, the Government Secretary, later views the cigarette remains with good-natured bafflement.

DART-FIRING MIRROR

APPEARANCE
Live And Let Die (1973)
USED BY **Whisper**

Inside a white "pimpmobile," Dr. Kananga's henchman Whisper has a side-view mirror with a camera sight, a remote control aiming and firing device, and a metal dart that, when fired into the target's temple, causes the victim's right foot to involuntarily stomp the accelerator as he dies. Whisper uses this to send Charlie, 007's CIA driver, speeding out of control.

DA VINCI MACHINE

APPEARANCE
Die Another Day (2002)
USED BY **MI6**

The Da Vinci Machine is a $1.3 million surgical system that allows doctors to examine or perform surgery on a patient using the machine's robotic arms. MI6 uses this apparatus to examine Bond after his 14-month incarceration in a North Korean prison. The machine's four arms scour Bond's body, and an MI6 doctor monitors 007's condition. The machine discovers indications of neurotoxins, histamines, serotonin, enzyme inhibitors, and scorpion venom, as well as venom antiserum. The North Koreans stung 007 with scorpions and then administered the antidote. Bond's pulse is 72, and his blood pressure is 120 over 80. His internal organs remain unaffected, but his liver is not in great condition.

MASTERPIECE *The Da Vinci Machine allows physicians to perform delicate surgery via robotic arms that move with exact precision.*

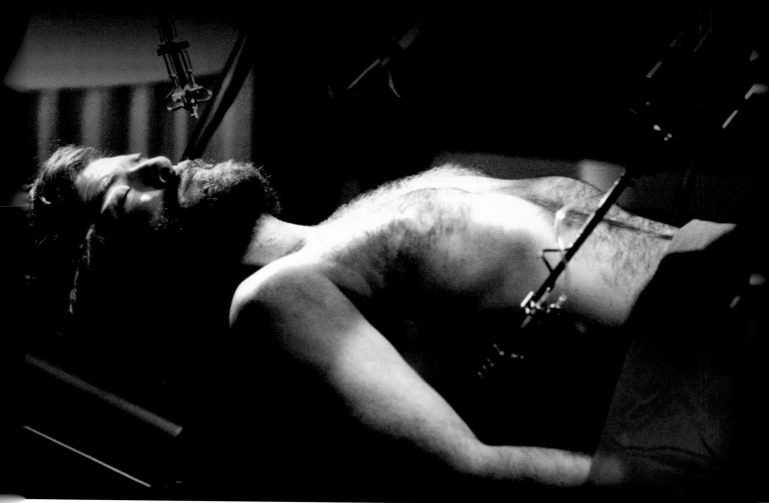

DECOMPRESSION CHAMBER

APPEARANCE
Licence To Kill (1989)
USED BY Franz Sanchez, Milton Krest

A decompression chamber allows a diver to return to regular atmospheric pressure on the surface rather than underwater. Milton Krest's ship the *Wavekrest* has one in the vessel's launch area. After Bond and Pam Bouvier plant money in the decompression chamber to frame Krest, Franz Sanchez kicks Krest into the chamber and turns the pressure inlet valve to maximum. As the depth gauge drops to 500 ft (152 m) below sea level, Sanchez smashes the vent with a fire ax, causing the pressure to drop instantly and Krest's head to explode.

DENTONITE TOOTHPASTE

APPEARANCE
Licence To Kill (1989)
USED BY James Bond

This looks like an ordinary tube of toothpaste, but it is actually filled with plastique explosive. As part of his plan to assassinate drug lord Franz Sanchez, Bond squeezes the plastique from the tube along the ledge of Sanchez's study, which is protected by armored glass. Bond then places a remote-controlled cigarette-package detonator amidst the plastique. He later blows out the windows of Sanchez's office using a remote control switch and sets his signature gun's sights on Sanchez.

DETONATOR

APPEARANCES
The Spy Who Loved Me (1977),
A View To A Kill (1985),
Tomorrow Never Dies (1997)
USED BY James Bond, Max Zorin,
May Day, Wai Lin

STEADY HAND *Bond extracts a missile's detonator in* **The Spy Who Loved Me.**

Detonators often feature in Bond's adventures. In some cases, the detonator itself is used as a weapon.

In *The Spy Who Loved Me*, Bond works with the USS *Wayne* crew to remove a detonator from a sea-launched ballistic missile. He then blasts open the control room shutters on the *Liparus* in an attempt to stop shipping magnate Karl Stromberg from initiating nuclear Armageddon.

A View To A Kill sees microchip mogul Max Zorin place a detonator atop several tons of explosives within his Main Strike Mine, hoping to trigger a double earthquake. Unable to stop the timer on the detonator, Bond works with Zorin's lover, May Day, to remove the detonator from the explosives. The pair uses a rail car to push the detonator out of the mine. However, a faulty handbrake on the rail car leads May Day to ride the rail car out of the mine, blowing herself up to ensure the detonator does not set off the explosives.

While trying to stop media mogul Elliot Carver from launching a war between Britain and China in *Tomorrow Never Dies*, 007 uses a small detonator from his watch to set off a hand grenade remotely. Later, Wai Lin tosses Bond a set of magnetized detonators that, when ignited by a missile's tailfire, will cause the missile to blow apart before taking flight.

DIAMOND SATELLITE WEAPON

APPEARANCE
Diamonds Are Forever (1971)
USED BY Ernst Stavro Blofeld,
Professor Dr. Metz

Blofeld engages Professor Dr. Metz to build him a diamond satellite weapon. The weapon uses light refracted through diamonds to create a massive laser beam that can cook submarines, ignite ICBM missiles, and even destroy entire cities. Blofeld uses the weapon to demand nuclear disarmament, hold the world's superpowers hostage, and offer the satellite's unconquerable power to the highest bidder.

To create the satellite, Blofeld and Metz need a huge cache of diamonds. When he only needs one last packet of diamonds to complete the satellite's array, Blofeld orders the assassins Wint and Kidd to kill the smugglers as soon as they have completed their work. When Bond impersonates Peter Franks, a new member of the smuggling team, he temporarily prevents them from obtaining the last diamonds.

Soon, smuggler Tiffany Case delivers the diamonds to Metz. Blofeld then orders the launch of the satellite and takes control of it from his oil rig headquarters. When the US government fails to respond to Blofeld's demands, he threatens to incinerate Washington DC. Bond uses Blofeld's bath-o-sub to destroy the computers controlling the satellite. Later, 007 ponders the difficult task of how to bring the diamonds safely back to Earth.

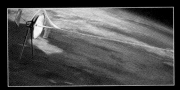

LASER SHOW *Blofeld demonstrates the power of his superweapon by destroying a US ICBM, a Soviet sub, and Chinese missiles.*

DICE, LOADED

APPEARANCE
Octopussy (1983)
USED BY Kamal Khan, James Bond

This pair of dice contains a small mercury load in the center cavity, which, when struck properly, shifts to force a roll of six.

Exiled Afghan prince Kamal Khan wins 220,000 rupees from retired Major Clive while playing backgammon at the Shiv Niwas Palace Hotel casino with loaded dice that always reveal a winning double six. When Clive refuses Khan's proposal to increase the stakes to 100,000 rupees, Bond takes his place, betting a real Fabergé egg, which Khan desperately wants. Bond then uses player's privilege and rolls Khan's loaded dice, winning 200,000 rupees and arousing Khan's interest and wrath.

DREAM MACHINE

APPEARANCE
Die Another Day (2002)
USED BY Gustav Graves/Colonel
Moon, Zao

The Dream Machine consists of a
face-enveloping mask that, with other
components, produces a sleep-like
state, allowing a body to repair and
regenerate at a faster rate than normal.
It is used as part of the DNA
replacement therapy offered by Dr.
Alvarez at his beauty parlor clinic in
Cuba. Gustav Graves/Colonel Moon,
who suffers from permanent insomnia
as a result of his DNA replacement,
uses the machine privately. Graves/
Moon says an hour a day in the
Dream Machine keeps him sane.

CURE FOR INSOMNIA *Zao arrives at Graves's
base while Graves uses the Dream Machine.*

DUNHILL CIGARETTE LIGHTER GRENADE

APPEARANCE
Tomorrow Never Dies (1997)
USED BY James Bond

This gold Dunhill lighter has a hidden
switch, which, when flicked, arms a
grenade. In order to infiltrate a
terrorist supermarket at the Khyber
Pass, Bond flicks the hidden switch,
and a red light flashes on the side of
the lighter. Bond throws it behind a
pile of oil drums, and it explodes. An
automatic radar-guided Gatling gun
spins and directs fire at Bond's grenade
diversion, allowing Bond to race to
an L39 Albatross jet and escape.

FIREBALL *Bond's Dunhill grenade lands near
an oil depot at the terrorist arms bazaar.*

ELECTRIFIED CHAIR

APPEARANCE
Thunderball (1965)
USED BY Ernst Stavro Blofeld

When Blofeld discovers that SPECTRE's income from the distribution of Red China narcotics in the United States has been short-changed, he exacts an extremely heavy price. Blofeld electrocutes SPECTRE No. 9 in his seat, has the chair with the smoking corpse lowered, and forces those working below to dispose of the body. Afterward, the smoking chair is raised back through the floor into its proper position.

ELEVATOR GAS CHAMBER

APPEARANCE
Diamonds Are Forever (1971)
USED BY Ernst Stavro Blofeld

When 007 enters the penthouse office of Willard Whyte, he finds himself in the presence of Blofeld. Surprisingly, Blofeld invites Bond to exit via his personal elevator. Bond does as suggested and soon finds himself trapped in a descending gas chamber. The gas does not kill Bond but knocks him out for many hours. When the elevator stops, Wint and Kidd collect 007's unconscious body and dump it in a pipeline that is soon buried underground.

ELECTRIFIED HEADSET

APPEARANCE
For Your Eyes Only (1981)
USED BY Ernst Stavro Blofeld?

Sending a shock through a headset is an unusual way to kill a helicopter pilot. A man who resembles Ernst Stavro Blofeld takes advantage of the electricity generated by the Augusta/Bell 206B's Allison 250 turboshaft engine. "Blofeld" uses a remote control unit to pump that charge into the temples of the pilot. This leaves the passenger, James Bond, at the mercy of "Blofeld's" remote-control flying skills.

ERICSSON MOBILE PHONE

APPEARANCES
Tomorrow Never Dies (1997),
Quantum Of Solace (2008)
USED BY James Bond, Dr. Kaufman

In *Tomorrow Never Dies*, the Ericsson JB988 mobile phone, saves Bond's life numerous times in Hamburg. It boasts several special features installed by Q Branch. These include a 20,000 volt stun gun, a fingerprint scanner, and an unlock Bond's 750iL is by hitting "recall–3–send." The sequence actually activates the stun gun in the mobile, shocking Kaufman.

Bond also uses the phone to drive and deploys the gadgets of the 750iL, using the phone, mostly from the backseat.

In *Quantum of Solace*, Bond tricks Elvis into calling his Sony Ericsson C902 cybershot phone, triggering a

Q: Your new telephone. Talk here, listen here.

007: So that's what I've been doing wrong all these years.

electronic lock pick hidden in the antenna. When opened, the phone reveals a touchpad and a color LCD screen. Together they can be used to remotely drive Bond's BMW 750iL.

When the British frigate HMS *Devonshire* sinks, M instructs Bond to investigate media mogul Elliot Carver's involvement. Bond uses the electronic lock pick in the mobile to enter techno-terrorist Henry Gupta's secret lab on the top floor of Carver's Media Group Network headquarters. He also engages the stun gun terminals and fries the electronic access panel outside Gupta's private office. Bond uses the phone to scan Gupta's fingerprint and then uses that scan to gain entry into Gupta's safe.

007 later gains the upper hand against assassin Dr. Kaufman by convincing him the only way to

trace and allowing Bond to put a GPS track on Elvis's movements. Bond follows Elvis and Dominic Greene from Haiti to Bregenz, Austria, disrupting their Quantum meeting at the opera. Bond uses the phone to snap close-up shots of the departing Quantum members, including British government advisor Guy Haines.

OPEN SESAME *(above right)* Bond uses the lock pick function of his Ericsson phone to gain access to Elliot Carver's Hamburg headquarters.

STUN GUN *(right)* Bond disables the electronic lock with his phone's stun function to enter Gupta's office.

WORK OF ART *This Imperial green-gold Easter Egg by Carl Fabergé contains a model of the state coach used by Tsar Nicholas II at his coronation in 1897.*

FABERGÉ EGG

APPEARANCE
Octopussy (1983)
USED BY James Bond

A forgery of an Imperial Fabergé Easter Egg places James Bond on the trail of a nuclear sabotage plot.

Rogue Soviet General Orlov pilfers the Fabergé egg and other valuable jewels from the Kremlin Art Repository in order to finance a plot to detonate a nuclear weapon on a US Airbase in West Germany. The Fabergé takes on great importance when agent 009 steals the forgery in East Germany. He reaches the residence of the British Ambassador but dies before he can explain its significance.

With the fake egg gone, General Orlov tells his accomplices, exiled Afghan prince Kamal Khan and smuggler Magda, that he needs the real egg back. They must buy it at auction so it can be returned to the Kremlin in time for an inventory of the repository. During the auction, James Bond switches the real egg for the fake obtained from 009. Bond then uses the real egg as bait for Khan in India. Magda steals the real egg from Bond and gives it to Khan, unaware that it has a homing device and transmitter from Q Branch inside. This addition allows 007 to gain valuable information about Orlov and Khan's plan. General Orlov, believing the real egg to be the fake, smashes it with the butt of his gun.

FAKE ASSASSINATION KIT

APPEARANCE
The Living Daylights (1987)
USED BY General Leonid Pushkin

This fake assassination kit is perfect for spies who want to convince their

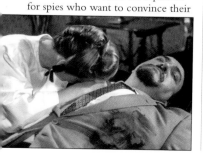

enemies they are dead. In order to convince General Koskov and Brad Whitaker that General Leonid Pushkin is out of the picture, 007 teams with Pushkin to "fake" his death using a bulletproof vest, a clear plastic bag containing "blood" or red dye, and a blood capsule for Pushkin to bite into at the time of the shooting. Bond fires at Pushkin at the North African Trade Convention in Tangier. The bullets burst the blood bag but are stopped by the vest. The fake assassination proves so convincing that everyone, including Pushkin's mistress, Rubavitch (shown grieving), is taken in.

FAKE FINGERPRINTS

APPEARANCE
Diamonds Are Forever (1971)
USED BY James Bond

Fake fingerprints allow an agent to undergo a rigorous background check without blowing his cover. To pose as smuggler Peter Franks, Bond covers his fingertips with false skin imprinted with the smuggler's own prints. When Bond meets smuggler Tiffany Case, she checks the prints and finds they match. Bond calls Q to congratulate him only to discover that the real Franks has escaped custody.

SHEDDING SKIN *Bond removes Q's ingenious fake fingerprints after passing muster with Tiffany Case.*

FAKE LEG CAST

APPEARANCE
Octopussy (1983)
USED BY James Bond

Bond apparently sustains several injuries while rescuing jewel smuggler Octopussy from exiled Afghan prince Kamal Khan's Beech 18 plane. Unable to travel from India to London, Bond retires to the bedroom on Octopussy's lake barge with a plastic cast on his right arm, a sling on his left, and one leg in traction. When Octopussy complains that she wishes he wasn't in such a weakened condition, the cast, the sling, and the traction suddenly fall apart, and Bond takes Octopussy in his arms. It has all been an elaborate ruse of Bond's to avoid returning to London.

FELIX LIGHTER

APPEARANCE
Live And Let Die (1973)
USED BY Harold Strutter, James Bond

A push-in car cigarette lighter doubles as a two-way radio for CIA agent Harold Strutter. Sitting in Strutter's car in Harlem, James Bond is surprised to hear CIA agent Felix Leiter joining in their conversation about a possible connection between dictator Dr. Kananga and businessman Mr. Big, because Felix is a few miles away in Midtown Manhattan. A built-in speaker allows Bond to hear Felix, and through a microphone, 007 informs his colleague that the gadget must be "a genuine Felix Lighter."

FINGER CLAMP

APPEARANCE
Diamonds Are Forever (1971)
USED BY James Bond

A finger clamp from Q's lab allows an agent being searched for a weapon to quickly gain the advantage. When Bond travels to Mexico to hunt down Ernst Stavro Blofeld, he infiltrates Blofeld's lab. Blofeld's double and two guards soon confront him. Bond raises his hands in surrender and that allows a guard to retrieve his Walther PPK from its shoulder holster. What the guard finds instead is a mousetrap-like device that clamps three of his fingers, slicing into them with razor-sharp teeth and giving Bond the upper hand.

FINGERPRINT SCANNER

APPEARANCE
Diamonds Are Forever (1971)
USED BY Tiffany Case

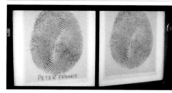

To infiltrate Blofeld's diamond smuggling ring, Bond poses as smuggler Peter Franks and makes contact with Tiffany Case. A smuggler herself, Tiffany doesn't take unnecessary chances and uses a fingerprint viewer to verify the identity of her new contact. She dusts Bond's glass for fingerprints and takes a Polaroid photograph. She then slides the photo of Bond's thumbprint into the fingerprint scanner viewer hidden in her closet where it appears on a screen next to the real thumbprint of Peter Franks. When the prints match, Tiffany accepts Bond as the real Franks and gives him his mission. Little does she know that Q has supplied Bond with a set of fake fingerprints for the occasion.

FIVE-BLADED KNIFE

APPEARANCE
Octopussy (1983)
USED BY Gobinda's men

Among the many weapons used by Kamal Khan's henchman, Gobinda, and his goons is a five-bladed knife, that allows an assailant to swing,

thrust, or throw the weapon with potentially deadly results.

One of Gobinda's goons uses the five-bladed knife when chasing Bond through the streets in Udaipur, India. Bond, riding in a tuk-tuk taxi, has no room to escape when the thug leaps from a jeep and seemingly pushes one of the knife's blades deep into Bond's chest. Bond knocks his attacker off the speeding vehicle and reveals that a thick wad of rupees stashed in his jacket has just saved his life.

FLASH PAPER

APPEARANCE
You Only Live Twice (1967)
USED BY James Bond

Magicians commonly use flash paper because, once ignited, it burns so completely as to leave virtually no ash and no smoke. Because of this, it is perfect for passing written information that must be destroyed without a trace. Flash paper is treated with nitric acid and sulfuric acid to create a sheet of nitrocellulose, allowing it to self-oxidize when lit. When M sends Bond to Japan to hunt for clues to the loss of an American spacecraft, he gives 007 the name of his contact on a sheet of flash paper. Bond memorizes it, then sets the sheet aflame with his lighter.

GEIGER COUNTER

APPEARANCE
Dr. No (1962)
USED BY James Bond

WATCH FACTOR The tiny amount of radiation in the luminous dial of Bond's Rolex is enough to activate a Geiger counter.

GEIGER COUNTER
This piece of scientific hardware provides vital evidence toward uncovering Dr. No's network and plans.

A Geiger counter is a particle detector that measures ionizing radiation. One arrives for 007 in Kingston in the diplomatic pouch. Bond demonstrates the Geiger counter's effectiveness to local fisherman Quarrel by running it over his Rolex watch and explaining how the luminous dial activates it. Bond then runs the Geiger counter over the exact spot in Quarrel's boat where the assassinated British Secret Service representative Commander Strangways placed rock samples from Crab Key.

The Geiger counter indicates a strong radioactive count. Professor Dent's claim that the rocks were merely worthless chunks of iron ore confirms Bond's suspicions that Dent is working for the enemy. The presence of radioactivity in the rock samples also leads Bond to investigate Dr. No's base on Crab Key.

GEIGER COUNTER CAMERA

APPEARANCE
Thunderball (1965)

USED BY Domino Derval

Bond provides Domino Derval with a Q Branch Geiger counter camera to help her locate two atomic weapons stolen by her lover Emilio Largo. 007 gives Domino the fake camera believing Largo will bring the bombs aboard the *Disco Volante*. Bond tells Domino to go on deck if the signal indicates strong radiation. Largo confronts Domino when she leaves her cabin, discovers the camera, and tortures her for betraying him.

GLASSES DETONATOR

APPEARANCE
The World Is Not Enough (1999)

USED BY James Bond

These Calvin Klein 718F glasses (with clear lenses; 007 has 20/20 vision) boast a small protrusion, which, when pressed, triggers a blinding flash from 007's Walther P99 handgun. When Lachaise's men trap Bond in the Swiss banker's Bilbao office, 007 presses the protrusion, triggering the flash from the Walther P99 and temporarily blinding Lachaise's men. This flash allows Bond to gain the upper hand, take out Lachaise's men, and confront the Swiss banker.

GOLD INGOT

APPEARANCE
Goldfinger (1964)

USED BY James Bond, Goldfinger

007 uses a solid gold ingot, reputedly from the Nazi hoard at the bottom of Lake Toplitz (Toplitzsee) in Saltzkammergut, Austria, to entice Goldfinger into a £5000 wager on their golf match, which Bond wins. Goldfinger pays off gangster Mr. Solo with gold ingots in Kentucky, but then extracts them from the crushed remains of his Lincoln Continental. Bond later ineffectively uses a gold ingot as a weapon against Oddjob.

GOLDENEYE

APPEARANCE
GoldenEye (1995)

USED BY General Ourumov, Alec Trevelyan

GoldenEye is a space-based nuclear weapons system designed to hit a large target on earth with a tremendous electromagnetic pulse. MI6 statistical analysis determined incorrectly during the Cold War that the Soviets had neither the finances nor technology to implement the system. The Soviets did, and the system consists of two satellites—Petya and Mischa—and two control stations in Russia and Cuba. Janus crime syndicate leader Alec Trevelyan takes control of GoldenEye. General Ourumov uses Petya to devastate Severnaya, and Trevelyan attempts to destroy London with Mischa. The Mischa weapon burns up in the atmosphere after programmer Natalya Simonova resets its orbit. James Bond destroys the Cuban control center through a series of sabotage efforts.

GOLDEN GUN

APPEARANCE The Man
With The Golden Gun (1974)
USED BY Scaramanga

Master assassin Francisco Scaramanga uses a unique 4.2 mm golden gun that is likely to have been designed by Lazar, a specialist Portuguese weapons maker in Macau. The gun consists of components that can be disassembled and smuggled disguised as everyday objects. The pistol consists of a cigarette lighter, a cigarette case, cuff links, and a fountain pen. These items fit together to make a single-shot weapon. Lazar also makes the soft 23-karat golden bullets the gun fires. He uses nickel to strengthen the gold, which flattens on impact like a dum dum for maximum wounding effect. Lazar delivers these bullets in a cigarette box to an unknown contact at the Casino de Macau. The bullets and gun seal Scaramanga's reputation as the greatest living assassin.

Scaramanga uses the gun to kill 002 Bill Fairbanks in Beirut and dispatch hitman Rodney in his island fun house. He shoots Gibson outside the Bottoms Up Club in Hong Kong. Later, he turns the gun on his business partner Hai Fat in Fat's estate office. When 007 arrives at Scaramanga's island, the assassin engages him in a duel—Bond's Walther PPK against his golden gun. With a little subterfuge, Bond wins. Scaramanga also has a golden Colt .45, which he uses to shoot the top off a bottle of champagne offered to Bond by Nick Nack.

A SINISTER MESSAGE *The arrival of a golden bullet inscribed "007" prompts M to send Bond on a mission to kill the world's most feared assassin.*

GPS ENCODER

APPEARANCE
Tomorrow Never Dies (1997)
USED BY Elliot Carver, Henry Gupta,
James Bond, Dr. Greenwalt

This US military Global Positioning System (GPS) encoder sends a time signal to space-based navigation satellites equipped with atomic clocks. The GPS system calculates positions based on time-differences between signals received from multiple satellites.

Media mogul Elliot Carver instructs techno-terrorist Henry Gupta to alter the time signal on an encoder purchased at a terrorist swap meet. The HMS *Devonshire* receives a signal transmitted from a Carver Media Group satellite, which sends the ship off course. The Chinese believe the British are in Chinese waters, and the British think they are in international waters. In reality, the British have strayed into Vietnamese waters. Bond steals the encoder from Gupta's safe and takes it to GPS expert Dr. Dave Greenwalt, who uses it to pinpoint where the *Devonshire* sank.

GRAPPLING HOOK GUN

APPEARANCE
Goldfinger (1964)
USED BY James Bond

To allow quick entry into a walled compound, Q develops a grappling hook gun. The gun propels a grappling hook and the spooled high-test nylon ultra-thin climbing rope 40 ft (12 m) into the air. The use of the gun eliminates the problem of the climbing rope becoming tangled. Bond uses this device to enter the oil storage depots owned by heroin-manufacturer Mr. Ramirez in Mexico.

GRAVITY CONTROL UNIT

APPEARANCE
Moonraker (1979)
USED BY Hugo Drax

Drax's space station has a radar-jamming system and an artificial gravity unit. The gravity control unit causes the station to rotate, creating a simulated gravitational pull. When Drax's men commence Operation Orchid, firing globes of nerve gas into the Earth's atmosphere, Bond and Dr. Holly Goodhead disable the radar-jamming system and make the space station visible from Earth. Drax orders the station's laser to destroy a fast-approaching US space shuttle, but Bond prevents this by engaging the gravity control unit's emergency stop and creating weightless chaos inside the station.

GRAVITY NORMAL *On arrival at the station, one of Drax's men engages the gravity control, enabling others to disembark with ease.*

QUICK THINKING *To save the attacking US shuttle, Bond flips open the cover on the emergency stop device and presses a button that shuts down the system.*

HAIRBRUSH TRANSMITTER

APPEARANCE
Live And Let Die (1973)
USED BY James Bond

In his hotel in San Monique, Bond unpacks a high-tech grooming kit. Removing the false back of a hairbrush, 007 reveals that it is also a radio transmitter. Before using it, Bond uses a bug-detector, disguised as a shaving kit, to sweep the room. Having located two hidden microphones, Bond employs the transmitter, using Morse code to send his message. To whom he communicates remains a mystery.

HANDBAG WALKIE-TALKIES

APPEARANCES
You Only Live Twice (1967), Moonraker (1979)
USED BY Japanese SIS agents, Dr. Holly Goodhead

When 007 enters the Ginza district of Tokyo looking for his initial contact in *You Only Live Twice*, two Japanese women watch him and radio his progress to an unknown person. It is likely they radio either Tiger Tanaka, the head of the Japanese Secret Service, or agent Aki, whom 007 is soon to meet at a Sumo wrestling arena.

In *Moonraker*, 007 discovers Dr. Holly Goodhead is really a CIA agent. In her hotel room in Venice, he finds a purse radio with a spring-loaded aerial among her standard CIA-issue equipment.

HANDCUFF CHAIR

APPEARANCE
Live And Let Die (1973)
USED BY Tee Hee, Mr. Big/ Dr. Kananga

With the pull of a switch on the back, this chair flips two arm shackles in place, pinning the unfortunate occupant. Tee Hee locks 007 in the chair for questioning from Mr. Big/ Dr. Kananga about the state of Solitaire's virginity, which apparently affects her ability to tell the future. This proves to be a subject Bond remains eager to avoid. Despite a threat to have Tee Hee clip off Bond's little finger, Kananga releases 007 so he can be fed to crocodiles.

HELICOPTER REMOTE UNIT

APPEARANCE
For Your Eyes Only (1981)
USED BY A Blofeld-like villain

The helicopter remote unit consists of a console equipped with levers, buttons, switches, a joystick, and two TV screens. A man who could be Blofeld uses the unit to electrocute the pilot of his helicopter and eliminate 007. Bond climbs out of the helicopter, moves to the front seat, and pulls out a cable running into a black box near the instrument panel, disabling the remote unit. He then takes control of the chopper and goes after the villain.

HOLOGRAM MACHINE

APPEARANCE
The World Is Not Enough (1999)
USED BY MI6

This machine is based at MI6's Remote Operations Centre at Castle Thane, Scotland. It generates a huge 3-D image of the head of terrorist Renard. This hologram allows MI6 doctor Molly Warmflash to explain how a bullet fired by agent 009 is moving through the medulla oblongata in Renard's brain, gradually killing off his senses. This allows him to feel no pain and to push himself harder and longer than any normal man until the bullet finally kills him.

HECKLER & KOCH GUNS

APPEARANCES
Five James Bond films
USED BY Bond, Dr. Kaufman, Elliot Carver's men, Gettler's men, Quantum agents, General Medrano's men, Raoul Silva's men

James Bond and his enemies have used a variety of German-made Heckler & Koch guns.

In *Tomorrow Never Dies*, assassin Dr. Kaufman kills Paris Carver with a Heckler & Koch 9 mm P7 pistol; Bond later turns the gun on him. Media mogul Elliot Carver's stealth ship is loaded with Heckler & Koch MP5A3 submachine guns, which Bond, Wai Lin, and Carver's men use.

In *The World Is Not Enough*, the Cigar Girl fires at Bond with a Heckler & Koch G36K, then fires a Heckler & Koch HK21 machine gun at his Q Boat.

Casino Royale sees Gettler's men fire UMP45 submachine guns at Bond as he tries to rescue Vesper Lynd and reclaim the stolen winnings from the poker game. Bond fires a bullet from a Heckler & Koch UMP9 9 mm into Quantum agent Mr. White's leg.

Quantum of Solace features Bond using a UMP9 to send an Alfa Romeo, filled with assassins firing Heckler & Koch G36C assault rifles, crashing off a cliffside Italian road. General Medrano's men also fire G36C assault rifles at Bond and Camille off Kings Quay in Haiti.

Skyfall sees Silva's men using Heckler & Koch HK416 assault rifles during their attack on Bond's childhood home Skyfall. Bond uses these weapons himself when he disarms Silva's henchmen.

HOMER SYSTEM

APPEARANCE
Goldfinger (1964), The Man With The Golden Gun (1974)
USED BY James Bond, Felix Leiter, Mary Goodnight

The homer system consists of a small radio transmitter that works with a unique rotating receiver. This receiver fixes the direction of the homer signal. The homer emits signals enabling the receiving unit to calculate its distance, allowing for a continuous fix on the homer's location. The CIA and British Secret Service developed the homer, and both James Bond and Felix Leiter use the device during their pursuit of Goldfinger.

Bond plants a large, magnetized version of the transmitter in Goldfinger's Rolls-Royce in England, allowing him to follow the car to Switzerland. Leiter reports Bond's whereabouts to M when the CIA picks up the signal from Bond's own homer, secreted in the heel of his shoe. Bond plants the homer on gangster Mr. Solo at Goldfinger's stud farm with a note to the CIA alerting them to Goldfinger's plans.

In *The Man With The Golden Gun*, staff intelligence officer Mary Goodnight has a homer on her in Bangkok. When Scaramanga kidnaps Goodnight, the signal reveals his location.

HYDRAULIC DETONATOR

APPEARANCE
The Living Daylights (1987)
USED BY Necros

The hydraulic system that operates the sliding glass doors of the Prater Café in Vienna is rigged by former KGB assassin Necros so that it will work with unexpected speed when triggered by remote control.

As Saunders, head of Section V, exits the café, Necros presses one of the walkman's buttons, causing the doors to slam shut. The glass door slices Saunders in half. As Bond reaches Saunders, a balloon drifts past with the words *smiert spionam* on it.

ICARUS

APPEARANCE
Die Another Day (2002)
USED BY Gustav Graves/Colonel Moon

The Icarus satellite, launched by billionaire Gustav Graves, has a reflective surface that spans 437 yd (400 m). It is purportedly designed to reflect the sun's light to allow crops to be grown at any time of the year in areas facing potential famine. However, Icarus also has another level of power, where the sun's light can be focused on a particular target, creating a deadly beam of high-intensity heat.

Graves attempts to use the Icarus to kill Bond in Iceland. He also tries to melt his Ice Palace and drown NSA agent Jinx. Graves later uses Icarus to devastate the DMZ minefield between North and South Korea hoping to trigger a war with South Korea and ultimately Japan.

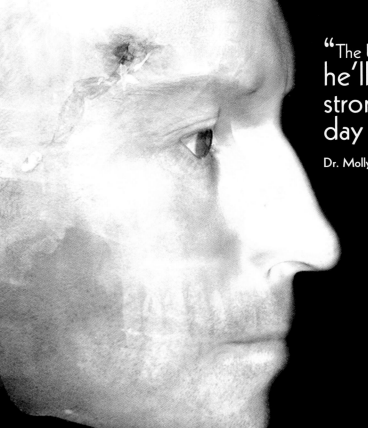

"The bullet will kill him, but **he'll grow stronger every day** until the day he dies."

Dr. Molly Warmflash

IDENTIGRAPH, VISUAL

APPEARANCE
For Your Eyes Only (1981)
USED BY James Bond, Q

The Visual Identigraph is an early digital imaging computer used by MI6 to identify suspects by matching facial features to photographs in the files of MI6, the Surete, Interpol, the Mossad, and the West German police.

Bond visits Q's workshop to use the Visual Identigraph and discovers the man who paid off Gonzales is Emile Leopold Locque.

INCENDIARY BOMBS

APPEARANCES
Live And Let Die (1973),
Skyfall (2012)
USED BY Quarrel Jr., Silva

When Bond goes to rescue Solitaire from the island of San Monique, Quarrel Jr. plants incendiary bombs with thirty second fuses. As Bond cuts Solitaire free from the sacrificial altar, the bombs blast Kananga's poppy fields, destroying his billion-dollar crop.

During his attack on Skyfall, Raoul Silva tosses several AN/MI4 grenades into the building, hoping to draw Bond and M out of hiding.

INHALER BUG

APPEARANCE
Casino Royale (2006)
USED BY James Bond

Bond notices that Le Chiffre uses an inhaler during their high-stakes poker game at Casino Royale. When Le Chiffre steps away from the table for a moment, 007 inserts a minuscule bugging and tracking device into the inhaler's base. With the aid of his Sony Ericsson phone, Bond tracks Le

JIM DIVING SUIT

APPEARANCE
For Your Eyes Only (1981)
USED BY Kristatos henchman

The JIM Atmospheric Diving Suit is larger than a normal diving suit. It has four windows in the headpiece as well as huge legs and arms fitted with deadly-looking pincers. The suit is named after Jim Jarratt who, wearing an "Iron Man" armored diving suit, located the sunken liner *Lusitania* 330 ft (100 m) down off the coast of Ireland in 1935. The modern JIM suit's purpose is for salvage work at depths exceeding 300 ft (91 m).

After Bond and Melina recover the ATAC transmitter from the command cabin of the sunken *St. Georges* spy ship, a Kristatos henchman in the JIM suit bursts into the cabin and uses the pincer arms to seize the ATAC from Melina. Bond removes the magnetic timer and thermite bomb from the ATAC console, attaches it to the back of the diving suit, and sets the timer for one minute. Kristatos's henchman pushes a console onto Bond's legs and traps him. Bond extricates himself, grabs the ATAC, and escapes with Melina from the wreck as the JIM diving suit explodes.

Chiffre back to his hotel room and overhears the part of the violent encounter between Le Chiffre and African terrorist Steven Obanno.

KEVLAR VEST

APPEARANCES
The Living Daylights (1987), Licence To Kill (1989), Die Another Day (2002)

USED BY General Pushkin, Pam Bouvier, James Bond

The high-strength polymer Kevlar was invented in 1965 to reinforce car tires, and became a key material used in bulletproof vests. In *The Living Daylights*, General Pushkin wears a Kevlar vest when he and 007 fake his death.

In *Licence To Kill*, Dario fires a bullet into Pam Bouvier's back. Bond thinks she's fatally wounded, but she's protected by Kevlar beneath her vest.

In *Die Another Day*, during a battle aboard a hovercraft, Bond blocks General Moon's bullets by holding a Kevlar vest in front of his body.

KEY FOB

APPEARANCES
The Living Daylights (1987), The World Is Not Enough (1999), Die Another Day (2002), Casino Royale (2006)

USED BY James Bond, Kara Milovy, Carlos

An innocent-looking key fob has saved James Bond's life on numerous occasions. In *The Living Daylights*, Q presents Bond with a Philips key fob with keys and a plastic rectangular box attached. Pressing a button on the box activates it. By whistling the first bars of "Rule Britannia," stun gas is released to a range of 5 ft (1.5 m), disorienting a person for about 20 seconds. The fob is also packed with a highly concentrated plastic explosive sufficient to remove the door of any safe. The activating signal is personalized, and Bond's code is a wolf whistle. The skeleton keys also open 90 percent of the world's locks.

Bond later whistles "Rule Britannia" to release the stun gas to disable the jailer and escape a Soviet air base jail in Afghanistan. Kara Milovy then uses one of the keys to unlock Bond's handcuffs.

In Tangier, while confronting Brad Whitaker in his military museum home, Bond attaches the

WRONG NUMBER *Carlos sends a signal from his cell phone that will detonate his exploding key fob.*

magnetic key fob to a bust of the Duke of Wellington. When 007 emits a wolf whistle, the bust explodes and crushes Whitaker to death.

In *The World Is Not Enough*, Bond uses his key fob to remotely drive his BMW Z8 along Valentin Zukovsky's caviar factory walkways in Baku. In *Die Another Day*, 007 presses a button on his key fob to engage the "adaptive camouflage" feature of his Aston Martin Vanquish. Bond also uses the fob to remotely drive the vehicle in his direction.

In *Casino Royale*, terrorist Carlos attaches a key fob detonator to the undercarriage of a Texron fuel truck, which he plans to crash into a Skyfleet S570 plane. Unbeknownst to Carlos, 007 attaches the key fob detonator to Carlos's belt buckle. Carlos triggers the detonator and obliterates himself.

KNOCKOUT CIGARETTE

APPEARANCE
The Spy Who Loved Me (1977)

USED BY Anya Amasova

As James Bond and Russian agent Anya Amasova travel on a traditional Nile felucca back to Cairo, Amasova interrupts a possible romantic interlude by putting Bond to sleep with a cigarette filled with narcotic dust. She then removes, from the inside pocket of Bond's tuxedo, a microfilm of blueprints detailing shipping tycoon Karl Stromberg's submarine tracking technology. When Bond meets Anya again in MI6's Egyptian headquarters, he says he wishes to know which brand of cigarettes she smokes.

LAPEL PIN

APPEARANCE
The World Is Not Enough (1999)

USED BY Sir Robert King, Elektra King

Sir Robert King wears a lapel pin, a Scottish heirloom called "The Eye of the Glens." His daughter, Elektra, replaces it with one that contains a transmitter. When King approaches his case of money, the urea-dipped cash and the metal anti-counterfeit strip serve as a detonator, blowing him up and devastating MI6 HQ.

LASER, INDUSTRIAL

APPEARANCES
Goldfinger (1964), Die Another Day (2002)

USED BY Goldfinger, Mr. Kil, James Bond

Goldfinger maintains an industrial laser for precision cutting sheets of gold at Auric Enterprises A. G. This laser, one of the first of its strength ever produced, is capable of projecting a beam of light to the surface of the moon or cutting through the metal security doors at the loading docks of Fort Knox. Goldfinger threatens to bisect 007 with the laser in Switzerland. He later hides it in the back of a disguised Army ambulance and uses it to enter the loading bay at the Bullion Depository vault.

Die Another Day sees 007 use another industrial laser. In the diamond cutting area of billionaire Gustav Graves's Icelandic mine, henchman Mr. Kil attempts to

DEATH RAYS *Bond battles Mr. Kil as deadly laser beams whirl around them in* Die Another Day.

eliminate spy Jinx, who is chained to a table, with a laser beam. Bond arrives and stops the laser with a remote device. Kil attacks and 007 knocks the remote against his face, switching on several lasers fired from a powerful robotic arm. Bond and Kil fight between the beams until Bond switches off the remote again. When Kil tries to stab Bond with a Maori bone hair comb, Jinx grabs the swinging remote and fires a laser beam into the back of Kil's head. The pair then cuts off Mr. Kil's hand with a laser to allow them to use his palm print to gain access to secure areas.

FINAL CUT *Goldfinger finds a novel use for his industrial laser— eliminating Bond.*

LASER CAMERA

APPEARANCE
Licence To Kill (1989)
USED BY Pam Bouvier

Pressing the shutter on this Polaroid camera shoots a brilliant red laser from the flash and takes an X-ray portrait of the subject. In Bond's hotel room in Isthmus City, Pam takes a photo of Bond and Q with the camera and is amazed when the laser shoots from the flash, burning a hole through a framed photograph of President Lopez. The X-ray portrait shows Bond and Q leaping out of the way of the laser.

NEAR MISS *Pam's Polaroid captures Bond and Q taking evasive action.*

LASER GUNS

APPEARANCE
Moonraker (1979)
USED BY Q Branch, James Bond, Hugo Drax's astronauts, space marines

One of Q's assistants demonstrates a laser rifle at Q's Brazilian laboratory.

The beams emitted by the laser rifle generate a heat great enough to melt the face of a mannequin in tests. Apparently, Q has shared the design with the US military, who go on to use similar weapons in their battle with Hugo Drax's men when they raid Drax's space station.

Drax himself has a laser cannon that can destroy approaching American space shuttles, but his plans are foiled before he can activate it.

The American space marines have lasers mounted over their shoulders on their life support packs and carry laser rifles. Drax's men are armed with chest-mounted laser weapons in the space battle, but on Drax's station, they have laser pistols. CIA agent Dr. Holly Goodhead commandeers one of these pistols as the battle ensues.

Drax's shuttle, Moonraker 5, is armed with a laser that Bond and Holly use to destroy Drax's nerve gas globes.

LEKTOR, THE

APPEARANCE
From Russia With Love (1963)
USED BY Soviet Intelligence,

The Soviet-built Lektor enables Eastern bloc intelligence agencies to communicate easily with each other. James Bond's mission is to bring the machine to the British Secret Service. The Lektor weighs approximately 22 lbs (10 kg) and is slightly larger than a typewriter. It can be easily carried in a brown case. It works using a series of rotating perforated disks, a light, and a mirror. Coded messages arrive via punch cards, which are then inserted into the machine, deciphered, and printed out. Fleming based the machine on the Enigma encoder used by the Nazis in World War II. In the novel, it is called the Spektor, but the name was changed for the film to avoid confusion with SPECTRE.

OPPORTUNIST THEFT *Tania steals the Lektor from the Soviet embassy.*

LIMPET MINES

APPEARANCE
From Russia With Love (1963), You Only Live Twice (1967), The Spy Who Loved Me (1977), A View To A Kill (1985), GoldenEye (1995) Tomorrow Never Dies (1997)
USED BY The Soviets, Japanese SIS ninjas, Karl Stromberg, Liparus crew, Klotkoff, Pola Ivanova, James Bond, Wai Lin

PRIMED TO KILL *Bond prepares to mine Carver's ship in* Tomorrow Never Dies.

A limpet mine is a magnetized explosive device that is attached to a ferrous object, then set off by remote control or via a timer. Soviet operatives set a limpet mine to kill Head of Station T, Kerim Bey, in *From Russia With Love*.

Japanese SIS ninjas use a limpet mine to blast a hole in the false lake in Blofeld's volcano to destroy SPECTRE's rocket base in *You Only Live Twice*.

The Spy Who Loved Me sees Karl Stromberg's men attaching a limpet speaker to the hull of the nuclear submarine USS *Wayne*, along with a cyanide bolt that they fire through the hull.

In *A View To A Kill*, KGB agents Klotkoff and Pola Ivanova attach a limpet to the jetty below Zorin's oil pumping station in San Francisco.

When 007 and 006 break into the Arkangel Chemical Weapons Facility in *GoldenEye*, Bond plants three magnetic explosives with digital timers. Though 007 sets them to detonate after six minutes, by pressing a button he reduces the count on one to three minutes. Nine years later, Bond plants a refined version of the mine on a nitrogen tank in Janus's Cuban GoldenEye satellite control facility. The timer on this version can be shut off by pressing a button on Bond's watch.

Bond uses limpets in his assault on an arms bazaar and, with help from spy Wai Lin, attaches limpets to the stealth ship belonging to Elliot Carver to prevent him from starting World War III in *Tomorrow Never Dies*.

LIPSTICK MAGNESIUM FLARE

APPEARANCE
You Only Live Twice (1967)
USED BY Helga Brandt

The lipstick magnesium flare belonging to SPECTRE No. 11, Helga Brandt, almost spells doom for James Bond. Brandt agrees to fly Bond from Kobe to Tokyo in her Meyers 200A aairplane. Once at altitude, Brandt traps Bond in his seat and drops her lipstick compact, in reality a magnesium flare which starts to burn through the floor to the fuel lines. Helga bails out, and Bond soon breaks free. He struggles before it explodes.

LOCATOR CARD

APPEARANCE
The World Is Not Enough (1999)
USED BY M

Every Russian nuclear warhead contains a locator card, a device similar in size and shape to a credit card, which emits a high-pitched signal on Russian emergency frequencies and allows the warhead to be tracked anywhere. Bond spots one of Renard's men removing the locator card from a warhead in a Kazakhstan underground nuclear test facility. 007 later retrieves it from the dead man's pocket and gives it to M when she arrives at Elektra King's oil pipeline station. Elektra later kidnaps M and holds her captive at Maiden's Tower on the Bosphorus near Istanbul, Turkey. When Elektra places an alarm clock on the ledge of M's cell to show M how much time is left before she and most of Istanbul are blown to kingdom come, M opens the back of the clock, removes the batteries and connects the wires to the locator card. Bond thus tracks M to Maiden's Tower.

FINAL CARD *M uses all her resourcefulness to escape incarceration.*

MANNEQUIN

APPEARANCE
Live And Let Die (1973)

USED BY **Baron Samedi**

During the sacrificial ceremonies on the Caribbean island of San Monique, the voodoo god of cemeteries, Baron Samedi, is called by worshippers. As the Baron rises from a grave, Bond pulls his Smith & Wesson 29 .44 Magnum and shoots Samedi in the head. The head breaks like plaster as the onlookers gasp. Bond fires two more shots, exploding the mannequin and revealing the trick, until the Baron in all-too-human form rises up from an adjacent grave.

MANTA RAY DISGUISE

APPEARANCE
Licence To Kill (1989)

USED BY **James Bond**

James Bond needs to gain entry into marine researcher and drug smuggler Milton Krest's research vessel, the *Wavekrest*, off the coast of Cay Sal Bank just north of Cuba. In order to avoid discovery, Bond covers himself underwater with a manta ray disguise. He fashions this disguise using a dark gray tarpaulin and two of his fisherman friend Sharky's fishing poles bent in a loop. When Krest's underwater probe, the *Sentinel*, passes over Bond's head, Bond drops the camouflage and swims after the craft, which is returning to the well area of the *Wavekrest*. Bond proceeds to climb aboard the *Wavekrest* undetected.

MECHANICAL ARM

APPEARANCE
Live And Let Die (1973)
USED BY **Tee Hee**

Tee Hee's mechanical arm is a feat of engineering. On the exterior of the pincers's "thumb" is a serrated blade that can slice through thin metal, complemented by two cutting blades on the pincers's "fingers." The arm features a series of high-torque motors in the "wrist" that give the arm many times the strength of a human limb, enough for Tee Hee to bend the barrel of Bond's Walther PPK. Although less sophisticated than Dr. No's mechanical hands, the pincers are far more deadly. The metal-work is insulated from Tee Hee's body, allowing him to handle high-voltage. When Tee Hee attacks 007 on The Crescent passenger train, Bond severs the release wires of the pincers's claw, locking the arm on the car's window handle. Bond then tosses Tee Hee through the window, ripping the mechanical arm from his body.

> **"Tee Hee**—on the first wrong answer from Miss Solitaire, you will snip **the little finger** of Mr. Bond's right hand.**"**
>
> **Kananga**

MEDIPAC

APPEARANCE
Casino Royale (2006)
USED BY **James Bond, Vesper Lynd**

The Medipac, located in the glove compartment of Bond's Aston Martin DBS, can monitor 007's vital signs remotely via his mobile phone. The kit includes medicines that can be administered in combipen form and a Medtronic portable defibrillator.

Bond uses the Medipac when Le Chiffre's girlfriend Valenka poisons him. However, in his struggle to attach one of the defibrillator panels, 007 knocks a lead loose. As he slips into unconsciousness, treasury officer Vesper Lynd reattaches the wire and fires the defibrillator, saving Bond's life.

MICRO-COMPARATOR

APPEARANCE
A View To A Kill (1985)
USED BY James Bond

When James Bond returns from Siberia with a microchip recovered from 003's body, Q uses a micro-comparator to compare it to an electromagnetic pulse impervious chip developed by Zorin Industries for the British government. The chips are identical, proving that the KGB had access to the secret chip designed by Zorin Industries.

MICROFILM VIEWER

APPEARANCE
The Spy Who Loved Me (1977)
USED BY James Bond

On a Nile felucca, 007 uses a pocket microfilm viewer to inspect microfilm of shipping tycoon Karl Stromberg's submarine tracking system blueprint that he retrieved from Jaws.

The microfilm viewer is disguised as a cigarette case and lighter and has a top that slides back to reveal a tiny screen. The microfilm clips onto the projector unit, which is disguised as a cigarette lighter. This fits into the top of the microfilm viewer. Using this device, 007 sees that key information has been deleted from the blueprints photographed on the microfilm.

MILK BOTTLE GRENADES

APPEARANCE
The Living Daylights (1987)
USED BY Necros

These milk bottles are really high-powered concussion grenades based on the WWII German Model 24 or "Potato Masher" grenade.

Soviet assassin Necros disguises himself as a milkman and infiltrates MI6's Blayden safe house. Throwing the explosive milk bottles, Necros causes utter chaos. The grenades seriously damage the house, resulting in "two dead, two in hospital," according to M. Necros and a group of conspirators then seemingly kidnap General Georgi Koskov.

MINI CAMERAS

APPEARANCE
On Her Majesty's Secret Service (1969), Moonraker (1979)
USED BY James Bond

In *On Her Majesty's Secret Service*, Bond uses a miniature Minox A/IIIs camera during the raid on Piz Gloria in Switzerland to photograph Blofeld's world map. The map features the locations of all of Blofeld's Angels of Death.

During the *Moonraker* mission, Bond takes blueprints of the Moonraker shuttle out of billionaire Hugo Drax's safe and photographs them with a miniature camera. The camera is engraved with 007, with the middle "0" being the camera lens.

MINI-REBREATHER

APPEARANCE Thunderball (1965), On Her Majesty's Secret Service (1969), Die Another Day (2002)
USED BY James Bond

For use during short periods underwater when conventional Scuba gear is not available, Q developed the mini-rebreather, which can last for up to four minutes.

Bond first uses it in *Thunderball* during an underwater battle with a SPECTRE agent in a pool at Emilio Largo's Nassau home. Bond later uses the device during the fight with SPECTRE frogmen in Biscayne Bay.

In *On Her Majesty's Secret Service*, after 007 dictates a letter of resignation to Miss Moneypenny, he pulls the mini-rebreather out of his office drawer.

Bond utilizes an updated model when investigating activities at the Iceland diamond mine of Gustav Graves in *Die Another Day*.

MONT BLANC PEN

APPEARANCE
Octopussy (1983)
USED BY James Bond

This Solitaire Mont Blanc Pen writes poisoned pen letters as well as featuring state-of-the-art listening devices. A drop from the pen releases a mix of nitric and hydrochloric acid that can dissolve all metals. There is also a listening device in the pen's cap enabling one to listen in on a bug placed in the Fabergé Egg's coach model. 007 employs the acid to eat through the bars on the window of his room at Kamal Khan's Monsoon Palace and uses the listening device to eavesdrop on Khan and General Orlov, despite interference from Magda's hairdryer.

MURPHY BED

APPEARANCE
You Only Live Twice (1967)
USED BY Ling, James Bond

The British Secret Service stages Bond's death by using a spring-loaded Murphy bed that hurls Bond up against a wall at the touch of a button. Enemy machine gunners break in and spray the underside with bullets. The bed features a steel plate that protects 007, but fake blood convinces Hong Kong authorities that gunmen have killed Bond.

UP AGAINST THE WALL *Ling flips her Murphy bed back so that gunmen can "kill" Bond.*

NIGHT-VISION GOGGLES

APPEARANCES
The Living Daylights (1987), Die Another Day (2002)

USED BY Saunders, James Bond, South Korean agents

These goggles allow someone to view a person over 200 yd (183 m) away at night by amplifying tiny amounts of light so an image can be clearly seen. Saunders uses a pair in Bratislava as he and Bond watch for the sniper assigned to eliminate General Koskov. Bond and his South Korean colleagues later wear night-vision goggles as they surf into North Korea.

NINJA THROWING STARS

APPEARANCES
You Only Live Twice (1967), Tomorrow Never Dies (1997)

USED BY Tiger Tanaka, ninjas, Wai Lin

During You Only Live Twice, head of the Japanese Secret Service, Tiger Tanaka, gives 007 a tour of his training camp. Bond sees ninjas practicing with throwing stars. Later, Tanaka hurls a throwing star into Blofeld's wrist as he pulls the trigger to shoot Bond. Blofeld's shot goes wide, saving 007's life.

In Tomorrow Never Dies, Wai Lin throws a star into the neck of one of Elliot Carver's guards as she heads to the stealth ship's engine room.

ODDJOB'S HAT

APPEARANCE
Goldfinger (1964)

USED BY Oddjob, James Bond

DEADLY WARNING *For Bond's benefit, Oddjob's razor-sharp hat brim slices the head off a statue at Goldfinger's golf club.*

The deadly black hat with "a light but very strong alloy" ring for a brim is one of the most dangerous weapons in any henchman's arsenal. Oddjob's hat, which is a dressage top hat in the film, allows the manservant to accurately hit a target at a range of up to a hundred yards. He can hurl the hat with enough force to sever the head from a granite statue at 20 yd (18 m).

In Fleming's novel, Oddjob wears a flat-brimmed bowler. He uses the bowler to kill Tilly Masterton, the sister of Goldfinger's paid companion Jill Masterton, outside Fort Knox. In the film, Oddjob's dressage top hat snaps Tilly's neck while in Switzerland. Oddjob later throws the hat at Bond inside the US Treasury Bullion vault at Fort Knox but misses. A second throw sails high and severs a high-voltage cable behind Bond. 007 takes hold of the hat, causing Oddjob some level of concern. Oddjob ducks Bond's throw, then goes to retrieve the hat stuck between metal bars in the gold vault. As Oddjob grabs the hat, 007 shoves the high-voltage cable against the bars, sending a deadly charge through Oddjob's body.

TIP OF THE HAT *In the gold vault at Fort Knox, James Bond considers turning the tables on Oddjob by hurling his metal-rimmed hat back at him.*

007: Remarkable. But what does the club secretary have to say?
Goldfinger: Oh nothing, Mr. Bond. I own the club.

OMEGA SEAMASTER WATCH

APPEARANCES
GoldenEye (1995), Tomorrow Never Dies (1997), The World Is Not Enough (1999), Die Another Day (2002), Casino Royale (2006), Quantum Of Solace (2008)

USED BY James Bond

Beginning with *GoldenEye*, Bond's watch of choice is an Omega Seamaster.

In *GoldenEye*, wearing the Omega Seamaster 300M Diver Quartz, 007 uses a laser emitted from the watch to cut an escape hatch in the floor of the train belonging to Alec Trevelyan. Trevelyan confiscates the watch in Cuba; by pressing the watch's helium release valve, he disarms two limpet mines planted by Bond.

In *Tomorrow Never Dies*, Bond changes to an Omega Seamaster 300M Diver. Bond slips on a version of the watch modified by the Chinese People's External Security Force in agent Wai Lin's bicycle shop. On Elliot Carver's stealth ship, Bond extracts the helium release valve from the watch, which is part of a remote detonator. He uses the detonator to make a booby trap with a grenade and a glass jar. Twisting the watch bezel triggers the detonator, which shatters the jar and sets off the grenade, blowing a hole in the ship.

In *The World Is Not Enough*, Bond activates LEDs on the Seamaster watch face by pressing the screw-down crown. These illuminate the inside of his inflating ski jacket when he and Elektra King are buried under an avalanche. Later, in a nuclear bunker, Bond fires a miniature piton with retractable high-tensile wire from the watch and raises himself to a gantry.

In *Die Another Day*, Bond again uses the helium release valve of his Seamaster as a detonator (this time a smaller version), sticking it into the C4 explosive he hides in smuggler Van Bierk's briefcase beneath the diamonds. In Colonel Moon's compound, a twist of the bezel causes the detonator to explode

BRIGHT IDEA *Bond sheds some light by activating his Seamaster's LEDs in* The World Is Not Enough.

the C4. After his release from captivity in North Korea, Bond receives a new watch from Q—his twentieth. At the Gustav Graves's Ice Palace, Bond uses the watch's laser function to cut a hole in the ice and rescue Jinx.

Bond wears two different Omega watches in *Casino Royale*. He sports a black Seamaster Co-Axial Planet Ocean model before he earns his licence to kill. Afterwards, he wears the Omega Seamaster 300M Diver.

In *Quantum Of Solace*, Bond wears an Omega Seamaster Planet Ocean 600m Co-Axial Chronometer with a black dial.

TIMED TO PERFECTION *Bond's Seamaster is an integral part of his style in* Casino Royale.

OPIUM BOMB

APPEARANCE
The Living Daylights (1987)

USED BY James Bond

In Afghanistan, Bond places a bomb inside a Red Cross relief sack in the hope of blowing up a cache of

opium. Bond ends up traveling with the opium and places the bomb inside a transport plane at a Soviet airbase. Bond sets the timer to explode in ten minutes and thirty seconds, shortly after Soviet General Koskov and his minions get airborne, but Koskov spots 007 before he can escape. Bond takes over the plane as the mujaheddin's Kamran Shah and his fighters attack the base. When 007 tries to defuse the bomb, Koskov's henchman, Necros, attacks. Bond throws Necros from the plane, resets the timer on the bomb to ten seconds, then uses it to blow up a bridge where Soviet troops pursue Shah and his men.

PARACHUTES

APPEARANCES

Goldfinger (1964), You Only Live Twice (1967), The Spy Who Loved Me (1977), Moonraker (1979), Octopussy (1983), A View To A Kill (1985), The Living Daylights (1987), Licence To Kill (1989), Tomorrow Never Dies (1997), Die Another Day (2002), Quantum Of Solace (2008)

USED BY James Bond, Pussy Galore, Helga Brandt, Jaws, Colonel Toro's paratroopers, May Day, 002, 004, Felix Leiter, Gustav Graves, Camille

Bond's penchant for jumping or falling from great heights, and his enemies' tendency to do the same, has made a parachute a vital piece of equipment in many adventures.

In *Goldfinger*, Bond and Pussy Galore parachutee from a Lockheed US VC–140B after it goes into a nosedive.

When Helga Brandt flies Bond to Tokyo in *You Only Live Twice*, she drops a magnesium flare in her Meyers 200A plane and parachutes out in mid-flight.

The Spy Who Loved Me sees Bond base jump, or base ski, off a precipice near Berngarten, Austria, unfurling a Union Jack parachute to escape from KGB agents.

In *Moonraker*, Jaws pushes 007 out of a jet. Bond intercepts the free-falling pilot and steals his ram-air parachute. He then fends off an

ESCAPE CHUTE *May Day glides away from Bond after killing a detective in the Eiffel Tower's Le Jules Verne restaurant.*

RULE BRITANNIA *(from left to right) KGB assassins pursue Bond; 007 performs a back-twist somersault after shooting Sergei Barsov; Bond sails to safety with his patriotic parachute.*

attack from Jaws, whose parachute fails to open.

During the action of *Octopussy*, Bond pulls the ripcords of Colonel Toro's guards in the back of a jeep in order to escape.

In *A View To A Kill*, May Day performs a base jump from the Eiffel Tower, parachuting down to Zorin's boat with a square ram-air parachute.

The Living Daylights begins with agents 002, 004, and 007 parachuting onto the Rock of Gibraltar to participate in war games with the SAS.

In *Licence To Kill*, 007 and Leiter parachute to the St. Mary's Star of the Sea Church in Key West after

capturing drug lord Franz Sanchez's plane.

Bond pops his square ram-air parachute below the Chinese radar when he makes a HALO jump to investigate the sunken HMS *Devonshire* in *Tomorrow Never Dies*.

Die Another Day sees billionaire Gustav Graves parachuting in to a London press conference with a square ram-air Union Jack canopy.

In *Quantum of Solace*, Bond and Camille share a parachute to land in a Bolivian desert sinkhole.

PARKER PEN GRENADE

APPEARANCE
GoldenEye (1995)
USED BY James Bond, Boris Grishenko

Bond's stainless steel Parker Jotter pen is actually a Class 4 grenade. Three clicks arm the four-second fuse; another three clicks disarm it.

At the GoldenEye control station in Cuba, computer programmer Boris Grishenko nervously clicks the pen. Mentally keeping track of the clicks, Bond slaps the pen from Grishenko's hand just before detonation; it explodes next to a fuel tank, setting off a chain reaction that devastates the control station.

PEN PAL *Boris Grishenko unknowingly plays with fire.*

PERISCOPE

APPEARANCE
From Russia With Love (1963)
USED BY Kerim Bey, James Bond

Head of Station T, Kerim Bey, manages to have a submarine periscope installed beneath the Soviet Consulate in Istanbul. The lens allows him to see into the high-level security meetings at the consulate. The periscope is accessed through a great drainage tunnel that leads from the Yerebatan Saray Sarniçi, the sunken palace cistern.

PIPELINE PIGS

APPEARANCES
Diamonds Are Forever (1971),
The Living Daylights (1987),
The World Is Not Enough (1999)

USED BY Mr. Wint and Mr. Kidd,
James Bond, Rosika Miklos, General
Georgi Koskov, Dr. Christmas Jones

A "pig" is a device that travels
through pipelines to seal them, check
for cracks, or clean them.

In *Diamonds Are Forever*, 007 is
buried alive in a section of pipeline
in Nevada. He sees a pig approaching,
manages to leap on top of it, then
short-circuits the machine by
touching the welding wires together.

In *The Living Daylights*, MI6
devises a pig for the Trans-Siberian
pipeline that can carry a man. It is
used by Bond and Czech technician
Rosika Miklos to help Soviet
General Koskov reach Austria from
Czechoslovakia and defect to the West.

In *The World Is Not Enough*,
terrorist Renard places a bomb on a
pig in Elektra King's pipeline. 007
and nuclear scientist Dr. Christmas
Jones use an observation rig to catch
up to the speeding pig. When the pig
and the rig lock together, Jones uses
her HP Jornada 430SE computer to
discover that half of the plutonium is
missing from the bomb. Bond and
Jones leap from the rig to the pipe
and allow the pig bomb to explode
in an attempt to convince Elektra
that they are both dead.

CAPITALIST PIG *Bond and Rosika Miklos
convince Koskov to ride the pig to Austria.*

RIDING THE PIPE *Dr. Jones prepares to speed
through Elektra King's pipeline.*

PITON BELT

APPEARANCE
GoldenEye (1995)

USED BY James Bond

Though it appears to be a typical size
34 in (86.3 cm) leather belt, the
buckle in this bit of wardrobe from
Q Branch has a 75-ft (22.8-m)
rappelling cord built in.

When fired, the piton shoots
out at high-velocity, pulling a
high-tensile wire designed to
support Bond's weight. Bond
uses it to escape from the
Russian Military Intelligence
Archives in St. Petersburg. He fires the
piton into the cement ceiling, swings
across an atrium, kicks a stunned
soldier out of the way, and
smashes through a window.
Bond lands on a supply
truck parked below the
window in the
compound's vehicle yard.

PITON GUN

APPEARANCE
Diamonds Are Forever (1971)

USED BY James Bond

Bond uses a piton-firing gun to gain
entry into Willard Whyte's private
suite at the Whyte House casino
hotel in Las Vegas. Bond rides on top
of the exterior express glass elevator
to the Starlight Lounge. He uses the
gun to shoot pitons with attached
climbing ropes. Fastening the ropes to
a climbing harness beneath his tuxedo,
he pulls himself up to the otherwise
inaccessible penthouse. Later, when
confronted with two Blofelds in
Whyte's office, Bond uses the piton
gun to shoot one in the head.

PITON LASER GUN

APPEARANCE
GoldenEye (1995)

USED BY James Bond

The piton laser gun is a multi-
purpose tool, able to fire its tempered
ultra-high carbon steel mini-piton
into granite. The 397 lb (180 kg) test
cable attached to the piton retracts
on an internal wrench as soon as the
user gives the trigger a second
squeeze. The laser can, at short-range,
melt most ductile metals.

James Bond employs the gun when
he infiltrates the Arkangel Chemical
Weapons Facility in the USSR. Bond
bungee jumps from a high dam
above the plant and uses the cable
from the gun to lower himself down
to a ledge. From this point, he cuts
through a metal plate on the
roof and slips undetected
into the interior.

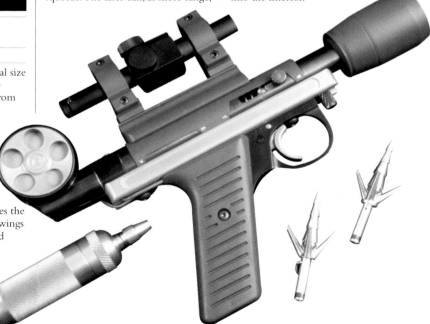

POISON GAS

APPEARANCES
Goldfinger (1964), You Only Live Twice (1967), The Spy Who Loved Me (1977), Moonraker (1979)

USED BY Goldfinger, Kisch, Blofeld, Stromberg, Hugo Drax

Poison gas remains a potent weapon of the megalomaniac villain. While any criminal might use stun gas, tear gas, or knockout gas, only a select few employ deadly vapors.

Goldfinger reduces organized crime in the United States when he gasses the leaders of America's foremost crime families with Delta 9. James Bond convinces Pussy Galore to contact the CIA in order to switch the gas before her pilots spray Delta 9 over Fort Knox in Kentucky.

In You Only Live Twice, Blofeld protects his volcano rocket base by pumping phosgene gas into the venting caves that lead to the sea. However, when he launches *Bird*

DEADLY GLOBE *Drax's satellite is designed to distribute a poison lethal only to humans.*

1, the rocket's exhaust must travel out of the caves, and fans apparently disperse the gas, allowing Bond, Japanese agent Kissy Suzuki, and the ninjas to escape safely after a battle with SPECTRE operatives.

In *The Spy Who Loved Me,* shipping magnate Karl Stromberg threatens to fill the *USS Wayne* with cyanide if Commander Carter refuses to surrender the submarine.

In *Moonraker,* billionaire Sir Hugo Drax rings the earth with satellite weapons filled with a deadly gas made from the plant Orchidea Negra. The gas made from this plant kills only humans. Bond must blast the weapons out of the sky before they enter the atmosphere.

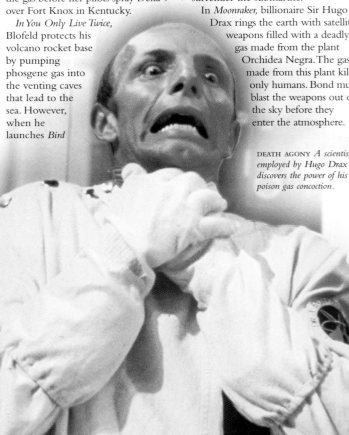

DEATH AGONY *A scientist employed by Hugo Drax discovers the power of his poison gas concoction.*

POISON STRING

APPEARANCE
You Only Live Twice (1967)

USED BY SPECTRE assassin

When SPECTRE attempts to kill James Bond, it sends an assassin armed with a deadly poison. As Bond sleeps with Japanese agent Aki, the assassin slithers into the attic, finds a gap in the ceiling, and lowers a black string. He then opens a bottle of a powerful poison that he pours down the string intending that drops will land in Bond's mouth. Before the drops can find their mark, Bond and Aki shift in their sleep. The drops spill into Aki's mouth and cause rapid death. Bond shoots the SPECTRE assassin, killing him instantly.

POLARIZING SUNGLASSES

APPEARANCE
A View To A Kill (1985)

USED BY James Bond

Standard sunglasses may have polarized lenses, but few offer adjustable settings that allow the wearer to cut glare and reflections from windows at almost any angle.

Q Branch provides these glasses to James Bond, allowing him to witness industrialist Max Zorin writing state geologist Stacey Sutton a check for $5 million at his French chateau. By moving the sliders at the bottom of the sunglasses frame, Bond can cut out the glare on the window of Zorin's room and see what is going on perfectly. On a sunny day at a garden party, nobody appears suspicious of the seemingly ordinary looking pair of sunglasses.

PUSHKIN'S WATCH

APPEARANCE
The Living Daylights (1987)

USED BY General Leonid Pushkin

By pushing the dial on the side of this watch, Pushkin can signal to the wearer of a receiver watch that he is in trouble with a low bleeping sound.

Bond confronts KGB head General Leonid Pushkin in his suite at the Hotel Isla De France in Tangier regarding Operation *Smiert Spionam.* Staring into the barrel of Bond's Walther PPK, Pushkin pushes the button on his watch to alert his bodyguard. Realizing what has happened, 007 knocks the bodyguard unconscious as he enters the suite.

RADAR-GUIDED GATLING GUN

APPEARANCE
Tomorrow Never Dies (1997)

USED BY Various terrorists

The Type 730 Chinese 30 mm Gatling gun is designed to be foolproof, firing at targets selected by radar.

When Bond encounters one at a terrorist supermarket on the Khyber Pass he easily distracts it by tossing a Dunhill cigarette lighter grenade behind a set of oil drums. When they explode, the 730 automatically turns and unleashes gunfire, allowing Bond to hijack an L39 Albatross fighter plane carrying Soviet SB-5 nuclear torpedoes. Once taxiing on the airfield, Bond fires a missile at the 730, destroying it instantly.

SECRET SIGNAL *Bond reveals the transmitter that brought the authorities to Silva's base.*

RADIO TRANSMITTER

APPEARANCE
Skyfall (2012)
USED BY James Bond

Q issues James Bond with a radio transmitter to broadcast his location in the event of an emergency.

Bond activates the transmitter on the yacht *Chimera* as he is taken to Silva's island off Macau and soon three Royal Navy Agusta Westland AW159 Lynx Wildcats hover above the island, aiding Bond's rescue and Silva's capture.

RADIOACTIVE PILL

APPEARANCE
Thunderball (1965)
USED BY James Bond

Q presents a radioactive pill to James Bond during Operation Thunderball. When swallowed, the pill sends out a signal to a special

BITTER PILL
When Q presents Bond with "a recently developed harmless radioactive device," Bond is unsure what to do with it. "Swallow it," Q replies.

receiver, allowing the person's position to be tracked. When 007 finds himself trapped in the coral cavern that SPECTRE uses to store the stolen atomic weapons, he swallows the pill, allowing CIA agent Felix Leiter to guide a Coast Guard helicopter to Bond.

RAKE METAL DETECTOR

APPEARANCE
The Living Daylights (1987)
USED BY MI6 "Gardener" agent

This 60 in (152.4 cm) garden rake not only provides grounds maintenance, but its prongs also contain a metal detector to track armed intruders to the Blayden safe house.

When Bond arrives at the safe house to aid in the questioning of Soviet defector General Georgi Koskov, the prongs of the standing rake turn and beep. This alerts one of the MI6 agents posing as a gardener that Bond is carrying his Walther PPK. The agent disarms Bond and allows him to enter the safe house.

RAPPELLING CUMMERBUND

APPEARANCE
Licence To Kill (1989)
USED BY James Bond

This broad sash, worn with a tuxedo, hides a nylon rappelling rope.

On top of the Isthmus casino, Bond removes his cummerbund, revealing a climber's rappelling rope. He ties the rope to the flagpole and rappels to the ledge outside of drug baron Franz Sanchez's office. Bond squeezes plastic explosive from a Dentonyte toothpaste tube and places a detonator from a cigarette package beneath Sanchez's office window, vital parts of a planned assassination attempt.

RAPIER MISSILE LAUNCHER

APPEARANCE
Octopussy (1983)
USED BY Colonel Toro's officers

The British Army and Royal Air Force began using this command-guided surface-to-air missile in 1967 to combat low-flying craft with high maneuverability.

After Bond escapes from Latin American officer Colonel Toro's paratroopers, he flies off in an Acrostar Bede jet. But a telephone call from one of Toro's officers has troops launching a rapier surface-to-air missile at 007. No matter what maneuver Bond makes, the missile remains locked on his tail. In a final attempt to rid himself of the missile, Bond flies the Bede jet through a spy plane hangar as Toro's men race to close the hangar doors. Bond makes it out safely through the other doors before they close, but the missile does not, resulting in a dramatic explosion that obliterates the hangar with the spy plane inside.

REMOTE-TRIGGERED IMPLANT

APPEARANCE
A View To A Kill (1985)

USED BY Max Zorin

This remote-control transmitter, which fits into a cane or jockey's whip, programs an injection of natural horse steroids, allowing a horse to overcome

fatigue while racing.

Amoral scientist Dr. Mortner implants a microchip into the racehorse Pegasus and installs a remote control transmitter into the silver-topped cane belonging to Pegasus's owner Max Zorin. At the press of a button, Zorin programs the horse steroids injection into Pegasus, allowing the horse to beat the others. Zorin later uses the cane transmitter to send Bond's horse Inferno into a frenzy when 007 begins to pull ahead in a steeplechase competing with Zorin.

REVERSIBLE JACKET

APPEARANCES
Live And Let Die (1973),
Octopussy (1983)

USED BY James Bond

One of the keys to confusing the enemy is good camouflage. But an outfit that may suit one circumstance can easily stand out when the situation changes. On a number of occasions, Bond has used a reversible jacket to blend seamlessly from one situation to another.

When visiting Tarot card reader Solitaire via hang glider, Bond wears black, but upon arrival he turns his jacket inside out and removes his trouser covers to reveal a more appropriate off-white, tropical suit.

On another mission, Bond arrives in a Latin American country to destroy a spy plane. He removes his hacking jacket and turns it inside out, revealing an officer's coat. It comes complete with medals, and with the addition of a holstered revolver, it allows him to pose as Colonel Luis Toro and enter the spy plane hangar.

RING CAMERA

APPEARANCE
A View To A Kill (1985)

USED BY James Bond

By simply bending one's ring finger, one can take black and white photos with this signet ring.

Bond wears this Q Branch ring camera at a party held by industrialist Max Zorin at his French chateau where he snaps shots of Zorin employees Bob Conley and Dr. Carl Mortner. CIA agent Chuck Lee later supplies 007 with biographical details on these men.

ROCKET-FIRING CIGARETTE

APPEARANCE
You Only Live Twice (1967)

USED BY Tiger Tanaka, James Bond

Head of the Japanese Secret Service, Tiger Tanaka, presents 007 with a rocket-firing cigarette. The rocket embedded in the cigarette is a real Finjet rocket, originally designed to be fired from a much larger weapon and saturate an area like a giant shotgun blast. Tanaka claims the rocket, adapted to fire from a cigarette, is accurate up to 30 yd (27.4 m). Bond uses the weapon to blast the SPECTRE crater-roof control operator, letting him briefly open the crater and enabling Tanaka's ninjas to enter Blofeld's volcano rocket base.

ROCKET GUN

APPEARANCE
You Only Live Twice (1967)

USED BY Tiger Tanaka

The Japanese SIS provides one of the few markets for the remarkable Gyrojet rocket guns, manufactured by the now defunct MB Associates out of San Ramon, California.

Head of the Japanese Secret Service, Tiger Tanaka, shows 007 an array of Gyrojet carbines and handguns and demonstrates a 12 mm model with an explosive incendiary charge in the rocket ammo.

The gun fires jet-propelled rockets that can carry explosive charges. Rocket guns are quiet and fire with almost no recoil, but accuracy depends on the precision achieved in the manufacturing of the ammo.

ROLEX WATCH

APPEARANCE
Live And Let Die (1973)

USED BY James Bond

James Bond wears a Rolex watch in a number of films, but the one he wears in *Live And Let Die* is the most memorable. The Rolex Submariner watch comes with two very handy extra features. Firstly, by pulling out the cap or twisting the rotating 60 minute bezel, the watch can become a hyper-intensified magnetic field. According to Q, the magnet is powerful enough to deflect the path of a bullet. Secondly, the watch has a rotating saw blade built into its face.

Miss Moneypenny delivers the newly repaired watch to 007 at his home before Bond departs on a mission to investigate the deaths of three British agents. Bond demonstrates the watch's magnetism on a sceptical M.

When Dr. Kananga/Mr. Big wishes to know if Solitaire still has the power to predict the future, he asks her if he is correctly reading the registration number of Bond's watch.

When Kananga captures 007 and Solitaire, the Rolex comes in useful. Tied to a winch platform dangling over a shark pool. Bond engages the magnet, drawing a shark pellet to him. He then sets the saw blade spinning. It cuts through the rope bindings, freeing Bond. 007 soon shoves the pellet in Kananga's mouth, causing him to explode.

ROLLEIFLEX CAMERA

APPEARANCE
From Russia With Love (1963)

USED BY James Bond

James Bond uses this simple ¼ in (0.64 cm) tape recording device built into the back of a Rolleiflex T Type 2 camera body to record his conversation with Soviet cipher clerk Tatiana Romanova. It allows Bond to act as a tourist while documenting valuable information about the Lektor decoder. After listening to this tape, the British Secret Service instructs Bond to move forward with obtaining the Lektor.

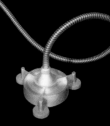

QUICK SPIN *The permutator checks every combination of Gumbold's safe.*

SAFE-CRACKER

APPEARANCES
You Only Live Twice (1967),
On Her Majesty's Secret Service (1969)

USED BY James Bond

In *You Only Live Twice*, James Bond employs a small pocket-sized safe-cracker unit to break into the office safe belonging to Blofeld's accomplice Mr. Osato. Although the unit detects the movement of the tumblers, it does not disengage the security alarm that sounds when 007 opens the safe. Bond grabs a few documents as Osato's guards approach, including a photo of the cargo ship *Ning-Po* and a paper with an explanatory microdot.

Bond also uses a safe-cracker/photocopy machine in Bern, Switzerland, in *On Her Majesty's Secret Service*. While lawyer Gumbold steps out to lunch, Bond infiltrates his office and collects a large tool chest sent over by a crane bucket. Bond opens the chest and removes a permutator programmed to electronically operate dials of a safe in all possible combinations. Bond attaches the permutator to a storage battery unit in the chest and places the permutator against the safe's dial. Once he cracks the safe, Bond removes papers concerning Blofeld and uses a photocopy machine located in the chest to make facsimiles of the documents. He packs up the chest, tosses it back in the crane bucket, and leaves the office as Gumbold returns.

CUTTING EDGE *Bond's Rolex proves not only stylish and durable, but in Dr. Kananga's grotto, it also saves him in the nick of time.*

SCARECROW CAMERA/GUN

APPEARANCE
Live And Let Die (1973)
USED BY **Tee Hee, Dr. Kananga**

Dr. Kananga uses scarecrows outfitted with video cameras and remote-fired guns to protect his poppy fields on San Monique. Kananga kills CIA double agent Rosie Carver with a shot fired from one of his scarecrows when he fears she might confess her duplicity to 007. Bond later uses the scarecrows to find Kananga's poppy fields. In turn, the scarecrows help Kananga keep watch on Bond.

SCARECROW SENTRY *Kananga's security cameras transmit pictures back to his base.*

SUDDEN DEATH *A gun in one of Kananga's scarecrows cuts short Rosie Carver's life.*

SEAGULL SNORKEL

APPEARANCE
Goldfinger (1964)
USED BY **James Bond**

When 007 must infiltrate the oil storage depots where Mr. Ramirez has his heroin manufacturing plant, he approaches underwater. Rather than use scuba gear, Bond employs a snorkel disguised as a seagull atop his head. The seagull also makes it appear that Bond's natural wake as he moves beneath the surface is its own.

SEA VAC

APPEARANCE
Tomorrow Never Dies (1997)
USED BY **James Bond, Elliot Carver**

Media mogul Elliot Carver uses the deep sea rotary drill known as the Sea Vac as a tool to provoke an international incident between Britain and China.

In Carver's stealth ship, this device, with 6-ft (1.8 m) conical bits, can be lowered into the water beneath Carver's stealth ship. The Sea Vac is controlled through a cable that guides speed, direction, and the intensity of the drill itself. Carver and his henchman Stamper use the Sea Vac to cut into the generator room of the British frigate HMS *Devonshire*, leading the crew to believe they have been hit by a Chinese aerial torpedo. Stamper then instructs the control technician to drill the Sea Vac into the frigate's mess room. After the *Devonshire* sinks, Carver's divers enter the missile room and steal a Tomahawk-class missile. Later, Carver aims a gun at 007 in the stealth ship's control room. Bond engages the motor of the Sea Vac behind Carver, and it chews the media baron to bits.

SECURITY CAMERA

APPEARANCE
You Only Live Twice (1967)
USED BY **SPECTRE No. 4**

In the office of Blofeld's accomplice Mr. Osato, a secretary works at a tabulating machine. In reality, the man is SPECTRE No. 4, and the tabulating machine controls a security camera and gun and conceals a video screen showing the weapon's target. When 007 visits Osato, SPECTRE No. 4 trains the camera and gun on Bond for the entire visit.

CHEWED UP *Carver battles Bond shortly before his Sea Vac drill shreds him to pieces.*

SEIKO WATCH

APPEARANCES
The Spy Who Loved Me (1977),
Moonraker (1979), For Your Eyes
Only (1981), Octopussy (1983),
A View To A Kill (1985)

USED BY James Bond

ON TRACK *The directional finder on Bond's watch comes in useful in* **Octopussy.**

James Bond wears a Seiko watch on five different missions.

In *The Spy Who Loved Me*, he wears a Seiko 0674, which can receive text messages that it prints on punch tape.

Moonraker sees Bond using a Seiko Digital LCD M354 Memory Bank Calendar watch. This watch includes detonating cord secreted in a rear compartment and a detonation cable attached to the start/stop timer button. It is detonated using the time/set button. 007 uses it to escape from the blast chute of the *Moonraker* shuttle.

In *For Your Eyes Only*, Bond wears a Seiko H357 Digital Analog Alarm watch with a display for scrolling

THE RIGHT TIME *The explosive device hidden in Bond's Seiko watch helps save his and Holly's lives in* **Moonraker.**

TEXT MESSAGE *Bond receives word from HQ in* **The Spy Who Loved Me.**

LED text messages and a radio transmitter for communication. At the end of the mission, Bond places the H357 near the macaw Max and lets him speak with the Prime Minister.

In *Octopussy*, Bond first wears a Seiko G757 Sports 100, containing a radio directional finder that allows him to track the fake Fabergé Egg, thanks to a homer in the egg. At the end of the mission, he wears a color model of the Seiko liquid crystal television watch, which allows him to see what Q's video cameras are filming from a hot air balloon.

Bond also wears a Seiko watch in *A View To A Kill*, but this watch has no known special features.

SHARK PELLET/GUN

APPEARANCE
Live And Let Die (1973)

USED BY James Bond, Dr. Kananga

The shark gun fires compressed CO2 pellets, which kill by filling the prey's body with gas.

Island dictator Dr. Kananga acquires the gun after it is found on the beach with Bond's gear in San Monique. Bond uses a pellet to kill Kananga. He shoves it into Kananga's mouth, causing him to inflate and explode.

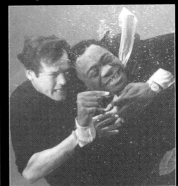

SHARK POOL SHOWDOWN *Bond shoves the shark gun's compressed-gas pellet into Kananga's mouth.*

SHARPER IMAGE CREDIT CARD

APPEARANCE
A View To A Kill (1985)

USED BY James Bond

In an attempt to ascertain a link between geologist Stacey Sutton and industrialist Max Zorin, Bond breaks into Stacey's house. Bond uses an electronic device disguised as a credit card from The Sharper Image, an electronics retailer. When placed between the jambs of a double-hung window, the card emits a signal that causes the window latch to rotate and unlock.

UNFORCED ENTRY *Bond breaks into Stacey Sutton's house with his special credit card.*

SHAVER BUG DETECTOR

APPEARANCE
A View To A Kill (1985)

USED BY Sir Godfrey Tibbett

This Norelco shaver conceals a sophisticated listening device locator

When James Bond travels to Max Zorin's French chateau, he poses as James St. John-Smythe, a rich British eccentric wishing to dabble in horses. He brings with him Sir Godfrey Tibbett, a horse trainer working with the British Secret Service. Tibbett sweeps the room for bugs with the shaver. Once found, the pair plays a taped conversation to throw off those eavesdropping. When the pair searches the grounds at night, they leave a tape of snoring playing to fool Zorin's men

SIGNATURE GUNS

APPEARANCE
Licence To Kill (1989), Skyfall (2012)
USED BY James Bond

An innocent-looking Hasselblad camera is actually a signature gun—a sniper's rifle that fires only if the handprint signature of the shooter matches the one programmed into the gun's optical palm reader grip.

Q, on leave from MI6, brings the weapon to Isthmus City to assist Bond, who has been removed from active duty by M. The gun's components include an infrared Bushnell gun sight, an extension tube, a Bolex bi-pod, and the right-hand signature pistol.

Bond attempts to use the gun to assassinate drug lord Franz Sanchez, but Hong Kong narcotics agents attack him. Unable to fire the weapon, the agents show it to British agent Fallon who confirms that the gun is government property.

In *Skyfall*, Q issues Bond with a Walther PPK/S 9mm short with a micro-dermal sensor in the grip. He has coded it to Bond's palm print. A panel flashes green when the gun is ready to fire. Bond uses the weapon in Shanghai. Later, at Macau's Floating Dragon Casino, one of Severine's bodyguards tries to shoot Bond with it. The panel flashes red, the gun doesn't fire, and a komodo dragon devours the villain (*see also* Walther PPK).

> Pam Bouvier: What kind of film does it take? 120?
> Q: No, .220 high-velocity.

SKI POLE ROCKET

APPEARANCE
The Spy Who Loved Me (1977)
USED BY James Bond

When Bond skis away from a cabin in Berngarten in the Austrian Alps, Sergei Barsov and three other KGB agents pursue him, armed with rifles and pistols. Though 007 appears to be unarmed, he is, in fact, well-prepared with an ingenious Q gadget. A twist of his ski pole causes a trigger to emerge. Skiing backwards, Bond aims the ski pole like a rifle and pulls the trigger, firing a four-bladed rocket dart into Barsov's chest, killing him instantly.

SKI SUIT ESCAPE POD

APPEARANCE
The World Is Not Enough (1999)
USED BY James Bond, Elektra King

By pulling a tab on this modified black ski suit jacket, an airbag inflates, enveloping the wearer in a protective cocoon. When an avalanche threatens Bond and Elektra King, 007 activates the airbag to protect them. He extracts a knife hidden in the jacket to cut through the airbag when the avalanche has finished, then punches through the snow to escape.

SNOWBALL *Bond and Elektra King find protection in his stylish yet functional ski jacket from Q Branch.*

SKYHOOK RESCUE SYSTEM

APPEARANCE
Thunderball (1965)
USED BY James Bond, Domino Derval

Developed by Robert E. Fulton, Jr., the Skyhook rescue system picks up 007 and Domino Derval after the *Disco Volante* explodes. The 90-lb (40.8-kg) kit consists of 500 ft (152.4 m) of nylon line, a harness, a helium tank, a balloon, and a jumpsuit.

Bond releases a balloon on a nylon line from a dinghy. A low-flying, unmarked CIA plane seizes the line and pulls Bond and Domino aloft. A crew member hooks the line into a winch, which allows Bond and Domino to be pulled into the plane.

HIGHFLIERS *The Skyhook rescue system allows James Bond and Domino to ascend to the skies.*

SMART TABLE

APPEARANCE
Quantum of Solace (2008)
USED BY MI6

The smart table at MI6 is a high-tech touch display screen that allows users to slide images—including surveillance footage, photos of suspects, maps, and other documents—by moving their hands

across the screen. Using this table, MI6 Forensics links bank bills found in Mitchell's apartment to Edmund Slate in Port-Au-Prince, Haiti.

SNAKE BRACELET/PITON

APPEARANCE
Tomorrow Never Dies (1997)
USED BY Wai Lin

This snake bracelet is not simply a beautifully-crafted piece of jewelry. The bracelet, which belongs to Chinese agent Wai Lin, also contains a piton and climbing wire that can be fired at a target.

Having broken into the Hamburg

headquarters of Elliot Carver's Media Group Network, Wai Lin is on the run from Carver's men. She fires the piton from her snake bracelet at a metal column and attaches it to a hook on the belt of her leather catsuit. She then walks confidently down the column in order to make her final escape from Carver's men, waving goodbye to James Bond as he attempts to flee from the guards.

SNOOPER

APPEARANCE
A View To A Kill (1985)
USED BY Q

This dog-like, remote-controlled robot has video cameras for eyes and antennae for ears, allowing one to conduct undercover surveillance operations.

When Bond is presumed missing in action, Q uses this prototype of a highly sophisticated surveillance machine to search the countryside home of state geologist Stacey Sutton to discover if Bond is actually alive. Q monitors the snooper from a

van outside the house and determines that Bond is indeed alive and otherwise engaged, sharing a shower with Sutton. When asked to report on Bond's status, Q replies that he's "just cleaning up a few details."

SOLAR-POWERED LASER CANNON

APPEARANCE
The Man With The Golden Gun (1974)
USED BY Scaramanga

Scaramanga has an unorthodox "golden gun" in his arsenal—a powerful solar-powered laser cannon, which, as Scaramanga explains to Bond, "Goes with the Solex—no extra charge." Emitting a focused beam of sunlight with a heat of 3,500 °F (1,927 °C), the laser cannon has the power to explode Bond's seaplane at the push of a button. Scaramanga observes that the cannon makes him and the protection it affords him "undeniably, the man with the golden gun."

SOLEX AGITATOR

APPEARANCE
The Man With The Golden Gun (1974)
USED BY Scaramanga

The British government believes the Solex Agitator could be the solution to the world's energy needs. Developed by British scientist Gibson, the Solex converts sunlight into energy with 95 percent efficiency. Gibson defects from Britain to develop the Solex and is assassinated by master assassin Francisco Scaramanga when he offers to return. Scaramanga takes possession of the Solex and plans to offer it up to the highest bidder. Bond saves the Solex before Scaramanga's island blows up, tucking it inside his shirt.

SONIC RING

APPEARANCE
Die Another Day (2002)
USED BY James Bond, Q

On a mission to Iceland, James Bond wears a ring, which by simply twisting it, turns into an ultra-high frequency, single-digit sonic agitator unit. Q demonstrates it on a sheet of bulletproof glass, placing his ringed hand on the glass and shattering it.

Bond first employs the ring at the fake diamond mine of Gustav Graves in Iceland. 007 uses it to shatter a glass floor of an office, allowing him to escape. Later, Bond uses the ring to rescue Jinx in the Ice Palace, shattering the windshield of his Aston Martin Vanquish to bring her inside the car.

SPEARGUNS

APPEARANCES
Thunderball (1965), For Your Eyes Only (1981), Licence To Kill (1989), Tomorrow Never Dies (1997)

USED BY
James Bond, Domino Derval, SPECTRE frogmen, aquaparas, Columbo's men, Stamper

Spearguns become more than tools to hunt fish in the adventures of James Bond. They serve as dangerous weapons above and below water.

During Operation Thunderball, Bond uses a CO_2-fired gun on Love Beach to impale assassin Vargas. On board the *Disco Volante*, Emilio Largo's mistress, Domino Derval, fires a fatal spear into Largo's back. SPECTRE frogmen and aquaparas use dozens of spearguns during underwater battles.

In *For Your Eyes Only*, one of smuggler Columbo's men fires a spear into the back of Claus, a henchman for smuggler Aris Kristatos.

SHOOT TO KILL *Claudine Auger (Domino) poses with a speargun at Lyford Cay, Bahamas.*

In *Licence To Kill*, Bond steals a speargun from an attacker below the *Wavekrest*, fires the harpoon line into the pontoon of a seaplane, and skis barefoot with the gun as his handle. *Tomorrow Never Dies* sees 007 witness Stamper shoot the pilot of Wai Lin's trawler with a speargun.

ADAPTABLE *Bond uses another diver's speargun as a ski-rope handle to barefoot ski behind a plane.*

STILETTO BOOT/SHOE

APPEARANCE
From Russia With Love (1963)

USED BY
Morzeny, Rosa Klebb

This SPECTRE-developed weapon of a retractable stiletto blade built into the right toe of a shoe or boot was used by henchman Morzeny to kill SPECTRE's planner, Kronsteen, and used by SPECTRE's Rosa Klebb in an attempt to kill 007.

The blade, upon deployment, is coated from a concealed reservoir with the lethal poison tetrodotoxin—in this case extracted from the sex organs of the pufferfish. There is no antidote.

Although tetrodotoxin is usually ingested, causing death in six to eight hours, direct application of a large amount into the cardiovascular system will result in death within seconds.

STILETTO FIGHTING STICK

APPEARANCE
You Only Live Twice (1967)

USED BY
SPECTRE assassin

A traditional bamboo fighting stick becomes a deadly weapon when a disguised SPECTRE assassin has it outfitted with a poison-tipped stiletto blade inside the hollow chute.

Tiger Tanaka, the head of the Japanese Secret Service, educates Bond in Japanese culture. While training in bojutsu stick fighting, the SPECTRE assassin knocks Bond's staff away. Twisting a section of his weapon, the assassin locks his stiletto in position. Bond snatches the weapon from the assassin's grasp and kills him. Tanaka reveals to Bond that the assassin is an outsider.

STINGER MISSILES

APPEARANCE
Licence To Kill (1989)

USED BY
Franz Sanchez, Perez

The shoulder-fired Stinger missiles allow ground troops to pose a serious threat to military aircraft as well as commercial aircraft. To that end, drug baron Franz Sanchez buys four infrared target lock Stinger missiles from the Contras and threatens to shoot down an American airliner if the DEA doesn't stop pursuing him. Heller, Sanchez's chief of security, makes a deal with CIA contract pilot and agent Pam Bouvier to return the Stingers if the US grants him immunity. When Bond tries to kill Sanchez, Heller tells Bouvier the deal is off. Sanchez and his henchman Perez fire two Stingers during their escape, one of which clips the tail of Bouvier's Piper PA-18 Super Cub.

SURFBOARD SABOTEUR KIT

APPEARANCE
Die Another Day (2002)

USED BY
James Bond

The surfboard Bond rides into the coast of Pukch'ong, North Korea contains a hidden saboteur kit. By twisting the surfboard fin, the surface of the board slides away to reveal a Walther P99 and ammunition, nylon rope, a tray of C-4 plastic explosive, a combat knife, and a GPS device. The knife conceals a radio beacon transmitter in its handle that deploys when Bond sticks the knife into the ground. The knife emits a duplicate beacon to one used to guide in a Mil Mi-8 helicopter, sending it off course. Bond later plants the plastic explosive in a case of conflict diamonds.

TANK BUSTER

APPEARANCE
Die Another Day (2002)
USED BY Colonel Moon

Korean Colonel Moon's Tank Buster is actually an OICW (Objective Individual Combat Weapon), which combines an assault rifle with semi-automatic, low velocity cannon-firing air-bursting munitions.

When Moon learns from henchman Zao that conflict diamond trader Mr. Van Bierk is, in fact, James Bond, he picks up his Tank Buster loaded with depleted uranium shells, which is located in his hovercraft mothership. He swings it around to aim at the Mil Mi–8 helicopter on which Bond flew into Moon's base. He fires the weapon, instantly blowing up the chopper. From his hovercraft mothership, he also detonates landmines in the DMZ with the Tank Buster in an effort to stop Bond.

FIRE POWER *Colonel Moon takes aim with his Objective Individual Combat Weapon, aka a tank buster.*

TAROT CARDS

APPEARANCE
Live And Let Die (1973)
USED BY Solitaire, James Bond

Solitaire uses tarot cards to foretell the future and discern the unseen. She sees Bond's journey to New York and his purpose, as well as his journey with double agent Rosie Carver. With the turn of a card, she can tell Bond is armed.

The cards originally brand 007 "The Fool," but when Solitaire invites Bond to choose a card to see his future, it is "The Lovers"—a card she will turn again in San Monique when asked by her boss, Kananga, about the future. Solitaire sends Bond an upside-down Queen of Cups tarot card to warn him that Rosie Carver will betray him.

Bond uses the tarot, too. He invites Solitaire to choose a card. Little does she know the deck is stacked with just one card: The Lovers. She considers the card she draws an omen, loses her virginity to 007, and with it her supposed powers. Baron Samedi later taunts her and Kananga with the Death card.

MARKED CARDS *The cards are fated in favor of 007—his number is visible on the card backs.*

THERMOS BOMB

APPEARANCE

A View To A Kill (1985)

USED BY Scarpine

Max Zorin's henchman Scarpine places a radio-triggered bomb disguised as a coffee thermos into an explosives-filled mining car in the Main Strike Mine. The bomb blows through the bottom of the San Andreas Lake, flooding the fault. This sets the stage for a larger explosion to trigger a double earthquake and flood Silicon Valley. The explosion and flood kill dozens of miners, Pan Ho and Jenny Flex. May Day survives and resolves to foil Zorin's plot.

THIRD NIPPLE

APPEARANCE

The Man With The Golden Gun (1974)

USED BY James Bond

The superfluous papilla appliance or third nipple ranks as one of the most unusual Q Branch equipment requests. Bond calls it "a little kinky," but he hopes it will serve a valuable purpose. Bond places it on his chest to pose as master assassin Francisco Scaramanga for an unscheduled meeting with industrialist Hai Fat. Bond counts on Fat never having met Scaramanga face to face. Fat plays along during their meeting, even inviting Bond back to his estate that evening. Hai Fat, in fact, does know Scaramanga, and he quickly plots to have Bond taken captive.

THREE-FINGERED SNIPER RIFLE

APPEARANCE

The Man With The Golden Gun (1974)

USED BY James Bond

In Macau, Portuguese gunsmith Lazar asks 007 to fire a custom-built bolt-action rifle made for a client who has lost two fingers. Bond shoots, but the bullet hits low. Lazar brags that the gun is balanced for a person with three fingers, not five. Bond decides to test this and threatens Lazar with the rifle. This gesture forces Lazar to reveal to 007 details of a new shipment of arch assassin Scaramanga's trademark golden bullets.

THROWING KNIVES

APPEARANCES

From Russia With Love (1963), Thunderball (1965), On Her Majesty's Secret Service (1969), Moonraker (1979), For Your Eyes Only (1981), Octopussy (1983), The World Is Not Enough (1999), Die Another Day (2002), Skyfall (2012)

USED BY Krilencu, Colonel Jacques Boitier, James Bond, Nick Nack, Venice assassin, Santos, Columbo, Mischka, Grischka, Cigar Girl, Jinx

Throwing knives have been used by Bond, his allies, and his enemies on numerous occasions.

Krilencu throws a knife into the stomach of a gypsy camp guard in *From Russia With Love*.

SPECTRE No. 6 Colonel Jacques Boitier attempts to eliminate 007 in *Thunderball* with a knife; instead, he pins Bond's wrist to a cabinet.

In *On Her Majesty's Secret Service,* Bond throws a knife in Marc Ange Draco's office, hitting the date September 14th on a calendar. Draco notes the date is actually the 13th. Bond replies, "I'm superstitious."

In *Moonraker*, Drax's Venice assassin rises from the coffin atop a funeral boat and throws a knife, which hits Bond's gondolier. He throws another at Bond but misses. Bond throws the knife back, killing the assassin.

In *For Your Eyes Only*, Columbo's man Santos throws a knife into a guard's stomach during a raid on a warehouse owned by smuggler Kristatos. Columbo later kills Kristatos with a throwing knife at an abandoned monastery in Greece.

In *Octopussy*, expert knife throwers Mischka and Grischka throw a knife into 009's back when he steals a fake Fabergé Egg from Octopussy's

Circus. Grischka later pins Bond to a cabin door with knives. Bond kills Grischka with one of his own blades.

In *The World Is Not Enough*, the assassin known as the Cigar Girl throws a knife into the neck of Swiss Banker Lachaise to stop him revealing information to 007.

In *Die Another Day*, NSA agent Jinx uses two knives aboard the Antonov flying command center. She throws one into the neck of a North Korean guard and one at double agent Miranda Frost. It misses her and hits a book, *The Art Of War*. Jinx grabs the knife-embedded book and stabs Miranda with it.

In *Skyfall*, James Bond throws a knife into Silva's back before the villain can kill M.

TORPEDO GUN

APPEARANCE
The Spy Who Loved Me (1977)

USED BY **Karl Stromberg**

Shipping tycoon Karl Stromberg has a gas-powered torpedo gun underneath his dining table onboard his *Atlantis* research laboratory. The gun fires an explosive missile through its long tube that runs almost the entire length of the table. When Stromberg fires at Bond, 007 dives out of the way as the missile destroys his chair. Bond then uses the tube to fire two Walther PPK bullets into Stromberg's abdomen, killing him.

TORTURE CHAIR

APPEARANCE
The World Is Not Enough (1999)

USED BY **Elektra King, James Bond**

The antique torture chair is a 19th century Ottoman Empire relic made of mahogany and inlaid with ivory. Elektra places Bond in this chair at her hideout at Maiden's Tower on the Bosphorus Sea. She secures 007's neck in a collar while he sits, shackled. A turn of the chair's wheel pushes a bolt into the back of 007's neck. Five turns will cause his neck to break.

Elektra is close to breaking Bond's neck when Russian casino owner Valentin Zukovsky enters the tower. Elektra shoots him, but Zukovsky lifts his walking stick (a single-action, single-shot rifle) and fires at a chair restraint, freeing one of 007's hands.

TRACKING DEVICE IMPLANT

APPEARANCE
Casino Royale (2006)

USED BY **James Bond**

INSIDE 007 *The portable sonic resonance unit allows an MI6 technician to see the placement of the tracking device in Bond's arm.*

At M's request, an MI6 technician fires a pea-sized tracking device from a syringe gun into the underside of James Bond's wrist. The device serves as both a longwave transmitter and 24 channel DGPS (Differential Global Positioning System) receiver. This allows it to transmit exceedingly accurate location data to MI6. After Le Chiffre and his accomplices force Bond into a car accident, they drag him from his wrecked Aston Martin DBS and dig the implant out of his arm with a knife. This prevents MI6 from locating 007 during the time Le Chiffre tortures him. Le Chiffre implies that he knew of the device's existence because Bond's contact René Mathis revealed this information.

HOLE IN ONE *Bond, fresh from receiving the tracking device implant, passes his hand through the Sonic Resonance Imaging unit.*

TRACTION TABLE

APPEARANCE
Thunderball (1965)

USED BY **James Bond**

At the Shrublands health clinic, osteopath Patricia Fearing suggests James Bond spend minutes on a motorized traction table—known by some patients as "the rack"—to help him recover from an injury to his lower back. While Bond is on the table, SPECTRE's Count Lippe enters. Lippe ratchets up the motor to full power. Bond passes out from the pain, but Patricia rescues him before he suffers possibly fatal injury.

TRANQUILIZER GUNS

APPEARANCES
Goldfinger (1964), Octopussy (1983)
USED BY Kisch, Pussy Galore, Octopussy and her army

Tranquilizer guns fire dart projectiles containing sedatives into wild animals, and in 007's adventures, into humans.

After James Bond talks his way out of being bisected by Auric Goldfinger with a laser beam in Switzerland, Goldfinger's henchman Kisch approaches with a tranquilizer gun and fires a projectile into Bond's side, knocking him unconscious. When 007 awakens on Goldfinger's Lockheed JetStar, he discovers Goldfinger is smuggling him into the United States. Pilot Pussy Galore shows him a similar gun and reveals it to be a tranquilizer.

During Operation Trove, jewel smuggler Octopussy's female army carries tranquilizer guns. Octopussy fires a tranquilizer dart into the neck of one of Mufti's thugs as they attack her and Bond in her floating palace. Later, when Octopussy and her army attack exiled Afghan prince Kamal Khan's Monsoon Palace, many of her gang fire tranquilizer darts into Kamal's remaining guards.

ANYTHING BUT TRANQUIL *One of Octopussy's gang takes aim with a tranquilizer gun.*

JUMP THE GUN *Pussy Galore discusses Bond's entry into the US with a Smith & Wesson .45. When Bond first wakes up, Miss Galore shows 007 a far less lethal tranquilizer gun.*

TRAPDOOR ELEVATOR

APPEARANCE
The Spy Who Loved Me (1977)
USED BY Karl Stromberg

When shipping tycoon Karl Stromberg surmises that his secretary has leaked his submarine tracking system plans, he casually asks her to excuse herself from his dining room. She steps into an elevator, and with the press of a button, Stromberg causes a trapdoor beneath her feet to open. The secretary falls through a chute into a pool where a shark eats her.

When Bond tries to rescue KGB agent Anya Amasova, Stromberg aims to dispose of 007 in the same way, but Bond saves himself by standing on the hinged edges of the trapdoor.

TRAPDOOR SLIDE

APPEARANCE
You Only Live Twice (1967)
USED BY Tiger Tanaka, Aki

Head of the Japanese Secret Service, Tiger Tanaka, uses a unique method of bringing guests into his office: a trapdoor slide hidden in the flooring of a Tokyo subway station hallway.

Bond chases agent Aki to get information about the murder of his contact, Dikko Henderson, pursuing her into a closed subway station. Aki suddenly stops and turns around; puzzled, Bond halts. At that moment, a trapdoor opens at his feet and 007 falls down a slide, landing in a chair in Tanaka's office.

TRAPDOOR TABLES

APPEARANCE
Live And Let Die (1973)
USED BY Dr. Kananga/Mr. Big

At Mr. Big's Fillet of Soul clubs, a special table exists for unwelcome visitors—one that places them in Mr. Big's private offices. In New York, a booth spins Bond into Mr. Big's lair. In New Orleans, Bond's table and chair drop into a French Quarter basement. The trapdoor table first appeared in the novel, where Bond and Felix Leiter are lowered into the basement below The Boneyard, a Harlem club owned by Mr. Big.

TABLE FOR ONE *Bond and Leiter at the Fillet of Soul shortly before the trapdoor opens.*

HIGH AND DRY *Sean Connery wearing the underwater drysuit costume in* **Goldfinger.**

UNDERWATER BREATHING UNIT/SHROUD

APPEARANCE
You Only Live Twice (1967)
USED BY James Bond

When assassins appear to shoot and kill James Bond, he receives a burial at sea with full military honors. What few know is that 007 remains very much alive, and his death has been staged to allow him to take on his next mission unnoticed. Wearing a rebreather to eliminate bubbles, packed inside a clear body bag, wrapped in a traditional sail-cloth shroud, and weighted with cannonballs, 007 endures his own funeral in Hong Kong Harbour before divers carry him to the M1 submarine to receive his assignment.

BURIAL AT SEA *James Bond disappears into the deep only to rise again in* **You Only Live Twice.**

UNDERWATER DRYSUIT

APPEARANCE
Goldfinger (1964)
USED BY James Bond

Developed by Q Branch, the underwater drysuit offers a light, waterproof covering for an agent, allowing them to use an aquatic approach to insert themselves into an area, then discard the drysuit to reveal ordinary clothes or even a dinner jacket and bow tie beneath. A series of one-way vents allow for the wearer to expel air bubbles that would otherwise remain trapped inside when putting on the suit. Bond uses the underwater drysuit when infiltrating the drug manufacturer Ramirez's heroin lab.

UNDERWATER GRENADE

APPEARANCE
Thunderball (1965)
USED BY James Bond

A part of 007's underwater arsenal, an underwater grenade is used by Bond to blow up two SPECTRE frogmen during the subaquatic battle at the conclusion of Operation Thunderball. A TNT charge triggers the grenade, killing with its concussive force rather than through the spread of shrapnel.

UNDERWATER INFRARED CAMERA

APPEARANCE
Thunderball (1965)
USED BY James Bond

The auto-film advance motor on this camera allows the user to take eight photos in rapid succession. With the use of infrared film, the camera can take photos in very low light situations. Bond uses the camera to photograph the underwater hatch in the bottom of the *Disco Volante* during Operation Thunderball.

UNDERWATER PROPULSION UNIT

APPEARANCE
Thunderball (1965)
USED BY James Bond

James Bond's most unusual weapon used during Operation Thunderball is a large underwater propulsion unit with forward-firing exploding torpedoes, complete with oxygen tanks. The unit comes with a yellow-green "smoke screen," which 007 sets off when he hits the water. The speed of the device allows Bond to swerve through the existing underwater battleground, ripping off enemy masks and dislodging air hoses. Bond kills a SPECTRE frogman with an underwater grenade, destroying the propulsion unit in the process.

IN THE DARK *Bond takes photos at night beneath the* Disco Volante *with Q's camera.*

VEREY PISTOL

APPEARANCES
From Russia With Love (1963), Thunderball (1965), On Her Majesty's Secret Service (1969), A View To A Kill (1985), Tomorrow Never Dies (1997), Skyfall (2012)
USED BY James Bond

When SPECTRE attacks Bond's Fairey Huntress speedboat in *From Russia With Love*, Bond releases the leaking fuel drums into the water and fires a Verey pistol. The flare ignites the fuel, engulfing the pursuing boats in flame.

During Operation Thunderball, SPECTRE frogmen trap Bond in an underwater cave. 007 fires his mini Verey pistol through an opening to alert Leiter and the US Coast Guard to his position.

On Her Majesty's Secret Service sees Blofeld using a flare to illuminate his night escape route from Piz Gloria during Operation Bedlam.

During an escape from Siberia in *A View To A Kill*, 007 fires a bright flare into the cabin of a Soviet helicopter, causing it to fill with smoke and crash.

Bond uses an underwater magnesium flare in a more conventional fashion while he is searching the wreck of HMS *Devonshire* in Vietnamese waters in *Tomorrow Never Dies*.

AND THE KITCHEN SINK *Bond's underwater propulsion unit turns him into a one-man navy.*

VIRTUAL REALITY GLASSES

APPEARANCE
Die Another Day (2002)
USED BY James Bond, Miss Moneypenny

Virtual reality glasses allow one to interact with a computer-simulated environment. In the virtual shooting range chamber located in MI6's disused London underground station, Bond dons these glasses, stands on a motion-sensing floor plate, and interacts with the computer-simulated MI6 offices and corridors. In the simulation, Bond finds himself sitting in his office cleaning his Walther P99. He hears gunshots and soon finds Moneypenny dead in her office with a bullet in her forehead. After taking out four gunmen, he joins Robinson, and they burst into M's office where a gunman holds M hostage. Two other gunmen stand in corners of the office. One shoots Robinson, and Bond takes out both of them. 007 then shoots M in the shoulder, and once she's out of the way with a flesh wound, fires his Walther into the chest of the gunman. Later, Moneypenny uses the glasses to enjoy her own romantic fantasy about Bond. When Q interrupts Moneypenny's simulation, she rises from the motion-sensing floor plate and quickly buttons her blouse.

VISA CARD SKELETON KEY

APPEARANCE
The World Is Not Enough (1999)
USED BY James Bond

Part of this ordinary-looking Visa credit card slides back, allowing a skeleton key to emerge. After spending a passionate evening with Elektra King, Bond approaches the office behind Elektra's mansion in Baku, uses the Visa credit card skeleton key to pick the lock, and searches for clues regarding an insider in the King Industries organization. The arrival of security chief Sasha Davidov soon interrupts his infiltration.

VOICE SIMULATOR

APPEARANCE
Diamonds Are Forever (1971)
USED BY Ernst Stavro Blofeld, James Bond

As well as using doubles, Blofeld has a voice box—which records voice patterns on tape—to complete his impersonation of Willard Whyte. A desktop unit allows Blofeld, or one of his doubles, to speak like Whyte on the phone. A miniature unit planted in the necks of the doubles also allows them to speak like Blofeld.

Q constructs a desktop unit in Las Vegas to help 007 sound like Bert Saxby on the phone. Using the unit, Bond calls Blofeld and discovers where the real Willard Whyte is being held.

WAI LIN'S BIKE SHOP

APPEARANCE
Tomorrow Never Dies (1997)
USED BY Wai Lin, James Bond

The bike shop spy Wai Lin enters in Saigon is actually a safe house for the Chinese People's External Security Force.

While at the safe house, Wai Lin and Bond battle goons sent by corrupt Chinese General Chang. Wai Lin also reveals the safe house's impressive armory of weapons and gadgets. At the push of a few buttons, old cabinets ascend to the ceiling and others swivel, revealing high-tech

PEDAL POWER Wai Lin of the Chinese Secret Service blends in with the Saigon crowd.

gadgets, guns, knives, and banks of computers. The gadgets include a dragon statue, which is really a flame thrower; a Chinese fan which, when unfolded, fires wire restraints across the room; a new Walther P99 (more powerful than Bond's Walther PPK 7.65), which Bond has been requesting from Q for some time; an Omega Seamaster watch, which 007 later uses as a detonator aboard Elliot Carver's stealth ship; and a stack of limpet mines.

The high-tech safe house also includes a computer (complete with Chinese keyboard) and several bike rickshaws, one of which can be fired as a projectile, as Wai Lin demonstrates by knocking out one of Chang's men.

HELL ON WHEELS Wai Lin battles Chang's goons in the bike shop safe house.

WALKIE-TALKIE FLUTE

APPEARANCE
Live And Let Die (1973)
USED BY Baron Samedi

When Bond and Solitaire search for Kananga's poppy fields, they discover an imposing man in peasant rags playing a flute in a graveyard. Unbeknownst to both of them, the man is Baron Samedi. He communicates to Kananga's hook-handed henchman, Tee Hee, via a walkie-talkie unit hidden in his reed flute, that Bond and Solitaire "are heading for the hill."

WALKING STICK GUN

APPEARANCE
The World Is Not Enough (1999)
USED BY Valentin Zukovsky

Russian casino owner Valentin Zukovsky's silver-handled walking stick conceals a .22 caliber single-shot rifle. Bursting into assassin Renard's hideout looking for his missing nephew, Zukovsky realizes he has been murdered and finds his enemy, Bond, shackled in Elektra King's torture chair. King shoots Zukovsky, but he finds the strength to aim his stick. He fires, not at 007, but at a chair restraint, freeing one of Bond's hands.

WALL-WALKING DEVICE

APPEARANCE
You Only Live Twice (1967)
USED BY James Bond

James Bond uses four large rubber suction cups to descend the sloping interior walls of Blofeld's volcano rocket base. When Bond discovers that the lake atop the volcano's crater is actually a metal roof, he sends agent Kissy Suzuki to alert head of the Japanese Secret Service Tiger Tanaka. Bond removes his fisherman's clothes to reveal a ninja suit. He places the large suction cups on his hands and knees and uses them to climb down from the roof to the floor of the rocket base.

WALTHER P99

APPEARANCES
Tomorrow Never Dies (1997),
The World Is Not Enough (1999),
Die Another Day (2002),
Casino Royale (2006)
USED BY James Bond

The Walther P99, introduced in 1996, is a semi-automatic pistol and an updated version of the Walther PPK 7.65 mm. With a magazine capacity of ten to sixteen rounds as opposed to the 7.65's seven rounds, this weapon offers more firepower.

Although Bond has repeatedly asked Q for a P99, it's not until he's in a safe house for the Chinese People's External Security Force in *Tomorrow Never Dies* that he acquires one for the first time. Attaching a silencer to the P99, he uses it to help him effectively attack media mogul Elliot Carver's stealth ship.

In *The World Is Not Enough*, the P99 includes a blinding flash mechanism, activated when Bond pushes a small protrusion on his Calvin Klein glasses. In *Die Another Day*, a P99 is hidden in Bond's surfboard saboteur kit.

Casino Royale sees Bond get into trouble with M when he shoots the terrorist Mollaka with his P99 in front of CCTV cameras at the Nambutu Embassy in Madagascar. When Bond arrives in Montenegro, he discovers a P99 fitted with a silencer in the glove compartment of his new Aston Martin DBS and places it in a brown envelope. During a break in the poker game with Le Chiffre, Bond returns to his hotel, collects the envelope from reception, and steps into the elevator with Vesper Lynd. Hearing angry voices coming from Le Chiffre's room (thanks to a bug), Bond pulls the P99 from the parcel (*opposite page, main picture*), though he never gets the chance to use it.

WALTHER PPK 7.65 MM

APPEARANCES
Dr. No (1962), From Russia With Love
(1963), Goldfinger (1964), Thunderball
(1965), You Only Live Twice (1967),
On Her Majesty's Secret Service
(1969), Diamonds Are Forever (1971),
Live And Let Die (1973), The Man
With The Golden Gun (1974), The
Spy Who Loved Me (1977),
Moonraker (1979), For Your Eyes
Only (1981), Octopussy (1983), A
View To A Kill (1985), The Living
Daylights (1987), Licence To Kill
(1989), GoldenEye (1995), Tomorrow
Never Dies (1997), Casino Royale
(2006), Quantum of Solace (2008),
Skyfall (2012)
USED BY James Bond

The Walther PPK 7.65 mm was introduced to German officers and police in 1931. It has become Bond's favored handgun in 21 missions.

In *Dr. No*, after Bond's Beretta jams, M assigns him the PPK. SPECTRE soon becomes aware of Bond's weapon of choice, as Blofeld points the gun out to his henchman Osato in *You Only Live Twice*.

Bond uses a PPK on nearly all his missions up to and including *Tomorrow Never Dies* (he does not fire it in *Moonraker*). The exception is *Octopussy* when Bond uses a Walther P5; while in India, he mentions to Q that he has mislaid his PPK.

In *Casino Royale*, Bond uses a PPK to kill Fisher in his first assassination assignment in Pakistan. After becoming a "00," a Walther P99 becomes his weapon of choice.

Bond returns to using a PPK full-time in *Quantum of Solace* and in *Skyfall*.

BOND'S NEW GUN *Major Boothroyd presents 007 with his new sidearm, a Walther PPK 7.65mm.*

WALTHER WA 2000 RIFLE

APPEARANCE
The Living Daylights (1987)
USED BY James Bond

Bond uses a Walther WA 2000 on a mission to protect a defecting Soviet General. Manufactured from the late 1970s to 1988, the WA 2000 uses .300 Winchester magnum cartridges, and is accurate to 1,000 m (3,281 ft). In Bratislava, Bond loads the rifle with steel-tipped bullets as he waits to shoot a KGB sniper posted to eliminate General Koskov as he defects to the West. Bond sees the sniper is the female cellist he noticed at a concert earlier in the evening. He senses she is not a professional assassin and, taking advantage of the WA 2000's accuracy, shoots her rifle out of her hands.

WATCH WITH GARROTE WIRE

APPEARANCE
From Russia With Love (1963)
USED BY Donald Grant

Concealed inside his ordinary-looking watch, SPECTRE assassin Donald "Red" Grant has 4 ft (1.2 m) of high-tensile strength garrote wire, accessed by pulling the crown out. Inside the watch, the wire feeds from a spring-loaded reel, which spools when tension is released. He uses the garrote to kill a James Bond double during a training exercise on SPECTRE Island. Grant later uses the garrote again in an attempt to kill 007 in their fight aboard the Orient Express but he becomes the victim, when 007 stabs him in the shoulder, then whips the garotte wire around Grant's neck.

KILLING TIME *Donald Grant awaits his moment to take the life of a James Bond double with his garrote wire watch.*

WAVE-WALKER

APPEARANCE
Diamonds Are Forever (1971)

USED BY James Bond

James Bond parachutes into the Pacific Ocean inside an icosahedron (20-sided) silver pod. The odd-looking device, made of water-proofed vinyl and supported by positive interior air pressure and inflated tubular ferrules, serves as a wave-walker. Ditching the chutes from an interior quick release, 007 walks within the pod, moving across the water's surface. He wave-walks to the base of an oil rig that houses Blofeld's control center. Blofeld's crew recovers the object, believing the occupant might have come to negotiate a peace deal.

UNIDENTIFIED OBJECT (above) A strange-looking silver pod lands near Blofeld's oil-rig base.

"Good morning, gentlemen. The Acme Pollution Inspection. We're cleaning up the world. We thought this was a suitable starting point."

Bond arrives at Blofeld's oil rig

WEIGHTED SKIRT

APPEARANCE
Octopussy (1983)

USED BY Magda

Magda wears a beautiful weighted Indian skirt, which she can remove from her body in an instant and use as a handy weapon. When Octopussy's army attacks Kamal Khan's Monsoon Palace, Magda uses her skirt to knock out one of Kamal's guards.

POWER DRESSING Magda adopts a traditionally peaceful pose, but her skirt is a dangerous weapon.

WRIST DART GUN

APPEARANCE
Moonraker (1979)
USED BY James Bond

The wrist dart gun is a unique weapon that can be used effectively and covertly against man and machine. Worn on a man's watch-style bracelet, the firing mechanism rests against the underside of the wrist. It is easily concealed, waterproof, and able to withstand the rigors of space travel. The gun senses nerve impulses when the hand rapidly flips upwards. For a short period, Q Branch offers it as standard issue with five red-tipped cyanide-coated darts that cause death in thirty seconds and five more blue-tipped darts with armor-piercing heads. Bond fires an armor-piercing dart to disable an out-of-control centrifuge at Hugo Drax's astronaut training facility. In Drax's secret space station, 007 fires a cyanide-coated dart into Drax's chest, before quickly ejecting the megalomaniac into orbit.

TRICK SHOT *(below) A dart from Bond's wrist dart gun finds its target.*

EYE OPENING *(above) Bond's X-ray glasses reveal a well-armed clientele at the bar.*

X-RAY SPECS

APPEARANCE
The World Is Not Enough (1999)
USED BY James Bond

Q Branch utilizes a transparent polymer video screen for interior coating of these light blue lenses. Filtered infra-red video reveals objects beneath a single layer of clothing, simulating X-ray vision capabilities. At Valentin Zukovsky's Casino Noir d'Or in Baku, Bond dons the glasses, which disclose that the patrons are concealing all manner of guns and weapons.

X-RAY DESK

APPEARANCE
You Only Live Twice (1967)
USED BY Mr. Osato

On a mission to investigate the disappearance of various space capsules, James Bond arranges to meet with Blofeld's accomplice, Mr. Osato. In the guise of Mr. Fisher, managing director of Empire Chemicals, Bond goes to Osato's office. Osato uses a fluoroscope built into his desk to X-ray 007's chest area. This provides Osato with a silhouette of Bond's Walther PPK. When Blofeld examines the X-ray film, he declares that only one man he knows uses this gun—James Bond.

YO-YO BUZZ SAW

APPEARANCE
Octopussy (1983)
USED BY Mufti's thugs

The weapon of choice for one of Mufti's thugs hired by Kamal Khan to kill Bond at Octopussy's Floating Palace is a large, steel-bladed yo-yo buzz saw attached to a steel wire. The thug first uses the weapon to kill Bond's contact Vijay. The gang then sneaks into Octopussy's palace, and attempts to murder Bond and Octopussy, who fight back and take refuge in a sitting room. The thug uses the saw to cut through the locked door. Bond and the thug, still clutching his saw, fall through a window and into the palace moat where a crocodile eats Bond's assailant.

"Take a giant step for **mankind!**"

007 to Drax, after shooting him with the wrist dart gun

THE
MOVIES

With every 007 film, there are two great stories. The first is the one viewers see on the screen—the intrigue, adventure, and spectacle that begin with the signature gun-barrel opening of each Bond movie. The other tale is far more complex but filled with just as many twists and turns and just as much excitement and suspense. This second tale is the story of the making of the film. The James Bond series is the longest-running and most successful in cinema history, and the credit for that rests on the shoulders not only of Ian Fleming and the producers and directors, but also on the thousands of individuals who have worked on the movies since 1962. On the following pages, take a look at the Bond films from the other side of the camera. View the adventures in the order they were made, through the perspective of the challenges the filmmakers faced. Meet 23 of the key creative talents who have contributed to the legacy of 007, from the producers, directors, and writers who shaped the series, to other key individuals who helped create the character of James Bond through music, stunts, and special effects. The following pages celebrate the stories behind the 007 cinematic adventures, the men and women who made the films, and the entertainment they have provided to billions around the world.

DR. NO (1962)

CAST Sean Connery (James Bond), Ursula Andress (Honey Ryder), Joseph Wiseman (Dr. No), Jack Lord (Felix Leiter), Bernard Lee (M), Anthony Dawson (Professor Dent), John Kitzmuller (Quarrel), Zena Marshall (Miss Taro), Eunice Gayson (Sylvia), Lois Maxwell (Miss Moneypenny), Lester Prendergast (Puss-Feller), Tim Moxon (Strangways), Marguerite LeWars (Photographer), Reginald Carter (Jones), Peter Burton (Major Boothroyd), William Foster-Davis (Duff), Louis Blaazer (Pleydell-Smith), Michel Mok (Sister Rose), Yvonne Shima (Sister Lily), Dolores Keator (Mary), Colonel Burton (General Potter), Eric Coverley, Charles Edghill, Henry Lopez (The Three Blind Mice), Adrian Robinson (Hearse driver)
PRODUCED BY Harry Saltzman & Albert R. Broccoli
DIRECTED BY Terence Young
SCREENPLAY BY Richard Maibaum, Johanna Harwood, Berkely Mather
BASED ON THE NOVEL BY Ian Fleming
MUSIC COMPOSED BY Monty Norman
ORCHESTRATED BY Burt Rhodes
"The James Bond Theme" played by the John Barry Orchestra, conducted by Eric Rodgers
DIRECTOR OF PHOTOGRAPHY Ted Moore, BSC
PRODUCTION DESIGNER Ken Adam
PRODUCTION MANAGER L. C. Rudkin
EDITOR Peter Hunt
MAIN TITLES DESIGNED BY Maurice Binder
ANIMATION Trevor Bond & Robert Ellis
ART DIRECTOR Syd Cain
MAKEUP John O'Gorman
SPECIAL EFFECTS Frank George
CONTINUITY Helen Whitson
ASSISTANT DIRECTOR Clive Reed
CAMERA OPERATOR John Winbolt
HAIR STYLIST Eileen Warwick
SOUND RECORDISTS Wally Milner & John Dennis
COSTUMES Tessa Welborn
SET DRESSING Freda Pearson
DUBBING EDITORS Archie Ludski & Norman Wanstall
ASSISTANT EDITOR Ben Rayner

MONTY NORMAN *The composer of "The James Bond Theme" on set.*

Throughout the 1950s, Ian Fleming flirted with the idea of bringing James Bond to the silver screen, but none of these ventures bore fruit. In 1961, Canadian producer Harry Saltzman optioned the rights to the Bond novels, but he could not find financing. Saltzman had all but given up on Bond when American producer Albert R. "Cubby" Broccoli, who was also interested in making 007 films, entered the picture. He secured financing with United Artists, and the pair set off with a budget of just under $1 million to make the first James Bond adventure.

Initially, Broccoli and Saltzman hoped *Thunderball* might be the first film, but legal battles over the film rights to the novel led to them selecting *Dr. No*, a story also set in a tropical location with plenty of action and a topical plot.

With strong support from United Artists, especially production executive David Picker, Broccoli and Saltzman assembled the cast and crew. For director, they selected Terence Young, whom Broccoli knew would bring style and elegance to the film. To adapt Fleming's sixth novel, they hired Wolf Mankowitz, who had introduced Broccoli to Saltzman, and Richard Maibaum, who had written Broccoli's first hit film, the Alan Ladd war adventure *The Red Beret* (1953). Maibaum and Wolf Mankowitz, however, raised eyebrows, when, in their first treatment, they made the chief villain Buckfield, a shipping magnate with a spider monkey named Li Ying perched on his shoulder. Disguised as the deceased, esoteric Dr. No, he plans to destroy the Panama Canal locks. Broccoli and Saltzman quickly demanded a more faithful adaptation of Fleming's text.

The most important question remained: who would play Bond? The producers considered everyone from Richard Burton to Cary Grant (the best man at Broccoli's wedding) but, in the end, they chose a young, dynamic Scottish actor named Sean Connery.

While Young helped to provide Connery with a more sophisticated image, the producers turned their attention to casting the leading lady, Honey Ryder. They soon focused their attention on the Swiss actress Ursula Andress and sent her the script. Prompted by her husband John Derek and the actor Kirk Douglas, Andress accepted the assignment. For the role of chief villain, Dr. No, Ian Fleming recommended friend and playwright Noel Coward. Coward answered Fleming with a telegram that read, "Dear Ian, the answer to Dr. No is No! No! No!" The producers soon

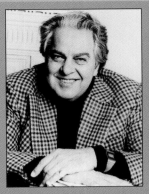

selected the classically trained New York actor Joseph Wiseman for the role.

Filming began in Jamaica on January 16, 1962 and moved along relatively smoothly. When the cast and crew returned to England, where production designer Ken Adam had constructed the film's imaginative sets, they realized they had something special on their hands. The film's polished look, sharp script, exotic settings, thrilling set-piece action sequences, and modern attitude to sex and violence elevated it far above the standard thriller of the time.

One important element remained—the music. Composer Monty Norman wrote some songs while visiting the production in Jamaica, working with the legendary Byron Lee to bring a Caribbean feel to the score. Yet the piece that would define Bond came from a discarded song from a musical version of V. S. Naipaul's novel *The House of Mr. Biswas*. Norman turned the music into "The James Bond Theme." During post-production, John Barry came in to orchestrate, arrange, and record a version of the theme that stepped away from the "Colonel Bogey" march sound of Norman's original, using a driving, reverb-laden electric guitar to play the tune. Editor Peter Hunt used Barry's recording throughout the film, and Barry soon became closely associated with the Bond sound.

The filmmakers' faith in their movie was fully vindicated when United Artists released *Dr. No* in England in October 1962. The film also performed excellently in the US, where it premiered six months later in April 1963. Quite simply, *Dr. No* was an extremely fresh film for its time, ushering in a new cinematic screen hero who would still delight audiences 52 years later.

VIP VISITOR *(below) Bond's creator, Ian Fleming, chats with Sean Connery in Jamaica during production.*

SHOOTING DR. NO *(left, top to bottom) Sean Connery, Terence Young, and Jamaican actor Reginald Carter discuss a shot at the start of production; the crew shoots near Ocho Rios, Jamaica, in early 1962; Ursula Andress being dressed by Tessa Welborn, who designed the film's famed white bikini; Ursula Andress being attended to by makeup artist John O'Gorman.*

ALBERT R. BROCCOLI

Albert R. "Cubby" Broccoli is one of the most legendary of all Hollywood producers; the James Bond series is the most successful film franchise in the history of cinema.

Broccoli's uncle, Pasquale, emigrated to the US from Italy in the 1870s, bringing a strain of broccoli seeds with him and establishing a successful vegetable farm. His father Giovanni immigrated at the turn of the century, and Cubby was born in Astoria, Queens, New York, in 1909.

In his youth, his resemblance to comic-strip character Abie Kabibble caused his cousins to call him Little Kabibbee, later shortened to Cubby.

After a stint as a coffin salesman, a vacation to Los Angeles in 1934 introduced him to Howard Hughes and Cary Grant, who would become lifelong friends. Deciding to stay in LA, Cubby worked several jobs over the next 15 years, including a jewelry and Christmas tree salesman; a talent agent; a studio mailroom runner; and an assistant director on The Black Swan (1942) and The Song Of Bernadette (1943). When World War II erupted, he joined the Navy and arranged for stars to appear in shows for servicemen.

Cubby's wonderful way with people paid off when he entered into a producing partnership with Irving Allen, forming Warwick Pictures and making movies with American actors in England to take advantage of British production subsidies.

After the death of his second wife, Nedra, Broccoli married actress/writer Dana Wilson. His partnership with Allen dissolved just before the birth of his daughter Barbara. A year later, in 1962, 007 came into his life, and the rest is history.

Cubby always believed that a film's budget should be reflected in the production values on the screen, and he consistently strove to attain the highest technical standards.

Albert R. Broccoli passed on the mantle of the Bond series with GoldenEye (1995) and died in 1996.

FROM RUSSIA WITH LOVE
(1963)

CAST Sean Connery (James Bond), Daniela Bianchi (Tatiana Romanova), Pedro Armendariz (Kerim Bey) Lotte Lenya (Rosa Klebb), Robert Shaw (Donald "Red" Grant), Bernard Lee (M), Eunice Gayson (Sylvia), Walter Gotell (Morzeny), Francis de Wolff (Vavra), George Pastell (Train conductor), Nadja Regin (Kerim Bey's Girlfriend), Lois Maxwell (Miss Moneypenny), Aliza Gur (Vida), Martine Beswick (Zora), Vladek Sheybal (Kronsteen), Leila (Gypsy dancer), Hansan Ceylan (Foreign agent), Fred Haggerty (Krilencu), Neville Jason (Kerim Bey's chauffeur), Peter Bayliss (Benz), Mushet Auaer (Mehmet), Peter Brayham (Rhoda), Desmond Llewelyn (Boothroyd), Jan Williams (Masseuse), Peter Madden (McAdams), Arlette Dobson (Hotel receptionist)
PRODUCED BY Harry Saltzman & Albert R. Broccoli
DIRECTED BY Terence Young
SCREENPLAY BY Richard Maibaum
ADAPTED BY Johanna Harwood
DIRECTOR OF PHOTOGRAPHY Ted Moore, BSC
EDITOR Peter Hunt
PRODUCTION MANAGER Bill Hill
ART DIRECTOR Syd Cain
TITLE SONG WRITTEN BY Lionel Bart
"FROM RUSSIA WITH LOVE" SONG PERFORMED BY Matt Munro
"THE JAMES BOND THEME" WRITTEN BY Monty Norman
ORCHESTRAL MUSIC COMPOSED AND CONDUCTED BY John Barry
ASSISTANT DIRECTOR David Anderson
SECOND UNIT CAMERAMAN Robert Kindred
CAMERA OPERATOR Johnny Winbolt
CONTINUITY Kay Mander
MAKEUP Basil Newall & Paul Rabiger
HAIRDRESSER Eileen Warwick
LOCATION MANAGER Frank Ernst
ISTANBUL PRODUCTION ASSISTANT Ilham Filmer
SPECIAL EFFECTS John Stears, assisted by Frank George
STUNT WORK ARRANGED BY Peter Perkins
SOUND RECORDISTS John W. Mitchell & C. le Messurier
ASSEMBLY EDITOR Ben Rayner
DUBBING EDITORS Norman Wanstall & Harry Miller
COSTUME DESIGNER Jocelyn Rickards
WARDROBE MISTRESS Eileen Sullivan
WARDROBE MASTER Ernie Farrer
ASSISTANT ART DIRECTOR Michael White
SET DRESSER Freda Pearson
TITLES DESIGNED BY Robert Brownjohn, assisted by Trevor Bond

The phenomenal success of *From Russia With Love* transformed James Bond from a literary spy to a cinematic hero. The film's integration of modern filmmaking techniques, Cold War ethics, elegance, gadgetry, adventure, and sex both defined Bond in the popular consciousness, and ushered in a new cinematic style that influences films to this day.

Producers Albert R. "Cubby" Broccoli and Harry Saltzman and the director Terence Young needed to make an October 1963 UK release date. They felt that since many readers and critics, including US President John F. Kennedy, saw the novel as one of Fleming's best, a screenwriter would only have to make minor changes. They did decide to shift the acts of villainy from the Soviet Union's SMERSH to the independent criminal organization SPECTRE, a conscious decision to, as Broccoli recalled, "steer 007 and the scripts clear of politics." Novelist Len Deighton worked briefly on the project before Richard Maibaum and then Joanna Harwood wrote drafts.

With a cast that included Academy Award-nominee and famed chanteuse Lotte Lenya, actor/novelist Robert Shaw, and Mexican character actor Pedro Armendariz (hired at the suggestion of John Ford), director Terence Young believed he could solve any remaining script issues during production. There was one remaining hurdle—finding the right actress for the role of Tatiana Romanova. Press releases went out around the world announcing that EON Productions was looking for a "young Greta Garbo." Italian actress Daniela Bianchi, a runner-up in the Miss Universe competition, won the role.

Shooting started on April 1, 1963 with Bond receiving his orders from M. On April 8-9, Terence Young shot Bond's meeting with Tatiana, a scene so perfectly realized filmmakers have used it to audition Bond actors and actresses for over 40 years. Harry Saltzman suggested shooting the SPECTRE training camp to parody the gladiator school scene in *Spartacus* (1960).

When the production moved to Istanbul in late April, Terence Young continued to alter the script on set. He brought Donald Grant into scenes that previously only included Bond and Soviet agents. The work to perfect the story proved difficult. Actor Peter Bayliss changed parts twice before Young cast him as Benz. Everywhere the crew set up to shoot, crowds gathered, causing delays. Young scrapped the climactic boat chase—scheduled for shooting off the coast of Turkey—because the boats moved too slowly. More seriously, Young noticed that Pedro Armendariz was masking a limp and at times appeared to be in great pain. Armendariz confessed he was dying of cancer.

Shaken by this news, the producers rearranged the schedule to immediately complete Armendariz's work at Pinewood Studios. Young worked hard to keep the film's energy high and demanded a chaotic and action-filled gun battle scene through which James Bond could move with seeming ease. Stunt coordinator Peter Perkins diligently rehearsed actresses Martine Beswick and Aliza Gur for the violent gypsy fight.

Armendariz completed filming in the early hours of Saturday, June 8. On Tuesday, June 18, he fatally shot himself at UCLA Medical Center. Armendariz's legacy to the Bond films did not end there. His son Pedro Armendariz Jr. appeared as a corrupt dictator in *Licence To Kill* (1989).

SCENE SETTING *(top to bottom) Terence Young directs Vladek Sheybal (Kronsteen); Lotte Lenya (Rosa Klebb) shows her true, sunny personality as her hair is touched up; Sean Connery and Daniela Bianchi (Tatiana Romanova) embrace under the direction of Terence Young.*

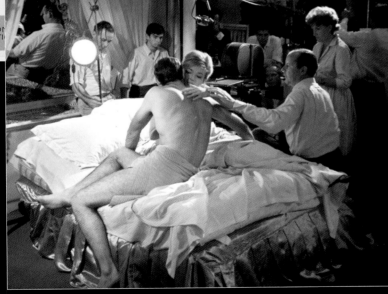

on just how well we have captured the split-second pace." Young and editor Peter Hunt worked closely to bring *From Russia With Love* together. They soon realized the film might be something quite remarkable. They rearranged the opening, and, at Hunt's suggestion, placed the scene of Grant apparently murdering 007 before the titles, creating the template of the pre-title sequence that has gone on to become a hallmark of the series. Hunt experimented with a faster, kinetic editing style that ignored traditional continuity in favor of movement and action. His influential innovations launched the modern style of action-film editing. Young's rapid shooting style worked perfectly with Hunt's cutting, drawing viewers into the action. Nowhere could this be better seen than the visceral fight between Bond and Donald "Red" Grant on the Orient Express. Using doubles in only two shots, shooting mostly handheld, Young captured what is still believed by many to be the most exciting fight scene in cinema history.

The completed cut proved remarkably entertaining. While filming had been every bit as challenging as an actual Bond adventure, the finished movie captured more excitement than most big-budget epics. The near-perfect pitch of Connery's performance as Bond, the staccato editing and the combination of suspense, wry humor, and action delivered a film experience like no other.

Composer John Barry delivered a lush, rich score that perfectly complemented the energy in film. The composer of the musical *Oliver!*, Lionel Bart, wrote the title song and hit singer and television personality Matt Munro provided silky vocals. John Barry combined Bart's melody with elements of "The James Bond Theme" and added a new composition, "007," that captured the soaring confidence of Bond's character. Barry's distinctive, modern score quickly became an audience favorite. The title song rose to #20 in the UK singles charts, and the soundtrack album charted on both sides of the Atlantic.

From Russia With Love premiered on October 10, 1963. Acclaimed by critics and public, it became the highest-grossing film ever released in the UK to that date, and broke records throughout Europe. Bond's place as the cultural phenomenon of the era had been secured.

ON LOCATION *(below, left to right) Sean Connery and Daniela Bianchi pose for publicity photos around the city of Istanbul; Pedro Armendariz enjoys the location work in Turkey.*

For the next month, the production moved to Scotland to film the speedboat chase as well as the helicopter assault on Bond. Disaster was narrowly averted when Terence Young and art director Michael White's helicopter ran into trouble. Thankfully, the lightning reactions of the pilot saved all those on board from serious injury or worse. When shooting the giant petrol explosion, a miscommunication caused the special-effects charges to explode during a rehearsal, causing a significant delay.

"Because of the violent action scenes," Young stated in a press release at the end of principle photography, "This has been a difficult film to shoot...of course, everything depends

HARRY SALTZMAN

Producer Harry Saltzman brought ideas, enthusiasm, and showmanship to the James Bond series. Born in Canada, Saltzman began booking vaudeville acts in New York. By 16, having already earned a small fortune, he left the US for France, where he managed a circus. During World War II, he served in the Royal Canadian Air Force and worked for the US in the Office of Strategic Services. After the war, Saltzman returned to New York and produced television shows such as *Captain Gallant Of The Foreign Legion*.

In the mid-1950s, Saltzman produced a Bob Hope comedy, *The Iron Petticoat* (1956). He soon joined director Tony Richardson and playwright John Osborne to form Woodfall Productions, producing dramas such as *Look Back In Anger* (1958) and *Saturday Night And Sunday Morning* (1960).

Wishing to make films with more commercial appeal, Saltzman left Woodfall and secured a six-month option on Ian Fleming's Bond novels. With Saltzman's option almost expired, he met Albert R. Broccoli. They formed a partnership and soon signed a six-picture deal with United Artists.

The partnership prospered, but Saltzman continued to produce films outside the realm of Bond. He spearheaded the Harry Palmer series of spy films and produced *Chimes At Midnight* (1965) and the World War II epic *The Battle Of Britain* (1969). In 1975, Saltzman sold his interest in 007 to United Artists, leaving Broccoli as sole producer of subsequent Bond films.

After producing 1980's *Nijinsky*, Saltzman became chairman of a theater management firm. He continued to be involved in financing international films, such as *Time of the Gypsies* (1988), nominated for a Palme d'Or. Saltzman died from a heart attack in 1994, at 78.

299

GOLDFINGER
(1964)

CAST Sean Connery (James Bond),
Honor Blackman (Pussy Galore), Gert Frobe
(Goldfinger), Shirley Eaton (Jill Masterson),
Tania Mallet (Tilly Masterson), Harold Sakata
[Tosh Togo] (Oddjob), Bernard Lee (M),
Martin Benson (Solo), Cec Linder (Felix Leiter),
Austin Willis (Simmons), Lois Maxwell (Miss
Moneypenny), Desmond Llewelyn (Q), Bill Nagy
(Midnight), Alf Joint (Capungo), Varley Thomas
(Swiss gatekeeper), Nadja Regin (Bonita),
Raymond Young (Sierra), Richard Vernon (Smithers),
Denis Cowles (Brunskill), Michael Mellinger (Kisch),
Burt Kwouk (Mr. Ling), Hal Galili (Strap), Lenny
Rabin (Henchman), Peter Cranwell (Johnny),
Mai Ling (Mei-Lei), Margaret Nolan (Dink),
Tricia Muller (Sydney), John McLaren (Brigadier),
Robert MacLeod (Atomic scientist),
Victor Brooks (Blacking), Gerry Duggan (Hawker)
PRODUCED BY
Harry Saltzman & Albert R. Broccoli
DIRECTED BY Guy Hamilton
SCREENPLAY BY
Richard Maibaum and Paul Dehn
PRODUCTION DESIGN BY Ken Adam
DIRECTOR OF PHOTOGRAPHY
Ted Moore, BSC
EDITOR Peter Hunt
PRODUCTION MANAGER L.C. Rudkin
ART DIRECTOR Peter Murton
"GOLDFINGER" TITLE SONG SUNG BY Shirley
Bassey
TITLE SONG LYRICS BY
Leslie Bricusse & Anthony Newley
MUSIC COMPOSED AND CONDUCTED BY
John Barry
ASSISTANT DIRECTOR Frank Ernst
CAMERA OPERATOR John Winbolt
CONTINUITY Constance Willis
MAKEUP Paul Rabiger & Basil Newall
ACTION SEQUENCES BY Bob Simmons
SPECIAL EFFECTS
John Stears, assisted by Frank George
ASSEMBLY EDITOR Ben Rayner
DUBBING EDITORS
Norman Wanstall & Harry Miller
SOUND RECORDISTS
Dudley Messenger & Gordon McCallum
HAIRDRESSER Eileen Warwick
WARDROBE SUPERVISOR Elsa Fennell
WARDROBE MISTRESS Eileen Sullivan
WARDROBE MASTER John Hilling
ASSISTANT ART DIRECTORS
Michael White & Maurice Pelling
SET DRESSER Freda Pearson
TITLES DESIGNED BY Robert Brownjohn

Goldfinger remains the most iconic of all Bond films,
certainly the film most referenced in popular culture.
Despite the tremendous financial success of both *Dr. No* and
From Russia With Love, *Goldfinger* did more to define the
cinematic James Bond than any other film. The story of its
creation shows the strength of the collaborative process that
has helped keep the Bond series going strong.

Screenwriter Richard Maibaum began adapting the novel
Goldfinger in April 1963, as *From Russia With Love* started
production. Maibaum immediately recognized plotting
problems for the film and set about strengthening Fleming's
original story. Maibaum let Bond discover Jill Masterson's
gilded body rather than hear about it from Jill's sister, Tilly.
He strengthened Goldfinger's motivation for keeping 007
alive. Most importantly, he changed Goldfinger's plot from
stealing the gold to destroying its value with an atomic blast.

Producers Broccoli and Saltzman approached Guy
Hamilton to direct the third Bond film. During pre-
production, Hamilton witnessed the tremendous success of
From Russia With Love in the UK, and was inspired to
develop an approach that would redefine the Bond series.
Working with British writer Paul Dehn and an uncredited
Berkeley Mather, Hamilton brought a greater emphasis on
humor to the film. Perhaps the clearest example of his
influence was the transformation of Bond's Aston Martin
DB Mk III from Fleming's novel into the film's gadget-filled
DB5, complete with machine guns and an ejector seat.
Viewers could both smile at the vehicle's outrageousness and
covet its deadly elegance.

Albert R. "Cubby" Broccoli brought in the accomplished
German actor Gert Frobe to play Goldfinger. To play Pussy
Galore, Hamilton suggested one of the most popular
actresses in England at the time, Honor Blackman, fresh
from playing judo expert Cathy Gale in the hit television
series *The Avengers*. Hamilton also spotted a wrestler by the
name of Tosh Togo, whom he realized would make a perfect
Oddjob. It turned out that Togo's real name was Harold
Sakata and he had won a Silver Medal in the 1948
Olympics. The filmmakers had to convince him that he
should use his real name in the credits. He insisted both
names appear on-screen.

While Hamilton and the producers were confident that
Goldfinger would be a huge success, other organizations were
still unaware of the Bond franchise's rapidly growing status.
Officials at the Bullion Depository at Fort Knox, were
reluctant to give the filmmakers access, despite the
production's well-connected technical advisor, US Air Force
Lt. Col. Charles Russhon. The aerial shots of Pussy Galore's
Flying Circus over the real Gold Depository attracted

particular protest from officialdom.

Although shooting began in late January in Miami, Sean
Connery was unable to join the production until mid-
March, leaving less than five months to complete the film.
Connery was then forced to miss a week of shooting when
Harold Sakata failed to pull his punch sufficiently while
slamming Bond with a karate chop.

Throughout the production, cast and crew felt sure they

DYNAMIC DUO *(facing page) Harold Sakata (Oddjob) and Gert Frobe (Goldfinger) on location at Stoke Poges Golf Club.*
GOLD FOR GOLDFINGER *(near left) Shirley Bassey with her Gold Record for the Goldfinger soundtrack. The album charted at #1 in the US in early 1965.*

THE MIDAS TOUCH *(clockwise from top left) Sean Connery (James Bond) and Honor Blackman (Pussy Galore) on the backlot set of Auric Stud at Pinewood Studios; Guy Hamilton directs Gert Frobe (Goldfinger) to shoot US soldiers; Hamilton and Blackman on the Rumpus Room set; Harry Saltzman and Albert R. Broccoli meet with Honor Blackman for photos of her signing her contract with EON Productions; Sean Connery and Shirley Eaton (Jill Masterson) meet Ian Fleming a few months before the author's death; Basil Newall paints Shirley Eaton gold for her iconic moment.*

were working on something special. Production designer Ken Adam created a series of magnificent sets, including a drug lab hidden in an oil storage tank, a rumpus room that transforms into a strategy center, and the Auric Enterprises laser room. For the climax inside the Fort Knox gold vaults, Cubby Broccoli declared that he wanted "a cathedral of gold." Adam rose to the challenge, creating a set fitting for the epic battle between Bond and Oddjob.

With its ingenious blend of humor, action, gadgets, sex, sophistication, and exotic locations, *Goldfinger* defined what audiences would come to expect from a Bond film. However the film was almost banned in the US because of the name Pussy Galore. Cubby Broccoli had to plead his case to MPAA chief Geoffrey Shurlock before the film gained a certificate of approval. The film went on to be ranked by the *Guinness Book of World Records* as the fastest-grossing film ever released.

Goldfinger also defined the "Bond sound." Composer John Barry convinced the producers he should not only write the score but also the title song. "Goldfinger," featuring vocals by the incomparable Shirley Bassey, became a worldwide hit (#8 in the US; #21 in the UK singles charts). Its success propelled the soundtrack album to the top of the US charts, replacing The Beatles. The film's other sounds drew praise, too, with the film winning the Academy Award for Best Sound Effects, awarded to Norman Wanstall.

Sadly, *Goldfinger*'s worldwide success came too late to be enjoyed by Ian Fleming, who died on August 12, 1964, barely a month before the film premiered in London. The creator had passed away but, with *Goldfinger*, James Bond was destined to live forever.

RICHARD MAIBAUM

Born in New York City in 1909, Richard Maibaum attended New York University and the University of Iowa. After receiving his master's degree, he returned to New York and performed in plays with the Shakespearean Repertory Theatre. Besides acting, he also wrote plays. His first produced, *The Tree*, an anti-lynching drama, opened in New York in April 1932 but closed within a week. Undeterred, he wrote other plays, including *Birthright* (1933), which tackled Hitler's anti-Jewish fanaticism; *Sweet Mystery Of Life* (1935), a comedy about life insurance; *The Lonely Man* (1935), suggested by Calvin Coolidge; and the musical *Catch-As-Catch-Can* (1935).

In 1935, agent Sam Marx signed Maibaum to a Hollywood contract and brought him to Los Angeles, where he became a screenwriter at MGM. While working on the 1940 spy thriller, *Foreign Correspondent*, the director, Alfred Hitchcock, advised Maibaum that he knew he had a film when the story had at least 13 "bumps," or big moments.

During World War II, Maibaum became the head of the US Army's Industrial Film Unit and later director of the Combat Films Division. Leaving the service as a lieutenant colonel, Maibaum became a writer and producer at Paramount Pictures on such films as *O.S.S.* (1946), the suspense classic *The Big Clock* (1948), and *The Great Gatsby* (1949). In the 1950s, he began writing scripts for Warwick Pictures, a venture begun by Irving Allen and Albert R. Broccoli, providing the screenplay for their first film, *The Red Beret* (1953), as well as *Hell Below Zero* (1954), *Cockleshell Heroes* (1955), and *Zarak* (1956).

When Broccoli went on to produce the Bond films, he turned to Maibaum to bring Ian Fleming's novels to the screen. Maibaum contributed to 13 Bond films. He claimed that he always tried to work 39 "bumps" into a 007 script. His final screen credit came in 1996, five years after his death, when his 1956 thriller *Ransom!* was remade starring Mel Gibson.

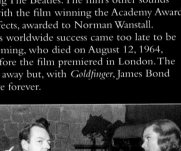

THUNDERBALL
(1965)

CAST Sean Connery (James Bond), Claudine Auger (Domino Derval), Adolfo Celi (Largo), Luciana Paluzzi (Fiona Volpe), Rik Van Nutter (Felix Leiter),
Bernard Lee (M), Martine Beswick (Paula), Guy Doleman (Count Lippe), Molly Peters (Patricia Fearing), Desmond Llewelyn (Q), Lois Maxwell (Miss Moneypenny), Ronald Culver (Foreign Secretary),
Earl Cameron (Pinder), Paul Stassino (Palazzi), Rose Alba (Madame Boitier), Philip Locke (Vargas), George Pravda (Kutze), Michael Brennan (Janni), Leonard Sachs (Group Captain Pritchard), Reginald Beckwith (Keniston), Anthony Dawson (Ernst Stavro Blofeld), Bob Simmons (Jacques Boitier), Bill Cummings (Quist), Maryse Guy Mitsouko (Mademoiselle La Porte), Edward Underdown (Air Vice Marshall)
PRODUCED BY Kevin McClory
PRESENTED BY Harry Saltzman & Albert R. Broccoli
DIRECTED BY Terence Young
SCREENPLAY BY Richard Maibaum and John Hopkins
BASED ON AN ORIGINAL SCREENPLAY BY Jack Whittingham
BASED ON THE ORIGINAL STORY BY Kevin McClory, Jack Whittingham & Ian Fleming
PRODUCTION DESIGN BY Ken Adam
DIRECTOR OF PHOTOGRAPHY Ted Moore, BSC
SUPERVISING EDITOR Peter Hunt
MUSIC COMPOSED AND CONDUCTED BY John Barry
TITLE SONG "THUNDERBALL" lyrics by Don Black, sung by Tom Jones
ART DIRECTOR Peter Murton
PRODUCTION SUPERVISOR David Middlemas
ASSISTANT DIRECTOR Gus Agosti
CAMERA OPERATOR John Winbolt
CONTINUITY Joan Davis
MAKEUP Paul Rabiger & Basil Newall
ACTION SEQUENCES BY Bob Simmons
SPECIAL EFFECTS John Stears
2ND UNIT CAMERAMAN Egil Woxholt
EDITOR Ernest Hosler
ASSEMBLY EDITOR Ben Rayner
DUBBING EDITORS Norman Wanstall & Harry Miller
SOUND RECORDISTS Bert Ross & Maurice Askew
HAIRDRESSER Eileen Warwick
COSTUMES DESIGNED BY Anthony Mendleson
WARDROBE MISTRESS Eileen Sullivan
WARDROBE MASTER John Brady
ASSISTANT ART DIRECTOR Michael White
SET DRESSER Freda Pearson
MAIN TITLE DESIGNED BY Maurice Binder
UNDERWATER SEQUENCES Ivan Tors Underwater Studios Ltd.
UNDERWATER DIRECTOR Ricou Browning
UNDERWATER CAMERAMAN Lamar Boren
UNDERWATER ENGINEER Jordan Klein

Thunderball has sold more tickets than any Bond film before or since. Its production history and legacy, however, remain controversial. When Harry Saltzman partnered with Albert R. Broccoli to produce James Bond films, they initially considered making *Thunderball*, which, having been published in 1961, was the most recent 007 novel. However, the novel was the subject of a lawsuit; a young director, Kevin McClory, claimed that work McClory and screenwriter Jack Whittingham had contributed to the story had been used by Fleming without credit or compensation.

Believing the lawsuit would soon be dismissed, Saltzman and Broccoli asked Richard Maibaum to write a script. When it became apparent that McClory's lawsuit against Ian Fleming and Fleming's friend Ivar Bryce would prove lengthy, Saltzman and Broccoli chose to adapt *Dr. No* as the first Bond adventure.

McClory settled his lawsuit in November 1963, as *From Russia With Love* broke box-office records in the UK. McClory gained screen rights to the novel and treatments and a credit in future editions of the novel. While McClory attempted to mount his own Bond film, Saltzman and Broccoli entered negotiations with Broccoli's old employer, agent-producer Charles K. Feldman, to make a film of the first Bond novel *Casino Royale*. When Feldman's terms proved too difficult, Saltzman and Broccoli struck a deal with McClory.

McClory had worked with the showman producer Michael Todd on *Around The World In 80 Days* (1956), and he pushed to make this Bond film an event movie with more of a "travelogue" feel. Thus, *Thunderball* became the first true widescreen Bond film.

In late 1964, Maibaum began rewriting *Thunderball*, this time with the knowledge of the success of the previous three Bond films. During production, respected British writer John Hopkins also contributed to the completed film's narrative polish and witty dialogue.

To direct, the producers returned to Terence Young, who quickly realized that *Thunderball*, as written, could not be shot without the addition of strong second-unit directors. He enlisted Ricou Browning, creator of *Flipper*, to direct the underwater scenes; underwater cameraman Lamar Boren shot the epic undersea battle. Broccoli's Hollywood friend, director André de Toth, filmed the aerial assault over Biscayne Bay.

Young wanted to keep 007's gadgetry from becoming a simple series of jokes. He and the filmmakers searched for real equipment for Bond's technological arsenal, including the Bell-Textron Jet Pack Bond uses to escape from SPECTRE agent Jacques Boitier's chateau in the film's opening sequence and the Skyhook rescue system that whisks Bond and Domino to safety at the film's close. Other gadgets proved so believable they even fooled military experts. After the film's opening, a Royal Navy representative called to inquire about Bond's mini-rebreather, only to be informed it wasn't real.

The film's cast was a testament to Bond's international appeal. Italian actors Adolfo Celi and Luciana Paluzzi led the villains. French actress Claudine Auger captured the role of Domino. Jamaican beauty Martine Beswick and British model/actress Mollie (Molly in the credits) Peters rounded out the cast.

The film required extensive work with sharks. Special effects supervisor John Stears found himself surrounded in a pool by frenzied sharks while working on one scene. On another occasion, Sean Connery found himself swimming through a plexiglass-walled tunnel in Largo's shark pool.

AQUATIC ADVENTURES *The crew prepares for a shot near Golden Cay, Bahamas.*

One missing piece of plexi allowed a lone shark to swim into the tunnel with Connery, resulting in a genuine expression of concern on Bond's face that one can see in the film. During scenes set in the open ocean, cameraman Lamar Boren used a unique way to fend off sharks he felt got too close—he rammed them with his 134-lb (61-kg) underwater camera. For the climactic underwater battle, 38 divers appeared on screen, requiring experienced scuba divers to be flown to Nassau from as far away as Richmond, Virginia.

The film's greatest challenge came during post-production. Young left the film as soon as shooting wrapped. At this point, the film was overlong. Editor Peter Hunt promised United Artists that he could bring the film together if they delayed the film's opening. Hunt helped to reshoot scenes, restructure the film's middle-third, and cut the movie down to 130 minutes from a first assembly that ran roughly 270 minutes.

Composer John Barry returned to score the film, creating a lush, mysterious soundtrack. He wrote the original opening credits song, "Mr. Kiss Kiss Bang Bang," the Italian nickname for 007, with Leslie Bricusse and recorded it twice: first with Shirley Bassey and then with Dionne Warwick. Concern that the song never mentioned the film's title resulted in Barry quickly writing "Thunderball" with Don Black, a hit in the US and UK for Tom Jones.

When the film opened in December 1965, audiences were awe-struck. *Thunderball* broke box-office records around the world and set a new standard for action-adventure films with its scale, scope, and amazing underwater battle sequences. John Stears won an Academy Award for the film's innovative special effects work.

For all its success, *Thunderball*'s legacy cast a small but troubling cloud over the Bond series from 1975 until 2000. During those years, McClory continually tried to parlay the rights he had into a James Bond series of his own. In 1983, Connery appeared in a non-EON produced *Thunderball* re-make, *Never Say Never Again*, based on McClory's rights. Then, in 1997, McClory struck a deal with Sony Pictures. After the settlement and disposition of the resulting lawsuits, McClory's Bond rights were severely limited. Sony severed their relationship with McClory and, most importantly, Sony ceded to the Bond producers the rights to *Casino Royale*. Every cloud has a silver lining.

OUT!

HERE COMES THE BIGGEST BOND OF ALL!

ZMAN and BROCCOLI present **SEAN CONNERY** in IAN FLEMING'S **"HUNDERBALL"** A UNITED ARTISTS

CLAUDINE AUGER · ADOLFO CELI · LUCIANA PALUZZI · RIK VAN NUTTER

N McCLORY Directed by TERENCE YOUNG **PANAVISION® TECHNICOLOR®**

AIBAUM & JOHN HOPKINS · Based on the original story by KEVIN McCLORY, JACK WHITTINGHAM and IAN FLEMING

TERENCE YOUNG

Born the son of an English police commissioner in the International Sector of Shanghai in 1915, Shaun Terence Young was educated in England. At Cambridge University, he excelled in rugby, tennis, and cricket. He also wrote film reviews for his college paper and had a summer job at BIP Studios. He gained a reputation as a talented screenwriter with the melodrama *Dangerous Moonlight* (1941).

During World War II, Young served with Britain's famed Guards Armoured Tank Division and was twice wounded in action. After the war, he returned to screenwriting and then became an assistant to directors Jacques Feyder, Alexander Korda, Josef von Sternberg, and King Vidor.

His directorial debut came in 1948 with *One Night With You*. His next film, *Corridor Of Mirrors* (1948), starring Lois Maxwell, won the "Best Film of the Year" award in France. *The Red Beret* (1953) marked his first teaming with 007 screenwriter Richard Maibaum and producer Albert R. Broccoli.

With an established reputation as an action director, Young was the ideal choice to helm *Dr. No* (1962). Many of those who worked with him thought he embodied the same qualities as 007—elegance, humor, and a knowledge of bespoke tailoring and fine wines. His staging of James Bond's introduction in *Dr. No* became a cinema classic, though he modestly claimed "it was really a steal of Paul Muni's introduction in *Juarez*." Young also directed the second film in the series, *From Russia With Love* (1963), and then, after a one film break, returned for his third and final Bond adventure, *Thunderball* (1965).

Young left Thunderball during post-production to direct a film for the United Nations, *The Poppy Is Also A Flower* (1966). His later films included *Wait Until Dark* (1967), *Mayerling* (1968), *Red Sun* (1971), *The Valachi Papers* (1972), *Bloodline* (1979), *Inchon* (1981), *The Jigsaw Man* (1983), and *Run For Your Life* (1988). In 1994, while preparing to direct a major European film, Young fell ill and died of a heart attack in hospital at Cannes, France.

ROCKET MAN *(left) One of the two stunt pilots flies the Bell Textron Rocket Belt in France.*
THE BIGGEST BOND OF ALL *(right) Crowds at the Paramount Theatre, Manhattan; like Goldfinger,* Thunderball *played 24 hours a day in New York throughout the Christmas holiday.*

WELCOME TO PARADISE *(above) Martine Beswick (Paula Caplan), Claudine Auger (Domino Derval), and Luciana Paluzzi (Fiona Volpe) during shooting on Paradise Beach.*
UNITED ARTISTS *(left) United Artists Exec. David Picker, Saltzman, and Broccoli at the Paramount Theatre.*
UNDERSEA SHOOT *(right) Lamar Boren shoots the beginning of the film's final battle.*

YOU ONLY LIVE TWICE
(1967)

CAST Sean Connery (James Bond), Akiko Wakabayashi (Aki), Mie Hama (Kissy Suzuki), Tetsuro Tamba (Tiger Tanaka), Teru Shimada (Mr. Osato), Karin Dor (Helga Brandt), Donald Pleasence (Blofeld), Bernard Lee (M), Lois Maxwell (Miss Moneypenny), Desmond Llewelyn (Q), Charles Gray (Dikko Henderson), Tsai Chin (Ling), Ronald Rich (Hans), Burt Kwouk (SPECTRE No.3), Michael Chow (SPECTRE No.4), Jeanne Roland (Bond's masseuse), David Toguri (Assassin [bedroom]), John Stone (Submarine Captain), Paul Carson, Norman Jones, Laurence Herder, Richard Graydon, Bill Mitchell, George Roubicek (Astronauts)
PRODUCED BY
Harry Saltzman & Albert R. Broccoli
DIRECTED BY Lewis Gilbert
SCREENPLAY BY Roald Dahl
ADDITIONAL STORY MATERIAL
Harold Jack Bloom
DIRECTOR OF PHOTOGRAPHY
Freddie Young, BSC
SUPERVISING EDITOR & 2ND UNIT DIRECTOR
Peter Hunt
PRODUCTION DESIGNED BY Ken Adam
ART DIRECTOR Harry Pottle
PRODUCTION SUPERVISOR
David Middlemas
SPECIAL EFFECTS John Stears
ACTION SEQUENCES BY Bob Simmons
MAIN TITLE DESIGNED BY
Maurice Binder
MUSIC COMPOSED, CONDUCTED AND
ARRANGED BY John Barry
TITLE SONG LYRICS BY Leslie Bricusse
TITLE SONG SUNG BY Nancy Sinatra
TECHNICAL ADVISOR Kikumaru Okuda
2ND UNIT CAMERAMAN Bob Huke
AERIAL UNIT CAMERAMAN
John Jordan
UNDERWATER CAMERAMAN
Lamar Boren
ASSISTANT DIRECTOR
William P. Cartlidge
LOCATION MANAGER Robert Watts
CAMERA OPERATOR Ernie Day
CONTINUITY Angela Martelli
MAKEUP Basil Newall & Paul Rabiger
DUBBING EDITORS
Norman Wanstall & Harry Miller
SOUND RECORDISTS
John Mitchell & Gordon McCallum
ASSEMBLY EDITOR Robert Richardson
WARDROBE MISTRESS Eileen Sullivan
HAIRDRESSER Eileen Warwick
SET DECORATOR David Ffolkes

You Only Live Twice became the Bond movie where the filmmakers first turned away from Ian Fleming's original plot. In its place, they created the most fantasy-laden Bond adventure of the 1960s, an epic film that reflected the immense global success of 007.

Producers Albert R. "Cubby" Broccoli and Harry Saltzman wanted *You Only Live Twice* to surpass the expectations of an audience flush with a glut of Bond competitors in movie theaters and on television. Initially, Broccoli and Saltzman hired television writer Harold Jack Bloom to adapt Fleming's novel. They then invited famed short-story writer Roald Dahl, who had been friends with Fleming and shared story ideas with him over the years, to write the final script. By 1966, the development of the Bond films had become a group effort. Ideas for gadgets, scenes, and stunts in *You Only Live Twice* came from all quarters. Dahl's job was to link these ideas into a coherent storyline.

To direct the film, Broccoli called Lewis Gilbert, who had recently won many accolades for *Alfie* (1966). Gilbert's expertise with epic films such as *Damn The Defiant!* (1962) and *The 7th Dawn* (1964) proved he could handle a production the size of a Bond adventure.

The filmmakers hired English-speaking Japanese actor Tetsuro Tamba to play Tiger Tanaka. German actress Karin Dor took the role of the leading villainess, Helga Brandt. Two leading Japanese actresses, Akiko Wakabayashi and Mie Hama, signed to play Kissy and Suki, respectively. Yet language difficulties prompted the filmmakers to switch their roles, and Akiko suggested that her character be renamed Aki. For the important role of Blofeld, the filmmakers initially cast Czech actor Jan Werich, but shortly after filming began, Gilbert suggested replacing him with a more sinister-looking figure, and Donald Pleasence, famed from *The Great Escape* (1963), took over the part. Pleasence wore a disfiguring scar on his face, with grafted skin stretched partially over one eye to complete the eerie look.

Production designer Ken Adam played a key role in the film's development, traveling to Japan with Broccoli, Saltzman, and Gilbert for location scouting. In Tokyo, they ran into former Bond editor Peter Hunt. Seizing the moment, Broccoli talked Hunt into returning as a second unit director.

The filmmakers searched Japan for a coastal castle similar to the one in Fleming's novel. A guide informed them that there are no castles by the sea in Japan. The filmmakers then began a search for a suitable location to serve as Blofeld's lair. While Harry Saltzman thought they should film in a series of vaults in a Japanese salt mine, Broccoli came up with a different idea.

While location scouting in a helicopter, the filmmakers spotted a string of volcanoes. Broccoli suggested that the

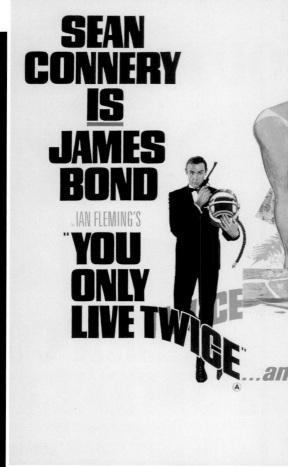

villain could be hiding a rocket base inside one of them. Ken Adam soon drew up plans for the largest enclosed set ever built, Blofeld's volcano rocket base, which would tower 120 ft (37 m) over Pinewood Studios in England. The set cost a million dollars, required more structural steel than the London Hilton, housed a working monorail and had a retractable roof large enough to allow a helicopter to fly in and out.

While building the volcano set, the filmmakers shot in Japan during the sweltering heat of the summer of 1966, beset by Japanese paparazzi. The press hounded Sean Connery, even on location at a remote fishing village.

Peter Hunt faced more significant problems directing the dogfight between the autogyro Little Nellie and four SPECTRE helicopters. Despite expert flying by Commander Ken Wallis and a group of Japanese helicopter pilots, the crew experienced a tragic accident when cameraman John Jordan lost his leg as two helicopters collided in mid-air. Aerial shooting in Japan ceased, and Hunt completed the scene in the Torremolinos Mountains in Spain months later.

Location work for the film included more than Spain. Off

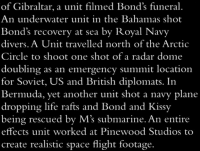

'ICE" is the only way to live!

SALTZMAN and ALBERT R. BROCCOLI · Directed by LEWIS GILBERT · Screenplay by ROALD DAHL

TZMAN and ALBERT R. BROCCOLI · Music by JOHN BARRY · Production designed by KEN ADAM · PANAVISION

COLOR · Released through UNITED ARTISTS

---

of Gibraltar, a unit filmed Bond's funeral. An underwater unit in the Bahamas shot Bond's recovery at sea by Royal Navy divers. A Unit travelled north of the Arctic Circle to shoot one shot of a radar dome doubling as an emergency summit location for Soviet, US and British diplomats. In Bermuda, yet another unit shot a navy plane dropping life rafts and Bond and Kissy being rescued by M's submarine. An entire effects unit worked at Pinewood Studios to create realistic space flight footage.

The battle in Blofeld's volcano proved another major challenge. First, the Academy Award-winning cinematographer Freddie Young had to light an area spanning more than 450 ft (137 m) for the wide shots. He needed virtually every light at Pinewood Studios to do it. The script called for invading Japanese ninjas to abseil down ropes from the top of the set, a 12-story drop. Future Bond second unit director Vic Armstrong, using a piece of rubber tubing around the rope to slow his descent, became the first to make the drop.

After completing second unit work, Hunt was asked by Broccoli and Saltzman to take over primary editing duties from Thelma Connell. Hunt cut approximately 15 minutes, tightening the film to a running length of under two hours.

John Barry returned to score the film, penning a haunting title song performed by Nancy Sinatra with lyrics by Leslie Bricusse. The score incorporated Japanese elements along with beautiful guitar and brass orchestrations. The title song became a minor hit for Sinatra and became a theme for her comeback tour in the 1990s.

The film opened only weeks after Charles K. Feldman's *Casino Royale* Bond spoof, but it was *You Only Live Twice* that triumphed at the box office. The film represented the culmination of a period of remarkable productivity for Broccoli and Saltzman. In just over four and a half years, the producers had premiered five 007 adventures, creating a phenomenon unequalled in film history. While the pace of making Bond films would shift to accommodate ever more complex movies, the dedication to exceeding audience expectations would continue.

ON LOCATION *(facing page, from top)* Kobe, Japan: Lewis Gilbert, Sean Connery, William P. Cartlidge and crew await the next shot; Tetsuro Tamba (Tiger Tanaka) and Mie Hama (Kissy) share a joke; Mie Hama has her hair reset after a plunge in the water.

ON SET *(this page, clockwise from above left)* Production Designer Ken Adam thoughtfully surveys the scene as his spectacular hollowed-out volcano set is constructed; the sheer scale of the volcano set stunned visitors; Sean Connery jokes between takes with his co-star Karin Dor (femme fatale Helga Brandt).

KEN ADAM

Born in Berlin in 1921, Ken Adam (real name Klaus Adam) left Germany with his family in 1934. After training as an architect at London University, he joined the RAF and took part in the Battle of Normandy. In 1946, Adam landed a job as a junior draftsman at Riverside Studios. Over the next decade, he became known as one of Europe's best film designers, earning his first Academy Award nomination for *Around The World In 80 Days* (1956).

In 1960, the producer Albert R. Broccoli hired Adam as production designer for *The Trials Of Oscar Wilde* (1960). Incidentally, Adam had already met Harry Saltzman, soon to be Broccoli's partner, while working in Italy. When Saltzman and Broccoli produced *Dr. No* (1962), they asked Adam to join the team. Adam set out to design imaginative sets using the very latest techniques and materials, setting the tone for the whole James Bond series.

Adam was unable to work on the second 007 film owing to a commitment to Stanley Kubrick's *Dr. Strangelove* (1964), but he returned for the next three, surpassing himself each time. Blofeld's hideout inside a volcano in 1967's *You Only Live Twice* resulted in a massive $1 million set on the Pinewood backlot. Greatly in demand, Adam only contributed to one of the next four Bond films, 1971's *Diamonds Are Forever*. After winning an Academy Award for his work on Kubrick's *Barry Lyndon* (1975), he returned for two more 007 assignments. His supertanker set for *The Spy Who Loved Me* (1977) required a space so huge that a special stage had to be constructed to house it. The resulting structure was christened the 007 Stage. Adam's designs for *The Spy Who Loved Me* earned him his third Academy Award nomination.

Adam continued to work on a variety of films in the 1980s and 1990s. He was nominated for an Oscar for 1993's *Addams Family Values* and scored his second win with *The Madness Of King George* (1994). In 2003, he was knighted by Queen Elizabeth II.

ON HER MAJESTY'S SECRET SERVICE (1969)

CAST George Lazenby (James Bond), Diana Rigg (Tracy Di Vicenzo), Telly Savalas (Blofeld), Gabriele Ferzetti (Draco), Ilse Steppat (Irma Bunt), Lois Maxwell (Miss Moneypenny), George Baker (Sir Hilary Bray), Bernard Lee (M), Bernard Horsfall (Campbell), Desmond Llewelyn (Q), Yuri Borienko (Grunther), Virginia North (Olympe), Geoffrey Cheshire (Toussaint), Irvin Allen (Che Che), Terry Mountain (Raphael), James Bree (Gumbold), John Gay (Hammond), Angela Scoular (Ruby Bartlett), Catherina von Schell (Nancy), Brian Worth (Manuel), Julie Ege (Scandinavian Girl), Mona Chong (Chinese Girl), Sylvana Henriques (Jamaican Girl), Dani Sheridan (American Girl), Joanna Lumley (English Girl), Zara (Indian Girl), Anoushka Hempel (Australian Girl), Ingrit Back (German Girl), Helena Ronee (Israeli Girl), Jenny Hanley (Irish Girl)
PRODUCED BY
Harry Saltzman & Albert R. Broccoli
DIRECTED BY Peter Hunt
ASSOCIATE PRODUCER Stanley Sopel
SCREENPLAY BY Richard Maibaum
ADDITIONAL DIALOGUE Simon Raven
DIRECTOR OF PHOTOGRAPHY
Michael Reed, BSC
PRODUCTION DESIGNED BY Syd Cain
MUSIC COMPOSED, CONDUCTED & ARRANGED BY John Barry
SONG "WE HAVE ALL THE TIME IN THE WORLD" SUNG BY Louis Armstrong
SONG "DO YOU KNOW HOW CHRISTMAS TREES ARE GROWN?" SUNG BY Nina
LYRICS BY Hal David
EDITOR & 2ND UNIT DIRECTOR John Glen
SPECIAL EFFECTS John Stears
ASSISTANT DIRECTOR Frank Ernst
CONTINUITY Joan Davis
PRODUCTION SUPERVISOR
David Middlemas
CAMERA OPERATOR Alec Mills
STUNT ARRANGER George Leech
2ND UNIT CAMERAMEN
Egil Woxholt & Roy Ford
AERIAL CAMERAMAN John Jordan
SKI CAMERAMEN
Willy Bogner Jr & Alex Barbey
MAIN TITLE DESIGNED BY Maurice Binder
DUBBING EDITORS
Nicholas Stevenson & Harry Miller
SOUND RECORDISTS
John Mitchell & Gordon McCallum
ART DIRECTOR Bob Laing
WARDROBE DESIGNER Marjory Cornelius
SET DECORATOR Peter Lamont
HAIRDRESSER Eileen Warwick
MAKEUP Paul Rabiger & Basil Newall
WARDROBE SUPERVISOR Jackie Cummins
STOCK CAR SEQUENCE DIRECTOR
Anthony Squire

THE STARS *(above) Diana Rigg (Tracy Di Vicenzo) and George Lazenby (James Bond) pose atop the Schilthornbahn in Switzerland.*

On Her Majesty's Secret Service is one of Ian Fleming's most complex and action-packed James Bond novels; it would also become one of the knottiest Bond adventures to bring to the screen.

Originally, producers Albert R. "Cubby" Broccoli and Harry Saltzman hoped to make the film after *Goldfinger*, and in early 1964, screenwriter Richard Maibaum worked on a script treatment. An agreement with producer Kevin McClory to make *Thunderball* in 1965 changed Broccoli's and Saltzman's plans.

When filming on *Thunderball* wrapped, the producers turned their attention to *OHMSS*. The plot required a mountaintop lair in the Swiss Alps, but the producers could not find a suitably snowy location, so *OHMSS* was postponed once more.

Near the start of filming *You Only Live Twice* in 1966, Sean Connery announced his retirement from the role of Bond. After the film's release in June 1967, the producers again chose to tackle *OHMSS*.

THE PRODUCER *(below) Producer Harry Saltzman on the lot at Pinewood Studios.*

THE DESIGNER *(bottom) Production Designer Syd Cain examines a large-scale model of Piz Gloria. Cain designed the sets for* **From Russia With Love,** *and* **Live And Let Die.** *He also contributed designs to* **GoldenEye,** *particularly the GoldenEye key.*

FAR UP! FAR OUT! FAR MORE! James Bond 007 is back!

ALBERT R. BROCCOLI and HARRY SALTZMAN present
JAMES BOND 007 in IAN FLEMING'S "ON HER MAJESTY'S SECRET SERVICE"

starring GEORGE LAZENBY · DIANA RIGG · TELLY SAVALAS as Blofeld
also starring GABRIELE FERZETTI and ILSE STEPPAT Produced by ALBERT R. BROCCOLI and HARRY SALTZMAN Directed by PETER HUNT · Screenplay by RICHARD MAIBAUM · Music by JOHN BARRY · PANAVISION® · TECHNICOLOR® United Artists

ORIGINAL MOTION PICTURE SOUNDTRACK ALBUM BY JOHN BARRY AVAILABLE ON UNITED ARTISTS RECORDS

B 70/9

Impressed by editor Peter Hunt's work on the previous five Bond films, the producers signed him to make his directorial debut with *OHMSS*. Broccoli and Saltzman believed that Hunt's quick cutting had helped set the style of the series. Hunt felt that, following the science fiction elements of *You Only Live Twice*, the Bond series needed to return 007 to his Ian Fleming roots. He asked Richard Maibaum to faithfully adapt Fleming's novel. His credo was, "We mustn't become imitators of our imitators." Hunt wanted to make a glossy film, but one that maintained the emotional rawness of Fleming's novel. He subsequently brought in British novelist and literary critic Simon Raven to sharpen and intellectualize the dialogue.

The filmmakers' first challenge was finding a new James Bond. One idea considered to account for the change of the lead actor was to have Bond undergo plastic surgery to fool his countless enemies, but this idea was dropped. Hunt and the producers narrowed the search to five actors, who were presented to the public in *Life* magazine: Hans De Vries, Anthony Rogers, Robert Campbell, John Richardson, and George Lazenby. After extensive screentesting, Lazenby won the role.

For the crucial role of Tracy, the woman who briefly becomes Mrs. Bond, the team selected Diana Rigg, an experienced actress who was as comfortable in action roles as playing Shakespeare. As the star of *The Avengers* television series, Rigg was also a worldwide name.

After Hunt declared he wanted a more powerfully built actor to play Ernst Stavro Blofeld, Broccoli's friend, American actor Telly Savalas, was cast. Saltzman had originally suggested the Italian actor Gabriele Ferzetti for the role of Blofeld, but Hunt and casting director Dyson Lovell convinced Saltzman that Ferzetti would be better suited to play Bond's ally, Marc Ange Draco. Completing

MAKING OHMSS *(below, left to right) Peter Hunt, on the set at Pinewood Studios, directs Lazenby and Rigg as they film Bond and Tracy's first night together; Telly Savalas (Blofeld) and producer Albert R. Broccoli socialize; Peter Hunt and Ilse Steppat (Irma Bunt) discuss the scene in Murren, Switzerland. Steppat never got to enjoy the success of the film. She passed away only four days after the release of* **OHMSS.**

the main casting, Hunt brought in German actress Ilse Steppat as Blofeld's evil accomplice, Irma Bunt.

Searching for the right location for Blofeld's hideout, Saltzman wondered if the tunnels at the Maginot Line could possibly be used. Then, above the tiny village of Murren, Switzerland, production designer Syd Cain and the Bond team learned that construction was nearly complete on a mountaintop restaurant that closely matched the location in Fleming's novel. The owners allowed the Bond crew to film in exchange for constructing a helipad and furnishing the restaurant.

Production began in October 1968, but the elaborate action sequences, bad weather, hard-to-access locations, and short daylight hours during winter contributed to *OHMSS* having the longest shooting schedule (nine months) and post-production schedule (over six months) of any Bond film to date. A foot chase over London rooftops and into the tunnels of the Royal Mail underground rail system was jettisoned altogether to save time.

Although the film itself contained remarkable action, the studio worried about the ending. Audiences expected to see 007 triumphant in the arms of a woman, not shattered, cradling a corpse. Hunt suggested ending the film with Bond's and Tracy's wedding and opening the next Bond film with Tracy's death. When Lazenby announced that he would not be returning as James Bond, the filmmakers decided the movie's finale would follow Fleming's novel.

John Barry's score was a triumph, perfectly reflecting the film's more serious tone. Barry used the newly invented Moog synthesizer to give a modern edge to the breathtaking action sequences. He composed an instrumental march for the title theme, since *On Her Majesty's Secret Service* didn't seem suited to a contemporary song. Barry suggested Louis Armstrong for the romantic ballad "We Have All The Time In The World," which serves as the theme for Bond and Tracy's relationship. Barry and lyricist Hal David also wrote a cheerful Christmas song, "Do You Know How Christmas Trees Are Grown?" performed by Danish singer Nina Van Pallandt (of the singing duo Nina & Frederik), which is part of the diegetic sound as Bond runs for his life in the village of Murren.

A month after the film's December 1969 opening, United Artists, Broccoli and Saltzman were all in agreement. While *OHMSS* had made money, the entire film had been a major risk which nobody wished to attempt again. The next film would need to adhere to the tried-and-true 007 formula. But the passing of time does something to movies, and time has been very good to *On Her Majesty's Secret Service*. Because of its memorable action and gripping emotional moments, many Bond aficionados and critics view the film as one of the best James Bond films ever made.

PETER HUNT

Born in 1928, Peter Hunt grew up in London's East End and spent school holidays at a documentary film company run by an uncle. He helped with the production of instructional films until 1942, when he joined the army and was sent to Italy. After the war, he worked in the cutting rooms of feature films, rising to the position of assembly editor of *The Man Who Watched The Trains Go By* (1952). He worked on *The Tall Headlines* (1952), directed by Terence Young, and became an editor with 1956's *A Hill In Korea*.

Hunt came to edit *Dr. No* (1962) through the recommendation of director Terence Young, giving the film a dynamic feel that suited 007. Hunt changed the way action films were edited by introducing a now widely imitated style called "crash cutting." Hallmarks of Hunt's editing style include jump cuts in a fight sequence; an abundance of insert shots to add suspense; the acceleration of certain shots for dramatic effect; a refusal to stop the film by fading in and fading out of a scene; and a dislike of close-ups, except when crucial to the story.

After editing and performing second unit director duties on *From Russia With Love* (1963), *Goldfinger* (1964), *Thunderball* (1965), and *You Only Live Twice* (1967), Hunt was announced as director of *On Her Majesty's Secret Service* in September 1967. Hunt gave the film a personal style and ensured the movie remained true to Fleming's novel.

In 1971, Hunt directed episodes of TV series *The Persuaders*, starring Roger Moore, and later directed Moore in *Gold* (1974) and *Shout at the Devil* (1976). His directing career in the 1980s included *Death Hunt* (1981), the miniseries *The Last Days Of Pompeii* (1984), and 1987's *Assassination*. In 1990, Michael Cimino hired Hunt to supervise editing of *Desperate Hours*. Afterward, Hunt retired to California, where he died in 2002.

DIAMONDS ARE FOREVER
(1971)

CAST Sean Connery (James Bond), Jill St. John (Tiffany Case), Charles Gray (Blofeld), Lana Wood (Plenty O'Toole), Jimmy Dean (Willard Whyte), Bruce Cabot (Bert Saxby), Putter Smith (Mr. Kidd), Bruce Glover (Mr. Wint), Norman Burton (Leiter), Joseph Furst (Dr. Metz), Bernard Lee (M), Desmond Llewelyn (Q), Leonard Barr (Shady Tree), Lois Maxwell (Moneypenny), Margaret Lacey (Mrs. Whistler), Joe Robinson (Peter Franks), David de Keyser (Doctor), Laurence Naismith (Sir Donald Munger), David Bauer (Mr. Slumber), Lola Larson (Bambi), Trina Parks (Thumper), Henry Rowland (Dr. Tynan), Edward Bishop (Klaus Hergersheimer), Leroy Hollis (Nevada sheriff), Denise Perrier (Marie)
PRODUCED BY Harry Saltzman & Albert R. Broccoli
DIRECTED BY Guy Hamilton
SCREENPLAY Richard Maibaum and Tom Mankiewicz
ASSOCIATE PRODUCER Stanley Sopel
MUSIC COMPOSED, CONDUCTED & ARRANGED BY John Barry
LYRICS BY Don Black
TITLE SONG SUNG BY Shirley Bassey
DIRECTOR OF PHOTOGRAPHY Ted Moore, BSC
PRODUCTION DESIGNED BY Ken Adam
EDITORS Bert Bates & John W. Holmes, ACE
PRODUCTION MANAGERS Claude Hudson & Milton Feldman
MAIN TITLE DESIGNED BY Maurice Binder
DUBBING EDITORS Teddy Mason, Jimmy Shields & Christopher Lancaster
DUBBING MIXER Gordon McCallum
SOUND RECORDISTS John Mitchell & Alfred J. Overton
SPECIAL EFFECTS Leslie Hillman & Whitney McMahon
WARDROBE SUPERVISORS Elsa Fennell & Ted Tetrick
VISUAL EFFECTS Albert Whitlock & Wally Veevers
STUNT ARRANGERS Bob Simmons & Paul Baxley
LOCATION MANAGERS Bernard Hanson & Eddie Saeta
MISS ST. JOHN'S COSTUMES BY Donfeld
2ND UNIT CAMERAMAN Harold Wellman
ART DIRECTORS Jack Maxsted & Bill Kenney
SET DECORATORS Peter Lamont & John Austin
PRODUCTION BUYER Ronnie Quelch
ASSISTANT DIRECTORS Derek Cracknell & Jerome M. Siegel
CONTINUITY Elaine Schreyeck & Del Ross
CAMERA OPERATORS Bob Kindred & Bill Johnson

SCENES FROM THE PRODUCTION
(clockwise from top) Sean Connery (James Bond) and Jill St. John (Tiffany Case) follow the direction of Guy Hamilton on stage at Pinewood Studios; Connery and St. John relax for a moment while shooting Bond and Tiffany's tense first meeting in Amsterdam; on location in San Pedro, California for the sailing of the Whyte Line's cruise ship; Sean Connery jokes with Jill St. John as producer Harry Saltzman and his son Steven look on.

Diamonds Are Forever became the first "make or break" 007 film with the fate of the series resting on its ability to reach an audience. The film's worldwide success lay not just with the decision to bring back director Guy Hamilton and star Sean Connery, but also with the skill of the filmmakers to adapt Bond to a changing audience and changing times.

In January 1970, producer Albert R. "Cubby" Broccoli met with United Artists to discuss the future of Bond. The studio and the producers felt that while *On Her Majesty's Secret Service* had been a good film, they needed to deliver the kind of entertainment *Goldfinger* provided, and they needed to do it for a reasonable budget.

First, United Artists wanted assurance that it was the old James Bond that the public wanted to see. They re-released *Thunderball* and *You Only Live Twice* as a major double-bill barely six months after *OHMSS*'s opening. Audiences packed theaters and cheered. The message was clear—cinemagoers wanted the return of the classic Bond.

Working with screenwriter Richard Maibaum, the filmmakers fashioned a first-draft script that involved Auric Goldfinger's twin brother and a boat chase set on Lake Mead. After searching for a new Bond, they selected John Gavin, an American actor who would become US Ambassador to Mexico during the 1980s. With no fanfare, they signed him to a contract, although the producers knew that United Artists President of Production David Picker hoped to cast a different actor as 007: Sean Connery.

Connery returned with the reluctant blessing of Broccoli and Saltzman for a world record salary, ten percent of the gross, and the right to green light two United Artists films of modest budgets.

Picker suggested hiring American writer Tom Mankiewicz, a writer he felt could bring wit and pace to the script while still capturing the essentially British tone of

Bond. After the first draft, all agreed to bring back Bond's nemesis, Ernst Stavro Blofeld, whose story it was felt had been left unresolved. To direct, the producers chose Guy Hamilton, who vowed to bring back the "*Goldfinger* touch" to the series. Mankiewicz's final script, developed with input from the producers and Hamilton, featured a return to intriguingly sinister henchmen—Wint and Kidd—a grand plot, and most of all, humor.

The filmmakers originally thought of shooting *Diamonds*, which was largely set in the US, in Hollywood. Pre-production work began at Universal Studios, but later the production moved back to Pinewood.

Shooting began on April 5, 1971 with the desert outside of Las Vegas doubling for South Africa. Cooperation from the billionaire Howard Hughes (whose reclusive behavior and use of doubles inspired the storyline) helped pave the way for an amazing car chase through downtown Las Vegas. The scene in which 007 turns a Ford Mustang on two wheels had to be shot three times: once at Universal Studios and then twice more with different stunt drivers in Las Vegas in order to properly capture the shot of the car emerging from the alley. The drivers performed the stunt on different sides of the car, resulting in much consternation on the part of the filmmakers. Most audience members never noticed.

The filmmakers staged the movie's climax at an oil rig off the coast of Oceanside, California. An assistant director miscued the explosions but, thankfully, one lone aerial cameraman captured nearly all the fireworks, saving the scene from a total re-shoot.

The biggest challenge occurred as the filmmakers moved back to Pinewood Studios, as every shot with Connery had to be completed in 18 weeks. On August 13, 1971, director Hamilton called cut on Connery's last shot. Everyone shook hands, and Connery left the role of 007 until his non-EON

ALBERT R. BROCCOLI and HARRY SALTZMAN present

Sean Connery
as James Bond 007
in IAN FLEMING'S

"Diamonds Are Forever"
Forever
Forever
Forever
Forever
Forever

ST. JOHN as 'Tiffany Case' · CHARLES GRAY

LANA WOOD as PLENTY O'TOOLE · JIMMY DEAN · BRUCE CABOT · Produced by ALBERT R. BROCCOLI and HARRY SALTZMAN · Directed by GUY HAMILTON
by RICHARD MAIBAUM and TOM MANKIEWICZ · Production Designed by KEN ADAM · Music by JOHN BARRY · PANAVISION® TECHNICOLOR®
©1971 UNITED ARTISTS CORPORATION

GP

United Artists

71/3

**PERSIANS AND PRODUCERS
(below, top to bottom)** The
cat trainer shows the many
doubles for Blofeld's white
Persian cat on set. The
name of his company?
"Pussies Galore"; on the
Moon set, producers Harry
Saltzman and Albert R.
Broccoli and director Guy
Hamilton discuss the
gravity of the situation.

GUY HAMILTON

The son of a British diplomat, Guy Hamilton was born in Paris in 1922 and spent his early childhood in France. At 16, he got his first film job as clapper boy for director Julien Duvivier. At the beginning of World War II, he was evacuated aboard a coal ship and found himself sleeping on coal piles near another refugee, Somerset Maugham. Arriving in London, he worked in the film library at Paramount News before joining the Royal Navy. After the war, he became an assistant director, working with such distinguished filmmakers as Carol Reed and John Huston. Reed helped Hamilton get his first directing job with 1952's *The Ringer*. While *The Intruder* (1953) and *The Colditz Story* (1955) showed that Hamilton was very adept with mostly male casts, he also branched out with a musical comedy, *Charley Moon* (1956), and the melodrama *Manuela* (1957).

By the end of the decade, he had proven himself a skilled director of big-budget films with spectacular action set-pieces, like *The Devil's Disciple* (1959) and *The Best of Enemies* (1962). He turned down an offer to direct *Dr. No* to make *The Party's Over*, a film about swinging London that wasn't released until 1965 due to censor issues. When Hamilton finally directed a Bond film, 1964's *Goldfinger*, he played up the humor and gadgetry, made Bond the most knowledgeable man alive, and set the template for the Bond films that followed. Hamilton directed two more films for Harry Saltzman, *Funeral In Berlin* (1966) and *The Battle Of Britain* (1969) before returning to the Bond series with *Diamonds Are Forever* (1971), *Live And Let Die* (1973), and *The Man With The Golden Gun* (1974), overseeing the transition from Sean Connery to Roger Moore.

After Bond, Hamilton directed the World War II action film *Force 10 From Navarone* (1978), the Agatha Christie mysteries *The Mirror Crack'd* (1980) and *Evil Under The Sun* (1981), and two 007-style adventures, *Remo Williams: The Adventure Begins* (1985) and *Try This One For Size* (1989), before retiring to the island of Mallorca.

appearance in *Never Say Never Again* 12 years later.

John Barry returned to score the music, bringing back Shirley Bassey to lend her seductive vocals to the title song. The score managed to capture in sound the glitter of diamonds sparkling in the light, adding a glamorous allure to Guy Hamilton's often humorous visuals.

The blend proved a perfect recipe for Bond's first film of the 1970s. Audiences flocked to cinemas, and the film sold 11 million more tickets in the US than its predecessor. The Oscars recognized *Diamonds Are Forever*'s brilliant use of sound, earning the film a nomination for Best Sound for Bond veterans Gordon K. McCallum, John Mitchell, and Alfred J. Overton.

James Bond had returned, but, with the role of 007 again up for grabs, further challenges lay ahead.

LIVE AND LET DIE (1973)

CAST Roger Moore (James Bond), Yaphet Kotto (Dr. Kananga/Mr. Big), Jane Seymour (Solitaire), Clifton James (Sheriff J. W. Pepper), Julius W. Harris (Tee Hee), Geoffrey Holder (Baron Samedi), David Hedison (Felix Leiter), Gloria Hendry (Rosie Carver), Bernard Lee (M), Lois Maxwell (Moneypenny), Tommy Lane (Adam), Earl Jolly Brown (Whisper), Roy Stewart (Quarrel Jr.), Lon Satton (Strutter), Arnold Williams (Kananga's cab driver), Ruth Kempf (Mrs. Bell), Joie Chitwood (Charlie), Madeline Smith (Miss Caruso), Michael Ebbin (Dambala), Kubi Chaza (Sales girl), Dennis Edwards (Baines), James Drake (Dawes), Robert Dix (Hamilton), Dan Jackson (Fillet of Soul waiter), B. J. Arnau (Fillet of Soul singer)
PRODUCED BY
Harry Saltzman & Albert R. Broccoli
DIRECTED BY Guy Hamilton
SCREENPLAY BY Tom Mankiewicz
MUSIC BY George Martin
TITLE SONG COMPOSED BY
Paul & Linda McCartney
TITLE SONG PERFORMED BY
Paul McCartney and Wings
DIRECTOR OF PHOTOGRAPHY
Ted Moore, BSC
PRODUCTION SUPERVISOR Claude Hudson
SPECIAL EFFECTS Derek Meddings
EDITORS Bert Bates, Raymond Poulton, GBFE & John Shirley
SOUND RECORDISTS
John Mitchell & Ken Barker
ASSISTANT DIRECTOR Derek Cracknell
LOCATION MANAGER Bernard Hanson
CHOREOGRAPHER Geoffrey Holder
COSTUME DESIGNER Julie Harris
MAIN TITLE DESIGNER Maurice Binder
CASTING DIRECTOR Weston Drury Jr.
STUNTS Bob Simmons, Joie Chitwood, Ross Kananga, Jerry Comeaux, Eddie Smith, Bill Bennet
DUBBING EDITORS Teddy Mason, Jimmy Shields, Chris Lancaster
SUPERVISING ART DIRECTOR Syd Cain
CO-ART DIRECTORS
Bob Laing, Peter Lamont
OPTICAL EFFECTS Charles Staffell
CONTINUITY Elaine Schreyeck
CAMERA OPERATOR Bob Kindred
SECOND UNIT CAMERAMAN John Harris
WARDROBE SUPERVISOR Laurel Staffell
MAKEUP SUPERVISOR Paul Rabiger
HAIRDRESSER Colin Jamison
CONSTRUCTION MANAGER Leon Davis
PROPS Patrick Weymouth
USA Crew
PRODUCTION MANAGERS
Stephen F. Kesten, Steven P. Skloot
ASSISTANT DIRECTOR Alan Hopkins
UNIT MANAGER Michael Rauch
LOCATION CO-ORDINATOR Jack Weis
ART DIRECTOR Stephen Hendrickson
CAMERA OPERATORS
George Bouillet & Warren Rothenberger
SHARK SCENES BY William Grefe

The success of *Live And Let Die* proved that the character of James Bond was a bigger star than the actor playing the role. With Sean Connery gone, producers Albert R. "Cubby" Broccoli and Harry Saltzman, working closely with United Artists President David Picker, began searching for a new 007. Although Broccoli and Saltzman considered many actors over the years, they always returned to the idea of bringing Roger Moore in to play 007. As Simon Templar in *The Saint* television series, Moore played a James Bond type: debonair, adventurous, unflappable. His success had made him a household name, and his reputation for professionalism was second to none. The studio approved the casting and also the producers' decision to bring back Guy Hamilton as director and Tom Mankiewicz as screenwriter.

Faced with the challenge of introducing a new actor as 007, Guy Hamilton suggested that Moore be careful not to in any way imitate Connery's Bond. "The fatal thing would be for Roger to step into Sean's shoes," Hamilton told TIME magazine. "He must have his own way." By stripping away the vestiges of the past, the filmmakers offered a Bond who felt fresh and new.

The early 1970s saw a vogue for blaxploitation films, and the filmmakers decided to place Bond in the modern world of African-American cinematic culture. The production team toured the Caribbean and plot elements soon fell into place—voodoo ceremonies in Haiti, talk of drug smuggling riches, a large crocodile farm in Jamaica whose gate bore a sign, "Trespassers will be eaten." Impressed with the crocodile farm's owner, Ross Kananga, the filmmakers set a major sequence on his property, hired him to perform a major stunt, and named the lead villain after him. Hamilton's fondness for jazz led to the suggestion of sending Bond to New Orleans, which dovetailed nicely with the film's voodoo subplot.

The filmmakers cast up-and-coming actor Yaphet Kotto in the dual role of Dr. Kananga/Mr. Big. Harry Saltzman cast

Jane Seymour as Solitaire. Seymour's career in movies and television after *Live And Let Die* would distinguish her as one of the most successful Bond actresses of her generation. Legendary choreographer Geoffrey Holder agreed to play Baron Samedi, a role he originated in Truman Capote's 1954 musical *House of Flowers*. He also staged the distinctive San Monique dance sequences in the film. Holder suggested the idea of closing the film on his character, the man who cannot die, riding on the front of Bond and Solitaire's train.

Filming began on Friday, October 13, 1972 in the Irish Bayou in Louisiana, shooting the boat chase between Bond and Mr. Big's men, the most complex and original ever conceived. The scene required 26 speedboats to leap over roadways and skid across lawns. Stuntman Jerry Comeaux set a world record leaping a Glastron GT-150 110 ft (33.5 m) over a road. Stunts destroyed 17 speedboats before the completion of filming.

The production filmed in Jamaica in late 1972, using some of the same locations seen in *Dr. No* a decade earlier. They also filmed at a set of banana boat docks adjacent to the late Ian Fleming's estate, Goldeneye, where the author wrote the novel *Live And Let Die*.

The emerald tree boa, used in the voodoo ceremonies, proved dangerous. While not poisonous, the snake sports very real fangs. After it bit Dambala actor Michael Ebbin, Dennis Edwards, playing Baines, was briefly overcome with nerves as Ebbin waved the snake in his face. The most serious case of jangled nerves, however, belonged to Ross Kananga, who dashed across the backs of three of his crocodiles five times while doubling 007. After the first take, the crocodiles began to anticipate Kananga's movements, snapping at him and nearly taking off his foot.

Bond composer John Barry could not schedule sufficient time to score *Live And Let Die*, so the producers sought out

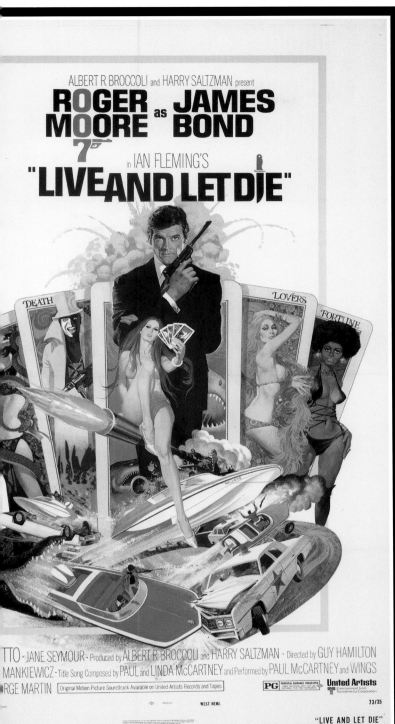

Barry's friend, the producer for The Beatles, George Martin. Martin worked with Paul and Linda McCartney and their band Wings to construct a brilliant title song that became the biggest Bond hit yet (#2 in the US; #7 in the UK). The song earned Paul and Linda McCartney an Academy Award nomination, and the score's richly produced sound helped create a new generation of Bond music fans.

Live And Let Die swept into theaters in the summer of 1973, becoming a solid success in the US and performing far better than the two previous Bond films overseas. It launched Roger Moore as a natural successor to Sean Connery and provided Bond fans with a new 007 for the next 12 years.

ARMED AND DANGEROUS *(facing page, top to bottom)* Roger Moore (James Bond), Tommy Lane (Adam), Jane Seymour (Solitaire), Arnold Williams (Cab Driver), and Yaphet Kotto (Dr. Kananga/Mr. Big) on location at Lakeside Airport in New Orleans; Roger Moore, the new 007, greets a bus full of young fans.

LOCATION, LOCATION, LOCATION *(right, top to bottom):* Robert Dix (Hamilton) awaits his fate in the French Quarter; the filmmakers shoot a key stunt on Jamaica's North Shore; producer Harry Saltzman and actress Jane Seymour on location in Louisiana.

TED MOORE

Ted Moore is remembered as one of the great widescreen cinematographers, equally adept at location and studio cinematography. His lavish color photography and clear compositions made him the perfect choice to realize James Bond's cinematic adventures. Moore's style set the photographic look of the Bond films, eschewing gritty realism for an elegance that mirrored the élan of Ian Fleming's writing.

Born in Cape Province, South Africa on August 7, 1914, Moore emigrated to England in 1930 with his family. Before the outbreak of World War II, Moore worked as a cameraman on films like *Sons Of The Sea* (1939) before joining the RAF. He flew combat missions during the war, earning a DFC from Britain and the Croix de Guerre from France. He worked with the RAF's Film Unit before deciding on a career in the movie industry after the war.

Moore's controlled work as a camera operator on difficult location films such as *The African Queen* (1951) won him widespread praise within the industry. Working on early films produced by Albert R. Broccoli and his then partner Irving Allen, such as *Hell Below Zero* (1954) and *The Black Knight* (1954), Moore graduated to cinematographer the following year, lensing *A Prize Of Gold* (1955) and *Cockleshell Heroes* (1955). Moore's speed and ability to capture complex shots particularly impressed Terence Young, who would go on to direct three Bond films shot by Moore.

Moore photographed using wide-angle lenses, frequently employing deep-focus techniques and emphasizing bold colors. His clear images allowed Bond editor Peter Hunt to cut action scenes with great speed. With Moore's images, the viewer could always clearly see what was happening, even in the briefest of shots.

Ted Moore shot seven James Bond film and won an Academy Award for 1966's *A Man For All Seasons.*

He died in 1987, at the age of 72.

THE MAN WITH THE GOLDEN GUN (1974)

CAST Roger Moore (James Bond),
Christopher Lee (Scaramanga), Britt Ekland
(Mary Goodnight), Maud Adams (Andrea Anders),
Hervé Villechaize (Nick Nack), Clifton James (Sheriff
J. W. Pepper), Richard Loo (Hai Fat), Soon-Taik Oh
(Lt. Hip), Marc Lawrence (Rodney), Bernard Lee
(M), Lois Maxwell (Moneypenny), Marne Maitland
(Lazar), Desmond Llewelyn (Q), James Cossins
(Colthorpe), Chan Yiu Lam (Chula), Carmen Sautoy
(Saida), Gerald James (Frazier), Michael Osborne
(Naval lieutenant), Michael Fleming (Communications
officer), Michael Goodliffe (Tanner), Gordon Everett
(Gibson), George Silver (Nightclub owner), Terry
Plummer (Rahman), Rocky Taylor (Hammud), Sonny
Caldinez (Kra), Françoise Therry (Chew Mee), Joie
Pacharintraporn (Cha), Cheung Chuen Nam, aka
Yuen Qiu (Nara), Jay Sidow (Maybelle Pepper)
PRODUCED BY
Harry Saltzman & Albert R. Broccoli
DIRECTED BY Guy Hamilton
SCREENPLAY BY
Richard Maibaum and Tom Mankiewicz
MUSIC COMPOSED, CONDUCTED &
ARRANGED BY John Barry
LYRICS BY Don Black
TITLE SONG PERFORMED BY Lulu
ASSOCIATE PRODUCER Charles Orme
DIRECTORS OF PHOTOGRAPHY
Ted Moore & Oswald Morris
PRODUCTION DESIGNER Peter Murton
PRODUCTION SUPERVISOR
Claude Hudson
LOCATION MANAGER (THAILAND)
Frank Ernst
LOCATION MANAGER (HONG KONG)
Eric Rattray
MAIN TITLE DESIGNED BY Maurice Binder
EDITORS John Shirley, Raymond Poulton, GBFE
DUBBING EDITORS Jimmy Shields,
Christopher Lancaster, Charles Crafford
DUBBING MIXER Ken Barker
SOUND RECORDIST Gordon Everett
ASSISTANT TO THE PRODUCERS
Reginald Barkshire
PRODUCTION ACCOUNTANT
Brian Bailey
PRODUCTION CO-ORDINATOR
(BANGKOK) Santa Pestonji
CASTING DIRECTORS
Maude Spector & Weston Drury Jnr.
WARDROBE SUPERVISOR Elsa Fennell
MAKEUP SUPERVISOR Paul Engelen
HAIRDRESSER Mike Jones
PROPS Patrick Weymouth
CO-ART DIRECTORS
Peter Lamont, John Graysmark
SPECIAL EFFECTS John Stears
MINIATURES Derek Meddings
CONSTRUCTION MANAGER Leon Davis
ASSISTANT DIRECTOR Derek Cracknell
CAMERA OPERATOR Bob Kindred
CONTINUITY Elaine Schreyeck
2ND UNIT CAMERAMAN John Harris

MAKING GOLDEN GUN
(clockwise from right) Director Guy Hamilton lines up a shot with Christopher Lee (Scaramanga) on the set of Hai Fat's office; Roger Moore (Bond), W. J. Milligan (the car stunt arranger), Albert R. Broccoli and Michael Redding (construction manager [location]) celebrate after the successful Astro Spiral jump; Maud Adams (Andrea Anders) listens to Christopher Lee (Scaramanga) discuss his golden gun; Guy Hamilton offers direction to Britt Ekland (Mary Goodnight) on location in Bangkok.

Best remembered for its flamboyant villains and spectacular locations, *The Man With The Golden Gun* was the last Bond film made under the partnership of producers Albert R. Broccoli and Harry Saltzman. After the great success of *Live And Let Die*, Saltzman and Broccoli dove into pre-production on *The Man With The Golden Gun*, which had originally been conceived as the follow-up to *You Only Live Twice* in 1968, with production slated for Cambodia. When civil war broke out in 1967, *Golden Gun* was shelved for six years.

Broccoli and Saltzman brought back director Guy Hamilton, writer Tom Mankiewicz, and much of the production crew of *Live And Let Die*. Peter Murton, who had worked with Ken Adam during much of the 1960s, signed on as production designer. The team originally visited Iran to scout locations, but the outbreak of the Yom Kippur–Ramadan War in October 1973 convinced the filmmakers not to shoot in the Middle East. Yet that very war did create the OPEC oil embargo, which launched the mid-1970s energy crisis, two events that inspired the film's plot. Broccoli's stepson, future Bond producer Michael G. Wilson, an engineer by training, was engaged to clarify the solar energy elements in the story for Richard Maibaum, who was rewriting Tom Mankiewicz's first draft script.

Guy Hamilton hoped to set the film's climax in Ha Long Bay in Vietnam. Although a peace accord had ended US involvement in the Vietnam War in January 1973, shooting in North Vietnamese territory proved impossible. Production designer Peter Murton saw a poster on the London Underground of similar spires near Phuket, Thailand, and the filmmakers soon departed to scout the location. They were impressed and decided to return the story to Southeast Asia, setting it largely in Hong Kong, Macau, and Thailand. On the Hong Kong location recce, Broccoli came up with the idea of using the hulk of the *Queen Elizabeth* in the harbor as M's Far East base.

The filmmakers did not have to look far to cast Mary Goodnight. Even before the script was written, Britt Ekland discussed the role with Broccoli. Swedish model Maud Adams

was chosen for the role of Andrea Anders. Guy Hamilton declared he wanted a miniature Oddjob for the henchman, leading to the casting of Hervé Villechaize as Nick Nack. Mankiewicz, who returned to rewrite Maibaum's draft before shooting began, originally suggested Jack Palance for Scaramanga, but Guy Hamilton soon turned to Christopher Lee. He proved ideal for the role, having also been a cousin by marriage to Ian Fleming. To round out the cast, flush from the success of *Live And Let Die*, the producers decided to bring back Clifton James as Sheriff J. W. Pepper.

The cast assembled in Bangkok in mid-April, proceeding to the village of Phang Nga. The remote village offered only the most rugged accommodation for cast and crew. Shooting began on Khow-Ping-Kan island, the setting for the exteriors of Scaramanga's lair. In Bangkok, the filmmakers shot a complex chase with longtail boats speeding through the city's famed floating market. This scene proved easy compared to the car chase involving Bond and Scaramanga, which involved the most harrowing car stunt ever conceived. The producers licensed a stunt designed by Raymond McHenry on a computer, inspired by his work on simulations of single-vehicle accidents. Perfected through trial and error by W. J. Milligan, Jr. and his stunt show crew, the Astro Spiral Jump had awed audiences in shows across America. Milligan worked with Peter Murton to create precisely built ramps that could look like a collapsed wooden bridge. Stunt driver Loren "Bumps" Willard performed the leap perfectly in one take; he had never attempted the stunt before.

Riots in Bangkok forced the second unit to leave earlier than scheduled, but other large challenges faced the first unit when it returned to England to complete the studio work. Broccoli, while in Thailand, found veteran Bond cinematographer Ted Moore was unable to complete the film. Upon arriving in London, Broccoli convinced Academy-Award-winning cinematographer Oswald Morris to replace him, a difficult task as Moore had shot seven of the previous Bond films. Despite the use of large pyrotechnic explosions on

Khow-Ping Kan island, the filmmakers needed to create images of a solar array rising from a rock spire and the island itself disintegrating. Miniature effects supervisor Derek Meddings built amazingly accurate copies of the island at Pinewood Studios. His most challenging effect proved to be creating shots of the sun passing behind clouds.

John Barry had only three weeks to score the film.

To reflect Guy Hamilton's style, his score had some humorous touches, including a penny whistle heard during the Astro Spiral jump. To create the flavor of Southeast Asian music, Barry worked with a Southern European instrument, the cymbalom, which he had used extensively for his score of *The Ipcress File* (1965). Barry lined up Scottish singer Lulu to perform Don Black's lyrics for the title song.

Soon after completion of *The Man With The Golden Gun*, Harry Saltzman sold his share of the Bond franchise to United Artists, leaving Broccoli as sole producer. The film opened on December 19, 1974 but, for a combination of reasons, sold fewer tickets in the US than any previous Bond film. Although the film made a profit, some thought it portended the end of the Bond franchise. Broccoli had different ideas.

JOHN STEARS

John Stears made the most outlandish concepts in the early Bond films a reality. He was the real Q, the man who devised the inner workings of gadgets, built 007's deadly toys and, when the time came, he was the man who blew them all up. His clever, convincing, and spectacular effects gave the Bond movies a grand sense of scale.

Born in Middlesex in 1934, John Stears developed an interest in pyrotechnics and ballistics while serving in the British Army. When he returned to civilian life, he landed a job making a model of a Bristol Bulldog biplane for the film *Reach For The Sky* (1956), the true story of airman Douglas Bader. He then went to work for the Rank Organization as a matte artist.

Stears began his association with James Bond when he built and destroyed a miniature of the bauxite wharf for *Dr. No* (1962). Impressed with his work, the producers asked him to become the special effects supervisor on the next 007 film. Stears blew up a miniature model of a SPECTRE helicopter and set the sea afire for *From Russia With Love* (1963), as well as packing an arsenal of weapons inside an Aston Martin for *Goldfinger* (1964). While working on *Thunderball* (1965), he managed to obtain a quantity of rocket fuel to boost the explosion of the *Disco Volante*. This film saw Stears take home an Academy Award for special effects. He provided more miniatures and explosions and attached missiles to the Little Nellie one-seater autogyro for *You Only Live Twice* (1967) and destroyed a model Piz Gloria for *On Her Majesty's Secret Service* (1969). Work on other films kept him absent from subsequent 007 films until *The Man With The Golden Gun* (1974), for which he provided a radio-controlled model of Scaramanga's flying car.

Stears won a second Academy Award in 1977 for his work on *Star Wars*. He remained busy throughout the 1980s, working on films such as *Outland* (1981), *The Bounty* (1984), and *F/X* (1986). Stears died of a stroke a year after the release of his last film *The Mask Of Zorro* (1998), directed by Martin Campbell.

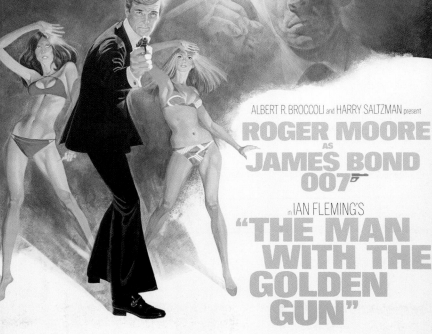

THE WORLD'S GREATEST VILLAINS TRIED TO KILL JAMES BOND

DR. NO. He couldn't kill Bond with a cyanide cigarette and the world's largest tarantula.

ROSA KLEB. She couldn't kill Bond with an assassin trained from birth.

GOLDFINGER AND ODD JOB. They couldn't split Bond in half with a laser beam or with the world's deadliest hat.

BLOFELD. He tried to kill Bond with a deadly virus and ten of the most beautiful women in the world.

NOW IT'S SCARAMANGA'S TURN TO TRY

ALBERT R. BROCCOLI and HARRY SALTZMAN present

ROGER MOORE AS JAMES BOND 007

in IAN FLEMING'S "THE MAN WITH THE GOLDEN GUN"

with CHRISTOPHER LEE · BRITT EKLAND · Produced by ALBERT R BROCCOLI and HARRY SALTZMAN
Directed by GUY HAMILTON · Screenplay by RICHARD MAIBAUM and TOM MANKIEWICZ · Music by JOHN BARRY

PG PARENTAL GUIDANCE SUGGESTED · ORIGINAL MOTION PICTURE SOUNDTRACK AVAILABLE ON UNITED ARTISTS RECORDS AND TAPES · COLOR· United Artists

THE SPY WHO LOVED ME
(1977)

CAST Roger Moore (James Bond), Barbara Bach
(Major Anya Amasova), Curt Jurgens (Karl
Stromberg), Richard Kiel (Jaws), Caroline Munro
(Naomi), Walter Gotell (General Gogol), Geoffrey
Keen (Minister of Defence), Bernard Lee (M),
George Baker (Captain Benson), Michael Billington
(Sergei Barsov), Olga Bisera (Felicca), Desmond
Llewelyn (Q), Edward de Souza (Sheik Hosein),
Vernon Dobtcheff (Max Kalba), Valerie Leon (Hotel
Receptionist), Lois Maxwell (Miss Moneypenny),
Sydney Tafler (Liparus Captain), Nadim Sawalha
(Fekkesh), Sue Vanner (Log cabin girl), Eva Rueber-
Staier (Rublevich), Robert Brown (Admiral
Hargreaves), Marilyn Galsworthy (Stromberg's
assistant), Milton Reid (Sandor), Cyril Shaps
(Bechmann), Milo Sperber (Markovitz), Albert
Moses (Barman), Rafiq Anwar (Cairo Club waiter),
Felicity York, Dawn Rodrigues, Anika Pavel, Jill
Goodall (Arab beauties), Shane Rimmer
(Commander Carter), Bryan Marshall
(Commander Talbot)
PRODUCED BY Albert R. Broccoli
DIRECTED BY Lewis Gilbert
SCREENPLAY BY
Christopher Wood and Richard Maibaum
ASSOCIATE PRODUCER William P. Cartlidge
SPECIAL ASSISTANT TO PRODUCER
Michael Wilson
PRODUCTION DESIGNED BY Ken Adam
MAIN TITLE DESIGNED BY Maurice Binder
MUSIC BY Marvin Hamlisch
TITLE SONG "NOBODY DOES IT BETTER"
performed by Carly Simon; lyrics by Carole Bayer
Sager; composed by Marvin Hamlisch; produced by
Richard Perry
DIRECTOR OF PHOTOGRAPHY Claude Renoir
EDITOR John Glen
PRODUCTION CONTROLLER
Reginald A. Barkshire
PRODUCTION MANAGER David Middlemas
ART DIRECTOR Peter Lamont
ASSISTANT ART DIRECTORS
Ernie Archer, John Fenner & Michael Lamont
ASSISTANT ART DIRECTOR (SET) Charles Bishop
CHIEF DRAUGHTSMAN Brian Savegar
SPECIAL EFFECTS SUPERVISOR Derek Meddings
Special Optical Effects Alan Maley
SPECIAL EFFECTS (STUDIO) John Evans
2ND UNIT DIRECTORS Ernest Day, John Glen
ACTION ARRANGER Bob Simmons
SKI JUMP PERFORMED BY Rick Sylvester
SET DRESSER Hugh Scaife
MAKEUP Paul Engelen
HAIRDRESSING Barbara Ritchie
FASHION CONSULTANT Ronald Paterson
WARDROBE SUPERVISOR Rosemary Burrows
SCRIPT SUPERVISOR Vernon Harris
CAMERA OPERATOR Alec Mills
CONTINUITY June Randall
ASSEMBLY EDITOR Alan Strachan
ASSISTANT EDITOR John Grover
SOUND RECORDIST Gordon Everett
PRODUCTION ACCOUNTANT Brian Bailey
PRODUCTION ASSISTANT Marguerite Green
CASTING DIRECTORS
Maude Spector & Weston Drury Jr.
UNDERWATER PHOTOGRAPHY Lamar Boren
CONSTRUCTION MANAGER Michael Redding
ASSISTANT DIRECTOR Ariel Levy
ASSISTANT DIRECTOR (2ND UNIT) Chris Kenny

The Spy Who Loved Me became Albert R. "Cubby" Broccoli's first Bond film as sole producer. Its success helped define the legacy of one of the film industry's most beloved figures.

In Spring 1975, Broccoli, Harry Saltzman, and director Guy Hamilton began preparing the tenth Bond film. For the first time, the filmmakers only had a title as Ian Fleming did not wish this novel, written from the perspective of a woman who meets James Bond for one harrowing night, to be used for a film plot. Many talented writers took a shot at developing the story, including veteran Richard Maibaum, *A Clockwork Orange* author Anthony Burgess, and writer/director John Landis.

Harry Saltzman's outside investments had created large debts, and the banks saw Saltzman's share of EON Productions as his largest asset. Saltzman sold his share to United Artists, leaving Albert R. "Cubby" Broccoli as sole producer of *The Spy Who Loved Me*.

Resolving these matters resulted in delays to pre-production. Guy Hamilton left the project, requiring Broccoli to find a new director and, despite the number of writers involved, the numerous scripts and treatments had yet to coalesce.

Broccoli sought out *You Only Live Twice* director Lewis Gilbert to bring the project back on track. Gilbert brought in Christopher Wood to complete the screenplay. Gilbert also brought John Glen onboard as an editor and additional unit director. Gilbert introduced the key script element of Bond killing Anya Amasova's lover late in the pre-production stage, helping to create a solid story underpinning the action. The production draft of the script reflected the additional humor Gilbert wanted and the craftmanship sought by special assistant to the producer Michael G. Wilson.

Curt Jurgens, co-star of Gilbert's *Ferry To Hong Kong* (1958), landed the role of Karl Stromberg. An assistant saw Richard Kiel on the American television series *The Barbary Coast* and suggested him for the part of Jaws. The filmmakers searched for an appropriate actress to play Anya Amasova. When United Artists Executive Danton Rissner asked if there was a small role for his friend Barbara Bach, he was surprised to discover that Broccoli wanted her for the lead.

While brainstorming for an idea for the opening sequence, all eyes fell on a TV advert for Canadian Club featuring a skier sailing off El Capitan in California and then unfurling a parachute to land safely. Research showed the ad was faked, but the parachutist, Rick Sylvester, said the stunt could be done on Baffin Island. Weather threatened to scotch the stunt, but finally the winds died down and the clouds parted. Out of three cameras rolling, fortunately one captured the shot.

Location work in Egypt proved an ordeal. Despite location

FLYING THE FLAG *Stuntman Rick Sylvester performs Bond's amazing ski and parachute jump in the opening scene.*

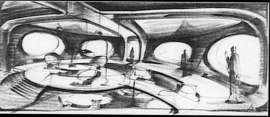

MAKING SPY *(clockwise from above far left) Barbara Bach and Roger Moore sit with Albert R. Broccoli on the set of the interior of the Liparus supertanker; Lamar Boren and his underwater crew prepare to film the Atlantis miniature off Coral Harbour, Bahamas; Ken Adam's design sketch of Stromberg's Atlantis lair; production designer Ken Adam stands on his magnificent Liparus set.*

ALBERT R. BRO
pre
ROGE
MOOR
IAN FLEM
JAME
BON
007
"TH
starring BARBARA B
and CURT JURGENS as "Stro

IT'S THE BIGGEST. IT'S THE BEST. IT'S BOND. AND BEYOND.

SPY WHO LOVED ME" A

Produced by ALBERT R. BROCCOLI
Directed by LEWIS GILBERT
Screenplay by CHRISTOPHER WOOD
& RICHARD MAIBAUM
Music by MARVIN HAMLISCH
Filmed in PANAVISION ®

United Artists
A Transamerica Company

ORIGINAL MOTION PICTURE SOUNDTRACK ALBUM
AND TAPE AVAILABLE ON UNITED ARTISTS RECORDS

LEWIS GILBERT

Lewis Gilbert brought scope and an incredibly wry sense of humor to the James Bond films, injecting his 007 adventures with a layer of elegant and exotic fantasy.

Born into a family of music-hall performers, Lewis Gilbert began his career as a child actor, appearing in such films as *Dick Turpin* (1933). Legendary British producer Alexander Korda offered to send him to the Royal Academy of Dramatic Arts, but Gilbert had his sights set on directing. In 1939, he worked as an assistant on Alfred Hitchcock's *Jamaica Inn*.

When World War II broke out, he joined the Royal Air Force. Attached to the US Air Corps Film Unit, he directed several documentaries such as *Sailors Do Care* (1944) and *Arctic Harvest* (1946). He continued to write and direct documentary shorts after the war, before directing low-budget features starting with *The Little Ballerina* (1948). By the end of the 1950s, he had graduated to directing more expensive productions, like *Reach For The Sky* (1956) and *Carve Her Name With Pride* (1958). He was particularly adept at war and action films like *Sink The Bismarck!* (1960) and *H.M.S. Defiant* (1962), and he had a knack for translating plays to the big screen, scoring a hit with *Alfie* (1966), which made an international star of Michael Caine.

When Albert R. Broccoli approached Gilbert to direct *You Only Live Twice* (1967), Gilbert was reluctant to take the job, but Broccoli eventually persuaded him. Gilbert brought a fresh eye to the series and returned a decade later to direct *The Spy Who Loved Me*, capitalizing on Roger Moore's 007 persona in the process. The immensely profitable *Moonraker* (1979) followed, after which Gilbert returned to making contained dramatic comedies.

In the 1980s, he had two major successes, *Educating Rita* (1983) and *Shirley Valentine* (1989). More recently, he directed the drama *Before You Go* (2002).

filming at some of the greatest temples along the Nile, including Karnak, Edfu and Abu Simbel, the day to day needs of the production were often difficult to meet. Communications with London were unreliable. The crew found the catering abysmal. Broccoli earned great goodwill by finding the supplies to cook a homemade pasta dinner for the cast and crew. At the *Son et Lumière* show at the pyramids, the crew discovered that they could not direct enough light onto the giant structures at night to get an exposure; as a result, all the pyramid shots were later created with mattes and miniatures back at Pinewood Studios in England.

Sardinia provided the perfect backdrop for second unit director Ernie Day to film much of the car chase with the Lotus Esprit. Special visual effects supervisor Derek Meddings made a shell car to be fired into the sea from an air cannon. In the clear waters of the Bahamas, three additional cars showed the Lotus transforming into a submarine. Perry Oceanographics built a fifth effects Lotus, a true submarine in the shape of an Esprit, for the Nassau shoot. Meddings supervised a cable pulling a final Lotus body onto a Sardinian beach to end the scene. Meddings also built models of the Liparus supertanker and Stromberg's *Atlantis* laboratory, both shot in the Bahamas.

At Pinewood, production designer Ken Adam broke new ground with sets that deftly combined sweeping curves, burnished metal finishes, and beautiful antiques. Yet no stage or location could be found for the interior of the *Liparus*, so Adam designed a permanent stage at Pinewood. Built in only 13 weeks, including the tanker interior, the 007 Stage became the largest film stage in the world. Adam secretly contacted the director Stanley Kubrick to help him devise a lighting design for the set. The 007 Stage opened with great fanfare, including a visit by former Prime Minister Harold Wilson.

John Barry was unavailable to score the film and suggested Marvin Hamlisch, then famed for his score for the 1976 Pulitzer-prize-winning musical *A Chorus Line*. Hamlisch wanted to create a big sound in keeping with the 007 style created by Barry. For the title song, Hamlisch thought, "Everything is bigger than life on a Bond film. So, I went right to Mozart, thinking, 'Go just the opposite.'" Hamlisch started the title song with a lone piano, waiting a full 30 seconds before introducing the sweeping orchestra. Lyricist Carole Bayer Sager came up with the title "Nobody Does It Better," a phrase that still defines Bond. Perfomed by Carly Simon, the song reached # 2 in the US and #7 in the UK. Both song and score earned Academy Award nominations, as did the art direction.

With a budget higher than any Bond film before it, *The Spy Who Loved Me* became a tremendous box office success and a touchstone film in the Bond series.

MOONRAKER
(1979)

CAST Roger Moore (James Bond), Lois Chiles (Holly Goodhead), Michael Lonsdale (Drax), Richard Kiel (Jaws), Corinne Clery (Corinne Dufour), Toshiro Sauga (Chang), Bernard Lee (M), Geoffrey Keen (Frederick Gray), Desmond Llewelyn (Q), Lois Maxwell (Miss Moneypenny), Emily Bolton (Manuela), Blanche Ravalec (Dolly), Irka Bochenko (Blonde beauty), Michael Marshall (Colonel Scott), Leila Shenna (Hostess private jet), Anne Lonnberg (Museum guide), Jean-Pierre Castaldi (Pilot private jet), Walter Gotell (General Gogol), Douglas Lambert (Mission Control Director), Arthur Howard (Cavendish), Alfie Bass (Consumptive Italian), Brian Keith (US Shuttle Captain), George Birt (Captain Boeing 747) Guy Delorme (Tree assassin)
PRODUCED BY Albert R. Broccoli
DIRECTED BY Lewis Gilbert
SCREENPLAY BY Christopher Wood
EXECUTIVE PRODUCER Michael G. Wilson
ASSOCIATE PRODUCER William P. Cartlidge
MUSIC BY John Barry
TITLE SONG "MOONRAKER"
performed by Shirley Bassey
composed by John Barry
lyrics by Hal David
PRODUCTION DESIGNED BY Ken Adam
MAIN TITLE DESIGNER Maurice Binder
EDITOR John Glen
DIRECTORS OF PHOTOGRAPHY
Claude Renoir, Jean Tournier
VISUAL EFFECTS SUPERVISOR Derek Meddings
VISUAL EFFECTS ART DIRECTOR Peter Lamont
LOCATION MANAGERS Frank Ernst (Brazil), Phillippe Modave (Italy), John Comfort (USA)
UNIT MANAGERS Robert Saussier (France), Chris Kenny (UK)
ASSISTANT DIRECTOR Michel Cheyko
ACTION SEQUENCES Bob Simmons
PRODUCTION CONTROLLER
Reginald A. Barkshire
PRODUCTION ACCOUNTANT Brian Bailey
ART DIRECTORS
Peter Lamont, Max Douy & Charles Bishop
CASTING DIRECTORS
Margot Capelier & Budge Drury
SET DECORATOR Peter Howitt
2ND UNIT CAMERAMAN Jacques Renoir
VISUAL EFFECTS CAMERAMAN Paul Wilson
OPTICAL EFFECTS CAMERAMAN
Robin Browne
ASSEMBLY EDITOR John Grover
2ND UNIT DIRECTORS Ernest Day & John Glen
SPECIAL EFFECTS John Evans, John Richardson, René Albouze, Serge Ponvianne
PRODUCTION MANAGERS Jean-Pierre Spiri-Mercanton (France), Terence Churcher (UK)
CAMERA OPERATORS Alex Mills, Michel Deloire, John Morgan
STUNT ARRANGER Bob Simmons
CONTINUITY Elaine Shreyeck
DUBBING EDITOR Allan Sones
DUBBING MIXER Gordon K. McCallum
SOUND MIXER Daniel Brisseau
SCRIPT EDITOR Vernon Harris
SPACE CONSULTANT Eric Burgess
COSTUME DESIGNER Jacques Fonteray
WARDROBE MASTER Jean Zay
MAKEUP ARTISTS
Monique Archambault & Paul Engelen
HAIRDRESSERS Mike Jones, Pierre Vade
STILLS CAMERAMAN Patrick Morin

THE GIRLS ARE OUT OF THIS WORLD

Albert R. Broccoli presents ROGER MOORE as JAMES BOND 007 in Ian Fleming's MOONRAKER

Co-starring Lois Chiles Richard Kiel as 'Jaws'
Michael Lonsdale as 'Drax' and Corinne Clery
Produced by Albert R. Broccoli Directed by Lewis Gilbert
Screenplay by Christopher Wood Music by John Barry Lyrics by Hal David
Production Design by Ken Adam Executive Producer Michael G. Wilson
Associate Producer William P. Cartlidge Title Song Performed by Shirley Bassey
Filmed in Panavision® United Artists A Transamerica Company

The eleventh EON James Bond film, made at the height of the worldwide science-fiction craze brought on by the success of *Star Wars* (1977), remains the most fantasy-laden Bond adventure ever. Its scope, scale, and sense of spectacle provided unique challenges to the Bond team.

At the end of *The Spy Who Loved Me* (1977), the title card announced James Bond would return in *For Your Eyes Only*. Within weeks of the release, producer Albert R. "Cubby" Broccoli and United Artists felt Bond's next adventure should be an adaptation of Ian Fleming's third novel, *Moonraker*. The concept was simple: take James Bond into space. Realizing that *Moonraker* could be made to coincide with the launch of the first NASA space shuttle, Broccoli declared he wanted *Moonraker* to be "science fact," not science fiction.

As with all the Bond films since *Live And Let Die* (1973), the script flowed from extensive location scouting. When Broccoli visited Brazil during the opening of *The Spy Who Loved Me*, his hosts took him to Iguazu Falls. Broccoli decided that the next Bond film would shoot in Brazil taking advantage of the unique opportunities provided by the location. The creative team returned, dreaming up a scene to take place during the Rio Carnival.

For financial reasons, Broccoli decided to move the production of *Moonraker* from Pinewood to Paris. With an early draft of the script in hand, production designer Ken Adam agreed this was feasible, but suggested that Broccoli book every studio in Paris to house the film. For months, the French film industry came to a standstill as *Moonraker* monopolized the stages and studio crafts departments.

Broccoli's desire to make, as executive producer Michael G. Wilson termed it, "an extravagant film" brought on a flurry of expensive scenes and ideas, not all of which could be included. A scene with microlight jets ended up being reworked for *Octopussy* (1983). Another scene at the Eiffel Tower was dropped, only to be transformed into the spectacular base jump in *A View To A Kill* (1985).

One element that could not be dropped was the climax in space. Broccoli turned to visual effects supervisor Derek Meddings to solve the problem. With limited time available, Meddings proposed a risky plan to create all the effects in the camera by shooting one element, winding back the film, and then shooting the next.

When the numbers came in, Broccoli discovered this film would cost more than twice the amount of any previous Bond film. Looking at the profits of *The Spy Who Loved Me*, both Broccoli and United Artists signed off. Never had more been riding on one of 007's cinematic adventures.

For the opening sequence, Michael G. Wilson wanted Bond to be pushed from a plane without a parachute. Locating some of the best parachutists in the world, the filmmakers overcame two problems: how to hide the parachutes and how to mount a 35mm camera on a helmet that would not injure the cameraman when his chute opened. Wilson and second unit director and editor John Glen traveled to California to film the sequence using an ultra-light titanium camera body and an experimental plastic Panavision lens, capturing amazing footage.

The filmmakers cast French actor Michael Lonsdale as Hugo Drax, American actress Lois Chiles as Dr. Holly Goodhead, and French actress Corinne Clery as Corinne Dufour. To play Drax's henchman Chang, the filmmakers cast Michael G. Wilson's aikido teacher, Toshiro Suga. Following his popularity in *The Spy Who Loved Me*, Richard Kiel returned as Jaws. Sadly, *Moonraker* would prove to be the last Bond film to feature Bernard Lee as M.

Filming was an endurance test, with complex shooting across the globe. In Brazil, stuntman Richard Graydon hurled himself over the edge of a cable car for a shot that took everyone's breath away. At Iguazu Falls, neither Bond's speedboat nor the hang glider could be filmed properly for the sequence, requiring miniatures to be built in England. In Venice, careful negotiations took place to allow the high-speed boat chase through the centuries-old canals. In France, weightless sequences required days of rigging wires for over a dozen performers.

DEREK MEDDINGS

Both parents of Derek Meddings worked for producer Alexander Korda; his father was a master carpenter, and his mother was a stand-in for actress Merle Oberon. Born in 1931, Meddings attended art school and, after a stint in the RAF, tried to break into the film industry. He eventually landed a job at Denham Labs creating movie titles and met matte painter Les Bowie. Bowie took him under his wing, and Meddings worked as a matte painter until he discovered that he was slightly color-blind. However, by then, he had discovered a talent for building miniatures.

While working with Bowie at Bray Studios, Meddings began moonlighting for TV producer Gerry Anderson in the evenings, painting backdrops and doing special effects work. Anderson soon had a hit with the *Thunderbirds* television series, and Meddings was busier than ever.

Meddings later did special effects for Anderson's feature film *Doppelgänger* (aka Journey To The Far Side Of The Sun, 1969). Next came *UFO* (1970), a live-action TV series. When that ended, Meddings returned to film work.

Production designer Syd Cain recommended Meddings to the Bond producers, and he soon began what would become a six-film affiliation with James Bond. He was responsible for the exploding poppy fields in *Live And Let Die* (1973); the destruction of Scaramanga's island for *The Man With The Golden Gun* (1974); the extensive models built for *The Spy Who Loved Me* (1977); the outer space models and effects for *Moonraker* (1979); and he created the illusion of Roger Moore and Carole Bouquet's underwater scenes in *For Your Eyes Only* (1981). He won an Oscar for his work on 1978's *Superman* and was nominated for *Moonraker*. He returned to Bond with *GoldenEye* (1995), where he did extensive miniature work.

Sadly, Meddings died from cancer before the film's premiere. *GoldenEye* is dedicated to his memory.

The pressure on Derek Meddings and his crew at Pinewood was great. Hundreds of effects shots needed to be completed. Meddings and his team created dozens of models of space shuttles, the space station, and space debris customized for each individual shot. Any mistakes meant starting again. For one shot of the space battle, a single piece of film endured 48 exposures. The slightest lens flare or speck of dirt would have ruined the work. To create the effect of the space station disintegrating, the team obtained two shotguns, closed the stage at Pinewood, and blew the model part. The effects work earned Meddings an Oscar nomination.

John Barry returned to the series to score the film. Shirley Bassey once again sang the title song, which featured lyrics by Hal David. *Moonraker* marked the last time the "007 Theme" would be heard in a John Barry Bond score, and Barry's use of it in the boat chase sequence is magisterial.

Moonraker's technical achievements and sense of grandeur make it a memorable addition to the Bond canon. The film broke numerous box-office records upon its release in the summer of 1979. *Moonraker* literally took 007 to new heights, but it also signaled a close to an era of introducing elements of science-fiction fantasy into the world of James Bond.

FOR YOUR EYES ONLY
(1981)

CAST Roger Moore (James Bond), Carole Bouquet (Melina Havelock), Topol (Columbo), Lynn-Holly Johnson (Bibi Dahl), Julian Glover (Kristatos), Cassandra Harris (Countess Lisl Von Schlaf), Jill Bennett (Jacoba Brink), Michael Gothard (Emile Locque), John Wyman (Kriegler), Jack Hedley (Havelock), Lois Maxwell (Moneypenny), Desmond Llewelyn (Q), Walter Gotell (General Gogol), Geoffrey Keen (Minister of Defence), James Villiers (Tanner), John Moreno (Ferrara), Charles Dance (Claus), Paul Angelis (Karageorge), Toby Robins (Iona Havelock), Jack Klaff (Apostis), Alkis Kristikos Santos (Nikos), Stag Theodore (Nikos), Stefan Kalipha (Hector Gonzales), Graham Crowden (First Sea Lord), Noel Johnson (Vice Admiral), William Hoyland (McGregor), Eva Rueber-Staier (Rublevich), Janet Brown (Prime Minister), John Wells (Denis)
PRODUCED BY Albert R. Broccoli
DIRECTED BY John Glen
SCREENPLAY BY Richard Maibaum & Michael G. Wilson
EXECUTIVE PRODUCER Michael G.Wilson
ASSOCIATE PRODUCER Tom Pevsner
MUSIC BY Bill Conti
TITLE SONG performed by Sheena Easton; music by Bill Conti; lyrics by Michael Leeson; produced by Christopher Neil
PRODUCTION DESIGNED BY Peter Lamont
MAIN TITLE DESIGNED BY Maurice Binder
DIRECTOR OF PHOTOGRAPHY Alan Hume
EDITOR John Grover
SPECIAL EFFECTS SUPERVISOR Derek Meddings
PRODUCTION SUPERVISOR Bob Simmonds
PRODUCTION MANAGERS Mara Blaseti, Phil Kohler, Aspa Lambrou
PRODUCTION CONTROLLER Reginald A. Barkshire
PRODUCTION ACCOUNTANT Douglas Noakes
DIRECTOR OF PUBLICITY Charles Juroe
ASSISTANT DIRECTOR Anthony Waye
CAMERA OPERATOR Alec Mills
VISUAL EFFECTS PHOTOGRAPHY Paul Wilson
CONTINUITY Elaine Schreyeck
SOUND MIXER Derek Ball
ART DIRECTOR John Fenner
SET DECORATOR Vernon Dixon
ACTION SEQUENCES Bob Simmons
DRIVING STUNTS Rémy Julienne
2ND UNIT DIRECTION & PHOTOGRAPHY Arthur Wooster, BSC
UNDERWATER PHOTOGRAPHY Al Giddings
AERIAL PHOTOGRAPHY James Devis
SKI PHOTOGRAPHY Willy Bogner
UNIT AND LOCATION MANAGERS Vincent Winter, Peter Bennett, Michaelis Lamrinos, Redmond Morris, Umberto Sambuco
2ND UNIT ASSISTANT DIRECTOR Gerry Gavigan
2ND UNIT CONTINUITY Phyllis Townshend
2ND ASSISTANT DIRECTORS Terry Madden, Michael Zimbrich, Gareth Tandy, Tony Broccoli
CASTING BY Maude Spector & Deborah McWilliams
COSTUME DESIGNER Elizabeth Waller
WARDROBE MASTER Tiny Nicholls
MAKEUP George Frost & Eric Allwright
HAIRDRESSERS Stephanie Kaye & Marsha Lewis
SPECIAL EFFECTS John Evans

Following *Moonraker*'s enormous success, producers Albert R. "Cubby" Broccoli and Michael G. Wilson decided it was time to bring 007 back to earth and closer to Ian Fleming's conception of the character.

Although Broccoli had considered producing non-007 features from time to time, including *The Detective* in 1979, he decided to stick with James Bond. To help shape the 12th 007 adventure, Broccoli brought back Bond screenwriting veteran Richard Maibaum, who began collaborating with Michael G. Wilson. For inspiration they turned to Fleming's short stories, *For Your Eyes Only* and *Risico*, as well as an unused keelhauling scene from the novel *Live And Let Die*, which was originally scripted to follow the cable car sequence in *Moonraker*.

To direct the new film, Broccoli turned to Bond editor and second unit director alumnus John Glen. With Roger Moore on board, attention turned to casting. Publicity director Charles "Jerry" Juroe recommended French actress Carole Bouquet for the revenge-seeking Melina Havelock. Broccoli's wife, Dana, suggested Israeli-born actor Topol of *Fiddler On The Roof* fame for pistachio-chewing rogue Columbo. American ice-skating champion and actress Lynn-Holly Johnson took the role of Olympic hopeful Bibi Dahl. British actor Julian Glover, once considered for the role of Bond, starred as the villainous Kristatos. British actress Jill Bennett, who starred in the early Broccoli production *Hell Below Zero* (1954), portrayed Bibi's coach Brink.

Budgeted at $28 million, *For Your Eyes Only* began filming on September 15, 1980 at the Villa Sylva at Kanoni above Corfu Town, which doubled as the villa of hitman Gonzales. Nearby, driving-stunts arranger Rémy Julienne and second unit director Arthur Wooster filmed a thrilling, gadget-free car chase involving Melina's Citroen 2CV.

When it came time to film Locque's Mercedes sliding off a cliff, Moore debated with Michael G. Wilson and John Glen how best to complete the scene. Should Bond just drop an incriminating pin to tip the balance? Or should Bond kick the car over the edge? The filmmakers chose to have Bond deliver the kick, signaling a harder-edged interpretation of the role.

Filming moved to the Meteora region of Greece, where Bond scales the mountain to the monastery hideout used by Kristatos. The local monks tried to disrupt filming by hanging their laundry from the windows. This didn't stop the filmmakers from shooting the sequence, in which Kristatos henchman Apostis kicks Bond over a cliff. Climber Rick Sylvester, doubling Moore, performed a 300 ft (91.4 m) fall from the mountain, and special effects wizard Derek Meddings built a 30-ft (9-m) trough partially filled with sandbags to ease the jarring impact on his body as the climbing rope pulled taut. To capture the death of Apostis, Glen filmed an empty patch of ground and then cut to a shot of actor Jack Klaff lying on the ground. With a harsh sound effect, it created the effect of Apostis violently hitting the ground.

Back in England, Glen filmed the remote-controlled helicopter pre-credits sequence at Becton Gas Works in East London. The idea for the scene originated one day when he saw a technician's son playing with a remote-controlled car at Pinewood Studios.

New Year arrived with mixed emotions. Beloved actor Bernard Lee proved too ill to shoot his scenes as M, so the filmmakers, hopeful that Lee would eventually recover, brought in James Villiers to play Tanner for the film. Sadly, Lee passed away shortly afterwards.

When the crew arrived in the Italian Alpine resort of Cortina d'Ampezzo, they discovered the town and mountains

in the midst of a snow drought. Twenty-five truckloads of virgin snow had to be brought in for the street scenes. Ski champion and filmmaker Willy Bogner returned for his third Bond film. Using a pair of skis that allowed him to ski both forward and backward, Bogner filmed breathtaking action. Actor John Wyman, playing ski champion Erich Kriegler, spent many hours learning the sport to convincingly play the role.

Another challenge occurred when the production team learned Carole Bouquet wasn't comfortable filming underwater. Again, Derek Meddings came to the rescue. Bouquet and Moore filmed on a dry sound stage with wind machines. Meddings then wound the film back in the camera, and superimposed bubbles onto the film negative.

ALBERT R. BROCCOLI
presents

ROGER MOORE
as
IAN FLEMING'S

JAMES BOND 007
in

FOR YOUR EYES ONLY

Starring CAROLE BOUQUET · TOPOL · LYNN-HOLLY JOHNSON · JULIAN GLOVER
Produced by ALBERT R. BROCCOLI · Directed by JOHN GLEN
Screenplay by RICHARD MAIBAUM and MICHAEL G. WILSON · Executive Producer MICHAEL G. WILSON
Music by BILL CONTI · Production Designer PETER LAMONT
Associate Producer TOM PEVSNER · PANAVISION® · TECHNICOLOR®
United Artists

Title Song Performed by SHEENA EASTON

THE EYES HAVE IT *(clockwise, starting below) Roger Moore (James Bond) and his son Christian during production; Moore gives Lynn-Holly Johnson (Bibi Dahl) a hug during rehearsals at the indoor ice rink at Cortina d'Ampezzo; Maurice Binder directs the title sequence with singer Sheena Easton; Al Giddings and his crew work on the Greek temple set off the coast of the Bahamas; Albert R. Broccoli, Sheena Easton, John Glen, and Michael G. Wilson pose for a publicity photo following the announcement that Easton would sing the film's title song; Roger Moore and Carole Bouquet (Melina Havelock) share a joke during a break on location in Cortina.*

Bill Conti composed and recorded the title song with Scottish singer Sheena Easton, who became the only singer to date to appear in the main titles. Easton scored a major hit on both sides of the Atlantic (#4 in the US; #8 in the UK), and the song earned an Academy Award nomination. Conti's score employed a bazouki, a Greek-Turkish stringed instrument, to add an ethnic flavor to several tracks.

For Your Eyes Only set a new direction for James Bond in the 1980s: less fantasy-laden and based upon more realistic premises. The film proved a major success during the summer of 1981.

BOB SIMMONS

Born in Fulham, London, in 1933, Bob Simmons first teamed with Bond producer Albert R. Broccoli on the film *The Red Beret* (1953). He became a legend in the world of film action stunts; his work on many Bond films, from *Dr. No* (1962) to *A View To A Kill* (1985), raised the bar for fight and action scenes.

Simmons holds the distinction of being the first actor to portray 007 on the big screen, as it is he who appears in the famed gun barrel opening at the beginning of *Dr. No*. Simmons did not work on *From Russia With Love* (1963), but his work on *Goldfinger* (1964) through *You Only Live Twice* (1967) contained innovative and exciting stunts seamlessly designed to make audiences believe that Sean Connery himself was taking incredible risks. A double high-fall at the Japanese Kobe docks in *You Only Live Twice* illustrates the stunt arranger's skill. When Simmons disappears behind a container for a fraction of a second, Connery steps into view to replace him.

Bob Simmons' preparation and skill helped save him when an explosion blew through the back of Count Lippe's Ford Skyliner in *Thunderball* (1965). Simmons kept his cool as flames poured into the driver's compartment, hurling himself out at the last moment to ensure not only his safety but also that director Terence Young got the shot.

Simmons passed away in 1988, but his legacy of hard-hitting action and stunts done for real lives on in the Bond films to this day.

DRY RUN *Bob Simmons rehearses with Roger Moore and stuntman Tom Haggerty in Greece while shooting* For Your Eyes Only.

OCTOPUSSY
(1983)

CAST Roger Moore (James Bond), Maud Adams (Octopussy), Louis Jourdan (Kamal Khan), Kristina Wayborn (Magda), Kabir Bedi (Gobinda), Steven Berkoff (General Orlov), David Meyer (Mischka), Tony Meyer (Grischka), Vijay Amritraj (Vijay) Desmond Llewelyn ("Q"), Robert Brown ("M"), Walter Gotell (Gogol), Geoffrey Keen (Minister of Defence), Suzanne Jerome (Gwendoline), Cherry Gillespie (Midge), Albert Moses (Sadruddin), Douglas Wilmer (Fanning), Andy Bradford (009), Lois Maxwell (Miss Moneypenny), Michaela Clavell (Penelope Smallbone), Philip Voss (Auctioneer), Bruce Boa (US General), Richard Parmentier (US aide), Paul Hardwick (Soviet Chairman), (Dermot Crowley (Kamp), Peter Porteous (Lenkin), Eva Rueber-Staier (Rublevich), Tina Hudson (Bianca), William Derrick (Thug with yo-yo), Stuart Saunders (Major Clive), Ken Norris (Colonel Toro), Gabor Vernon (Borchoi), Tony Arjuna (Mufti)
PRODUCED BY Albert R. Broccoli
DIRECTED BY John Glen
SCREEN STORY AND SCREENPLAY BY George MacDonald Fraser and Richard Maibaum & Michael G. Wilson
EXECUTIVE PRODUCEr Michael G. Wilson
ASSOCIATE PRODUCER Thomas Pevsner
MUSIC COMPOSED AND CONDUCTED BY John Barry
THE SONG "All Time High," performed by Rita Coolidge; music by John Barry; lyrics by Tim Rice
PRODUCTION DESIGNED BY Peter Lamont
MAIN TITLE DESIGNER Maurice Binder
DIRECTOR OF PHOTOGRAPHY Alan Hume
SUPERVISING EDITOR John Grover
SPECIAL EFFECTS SUPERVISOR John Richardson
2ND UNIT DIRECTOR AND PHOTOGRAPHER Arthur Wooster
COSTUME DESIGNER Emma Porteous
CASTING Debbie McWilliams
PRODUCTION SUPERVISOR Hugh Harlow
PRODUCTION MANAGERS Philip Kohler, Barrie Osborne, Leonhard Gmür, Gerry Levy
PRODUCTION ACCOUNTANT Douglas Noakes
ASSISTANT DIRECTOR Anthony Waye
CAMERA OPERATOR Alec Mills
CAMERA GRIPS W.C. "Chunky" Huse, Colin Manning
SOUND RECORDIST Derek Ball
CONTINUITY Elaine Schreyeck
ACTION SEQUENCES ARRANGED BY Bob Simmons
DRIVING STUNTS ARRANGED BY Rémy Julienne
AERIAL TEAM DIRECTOR Phil Wrestler
ART DIRECTOR John Fenner
SET DECORATOR Jack Stephens
MAKEUP SUPERVISOR George Frost
HAIRDRESSING SUPERVISOR Christopher Taylor
PRODUCTION CONTROLLER Reginald A. Barkshire
DIRECTOR OF PUBLICITY Charles Juroe
EDITORS Peter Davies, Henry Richardson
SOUND EDITOR Colin Miller
LOCATION MANAGERS Peter Bennett, Rashid Abassi
2ND UNIT ASSISTANT DIRECTOR Gerry Gavigan
ADDITIONAL ASSISTANT DIRECTORS Baba Shaikh, Don French
EXECUTIVE ASSISTANT Barbara Broccoli

In 1967, *You Only Live Twice* beat the spoof version of *Casino Royale* at the box office by advertising "Sean Connery IS James Bond." In 1983, producers Albert R. "Cubby" Broccoli and Michael G. Wilson faced another rival Bond film, *Never Say Never Again*, but this time the rivals had Connery. *Octopussy* rose to the challenge, exciting audiences worldwide with a winning mixture of audacity, romantic adventure, humor, and suspense.

Scripting for *Octopussy* began with a new Bond writer, George MacDonald Fraser, author of the Flashman novels. His first draft included a pre-titles sequence set at the Isle of Man Tourist Trophy car races as well as a story based in India. Richard Maibaum and Wilson rewrote Fraser's script, retaining some of his ideas, including a deadly yo-yo buzz saw and Bond evading capture by hiding in a gorilla suit.

John Glen returned to direct hi[s]
with Roger Moore agreeing to te[
focus shifted to casting other role[s]
Adams as Octopussy, bringing he[r]
starring role in a Bond film. Fren[ch]
friend of Broccoli's, secured the r[
Swedish actress Kristina Wayborn[.]
Garbo in a television mini-series,[
George MacDonald Fraser sugges[ted]
Bedi for Khan's henchman Gobin[
crazed Soviet General Orlov, Bar[
British actor/director Steven Ber[
Los Angeles. Moore recommende[d]
co-star from the television series [
his daughter Deborah, for the cru[

great tennis fan, cast Davis Cup champion Vijay Amritraj in his screen debut as Bond's Indian contact, Vijay.

Second unit and aerial unit work on *Octopussy* began weeks before principle photography, with *Moonraker* skydiving experts B. J. Worth, Jake Lombard and cameraman Randy DeLuca filming a mid-air fight on top of Kamal Khan's Beech 18 airplane. In addition, J. W. "Corkey" Fornof piloted his Acrostar Bede jet over Southern Utah for much of the pre-credit sequence. In fact, the Bede jets had originally appeared in an early *Moonraker* script draft. While in Utah, aerial team director Phil Wrestler attempted to film the destruction of Khan's plane for the movie's climax. He projected a full-sized plane along a railroad track and shot it off a cliff, hoping the plane would fall 1,000 ft (304 m) to its destruction. The plane, filled with explosives, leveled out and began flying on its own. Wrestler was horrified that it might fly into Utah State Route 9 but, thankfully, the plane banked and crashed into a nearby gully out of camera range. Special effects supervisor John Richardson subsequently blew up a model plane at Pinewood Studios.

First unit filming then began in West Berlin on August 10, 1982, with production designer Peter Lamont's crew painting a section of the graffiti-covered Berlin Wall to make it look like the East Berlin side. At RAF Northolt in England, the producers shot the Acrostar's trip through a military hangar. John Richardson stripped an old Jaguar down to its chassis and attached a pole from the car to a mock-up of the jet. As the Jaguar sped through the hangar, Glen had soldiers running in front of the car to conceal it. Moore even sat in the cockpit. Richardson then blew up a miniature of the hangar. For the closer shots of the plane and the missile pursuing it, Richardson built a model plane and attached a flaming firework behind it.

To film the Germany train scenes, the team traveled to the Nene Valley Steam Railway near Peterborough, England. For close shots of Moore hanging from the undercarriage of the train, Peter Lamont used an old silent film trick. He had two of the Nene Valley carriages delivered to stages at Pinewood. He suspended the carriages from cranes and placed a looped painting of railway track beneath the rail cars. With Moore hanging on beneath the train, and the painting moving, it appeared the star was really beneath a speeding train.

At the end of September, filming moved to one of the most exotic Bond locations yet, Udaipur, India, where the Maharana rolled out the red carpet for the crew. One of Lamont's most difficult tasks was the creation of Octopussy's barge. He found two derelict ceremonial barges in Bombay, and the Maharana gave permission to destroy both of them to make one working barge. The Maharana also gave the filmmakers permission to film the tiger hunt sequence in his overgrown garden. To create the effect of a tiger leaping out at Bond, Glen borrowed the Maharana's stuffed tiger, had it placed it in a wheelbarrow and then pushed through the bushes at Moore.

ON THE SET *Peter Lamont with his design for Octopussy's bedroom.*

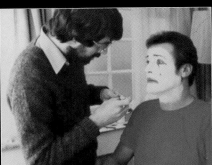

For the tuk-tuk taxi chase, local crowds descended upon the set, much to the distress of the stunt drivers. One man on a bicycle got past the security and rode through a shot that remained in the film.

John Barry returned to compose his ninth Bond film score. He collaborated with Tim Rice on six different songs, and "All Time High" was the one selected by the production team, despite not mentioning the title of the film in its lyrics. Rita Coolidge performed the song, which reached #36 on the US charts.

In the end, production delays caused the rival Connery Bond film, Never Say Never Again to be pushed back to an October 1983 release date. Octopussy premiered in June 1983 and became the biggest Bond film of the 1980s in the US, out-grossing Connery's by a large margin.

DRESSED TO KILL
(clockwise from top)
The crew filming on location in Iceland; Christopher Walken (Max Zorin), Grace Jones (May Day) and producer Michael G. Wilson listen to director John Glen set the scene on the Seine; Broccoli and Moore relax during shooting of the Renault taxi chase in Paris.

A VIEW TO A KILL (1985)

CAST Roger Moore (James Bond), Christopher Walken (Max Zorin), Tanya Roberts (Stacey Sutton), Grace Jones (May Day), Patrick Macnee (Tibbett), Patrick Bauchau (Scarpine), David Yip (Chuck Lee), Fiona Fullerton (Pola Ivanova), Manning Redwood (Bob Conley), Alison Doody (Jenny Flex), Willoughby Gray (Dr. Carl Mortner), Desmond Llewelyn (Q), Robert Brown (M), Lois Maxwell (Miss Moneypenny), Walter Gotell (General Gogol), Geoffrey Keen (Minister of Defence), Jean Rougerie (Achille Aubergine), Daniel Benzali (Howe), Papillon Soo Soo (Pan Ho), Mary Stavin (Kimberley Jones), Dominique Risbourg (Butterfly Act compere), Carole Ashby (Butterfly girl), Lucien Jerome (Paris taxi driver), Joe Flood (SFPD Captain), Bogdan Kominowski (Klotkoff), Dolph Lundgren (Venz)
PRODUCED BY Albert R. Broccoli & Michael G. Wilson
DIRECTOR John Glen
SCREENPLAY BY Richard Maibaum & Michael G. Wilson
ASSOCIATE PRODUCER Thomas Pevsner
MUSIC COMPOSED AND CONDUCTED BY John Barry
TITLE SONG performed by Duran Duran composed by Duran Duran and John Barry produced by Bernard Edwards
PRODUCTION DESIGNED BY Peter Lamont
MAIN TITLE DESIGNED BY Maurice Binder
DIRECTOR OF PHOTOGRAPHY Alan Hume
2ND UNIT DIRECTOR & PHOTOGRAPHER Arthur Wooster, BSC
SKI SEQUENCES DIRECTED & PHOTOGRAPHED BY Willy Bogner
COSTUMES Emma Porteous
CASTING Debbie McWilliams
EDITOR Peter Davies
SOUND EDITOR Colin Miller
SPECIAL EFFECTS SUPERVISOR John Richardson
PRODUCTION SUPERVISOR Anthony Waye
PRODUCTION MANAGERS Philip Kohler, Serge Touboul, Leonhard Gmür, Ned Kopp & Company, Jón Thor Hannesson
UNIT MANAGER Iris Rose
PRODUCTION ACCOUNTANT Douglas Noakes
ASSISTANT DIRECTOR Gerry Gavigan
CAMERA OPERATOR Michael Frift
SOUND RECORDIST Derek Ball
CONTINUITY June Randall
ELECTRICAL SUPERVISOR John Tythe
ACTION SEQUENCE ARRANGER Martin Grace
DRIVING STUNTS ARRANGER Rémy Julienne
ART DIRECTOR John Fenner
SET DECORATOR Crispian Sallis
CONSTRUCTION MANAGER Michael Redding
MAKEUP SUPERVISOR George Frost
HAIRDRESSING SUPERVISOR Ramon Gow
PRODUCTION CONTROLLER Reginald A. Barkshire
DIRECTOR OF MARKETING Charles Juroe
LOCATION MANAGERS Nick Daubeny, Agust Baldursson, Stefan Zürcher, Jean-Marc Deschamps, Steph Benseman, Rory Enke
2ND UNIT ASSISTANT DIRECTOR Peter Bennett
2ND UNIT CONTINUITY Penny Daniels, Daphne Carr
ADDITIONAL ASSISTANT DIRECTORS Edi Hubschmid, Laurent Bregeat, Serge Menard, Terry Madden, Andrew Warren, Simon Haveland, Nick Heckstall-Smith, Barbara Broccoli

A View To A Kill marked the end of Roger Moore's 12-year tenure as Bond. The film's blend of humor and action exemplifies the qualities Moore brought to the role. Richard Maibaum and Michael G. Wilson returned to co-write their third Bond film. It was Wilson's idea to set the film's story around Silicon Valley, and the pair decided to have the villain attempt to destroy this high-tech center by flooding the San Andreas Fault and creating a double earthquake.

To flesh out the script, the writers looked to unused ideas from previous Bond films. One such idea came from *Moonraker* (1979) and involved a poisonous bee brooch killing Bond's contact at the Eiffel Tower's Le Jules Verne Restaurant. For this film, director John Glen suggested the deadly insect should be a butterfly marionette.

The producers cast Oscar-winner Christopher Walken as Max Zorin, chose Tanya Roberts to play geologist Stacey Sutton, signed disco diva Grace Jones as the villainous May

In August, filming began in Paris. To perform May Day's jump off the Eiffel Tower, parachute/skydiving expert B. J. Worth made 22 test jumps from a hot-air balloon. When, after lengthy negotiations, the French authorities finally approved the stunt, a man and woman suddenly parachuted off the Eiffel Tower. The production team worried that the authorities might revoke their permission, but the thrillseekers actually showed that the jump could be performed safely. B. J. Worth successfully executed the stunt in a single take with numerous cameras rolling, creating one of the iconic images from the film. Filming continued at Chantilly Chateau outside Paris. The Silver Cloud Rolls-Royce driven by Patrick Macnee in the film actually belonged to Broccoli. When it came time to sink the Rolls back in England, the crew used a duplicate car.

After filming at the Amberley Chalk Pits Museum in West Sussex, which served as the exterior to Zorin's mine, the production moved to San Francisco. Mayor Dianne Feinstein gave the crew unprecedented permission to film in the city, including simulating a real fire at City Hall and capturing a fire truck chase over three weeks of night shooting.

For the film's climactic battle atop the Golden Gate Bridge, action sequence arranger Martin Grace supervised shots of stuntmen fighting on one of the main suspension cables. With two VistaVision cameras, the crew filmed plate shots to be used in the studio. At Pinewood, Lamont built full-scale replicas of the bridge. Front projectionist Charles Staffel projected the VistaVision footage below the actors on the studio floor. Editor Peter Davies then assembled location, model, and studio shots into a seamless whole.

The production celebrated the rebuilding of the 007 Stage on January 7, 1985. At a special ceremony, Pinewood renamed

Day, and awarded the role of Bond's ally Sir Godfrey Tibbett to Patrick Macnee, star of *The Avengers* television series.

Ski unit director Willy Bogner's plans to film the Siberian pre-titles sequence in Scotland ended when, after five weeks of planning, the snow melted. Bogner turned to alternative locations in Iceland and Switzerland. In Iceland, it took the production team three tries before they successfully crashed the model helicopter into a glacier.

In June 1984, disaster struck: the 007 soundstage at Pinewood Studios burned down during production of *Legend* (1985). EON Productions set about rebuilding the stage, but this meant that production designer Peter Lamont's mine set could not be completed until the end of the shooting schedule. Any delay would mean postponing the film's release.

it the Albert R. Broccoli 007 Stage in honor of the producer's contribution to the British film industry.

John Barry returned to compose his tenth Bond film score. John Taylor of the rock group Duran Duran asked Broccoli if the group could create the title song. Broccoli agreed, and Duran Duran, working with Barry, created the most successful Bond movie theme to date, hitting #1 on the US charts and reaching #2 in the UK

A View To A Kill marked the end of an era for the Bond series. After this, his seventh film as James Bond, Roger Moore stepped aside from the role. His tremendously successful tenure brought legions of fans to the series, making 007 just as much a popular culture icon of the 1970s and 1980s as he had been in the 1960s.

HAS JAMES BOND FINALLY MET HIS MATCH?

ALBERT R. BROCCOLI Presents

ROGER MOORE
as IAN FLEMING's

JAMES BOND 007

A VIEW TO A KILL

Starring TANYA ROBERTS · GRACE JONES · PATRICK MACNEE
and CHRISTOPHER WALKEN Music by JOHN BARRY Production Designer PETER LAMONT
Associate Producer TOM PEVSNER Produced by ALBERT R. BROCCOLI and MICHAEL G. WILSON
Directed by JOHN GLEN Screenplay by RICHARD MAIBAUM and MICHAEL G. WILSON

JOHN BARRY

John Barry created the musical sound of James Bond. His arrangement and orchestration of "The James Bond Theme" combined his own twangy-guitar signature (from his earlier career as leader of the British rock-instrumental group The John Barry Seven) with a jazzy big-band kick. Recurring throughout *Dr. No* (1962), it guaranteed Barry's subsequent involvement with 007.

Barry's innovative approach combined pop, jazz, and classical styles to create a genre of movie music that was exciting, romantic, and suspenseful. After he scored the next Bond film, *From Russia With Love* (1963), *Goldfinger* (1964) became the first of many Bond films for which Barry wrote title song and score.

He was born John Barry Prendergast in York, England, in 1933. His father ran a chain of theaters, and Barry gravitated toward a career that combined movies and music. While on national service in the early 1950s, Barry studied playing the trumpet, via a correspondence course, with famed Stan Kenton arranger Bill Russo. By the late 1950s, he was a prominent figure on the British rock 'n' roll scene. His group backed the popular singer Adam Faith, and Barry duly supplied the music for Faith's film debut, *Beat Girl* (1960). Barry's future as a film composer was assured.

Barry composed the scores for 11 Bond films (and, with *Dr. No*, contributed to a 12th). He continually updated his style, incorporating a Moog synthesizer in *On Her Majesty's Secret Service* (1969) and the rock sounds of The Pretenders on 1987's *The Living Daylights*. He collaborated with top pop vocalists and bands, from Shirley Bassey (*Goldfinger*, 1971's *Diamonds Are Forever*, 1979's *Moonraker*) to Duran Duran (*A View To A Kill*, 1985) and a-ha (*The Living Daylights*, 1987); and established a musical framework for Bond to which composers David Arnold and Thomas Newman adhere to this day.

Beyond Bond, Barry's film career encompassed many significant films. He won Academy Awards for *Born Free* (1966, song and score), *The Lion In Winter* (1968), *Out Of Africa* (1985) and *Dances With Wolves* (1990). He sadly passed away in 2011.

THREE POINTS OF VIEW *(below, left to right) Director John Glen on the set; director of marketing Charles "Jerry" Juroe. Princess Diana attends the London premiere of A View To A Kill, meeting members of Duran Duran who performed the film's title song.*

THE LIVING DAYLIGHTS
(1987)

CAST Timothy Dalton (James Bond), Maryam d'Abo (Kara Milovy), Jeroen Krabbe (General Georgi Koskov), Joe Don Baker (Brad Whitaker), John Rhys-Davies (General Leonid Pushkin), Art Malik (Kamran Shah), Andreas Wisniewski (Necros), Thomas Wheatley (Saunders), Desmond Llewelyn (Q), Robert Brown (M), Geoffrey Keen (Minister of Defense), Walter Gotell (General Gogol), John Terry (Felix Leiter), Caroline Bliss (Miss Moneypenny), Nadim Sawalha (Chief of Security, Tangier), Virginia Hey (Rubavitch), John Bowe (Col. Feyador), Julie T. Wallace (Rosika Miklos), Kell Tyler (Linda), Catherine Rabett (Liz), Dulice Liecier (Ava), Carl Rigg (Imposter 00 Agent), Tony Cyrus (Chief of Snow Leopard Brotherhood), Ken Sharrock (Jailer) Frederick Warder (004), Glyn Baker (002)
PRODUCED BY Albert R. Broccoli & Michael G. Wilson
DIRECTOR John Glen
SCREENPLAY BY
Richard Maibaum & Michael G. Wilson
ASSOCIATE PRODUCERS
Tom Pevsner & Barbara Broccoli
TITLE SONG performed by a-ha; composed by Pal Waaktaar and John Barry; produced by Jason Corsaro, a-ha, and John Barry
SONGS "Where Has Everybody Gone?" & "If There Was A Man" performed by The Pretenders; music by John Barry; lyrics by Chrissie Hynde; produced by John Barry and Paul O'Duffy
MUSIC COMPOSED AND CONDUCTED BY John Barry
PRODUCTION DESIGNER Peter Lamont
MAIN TITLE DESIGNED BY Maurice Binder
DIRECTOR OF PHOTOGRAPHY Alec Mills
2ND UNIT DIRECTOR & PHOTOGRAPHER Arthur Wooster, BSC
COSTUME DESIGNER Emma Porteous
CASTING Debbie McWilliams
EDITORS John Grover & Peter Davies
SOUND EDITOR Colin Miller
SPECIAL EFFECTS SUPERVISOR John Richardson
PRODUCTION SUPERVISOR Anthony Waye
PRODUCTION ACCOUNTANT Douglas Noakes
DIRECTOR OF MARKETING Charles Juroe
PRODUCTION MANAGERS Philip Kohler, Sparky Greene, Arno Ortmair, Leonhard Gmür, Denise O'Dell
UNIT MANAGER Iris Rose
ASSISTANT DIRECTOR Gerry Gavigan
CAMERA OPERATOR Michael Frift
SOUND RECORDIST Derek Ball
CONTINUITY June Randall
ELECTRICAL SUPERVISOR John Tythe
STUNT SUPERVISOR Paul Weston
DRIVING STUNTS ARRANGER Rémy Julienne
AERIAL STUNTS ARRANGER B. J. Worth
ART DIRECTOR Terry Ackland-Snow
SET DECORATOR Michael Ford
CONSTRUCTION MNGR. Anthony Graysmark
MAKEUP SUPERVISOR George Frost
HAIRDRESSING SUPERVISOR Ramon Gow
PRODUCTION CONTROLLER
Reginald A. Barkshire
LOCATION MANAGERS Nick Daubeny, John Bernard, Arie Bohrer, Stefan Zuercher, Driss Gaidi
ACTION UNIT ASSISTANT DIR. Terry Madden
ACTION UNIT CONTINUITY Jean Bourne
ADDITONAL ASSISTANT DIRS. Callum McDougall, Crispin Reece, Nick Heckstall-Smith, Terry Blyther, Urs Egger, Ahmed Hatimi, Mohamed Hassini

MAKING DAYLIGHTS *(below, left to right) Associate producer Barbara Broccoli studies the next shot on location in Weissensee, Austria; Maryam d'Abo (Kara Milovy) discusses a scene with director John Glen at Pinewood Studios; Producer Albert R. Broccoli and Timothy Dalton (James Bond) give a tour of Q's lab set to HRHs Princess Diana and Prince Charles. Desmond Llewelyn (Q), Maryam d'Abo, and John Glen stand in the background.*

The Living Daylights, the 15th Bond film, proved to be a watershed for the series. The film offered insightful moments exploring the character of 007, a sign of the increasing awareness on the part of the filmmakers of the dramatic potential in the James Bond stories.

Once the decision came from producer Albert R. "Cubby" Broccoli to recast the role of James Bond, Michael G. Wilson and Richard Maibaum began hammering out story ideas. The pair initially looked at exploring 007's roots and developed a story involving Bond as a rebellious young naval officer, who lives his life according to the family motto "The World Is Not Enough." Broccoli rejected the concept, feeling audiences wanted to see Bond as a professional, not an amateur. He also felt it was too soon to re-launch the Bond storyline. Wilson and Maibaum turned to the Fleming short story *The Living Daylights* as a launching point for the script. As inspiration for

the character of Koskov, the writers looked to the real-life story of KGB officer Vitaly Yurchenko, who defected to the CIA for a short time in 1985, then re-defected to the Soviet Union. Leadership changes in the Soviet Union helped define the story, and the increasingly grim war in Afghanistan provided a unique setting.

As the script took shape, Bond screen tests continued. With top choice Timothy Dalton unavailable, the producers settled on Pierce Brosnan, but NBC renewed Brosnan's contract to appear in the television series *Remington Steele* at the last moment. With some shifts to the shooting schedule, Dalton was able to take the role.

To fill out the cast, the filmmakers drew together an assortment of international actors. European actress Maryam d'Abo took the role as Czech cellist Kara Milovy. For Russian defector villain Georgi Koskov, the producers cast Dutch

THE NEW JAMES BOND...
LIVING ON THE EDGE

ALBERT R. BROCCOLI
presents
TIMOTHY DALTON
as IAN FLEMING'S
JAMES BOND 007

THE LIVING DAYLIGHTS

PG

STARRING MARYAM d'ABO
OE DON BAKER ART MALIK AND JEROEN KRABBÉ
UCTION DESIGNER PETER LAMONT MUSIC BY JOHN BARRY
IATE PRODUCERS TOM PEVSNER AND BARBARA BROCCOLI
UCED BY ALBERT R. BROCCOLI AND MICHAEL G. WILSON
DIRECTED BY JOHN GLEN
ENPLAY BY RICHARD MAIBAUM AND MICHAEL G. WILSON

DESIGNS FOR LIVING
(above and left) Art
department concept
drawing of Bond's new
Aston Martin; a sketch
by costume designer
Emma Porteous of an
elegant evening gown for
Kara Milovy.

actor Jeroen Krabbe, who had previously impressed them in the film *Soldier Of Orange* (1979). American actor Joe Don Baker of *Walking Tall* (1973) fame landed the role of arms dealer Brad Whitaker. The filmmakers originally hoped series regular Walter Gotell could play a larger role as KGB chief General Gogol, but health insurance restrictions led to the creation of a new KGB chief, General Pushkin. Welsh character actor John Rhys-Davies took the part. Caroline Bliss also landed the role of Miss Moneypenny.

Second unit filming began on Gibraltar on September 17, 1986. When Dalton later joined the Gibraltar second unit, he impressed everyone by performing many of his own stunts atop a speeding Land Rover.

Production quickly moved to Vienna, where a major press conference introduced the new James Bond to the world. Glen and his crew filmed in the Viennese opera houses, the Volksopera and the Schönbrunn Palace concert hall. Glen also shot at the Prater Amusement Park, the scene of the memorable confrontation between Orson Welles and Joseph Cotton in the classic thriller, *The Third Man* (1949), on which Glen had been a junior editor.

In the US, above California's Mojave Desert, parachute experts B. J. Worth and Jake Lombard filmed the fight sequence in which a cargo net falls out of the back of a plane in flight with Bond and henchman Necros hanging on for dear life.

The first unit moved to Morocco, shooting in the Forbes Museum in Tangier, where publisher Malcolm Forbes housed his lavishly detailed dioramas of important battles. They also shot exteriors in the city, including the rooftop chase when Bond eludes the Moroccan police. Filming continued in Ouarzazate, the location doubling for the Soviet airbase in Afghanistan. The film's climactic battle remains the largest ever in a Bond movie.

The crew returned to Pinewood Studios, where Prince Charles and Princess Diana paid a visit to the set in December. Jeroen Krabbe suggested to Diana that she smash a prop bottle over the head of the Prince as a joke. The next day, the picture landed on the front pages of newspapers around the globe.

In Weissensee, Austria, 007's new Aston Martin led a chase on an ice lake. Glen suggested that, at the end of the sequence, Bond and Kara should abandon the crashed car and use Kara's cello case as a sled to escape across the border. Steering the modified case as it sped across the snow became quite a challenge for actress Maryam d'Abo.

Filming wrapped at Pinewood Studios on February 13, 1987. One week later, Broccoli was awarded an honorary Order of the British Empire.

Ray Still, director of Warner Brothers Records, suggested the Norwegian pop trio a-ha, and their title song, written with John Barry, reached #5 in the UK. Barry returned to score his 11th and final film score, writing 57 minutes of music in just four weeks and using a synthesizer to give the score a fresh sound. He also co-wrote two additional songs which The Pretenders performed. Barry fittingly made a cameo as a conductor at the end of the film, an appearance that served as a coda to his career with 007.

The Living Daylights was a worldwide smash when released in the summer of 1987. It proved once again to Cubby Broccoli that the star of the picture is James Bond, not the actor who portrays him.

JOHN GLEN

John Glen holds the record for helming five James Bond films, the most of any director. He is responsible for bringing a more realistic, espionage-driven feel to the films.

Born on May 15, 1932, in Sunbury-on-Thames, England, Glen began work in the film industry as a messenger at Shepperton Studios under director Alexander Korda. In 1947, he worked as a runner in the cutting room and then as an assembly editor on such films as *The Third Man* (1949) and *The Wooden Horse* (1950). After two years in the Royal Air Force, he entered the business once again as a sound editor. Glen then worked his way up to second unit director and editor on such British television series as *Danger Man* and *Man In A Suitcase*.

Peter Hunt, director of *On Her Majesty's Secret Service* (1969), gave Glen the opportunity of a lifetime to direct second unit and edit the film. They had been assistants in the editing room at Shepperton Studios. His work on the bob-run sequence for *OHMSS* greatly impressed Bond producer Albert R. "Cubby" Broccoli.

Throughout the 1970s, Glen's services as a second unit director and editor were in constant demand on such films as *Murphy's War* (1971), *Catlow* (1971), *Gold* (1974), *Shout At The Devil* (1976), *The Wild Geese* (1978), the Bond film *Moonraker* (1979) and *The Sea Wolves* (1980). He also edited the films *Pulp* (1972), *Dead Cert* (1974), and Bond director Lewis Gilbert's *Seven Nights in Japan* (1976). Glen's work on the classic ski parachute jump in *The Spy Who Loved Me* (1977) established him as a master of filming action material.

In 1980, Cubby Broccoli gave Glen the opportunity to make his feature film directing debut with the 12th James Bond film, *For Your Eyes Only*. After that film's enormous success, Glen directed four more Bond films.

Since leaving the series, he has directed the films *Aces: Iron Eagle III* (1992), *Christopher Columbus: The Discovery* (1992), and *The Point Men* (2001).

LICENCE TO KILL (1989)

CAST Timothy Dalton (James Bond), Carey Lowell
(Pam Bouvier), Robert Davi (Franz Sanchez), Talisa
Soto (Lupe Lamora), Anthony Zerbe (Milton Krest),
Frank McRae (Sharkey), Everett McGill (Killifer),
Wayne Newton (Professor Joe Butcher), Benicio del
Toro (Dario), Anthony Starke (Truman-Lodge), Pedro
Armendariz, Jr. (Hector Lopez), Desmond Llewelyn
(Q), David Hedison (Felix Leiter), Priscilla Barnes
(Della Churchill), Robert Brown (M), Caroline Bliss
(Miss Moneypenny), Don Stroud (Heller), Grand L.
Bush (Hawkins), Cary-Hiroyuki Tagawa (Kwang),
Alejandro Bracho (Perez), Guy de Saint Cyr (Braun),
Rafer Johnson (Mullens), Diana Lee-Hsu (Loti),
Christopher Neame (Fallon)
PRODUCED BY
Albert R. Broccoli & Michael G. Wilson
DIRECTED BY John Glen
WRITTEN BY
Michael G. Wilson & Richard Maibaum
ASSOCIATE PRODUCERS
Tom Pevsner & Barbara Broccoli
PRODUCTION DESIGNED BY Peter Lamont
DIRECTOR OF PHOTOGRAPHY Alec Mills
VISUAL EFFECTS John Richardson
ORIGINAL SCORE COMPOSED AND
CONDUCTED BY Michael Kamen; title song lyrics
by Narada Michael Walden, Jeffrey Cohen, Walter
Afanasieff, performed by Gladys Knight
CASTING BY Jane Jenkins & Janet Hirshenson
MAIN TITLE DESIGNED BY Maurice Binder
COSTUME DESIGNER Jodie Tillen
2ND UNIT DIRECTED & PHOTOGRAPHED BY
Arthur Wooster, BSC
EDITOR John Grover
SOUND EDITOR Vernon Messenger
ART DIRECTOR Michael Lamont
SET DECORATOR Michael Ford
CONSTRUCTION MANAGER Tony Graysmark
MAKEUP SUPERVISORS
George Frost & Naomi Donne
HAIRDRESSING SUPERVISOR Tricia Cameron
ELECTRICAL SUPERVISOR John Tythe
CONTINUITY Jean Randall
ASSISTANT DIRS Miguel Gil, Miguel Lima
CAMERA OPERATOR Michael Frift
SOUND RECORDIST Edward Tise
CONTINUITY June Randall
DIRECTOR OF MARKETING Charles Juroe
PRODUCTION SUPERVISOR MEXICO
Hector Lopez
PRODUCTION MANAGER Philip Kohler
UNIT MANAGER Iris Rose
STUNT CO-ORDINATOR Paul Weston
DRIVING STUNTS ARRANGER Rémy Julienne
AERIAL STUNT SUPERVISOR "Corkey" Fornof
PRODUCTION SUPERVISOR Anthony Waye
UNDERWATER SCENES DIRECTED &
PHOTOGRAPHED BY Ramon Bravo
PRODUCTION ACCOUNTANT
Douglas Noakes
PRODUCTION COORDINATOR
Coolee Deleon
2ND ASSISTANT DIRECTOR Callum McDougall
PRODUCTION ASSISTANTS Ignacio Cervantes,
Marcia Perskie, Gerardo Barrera, Monica Greene
PRODUCTION SECRETARY Ileana Franco
ACCOUNTANTS
Jane Meagher, Rosa Maria Gomez
ASSISTANT ACCOUNTANT Andrew Noakes
ASSEMBLY EDITOR Matthew Glen
SOUND EDITORS Peter Musgrave, Mark Auguste

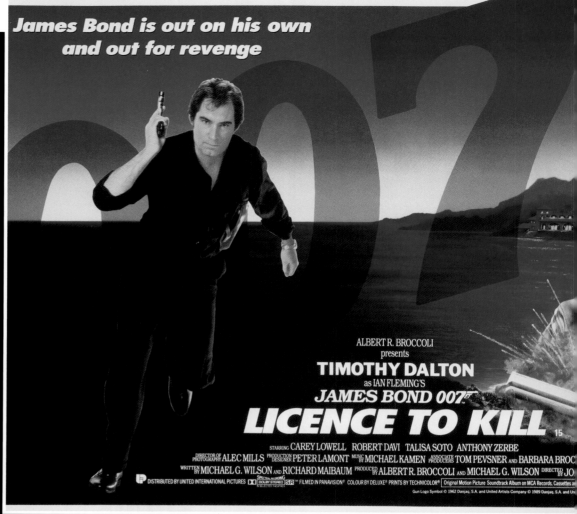

James Bond is out on his own and out for revenge

ALBERT R. BROCCOLI presents TIMOTHY DALTON as IAN FLEMING'S JAMES BOND 007 LICENCE TO KILL 15 STARRING CAREY LOWELL ROBERT DAVI TALISA SOTO ANTHONY ZERBE DIRECTOR OF PHOTOGRAPHY ALEC MILLS PRODUCTION DESIGNER PETER LAMONT MUSIC BY MICHAEL KAMEN ASSOCIATE PRODUCERS TOM PEVSNER AND BARBARA BROC WRITTEN BY MICHAEL G. WILSON AND RICHARD MAIBAUM PRODUCED BY ALBERT R. BROCCOLI AND MICHAEL G. WILSON DIRECTED BY JO DISTRIBUTED BY UNITED INTERNATIONAL PICTURES DOLBY STEREO SR IN SELECTED THEATRES FILMED IN PANAVISION COLOUR BY DELUXE PRINTS BY TECHNICOLOR Original Motion Picture Soundtrack Album on MCA Records, Cassettes an Gun Logo Symbol © 1962 Danjaq, S.A. and United Artists Company © 1989 Danjaq, S.A. and Uni

The success of Timothy Dalton's first Bond film, *The Living Daylights*, led producer Albert R. "Cubby" Broccoli to tailor his 16th 007 film to Dalton's harder-edged persona.

During Fall 1987, the filmmakers went on a recce to China, where they imagined a chase sequence on the Great Wall and a fight scene involving the uncovered terracotta soldiers at Xian. Screenwriter Richard Maibaum and writer/producer Michael G. Wilson wrote two treatments concerning a drug warlord in the Golden Triangle, but plans to film in the country fell through.

The filmmakers soon decided that Mexico provided an array of locations and production services with which they could mount a new incarnation of the film. Wilson and Maibaum recast their story with a Central American drug lord. They chose to shoot the film's interiors at the famed Churubusco Studios in Mexico City. The writers used Milton Krest, a character from Fleming's short story *The Hildebrand Rarity*, as one of the villain's main henchmen. They also took unused scenes from Fleming's novel *Live And Let Die* and incorporated those into the plot.

After Cubby Broccoli and Maibaum saw Robert Davi in the 1988 TV movie *Terrorist on Trial—The U.S. Vs. Salim Ajami*, they decided he would make the perfect Franz Sanchez. Davi researched drug lords and had the script translated into Spanish to learn his lines with the proper cadence. Davi also performed the role of 007 to help audition actresses for the role of Sanchez's mistress, Lupe. Brooklyn-born actress Talisa Soto won the part. Carey Lowell

landed the role of CIA pilot Pam Bouvier, while David Hedison reprised the role of Felix Leiter, which he played in *Live And Let Die*. Future Academy Award-winner Benicio del Toro secured one of his first roles as the knife-wielding henchman Dario. Desmond Llewelyn returned for his largest role ever as Q, providing a welcome sense of familiarity to this darker-than-usual film. Las Vegas entertainer Wayne Newton always wanted to be in a Bond film, and Broccoli cast him as the oily televangelist Professor Joe Butcher. Pedro Armendariz Jr., whose father Pedro Armendariz played Kerim Bey in *From Russia With Love* (1963), portrayed Isthmus City's puppet President Hector Lopez.

Upon arriving in Mexico, production designer Peter Lamont found he needed to totally refurbish the studio to make it operational for a Bond film. Filming began on July 18, 1988, at Churubusco. On August 1st, the production moved to Key West, Florida, where second unit director Arthur Wooster supervised the filming of Bond lassoing Sanchez's plane in mid-air with Jake Lombard doubling Dalton. Special consultants Sparky Greene and Jillian Palenthorpe suggested the sequence involving Bond's escape from the Wavekrest underwater and then via plane to Wilson. Waterskiing champion David Reinhardt doubled for Bond barefoot skiing behind a plane. Skydiving experts Lombard and B. J. Worth, along with aerial supervisor J.W. "Corkey" Fornof, took over for the Cessna plane hijacking. Famed underwater photographer Ramon Bravo filmed the underwater scenes at Isla Mujeres near Cancun, Mexico.

challenge of performing the grueling stuntwork on the dangerous location. The curving road had seen so many fatal accidents that locals claimed the area was cursed. Each accident on the location set off new rounds of speculation as to possible supernatural causes.

During post-production, MGM changed the film's title from *Licence Revoked* to *Licence To Kill*. It became the first Bond film to receive a PG-13 rating in the US and, in many countries, several cuts for violence were made to achieve a more family-friendly rating. In the UK, the film received a 15 certificate, the only James Bond film to receive that rating.

Composer Michael Kamen, hot off the action films *Lethal Weapon* (1987) and *Die Hard* (1988), scored *Licence To Kill*, working closely with Glen to give the film a Bond feel. Soul singer Gladys Knight performed the title song (which reached #6 in the UK), and Patti Labelle sang the end title song "If You Asked Me To," which became a hit for Celine Dion almost three years later.

Despite receiving high test screening ratings, *Licence To Kill* failed to achieve a breakout American audience when it was released during the summer of 1989. Sadly, *Licence To Kill* would prove to be the last Bond film for many veterans of the series: Maurice Binder, Richard Maibaum, John Glen, and Alec Mills.

ADVENTURE IN MEXICO
(top to bottom) Timothy Dalton (James Bond) receives instruction from stunt coordinator Paul Weston and director John Glen; director John Glen on location in the Florida Keys with (from left to right) camera grip W. C. "Chunky" Huse, camera trainee Tom Kopp, camera operator Michael Frift, script supervisor June Randall, camera focus Frank Elliot, director of photography Alec Mills, and clapper boy Simon Mills; producer Albert R. Broccoli holds the slate for a scene shot on 25th October, 1988. Peter Lamont stands in front of his spectacular set for the second floor of the Casino d'Isthmus, Sanchez's headquarters.

Other key Mexico locations were utilized to ensure this film would be as exotic as its predecessors. For Sanchez's mansion, Broccoli's close relationship with Baron Ricky di Portanova allowed for filming at his palatial home in Acapulco known as Arabesque. The Centro Ceremonial Otomi near Toluca, built for the Otomi Indians but now deserted, was chosen as the site of Professor Joe Butcher's Meditation Institute.

A Coast Guard law enforcement friend of Wilson's told him that one way drug dealers smuggled cocaine was to dissolve it in airplane fuel and then recover it once in the US. Wilson took this idea and had the villain Sanchez dissolve his cocaine in four tanker trucks. During the film's climax, Bond must destroy the tankers. In order to perform the incredible tanker side and back wheelies of the chase, vehicle stunt supervisor Rémy Julienne contacted Larry Orr, chief engineer of Kenworth Trucks, who modified and sent the stunt trucks, known as Pamela 1, 2, and 3 (after the film's heroine), to Rumorosa Pass, an hour from Mexicali. There, the first and second unit faced the seven-week shooting

MAURICE BINDER

The main title designs of Maurice Binder are true works of art and contain many of the signature images of the James Bond films. His feeling for color, shape, and mood helped define the world of 007. His sense of humor, seen in the trailers he cut for the Bond films, helped build anticipation for Bond adventures all over the globe.

Born in 1925, Binder studied engineering and attended the Art Students' League. He started as a teaboy at Macy's department store in New York City but soon became their art director. During World War II, Binder served on an army salvage ship. On a stop near Hollywood, Binder made some contacts in the film studios leading to work as a stills photographer. After the war, he moved into movie advertising and designed opening film credits, especially for director Stanley Donen. His titles on the 1961 film *The Grass Is Greener* received a tremendous reaction from the audience at the premiere. The next day, Binder received a phone call asking him to design the titles and trailer for a film called *Dr. No*. Binder showed the producers his idea for the opening gunbarrel logo, which became a signature image on all the Bond films to follow. Although absent from *From Russia With Love* (1963) and *Goldfinger* (1964), he designed the titles for *Thunderball* (1965) through to *Licence To Kill* (1989), using a combination of the most sophisticated and basic filmic techniques to create stunning, dreamlike visuals.

Binder became one of the most sought-after title designers, working on films as diverse as *Billion Dollar Brain* (1967), *Barbarella* (1968), *The Private Life of Sherlock Holmes* (1970), *The Wild Geese* (1978), and *The Last Emperor* (1987). In 1980, Binder used his optical printing experience to create the special visual effects for the time travel movie, *The Final Countdown*.

In addition to his work on titles, Binder owned a remarkable modern art collection. He died in 1991.

GOLDENEYE
(1995)

CAST Pierce Brosnan (James Bond), Sean Bean (Alec Trevelyan), Izabella Scorupco (Natalya Simonova), Famke Janssen (Xenia Onatopp), Joe Don Baker (Jack Wade), Judi Dench (M), Robbie Coltrane (Valentin Zukovsky), Tchéky Karyo (Dimitri Mishkin), Gottfried John (General Ourumov), Alan Cumming (Boris Grishenko), Desmond Llewelyn (Q), Samantha Bond (Moneypenny), Michael Kitchen (Bill Tanner), Serena Gordon (Caroline), Billy J. Mitchell (Admiral Farrel), Michelle Arthur (Anna), Minnie Driver (Irina)
PRESENTED BY Albert R. Broccoli
PRODUCED BY Michael G. Wilson & Barbara Broccoli
DIRECTED BY Martin Campbell
SCREENPLAY BY Jeffrey Caine and Bruce Feirstein
STORY BY Michael France
EXECUTIVE PRODUCER Tom Pevsner
"GOLDENEYE" performed by Tina Turner; written by Bono & The Edge; produced by Nellee Hooper
MUSIC BY Eric Serra
PRODUCTION DESIGNER Peter Lamont
DIRECTOR OF PHOTOGRAPHY Phil Méheux, BSC
EDITOR Terry Rawlings
COSTUME DESIGNER Lindy Hemming
2ND UNIT DIRECTOR Ian Sharp
2ND UNIT CAMERAMAN Harvey Harrison, BSC
ADDITIONAL UNIT DIRECTED & PHOTOGRAPHED BY Arthur Wooster, BSC
SPECIAL EFFECTS SUPERVISOR Chris Corbould
MINIATURE EFFECTS SUPERVISOR Derek Meddings
STUNT COORDINATOR Simon Crane
CASTING Debbie McWilliams
MAIN TITLE DESIGNED BY Daniel Kleinman
VISUAL EFFECTS PHOTOGRAPHY Paul Wilson, BSC
SUPERVISING SOUND EDITOR Jim Shields
SUPERVISING ART DIRECTOR Neil Lamont
SET DECORATOR Michael Ford
CONSTRUCTION COORDINATOR Tony Graysmark
PROPERTY MASTER Barry Wilkinson
MODEL UNIT ART DIRECTOR Michael Lamont
MODELLER HEAD OF DEPARTMENT Brian Smithies
MAKEUP SUPERVISOR Linda Devetta
HAIRDRESSING SUPERVISOR Colin Jamison
WARDROBE SUPERVISOR John Scott
STILLS PHOTOGRAPHER Keith Hamshere
PUBLICITY & MARKETING Gordon Arnell
PARACHUTE COORDINATOR B. J. Worth
CAR CHASE STUNTS Rémy Julienne
PRODUCTION MANAGER Philip Kohler
UNIT MANAGER Iris Rose
LOCATION PRODUCTION MANAGERS Serge Toubol, Valery Yermolaev, Ellen Gordon, Leonard Gmür, Stefan Zürcher
ASSISTANT DIRECTOR Gerry Gavigan
CAMERA OPERATOR Roger Pearce
SOUND RECORDIST David John
SCRIPT SUPERVISOR June Randall
ELECTRICAL SUPERVISOR Terry Potter
2ND UNIT ASSISTANT DIR. Terry Madden
ASSOCIATE PRODUCER Anthony Waye
FINANCIAL CONTROLLER Douglas Noakes
PRODUCTION ACCOUNTANT Andrew Noakes
COSTINGS ACCOUNTANT John Roebuck
ADDITIONAL PRODUCTION MANAGER Callum McDougall
DANJAQ VP OF MARKETING John Parkinson
LEGAL SERVICES David Pope

No limits. No fears. No substitutes.

After the release of *Licence To Kill* in 1989, Albert R. "Cubby" Broccoli and Michael G. Wilson decided that a new team should write and direct the next 007 adventure. Within months, the Berlin Wall fell, Communism in Europe collapsed, and the Cold War that spawned Bond ceased to exist. Was James Bond still relevant? The producers developed a new script, but MGM/UA began a painful financial journey that resulted in lawsuits and a lengthy delay for 007.

When the dust settled in 1992, Broccoli and Wilson declared they wanted to make a new Bond film. The pair brought in a new producer who had known Bond all her life. Barbara Broccoli took on the job of producing her first Bond film with a determination to make the characters in the film as rich and varied as in the Ian Fleming novels.

Working with screenwriter Michael France, the producers developed the premise of Bond facing his MI6 mentor, Alec Trevelyan, 006, who has now turned into a master criminal in control of a devastating space weapon. Screenwriter Jeffrey Caine introduced the motivation for the former 006: the purported betrayal of the Leinz Cossacks by the British army at the end of World War II.

Although Cubby was still very much part of the key decisons made during this vital period, he had passed on the day-to-day film production to Michael G. Wilson and Barbara Broccoli. As the script developed, Timothy Dalton announced he would not return as Bond. Pinewood Studios booked other films, forcing the filmmakers to look for another studio.

Michael G. Wilson and Barbara Broccoli confronted these challenges head-on. They discovered an abandoned Rolls Royce aircraft factory that production designer Peter Lamont transformed into a new film studio dubbed Leavesden. They brought in the experienced New Zealand director Martin Campbell and cast Pierce Brosnan as the new James Bond. By late summer 1994 the filmmakers were ready to start; however the producers and the studio decided to do more work on the script. Writer Bruce Feirstein joined the team, honing dialogue and tightening the story. During this time, the idea of a female M came to pass.

To play the vengeful Alec Trevelyan, the filmmakers turned to an actor they felt could have been a contender for the role of Bond, Sean Bean. Casting director Debbie McWilliams searched all over the world before finding Izabella Scorupco in Sweden to play Russian programmer Natalya Simonova. Dutch actress Famke Janssen landed the part of Xenia Onatopp, Joe Don Baker returned to play CIA agent Jack Wade, and Judi Dench became the new M.

With a budget more than twice that of any previous 007 film, production began on January 16, 1995, the exact month and day *Dr. No* began lensing in Jamaica 33 years before. The filmmakers sent Ian Sharp and his second unit to St. Petersburg, Russia, to film the location shots for the tank chase. The city authorities worried about damage to streets and the foundations of historic buildings, so the filmmakers undertook an engineering study to see if the chase could be completed safely. Working with the utmost care, the crew staged stunts and explosions in the heart of the city. To complete the sequence, production designer Peter Lamont built a two-block stretch of a St. Petersburg street at Leavesden. There, the filmmakers used a real T-55 tank to smash through a wall, roll over cars, grind through narrow alleys, and ram into a statue.

The film's opening sequence featured two incredible stunts.

Firstly, stuntman Wayne Michaels performed the world's highest bungee jump off a fixed point, the Verzasca dam in Switzerland. Secondly, parachutist Jacques "Zoo" Malnuit drove a motorcycle off a cliff-face in Switzerland, launching into a free-fall after a plane. In another Swiss valley, B. J. Worth and his team tried to actually have a freefalling jumper catch a diving plane. Unable to complete the stunt, the filmmakers created the effect using a digital composite image.

Location work in Puerto Rico and Monaco included not only Bond's classic Aston Martin DB5, but the BMW Z3, a sleek sports car that was only in the prototype stage.

In Puerto Rico, the filmmakers shot at the giant Arecibo Observatory, the world's largest single-dish radio telescope. To shoot the scripted scene of the observatory appearing from beneath a draining lake, the filmmakers turned to miniature effects supervisor Derek Meddings. The stunning array of miniatures created by Meddings included a vast stretch of Siberian wilderness, Alec Trevelyan's armored train, several fighter jets, both giant satellite dishes, and the entire Soviet chemical weapons facility, seen in the opening sequence as it explodes.

For the music, the filmmakers chose Eric Serra, composer of the music for *La Femme Nikita* (1990), and asked John Altman to record a version of "The James Bond Theme" to accompany the tank chase through the streets of St. Petersburg. The filmmakers asked Bono and The Edge of U2 to compose the title number. Sung by Tina Turner, "GoldenEye," reached #10 in the UK.

Audiences embraced Pierce Brosnan as Bond in overwhelming numbers. In the US, the film sold just shy of three times the number of tickets as *Licence to Kill*, the best box-office of any Bond film since *Moonraker*. The success of *GoldenEye* emphasized Bond's relevance in the post-Cold War world and marked the passing of the torch from Albert R. Broccoli to a new generation of producers: Michael G. Wilson and Barbara Broccoli.

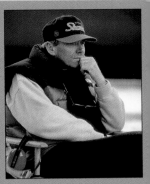

MARTIN CAMPBELL

Few directors bring such energy and passion to a film set as Martin Campbell. His desire to glean the most from every shot has helped launch both Pierce Brosnan and Daniel Craig in the role as James Bond.

Born in New Zealand in 1940, Martin Campbell moved to England in 1966 to become a cinematographer. He graduated to assistant director with the 1972 exploitation film *The Love Box*. The following year, he made his directing debut with an adult comedy, *The Sex Thief*, followed in 1975 by *Eskimo Nell*, a satire of the adult comedy genre. He produced the film *Black Joy* (1977) and was associate producer of *Scum* (1979), a tough and controversial exposé of the British borstal system for young offenders.

Moving into television in the late 1970s, Campbell made his name as a superior director of action dramas, helming episodes of *Minder*, *Shoestring*, and *The Professionals*. In the early 1980s, he directed two critically acclaimed miniseries, *Reilly: Ace of Spies* (1983) and *Edge Of Darkness* (1985), the latter winning a BAFTA TV Award for Best Drama Series.

Campbell returned to feature directing with the American thriller *Criminal Law* (1988), starring Gary Oldman and Kevin Bacon, followed by *Defenseless* (1991) and *No Escape* (1994). His work in the spy genre with *Reilly* and *Edge Of Darkness* impressed producers Michael G. Wilson and Barbara Broccoli, who chose him to introduce Pierce Brosnan as 007 in *GoldenEye* (1995). The result was an exciting and hugely profitable film that relaunched the franchise after a six-year hiatus.

After *GoldenEye*, Campbell directed *The Mask Of Zorro* (1998), *Vertical Limit* (2000), *Beyond Borders* (2003), and *The Legend Of Zorro* (2005). He returned to the world of Bond for 2006's *Casino Royale*.

MAKING GOLDENEYE *(clockwise from above left) Pierce Brosnan (James Bond) performs a slide on a set re-creation of the Arecibo radio telescope; Derek Meddings poses on his miniature of the area surrounding the Severnaya Space Weapons Centre; Sean Bean (Alec Treveylan) and Pierce Brosnan shoot the film's climax (turned 90°) on a green screen stage at Leavesden Studios; script writer Bruce Feirstein; Pierce Brosnan with Desmond Llewelyn on the set of Q's lab.*

TOMORROW NEVER DIES (1997)

CAST Pierce Brosnan (James Bond), Jonathan Pryce (Carver), Michelle Yeoh (Wai Lin), Teri Hatcher (Paris Carver), Ricky Jay (Gupta), Götz Otto (Stamper), Joe Don Baker (Wade), Vincent Schiavelli (Dr. Kaufman), Judi Dench (M), Desmond Llewelyn (Q), Samantha Bond (Moneypenny), Colin Salmon (Robinson), Geoffrey Palmer (Admiral Roebuck), Julian Fellowes (Minister of Defense), Terence Rigby (General Bukharin), Cecilie Thomsen (Professor Inga Bergstrom), Nina Young (Tamara), Daphne Deckers (Carver's PR), Mark Spalding (Stealth Boat Captain), Bruce Alexander (Captain, HMS *Chester*), Anthony Green (Firing Officer, HMS *Chester*), Christopher Bowen (Commander Richard Day), Michael Byrne (Admiral Kelly), Pip Torrens (Captain, HMS *Bedford*)
PRODUCED BY Michael G. Wilson & Barbara Broccoli
DIRECTOR Roger Spottiswoode
SCREENPLAY BY Bruce Feirstein
LINE PRODUCER Anthony Waye
"TOMORROW NEVER DIES" written by Sheryl Crow & Mitchell Froom; produced by Mitchell Froom; performed by Sheryl Crow
MUSIC BY David Arnold
PRODUCTION DESIGNER Allan Cameron
DIRECTOR OF PHOTOGRAPHY Robert Elswitt
EDITORS Dominique Fortin, Michael Arcand
COSTUME DESIGNER Lindy Hemming
2ND UNIT DIRECTOR & STUNT COORDINATOR Vic Armstrong
SPECIAL EFFECTS SUPERVISOR Chris Corbould
STUNT SUPERVISOR Dickey Beer
CASTING Debbie McWilliams
MAIN TITLE DESIGNED BY Daniel Kleinman
MINIATURE EFFECTS John Richardson
AERIAL COORDINATOR Marc Wolff
HALO JUMP COORDINATOR B. J. Worth
2ND UNIT CAMERAMAN Jonathan Taylor
MINIATURE PHOTOGRAPHY Paul Wilson
UNDERWATER PHOTOGRAPHY Pete Romano
ADDITIONAL PHOTOGRAPHY Eddie Collins
AERIAL PHOTOGRAPHY Adam Dale
SET DECORATOR Peter Young
CONSTRUCTION COORDINATOR Ray Barrett
PROPERTY MASTER Ty Tieger
ART DIRECTORS Stephen Scott, Giles Masters, Tony Reading, Jonathan Lee, Ken Court
MAKEUP SUPERVISOR Norma Webb
HAIRDRESSING SUPERVISOR Eithne Fennell
WARDROBE SUPERVISOR John Scott
ELECTRICAL SUPERVISOR John Higgins
STILLS PHOTOGRAPHER Keith Hamshere
PUBLICITY & MARKETING Gordon Arnell
FAR EAST PROD. SUPERVISOR Philip Kohler
UNIT MANAGER Iris Rose
PRODUCTION MANAGER Janine Modder
LOCATION PRODUCTION MANAGERS Terry Bamber, John Bernard, Leonhard Gmür, Neil Ravan
ASSISTANT DIRECTOR Gerry Gavigan
CAMERA OPERATOR Ian Foster
SCRIPT SUPERVISOR Angela Wharton
SOUND MIXER Chris Munro
SUPERVISING SOUND EDITOR Martin Evans
2ND UNIT ASSISTANT DIR. Terry Madden
PRODUCTION SUPERVISOR Callum McDougall
SUPERVISING PRODUCTION ACCOUNTANT Andrew Noakes
LEGAL & BUSINESS AFFAIRS David Pope

ALBERT R. BROCCOLI'S EON PRODUCTIONS PRESENTS PIERCE BROSNAN AS IAN FLEMING'S JAMES BOND 007 IN "TOMORROW NEVER DIES" JONATHAN PRYCE MICHELLE YEOH TERI HATCHER JOE DON BAKER AND JUDI DENCH
COSTUME DESIGNER LINDY HEMMING MUSIC BY DAVID ARNOLD DIRECTED BY PHOTOGRAPHY ROBERT ELSWITT PRODUCTION DESIGNER ALLAN CAMERON LINE PRODUCER ANTHONY WAYE WRITTEN BY BRUCE FEIRSTEIN TITLE SONG PERFORMED BY CHERYL CROW PRODUCED BY MICHAEL G. WILSON AND BARBARA BROCCOLI DIRECTED BY ROGER SPOTTISWOODE

"How do we make the 18th Bond an event?" United Artists production executive Jeff Kleeman asked producers Michael G. Wilson and Barbara Broccoli in May 1995, while *GoldenEye* was still shooting.

Bruce Feirstein, the final contributing writer to the *GoldenEye* script, had a nine-word pitch about a media baron villain, "Words are the new weapons; satellites, the new artillery." Wilson and Broccoli were intrigued and commissioned Feirstein to write a first draft.

Numerous rewrites followed as the producers brought in director Roger Spottiswoode, who began as an editor for directors Sam Peckinpah and Walter Hill in the 1970s. Spottiswoode brought a strong sense of pace to the film, which became the first 007 adventure to run less than two hours since 1971's *Diamonds Are Forever*.

Hong Kong action star Michelle Yeoh accepted the role of Wai Lin, a Chinese secret agent and very much Bond's equal. For the role of power-hungry Elliot Carver, the filmmakers recruited British actor and *Miss Saigon* star Jonathan Pryce. American Teri Hatcher, from the hit television series *Lois and Clark*, signed to play Paris Carver, Bond's former lover-turned-villain's wife. The filmmakers shot the emotional love scene between Bond and Paris in a suite at Stoke Poges Golf Club, the setting of the golf game in *Goldfinger* (1964).

With both Pinewood and Leavesden Studios completely booked, the filmmakers once again needed to create a new studio. They turned a former grocery warehouse in Frogmore, England into a production facility.

Long-time production designer Peter Lamont could not work on the film due to his commitment to James Cameron's *Titanic* (1997); production designer Allan Cameron was hired and gave the film very high-tech yet realistic sets.

Second unit director Vic Armstrong filmed many remarkable action scenes, including the pre-titles sequence, set at a Khyber Pass terrorist arms bazaar. The cameras rolled in January 1997 in the French Pyrenees to take advantage of the snow. Armstrong and his crew later filmed a spectacularly contained car chase with the Brent Cross Shopping Centre car park doubling for a multi-story car park in Hamburg. To create the effect of Bond driving his car via a touchpad on his cell phone, special effects supervisor Chris Corbould's crew rebuilt four BMW 750iLs to be driven by hidden stunt driver Steve Griffin crouched on the back floorboard watching video monitors. In the end, 17 BMW 750iLs were used by the production to put the four minute car chase on film. The filmmakers also staged a hair-raising motorcycle-helicopter chase seamlessly melding Bangkok locations and English sets. At Frogmore, French motorcycle expert Jean-Pierre Goy, astride a BMW R1200 motorbike, insisted on performing an incredible leap between two buildings over a prop helicopter.

Simultaneously, miniature effects supervisor John Richardson commandeered the Baja Studios tank in Mexico after *Titanic* finished production to film models of the stealth ship and HMS *Devonshire*. To perform the film's spectacular HALO jump, parachute specialist B. J. Worth conducted 80 parachute jumps, falling 12,000 ft (3,658 m) over Arizona and 14,000 ft (4,267 m) over Florida. Spottiswoode's editing

MAKING TOMORROW *(below top left) Roger Spottiswoode directs Pierce Brosnan (Bond) and Michelle Yeoh (Wai Lin) on a rooftop in Bangkok.*
OUR MAN IN FROGMORE *(below top right) Production designer Allan Cameron on his recreated Saigon street at Frogmore Studios.*
EVERY PICTURE TELLS A STORY *(below bottom left): Original storyboards of the helicopter attack on Bond and Wai Lin.*
CITYSCAPE *(below, middle right) A scenic artist touches up a photographic transparency of Saigon used for the sequence in Carver's media headquarters in Vietnam.*

skills were invaluable in designing these sequences so they would cut smoothly. When Bond and Wai Lin leap from a Saigon skyscraper and rip a banner of Carver's face, Spottiswoode combined shots of the lead actors, stunt performers, miniatures of the actors, the real location at Sinn Sathorn Tower in Bangkok, a 60 ft (18.3 m) replica of the building and banner on the Frogmore backlot, and digital compositing to create the finished sequence.

During the final weeks of production, the crew filmed the interior of the stealth ship climax inside the Albert R. Broccoli 007 Stage at Pinewood Studios during the day. At night, the crew switched to filming the underwater sequences beneath the ship interior in the 007 stage tank. The sequences had to be filmed with different electrical power setups and at different times of the day to avoid injuring anybody.

To make the December 9, 1997 premiere date, David Arnold composed and recorded the score in sections during production. When the filmmakers first heard the opening bars from Arnold's outstanding "White Knight" cue, they knew they had found the heir apparent to John Barry. With one foot in the 1960s and the other set firmly in the 1990s, Arnold created a fresh-sounding score with several references to Bond music of the past. Sheryl Crow wrote and performed the brooding title song, which received Golden Globe and Grammy nominations, and Arnold, David McAlmont, and Bond lyricist alumnus Don Black wrote the haunting end-title song "Surrender," a sexy, brassy number belted out by k.d. lang in the style of Shirley Bassey.

Tomorrow Never Dies opened to a whirlwind of publicity during the 1997 Christmas season. It topped *GoldenEye*'s grosses in the US and played to packed cinemas around the world, solidifying Pierce Brosnan's place as the perfect James Bond for the 1990s.

DAVID ARNOLD

David Arnold made James Bond music exciting for a new generation of fans. He is the first composer since John Barry to score more than one Bond film. Like Barry, he has an inherent sense of the James Bond sound. Born in Luton in 1962, Arnold saw his first Bond movie, *You Only Live Twice* (1967), as a child and was mesmerized by the film and its music. Years later, he taught himself to write, orchestrate, and compose scores for filmmaker Danny Cannon and scored with the hit Bjork-performed song "Play Dead" for the film *The Young Americans* (1993). After winning a Grammy for his rousing score for the sci-fi blockbuster *Independence Day* (1996), he set to work on an album entitled *Shaken And Stirred*, for which modern artists performed new interpretations of classic Bond songs. As he finished these recordings, he sent them to MGM Music and the Bond producers. They were extremely impressed with what they heard, and, when John Barry proved unable to score *Tomorrow Never Dies* (1997), the film was offered to Arnold with Barry's blessing. Arnold has gone on to compose soundtracks for *The World Is Not Enough* (1999), *Die Another Day* (2002), *Casino Royale* (2006), and *Quantum of Solace* (2008).

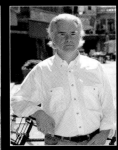

STREET PERFORMERS *An extra prepares for his moment on the Frogmore backlot (below left); Pierce Brosnan and Michelle Yeoh shoot close ups for the motorcycle chase in a Saigon market (below right).*

IE BLADE SLIDES UNDER THE WHIRLING BLADES.

RD. BOND & LIN MAKE THEIR ESCAPE.

T DOWN FROM HELICOPTER TO FIND ON THROUGH THE WASHING LINE

COOL CUSTOMER *(right) Vic Armstrong directs Bond and Elektra's ski tour.*

ELECTRIFYING *(far right) Original design sketch by Lindy Hemming of Elektra King's red gown.*

THE MEN BEHIND THE MAYHEM *(clockwise from right) Michael Apted discusses motivation with Robert Carlyle (Renard) at Pinewood Studios; Special Effects Supervisor Chris Corbould poses by Bond's BMW Z8; Desmond Llewelyn (Q) talks with Apted.*

THE WORLD IS NOT ENOUGH
(1999)

CAST Pierce Brosnan (James Bond), Sophie Marceau (Elektra King), Robert Carlyle (Renard), Denise Richards (Christmas Jones), Robbie Coltrane (Valentin Zukovsky), Judi Dench ("M"), Desmond Llewelyn ("Q"), John Cleese (Q's Assistant), Samantha Bond (Miss Moneypenny), David Calder (Sir Robert King), Michael Kitchen (Tanner), Colin Salmon (Robinson), Serena Scott Thomas (Dr. Molly Warmflash), John Seru (Gabor), Claude-Oliver Rudolph (Colonel Akakievich), Ulrich Thomsen (Sacha Davidov), Goldie (The Bull), Maria Grazia Cucinotta (Cigar Girl), Patrick Malahide (Lachaise), Jeff Nuttall (Dr. Arkov), Diran Meghreblian (Priest)
PRODUCERS Michael G. Wilson & Barbara Broccoli
DIRECTOR Michael Apted
WRITTEN BY Neal Purvis & Robert Wade and Bruce Feirstein
LINE PRODUCER Anthony Waye
'THE WORLD IS NOT ENOUGH' PERFORMED BY Garbage
MUSIC BY David Arnold
PRODUCTION DESIGNER Peter Lamont
DIRECTOR OF PHOTOGRAPHY Adrian Biddle, BSC
EDITOR Jim Clark
COSTUME DESIGNER Lindy Hemming
2ND UNIT DIRECTED BY Vic Armstrong
SPECIAL EFFECTS SUPERVISOR Chris Corbould
STUNT CO-ORDINATOR Simon Crane
CASTING Debbie McWilliams
MINIATURES John Richardson
VISUAL EFFECTS SUPERVISOR Mara Bryan
MAIN TITLE DESIGNED BY Daniel Kleinman
2ND UNIT PHOTOGRAPHY Jonathan Taylor
MINIATURE PHOTOGRAPHY Paul Wilson, BSC
UNDERWATER PHOTOGRAPHY Tim Wooster
AERIAL COORDINATOR Marc Wolff
ADDITIONAL UNIT DIRECTED & PHOTOGRAPHED BY Arthur Wooster, BSC
SUPERVISING ART DIRECTOR Neil Lamont
SET DECORATOR Simon Wakefield
CONSTRUCTION CO-ORDINATOR Peter G. Williams
PROPERTY MASTER Barry Wilkinson
ART DIRECTORS Andrew Ackland-Snow, Steve Lawrence, Fred Hole, Simon Lamont, Mark Harris, Jim Morahan
MAKEUP SUPERVISOR Linda De Vetta
HAIRDRESSING SUPERVISOR Colin Jamison
WARDROBE SUPERVISOR John Scott
ELECTRICAL SUPERVISOR Kevin Day
STILLS PHOTOGRAPHER Keith Hamshere
PUBLICITY & MARKETING Anne Bennett
UNIT MANAGER Iris Rose
PRODUCTION SUPERVISORS Philip Kohler, Janine Modder, Hugh Harlow
LOCATION PRODUCTION MANAGERS Terry Bamber, John Bernard, Tim Lewis, Ali Akdeniz, Yousaf Bokhari, Carlos Taillefer
ASSISTANT DIRECTOR Gerry Gavigan
2ND UNIT ASSISTANT DIRECTOR Terry Madden
SCRIPT SUPERVISOR Nikki Clapp
SOUND MIXER Chris Munro
SUPERVISING SOUND EDITOR Martin Evans
CAMERA OPERATOR David Worley
ASSOCIATE PRODUCER Nigel Goldsack
FINANCIAL CONTROLLER Andrew Noakes
PRODUCTION EXECUTIVE David Pope

The World Is Not Enough brought James Bond's adventures in the 20th century to a close, and the producers were determined to create a dramatic plot with emotionally complex characters that would twist the audience's preconceptions of 007 at every turn.

In November 1997, Bond producer Barbara Broccoli watched an episode of *Nightline* that detailed how the untapped oil in the Caspian Sea was ripe for the taking after decades of Soviet control. Every major oil company now had a stake there. Broccoli wondered what might happen if the next Bond villain tried to eliminate all the competition to provide the only pipeline from the Caspian to the West.

Broccoli and her producing partner Michael G. Wilson approached British screenwriters Neal Purvis and Robert Wade. The duo pitched two villains: one who was close to death and the other a woman; the characters of Renard and Elektra King grew from these early conversations. During the scripting process, Broccoli reminded the writers, "With Elektra, Bond thinks he has found Tracy [his short-lived wife from OHMSS] but he's really found Blofeld."

Since Elektra was the key to making the film work, the producers wanted a filmmaker skilled at eliciting strong performances from women. They appointed Michael Apted to helm *The World Is Not Enough*, a title taken from the family motto of a branch of the Bond family in the novel *On Her Majesty's Secret Service*. Apted had directed Sissy Spacek in an Academy Award–winning performance and Sigourney Weaver and Jodie Foster to Academy Award nominations. He immediately saw great potential in involving M more in the plot. To strengthen the women's roles, Apted brought in his screenwriter wife Dana Stevens. To strengthen Bond's role, Apted brought screenwriter Bruce Feirstein back to the fold.

With the script complete, the producers focused on casting. French actress Sophie Marceau was chosen for the central role of Elektra and, after a mesmeric performance as a psychopath in the British television crime series *Cracker*, Scottish actor Robert Carlyle was chosen to play terrorist

Renard. American actress Denise Richards landed the role of nuclear physicist Dr. Christmas Jones. Robbie Coltrane reprised his popular character from *GoldenEye*, Russian arms dealer Valentin Zukovsky. In this film, Zukovsky owns a casino and caviar factory in Baku.

Filming began at Pinewood Studios on January 11, 1999, the first 007 film to be based at the studio since 1987's *The Living Daylights*. Filming continued in Bilbao, Spain, which Apted chose for the backdrop of the Guggenheim Museum. When the crew arrived, 100,000 excited Spaniards came to view the production. Apted and his crew returned to Spain later in the shoot after the cancellation of extensive filming in Turkey. Second unit director Vic Armstrong and stunt coordinator Simon Crane had their hands full with two major stunt sequences: the boat chase on the River Thames and the parahawk—ski chase (filmed in Chamonix, France). Production designer Peter Lamont's team built the set of Zukovsky's caviar factory—a complicated set of walkways and night walls complete with fiber-optic stars—in the Paddock Tank at Pinewood. The set was now ready to film the difficult sequence where Bond is pursued by Elektra's helicopters equipped with murderous buzzsaws. Since the local community would not allow real helicopters to be flown above the studio, a unit shot footage of helicopters at

Long Valley, later enhanced with CGI effects. Miniature helicopters also appeared in shots. For realism, special-effects supervisor Chris Corbould and his team suspended an Aerospatiale Squirrel helicopter sans rotors on a computer programmed gimble arm to swoop over the set. In the Bahamas, miniature effects supervisor John Richardson shot the 45-foot (13.7 m) submarine model for the film's climax.

During the film's test screening, the Thames boat chase followed the main titles. But audience feedback indicated that the pre-titles sequence needed to be bigger. Apted and the producers decided to do some tight editing and move the boat chase so that it came before the main titles, resulting in the longest pre-titles sequence to date.

David Arnold returned to compose the film's electronic-driven score, using an Arabic string instrument, the qanun, to give a Middle Eastern feel. Since the lyrics of the title song, written with Don Black, were from Elektra's point-of-view, Arnold chose Shirley Manson of the rock band Garbage, since he felt her voice had a "steel fist in a velvet glove" quality. The song reached #11 on the UK charts.

The World Is Not Enough premiered in November 1999 and proved a huge worldwide success. The producers had gambled on a more complex storyline and won.

DANIEL KLEINMAN

After Maurice Binder died in 1991, director Daniel Kleinman faced the unenviable task of stepping into his shoes as the designer and creator of one of the most important sequences in every Bond film: the main titles. His first assignment was *GoldenEye* in 1995, and he has remained with the Bond team ever since.

After graduating from art school in 1977, Kleinman worked as an illustrator of album covers. His work caught the attention of music video directors, and he became one himself in 1983 when he directed the video "Crushed By The Wheels Of Industry" for Heaven 17. Over 100 music video directing assignments followed, including one-hour HBO specials for Madonna, Prince, and Van Halen. He came to the notice of the Bond producers when he directed Gladys Knight's video for *Licence To Kill* (1989).

Kleinman has used digital technology to update the look of the titles, choosing images that reflect the themes of each film. For *GoldenEye*, he used falling Soviet statues to symbolize the end of Communism. For *Tomorrow Never Dies* (1997), he took viewers behind video screens into a seemingly transparent world where everything is visible. In the titles for *The World Is Not Enough* (1999), Kleinman showcased Elektra King's obsession with oil. For *Die Another Day* (2002), Kleinman broke new ground by intercutting the film's motifs of ice and fire with Bond's grueling 14 months of torture in a North Korean prison.

For *Casino Royale* (2006), Kleinman found inspiration in a first edition cover of Ian Fleming's novel that featured red hearts dripping blood. In *Skyfall* (2012), Kleinman followed director Sam Mendes' brief that Bond should travel into the underworld like Alice going into the rabbit hole and experience the story in his unconscious.

One of the world's top commercial directors, Kleinman has stayed true to his dictum that he only creates titles for 007.

ALBERT R. BROCCOLI'S EON PRODUCTIONS PRESENTS
PIERCE BROSNAN AS IAN FLEMING'S JAMES BOND 007 IN

The WORLD Is Not Enough
007

DIE ANOTHER DAY (2002)

CAST Pierce Brosnan (James Bond), Halle Berry (Jinx), Toby Stephens (Gustav Graves), Rosamund Pike (Miranda Frost), Rick Yune (Zao), Judi Dench (M), John Cleese (Q), Michael Madsen (Falco), Will Yun Lee (Colonel Moon), Kenneth Tsang (General Moon), Emilio Echevarría (Raoul), Mikhail Gorevoy (Vlad), Lawrence Makoare (Mr. Kil), Colin Salmon (Robinson), Samantha Bond (Moneypenny), Ben Wee (Snooty desk clerk), Ho Yi (Hotel Manager), Rachel Grant (Peaceful), Ian Pirie (Creep), Simón Andreu (Dr. Alvarez), Mark Dymond (Van Bierk), Deborah Moore (Air hostess), Tymarah (Scorpion Guard)
PRODUCED BY
Michael G. Wilson & Barbara Broccoli
DIRECTED BY Lee Tamahori
WRITTEN BY Neal Purvis & Robert Wade
EXECUTIVE PRODUCER Anthony Waye
CO-PRODUCER Callum McDougall
"DIE ANOTHER DAY" PERFORMED BY Madonna
MUSIC David Arnold
PRODUCTION DESIGNER Peter Lamont
DIRECTOR OF PHOTOGRAPHY
David Tattersall, BSC
EDITOR Christian Wagner
COSTUME DESIGNER Lindy Hemming
2ND UNIT DIRECTOR Vic Armstrong
SPECIAL EFFECTS SUPERVISOR Chris Corbould
STUNT COORDINATOR George Aguilar
CASTING Debbie McWilliams
MAIN TITLE DESIGNED BY Danny Kleinman
MODEL EFFECTS SUPERVISOR John Richardson
VISUAL EFFECTS SUPERVISOR Mara Bryan
2ND UNIT PHOTOGRAPHY Jonathan Taylor
MODEL PHOTOGRAPHY Paul Wilson
ADDITIONAL UNITS PHOTOGRAPHY BY
Shaun O'Dell, Arthur Wooster BSC, Don King
SUPERVISING ART DIRECTOR Simon Lamont
SET DIRECTOR Simon Wakefield
CONSTRUCTION MANAGER Paul Hayes
PROPERTY MASTER Ty Tieger
ELECTRICAL SUPERVISOR Eddie Knight
ART DIRECTORS James Hambidge, Mark Harris, Fred Hole, Stephen Scott, Alan Tomkins
PUBLICITY & MARKETING Anne Bennett
MAKEUP SUPERVISOR Paul Engelen
HAIRDRESSING SUPERVISOR Colin Jamison
WARDROBE SUPERVISOR Graham Churchyard
STILLS PHOTOGRAPHER Keith Hamshere
PRODUCTION MANAGERS
Terry Bamber, Tim Lewis
UNIT MANAGER Iris Rose
PRODUCTION SUPERVISOR Janine Modder
LOCATION PRODUCTION SUPERVISORS
Philip Kohler, Mark Albela, Chris Brock, Glenn Beadles
ASSISTANT DIRECTOR Gerry Gavigan
2ND UNIT ASSISTANT DIRECTOR
Terry Madden
SCRIPT SUPERVISOR Anna Worley
SOUND MIXER Chris Munro
SUPERVISING SOUND EDITOR Martin Evans
CAMERA OPERATOR Peter Robertson
POST PRODUCTION SUPERVISOR
Michael Solinger
FINANCIAL CONTROLLER Andrew Noakes
PRODUCTION EXECUTIVE David Pope

Die Another Day in 2002 marked the release of the 20th James Bond film, the 40th anniversary of the 007 film series. Screenwriters Neal Purvis and Robert Wade began work on "Bond 20" in the summer of 2000, brainstorming ideas with producers Michael G. Wilson and Barbara Broccoli. Agreeing they wanted the new film to be on a grand scale, similar to 1967's *You Only Live Twice.* Purvis and Wade suggested structuring the film around Ian Fleming's third novel, *Moonraker,* with a villain who transforms his identity, becomes a knighted industrialist, and plans to use a space weapon in a mad act of vengeance. Choosing the long-running political tensions between North and South Korea as the film's main theme, they plotted a grand, globe-hopping adventure on a scale never before seen in a Bond movie.

To direct, the producers chose New Zealand-born Lee Tamahori, who had helmed *Once Were Warriors* (1994), a movie Broccoli called "one of the best films made in the last 50 years." Tamahori brought a sense of spectacle and history to *Die Another Day,* peppering it with clever nods to James Bond's past. Eagle-eyed viewers will note, for example, the name of the Hong Kong hotel, The Rubyeon Royale, which pays homage to the Ruby Anniversary of EON Productions as well as the first Bond novel *Casino Royale.*

The producers cast Halle Berry as NSA agent Jinx; British stage actor Toby Stephens joined the cast to play the villain Graves; and newcomer Rosamund Pike took the role of duplicitous MI6 agent Miranda Frost. Rick Yune pursued the smaller role of Colonel Moon, but Tamahori cast him in the larger role of terrorist Zao.

On Christmas Day, 2001, a small unit began work off the coast of Maui, Hawaii, where Laird Hamilton and his surfing team rode some of the world's largest waves for the film's opening scene—a sign of the scale to come. The precredits sequence alone required a small fleet of hovercraft, bounding mines, the destruction of several sports cars, and a miniature

of a vast waterfall. Everyone involved wanted this film to be the biggest Bond ever: the filmmakers changed the climax from an indoor Japanese beach to an out-of-control Antonov plane, the largest aircraft in the world, and Tamahori continued a car chase that began on a frozen lake into Peter Lamont's magnificent, melting Ice Palace set. Filming also took place in the largest greenhouse in the world, The Eden Project, in Cornwall, England.

Five weeks into filming, Pierce Brosnan injured his knee while sprinting on the set of Colonel Moon's compound on the Pinewood backlot. Brosnan flew to Los Angeles for emergency surgery, which ignited worries about the schedule. However, according to Broccoli, Pierce "was almost bionic in his recovery."

The production received some morale-boosting news in March when Halle won the Best Actress Academy Award for

Monster's Ball and sound mixer Chris Munro won the Oscar for Best Sound for *Black Hawk Down*. The Academy Awards also featured nominations for Dame Judi Dench and Dame Maggie Smith, mother of Toby Stephens, for *Iris* and *Gosford Park* respectively.

Halle Berry soon returned to the production to shoot Jinx's dramatic emergence from the sea in an orange bikini, deliberately recalling Ursula Andress's iconic first appearance as Honey Ryder in *Dr. No* (1962). The scene was shot in Cadiz, Spain (doubling for Havana, Cuba) during a cold but thankfully clear day after five days of steady rain.

By June 2002, seven units were filming simultaneously to deliver the movie by November 2002. Aerial, underwater, and miniature units, as well as first, second, and third units pulled together to create remarkable

fencing instructor Verity; she thus became the first title-song performer to play a role in a Bond film.

On November 18, 2002, *Die Another Day* premiered at London's Royal Albert Hall. Her Majesty Queen Elizabeth II made this the only film premiere of her Jubilee year celebrations, viewing the movie with former James Bond actors George Lazenby, Sir Roger Moore, Timothy Dalton, and 3,000 guests.

Die Another Day thrilled audiences around the globe. However, while the film successfully brought James Bond into the new century, it also marked the end of an era. It would prove to be Pierce Brosnan's last performance as James Bond.

PAUSE FOR THOUGHT *(facing page, top left) Senior vice president of marketing and publicity Anne Bennett confers with producer Michael G. Wilson.*

ON AND OFF SET *(clockwise from left) Pierce Brosnan shoots in front of a blue screen for close ups during the hovercraft sequence; costume designer Lindy Hemming warms Halle Berry (Jinx) on a chilly location shoot in Spain; assistant director Gerry Gavigan lines up the background action for a major shot; supervising art director Simon Lamont with his uncle, production designer Peter Lamont.*

THE DIE IS CAST *(far left and left) Casting director Debbie McWilliams; Lee Tamahori directs John Cleese (Q) and Pierce Brosnan.*

KEEPING COOL *Pierce Brosnan and producer Michael G. Wilson await the next shot.*

images of action.

Special effects supervisor Chris Corbould provided numerous practical special effects, including one shot for the film's climax that involved a staggering 70 explosions.

David Arnold returned to compose his third Bond film score, this time experimenting by recording an orchestra playing sections of his score in reverse. He also used a Korean stringed instrument, the yanggeum, to give the Korean scenes a distinctive feel. Madonna wrote and performed the title song and also had a cameo role as

NEAL PURVIS & ROBERT WADE

Screenwriters Neal Purvis and Robert Wade have contributed highly inventive plots, characters, and action scenes to the James Bond film series and have succeeded in giving the stories of the recent 007 adventures a highly modern feel while simultaneously tipping their hats to Bond's creator Ian Fleming. They are noted for creating rich villains and exploring the complex character of 007.

Purvis, born outside London, and Wade, born in Cardiff, Wales, met at the University of Kent at Canterbury, where Purvis studied philosophy and Wade studied English. They subsequently began collaborating on film scripts, enjoying their first success in 1991 when their script *Let Him Have It*, the story of the Craig-Bentley murder case, was made into a feature film by director Peter Medak. The film was screened for Parliament and played a role in Derek Bentley's posthumous pardon. Purvis and Wade continued to work in a variety of genres, and one of their scripts for the highwayman adventure *Plunkett And MacLeane* (1999) came to the attention of Bond producers Michael G. Wilson and Barbara Broccoli.

The pair wrote the storyline and co-wrote the screenplay of *The World Is Not Enough* (1999) and were the only writers on *Die Another Day* (2002). They took time off from the Bond series to co-write the spy spoof *Johnny English* (2003) starring Rowan Atkinson, and then wrote the story outlines and formative drafts of *Casino Royale* (2006) *Quantum of Solace* (2008), and *Skyfall* (2012). They also wrote and co-produced both *Return to Sender* (2004) and *Stoned* (2005).

WRITTEN IN ICE *(above) Neal Purvis and Robert Wade discuss the script with Lee Tamahori on the ice palace set.*

CASINO ROYALE (2006)

CAST Daniel Craig (James Bond), Eva Green (Vesper Lynd), Mads Mikkelsen (Le Chiffre), Judi Dench (M), Jeffrey Wright (Felix Leiter), Giancarlo Giannini (Mathis), Caterina Murino (Solange), Simon Abkarian (Dimitrios), Isaach De Bankole (Obanno), Jesper Christensen (Mr. White), Ivana Milicevic (Valenka), Tobias Menzies (Villiers), Claudio Santamaria (Carlos), Sébastien Foucan (Mollaka), Malcolm Sinclair (Dryden), Richard Sammel (Gettler), Ludger Pistor (Mendel), Joseph Millson (Carter), Daud Shah (Fisher), Clemens Schick (Kratt), Obanno's lieutenant (Michael Offei), Ade (Infante), Urbano Barberini (Tomelli), Tsai Chin (Madame Wu), Charlie Levi Leroy (Gallardo), Lazar Ristovski, (Kaminofsky), Tom So (Fukutu), Veruschka (Gräfin Von Wallenstein)
PRODUCERS Michael G. Wilson & Barbara Broccoli
DIRECTOR Martin Campbell
SCREENPLAY WRITERS Neal Purvis & Robert Wade and Paul Haggis
BASED ON THE NOVEL BY Ian Fleming
EXECUTIVE PRODUCERS Anthony Waye & Callum McDougall
"YOU KNOW MY NAME" PERFORMED BY Chris Cornell
"YOU KNOW MY NAME" WRITTEN & PRODUCED BY Chris Cornell & David Arnold
MUSIC BY David Arnold
PRODUCTION DESIGNER Peter Lamont
DIRECTOR OF PHOTOGRAPHY Phil Méheux, BSC
EDITOR Stuart Baird, ACE
COSTUME DESIGNER Lindy Hemming
2ND UNIT DIRECTOR Alexander Witt
SPECIAL EFFECTS & MINIATURE EFFECT SUPERVISOR Chris Corbould
MAIN TITLE DESIGNER Daniel Kleinman
CASTING Debbie McWilliams
STUNT COORDINATOR Gary Powell
UNIT PRODUCTION MANAGER Jeremy Johns
2ND UNIT PRODUCTION MANAGER Terry Bamber
1ST ASSISTANT DIRECTOR Bruce Moriarty
VISUAL EFFECTS & MINIATURE SUPERVISOR Steve Begg
SUPERVISING ART DIRECTOR Simon Lamont
PROPERTY MASTER Ty Teiger
CONSTRUCTION MANAGER Stephen Bohan
POST PRODUCTION SUPERVISOR Michael Solinger
SOUND RECORDIST Chris Munro
ELECTRICAL SUPERVISOR Eddie Knight
STILLS PHOTOGRAPHER Jay Maidment
MAKEUP SUPERVISOR Paul Engelen
HAIRDRESSING SUPERVISOR Christine Blundell
WARDROBE SUPERVISOR Dan Grace
CAMERA OPERATOR Roger Pearce
2ND UNIT ASSISTANT DIRECTOR Terry Madden
SCRIPT SUPERVISOR Jean Bourne
PUBLICITY & MARKETING Anne Bennett
PROMOTIONS Keith Snelgrove
ASSISTANT PRODUCER David G. Wilson
ASSOCIATE PRODUCER Andrew Noakes
PRODUCTION EXECUTIVE David Pope

ALBERT R. BROCCOLI'S EON PRODUCTIONS PRESENTS DANIEL CRAIG as IAN FLEMING'S JAMES BOND 007 in

CASINO ROYALE
007

NOVEMBER 16
casinoroyale-movie.co.uk

After the completion of *Die Another Day* (2002), producers Michael G. Wilson and Barbara Broccoli discussed the future of James Bond. They decided to make a film of *Casino Royale*, the first, darkest, and most literary of the Bond novels, which had been previously unavailable to EON Productions. Wilson and Broccoli felt the storyline of Bond going after a Soviet operative who has squandered money and now desperately needs to win it back at the gaming tables could be adapted to the world of modern terror networks and those that finance terrorist attacks.

To film Ian Fleming's first novel and the story of how Bond became a "00" presented the producers with many new

FUN IN THE SUN *(clockwise from above right) Daniel Craig (James Bond) prepares for his entrance from the sea in the Bahamas; Sébastien Foucan receives weapons training on location; director Martin Campbell in his element.*

challenges. Not only did they need to find a new actor to play James Bond, but MGM was soon sold to a consortium that included Sony Pictures. Sony would now finance and distribute the new Bond film. The careful development of the script, the change of studios, and the long process of casting contributed to a four-year gap between Bond films.

Screenwriters Neal Purvis and Robert Wade returned to adapt Fleming's novel. The filmmakers worked to capture the spirit of Fleming's novel while focusing on the story of "how James became Bond." In early 2005, Martin Campbell signed to direct the film. His success with *GoldenEye* (1995) had launched Pierce Brosnan as 007; he now faced the task of launching another actor to take on the character of James Bond. Paul Haggis, soon to win an Oscar for producing *Crash*

(2004), joined to work on the script. With a script finally in place, Campbell and the producers conducted two days of screen testing and formally approached their first choice to play 007—Daniel Craig.

The filmmakers assembled an international cast to fill the key remaining roles. French actress Eva Green signed on for the critical role of Vesper Lynd, and Danish actor Mads Mikkelsen took the part of Le Chiffre. To play Bond's liaison in Montenegro, the filmmakers chose Italian acting legend Giancarlo Giannini. African-American actor Jeffrey Wright became the seventh actor to portray Felix Leiter.

Production began on the 27th January 2006 at Modrany Studio, outside Prague. The rigorous fitness regime Daniel Craig had embarked on in preparation for the shoot immediately paid off: Craig's first scene was the pulse-pounding chase sequence in which Bond pursues would-be bomber Mollaka through the Nambutu Embassy.

On the 17th February, the production moved to the Bahamas. A derelict hotel in Coral Harbour provided the perfect location for the filmmakers to stage an amazing foot chase through a construction site. The scene was inspired by footage Purvis and Wade had seen of Sébastien Foucan demonstrating his sport of free running, also known as parkour, in the 2003 documentary *Jump London*. The filmmakers cast Foucan as the bomb-maker Mollaka and employed his amazing skills to make the stunts as real as possible. The jaw-dropping leap from one construction crane to another and then to a roof below was done in one shot. While the jumpers wore safety harnesses connected to an even higher crane and a 15 in by 28 in (38 cm by 7 cm) landing platform was digitally removed from the shot, the leap was done for real.

Back at the Barrandov Studios in Prague, the filmmakers shot the poker game between Bond and Le Chiffre on one of Peter Lamont's most beautifully designed sets. Producer Michael G. Wilson, along with poker expert Thomas

Sambrook taught the actors the intricacies of Texas Hold'em poker, a game requiring a great deal more strategy than baccarat, the game Fleming chose for the novel.

In England, the stunt team tested ways to somersault one of the few Aston Martin DBS models then in existence. Stunt co-ordinator Gary Powell and driver Adam Kirley used an 18-in (46-cm) ramp to launch the $200,000-plus car into a roll, but the vehicle quickly slammed back down, shattering a mannequin of Vesper used in the shot. Special-effects supervisor Chris Corbould's team then mounted an air cannon in the car, hoping it would launch the vehicle into the air. The car flipped over seven times, a new world record.

At Dunsfold Aerodrome in Surrey, England, second unit director Alexander Witt staged other major stunts, including launching a car into the air as if it had been blasted by the slipstream of a 747 airliner. On the Albert R. Broccoli 007 Stage at Pinewood, special and visual effects supervisors Chris Corbould and Steve Begg helped create the most complex set ever built for a Bond film, the interior of a Venetian villa that crumbles into the Grand Canal. They also created the villa in miniature at 1/3 scale—26 ft (7.9 m) tall—in Pinewood's 800,000-gallon (3,636,872-liter)

HOW JAMES BECAME BOND
(top to bottom, left to right)
Second unit director Alexander Witt; Martin Campbell discusses an important cinematic moment with Eva Green (Vesper Lynd) and Daniel Craig; executive producer Callum McDougall; Eva Green, Daniel Craig and Caterina Murino (Solange) pose for a publicity photo in the Bahamas; associate producer Andrew Noakes and executive producer Tony Waye on location; screenwriter Paul Haggis.

Paddock Tank.

Throughout the physically gruelling shoot, Daniel Craig continued to surpass the crew's expectations. The three months of training he undertook before filming had given his body a lean, dangerous look. His performance did not echo his predecessors as much as it brought Fleming's words to life. But would audiences accept a harder, colder Bond? Would they endure the stomach-wrenching torture scene from Fleming's novel? Would they feel betrayed by a Bond film where 007 does not get the girl, but only ends up with the bitter taste of her death and betrayal? As with the film's poker game, the stakes for the filmmakers were enormous.

Composer David Arnold faced a unique challenge with his fourth 007 score. The script specifically stated that the Bond theme would not be played until the end credits. Arnold and title song performer Chris Cornell, formerly of the rock band Soundgarden and later Audioslave, co-wrote a theme, "You Know My Name," which they felt contained the musical DNA of James Bond without relying on Monty Norman's "The James Bond Theme." The result was a hard-driving theme song that celebrated the essence of Bond's character in the film.

Casino Royale premiered on Tuesday, 14th November 2006, at the Odeon Leicester Square, London. The premiere had been chosen as the 60th Royal Film Performance, and was attended by Her Majesty, Queen Elizabeth II. The response around the globe was phenomenal: *Casino Royale* became the highest-grossing Bond film ever. In the UK, it became the first Bond film to earn more than $100 million at the box office. Daniel Craig's performance won universal praise and a BAFTA nomination for Best Actor. For producers Wilson and Broccoli, the gamble of making *Casino Royale* had paid off: a new standard had been set and a path for 007's future had been laid.

MICHAEL G. WILSON & BARBARA BROCCOLI

Michael G. Wilson and Barbara Broccoli have been the producers of the James Bond films since 1995. Their vision has kept the 007 series and the character of James Bond both exciting and relevant.

Born in New York to actress-writer Dana Wilson, Michael G. Wilson studied engineering and then law. His mother married Bond producer Albert R. "Cubby" Broccoli in 1960, allowing Michael to witness firsthand Bond's success and development. In 1972, Wilson began working for his stepfather and Harry Saltzman in a legal-administrative capacity. He worked on many aspects of *The Spy Who Loved Me* (1977), earning the title, Special Assistant to the Producer. Wilson became executive producer on *Moonraker* (1979). For the next five Bond films, Wilson collaborated on the screenplays. With *A View To A Kill* (1985), Wilson became a full producing partner with Albert R. "Cubby" Broccoli. Michael G. Wilson is the Chairman of the National Media Museum of Photography, Film and Television.

Barbara Broccoli grew up with the Bond films. After earning a film degree from Loyola University in Los Angeles, she became an assistant director on *A View To A Kill*, although also she worked on the crew of both *For Your Eyes Only* (1981) and *Octopussy* (1983). With the next two films in the series, Broccoli graduated to associate producer, and first became a producer with Michael G. Wilson on *GoldenEye* in 1995.

Outside of Bond, Broccoli executive produced the acclaimed *Crime Of The Century* for HBO in 1996. Broccoli is also Chair of First Light, the UK Film Council's filmmaking initiative for young people.

QUANTUM OF SOLACE
(2008)

CAST Daniel Craig (James Bond), Olga Kurylenko (Camille), Mathieu Amalric (Dominic Greene), Judi Dench (M), Giancarlo Giannini (Mathis), Gemma Arterton (Agent Fields), Jeffrey Wright (Felix Leiter), David Harbour (Gregg Beam), Jesper Christensen (Mr. White), Anatole Taubman (Elvis), Rory Kinnear (Tanner), Tim Pigott-Smith (Foreign Secretary), Joaquín Cosio (General Medrano), Fernando Guillén Cuervo (Colonel of Police), Jesús Ochoa (Lt. Orso), Glenn Foster (Mitchell), Paul Ritter (Guy Haines), Simon Kassianides (Yusef), Stana Katic (Corinne), Neil Jackson (Mr. Slate), Oona Chaplin (Receptionist)
PRODUCERS Michael G. Wilson & Barbara Broccoli
DIRECTOR Marc Forster
WRITTEN BY Paul Haggis and Neal Purvis & Robert Wade
EXECUTIVE PRODUCERS Anthony Waye & Callum McDougall
'ANOTHER WAY TO DIE' Performed by Jack White & Alicia Keys
WRITTEN & PRODUCED BY Jack White
MUSIC BY David Arnold
PRODUCTION DESIGNER Dennis Gassner
DIRECTOR OF PHOTOGRAPHY Roberto Schaefer A.S.C.
EDITORS Matt Chessé A.C.E.
Richard Pearson A.C.E.
COSTUME DESIGNER Louise Frogley
SECOND UNIT DIRECTOR Dan Bradley
STUNT COORDINATOR Gary Powell
SECOND UNIT BOAT SEQUENC DIRECTED BY Simon Crane
SPECIAL EFFECTS SUPERVISOR Chris Corbould
VISUAL EFFECTS DESIGNER Kevin Tod Haug
UNIT PRODUCTION MANAGER Jeremy Johns
SECOND UNIT PRODUCTION MANAGER Terry Bamber
FIRST ASSISTANT DIRECTOR Michael Lerman
CASTING Debbie McWilliams
MAIN TITLES DESIGNED BY MK12
PUBLICITY AND MARKETING Anne Bennett
PROMOTIONS Keith Snelgrove
POST PRODUCTION SUPERVISOR Michael Solinger
VISUAL EFFECTS PRODUCER Leslie McMinn
ASSISTANT PRODUCER Gregg Wilson
SUPERVISING ART DIRECTOR Chris Lowe
SET DIRECTOR Anna Pinnock
PROPERTY MASTER Barry Gibbs
CONSTRUCTION MANAGER Stephen Bohan
STILLS PHOTOGRAPHER Karen Ballard
PRODUCTION MANAGER UK Janine Modder
MAKEUP SUPERVISOR Paul Engelen
HAIRDRESSING SUPERVISOR Zoe Tahir
BOND GIRLS MAKEUP & HAIR Naomi Donne
WARDROBE SUPERVISOR Lindsay Pugh
CAMERA OPERATOR George Richmond
SCRIPT SUPERVISOR Nikki Clapp
SECOND UNIT DIRECTOR OF PHOTOGRAPHY Shaun O'Dell
SECOND UNIT ASSISTANT DIRECTOR Terry Madden
SOUND RECORDIST Chris Munro
ELECTRICAL SUPERVISOR Eddie Knight
ASSISTANT PRODUCER Andrew Noakes
PRODUCTION EXECUTIVE David Pope

Quantum Of Solace, the 22nd Bond adventure, began principal photography on 7th January 2008. The film picked up the story one hour after the end of *Casino Royale*, making *Quantum* the first direct sequel produced by EON. The producers chose Marc Forster, acclaimed director of *The Kite Runner* (2007), *Finding Neverland* (2004), and *Monsters Ball* (2001) to direct, and the script was once again written by Paul Haggis, Neal Purvis, and Robert Wade.

Daniel Craig reprised the role of Bond, having won rave reviews for his debut as 007 in *Casino Royale*. Starring alongside him as the vengeful Camille was Olga Kurylenko, a former fashion model who had effortlessly crossed over to film acting with starring roles in the French thriller *Le Serpent* (2006) and the graphic novel adaptation *Hitman* (2007). Rising British star Gemma Arterton played Agent Fields.

The cast of villains was led by Mathieu Amalric, one of France's leading screen stars, as Dominic Greene, with Elvis at his side, played by Anatole Taubman. Joaquín Cosio took the role of General Medrano, Camille's bitter enemy.

The indispensable Judi Dench returned as M, and other welcome faces reprising their *Casino Royale* roles were Jeffrey Wright (Felix Leiter), Jesper Christensen (Mr. White), and Giancarlo Giannini (Mathis).

The production team filmed in more overseas locations than any other Bond movie to date. Filming began at Pinewood Studios before traveling to Panama City and Colon in Panama, the Atacama Desert in Chile, Sienna, Carrara, Lake Garda and Fonteblanda in Italy, and Bregenz, Austria, with an additional unit filming an aerial sequence in Mexico.

At Pinewood, the production used the 007 stage and five other sound stages to build the interiors of over 14 different sets. The "Back Lot" was also utilized to build the exterior of

Perla De Las Dunas, the hotel Medrano chooses for the money exchange with Greene. The hotel's interior was built on the 007 Stage and fitted with over 50 explosive charges for Bond's violent clash with Greene.

Bruneval Barracks, Montgomery Lines in Aldershot, Hampshire, doubled for snowy Moscow, where Bond tracks down Yusef Kabira, the man who betrayed Vesper.

Bodyflight, Bedford, the world's largest skydiving wind tunnel, was used by the visual effects department to film Bond and Camille's freefall from the DC-3 plane in Bolivia. The facility was originally built by the MOD to research aircraft control. The tunnel simulates the experience of freefalling at 170 mph. Craig and Kurylenko trained with Gary Powell and his stunt team for several weeks before filming. The sinkhole Bond and Camille freefall into was created on a Pinewood set.

Panama City doubled for the streets and buildings of La Paz, Bolivia. Filming began at Howard Airport, dressed by the art department to serve as La Paz Airport, where Agent Fields greets Bond and Mathis. The production chose two remarkable buildings for the film: the Inac Building and The Old Union Club. The Inac Building in Casco Viejo (usually the offices of the Institute Nationale Du Culture) became the set of the Andean Grand Hotel, Bond's choice on arrival in La Paz. The art department gave the Inac new awnings, polished floors, and a full paint job inside and out. In the film, Bond stays here with Agent Fields, who meets a sticky end in the hotel's honeymoon suite.

NOTE PERFECT *1st assistant director Michael Lerman and* **Quantum Of Solace's** *director Marc Forster plan the day's shoot in northern Chile's desert region.*

Two minutes walk away is The Old Union Club. This became the location for Greene's fundraising party. The production team took months to clean the area of rubble and rubbish before the art department built an illuminated bar, hung peach drapes within the building's arches and installed elegant white lights. Filming of the scene took place over four nights.

The production then moved to Colón, Panama. The huge Arboix Building in downtown Colón became the Hotel

DRESS REHEARSAL *Marc Forster directs the confrontation between Greene (Mathieu Amalric), Camille (Olga Kurylenko), and Bond (Daniel Craig) at the Greene Planet fundraiser.*

Dessalines, Haiti. In the film, this is Bond's first stop on his mission, and he battles Quantum agent Mr. Slate in one of the top-floor rooms. In Colón, the crew often engaged in extensive renovation projects, for much of the city's beautiful architecture is in decay. A third action unit joined the main unit in Colón to shoot the boat chase, much of which took place at Jetty 3 and Jetty 6. The final part of the sequence was filmed at Cabra Island, where Bond disembarks at a paradise island with Camille in his arms. A hundred years ago the island was used by neighbouring Isle Grande as a cemetery. Today, it is privately owned—two and a half hectares of palm trees, macaws, wild deer, and butterflies.

Northern Chile possesses the vast, barren landscapes envisioned by Marc Forster for the film's climax. Based in a hotel in Antofagasta, the crew traveled for up to two hours each morning to reach filming locations. The ESO Paranal (the European Organization for Astronomical Research in the

DESERT SHOOT
Director Marc Forster and Daniel Craig (James Bond) in conference in Chile.

Southern Hemisphere) was the setting for the exterior scenes at Perla de las Dunas, Bolivia. The observatory is sited 6,000 ft up on a mountain crest bordering the Atacama desert—a perfect place for studying the stars. Other remote locations in Chile were used for the drought-stricken village Bond and Camille walk through, the train station where they part ways, and the desert where Bond abandons Greene.

Quantum's aerial sequences were shot in the mountains of Baja California, Mexico. A crew of 66, led by 2nd unit director Dan Bradley, filmed for 17 days from a small airport near the town of San Felipe. In the sequence, Bond flies a vintage DC-3 plane (made in 1939) and is attacked by an acrobatic Marchetti and a Huey helicopter. For environmental and safety reasons, gunfire and smoke was added later as a visual effect. The aircraft were filmed by an Aerostar fitted with Snakehead nose and tail cameras and by an Astar helicopter carrying a Spacecam. Two ground camera crews covered the action from the mountains.

The film's thrilling opening sequence was shot by the second unit over eight weeks in three different Italian locations. Lake Garda, in the north, marked the start of the Aston Martin vs. Alfa Romeo car chase. The crew moved from Lake Garda to Carrara to continue filming the chase

READY TO ROLL *(left to right)) production designer Dennis Gassner; director of photography Roberto Schaefer.*

through the 2000-year-old marble quarry; Michelangelo sculpted his "David" from this gleaming white stone.

Filming the car chase concluded in the historic centre of Siena where shots of the world-famous Palio horse race were filmed the previous year. The second unit shot Bond's chase on foot through the Piazza Il Campo and over the city's sprawling rooftops. The chase culminates in an art gallery, which was built on the 007 Stage at Pinewood Studios.

The opera house scene, where Bond discovers Greene in a secret meeting with Quantum, was shot over two weeks of night shoots at the Bregenz Festival House in Austria, during the 2007/8 production of *Tosca*, performed on the famous floating stage, surrounded by Lake Constance, on a spectacular giant eye set.

For his fifth 007 score, composer David Arnold used darker, more ambiguous electronic sounds alongside the orchestra than in *Casino Royale* to reflect Bond's emotional state. He also used South American percussion instruments and charango and pan pipes to reflect the exotic locations and a creeping, poisonous theme for the Quantum Organization. American rocker Jack White wrote and produced the theme song "Another Way To Die" and performed it with R&B singer Alicia Keys, marking the first duet for a Bond title song.

On 29th October 2008, Princes William and Harry attended the star-studded Royal World Charity Premiere of *Quantum* of Solace in Leicester Square, London. The film would gross a phenomenal $576 million worldwide, the most successful Bond film to date.

CHRIS CORBOULD

Chris Corbould has made essential contributions to the special effects featured in many Bond films. He comes from a special effects family—his uncle Colin Chilvers and brothers Neil and Paul are also prolific special-effects coordinators.

Corbould's career started in 1977 as a technician on *The Spy Who Loved Me*. After *Moonraker* (1979). He was senior technician on *For Your Eyes Only* (1981) and *A View To A Kill* (1985), floor supervisor on *The Living Daylights* (1987), and supervisor for the 2nd unit on *Licence To Kill* (1989).

In 1995, when Pierce Brosnan took the role of Bond in *GoldenEye*, Corbould worked on his first 007 film as supervisor and he has been responsible for the special effects on every Bond film since, including 2012's *Skyfall*. Corbould and his team were BAFTA nominated for *GoldenEye*, *Casino Royale* (2006), and *Quantum of Solace* (2008).

Corbould's other film credits include: *The Mummy* (1999); *102 Dalmations* (2000), *Lara Croft: Tomb Raider* (2001), *Lara Croft Tomb Raider: Cradle Of Life* (2003), *Batman Begins* (2005), and *The Dark Knight* (2008), *Inception* (2010), for which he won the Academy Award for Best Achievement in Visual Effects, *The Dark Knight Rises* (2012), the upcoming *Star Wars VII* (2015), and *Bond 24* (2015).

In 2014 Corbould was awarded the Order of the British Empire for services to film.

BIG BANG *Corbould and his team create a spectacular explosion on the Perla de las Dunas set in Pinewood; Mathieu Amalric takes cover.*

SKYFALL (2012)

CAST Daniel Craig (James Bond), Judi Dench (M),
Javier Bardem (Silva), Ralph Fiennes (Gareth
Mallory), Naomie Harris (Eve), Bérénice Lim
Marlohe (Severine), Albert Finney (Kincade),
Ben Whishaw (Q), Rory Kinnear (Tanner),
Ola Rapace (Patrice), Helen McCrory (Clair Dowar
MP), Nicholas Woodeson (Dr. Hall), Bill Buckhurst
(Ronson).
DIRECTOR Sam Mendes
PRODUCERS
Michael G. Wilson and Barbara Broccoli
WRITTEN BY
Neal Purvis & Robert Wade and John Logan
EXECUTIVE PRODUCER
Callum McDougall
"SKYFALL" Performed by Adele
WRITTEN BY Adele and Paul Epworth
PRODUCED BY Paul Epworth
MUSIC BY Thomas Newman
PRODUCTION DESIGNER Dennis Gassner
DIRECTOR OF PHOTOGRAPHY
Roger Deakins A.S.C., B.S.C.
EDITORS Stuart Baird A.C.E., Kate Baird
COSTUME DESIGNER Jany Temime
SECOND UNIT DIRECTOR Alexander Witt
SPECIAL EFFECTS AND MINIATURE EFFECTS
SUPERVISOR Chris Corbould
STUNT COORDINATOR Gary Powell
CASTING Debbie McWilliams
MAIN TITLES DESIGNED BY Daniel Kleinman
UNIT PRODUCTION MANAGERS
Callum McDougall, Jeremy Johns
FIRST ASSISTANT DIRECTOR Michael Lerman
VISUAL EFFECTS AND MINIATURE
SUPERVISOR Steve Begg
ASSOCIATE PRODUCER Gregg Wilson
PRODUCTION SUPERVISOR Janine Modder
LOCATION PRODUCTION MANAGERS
Chris Brock, Angus More Gordon, Anthony Waye
SECOND UNIT PRODUCTION MANAGER
Terry Bamber
POST PRODUCTION SUPERVISOR
Michael Solinger
SUPERVISING ART DIRECTOR Chris Lowe
SET DECORATOR Anna Pinnock
PROPERTY MASTER Jamie Wilkinson
CONSTRUCTION MANAGER Stephen Bohan
STILLS PHOTOGRAPHER François Duhamel
VISUAL EFFECTS PRODUCER Leslie Lerman
MAKEUP DESIGNER Naomi Donne
HAIR DESIGNER Zoe Tahir
MR. CRAIG'S MAKEUP Donald Mowat
WARDROBE SUPERVISOR Gordon Harmer
PUBLICITY AND MARKETING
Stephanie Wenborn
PROMOTIONS Keith Snelgrove
SCRIPT SUPERVISOR Jayne-Ann Tenggren
SOUND RECORDIST Stuart Wilson
ELECTRICAL SUPERVISOR John Higgins
SECOND UNIT ASSISTANT DIRECTOR
Terry Madden
CO-PRODUCERS Andrew Noakes, David Pope

On April 19, 2010, Bond producers Michael G. Wilson and Barbara Broccoli issued a statement that the latest film, then-titled *Bond 23*, was on hold as MGM Studios, co-owners of Bond, was on the brink of bankruptcy.

By this stage, development on *Bond 23* was well advanced. Bond screenwriters Neal Purvis and Robert Wade, together with Peter Morgan, had worked on a treatment that was delivered in November 2009. In addition, Sam Mendes, impressed with the franchise's direction since *Casino Royale*, had accepted Wilson and Broccoli's offer of the director's chair.

Deciding that the treatment wasn't quite right, Mendes worked with Purvis and Wade on a script featuring a villain named Raoul Sousa seeking revenge on M for betraying him. This draft also reintroduced the character of Q. Purvis and Wade set the climax at Bond's Scottish ancestral home, which they named Skyfall.

MGM emerged from bankruptcy in December 2010, and Sony Pictures agreed to co-fund the film. With *Bond 23* officially back on track, the focus was on a 2012 release, marking the 50th anniversary of the James Bond film series. Mendes invited John Logan to revise the script. Logan decided to reintroduce the character of Moneypenny as a field agent and give her a first name: Eve. Mendes also brought in famed cinematographer Roger Deakins. Production designer Dennis Gassner, who had worked on *Quantum of Solace* and previously with Mendes on *Road to Perdition* (2002) and *Jarhead* (2005), also came onboard.

A press conference on November 3, 2011 (50 years to the day that Sean Connery was announced as James Bond) at London's Corinthia Hotel confirmed the title of the film as *Skyfall*. The stellar cast would include: Javier Bardem as the villain, now-named Silva; Ralph Fiennes as Gareth Mallory, Naomie Harris as Eve Moneypenny; Bérénice Lim Marlohe as Severine; Ben Whishaw as Q; Rory Kinnear returning as Chief of Staff Tanner; Ola Rapace as the assassin Patrice; Albert Finney as Skyfall's gamekeeper Kincade; and with Judi Dench returning as M. During the conference, Craig expressed his desire to make a "Bond film with a capital B."

The pre-titles sequence, in which Daniel Craig's Bond chases Ola Rapace's Patrice onto a fast-moving train was filmed in the Turkish cities of Istanbul and Adana. Attached to safety wires, Craig and Rapace performed their own stunts atop the train, which was traveling at over 30 miles per hour above a 300-foot drop.

The first unit filmed at a variety of London locations with a splinter unit filming exteriors in Shanghai. The waterfront Macau casino was a spectacular set built on Pinewood's Paddock Tank. On the studio back lot, the production team

![SKYFALL poster]

FIRST STEPS *(far left) Shooting begins with Daniel Craig in costume as James Bond; (left) Javier Bardem wearing blue overalls for a costume test with costume designer Jany Temime and key set costumer Kevin Pratten.*

BEHIND THE SCENES *(clockwise from above)* Stunt co-ordinator *Gary Powell rehearses the bike chase in Istanbul's Grand Bazaar; Javier Bardem (Silva), director Sam Mendes and Bérénice Marlohe (Severine) on the dead city set; screenwriter John Logan and producer Michael G. Wilson on the set of Q's lab.*

had worked with Judi Dench in seven James Bond films over 17 years.

Long-time Mendes composer Thomas Newman wrote the score for *Skyfall*, winning a BAFTA Award for Best Film Music. Singer-songwriter Adele and record producer Paul Epworth provided the title song, "Skyfall," which debuted on Global James Bond Day October 5, 2012, a day-long series of events for 007 fans around the world celebrating James Bond's golden anniversary on film. Performed by Adele, "Skyfall" won Best Original Song at the 85th Academy Awards®.

After much fanfare, including a popular segment that filmmaker Danny Boyle shot with Daniel Craig and Queen Elizabeth II for the 2012 Summer Olympics Opening Ceremony in London, *Skyfall* had its Royal Premiere at the Royal Albert Hall on October 23, 2012. *Skyfall*, the first Bond film to be shown on Imax screens, became the highest-grossing film in the UK to date.

erected Silva's "Dead City" lair. On Pinewood's 007 Stage, special effects supervisor Chris Corbould's concept of a London underground train crashing into a service chamber became a reality when Corbould and his team fitted an overhead track with two full-size carriages hung underneath and linked to a powerful truck and cable system. This allowed the two carriages, which had a combined weight of roughly 15 tons, to get up to speed and then dip down into the set. Ten remotely operated cameras covered this thrilling, one-time stunt from various angles.

For the film's climax, production designer Dennis Gassner constructed a façade of Skyfall Lodge on Hankley Common, Surrey, with interiors filmed at Pinewood. For the scene in which Silva's helicopter crashes into the lodge, Corbould and visual effects and miniature supervisor Steve Begg created a ⅓-scale helicopter and lodge at Longcross Studios and controlled the helicopter with a motion base on a hydraulic arm.

M's death scene proved an emotional day on set, especially for producers Michael G. Wilson and Barbara Broccoli, who

AT THE BAFTAS *(left to right) Screenwriter Robert Wade, director Sam Mendes, producers Barbara Broccoli and Michael G. Wilson, and screenwriter Neal Purvis with the BAFTA for Outstanding British Film.*

AWARD WINNER *British singer-songwriter Adele proudly displays her Academy Award® for Best Song.*

SAM MENDES

Sam Mendes' work directing theatre and film spans 25 years. At 24, he became the first Artistic Director of the Minerva Theatre in Chichester. At 27, he founded the Donmar Warehouse in London, which he ran for ten years. It is now one of the world's leading playhouses. Mendes' other theatre work includes numerous acclaimed productions, ranging from classical drama to modern plays and musicals, for the Royal Shakespeare Company, the National Theatre and London's West End. His latest production, *Charlie and the Chocolate Factory* is running at the Theatre Royal Drury Lane.

In 2009, Mendes founded the Bridge Project, a transatlantic classical theatre company. His many theatre awards include: four Olivier Awards, two Tony Awards, four Evening Standard Awards, several Critics' Choice Awards and the Hamburg Shakespeare Prize.

In 1998 Mendes directed his first film, *American Beauty*, winning the Academy Award® for Best Director and Best Picture, as well as the Golden Globe and Directors' Guild Awards. He has since directed the Academy Award®-winning *Road To Perdition* (2002), *Jarhead* (2005), *Revolutionary Road* (2008), *Away We Go* (2009), and the BAFTA and Academy Award®-winning *Skyfall* (2012), one of the most successful films of all time.

In 2003 Mendes founded Neal Street Productions with Pippa Harris and Caro Newling. Neal Street has produced the BAFTA award-winning television series *Call The Midwife* and *The Hollow Crown*; several movies including *Starter for 10* (2006), *Things We Lost in the Fire* (2007), *Stuart: A Life Backwards* (2007) and, in the theatre, the long-running *Shrek The Musical*.

Mendes was awarded a CBE in 2000 and a Directors' Guild Lifetime Achievement Award in 2005.

NB Numbers in **bold** indicate main entries.

A

Acrostar Bede jet 101, 112, **198**, 319
Adam, Ken 302-303, 306, 310, 312-313, 314
Adam **38**, 219
Aerospatiale helicopters **198**, 331
aerosol can 166, **244**
AgustaWestland AW101 helicopter 97
airships 95, 188, **200**
Akakievich, Colonel **148**
Aki **110**, 161, 191, 240, 260, 272, 302
Alvarez, Dr. **38**, 48, 57, 92, 128, 130, 166, 186, 238, 247, 254
Amasova, Major Anya 62, 79, 99, 109, **110–11**, 163, 183, 207, 216, 222, 226, 227, 236, 241, 246, 250, 263, 285, 312-313
ambulance **233**, **241**, 263
AMC Hornet X hatchback 180, **200**, **201**
AMC Matador **201**
Anders, Andrea 95, **111**, 126, 246, 310
Anderson Wheeler 500 NE double rifle **244**
Antonov AN-124 plane 57, 104, **201**, 246, 283
Apollo Jet Crew **38**
Apostis **38**, 316
AR-7 folding sniper's rifle 134
Arkov, Prof. Mikhail **38**, 48, 129, 148, 231
Arnold, David 320, 328-29, 330-31, 332-333, 334-35 336-37
ASAT (anti-satellite) missile **244**
Asian Cartel **38**
assault rifle 105, **244**
Aston Martin DB5 75, 83, 100, 115, 134, 142, **202–03**, 204, 217, 219, 228, 234, 327
Aston Martin DBS **204**, 266, 283, 289, 335
Aston Martin DB Mk III **202**, 298
Aston Martin Silver Birch 202, 203
Aston Martin V8 **205**
Aston Martin Vanquish V12 106, **205**, 222, 236, 263, 279
astronauts **149**, 222
ATAC 70, 71, 127, 154, 158 , 175, 229, 235, 241, **244**, 262
atomic devices 67, 75, 77, 137, 220, 242, **244–45**, 258
attaché case 134, **244**, **245**
Aubergine, Achille 49, 107, 145, **149**, 151, 217, 233
Audi 200 Quattro **206**
avalanche-rescue receiver **245**

B

Baines 48, 64, **149**, 308
Bambi **39**
Barry, John 296-97, 298-99, 300, 302-03, 310-11, 314-15, 318, 3020-21,

322-23, 329
Barsov, Sergei **39**, 75, 110-11, 278
Bartlett, Ruby **112**
bath-o-sub submarine **206**
battlesuit **244**
Beam, CIA Chief Gregory 58, **149**, 169
Bechmann, Dr. **77**, 99, 190, 207
Beech 18 plane **206**, 319
Bell, Mrs. **149**, 211
Bell helicopters **206-207**
Bell 206 JetRangers **206**, **207**
Bell 206B helicopter 77, 137, **206**, 244
Bell-Textron Jet Pack **246**
Benson, Capt. **149**
Bentley Continental **207**
Bentley Mark IV **207**
Bentley Mark VI **207**
Benz 56, **149**, 166, 231, 297
Bergstrom, Prof. Inga **112**
Beretta .25 automatic 183, **246-47**, 289
Beretta 84FS Cheetah **247**
Beretta 950 (Jetfire) **246-47**
Beretta Tomcat **247**
Bey, Kerim 56, 70, 138, 145, 149, **150**, 167, 192, 193, 231
Bianca 101, **112**
Big, Mr. see Kananga, Dr. (aka Mr Big)
Binder, Maurice 300, 302, 304, 306, 308, 310, 312, 314, 316–317, 318, 320, 324-25, 331
binocular/monocular camera **247**
Bird 1 61, 149, **207**, 222, 228, 272
Bleeker Flying School 149, 211
Blofeld, Ernst Stavro 36, 40–41, 60, 77, 93, 95, 98, 101, 106, 112, 113, 121, 151, 153, 155, 159, 204, 210, 228, 251, 267, 286, 305, 306
Blofeld's Angels of Death **112-13**, 251, 267
blunderbuss 251
BMW 750iL 199, **208**, 255
BMW R1200 **209**
BMW Z3 **208**
BMW Z8 **208-09**, 216, 263
Bob, Billy 219
bobsleds **210**
Boitier, Col. Jacques **42**, 98, 166, 246, 282
Bombardier Ski-Doo MX Z-REV snowmobiles **236**
Bombe Surprise 106, **247**
bomb sled **210**
Bond (and)
    actors playing 24–35
    curriculum vitae 14–15
    lifestyle 20–21
    skills 16–17
    wardrobe 16–17
Bondola **210**
Bond's belt 271
Bonita **42**, 89
book/tape recorder **247**
Boothroyd, Major 182-83 see also Q
Borchoi **150**, 169
bounding mines **247**

Bouvier, Pam 48, 61, 85, 92, **114**, 130, 223, 241, 247, 248, 253, 263, 265, 278, 280
Brandt, Helga **42**, 84, 98, 228, 229, 270, 302
Braun **43**, 61, 85
Bray, Sir Hilary 114, **151**, 159
Breitling diver's watch **247**
briefcase bomb compartment **248**
Brink, Jacoba 119, **151**, 316
Broccoli, Albert R. "Cubby" 25, 26, 29, 30–31, 32, 35, 294-95, 296-97, 298-99, 300-01, 302-03, 304-05, 306-07, 308-09, 310-11, 312-13, 314-15, 316-17, 318-19, 320, 322-23, 324-25
Broccoli, Barbara 35, 294, 320, 322, 328, 330, 332-33, 334-35, 336, 338, 339
broom radio **248**
Brosnan, Pierce **32–33**, 322, 326-27, 328-29, 330, 332-33, 334, 337
BSA A65L Lightning motorbike 204, **210**, 219
bug detector **248**, 260 see also shaver bug detector
Bukharin, General **151**
Bull, The **43**
Bunt, Irma **43**, 98, 121, 155, 206, 228, 305
Butcher, Professor Joe **44**, 92
Butterfly Girl **151**

C

cable cars 60, 63, **210-211**
Cagiva motorcycle **211**, 231
cameras 61, 88, 120, 244, 251, 258, 264, 267, 274, 275, 276, 286, 300-301
Camille 58–59, 76, 89, 95, **116–117**, 174, 181, 206, 215, 238, 336-37
Campbell, Martin 35, 60, 151, 301, 311, 326-27, 334
Campbell 60, **151**, 304
Caplan, Paula 62, 103, 104, **152**
captured trawler 211
Capungo **44**
Caroline **115**, 118, 205, 217
Carter, Commander 78, **152**, 224, 233, 241, 272
Caruso, Miss **115**
Carver, Elliot **45**, 60–61, 65, 98, 115, 130-31, 152, 159, 163, 187, 194, 199, 206, 208, 212, 222, 237, 249, 251, 253, 254, 255, 259, 260, 269, 276, 279, 287
Carver's PR **152**
Carver, Paris 61, **115**, 210, 260
Carver, Rosie **46**, 64, 141, 149, 244, 277, 281
Case, Tiffany 106, **118-19**, 136, 218, 220, 229, 247, 248, 253, 256, 257
Casino Royale 11, 14, 19, 20, 34, 35, 44, 50, 51, 52, 53, 69, 74, 78, 82, 88, 102, 105, 132-33, 142, 152, 168, 169, 171, 172, 173, 181, 194, 205, 206, 230, 236, 237, 238, 260, 263, 266, 269, 283, 289, 300, 303, 319, 327, 329, 331, 332,

333, **334–35**, 336-37
Bond villains
    Carlos **44**, 78, 174, 236, 237, 238, 263
    Dimitrios, Alex **50**, 78, 142, 205, 230, 236, 238
    Dryden **51**
    Fisher **52**, 289
    Gettler **53**, 132, 237, 260
    Kratt **69**
    Le Chiffre 69, **74**, 82, 88-89, 103, 104, 132-33, 142 152, 169, 174, 204, 236, 238, 262, 267, 271, 277
    Mollaka 69, **78**, 152, 238, 239
    Obanno, Steven 69, 74, **82**, 103, 104, 132, 262
    Valenka **82**, **103**, 132, 204, 266
    White, Mr. 69, 74, 82, 88, 103, **105**, 132, 260
Bond women
    Lynd, Vesper 88, 103, 104, **132-33**, 169, 174, 175, 204, 237, 260, 266, 289
    Solange **142**
Supporting cast
    Carter 78, **152**
    Casino Royale players **152**
    Letter, Felix 132, 152, 168, 169
    M 132, 171, 173, 194, 237, 283, 289
    Mathis, René **174**, 283
    Mendel **175**
    Mitchell 105
    unnamed foreign agent **193**
    Villiers **194**, 230
Vehicles
    Aston Martin 105
    Aston Martin DB5 142, **202**
    Aston Martin DBS **204**, 266, 283, 289
    Aston Martin Silver Birch (1964) 203
    Notar MD-600N helicopter **230**
    Skyfleet S570 prototype airliner 74, 78, 142, **236**, **237**, 238, 263
    Spirit 54 yacht **237**
    Sunseeker yacht 238
    Texron tanker 236, 237, 263
Weapons & equipment
    Heckler & Koch guns **260**
    inhaler bug **262**
    key fob detonator 237, 263
    Medipac **266**
    Omega Seamaster watches **269**
    Sony Ericsson phone 262
    tracking device implant 69, **283**
    Walther P99 **288-89**
    Walther PPK 204, **289**
Casino Royale players **152**
cassette tape **248**
cello case **248**
cement sprayer 226
centrifuge trainer **249**
Cessna 140 N77029 plane 149, 211
Cessna 185 seaplane 198, **211**, 235
Cha **153**
chakra torture kit 98, **249**
Chang, Mr. 46, 137, **153**, 249, 314

Chang, General 130, 287
Charlie 91, **153**
Che Che 153, 234
check copier **249**
Chester, HMS 187, **212**
Chevrolet delivery truck **212**
Chew Mee **119**
Chula 47, 190, 206
CIA Standard Issue Equipment **249**
Cigar Girl 47, 72, 221, 232, 238, 283
cigarette case remote control (Largo's) **249**
cigarette case safecracking unit **250**
cigarette lighter 92, 248, **250**
cigarette lighter (gift from Felix) **250**
cigarette package detonator **250**, 263
Citroën 2CV 127, **212**, 316
Claus 145, 280
Clive, Major **153**, 253
code-cracking device **250**
coffin body collector **250**
Colonel of Police 44, **48**, 174, 236, 237, 238, 263
Colthorpe **154**
Columbo, Milos 70–71, 75, 119, 127, 145, **154**, 157, 251, 280, 282, 316
commando kit **251**
commando knife beacon **251**, 280
compact communicator **251**
computer mirror camera **251**
Conley, Bob **48**, 166, 268
Connery, Sean **24–25**, 294–95, 296–97, 298–99, 300–01, 302–03, 206–07
Corbould, Chris 326, 328, 330–31, 332, 333, 334–35, 336–37
Corinne 61, 154
Coward, Noel 294
Craig, Daniel **34–35**, 48, 327, 331, 333, 334–35, 336–37
crocodile mini-submarine **213**
crossbow 126, 191, **251**
cyanide cigarette 63, **252**

D

Da Vinci machine **252**
Dahl, Bibi 70, 71, **119**, 151, 154, 316
Dalton, Timothy **30–31**, 35, 322–23, 324–25, 326, 333
Dambala **48**, 65, 149, 308
Dario **48**, 85, 198, 263
dart-firing mirror **252**
Davidov, Sasha **48**, 286
Dawes 64, **154**
Day, Commander **155**, 213
Day, May **48**, 49, 61, 106, 149, 151, 166–67, 192, 193, 200, 219, 233, 234, 251, 253, 270, 282
decompression chamber **253**
Defence, Minister of 110, 175, 187
Delta-9 nerve gas *see* nerve gas *and* poison gas
Dent, Prof. **49**, 80, 143
Dentonite toothpaste 250, **253**, 273
Derval, Domino 72, 89, 103, 120, 152, 214, 258, 278, 280, 300
Derval, Major François 72, 75, 85, 104, 120, 241
detonator 49, 107, 131, 242, 253
  cigarette package **250**, 263
  glasses 258, 289
  hydraulic 261
  key fob 237, 263
Devonshire, HMS 60, 98, 130, 155, 159, 175, 187, 194, 211, **213**, 237, 240, 259, 270, 276, 286
Di Vicenzo, Tracy 60, 112, **120–21**, 153, 155, 204, 228, 234, 305
diamond satellite weapon/laser 77, 223, **253**
Diamonds Are Forever 19, 20, 24, 39, 40, 52, 77, 93, 95, 98, 101, 106, 118–19, 136, 161, 168, 169, 177, 180, 192, 194, 204, 206, 218, 219, 220, 229, 247, 248, 253, 255, 256, 257, 271, 290, 303, **306–07**, 321, 328

Bond villains
  Bambi 39
  Blofeld, Ernst Stavro 40–41, 77, 93, 95, 101, 106, 118–19, 136, 194, 206, 248, 253, 255, 256, 271, 286, 290
  Franks, Peter **52**, 256–57
  Metz, Prof. 57, **77**, 229, 248, 253
  Saxby, Bert **93**, 101, 194, 286
  Slumber, Morton **95**, 136
  Thumper **39**, 194
  Tree, Shady 95, **101**
  Wint, Mr. & Kidd, Mr. 95, 101, **106**, 136, 192, 194, 219, 235, 253, 271

Bond women
  Case, Tiffany 106, **118–19**, 136, 218, 220, 229, 247, 248, 253, 256, 257
  Marie **133**
  O'Toole, Plenty 118, **136**

Supporting cast
  Hergersheimer, Klaus **161**
  Leiter, Felix **168–69**, 206
  M **170**
  Moneypenny, Miss **177**
  Munger, Sir Donald **180**
  Nevada Sheriff **180**
  Q 204, 256, 257, 286
  Tynan, Dr. 106, **192**
  Whistler, Mrs. 106, 192, **194**
  Whyte, Willard 93, 106, **194**, 206, 247, 248, 255, 271, 286

Vehicles
  Aston Martin DBS 204
  bath-o-sub submarine **206**, 253
  Bell 206B helicopter 206
  cruise ship 106
  Ford Thunderbird (1965) **219**
  helicopters 169, 206

Honda ATC 3-wheelers **220**, 229
moonbuggy 180, 222, **229**
Mustang Mach I "Fastback" 180, 218

Weapons & equipment
  Bombe Surprise 106, **247**
  cassette tape 248
  diamond satellite laser 77, **253**
  elevator gas chamber **255**
  fake fingerprints **256**
  finger clamp **256**
  fingerprint scanner **257**
  pipeline pig **271**
  piton gun **271**
  shield 169
  space weapon 194
  voice simulator **286**
  wave-walker **290**
  Walther PPK 7.65 mm 256, **289**
dice, loaded **253**
Die Another Day 16, 32, 38, 52–53, 57, 65, 78, 81, 95, 103, 104, 106, 128–29, 137, 153, 156, 166, 177, 186, 187, 193, 199, 201, 205, 219, 221, 222, 230, 231, 236, 238, 244, 245, 246, 247, 251, 254, 261, 268, 269, 270, 279, 281, 329, 331, **332–33**, 335

Bond villains
  Alvarez, Dr. **38**, 57, 128, 166, 186, 238, 247, 254
  Frost, Miranda **52–53**, 57, 129, 193, 201, 283
  Graves, Gustav/Moon, Colonel Tan-Sun **57**, 65, 78, 81, 128–29, 156, 185, 193, 199, 201, 205, 219, 221, 231, 244, 247, 251, 254, 261, 263, 267, 269, 270, 279, 281
  Kil, Mr. **65**, 263
  Moon, General 57, **78**, 81, 245
  North Korean generals **81**
  Scorpion guard 95
  Van Bierk, Mr. **104**, 198, 251, 269, 281
  Vlad **104**, 245
  Zao 57, 78, **106**, 128, 153, 186, 205, 222, 281

Bond women
  Jinx **128–29**, 153, 187, 201, 219, 230, 238, 247, 251, 261, 263, 269, 279, 283

Peaceful Fountains of Desire **137**
Supporting cast
  Chang, Mr. 137, **153**
  Falco, Damian **156**
  Krug, Mr. **166**
  M 156, 187, 246, 286
  Moneypenny, Miss **177**, 286
  Q 205, 246, 269, 279
  Raoul **187**
  Robinson, Charles **187**, 286
  unnamed foreign agent **193**
  Verity 193
  Villiers 230
Vehicles
  Antonov An-124 plane 57, 104, 101, 246, 283
  Antonov transport plane 129
  Aston Martin Vanquish V12 106, **204**, 222, 236, 263, 279
  Bombardier Ski-Doo MX Z-REV snowmobiles 236
  Ford Fairlane 185
  Ford Thunderbird **219**
  helicopter 101, 106
  hovercraft 57, 231, 247
  ice dragster **221**
  Jaguar XKR 205, **222**
  Mil Mi-8 helicopter 199, 251, 280, 281
  Notar MD-600N helicopter 201, **230**
  Osprey hovercraft **231**
  Sunseeker 48–50 speedboat **238**
  Superhawk 48 powerboat 128
  switchblade gliders 129, **238**
Weapons & equipment
  ASAT missile **244**
  battlesuit 57, **245**
  Bell-Textron Jet Pack 246, 302
  Beretta 84FS Cheetah **247**
  Beretta Tomcat **247**
  bounding mines **247**
  cell phone bomb 128
  commando kit **251**
  commando knife beacon **251**, 280
  Da Vinci machine **252**
  diamond-cutting laser 65
  Dream Machine **254**
  ejector seat 222
  Gatling gun 222

heat-seeking missiles 222
Icarus satellite 57, 81, 128, 129, 245, **261**
Kevlar vest 263
key fob **263**
laser, industrial **263**
Llama Especial pistol 137
Maori bone hair comb 65, 263
mini rebreather **267**
mortar bomb 222
night vision goggles **268**
parachutes 221, 228, 240
PDA mobile phone 57
rocket belt **246**
rocket launcher 222
rockets 231
Seamaster Omega watch 231, **269**
sonic ring **279**
surfboard saboteur kit **280**, 289
sword 129
tank buster **281**
throwing knives 283
virtual reality glasses **286**
Walther P99 81, 104, 280, 286, **289**
Dimitrios, Alex **50**, 78, 142, 205, 230, 236, 238
Dink **120**
Disco Volante 62, 72, 103, 120, **214**, 244, 258, 278, 280, 286, 311
Dolly 63, **155**, 188, 211
Douglas DC-3 aircraft 117, **215**, 335
Dr. No 11, 19, 20, 24, 80–81, 88, 95, 101, 139, 143, 144, 156, 168, 170, 174, 177, 181, 185, 190, 215, 238, 246, 252, 257, **294–95**, 299, 300, 301, 305, 317
 Bond villains
  Dent, Prof. **49**, 80, 143
  Jones, Mr. 49, **63**, 80, 156, 252, 257
  No, Dr. 49, 63, 71, **80**, 95, 100, 139, 168, 181, 215, 238, 257, 262, 266, 294, 311
  photographer, the 80, **88**
  Sister Lily & Sister Rose **95**
  SPECTRE 80, 289
  Three Blind Mice, The 80, **101**, 143, 174, 238
 Bond women
  Ryder, Honey 95, **139**, 168, 181, 185, 215
  Taro, Miss 49, 80, **143**, 156, 181, 190, 238
  Trench, Sylvia **144**
 Supporting cast
  Duff, Supt. **156**
  Leiter, Felix 88, 185
  M **170**, 246, 289
  Moneypenny, Miss **177**
  Pleydell-Smith 63, **181**, 252
  Prescott, Mary 49, 80, 101, 156, **174**, 190
  Puss-Feller 88, **181**, 185
  Q **182–83**, 185
  Quarrel 80, 88, 139, 156, 181, **185**, 215, 257
  Ryder, Mr. 80, 139

Strangways, John 49, 80, 101, 156, 174, 186, **190**, 257
 Vehicles
  dragon tank 185, **215**
  hearse 101, 238
  Sunbeam Alpine 101, 190, **238**
 Weapons & equipment
  Beretta .25 automatic 183, **246**, 289
  cyanide cigarette 63, **252**
  Geiger counter **257**
  Rolex watch **257**
  Walther PPK 7.65 mm **289**
Dowar, Clair **155**, 173
Draco, Marc Ange 112, 120–21, 153, **155**, 159, 206, 210, 228 233, 234, 251, 282, 305
dragon tank 185, **215**
Drax, Hugo 36, **50–51**, 57, 63, 101, 104, 122, 125, 133, 155, 158, 159, 188, 207, 210, 219, 229, 249, 250, 259, 260, 264, 267, 270, 272, 282, 291, 314
dream machine **254**
Dryden 14, **51**
Dunhill cigarette lighter grenade **254**
Duff, Supt. **156**
Dufour, Corinne **122**, 207, 314

E

Eden, Sir Anthony 10
ejector seat 202, 222, 223, 239
electrified chair **255**
electrified headset **255**, 260
elevator gas chamber **255**
Ericsson JB988 mobile phone 208, **255**
escape pod (Stromberg's) 115, **216**
Eurocopter helicopters 199, 209
Eurocopter 355 Twin Star tree-cutters 209, **216**
Eurocopter AS-365N Dauphin 199, 263

F

Fabergé egg 77, 133, 148, 157, 169, 253, **256**, 267, 283
Fairey Huntress speedboat 91, 216, 286
fake assassination kit **256**
fake fingerprints **256**
fake leg cast **256**
Falco, Damian **156**
Fallon **157**, 278
Fanning, Jim **157**
Farrel, Admiral **157**, 217, 239, 247
Fat, Hai **51**, 95, 119, 153, 158, 161, 206, 259, 282
Fearing, Patricia **122**, 283
Fekkesh, Aziz 93, 111, 122, **157**, 162, 163
Felicca 93, **122**
Felix lighter **256**
Ferrara, Luigi 71, 75, **157**, 227
Ferrari Spider F355 GTS 83, 115, **217**
Feyador, Col. **52**, 62, 68, 188
Fields, Agent 59, **123**, 171

Fillet of Soul 159, 190, 285
Fillet of Soul waiter **52**
finger clamp **256**
fingerprint scanner **257**
fire extinguisher 95, 233
fire truck 142, **217**
Fisher, **52**, 289
five-bladed knife **257**
flash paper **257**
Fleming, Ian **10–11**, 16, 168, 170, 176, 182, 197, 264, 294–95, 298, 300, 301, 302, 305, 310, 314 *see also novels and short stories*
Flex, Jenny **52**, 61, 282
For Your Eyes Only 16, 28, 38, 40, 56, 70–71, 75, 119, 121, 127, 145, 151, 154, 157, 158, 159, 160, 175, 183, 187, 191, 207, 212-13, 227, 229, 235, 241, 244, 247, 251, 255, 262, 280, 282, 314–15, **316–17**, 319, 323, 335, 337
 Bond villains
  Apostis 38
  Blofeld, Ernst Stavro 40–41, 207, 255
  Claus 145, 280
  Gonzales, Hector **56**, 75, 127, 160, 191, 212, 235, 246, 251, 262
  Kriegler, Erich **70**, 119
  Kristatos, Aris **70–71**, 75, 119, 127, 145, 151, 154, 157, 158, 175, 235, 241, 244, 251, 280, 282
  Locque, Emile Leopold 56, **75**, 145, 157, 247, 262
 Bond women
  Dahl, Bibi 70, 71, **119**, 151, 154
  Havelock, Melina 56, 71, **127**, 154, 181, 191, 212, 227, 229, 235, 241, 244, 251, 262
  Von Schlaf, Countess Lisl **145**, 154
 Supporting cast
  Brink, Jacoba 119, **151**
  Columbo, Milos 70–71, 75, 119, 127, 145, **154**, 157, 251, 280, 282
  Ferrara, Luigi 71, 75, **157**, 227
  Gogol, General 71, **158**, 187, 244
  Gray, Sir Frederick 159
  Havelock, Iona 56, 75, 127, **160**, 175, 235, 241
  Havelock, Timothy 56, 71, 75, 127, 154, **160**, 175, 229, 235, 241
  M 159, 191
  Max **175**, 277
  Moneypenny, Miss **176**
  Prime Minister **181**, 277
  Q 191, 262
  Rublevitch **187**
  Tanner, Bill **191**
  unnamed foreign agent **193**
 Vehicles
  Bell helicopter **207**
  Citroën 2CV 127, 232-33
  dune buggies 145
  Lotus Esprit Turbo (1980) **227**
  Mercedes (Locque's) 157
  Neptune submarine 127, 227, **229**, 244
  Osel "Mantis" one-man

atmospheric submersible **227**, 229
Peugeot 504 sedans 212
Rolls-Royce 145
Santa Mavra **235**
Seabee seaplane **235**
seaplane (Gonzales's) **235**
St. Georges 70, 71, 127, 154, 160, 227, 229, **235**, 244, 262
Triana 127, 160, 181, 235, **241**
Yamaha XJ 500 motorcycle 70
 Weapons & equipment
  automatic targeting attack communicator (ATAC) 70, 71, 127, 154, 158, 175, 229, 235, 241, **244**, 262
  binocular/monocular camera **247**
  contact mine 71
  crossbow 127, 191, **251**
  electrified headset **255**, 260
  helicopter remote unit **262**
  Identigraph, Visual **262**
  JIM diving suit **262**
  knives/throwing knives 71, 127, 251, 282
  machine gun 70, 127
  Seiko H357 watch 181, **277**
  spearguns **280**
  spiked candelabra 70
  Walther PPK 7.65 mm 150, **289**
Ford Mustang 306
Ford Mustang (1965) (Fiona Volpe's) **218**
Ford Mustang convertible 134, **218**
Ford Mustang Mach I "Fastback" 180, **218**
Ford Skyliner 203, 209, **219**
Ford Thunderbird **219**
Foreign Secretary **157**
Forster, Marc 336, 337
Franks, Peter **52**, 95, 101, 118
Frazier, Professor **157**
From Russia With Love 20, 24, 40, 68, 70, 71, 79, 91, 98, 138, 144-45, 149, 150, 159, 163, 167, 177, 183, 192, 193, 207, 212, 216, 220, 231, 245, 264, 270, 275, 280, 282, **296–97**, 299, 300, 301, 305, 310, 314, 317, 319, 321, 324, 325
 Bond villains
  Blofeld, Ernst Stavro 40–41, 68, 71, 79
  Grant, Donald "Red" **56**, 68, 79, 91, 138, 149, 150, 159, 212, 220, 231, 245, 289, 297, 298
  Klebb, Rosa 56, **68**, 79, 98, 138, 150, 162, 220, 280
  Krilencu **70**, 145, 150, 245, 282
  Kronsteen 56, 68, **72**, 79, 231
  Morzeny **79**, 280
  Rhoda 91, 212
  SMERSH 56, 68, 71, 79, **98**, 138
  SPECTRE 56, 68, 71, 79, 91, 149, 159, 162, 192, 212, 216, 231, 245, 264, 280, 286, 289
 Bond women
  Romanova, Tatiana 56, 68, 71, 79, **138**, 149, 162, 216, 220, 231, 275,

297
  Trench, Sylvia 144
  Vida & Zora 145, **193**
Supporting cast
  Benz 56, **149**, 166, 230
  Bey, Kerim 56, 70, 138, 145, 149,
   150, 167, 192, 193, 231
  Grant's masseuse **159**
  hotel receptionist **162**
  Kerim Bey's girlfriend **167**
  Leila **167**
  M 56, 68, 144
  Moneypenny, Miss 144, **177**, 207
  Q 183, 245
  train conductor **192**
  Vavra 145, **193**
Vehicles
  Bentley Continental 207
  Bentley Mark IV **207**
  Bentley Mark VI convertible 207
  Chevrolet delivery truck **212**
  Fairey Huntress speedboat 91, 216,
   286
  helicopter 212
  Hiller UH-12C helicopters **220**
  Orient Express 56, 68, 91, 138, 149,
   212, 220, **231**, 289
  SPECTRE escape boat 212
  truck 91
Weapons & equipment
  Armalite sniper rifle 245
  attaché case **245**
  bug detector **248**
  hand grenades 212
  Lektor decoder 68, 71, 91, 138,
   150, 216, 231, 264, 275
  limpet mines 70, 150, 161, **264**
  periscope **270**
  poisoned knitting needles 68
  Rolleiflex camera **275**
  stiletto boot/shoe 68, **280**
  tear-gas canister 56
  throwing knives 245, 282
  trick briefcase 183
  Verey pistol 286
  Walter PPK 7.65 mm 286
  watch with garrote wire 56, **289**
Frost, Miranda **52–53**, 57, 129, 193,
  201, 283

G

Gabor 53
Galore, Pussy **124–25**, 175, 220, 226,
  270, 272, 284, 300
  and Flying Circus 124, 232, 299
Geiger counter **257**
Geiger counter camera 120, **258**
Gettler 53, 132, 237, 260
Gibson 79, 95, 126, **158**, 158, 161, 259,
  279
glasses detonator 258
Glastron CVX-19 Intimidator 219
Glastron speedboat **219**
Glen, John 304–05, 312, 314, 316–17,
  320, 322–23
Gobinda **54**, 77, 137, 194, 206, 230,

241, 257
Godfrey, Admiral John 11
Gogol, General 71, 83, 107,
  128, 135, 150, **158**, 159, 166,
  168, 181, 187, 193, 198, 219
gold ingot **258**
golden gun/bullets 94, 95,
  154, 166, 187, 188, **259**, 282
GoldenEye 14, 19, 32, 60,
  83, 84–85, 102, 115, 140,
  148, 157, 162, 171, 175, 177,
  191, 194, 195, 198–99, 205,
  208, 211, 217, 238, 239,
  240, 241, 247, 250, 258,
  264, 270,
  271, 295, 205, 315, **326–27**,
  328, 329, 330, 331, 334,
  335, 337
  Bond villains
   Grishenko, Boris **60**, 84,
    102, 140, 270
   Onatopp, Xenia 60, **83**,
    84–85, 102, 115, 140, 162,
    198–99, 203, 217, 239, 240, 247
   Ourumov, General 60, **83**, 84–85,
    102, 140, 175, 238, 239, 240, 258
   Trevelyan, Alec 60, 83, 84, **102**, 140,
    148, 157, 195, 238, 239, 240, 250,
    258, 269
  Bond women
   Caroline **115**, 203, 217
   Simonova, Natalya 60, 83, 84, 102,
    140, 175, 194, 199, 238, 239, 240,
    258
  Supporting cast
   Farrel, Admiral Chuck **157**, 217,
    239, 247
   Irina **162**
   M 115, 171, 191, 239
   Mishkin, Dimitri 84, **175**
   Moneypenny, Miss **177**
   Q 208
   Tanner, Bill 171, **191**, 239
   unnamed foreign agent **193**
   Wade, Jack **194**, **195**, 208, 241
   Zukovsky, Valentin 162, **194**, **195**,
    241
  Vehicles
   Aston Martin DB5 83, 115, **203**,
    217
   BMW Z3 **208**
   Cagiva motorcycle **211**, 231
   Cessna 172 plane 194, 208
   Eurocopter 355 Twin Star 198–99
   Ferrari 157
   Ferrari Spider F355 GTS 83, 115,
    217
   helicopters 140, 198
   Manticore 217
   MiG-29 jet fighters 239
   Pilatus PC-6/B2-H4 Turbo-Porter
    231
   T-55 tank **238**, 240
   Tiger helicopter 83, 157, **239**
   Trevelyan's train 84, 238, 240, 269
   Zaporozhets 965 car **241**
  Weapons & equipment

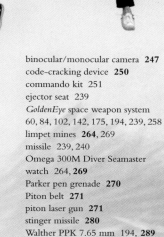

   binocular/monocular camera **247**
   code-cracking device **250**
   commando kit 251
   ejector seat 239
   GoldenEye space weapon system
    60, 84, 102, 142, 175, 194, 239, 258
   limpet mines **264**, 269
   missile 239, 240
   Omega 300M Diver Seamaster
    watch 264, **269**
   Parker pen grenade **270**
   Piton belt **271**
   piton laser gun **271**
   stinger missile **280**
   Walther PPK 7.65 mm 194, **289**
gold-plated Colt .45, 226
Goldfinger 54, 67, 89, 98 100, 161,
  168, 175, 177, 183, 189, 193, 202, 219,
  220, 224, 225, 226, 232, 234, 241, 244,
  251, 258, 259, 261, 263, 268, 270, 276,
  284, 285, **298–99**, 305, 306, 307, 310,
  311, 317
  Bond villains
   Bonita **42**, 89
   Capungo 44
   Goldfinger, Auric 16, 36–37,
    54–55, 67, 75, 82, 98, 124, 134, 161,
    168, 189, 202, 218, 219, 220, 224,
    225, 226, 241, 244, 258, 261, 263,
    272, 284, 298–99, 301, 306, 311
   Kisch **67**, 82, 161
   Ling, Mr. **75**, 220
   Oddjob 67, **82**, 98, 134, 161, 224,
    258, 268
   Ramirez, Mr. **89**, 120, 189, 259,
    276, 285
   Solo, Mr. 82, **98**, 161, 224, 258, 261
   Swiss gatekeeper **100**
  Bond women
   Dink **120**
   Galore, Pussy **124–25**, 175, 220,
    226, 270, 272, 284
   Masterson, Jill **134**, 202, 218, 268
   Masterson, Tilly 82, **134**, 268
  Supporting cast
   Hawker **161**
   Hoods Convention **161**

  Leiter, Felix 120, 124, **168**, 219, 261
  M 148, 189, 261
  Mei-Lei **175**, 245
  Moneypenny, Miss **177**
  Q 183, 202, 259
  Sierra **189**
  Simmons, Mr. 134, **189**
  Smithers, Colonel **189**
  unnamed foreign agent **193**
Vehicles
  Aston Martin DB5 100, 134, **202**,
   234
  Hiller UH-12C helicopter **220**
  Ford Mustang convertible 134, **218**
  Ford Thunderbird (Leiter's) **219**
  Lincoln Continental 82, 236, 272
  Lockheed JetStar plane 175, **225**,
   226, 284
  Lockheed US VC-140B plane **226**,
   270
  Piper PA-28 Cherokee 232
  Rolls-Royce Silver Phantom (1937)
   202, **234**, 261
  US Army ambulance **241**, 263
Weapons & equipment
  ArmaLite Ar-7 case 134
  atomic devices 67, 75, 220, **244**
  attaché case 134, **244**
  Colt .45 (Bond's) 250
  commando kit 251
  Delta 9 nerve gas 124, 232
  ejector seat 202
  gold ingot **258**
  gold-plated Colt .45 226
  grappling hook gun **259**
  homer system 202, **261**
  laser, industrial 241, **263**, 284
  machine gun 100
  nerve gas 161
  Oddjob's hat **268**
  parachutes 226
  poison gas **272**
  seagull snorkel **276**
  tranquilizer guns 67, **284**
  underwater drysuit **285**
  Walther PPK 7.65 mm **289**
Gonzales, Hector **56**, 75, 127, 160,
  191, 212, 235, 247, 251, 262
Goodhead, Dr. Holly 63, 122, **125**,
  210-11, 229, 233, 249, 259, 260, 264,
  312
Goodnight, Mary 69, 79, 95, **126**, 161,
  176, 200, 201, 222, 235, 261, 310
GPS encoder 60, 159, 194, 208, **259**
Grant, Donald "Red" 20, **56**, 68, 79,
  91, 98, 138, 149, 150, 159, 212, 220,
  231, 245, 289
Grant's masseuse **159**
grappling hook gun **259**
Graves, Gustav/Moon, Colonel
  Tan-Sun **57**, 65, 78, 81, 128-29, 156,
  186, 193, 199, 201, 205, 219, 221, 231,
  244 247, 251, 254, 261, 265, 267, 269,
  270, 279, 281
gravity control unit **259**
Gray, Sir Frederick 159
Green, Eva 35

Greene, Dominic 48, **58–59**, 63, 76, 88-89, 95, 117, 123, 149, 157, 169, 174, 207, 215, 255, 336-37
Greenwalt, Dr. **159**, 259
Grischka **77**, 230, 282-83
Grishenko, Boris **60**, 84, 102, 140, 270
Grunther **60**, 151
Gumbold, Gebrüder 151, 155, **159**, 234, 275
Gupta, Henry **60–61**, 159, 259

H

Haines, Guy 61, 88, 171, 255
hairbrush transmitter **260**
Hall, Dr. **159**
Hamilton 64, **159**, 190, 309
Hamilton, Guy 175, 177, 298-99, 306, 308-09, 310, 312
handbag walkie-talkie **260**
handcuff chair **260**
Hans **61**
Hargreaves, Admiral **160**
Havelock, Iona 56, 75, 127, **160**, 175, 235, 241
Havelock, Melina 56, 71, **127**, 154, 160, 181, 191, 212, 227, 229, 235, 241, 244, 251, 262, 316, 317
Havelock, Timothy 56, 71, 75, 127, 154, **160**, 175, 229, 235, 241
Hawker **161**
Hawkins **161**
hearse 101, 238
heat-seeking missiles 222
Heckler & Koch guns 238, **260**
helicopter remote unit **262**
Heller **61**, 114, 157, 166, 169, 198, 280
Henderson, Dikko 84, 110, **161**, 240, 285
Hercules C-130 cargo plane **220**
Hergersheimer, Klaus **161**
HH-65A Dauphin helicopter 198
Hiller UH-12C helicopter **220**
Hip, Lt. 126, 153, 157, **161**
Ho, Pan **61**, 282
hologram machine 145, **260**
Home Secretary **161**
homer system 202, **261**
Honda ATC 3-wheelers **220**, 229
Hoods Convention **161**
Hosein, Sheik **162**
hot air balloon **220-21**
hotel receptionist **162**
Howe, W. G. **61**, 107, 188
Hudson, Hugh 35, 306
Hunt, Peter R. 294, 296-97, 298, 300, 302-03, 304-05, 309, 323
hydraulic detonator **261**

I

Icarus satellite 57, 81, 128, 129, 245, **261**
ICBM train *see* Trevelyan's Train, **240**
ice dragster **221**
Iceberg submarine 129, **221**
Identigraph, Visual **262**

Imposter 00 Agent **61**
incendiary bombs 184, **262**
inhaler bug **262**
Irina **162**
Ivanova, Pola **128**, 174, 219, 264

J

Jaguar XKR 204, **222**
Jailer **62**
Janni **62**
Janus crime syndicate 157, 198, 239, 258
Jaws **62**, 93, 99, 111, 125, 133, 155, 157, 163, 188, 201-11, 219, 233, 236, 267, 270, 314
JIM diving suit **262**
Jinx 109, **128-29**, 153, 185, 201, 219, 230, 238, 247, 251, 261, 263, 269, 279, 283
Jones, Dr. Christmas 91, **129**, 148, 209, 216, 238, 301
Jones, Kimberley **129**, 221
Jones, Mr. 49, **63**, 80, 156, 252, 257
junk 95, 126, **222**
Jupiter 16 61, 149, **222**

K

Kalba, Max 62, 111, 157, **162**, 163
Kananga, Dr. (aka Mr Big) 48, **64–65**, 91, 100, 105, 140-41, 149, 154, 159, 169, 185, 190, 206, 211, 228, 250, 252, 256, 260, 262, 274, 276, 277, 281, 285, 287, 308
Kananga, Ross 308
Kananga's cab driver 65
Karakov, Gregor 88
Kaufman, Dr. **65**, 115, 249, 255, 260
Kawasaki 900 motorcycle **222**
Kawasaki-Verotol KV107 **222**
Kelly, Admiral **163**, 206
Kennedy, President John F. 11, 296
Kenworth W900B tanker trucks **223**
Kevlar vest 48, 253, **263**
key fob (Bond's) 62, 105, **263**
key fob detonator 236, 263
Khan, Kamal **65**, 77, 83, 133, 136-37, 153, 157, 194, 198, 206, 221, 230, 253, 256, 267, 284, 291
Kidd, Mr. 20, 95, 101, **106**, 136, 192, 194, 219, 247, 253, 271, 306
Kil, Mr. **65**
Killifer 64, **66**, 92, 189
Kincade 97, **164-5**, 173
King, Elektra 36, 48, **66-67**, 72, 90-91, 129, 165, 171, 180, 187, 195, 199, 208, 216, 231, 245, 263, 265, 269, 271, 278, 283, 286, 288
King, Sir Robert 66, 72, 90-91, **165**, 263
Kisch 67, 82, 161
Klebb, Rosa 56, **68**, 79, 98, 138, 150, 162, 220, 280
Kleinman, Daniel 326, 329, 330-31, 332, 334

Klotkoff 128, **166**, 193, 264
knife 48, 257 *see also* throwing knives
knockout cigarette **263**
Koskov, General 61, **68–69**, 79, 105, 135, 159, 175, 188, 189, 206, 207, 233, 256, 267, 268, 271, 273, 289
Kra **69**, 126
Kratt **69**
Krest, Milton 66, **69**, 130, 189, 235, 236, 241, 253, 265
Kriegler, Erich **70**, 119
Krilencu **70**, 145, 150, 245, 282
Kristatos, Aris **70–71**, 75, 119, 127, 145, 151, 154, 157, 158, 175, 235, 241, 244, 251, 280, 282, 316
Kronsteen 56, 68, **72**, 79, 98, 231
Krug, Mr. **166**
Kutze, Ladislav **72**, 120, 214, 244
Kwang 61, 157, **166**, 169

L

L39 Albatross jet 212, **223**, 254, 273
La Fayette yacht 239
La Porte, Mademoiselle **166**
Lachaise **72**, 258, 283
Lamont, Peter 304, 306, 308, 310, 312, 314, 316, 318-19, 320, 322, 324-25, 326-27, 328, 330, 332, 333, 334
Lamora, Lupe 48, 69, 92, 114, **130**, 169
Land Rover 61, **224**
lapel pin **263**
Largo, Emilio **72**, 73, 85, 89, 98, 103, 104, 152, 210, 214, 219, 224, 241, 244, 247, 249, 251, 258, 267, 280, 300
laser, industrial **263**
laser camera **264**
laser guns 125, 188, **264**, 271
Lazar 154, **166**, 259, 282
Lazenby, George **26–27**, 304-05
Le Chiffre 69, **74**, 77, 82, 88-89, 103, 104, 132-33, 142 152, 169, 174, 204, 236, 238, 262, 266, 283, 289
Lebanese gangsters **166**
Lee, Chuck 49, 107, **166**, 188, 274
Leila **167**
Leiter, Della 48, 87, 92, **167**, 189, 250
Leiter, Felix 48, 66, 88, 92-93, 114, 120, 124, 130, 149, 161, 167, **168-69**, 185, 189, 198, 206, 219, 250, 256, 261, 270, 273, 285, 286, 336
Lektor, The 68, 71, 91, 138, 150, 216, 231, **264**, 275
Lenkin 83, 150, **169**
Lewis, Gilbert 302, 312-13, 314-15, 323
Licence To Kill 16, 30, 38, 43, 44, 48, 61, 66, 69, 87, 92-93, 103, 114, 130, 157, 161, 166, 167, 168, 169, 183, 189, 198, 211, 223, 232, 235, 236, 241, 247, 248, 250, 253, 263, 264, 270, 280, 296, 310, **324-25**, 326, 327, 331, 337

Bond villains
Asian cartel **38**
Braun **43**, 61, 85
Butcher, Professor Joe **44**, 92
Dario **48**, 85, 188, 263

Heller **61**, 114, 17, 166, 169, 198, 280
Killifer, Ed **66**, 92, 189
Krest, Milton 66, **69**, 130, 189, 235, 236, 241, 253, 265
Perez **85**, 280
Sanchez, Franz 48, 61, 66, 69, 85, **92-93**, 114, 130, 161, 166, 167, 168, 169, 198, 211, 223, 235, 236, 241, 248, 250, 253, 270, 273, 278, 280
Truman-Lodge, William **103**

Bond women
Bouvier, Pam 48, 61, 85, 92, **114**, 130, 223, 241, 247, 248, 253, 263, 265, 278, 280
Lamora, Lupe 48, 69, 92, 114, **130**, 169

Supporting cast
Alvarez, Dr. 48, 92, 130
Fallon **157**, 278
Hawkins **161**
Kwang 61, 157, **166**, 169
Leiter, Della 48, 85, 92, **167**, 189, 250
Leiter, Felix 48, 66, 92-93, 114, 130, 161, 167, 189, 198, 250, 270
Lopez, Hector 92, 130, **169**
Loti 61, 157, 166, **169**
M 157, 161, 171
Moneypenny, Miss **176**
Mullens, Agent 161
Q 183, 248, 264, 278
Rasmussen 189
Sharky 66, **189**, 265
unnamed foreign agent **193**

Vehicles
Aerospatiale 350B A-Star helicopter **198**
Cessna 185 seaplane 198, 211, **235**
Kenworth W900B tanker trucks **223**
Pa Ja Ma 189
Piper PA-18 Super Cub crop-duster 223, 280
Sentinel submersible 66, 211, **235**, 265
Shark Hunter submersible 66, **236**
tanker trucks 85, 92
US Coastguard HH-65A Dauphin helicopter 198
Wavekrest 69, 130, 189, 211, 235, 236, **241**, 253, 265, 280

Weapons & equipment
Beretta 114
Beretta 950 Jetfire **246-47**
Bowie knife 48
broom radio **248**
cigarette lighter 92, 248, **250**
cigarette package detonator **250**, 263
decompression chamber **253**
Dentonite toothpaste 250, **253**, 273
insecticide powder 85
Kevlar vest 48, **263**
laser camera **264**
manta ray disguise **265**
parachutes **270**

pulverizer 48
Q's suitcase 183
rappelling cummerbund **273**
shark tank 66
signature gun **278**
spearguns 211, **280**
Stinger missiles 61, 85, 92, 223, **280**
stingray tail 69, 130
submachine gun 103
Walther PPK 7.64 mm **289**
limpet mines 70, 130, 150, 157, **264**, 269, 287
Lin, Wai 109, **130–31**, 198, 206, 209, 211, 213, 222, 249, 253, 268, 269, 279, 280, 287, 289
Lincoln Continental (1964) **224**
Lincoln Continental convertible **224**
Linda **131**
Ling, Mr. **75**, 220
Liparus 99, 111, 152, 190, **224**, 227, 241, 242, 253, 312, 313
Liparus captain **75**
Lippe, Count **75**, 98, 104, 203, 209, 210, 219, 283
lipstick magnesium flare **264**
Little Nellie **224–25**, 302, 310
Live And Let Die 20, 28, 38, 46, 48, 64–65, 91, 100, 105, 115, 140–41, 149, 153, 154, 159, 168, 169, 177, 180, 185, 190, 206, 211, 219, 238, 234, 244, 250, 252, 256, 260, 262, 265, 274–75, 276, 277, 305, 307, **308–09**, 310, 314, 315, 324

  Bond villains
    Adam **38**, 219
    Carver, Rosie **46**, 64, 141, 149, 244, 277, 281
    Dambala **48**, 65, 149
    Fillet of Soul waiter **52**
    Kananga, Dr. 48, **64–65**, 91, 100, 105, 140–41, 149, 154, 159, 169, 185, 190, 206, 211, 228, 250, 252, 256, 260, 262, 274, 276, 277, 281, 285, 287
    Kananga's cab driver **65**
    sales girl **91**
    Samedi, Baron 64, 65, **91**, 185, 265, 281, 287
    Tee Hee **100**, 260, 266, 287
    Whisper 91, **105**, 252

  Bond women
    Caruso, Miss **115**
    Solitaire 48, 64–65, 91, **140–41**, 185, 206, 228, 260, 262, 274, 281, 287

  Supporting cast
    Baines 48, 64, **149**
    Bell, Mrs. **149**, 211
    Bob, Billy 287
    Charlie 91, **153**
    Dawes 64, **154**
    Hamilton 64, **159**, 190
    Leiter, Felix 168, 169, 256, 285
    M 115, 154, 274
    Moneypenny, Miss 115, **177**, 274
    Pepper, Sheriff J.W. **180**, 287
    Q 274

Quarrel Jr. **185**, 262
Strutter, Harold **190**, 256
Vehicles
  Bell 206 JetRanger helicopter 206
  Cadillac 91
  Cessna 140 plane 149
  Cessna 140 N77029 plane 211
  Corvorado 91, 105, 153
  Crescent train 91, 100, 266
  Glastron speedboats **219**
  monorail **228**
  Routemaster bus **234**
  V-145 Fireflite 219
  V-156 Sportster 219
  V-162 Futura 219
  V-185 Crestflite 219
Weapons & equipment
  aerosol can **244**
  bug detector **248**, 260
  coffin body collector **250**
  commando kit 251
  dart-firing mirror **252**
  Felix lighter **256**
  hairbrush transmitter **260**
  handcuff chair **260**
  incendiary bombs 185, **262**
  mannequin (Baron Samedi) **265**
  mechanical arm 100, **266**
  metal dart 153
  reversible jacket **274**
  Rolex watch **274–75**
  scarecrow camera/gun **276**
  shark pellet/gun 65, 105, 185, **275**, 277
  Smith & Wesson 29.44 Magnum 265
  switchblade 159
  tarot cards 91, 141, **281**
  trapdoor tables **285**
  walkie-talkie flute **287**
  Walther PPK 100, 255, **289**
Living Daylights, The 16, 30, 52, 61, 62, 68–69, 79, 98, 105, 131, 135, 149, 158, 159, 168, 169, 175, 181, 187, 188, 189, 193, 205, 206, 207, 220, 224, 233, 237, 244, 248, 251, 256, 261, 263, 267, 268, 269, 270, 271, 273, 289, 321, **322–23**, 324, 325, 337

  Bond villains
    Feyador, Col. **52**, 62, 68, 188
    Imposter 00 Agent **61**
    Jailer **62**
    Koskov, General 61, **68–69**, 79, 105, 135, 159, 175, 188, 189, 206, 207, 233, 256, 267, 268, 269, 271, 273, 289
    Necros 68, **79**, 188, 207, 261, 267, 269
    Whitaker, Brad 61, 68–69, 79, **105**, 135, 169, 181, 188, 189, 244, 256, 263

  Bond women
    Linda **131**
    Milovy, Kara 62, 68, 69, **135**, 188, 205, 237, 248, 263

  Supporting cast
    "00" Section/agents 61, **148**, 220

Gogol, General 135, **158**, 181
Gray, Sir Frederick **159**
Leiter, Felix 168, 169
M 148, 181, 220
Max **175**
Miklos, Rosika **175**, 206, 271
Moneypenny, Miss 135
Pushkin, General Leonid 61, 68–69, **181**, 187, 256, 263, 273
Q 263
Rubavitch **187**, 256
Saunders 79, **188**, 206, 261, 268
Shah, Kamran 62, **188**, 269
Snow Leopard Brotherhood 69, **188**, **189**
unnamed foreign agent **193**
Vehicles
  Aston Martin V8 Volante **205**
  Audi 200 Quattaro **206**
  cargo plane 188
  Hercules C-130 cargo plane **220**
  Land Rover 61, **224**
  Moonraker II 131
  "Red Cross" Bell helicopters 207, **233**
  Soviet Army armored vehicle 188
  Soviet Army UAZ-469 army transport **237**
  Soviet Army transport plane 79, **237**
Weapons & equipment
  assault rifle 105, **244**
  cello case **248**
  commando kit 251
  fake assassination kit **256**
  hydraulic detonator **261**
  Kevlar vest **263**
  key fob 62, 105, **263**
  milk bottle grenades **267**
  night-vision goggles **268**
  opium bomb **269**
  parachutes 61, 131, 220, 224, 237, 251, **270**
  pipeline pigs 175, **271**
  Pushkin's watch **273**
  rake metal detector **273**
  Walkman headphone 79

Walther PKK 244, 273, **289**
Walther WA 2000 rifle **289**
locator card 75, 104, 203, 210, 219, **264**, 283
Lockheed JetStar plane 175, **225**, 226, 284
Lockheed US VC-140B **226**, 270
Locque, Emile Leopold 56, **75**, 145, 157, 247, 262
log cabin girl **75**
longtail boats 190, **206**, 310
Lopez, Hector 92, 130, **169**
Loti 61, 157, 166, **169**
Lotus Esprit 207, **226**, 236
Lotus Esprit Turbo (1980) **227**
Lynd, Vesper 19, 63, 88, 103, 104, **132–33**, 169, 171, 174, 175, 193, 204, 237, 260, 266, 289, 336

M

M 56, 63, 66, 68, 75, 77, 91, 95, 96, 97, 164, 165, 172-3 111, 115, 132, 143, 144, 145, 148, 154, 156, 157, 158, 159, 161, 165, 169, **170-73**, 175, 181, 185, 187, 189, 191, 194, 199, 220, 227, 237, 239, 246, 257, 261, 264, 274, 283, 286, 289, 297, 303, 310 314, 316, 336, 338
M1, HMS submarine 227, 285
machine guns 79
McWilliams, Debbie 35
Magda **133**, 256, 257, 290
Maglev train **227**
Maibaum, Richard 294, 296, 297, 298-99, 300-01, 304-05, 306-07, 310-11, 312-13, 316-17
Mallory, Gareth 172, **173**, 178, 185
Man With The Golden Gun, The 19, 28, 47, 51, 69, 79, 94-95, 111, 119, 126, 148, 153, 154, 157, 158, 161, 166, 180, 187, 188, 190, 191, 200-01, 206, 222, 235, 259, 261, 279, 282, 289, 305, 307, **310-11**, 315

Bond villains
Chula **47**, 190, 206
Fat, Hai **51**, 95, 119, 153, 158, 161, 206, 259, 282
Kra **69**, 126
Nick Nack **79**, 126, 187, 222, 259
Scaramanga, Francisco 69, 79, **94–95**, 111, 119, 126, 148, 157, |158, 161, 166, 180, 187, 188, 189, 200–01, 222, 235, 259, 261, 279, 282

Bond women
Anders, Andrea 95, **111**, 126, 246
Chew Mee **119**
Goodnight, Mary 69, 79, 95, **126**, 161, 200, 201, 222, 235, 261

Supporting cast
Cha & Nara **153**
Colthorpe 14, **154**
Fairbanks, Bill (002) 259
Frazier, Professor **157**
Gibson 79, 95, 126, 157, **158**, 161, 259, 279
Hip, Lt. 126, 153, 157, **161**
Lazar 154, **166**, 259, 282
Lebanese gangsters **166**
M 95
Moneypenny, Miss 148
Pepper, Sheriff J.W. **180**, 200
Q 154, 219, 282
Rodney **187**, 259
Saida 154, 166, **188**
street urchin **190**
Tanner, Bill **191**

Vehicles
AMC Hornet X hatchback 180, **200**, **201**
AMC Matador X coupé **201**
junk 95, 126, **222**
longtail boat 190, **206**

Seebee seaplane 235

Weapons & equipment
Beretta automatic **246**
golden gun/bullets 94, 95, 154, 166, 187, 188, **259**, 282
homer system **261**
solar-powered laser cannon 235, **279**
Solex Agitator 79, 95, 111, 126, 157, 158, 200, **279**
spanner 69, 126
third nipple **282**
three-fingered sniper rifle **282**
Walther PKK 259, **289**
Mankiewicz, Tom 306–07, 308–09, 310–311
manta ray disguise **265**
Manticore yacht 217
Manuela **133**
Marie **133**
Markovitz, Prof. **77**, 99, 190, 207
Mary *see* Prescott, Mary
Masterson, Jill **134**, 202, 218, 268, 299
Masterson, Tilly 82, **134**, 268, 299
Mathis, René 48, 171, **174**, 283, 336
Max **175**, 277
mechanical arm 100, **266**
Meddings, Derek 313, **314–15**, 316
Medrano, General 48, 58, 59, **76**, 88–89, 117, 169, 174, 181, 238, 336
Medipac **266**
Mei-Lei **175**, 245
Mendel **175**
Mendes, Sam 35
Mercedes 121, 157, 204, 316
Mercury Cougar 204, **228**
Metz, Prof. 57, **77**, 229, 248, 253
Meyers 200A **228**, 270
micro-comparator **267**

microfilm viewer **267**
MiG-29 jet fighter 239
Miklos, Rosika **175**, 206, 271
Mil Mi-8 helicopter 199, 251, 280, 281
milk bottle grenades **267**
Milovy, Kara 62, 68, 69, **135**, 188, 205, 237, 248, 263
mines 247 *see* also limpet mines
mini camera **267**
mini-rebreather 267
Minister of Defence 111, 175, 187
Mischka **77**, 282
Mishkin, Dimitri 84, **175**
Mitchell, Craig **77**, 88, 95, 171, 279
Mollaka 69, **78**, 152, 238, 239
Moneypenny, Miss 112, 115, 135, 144, 148, **176–77**, 189, 207, 226, 267, 286
Moneypenny, Eve 86, 172, 173, **178–9**
monorail **228**
Moon, Colonel *see* Graves, Gustav/ Moon, Colonel Tan-Sun
Moon, General 57, **78**, 81, 245
moonbuggy 180, 220, 180, 220, **229**
Moonraker 28, 38, 46, 101, 104, 122, 125, 133, 155, 158, 159, 170, 176, 188, 207, 210–11, 219, 229, 233, 249, 250, 259, 260, 264, 267, 270, 272, 282, 291, 313, **314–15**, 319, 320, 321, 323, 327, 332, 337
Bond villains
Apollo Jet Crew **38**
Chang **46**, 249
Drax, Hugo **50–51**, 101, 104, 122, 125, 133, 155, 158, 159, 188, 207, 210, 219, 229, 249, 250, 259, 260, 264, 267, 270, 272, 282, 291
Jaws 62, 125, 133, 155, 188, 210–11, 219, 233, 270
tree assassin **101**
Venice assassins **104**, 219, 282
Bond women
Dufour, Corinne **122**, 207
Goodhead, Dr. Holly 122, **125**, 210–11, 229, 233, 249, 259, 260, 264
Manuela **133**
Supporting cast
Dolly **155**, 188, 211
Gogol, General 158
Gray, Sir Frederick 159
M **170**
Moneypenny, Miss **176**
Q 264, 291
Scott, Colonel 155, 160, **188**
unnamed foreign agent **193**
Vehicles
ambulance **233**
Bell 206 JetRangers 207
Bondola **210**
cable car **210–11**
Glastron speedboats **219**
gondola 104
Moonraker space shuttle 122, 125, 155, **229**, 264, 277
Weapons & equipment
centrifuge trainer **249**
CIA Standard Issue Equipment **249**

cigarette case safecracking unit **250**
fire extinguisher 233
gravity control unit **259**
handbag walkie-talkie **260**
laser guns 125, 188, **264**
machine gun 104
mini camera **267**
Mont Blanc pen **267**
parachutes **270**
poison gas 125, 264, **272**
Seiko Digital LCD M354 watch 277
throwing knives/knives 104, **282**
Walther PPK 7.65 mm **289**
wrist dart gun 249, **291**
Moonraker space shuttle 63, 125, 155, 193, **229**, 264, 277
Moore, Roger **28–29**, 307, 308–09, 310–11, 312–13, 314–15, 316–17, 318–19, 320–21, 332–33
Moore, Ted 294–95, 296–97, 298–99, 300–01, 306–07, 308–09, 310–11
Morris, Oswald 210
Mortner, Dr. Carl **79**, 107, 192, 200, 274
Morzeny **79**, 280
Moskvich use pdfs
Munger, Sir Donald **180**
Murphy bed **267**
Murton, Peter 310

N

Naomi **79,** 207
Nara **153**
Necros 7, 68, **79**, 188, 207, 261, 267, 269
Neptune submarine 127, 227, **229**, 244
nerve gas 124, 161, 232 *see* also poison gas
Nevada Sheriff **180**
Nick Nack **79**, 126, 187, 222, 259, 310
night-vision goggles **268**
Nikoli, Capt. **180**, 195
Ning-Po 84, **229**, 240, 275
Ninja throwing knives *see* throwing knives
Ninja throwing stars **268**
No, Dr. 49, 63, 71, **80**, 95, 98
North Korean generals **81**
Notar MD-600N helicopter **230**
novels, the 11, 19, 30, 98, 139, 148, 207, 298 *see* also short stories
Casino Royale 11, 14, 74, 132–33, 142, 168, 174, 177, 181, 182
Diamonds Are Forever 98, 106, 119, 168
Dr. No 71, 80, 88, 139, 143, 181, 172–73, 185, 190, 215
From Russia With Love 16, 56, 68, 70, 71, 98, 138, 150, 159, 174, 231
Goldfinger 16, 44, **54–55**, 99, 105, 124, 134, 168, 189, 268, 299
Live And Let Die 52, 65, 141, 168, 185, 190, 316
Moonraker 51, 57

On Her Majesty's Secret Service 42, 112, 121, 126

The Man With The Golden Gun 95, 126, 139, 168, 170

Thunderball 72, 98, 120, 168, 176

You Only Live Twice 41, 42, 126, 143, 191, 197, 305

O

O'Toole, Plenty 118, **136**

Obanno, Steven 69, 74, **82**, 103, 104, 132, 262

Octopussy 14, 16, 28, 54, 65, 77, 83, 101, 112, 133, 136–37, 148, 150, 153, 157, 158, 168, 170, 187, 189, 193, 194, 198, 206, 213, 221, 230, 234, 241, 244, 248, 253, 256, 257, 267, 270, 273, 274, 283, 284, 290, 291, 312, **318–19**, 335

Bond Villains
Gobinda **54**, 77, 137, 194, 206, 230, 241, 257

Grischka **77**, 230, 282–83

Khan, Kamal **65**, 77, 83, 133, 136–37, 153, 157, 194, 198, 206, 221, 230, 253, 256, 267, 284, 291

Mischka **77**, 282

Orlov, General 65, 77, **83**, 137, 158, 169, 187, 198, 230, 244, 256, 267

Toro, Colonel **101**, 112, 198, 248, 270, 273, 274

Bond women
Bianca 101, **112**

Magda **133**, 256, 257, 290

Octopussy 65, 77, 83, **136–37**, 187, 194, 206, 213, 256, 284

Supporting cast
"00" Section **148**

Borchoi **150**, 169

Clive, Major **153**, 253

Fanning, Jim **157**

Gogol, General 83, 150, 158, 159, 169, 187, 198

Gray, Sir Frederick 159

Lenkin 83, 150, **169**

M 148, **170**, 171, 189

Moneypenny, Miss **176**, 189

Q 143, 194, 213, 221, 256

Rublevitch **187**

Sadruddin **187**, 194

Smallbone, Penelope **189**

unnamed foreign agent **193**

US general **193**

Vijay 187, **194**, 241

Vehicles
Acrostar Bede jet 101, 112, **198**, 273

Aerospatiale helicopters **198**

Beech 18 plane 137, **206**, 256

crocodile mini-submarine **213**

hot air balloon **221**

Kamal's plane 65, 137

Octopussy's barge 136, **230**

Octopussy's train/circus train 65, 77, 83, 137, **230**

Range Rover convertible 112, 198

Rolls-Royce Phantom III (KAM 1) (Kamal Kahn's) **234**

tuk-tuk taxi 194, **241**, 257

Weapons & equipment
atomic device/bomb 77, 137, **244**

Beretta automatic **246**

briefcase bomb compartment **248**

blunderbuss **241**

cannon 193, 230

dice, loaded **253**

Fabergé egg 77, 133, 148, 157, 169, 253, **256**, 267, 283

fake leg cast (Bond's) **256**

five-bladed knife **257**

Mont Blanc pen **267**

nuclear weapon 83, 133

parachutes 112, **270**

Rapier missile 198, **273**

reversible jacket **274**

Seiko G757 watch **277**

stun grenades 133

throwing knives/knives 77, 282–83

tranquilizer gun **284**

Walther PPK 7.65 mm **289**

weighted skirt 133, **290**

yo-yo buzz saw 194, **291**

Octopussy (and her) army 284, 290

barge 136, 137, 230

circus 77, 133, 136–37, 193

circus train 65, 77, 83, 230

Oddjob 67, **82**, 98, 134, 161, 224, 258, 268, 299, 300, 311

Oddjob's hat **268–69**

Olympe **180**

Omega 300M Diver Seamaster watch **269**

Omega Seamaster watch **269**

On Her Majesty's Secret Service 16, 19, 20, 26, 40, 43, 60, 98, 112, 120–21, 151, 153, 155, 159, 177, 180, 204, 206, 210–11, 228, 233, 234, 251, 267, 275, 286, **304–05**, 306, 311, 321, 323, 330

Bond villains
Blofeld, Ernst Stavro 40–41, 60, 68, 71, 79, 112, 113, 121, 151, 153, 155, 159, 204, 207, 210, 228, 251, 255, 267, 286, 302, 305, 311

Bunt, Irma **43**, 121, 155, 206, 228

Grunther **60**, 151

SPECTRE 121, 159

Bond women
Bartlett, Ruby **112**

Blofeld's Angels of Death **112–13**, 251, 267

Di Vicenzo, Tracy 60, 112, **120–21**, 153, 155, 204, 228, 234

Supporting cast
Bray, Sir Hilary 112, **151**, 159

Campbell 60, **151**

Che Che **153**, 234

Draco, Marc Ange 112, 120–21, 153, **155**, 159, 206, 210, 228, 233, 234, 251, 282, 305

Gumbold, Gebrüder 151, 155, **159**, 234, 275

M **170**

Moneypenny, Miss 181, 267

Olympe **180**

Q **182**

Raphael 234

Vehicles
Aston Martin DBS **204**, 228

Bell 206 JetRanger helicopter 206

bobsleds **210**

cable car 60, **210**

helicopter 155

Mercedes (Blofeld's) 121, 204

Mercury Cougar 204, **228**

"Red Cross" helicopters 206, **233**

Rolls-Royce coupé 234

Weapons & equipment
compact communicator **251**

grenade 210

mini camera **267**

mini-rebreather **267**

safe-cracker **275**

sniper rifle 94

submachine gun MP40 121

throwing knives 282

Verey pistol **286**

Walther PPK 7.65 mm **289**

Onatopp, Xenia 60, **83**, 84–85, 102, 115, 140, 162, 198-99, 203, 217, 239, 240, 247

opium bomb **269**

Orient Express 56, 68, 91, 138, 149, 212, 220, **231**, 289, 298

Orlov, General 65, 77, **83**, 137, 158, 169, 187, 198, 230, 244, 256, 267

Osato, Mr. **84**, 98, 191, 275, 276, 291

Osel "Mantis" one-man atmospheric submersible **227**, 229

Osprey hovercraft **231**

Ourumov, General 60, **83**, 84–85, 102, 140, 175, 238, 239, 240, 258

P

Palazzi, Angelo 72, 75, **85**, 104, 241, 244

parachutes 61, 112, 117, 131, 216, 220, 221, 224, 226, 228, 233, 237, 238, 240, 251, **270**

parahawks **231**

Parker pen grenade **270**

Pascal, Amy 35

Patrice **86-7**, 97, 172, 178

Peaceful Fountains of Desire **137**

Pepper, Sheriff J.W. 38, **180–81**, 310

Perez **85**, 280

Perla de las Dunas Hotel 59, 76, 117, 337

receptionist 181

photographer, the 80, 88

Pilatus PC-6/B2-H4 Turbo-Porter **231**

Pinder **181**

pipeline pigs **271**

Piper PA-18 Super Cub crop-duster 232

Piper Cherokee **232**

Pleydell-Smith 63, **181**, 252

piton belt **271**

piton gun **271**

piton laser gun **271**

poison gas **272**

poison string **272**

poisoned hook 149, 151

polarizing sunglasses **272**

Prescott, Mary 49, 80, 101, 156, 171, **174**, 178

Prime Minister 181, **277**

Pushkin, General Leonid 61, 68–69, **181**, 187, 256, 263, 273

Pushkin's watch **273**

Puss-Feller 88, **181**, 185

Q

Q 97, 113, 143, 149, 154, **182-83**, **184-85**, 191, 194, 202, 204, 205, 208, 213, 221, 226, 245, 246, 247, 248, 255, 256, 258, 259, 262, 264, 267, 269, 274, 277, 278, 279, 282, 286, 291

Q boat **232**

Quantum 58–59, 76, 88-89, 105, 255, 260, 337

Quantum of Solace 34, 35, 36, 48, 58–59, 61, 76, 77, 88-89, 95, 116-17, 123, 149, 157, 168, 171, 174, 181, 191, 193, 207, 215, 238, 255, 268, 289, **336-37**

Bond Villains
Beam, CIA Chief Gregory 58, **149**, 169

Carlos 48, 174

Elvis **51**, 123, 255

Greene, Dominic 48, **58–59**, 63, 76, 90, 99, 121, 127, 153, 161, 177, 186, 219, 227, 267

Haines, Guy 61, 88, 171, 255

Lynd, Vesper 63, 88, 171, 174, 193

Medrano, General 58, 59, **76**, 88–89, 117, 169, 174, 181, 238, 336

Slate, Edmund 58, 77, **95**, 117, 171, 279, 337

White, Mr. 77, 88, **105**, 204

Yusef 63, 88, 106, 171, 193

Bond Women
Camille 58–59, 76, 89, 95, **116–17**, 174, 181, 207, 215, 238

Fields, Agent 59, **123**, 171

Supporting Cast
Colonel of Police 59

Corinne 63, 154

Foreign Secretary **157**

Leiter, Felix 149, 169

M 63, 77, 157, 169, 171, 191

Mathis, René 48, 171, **174**

Mitchell, Craig **77**, 88, 95, 171, 279

Montes, Ernesto 76, 117

Perla de las Dunas' receptionist **181**

Q **255**

Vehicles
Alfa Romeo 159s 204, 337

Aston Martin DBS **204**, 337

Bell helicopter **207**

Bell UH-1H helicopter 207

Douglas DC-3 117, **215**, 337

Range Rover 215
SIAI-Marchetti SF260TP plane 215, 337
Sunseeker Superhawk 43 238
Sunseeker Sovereign 17 238
Weapons and Equipment
Ericsson mobile phone **255**
machine gun 215
nano-surveillance camera phone 61
Omega Seamaster watch **269**
parachutes 117
smart tables 279
Walther PPK 7.65 mm **289**
Quarrel 80, **185**
Quarrel Jr. **185**
Quist **89**, 247

R

radar-guided Gatling gun 273
radioactive pill **273**
Radio transmitter 184, **273**
rake metal detector **273**
Ramirez, Mr. **89**, 120, 189, 259, 276, 285
Range Rovers 112, 198, 215
Ranger, HMS 99, 149, 160, 190, 224, **233**
Raoul **186**
Raphael 234
rapier missile launcher **273**
rappelling cummerbund **273**
"Red Cross" helicopters 206, 207, **233**
remote-triggered implant **274**
Renard (Vicktor Zokas) 48, 66, 72, **90–91**, 129, 145, 148, 165, 180, 195, 231, 232, 238, 245, 260, 264, 271, 288
Renault 11 TXE taxi **233**
reversible jacket **274**
Rhoda **91**, 212
ring camera **274**
Robinson, Charles **187**, 286
rocket belt 301
rocket gun **274**
rocket-firing cigarette **274**
rockets 75, 203, 210, 219, 231
Rodney **187**, 259
Roebuck, Admiral 151, 175, **187**, 212
Rolex Submariner watch 247, 274–75
Rolleiflex camera **275**
Rolls-Royce coupé 115
Rolls-Royce Phantom II, (Goldfinger's) 234
Rolls-Royce Phantom III (KAM 1) (Kamal Khan's) **234**
Rolls-Royce Silver Cloud II **234**
Rolls-Royce Silver Shadow **234**
Romanova, Tatiana 56, 68, 71, 79, **138**, 149, 162, 216, 220, 231, 275
Ronson 86, **187**
Routemaster bus **234**
Rubavitch **187**
Rublevitch, Miss 158, **187**
Ryder, Honey 95, **139**, 168, 181, 185, 215
Ryder, Mr. 80, 139

S

Sadruddin **187**, 184
safe-cracker **275**
Saida 154, 166, **188**
St. Georges 70, 71, 127, 154, 160, 227, 229, **235**, 244, 262
sales girl **91**
Salzman, Harry 294, 296–97, 298–99, 300–01, 302–03, 304–05, 306–07, 308–09, 310–11 312
Samedi, Baron 64, 65, **91**, 185, 265, 281, 287
Sanchez, Franz 16, 48, 61, 66, 69, 85, **92–93**, 114, 130, 161, 166, 167, 168, 169, 198, 211, 223, 235, 236, 241, 244, 250, 253, 270, 273, 278, 280
Sandor **93**, 122
Santa Mavra **235**
Saunders 79, **188**, 206, 261, 268
Saxby, Bert **93**, 101, 194, 286
Scaramanga, Francisco 69, 79, **94–95**, 111, 119, 126, 148, 157, 158, 161, 166, 168, 180, 187, 188, 191, 200–01, 222, 235, 259, 261, 279, 282, 311
scarecrow camera/gun **276**
Scarpine 48, **95**, 224, 282
Scorpion guard 95
Scott, Colonel 155, 158, **188**
Sea Vac drill **98**, 213, 237, **276–77**
Seabee seaplane **235**
seagull snorkel **276**
seaplane (Gonzales's) **235**
security camera **276**
Seiko 0674 watch with text printout **277**
Seiko Digital LCD M354 watch 277
Seiko G757 Sports 100 watch 277
Seiko H357 Duo Display watch 181, 277
Sentinel submersible 66, 211, **235**, 265
Severine 97, **140**, 178
SFPD Captain 188
Shah, Kamran 62, **188**, 269
Shark Hunter submarine 66, **236**
shark pool 89, 103, 300
shark pellet/gun 65, 105, 185, **275**, 277
Sharky 66, **189**, 265
Sharper Image credit card **277**
shaver bug detector **277**
Sherpa van **236**
short stories
007 in New York 142
A View to a Kill 142
For Your Eyes Only 56, 127, 160, 316
Octopussy 14, 137
Risico 154, 316
The Hildebrand Rarity 69
Sierra **189**
Silva, 86, **96–7**, 140, 164, 165, 173, 184, 185
signature guns **278**
Simmons, Bob 316, 317
Simmons, Mr. 134, **189**
Simonova, Natalya 60, 83, 84, 102,

140, 175, 194, 199, 238, 239, 24 0, 258
Sister Lily **95**
Sister Rose **95**
Skyfall 34–5, 86–7, 96–7, 140, 155, 159, 164–5, 172–3, 173, 178–9, 184–5, 187, 191, 202–3, 212, 244, 273, 278, 289
Bond villains
Patrice **86–7**, 97, 172, 178
Silva 86, **96–7**, 140, 164, 165, 173, 184, 185
Bond women
Severine 97, **140**, 178
Supporting cast
Dowar, Clair **155**, 173
Hall, Dr. **159**
Kincade 97, **164–5**, 173
M 96, 97, 164, 165, **172–3**, 185
Mallory, Gareth 172, **173**, 178, 185
Moneypenny, Eve 86, 172, 173, **178–9**
Q 97, **184–5**
Ronson 86, **187**
Tanner 185, **191**
Vehicles
AgustaWestland AW101 helicopter 97
Aston Martin DB5 **202–3**
Audi 86
Caterpillar 320D L excavator 87
Chimera 140, 212
Honda motorcycle 35, 87
Land Rover Defender 86, 87, 178
Weapons & equipment
Anderson Wheeler 500 NE double rifle **244**
Glock 18 86
Radio transmitter 184, **273**
Signature gun 184, **278**
Walter PPK 184, 289
ski pole rocket **278**
ski suit escape pod **278**
Ski-Doos 236
Skyhook rescue system **278**
Slate, Edmund 58, 77, **95**, 117, 171, 279, 337
Slumber, Morton **95**, 136
Smallbone, Penelope **189**
smart tables 279
SMERSH 56, 65, 68, 71, 79, **98**, 138
Smithers, Colonel **189**
snake bracelet/piton **279**
snooper **279**
Snow Leopard Brotherhood **189**
snowmobiles **236**
Solange 142
Solex Agitator 79, 95, 113, 126, 157, 158, 200, **279**
Solitaire 48, 64–65, 91, **140–41**, 185, 206, 228, 260, 262, 274, 281, 287
Solitaire Mont Blanc pen **267**
Solo, Mr. 82, **98**, 161, 224, 258, 261
sonic ring **279**
Sony Ericsson phone 262
Soviet Army UAZ-469 transport plane **237**
spearguns **280**

SPECTRE 20, 56, 68, 71, 72, 75, 79, 80, 84, 91, **98**, 103, 104, 110, 121, 143, 149, 159, 161, 162, 166, 191, 202, 207, 210, 212, 216, 229, 231, 239, 240, 241, 244, 245, 246, 247, 249, 255, 264, 267, 274, 276, 277, 280, 283, 285, 286, 289, 297
SPECTRE helicopters 302, 311
Spirit 54 yacht **237**
Spy Who Loved Me, The 28, 39, 62–63, 75, 77, 79, 93, 99, 110–11, 122, 149, 152, 157, 158, 159, 160, 163, 187, 190, 207, 216, 222, 224, 226, 227, 233, 236, 241, 244, 250, 253, 263, 264, 267, 270, 272, 277, 278, 283, 285, 303, **312–13**, 314–15, 319, 323, 335, 337
Bond villains
Barsov, Sergei **39**, 75, 110–11, 278
Bechmann, Dr. **77**, 99, 190, 207
Dolly 63, **155**
Jaws **62**, 93, 99, 111, 157, 163, 236, 267
Liparus captain 75
log cabin girl 75
Markovitz, Prof. **77**, 99, 190, 207
Naomi **79**, 207
Sandor **93**, 122
Stromberg, Karl 62, 63, 75, 77, 79, 93, **99**, 111, 122, 152, 157, 162, 163, 190, 207, 216, 222, 224, 226, 227, 233, 236, 241, 242, 253, 263, 264, 267, 272, 283, 285
Bond women
Amasova, Major Anya 62, 79, 99, **110-111**, 163, 207, 216, 222, 226, 227, 236, 241, 246, 250, 263, 285
Felicca 93, **122**
Goodhead, Dr. Holly 63
Supporting cast
Benson, Capt. 149
Carter, Commander **152**, 224, 233, 241, 272
Drax, Hugo 63
Fekkesh, Aziz 93, 111, 122, **157**, 162, 163
Gogol, General 110, 111, 158, 187
Gray, Sir Frederick 159
Hargreaves, Admiral **160**
Hosein, Sheik 162
Kalba, Max 62, 111, 157, **162**, 163
M 75, 111, 158
Minister of Defence 111
Moneypenny, Miss **176**
Q 111, 149, 241
Rublevitch **187**
Stromberg's assistant 77, **190**
Talbot, Cmdr. **190**
Vehicles
Bell Jet Ranger helicopter 79, 206-07
Beretta automatic **246**
cable cars 63
charter jet 63
escape pod (Stromberg's) 111, **216**
helicopter 77, 99
Kawasaki 900 motorcycle **222**
Leyland Sherpa van **236**

Liparus 99, 111, 152, 190, **224**, 227, 241, 242, 253

Lotus Esprit 207, **226**, 236

Maglev train **227**

Moonraker shuttle 63

Nile felucca 263, 267

Potemkin 77, 99, 110, 224, 233

Ranger, HMS 99, 149, 160, 190, 224, **233**

Shark Hunter submarine 236

Wayne, USS 99, 111, 152, 216, 224, **241**, 253, 264, 272

wetbike **241**

Weapons & equipment

atomic devices **244**

cement sprayer 226

cigarette lighter 250

detonator 243

electromagnet 63

hand grenade 170

knockout cigarette **263**

limpet mines 263

machine guns 79

microfilm viewer **267**

nuclear missiles/missiles 75, 233, 236

parachutes **270**

poison gas **272**

Seiko 0674 watch with text printout 277

ski pole rocket **278**

submarine tracking system 162, 163, 236, 242, 285

torpedo gun **283**

torpedoes 152, 226, 241

trapdoor elevator 285

trick cigarette 111

Walther PPK 7.65 mm 99, 283, **289**

Stamper 65, **98**, 130-31, 211, 213, 249, 280

stealth ships 130, 163, **237**, 251, 269, 276, 287, 289

Stears, John 304-05, 311

stiletto boot/shoe **280**

stiletto fighting stick **280**

Stinger missiles 61, 85, 92, 208, 223, **280**

Strangways, John 49, 80, 101, 156, 174, 185, **190**, 257

street urchin **190**

Stromberg, Karl 36, 62, 63, 75, 77, 79, 93, **99**, 111, 122, 152, 157, 152, 163, 190, 207, 216, 222, 224, 226, 227, 233, 236, 241, 242, 253, 263, 263, 267, 272, 283, 285, 312, 313

Stromberg's assistant 77, **190**

Strutter, Harold **190**, 256

Sunbeam Alpine 3/A Series II **238**

Sunseeker motor boats 238

Sunseeker Superhawk speedboat 34, 43, 128, 232, **238**

Supporting cast 146–95 *see* also individual film titles

surfboard saboteur kit **280**

Sutton, Stacey 20, 61, 107, **142**, 167, 188, 198, 200, 218, 249, 272, 277, 279

Suzuki, Kissy **143**, 191, 227, 272, 288,

302, 303

Swiss gatekeeper **100**

switchblade gliders **238**

T

T-55 tank **238**

Talbot, Cmdr. **190**

Tanaka, Tiger 110, 143, **191**, 198, 222, 228, 239, 260, 268, 274, 280, 285, 288, 302

Tanaka's train **239**

tank buster gun **281**

Tanner, Bill 171, 185, **191**, 239, 316

Taro, Miss **143**, 177, 191, 239

tarot cards 91, 149, **281**

Tee Hee **100**, 260, 266, 287

Texron tanker 236, 237, 239, 263

thermal imaging system 282

Thermos bomb **282**

third nipple **282**

throwing knives 77, 282-83

Thumper **39**, 194

Thunderball 19, 20, 24, 40, 42, 72–73, 85, 89, 98, 103, 104, 120, 122, 148, 152, 161, 166, 168, 170, 176, 181, 183, 202, 210, 214, 218, 219, 224, 239, 241, 244, 246, 247, 249, 251, 255, 258, 267, 273, 278, 280, 281, 282, 285, 286, 294, **300-01**, 305, 306, 307, 311, 317, 325

Bond villains

Blofeld, Ernst Stavro **40–41**, 75, 219, 255

Boitier, Col. Jacques **42**, 166, 246, 282

Janni **62**

Kutze, Ladislav **72**, 120, 214, 244

Largo, Emilio **72**, 73, 85, 89, 103, 104, 152, 210, 214, 219, 224, 241, 244, 247, 249, 251, 258, 267, 280

Lippe, Count **75**, 104, 203, 210, 219, 283

Palazzi, Angelo 72, 75, **85**, 104, 241, 244

Quist **89**, 247

SPECTRE 72, 75, **98**, 103, 104, 161, 166, 202, 310, 239, 241, 244, 246, 247, 249, 255, 267, 277, 280, 283, 285

Vargas 62, **103**, 280

Volpe, Fiona 72, 73, 75, **104**, 203, 210, 218, 219, 246

Bond women

Derval, Domino 72, 89, 103, **120**, 152, 214, 258, 278, 280

Fearing, Patricia **122**, 283

Supporting cast

Caplan, Paula 62, 103, 104, **152**

Derval, Major François 72, 75, 85, 104, **120**, 241

Home Secretary **161**

Kenniston 161

La Porte, Mademoiselle **166**

Leiter, Felix 168-69, 273, 286

M **170**

Moneypenny, Miss **176**

Pinder **181**

Q 183, 247, 258, 267, 277

Vehicles

Aston Martin DB5 75, **202-03**, 210, 219

Beretta automatic **246**

bomb sled **210**

BSA A65L Lightning motorbike 203, **210**, 219

coastguard helicopter 273

Disco Volante 62, 72, 103, 120, **214**, 244, 258, 278, 280, 286

Ford Mustang (1965) (Fiona Volpe's) **218**

Ford Skyliner (Lippe's) 203, 209, **219**

Ford Thunderbird (1965) (Largo's) **219**

Lincoln Continental convertible **224**

NATO bomber 72

tow sled **239**

Vulcan bomber 85, 210, 239, **241**

Weapons & equipment

atomic devices/bombs 241, **244**, 258

Bell-Textron Jet Pack **246**

book/tape recorder **247**

Breitling diver's watch **247**

cigarette case remote control **249**

commando kit **251**

electrified chair **255**

Geiger counter camera 120, **258**

hydrogen bombs 72

mini-rebreather 267

motorized traction machine 75, 122

nuclear weapons 171

radioactive pill **273**

rockets 75, 203, 210, 219

shark pool 89,103

Skyhook rescue system **278**

spearguns 103, 120, 222, 239, **280**

steam cabinet 75

throwing knives **282**

traction table **283**

underwater grenade **285**

underwater infrared camera **286**

underwater propulsion unit **286**

Verey pistol **286**

Walther PPK 7.65 mm **289**

Tibbett, Sir Godfrey 49, 107, 149, **192**, 234, 277

Tiger helicopter 83, 157, **239**

Tomahawk–class missiles 98, 130-31

Tomorrow Never Dies 32, 45, 60–61, 65, 98, 112, 130–31, 151, 152, 155, 159, 163, 175, 177, 187, 194, 199, 206, 208, 209, 211, 212, 213, 222, 223, 237, 240, 249, 251, 259, 268, 270, 273, 276, 279, 287, 319, **328-29**, 331

Bond villains

Carver, Elliot **45**, 60–61, 65, 98, 115, 130-31, 152, 159, 163, 187, 194, 199, 206, 208, 213, 222, 237, 249, 251, 253, 254, 255, 259, 260, 269, 276, 279, 287

Chang, General 130, 287

Gupta, Henry **60–61**, 159, 259

Kaufman, Dr. **65**, 115, 249, 255, 260

Stamper 65, **98**, 130-31, 211, 213, 249, 280

Bond women

Bergstrom, Prof. Inga **112**

Carver, Paris 61, **115**, 211, 260

Lin, Wai **130-31**, 198, 206, 209, 211, 213, 222, 249, 253, 268, 269, 279, 280, 287, 289

Supporting cast

Bukharin, General **151**

Carver's PR **152**

Day, Commander **155**, 213

Greenwalt, Dr. **159**, 259

Kelly, Admiral **163**, 206

M 175, 187

Minister of Defence 175, 187

Moneypenny, Miss 112, 181

Q 199, 255, 287, 289

Robinson, Charles **187**

Roebuck, Admiral 151, 179, **187**, 212

unnamed foreign agent **193**

Wade, Jack 159, **194**, 240

Vehicles

Aston Martin DB5 **202-203**

BMW 750iL 199, **208**, 255

BMW R1200 **209**

Bedford, HMS 163, **206**, 237

captured trawler 211

Chester, HMS 187, **212**

Devonshire, HMS 60, 98, 130, 155, 159, 175, 187, 194, 211, **213**, 237, 240, 259, 270, 276, 286

Eurocopter helicopters 199, 209

junk **222**

L39 Albatross jet 212, **223**, 254, 273

M's limousine 187

MiGs, Chinese 155, 213

stealth ship 130, 163, **237**, 251, 269, 276, 287, 289

Transport Allianz C-160 plane **240**

Weapons & equipment

Beretta .25 automatic **246**

Chakra torture kit 98, **249**

commando kit 251

cruise missile 130, 213

detonators 131, **253**

Dunhill cigarette lighter grenade **254**, 273

Ericsson JB988 mobile phone 208, **255**

GPS encoder 60, 159, 194, 208, **259**

Heckler & Koch guns **260**

limpet mines 130, 287

machine gun 213

Ninja throwing stars **268**

nuclear torpedoes 151, 212

Omega 300M Diver Seamaster watch **269**, 287

parachutes 240, **270**

radar-guided Gatling gun 273

Sea Vac drill 98, 213, 237, **276-77**

seat ejector 223

snake bracelet/piton **279**

spearguns 211, **280**

Tomahawk-class missile 98, 130-31

torpedoes 155, 215, 273

Verey pistol **286**

Wai Lin's bike shop 269, **287**, 289

Walter P99 287, 289

Walther PPK **208**, **289**

Toro, Colonel **101**, 112, 198, 248, 270, 273, 274

torpedo gun **283**

torpedoes 151, 152, 155, 212, 223, 226, 232, 241, 273

tow sled **239**

Toyota 2000 GT 110, 222, **240**

Toyota Crown S40 222

tracking device im plant 69, **283**

tracking system 162, 163, 236, 242, 285

traction table **283**

train conductor **192**

tranquilizer gun 67, **284**

Transport Allianz C-160 plane **240**

trapdoor elevator **285**

trapdoor slide **285**

trapdoor tables **285**

Tree, Shady 95, **101**

tree assassin **101**

Trench, Sylvia **144**

Trevelyan, Alec 60, 83, 84, **102**, 140, 148, 157, 195, 238, 239, 240, 250, 258, 269

Trevelyan's train 84, 238, 240, 269

Triana 127, 160, 181, 235, **241**

Truman-Lodge, William **103**

tuk-tuk taxi 174, **241**, 257

Tynan, Dr. 106, **192**

underwater breathing unit/shroud **285**

camera 300

drysuit 285

grenade 285

infrared camera 286

propulsion unit 286

unnamed foreign agent 181, **193**

US Army ambulance **241**, 263

US general **193**

V

V-145 Fireflite 219

V-156 Sportster 219

V-162 Futura 219

V-185 Crestflite 219

Valenka 82, **103**, 132, 204, 266

Van Bierk, Mr. **104**, 199, 251, 269, 281

Vargas 62, **103**, 280

Vavra 145, **193**

Venice assassins **104**, 219, 282

Venz **193**

Verey pistol **286**

Verity 193

Vida **145**, 193

View To A Kill, A 16, 19, 20, 28, 48, 49, 61, 69, 95, 107, 128, 142, 148, 149, 151, 158, 159, 166, 170, 176, 188, 192, 198, 200, 218, 219, 233, 234, 236, 245, 249, 251, 253, 264, 267, 270, 272, 277, 314, 317, **320-21**, 335, 337

Bond villains

Conley, Bob 48, 166, 274

Day, May 48, 49, 67, 107, 149, 151, 166-67, 192, 193, 200, 219, 233, 234, 251, 253, 270, 282

Flex, Jenny **52**, 61, 282

Ho, Pan 61, 282

Howe, W.G. 61, 107, 188

Mortner, Dr. Carl/Hans Glaub 79, 107, 192, 200, 274

Scarpine 48, **95**, 234, 282

Zorin, Max 48, 49, 61, 79, 95, **107**, 130, 142, 149, 158, 159, 166, 192, 193, 198, 200, 218, 219, 233, 234, 245, 249, 251, 253, 264, 270, 272, 274, 277, 282

Bond women

Ivanova, Pola **128**, 166, 219, 264

Jones, Kimberley **129**, 221

Sutton, Stacey 61, 107, **142**, 167, 188, 198, 200, 218, 249, 272, 277, 279

Supporting cast

Aubergine, Achille 49, 107, **149**, 151, 219, 233

Butterfly Girl **151**

Gogol, General 107, 128, 158, 166, 193, 219

Gray, Sir Frederick 159

Klotkoff 130, **166**, 193, 264

Lee, Chuck 49, 107, **166**, 188, 274

M **170**

Moneypenny, Miss **176**

O'Rourke 166

Q 267, 279

SFPD Captain 188

Tibbett, Sir Godfrey 49, 107, 149, **192**, 234, 277

Venz **193**

Vehicles

Aerospatiale helicopter **198**

airships 95, 188, **200**

fire truck 142, **217**

Ford Thunderbird **219**

Glastron CVX-19 Intimidator 219

iceberg submarine 129, **221**

Renault 11 TXE taxi **233**

Rolls-Royce Silver Cloud II **234**

snowmobiles **236**

Weapons & equipment

avalanche-rescue receiver 245

check copier **249**

commando kit 251

computer mirror camera **251**

detonator 49, 107, **253**

fire extinguisher 95

limpet mines 264

micro-comparator **267**

parachutes 233, **270**

poisoned hook 149, 159

polarizing sunglasses **272**

remote-triggered implant **274**

ring camera **274**

Seiko watch **277**

Sharper Image credit card **277**

shaver bug detector **277**

snooper **279**

thermos bomb **282**

Verey pistol **286**

Walter PPK 7.65 mm 61, 289

waterproof Walkman 128

Vijay 187, **194**, 241

Villiers **194**, 230

virtual reality glasses **286**

Visa card skeleton key **286**

Vlad **104**, 245

voice simulator **286**

Volpe, Fiona 72, 73, 75, 98, **104**, 203, 210, 218, 219, 246

Von Schlaf, Countess Lisl **145**, 154

Vulcan bomber 85, 210, 239, **241**

Wade, Jack 159, **194**, **195**, 208, 240, 241

Wai Lin's bike shop 269, **287**, 289

walkie-talkie flute **287**

walking stick gun 25, 195, 283, **288**

Walkman, waterproof 128

Walkman headphone 79

wall-walking device **288**

Wallis, Wing Commander Ken 302

Walther P99 81, 104, 280, 286, **288-89**

Walther PPK 7.65 mm 61, 99, 154, 184, 195, 244, 256, 259, 273, 282, 283, **289**, 291

Walther WA 2000 rifle **289**

Warmflash, Dr. Molly **145**, 260

watch with wire garrote 56, **289**

Wavekrest 69, 130, 189, 211, 235, 236, **241**, 253, 265, 280

wave-walker **290**

Wayne, USS 99, 111, 152, 216, 224, **241**, 253, 264, 272

weighted skirt 133, **290**

wetbike **241**

Whisper 91, **105**, 252

Whistler, Mrs. 106, 192, **194**

Whitaker, Brad 61, 68–69, 79, **105**, 135, 169, 181, 188, 189, 244, 256, 263

White, Mr. 19, 69, 74, 77, 82, 88, 103, **105**, 132, 204, 260, 336

Whyte, Willard 93, 106, **194**, 206, 247, 248, 255, 271, 286

Wilson, Michael G. 35, 310, 314-15, 316-17, 336, 338, 339

Wint, Mr. 95, 103, **106**, 136, 192, 194, 219, 247, 253, 271, 306

Wood, Christopher 312, 314

World Is Not Enough, The 16, 32, 38, 43, 48, 53, 66–67, 72, 90–91, 129, 145,

148, 165, 171, 177, 180, 187, 193, 195, 199, 208–09, 216, 221, 231, 232, 234, 238, 244–45, 258, 260, 263, 264, 269, 271, 278, 283, 286, 289, 322, 329, **330–31**, 333

Bond villains

Arkov, Prof. Mikhail **38**, 48, 129, 148, 231

Bull, The **43**

Cigar Girl **47**, 72, 221, 232, 248, 283

Davidov, Sasha **48**, 286

Gabor **53**

King, Elektra Vavra 48, **66–67**, 72, 90–91, 129, 165, 171, 180, 187, 195, 199, 208, 216, 231, 245, 263, 265, 269, 271, 278, 283, 286, 288

Lachaise **72**, 258, 283

Renard (Vicktor Zokas) 48, 66, 72, **90–91**, 129, 145, 148, 165, 180, 195, 231, 232, 238, 245, 260, 264, 271, 288

Bond women

Jones, Dr. Christmas 91, **129**, 148, 209, 216, 238, 301

Warmflash, Dr. Molly **145**, 260

Supporting cast

Akakievich, Colonel **148**

King, Sir Robert 66, 72, 90–91, **165**, 263

M 66, 91, 145, 165, 187, 199, 264

Moneypenny, Miss **177**

Nikoli, Capt. **180**, 195

Q 208, 291

Robinson, Charles **187**

unnamed foreign agent **193**

Zukovsky, Valentin 66, 129, 180, **195**, 209, 216, 234, 263, 283, 288, 291

Vehicles

BMW Z8 **208–09**, 216, 263

Eurocopter AS-365N Dauphin 199, 263

Eurocopter tree-cutters 209, **216**

hot air balloon **221**

nuclear submarine 66, 91, 180, 195

parahawks **231**

Q boat **232**, 238

Rolls-Royce Silver Shadow 216, **234**

Sunseeker Manhattan 50 Flybridge yacht **238**

Sunseeker Superhawk speedboat 232, **238**

Weapons & equipment

atomic device **245**

glasses detonator 258, 289

Heckler & Koch G36 rifle 238

hologram machine 145, **260**

key fob 209, **263**

lapel pin **263**

locator card **264**

missile launcher 209

Omega Seamaster watch **269**

pipeline pig 129, **271**

plutonium rod 91, 129, 245

ski suit escape pod **278**

throwing knives 283

torpedoes 232

torture chair **283**, 288

Visa card skeleton key **286**

walking stick gun 195, 283, **288**

Walther P99 handgun 258, **289**

X-ray specs **291**

wrist dart gun 249, **291**

X

X-ray desk **291**
X-ray specs **291**

Y

Yamaha XJ-500 motorcycle 70

You Only Live Twice 20, 24, 40, 42, 61, 84, 98, 110, 143, 149, 161, 177, 187, 191, 198, 207, 222, 224–25, 227, 228, 229, 239, 240, 251, 257, 264, 267, 270, 272, 274, 275, 276, 280, 285, 288, 289, 291, **302–03**, 305, 306, 307, 310, 311, 313, 317, 318, 329, 332

Bond villains

Blofeld, Ernst Stavro 40–41, 61, 84, 143, 149, 161, 191, 207, 222, 224, 228, 229, 264, 268, 272, 274, 291

Brandt, Helga **42**, 84, 228, 229, 270

Hans **61**

Osato, Mr. **84**, 191, 275, 276, 291

SPECTRE 84, 110, 143, 149, 191, 207, 229, 240, 264, 272, 274, 276, 280

Bond women

Aki **110**, 161, 191, 240, 260, 272

Ling **131**

Suzuki, Kissy **143**, 191, 227, 272, 288

Supporting cast

astronauts **149**, 222

Henderson, Dikko 84, 110, **161**, 240, 285

M 143, 227, 257

Moneypenny, Miss **177**, 227

Q 183, 272

Tanaka, Tiger 110, 143, **191**, 198, 222, 228, 239, 260, 268, 274, 280, 285, 288

Vehicles

Aerospatiale Alouette 316B helicopter **198**

Bird 1 61, 149, **207**, 222, 228, 272

Jupiter 16 orbiter 61, 149, **222**

Kawasaki/Boeing KV107-11 **222**

Kawasaki-Verotol KV107 **222**

Little Nellie **224–25**

M1 submarine 227, 285

Meyers 200A **228**, 270

monorail **228**

Ning-Po 84, **229**, 240, 275

SPECTRE helicopters **224–25**

Tanaka's train **239**

Toyota 2000 GT 110, 222, **240**

Toyota Crown S40 222

Weapons & equipment

commando kit 251

flash paper **257**

handbag walkie-talkie **260**

industrial magnet 222

limpet mines 264

lipstick magnesium flare **264**

Murphy bed **267**

Ninja throwing stars **268**

parachutes 228, **270**

poison gas 272

poison string 272

rocket gun **274**

rocket-firing cigarette **274**

safe-cracker **275**

security camera **276**

stiletto fighting stick **280**

trapdoor slide **285**

underwater breathing unit/shroud **285**

wall-walking device **288**

Walther PPK 7.65 mm **289**, 291

X-ray desk **291**

Young, Terence **294–95**, 296–97, 300–01, 305, 309, 317

yo-yo buzz saw 194, **291**

Yusef **63**, 88, 104, 171, 193

Z

Zao 57, 78, **106**, 128, 153, 186, 205, 222, 281

Zaporozhets 965 car **241**

Zora 145, 193

Zorin, Max 16, 48, 49, 61, 79, 95, **107**, 128, 142, 149, 158, 159, 166, 192, 193, 198, 200, 218, 219, 233, 234, 245, 249, 251, 253, 264, 270, 272, 274, 277, 282

Zukovsky, Valentin 66, 129, 162, 180, **194**, **195**, 209, 216, 234, 263, 283, 288, 291

 DK Penguin Random House

SENIOR EDITOR	Alastair Dougall
SENIOR ART EDITORS	Jill Clark, Guy Harvey
SENIOR DESIGNER	Lisa Crowe, Anna Formanek
EDITORS	Julia March, Amy Junor
DESIGNERS	Hanna Ländin, Lynne Moulding
DESIGN ASSISTANT	Mika Kean-Hammerson
SENIOR PRODUCER	Kathleen McNally
MANAGING EDITOR	Sadie Smith
MANAGING ART EDITOR	Ron Stobbart
CREATIVE MANAGER	Sarah Harland
PUBLISHER	Julie Ferris
ART DIRECTOR	Lisa Lanzarini
PUBLISHING DIRECTOR	Simon Beecroft

First published 2007; reprinted 2008; revised 2009, 2014

This edition published in 2015 in Great Britain
by Dorling Kindersley Limited
80 Strand, London WC2R 0RL

001-270262-Sept/15

A WORLD OF IDEAS:
SEE ALL THERE IS TO KNOW

The authors would like to thank those who helped fact-check and research various bits
of info, including John and Laurie Barry, Anne Bennett at EON Productions,
Raymond Benson, James Burkart Jr., Martin Campbell, John Cox, Corinne Erard at
Omega SA, Bruce Feirstein, Gary Firuta, Julie Graham, Charles Helfenstein, Andrew
Lycett, Duncan Mac, Scott McIsaac, Tom Mankiewicz, Doug Redenius, Hillary
Saltzman, David Sulzberger, Michael Van Blaricum, and Dean Williams. Doug Oliver at
the Cessna Aircraft Company was extremely helpful in identifying some of the more
obscure aircraft seen in the Bond films. Brian and Ray McHenry verified the parameters
for the Astro-Spiral car jump as detailed in the AMC Hornet entry. There are
certainly more who need to be thanked, but whose names are, for the moment, lost in
a sea of emails related to this project.

This book, of course, would not exist without the novels of Ian Fleming,
the creator of James Bond. We have tried to note the characters, vehicles, and gadgets
that originally appeared in the literary universe. Just as importantly, the creators of this
book are in debt to all those who contributed ideas, performances, and labor to the
making of the Bond films. In particular, the great unit still photographers and the
cinematographers deserve special mention. The images presented inside are memorable
because of their skill and artistry. In the movie section, space has only been afforded to
highlight 23 of the artists and technicians who have greatly contributed to the 007
series. Many more could be included. Their contributions are just as vital to the success
of 007. In the end, this book is nothing more than a celebration of the creative work
of others. Ultimately, these films exist because of the guidance of four individuals:
Albert R. Broccoli, Harry Saltzman, Michael G. Wilson, and Barbara Broccoli.
Every character, every gadget, every vehicle was deemed Bond-worthy by at
least one of these individuals before it was ever committed to celluloid.
We may have typed the text, but they wrote the book on Bond.

DK would like to thank Dan Bunyan for design work; Catherine Saunders and Heather
Scott for editorial assistance; Guy Harvey and Robert Perry for color correction and
retouching; Santosh Kumar G, Viv Ridgeway, and Siu Yin Chan for additional DTP
work; Sarah Ashun for additional photography; Martin Copeland for picture research.
DK would also like to thank Jenni McMurrie at EON Productions for her
invaluable help. Thanks also to Nathan Clark.